Audi A4
Automotive
Repair
Manual

by Jeff Killingsworth
and John H Haynes

Member of the Guild of Motoring Writers

Models covered:

Audi A4 Sedan, Avant and Cabriolet - 2002 through 2008
1.8L/2.0L four-cylinder turbo and 3.0L/3.2L V6 engines
Does not include diesel engine, S4 or RS4 model information

(15030 - 12N1)

ABCDE
FGHIJ
KLMNO
PQ

Haynes Publishing Group
Sparkford Nr Yeovil
Somerset BA22 7JJ England

Haynes North America, Inc
861 Lawrence Drive
Newbury Park
California 91320 USA

Acknowledgements

Technical writers who contributed to this project include Jay Storer and Mike Stubblefield. Wiring diagrams provided exclusively for Haynes North America, Inc by Valley Forge Technical Information Services.

A book in the Haynes Automotive Repair Manual Series

Printed in the U.S.A.

ISBN-13: 978-1-56392-837-6
ISBN-10: 1-56392-837-X

Library of Congress Control Number: 2010928534

Contents

Introductory pages

About this manual	0-5
Introduction	0-5
Vehicle identification numbers	0-6
Recall information	0-7
Buying parts	0-8
Maintenance techniques, tools and working facilities	0-8
Jacking and towing	0-15
Anti-theft audio system	0-15
Booster battery (jump) starting	0-16
Automotive chemicals and lubricants	0-17
Conversion factors	0-18
Fraction/decimal/millimeter equivalents	0-19
Safety first!	0-20
Troubleshooting	0-21

Chapter 1
Tune-up and routine maintenance — **1-1**

Chapter 2 Part A
Four-cylinder engines — **2A-1**

Chapter 2 Part B
V6 engines — **2B-1**

Chapter 2 Part C
General engine overhaul procedures — **2C-1**

Chapter 3
Cooling, heating and air conditioning systems — **3-1**

Chapter 4
Fuel and exhaust systems — **4-1**

Chapter 5
Engine electrical systems — **5-1**

Chapter 6
Emissions and engine control systems — **6-1**

Chapter 7A
Manual transaxle — **7A-1**

Chapter 7B
Automatic transaxle — **7B-1**

Chapter 8
Clutch and driveline — **8-1**

Chapter 9
Brakes — **9-1**

Chapter 10
Suspension and steering systems — **10-1**

Chapter 11
Body — **11-1**

Chapter 12
Chassis electrical system — **12-1**

Wiring diagrams — **12-21**

Index — **IND-1**

Haynes mechanic and photographer with a 2006 Audi A4 Sedan

About this manual

Its purpose

The purpose of this manual is to help you get the best value from your vehicle. It can do so in several ways. It can help you decide what work must be done, even if you choose to have it done by a dealer service department or a repair shop; it provides information and procedures for routine maintenance and servicing; and it offers diagnostic and repair procedures to follow when trouble occurs.

We hope you use the manual to tackle the work yourself. For many simpler jobs, doing it yourself may be quicker than arranging an appointment to get the vehicle into a shop and making the trips to leave it and pick it up. More importantly, a lot of money can be saved by avoiding the expense the shop must pass on to you to cover its labor and overhead costs. An added benefit is the sense of satisfaction and accomplishment that you feel after doing the job yourself.

Using the manual

The manual is divided into Chapters. Each Chapter is divided into numbered Sections, which are headed in bold type between horizontal lines. Each Section consists of consecutively numbered paragraphs.

At the beginning of each numbered Section you will be referred to any illustrations which apply to the procedures in that Section. The reference numbers used in illustration captions pinpoint the pertinent Section and the Step within that Section. That is, illustration 3.2 means the illustration refers to Section 3 and Step (or paragraph) 2 within that Section.

Procedures, once described in the text, are not normally repeated. When it's necessary to refer to another Chapter, the reference will be given as Chapter and Section number. Cross references given without use of the word "Chapter" apply to Sections and/or paragraphs in the same Chapter. For example, "see Section 8" means in the same Chapter.

References to the left or right side of the vehicle assume you are sitting in the driver's seat, facing forward.

Even though we have prepared this manual with extreme care, neither the publisher nor the author can accept responsibility for any errors in, or omissions from, the information given.

NOTE

A **Note** provides information necessary to properly complete a procedure or information which will make the procedure easier to understand.

CAUTION

A **Caution** provides a special procedure or special steps which must be taken while completing the procedure where the Caution is found. Not heeding a Caution can result in damage to the assembly being worked on.

WARNING

A **Warning** provides a special procedure or special steps which must be taken while completing the procedure where the Warning is found. Not heeding a Warning can result in personal injury.

Introduction to the Audi A4

Audi A4 models are available in either a four-door sedan body style, four-door wagon body style (Avant), or a two-door Cabriolet (convertible).

Depending on year and model, A4 vehicles are powered by a 1.8L turbocharged four-cylinder, 2.0L turbocharged four-cylinder, 3.0L V6 or a 3.2L V6 engine.

Automatic transmission models come equipped with either a five-speed automatic transmission, a six-speed automatic transmission or a Continuously Variable Transmission (CVT), and manual transmission models are equipped with either a five-speed or six-speed manual transmission.

The front suspension on all models is independent, with four transverse links (control arms) per side, coil-over shock absorber assemblies and a stabilizer bar. The rear suspension uses two upper transverse links (control arms) and a lower control arm with tie-rod, individual coil springs, shock absorbers and a stabilizer bar.

The steering system consists of a rack-and-pinion steering gear and two adjustable tie-rods. Power assist is standard.

The brakes are disc at the front and rear, with power assist standard. An Anti-lock Brake System (ABS) is standard equipment.

Vehicle identification numbers

Modifications are a continuing and unpublicized process in vehicle manufacturing. Since spare parts lists and manuals are compiled on a numerical basis, the individual vehicle numbers are necessary to correctly identify the component required.

Vehicle Identification Number (VIN)

This very important identification number is stamped on a plate attached to the dashboard inside the windshield on the driver's side of the vehicle (see illustration). The VIN also appears on the Vehicle Certificate of Title and Registration. It contains information such as where and when the vehicle was manufactured, the model year and the body style.

VIN engine and model year codes

Two particularly important pieces of information found in the VIN are the engine code and the model year code. Counting from the left, the engine code letter designation is the 5th digit and the model year code letter designation is the 10th digit.

On the vehicles covered by this manual the model year codes are:

2	2002
3	2003
4	2004
5	2005
6	2006
7	2007
8	2008

On the vehicles covered by this manual the engine codes are:

C	1.8L four-cylinder turbo
H	3.0L V6 (2002)
T	3.0L V6 (2003 to 2006)
F	2.0L four-cylinder turbo
G	3.2L V6 (2006)
H	3.2L V6 (2007 and later)

Vehicle Certification Label

The Vehicle Certification Label is attached to the driver's side door post (see illustration). Information on this label includes the name of the manufacturer, the month and year of production and the Vehicle Identification Number.

Engine identification number

Locations of the engine identification number:

1.8L four-cylinder engine: At the left rear corner of the engine block.

2.0L four-cylinder engine: At the left rear of the engine block, next to the transaxle bellhousing.

3.0L V6 engine: At the front of the cylinder block, behind the power steering pump.

3.2L V6 engine: At the front of the cylinder block, below the right cylinder head.

The VIN number is visible through the windshield on the driver's side

The vehicle certification label is affixed to the driver's side door post

Recall information

Vehicle recalls are carried out by the manufacturer in the rare event of a possible safety-related defect. The vehicle's registered owner is contacted at the address on file at the Department of Motor Vehicles and given the details of the recall. Remedial work is carried out free of charge at a dealer service department.

If you are the new owner of a used vehicle which was subject to a recall and you want to be sure that the work has been carried out, it's best to contact a dealer service department and ask about your individual vehicle - you'll need to furnish them your Vehicle Identification Number (VIN).

The table below is based on information provided by the National Highway Traffic Safety Administration (NHTSA), the body which oversees vehicle recalls in the United States. The recall database is updated constantly. For the latest information on vehicle recalls, check the NHTSA website at www. nhtsa.gov, www.safercar.gov, or call the NHTSA hotline at 1-888-327-4236.

Recall date	Recall campaign number	Model(s) affected	Concern
March 11, 2005	05V096000	2003, 2004 Audi A4 Cabriolet	On some models, there is a possibility of xenon headlamp coating degradation over time. The luminous transmittance of the headlamp may decrease over a period of time. This condition could affect a driver's field of view, increasing the risk of a crash.
January 17, 2006	06V017000	2003 Audi A4	On some models produced from September 2002 to March 2003, equipped with a 1.8L four-cylinder turbo or a 3.0L engine, a change in the electrical motor components in the fuel pump can lead to an inoperative fuel pump, causing the engine to stall. This could present a potential risk of crash.
August 28, 2006	07V375000	2003 Audi A4	On some models produced from September 2002 to March 2003, equipped with a 1.8L four-cylinder turbo or a 3.0L engine, a change in the electrical motor components in the fuel pump can lead to an inoperative fuel pump, causing the engine to stall. This could present a potential risk of crash.

Buying parts

Replacement parts are available from many sources, which generally fall into one of two categories - authorized dealer parts departments and independent retail auto parts stores. Our advice concerning these parts is as follows:

Retail auto parts stores: Good auto parts stores will stock frequently needed components which wear out relatively fast, such as clutch components, exhaust systems, brake parts, tune-up parts, etc. These stores often supply new or reconditioned parts on an exchange basis, which can save a considerable amount of money. Discount auto parts stores are often very good places to buy materials and parts needed for general vehicle maintenance such as oil, grease, filters, spark plugs, belts, touch-up paint, bulbs, etc. They also usually sell tools and general accessories, have convenient hours, charge lower prices and can often be found not far from home.

Authorized dealer parts department: This is the best source for parts which are unique to the vehicle and not generally available elsewhere (such as major engine parts, transmission parts, trim pieces, etc.).

Warranty information: If the vehicle is still covered under warranty, be sure that any replacement parts purchased - regardless of the source - do not invalidate the warranty!

To be sure of obtaining the correct parts, have engine and chassis numbers available and, if possible, take the old parts along for positive identification.

Maintenance techniques, tools and working facilities

Maintenance techniques

There are a number of techniques involved in maintenance and repair that will be referred to throughout this manual. Application of these techniques will enable the home mechanic to be more efficient, better organized and capable of performing the various tasks properly, which will ensure that the repair job is thorough and complete.

Fasteners

Fasteners are nuts, bolts, studs and screws used to hold two or more parts together. There are a few things to keep in mind when working with fasteners. Almost all of them use a locking device of some type, either a lockwasher, locknut, locking tab or thread adhesive. All threaded fasteners should be clean and straight, with undamaged threads and undamaged corners on the hex head where the wrench fits. Develop the habit of replacing all damaged nuts and bolts with new ones. Special locknuts with nylon or fiber inserts can only be used once. If they are removed, they lose their locking ability and must be replaced with new ones.

Rusted nuts and bolts should be treated with a penetrating fluid to ease removal and prevent breakage. Some mechanics use turpentine in a spout-type oil can, which works quite well. After applying the rust penetrant, let it work for a few minutes before trying to loosen the nut or bolt. Badly rusted fasteners may have to be chiseled or sawed off or removed with a special nut breaker, available at tool stores.

If a bolt or stud breaks off in an assembly, it can be drilled and removed with a special tool commonly available for this purpose. Most automotive machine shops can perform this task, as well as other repair procedures, such as the repair of threaded holes that have been stripped out.

Flat washers and lockwashers, when removed from an assembly, should always be replaced exactly as removed. Replace any damaged washers with new ones. Never use a lockwasher on any soft metal surface (such as aluminum), thin sheet metal or plastic.

Fastener sizes

For a number of reasons, automobile manufacturers are making wider and wider use of metric fasteners. Therefore, it is important to be able to tell the difference between standard (sometimes called U.S. or SAE) and metric hardware, since they cannot be interchanged.

All bolts, whether standard or metric, are sized according to diameter, thread pitch and length. For example, a standard 1/2 - 13 x 1 bolt is 1/2 inch in diameter, has 13 threads per inch and is 1 inch long. An M12 - 1.75 x 25 metric bolt is 12 mm in diameter, has a thread pitch of 1.75 mm (the distance between threads) and is 25 mm long. The two bolts are nearly identical, and easily confused, but they are not interchangeable.

In addition to the differences in diameter, thread pitch and length, metric and standard bolts can also be distinguished by examining the bolt heads. To begin with, the distance across the flats on a standard bolt head is measured in inches, while the same dimension on a metric bolt is sized in millimeters (the same is true for nuts). As a result, a standard wrench should not be used on a metric bolt and a metric wrench should not be used on a standard bolt. Also, most standard bolts have slashes radiating out from the center of the head to denote the grade or strength of the bolt, which is an indication of the amount of torque that can be applied to it. The greater the number of slashes, the greater the strength of the bolt. Grades 0 through 5 are commonly used on automobiles. Metric bolts have a property class (grade) number, rather than a slash, molded into their heads to indicate bolt strength. In this case, the higher the number, the stronger the bolt. Property class numbers 8.8, 9.8 and 10.9 are commonly used on automobiles.

Strength markings can also be used to distinguish standard hex nuts from metric hex nuts. Many standard nuts have dots stamped into one side, while metric nuts are marked with a number. The greater the number of dots, or the higher the number, the greater the strength of the nut.

Metric studs are also marked on their ends according to property class (grade). Larger studs are numbered (the same as metric bolts), while smaller studs carry a geometric code to denote grade.

It should be noted that many fasteners, especially Grades 0 through 2, have no distinguishing marks on them. When such is the case, the only way to determine whether it is standard or metric is to measure the thread pitch or compare it to a known fastener of the same size.

Standard fasteners are often referred to as SAE, as opposed to metric. However, it should be noted that SAE technically refers to a non-metric fine thread fastener only. Coarse thread non-metric fasteners are referred to as USS sizes.

Since fasteners of the same size (both standard and metric) may have different strength ratings, be sure to reinstall any bolts, studs or nuts removed from your vehicle in their original locations. Also, when replacing a fastener with a new one, make sure that the new one has a strength rating equal to or greater than the original.

Tightening sequences and procedures

Most threaded fasteners should be tightened to a specific torque value (torque is the twisting force applied to a threaded component such as a nut or bolt). Overtightening the fastener can weaken it and cause it to break, while undertightening can cause it to eventually come loose. Bolts, screws and studs, depending on the material they are made of and their thread diameters, have specific torque values, many of which are noted in the Specifications at the beginning of each Chapter. Be sure to follow the torque recommendations closely. For fasteners not assigned a

Grade 1 or 2   Grade 5   Grade 8

Bolt strength marking (standard/SAE/USS; bottom - metric)

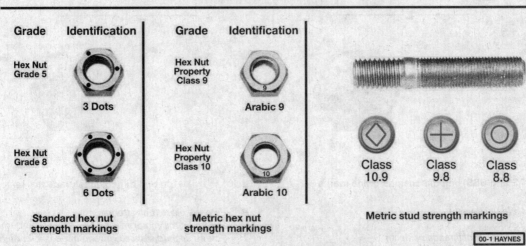

Standard hex nut strength markings

Metric hex nut strength markings

Metric stud strength markings

00-1 HAYNES

specific torque, a general torque value chart is presented here as a guide. These torque values are for dry (unlubricated) fasteners threaded into steel or cast iron (not aluminum). As was previously mentioned, the size and grade of a fastener determine the amount of torque that can safely be applied to it. The figures listed here are approximate for Grade 2 and Grade 3 fasteners. Higher grades can tolerate higher torque values.

Fasteners laid out in a pattern, such as cylinder head bolts, oil pan bolts, differential cover bolts, etc., must be loosened or tightened in sequence to avoid warping the component. This sequence will normally be shown in the appropriate Chapter. If a specific pattern is not given, the following procedures can be used to prevent warping.

Initially, the bolts or nuts should be assembled finger-tight only. Next, they should be tightened one full turn each, in a crisscross or diagonal pattern. After each one has been tightened one full turn, return to the first one and tighten them all one-half turn, following the same pattern. Finally, tighten each of them one-quarter turn at a time until each fastener has been tightened to the proper torque. To loosen and remove the fasteners, the procedure would be reversed.

Component disassembly

Component disassembly should be done with care and purpose to help ensure that

Metric thread sizes	Ft-lbs	Nm
M-6	6 to 9	9 to 12
M-8	14 to 21	19 to 28
M-10	28 to 40	38 to 54
M-12	50 to 71	68 to 96
M-14	80 to 140	109 to 154
Pipe thread sizes		
1/8	5 to 8	7 to 10
1/4	12 to 18	17 to 24
3/8	22 to 33	30 to 44
1/2	25 to 35	34 to 47
U.S. thread sizes		
1/4 - 20	6 to 9	9 to 12
5/16 - 18	12 to 18	17 to 24
5/16 - 24	14 to 20	19 to 27
3/8 - 16	22 to 32	30 to 43
3/8 - 24	27 to 38	37 to 51
7/16 - 14	40 to 55	55 to 74
7/16 - 20	40 to 60	55 to 81
1/2 - 13	55 to 80	75 to 108

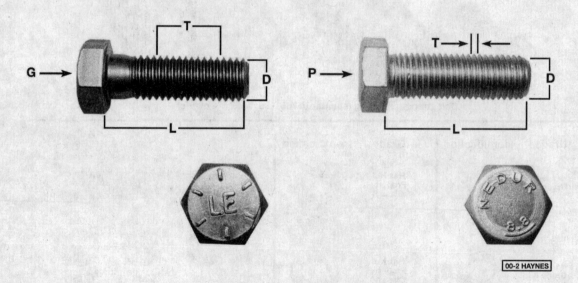

00-2 HAYNES

Standard (SAE and USS) bolt dimensions/grade marks

G   Grade marks (bolt strength)
L   Length (in inches)
T   Thread pitch (number of threads per inch)
D   Nominal diameter (in inches)

Metric bolt dimensions/grade marks

P   Property class (bolt strength)
L   Length (in millimeters)
T   Thread pitch (distance between threads in millimeters)
D   Diameter

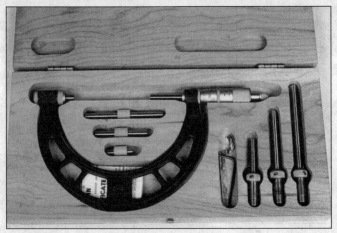

Micrometer set

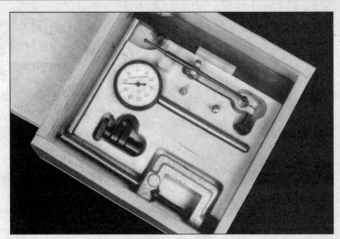

Dial indicator set

the parts go back together properly. Always keep track of the sequence in which parts are removed. Make note of special characteristics or marks on parts that can be installed more than one way, such as a grooved thrust washer on a shaft. It is a good idea to lay the disassembled parts out on a clean surface in the order that they were removed. It may also be helpful to make sketches or take instant photos of components before removal.

When removing fasteners from a component, keep track of their locations. Sometimes threading a bolt back in a part, or putting the washers and nut back on a stud, can prevent mix-ups later. If nuts and bolts cannot be returned to their original locations, they should be kept in a compartmented box or a series of small boxes. A cupcake or muffin tin is ideal for this purpose, since each cavity can hold the bolts and nuts from a particular area (i.e. oil pan bolts, valve cover bolts, engine mount bolts, etc.). A pan of this type is especially helpful when working on assemblies with very small parts, such as the carburetor, alternator, valve train or interior dash and trim pieces. The cavities can be marked with paint or tape to identify the contents.

Whenever wiring looms, harnesses or connectors are separated, it is a good idea to identify the two halves with numbered pieces of masking tape so they can be easily reconnected.

Gasket sealing surfaces

Throughout any vehicle, gaskets are used to seal the mating surfaces between two parts and keep lubricants, fluids, vacuum or pressure contained in an assembly.

Many times these gaskets are coated with a liquid or paste-type gasket sealing compound before assembly. Age, heat and pressure can sometimes cause the two parts to stick together so tightly that they are very difficult to separate. Often, the assembly can be loosened by striking it with a soft-face hammer near the mating surfaces. A regular hammer can be used if a block of wood is placed between the hammer and the part. Do

not hammer on cast parts or parts that could be easily damaged. With any particularly stubborn part, always recheck to make sure that every fastener has been removed.

Avoid using a screwdriver or bar to pry apart an assembly, as they can easily mar the gasket sealing surfaces of the parts, which must remain smooth. If prying is absolutely necessary, use an old broom handle, but keep in mind that extra clean up will be necessary if the wood splinters.

After the parts are separated, the old gasket must be carefully scraped off and the gasket surfaces cleaned. Stubborn gasket material can be soaked with rust penetrant or treated with a special chemical to soften it so it can be easily scraped off. **Caution:** *Never use gasket removal solutions or caustic chemicals on plastic or other composite components.* A scraper can be fashioned from a piece of copper tubing by flattening and sharpening one end. Copper is recommended because it is usually softer than the surfaces to be scraped, which reduces the chance of gouging the part. Some gaskets can be removed with a wire brush, but regardless of the method used, the mating surfaces must be left clean and smooth. If for some reason the gasket surface is gouged, then a gasket sealer thick enough to fill scratches will have to be used during reassembly of the components. For most applications, a non-drying (or semi-drying) gasket sealer should be used.

Hose removal tips

Warning: *If the vehicle is equipped with air conditioning, do not disconnect any of the A/C hoses without first having the system depressurized by a dealer service department or a service station.*

Hose removal precautions closely parallel gasket removal precautions. Avoid scratching or gouging the surface that the hose mates against or the connection may leak. This is especially true for radiator hoses. Because of various chemical reactions, the rubber in hoses can bond itself to the metal spigot that the hose fits over. To remove

a hose, first loosen the hose clamps that secure it to the spigot. Then, with slip-joint pliers, grab the hose at the clamp and rotate it around the spigot. Work it back and forth until it is completely free, then pull it off. Silicone or other lubricants will ease removal if they can be applied between the hose and the outside of the spigot. Apply the same lubricant to the inside of the hose and the outside of the spigot to simplify installation.

As a last resort (and if the hose is to be replaced with a new one anyway), the rubber can be slit with a knife and the hose peeled from the spigot. If this must be done, be careful that the metal connection is not damaged.

If a hose clamp is broken or damaged, do not reuse it. Wire-type clamps usually weaken with age, so it is a good idea to replace them with screw-type clamps whenever a hose is removed.

Tools

A selection of good tools is a basic requirement for anyone who plans to maintain and repair his or her own vehicle. For the owner who has few tools, the initial investment might seem high, but when compared to the spiraling costs of professional auto maintenance and repair, it is a wise one.

To help the owner decide which tools are needed to perform the tasks detailed in this manual, the following tool lists are offered: *Maintenance and minor repair, Repair/overhaul* and *Special.*

The newcomer to practical mechanics should start off with the *maintenance and minor repair* tool kit, which is adequate for the simpler jobs performed on a vehicle. Then, as confidence and experience grow, the owner can tackle more difficult tasks, buying additional tools as they are needed. Eventually the basic kit will be expanded into the *repair and overhaul* tool set. Over a period of time, the experienced do-it-yourselfer will assemble a tool set complete enough for most repair and overhaul procedures and will add tools from the special category when it is felt that the expense is justified by the frequency of use.

Dial caliper

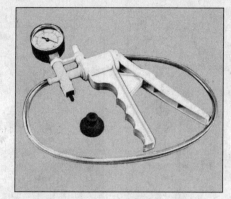

Hand-operated vacuum pump

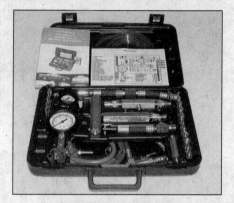

Fuel pressure gauge set

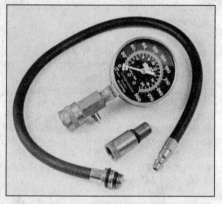

Compression gauge with spark plug hole adapter

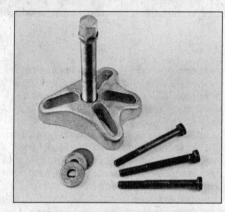

Damper/steering wheel puller

General purpose puller

Hydraulic lifter removal tool

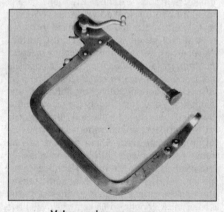

Valve spring compressor

Valve spring compressor

Ridge reamer

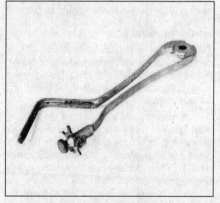

Piston ring groove cleaning tool

Ring removal/installation tool

Ring compressor

Cylinder hone

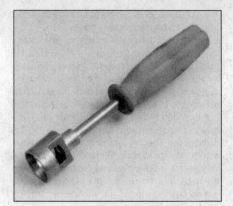

Brake hold-down spring tool

Torque angle gauge

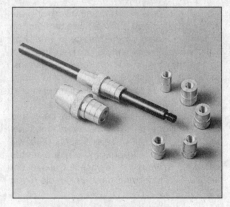

Clutch plate alignment tool

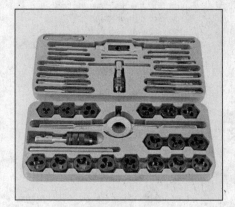

Tap and die set

Maintenance and minor repair tool kit

The tools in this list should be considered the minimum required for performance of routine maintenance, servicing and minor repair work. We recommend the purchase of combination wrenches (box-end and open-end combined in one wrench). While more expensive than open end wrenches, they offer the advantages of both types of wrench.

Combination wrench set (1/4-inch to 1 inch or 6 mm to 19 mm)
Adjustable wrench, 8 inch
Spark plug wrench with rubber insert
Spark plug gap adjusting tool
Feeler gauge set
Brake bleeder wrench
Standard screwdriver (5/16-inch x 6 inch)
Phillips screwdriver (No. 2 x 6 inch)
Combination pliers - 6 inch
Hacksaw and assortment of blades
Tire pressure gauge
Grease gun
Oil can
Fine emery cloth
Wire brush
Battery post and cable cleaning tool
Oil filter wrench
Funnel (medium size)
Safety goggles
Jackstands (2)
Drain pan

Note: *If basic tune-ups are going to be part of routine maintenance, it will be necessary to purchase a good quality stroboscopic timing light and combination tachometer/dwell meter. Although they are included in the list of special tools, it is mentioned here because they are absolutely necessary for tuning most vehicles properly.*

Repair and overhaul tool set

These tools are essential for anyone who plans to perform major repairs and are in addition to those in the maintenance and minor repair tool kit. Included is a comprehensive set of sockets which, though expensive, are invaluable because of their versatility, especially when various extensions and drives are available. We recommend the 1/2-inch drive over the 3/8-inch drive. Although the larger drive is bulky and more expensive, it has the capacity of accepting a very wide range of large sockets. Ideally, however, the mechanic should have a 3/8-inch drive set and a 1/2-inch drive set.

Socket set(s)
Reversible ratchet
Extension - 10 inch
Universal joint
Torque wrench (same size drive as sockets)
Ball peen hammer - 8 ounce
Soft-face hammer (plastic/rubber)
Standard screwdriver (1/4-inch x 6 inch)

Standard screwdriver (stubby - 5/16-inch)
Phillips screwdriver (No. 3 x 8 inch)
Phillips screwdriver (stubby - No. 2)
Pliers - vise grip
Pliers - lineman's
Pliers - needle nose
Pliers - snap-ring (internal and external)
Cold chisel - 1/2-inch
Scribe
Scraper (made from flattened copper tubing)
Centerpunch
Pin punches (1/16, 1/8, 3/16-inch)
Steel rule/straightedge - 12 inch
Allen wrench set (1/8 to 3/8-inch or 4 mm to 10 mm)
A selection of files
Wire brush (large)
Jackstands (second set)
Jack (scissor or hydraulic type)

Note: *Another tool which is often useful is an electric drill with a chuck capacity of 3/8-inch and a set of good quality drill bits.*

Special tools

The tools in this list include those which are not used regularly, are expensive to buy, or which need to be used in accordance with their manufacturer's instructions. Unless these tools will be used frequently, it is not very economical to purchase many of them. A consideration would be to split the cost and use between yourself and a friend or friends. In addition, most of these tools can be obtained from a tool rental shop on a temporary basis.

This list primarily contains only those tools and instruments widely available to the public, and not those special tools produced by the vehicle manufacturer for distribution to dealer service departments. Occasionally, references to the manufacturer's special tools are included in the text of this manual. Generally, an alternative method of doing the job without the special tool is offered. However, sometimes there is no alternative to their use. Where this is the case, and the tool cannot be purchased or borrowed, the work should be turned over to the dealer service department or an automotive repair shop.

> *Valve spring compressor*
> *Piston ring groove cleaning tool*
> *Piston ring compressor*
> *Piston ring installation tool*
> *Cylinder compression gauge*
> *Cylinder ridge reamer*
> *Cylinder surfacing hone*
> *Cylinder bore gauge*
> *Micrometers and/or dial calipers*
> *Hydraulic lifter removal tool*
> *Balljoint separator*
> *Universal-type puller*
> *Impact screwdriver*
> *Dial indicator set*
> *Stroboscopic timing light (inductive pick-up)*
> *Hand operated vacuum/pressure pump*
> *Tachometer/dwell meter*
> *Universal electrical multimeter*
> *Cable hoist*
> *Brake spring removal and installation tools*
> *Floor jack*

Buying tools

For the do-it-yourselfer who is just starting to get involved in vehicle maintenance and repair, there are a number of options available when purchasing tools. If maintenance and minor repair is the extent of the work to be done, the purchase of individual tools is satisfactory. If, on the other hand, extensive work is planned, it would be a good idea to purchase a modest tool set from one of the large retail chain stores. A set can usually be bought at a substantial savings over the individual tool prices, and they often come with a tool box. As additional tools are needed, add-on sets, individual tools and a larger tool box can be purchased to expand the tool selection. Building a tool set gradually allows the cost of the tools to be spread over a longer period of time and gives the mechanic the freedom to choose only those tools that will actually be used.

Tool stores will often be the only source of some of the special tools that are needed,

but regardless of where tools are bought, try to avoid cheap ones, especially when buying screwdrivers and sockets, because they won't last very long. The expense involved in replacing cheap tools will eventually be greater than the initial cost of quality tools.

Care and maintenance of tools

Good tools are expensive, so it makes sense to treat them with respect. Keep them clean and in usable condition and store them properly when not in use. Always wipe off any dirt, grease or metal chips before putting them away. Never leave tools lying around in the work area. Upon completion of a job, always check closely under the hood for tools that may have been left there so they won't get lost during a test drive.

Some tools, such as screwdrivers, pliers, wrenches and sockets, can be hung on a panel mounted on the garage or workshop wall, while others should be kept in a tool box or tray. Measuring instruments, gauges, meters, etc. must be carefully stored where they cannot be damaged by weather or impact from other tools.

When tools are used with care and stored properly, they will last a very long time. Even with the best of care, though, tools will wear out if used frequently. When a tool is damaged or worn out, replace it. Subsequent jobs will be safer and more enjoyable if you do.

How to repair damaged threads

Sometimes, the internal threads of a nut or bolt hole can become stripped, usually from overtightening. Stripping threads is an all-too-common occurrence, especially when working with aluminum parts, because aluminum is so soft that it easily strips out.

Usually, external or internal threads are only partially stripped. After they've been cleaned up with a tap or die, they'll still work. Sometimes, however, threads are badly damaged. When this happens, you've got three choices:

1) *Drill and tap the hole to the next suitable oversize and install a larger diameter bolt, screw or stud.*
2) *Drill and tap the hole to accept a threaded plug, then drill and tap the plug to the original screw size. You can also buy a plug already threaded to the original size. Then you simply drill a hole to the specified size, then run the threaded plug into the hole with a bolt and jam nut. Once the plug is fully seated, remove the jam nut and bolt.*
3) *The third method uses a patented thread repair kit like Heli-Coil or Slimsert. These*

easy-to-use kits are designed to repair damaged threads in straight-through holes and blind holes. Both are available as kits which can handle a variety of sizes and thread patterns. Drill the hole, then tap it with the special included tap. Install the Heli-Coil and the hole is back to its original diameter and thread pitch.

Regardless of which method you use, be sure to proceed calmly and carefully. A little impatience or carelessness during one of these relatively simple procedures can ruin your whole day's work and cost you a bundle if you wreck an expensive part.

Working facilities

Not to be overlooked when discussing tools is the workshop. If anything more than routine maintenance is to be carried out, some sort of suitable work area is essential.

It is understood, and appreciated, that many home mechanics do not have a good workshop or garage available, and end up removing an engine or doing major repairs outside. It is recommended, however, that the overhaul or repair be completed under the cover of a roof.

A clean, flat workbench or table of comfortable working height is an absolute necessity. The workbench should be equipped with a vise that has a jaw opening of at least four inches.

As mentioned previously, some clean, dry storage space is also required for tools, as well as the lubricants, fluids, cleaning solvents, etc. which soon become necessary.

Sometimes waste oil and fluids, drained from the engine or cooling system during normal maintenance or repairs, present a disposal problem. To avoid pouring them on the ground or into a sewage system, pour the used fluids into large containers, seal them with caps and take them to an authorized disposal site or recycling center. Plastic jugs, such as old antifreeze containers, are ideal for this purpose.

Always keep a supply of old newspapers and clean rags available. Old towels are excellent for mopping up spills. Many mechanics use rolls of paper towels for most work because they are readily available and disposable. To help keep the area under the vehicle clean, a large cardboard box can be cut open and flattened to protect the garage or shop floor.

Whenever working over a painted surface, such as when leaning over a fender to service something under the hood, always cover it with an old blanket or bedspread to protect the finish. Vinyl covered pads, made especially for this purpose, are available at auto parts stores.

Jacking and towing

Jacking

Warning: *The jack supplied with the vehicle should only be used for changing a tire or placing jackstands under the frame. Never work under the vehicle or start the engine while this jack is being used as the only means of support.*

The vehicle should be on level ground. Place the shift lever in Park, and block the wheel diagonally opposite the wheel being changed. Set the parking brake.

Remove the spare tire and jack from stowage **(see illustration)**. Remove the wheel cover and trim ring (if so equipped) with the tapered end of the wheel bolt wrench by inserting and twisting the handle and then prying against the back of the wheel cover. Loosen the wheel bolts about 1/4-to-1/2 turn each.

Place the jack under the side of the vehicle and adjust the jack height until it engages the vertical rocker panel flange nearest the wheel to be changed. There is a front and rear jacking point on each side of the vehicle **(see illustration)**.

Turn the jack handle clockwise until the tire clears the ground. Remove the wheel bolts and pull the wheel off, then install the spare.

Install the wheel bolts and tighten them snugly. Don't attempt to tighten them completely until the vehicle is lowered or it could slip off the jack. Turn the jack handle counterclockwise to lower the vehicle. Remove the jack and tighten the wheel bolts in a diagonal pattern.

Install the cover (and trim ring, if used) and be sure it's snapped into place all the way around.

Stow the tire, jack and wrench. Unblock the wheels.

Towing

The manufacturer states that the only safe way to tow these vehicles is with a flat-bed-type car carrier. Other methods could cause damage to the drivetrain.

The jack and factory tools are located in the well on the left and right of the spare tire in the luggage compartment

Place the jack so it engages the rocker panel nearest the wheel to be raised

Anti-theft audio system

General information

1   Models equipped with Chorus II+ and Symphony II+ radio systems have an anti-theft feature that will render the stereo inoperative if stolen or if the battery is disconnected. If the power source to the stereo is cut, the stereo will be inoperative. Even if the power source is immediately re-connected, the stereo will not function.

2   Do not disconnect the battery, remove the stereo or disconnect related components unless you have the individual ID (code) number for the stereo.

Unlocking the stereo after a power loss

3   When the power is restored to the stereo, the stereo won't operate. Enter your ID code to reactivate it, using the following Steps.

4   Turn the radio ON. The lower display window (where radio stations are displayed) should show "SAFE". After a few seconds, the SAFE message should go out and the numerals "1000" should display.

5   Press the upper left control button on the radio, until the first digit appears in the display.

6   Enter the three remaining code digits with the other three control buttons.

7   Press the ENTER control button and the radio security code is set.

Unlocking the navigation after a power loss

8   Turn the navigation system ON.

9   Enter the PIN number using the Speller keys.

10   Once the code is entered, press the OK button and the code is set.

Booster battery (jump) starting

Observe these precautions when using a booster battery to start a vehicle:

a) *Before connecting the booster battery, make sure the ignition switch is in the Off position.*
b) *Turn off the lights, heater and other electrical loads.*
c) *Your eyes should be shielded. Safety goggles are a good idea.*
d) *Make sure the booster battery is the same voltage as the dead one in the vehicle.*
e) *The two vehicles MUST NOT TOUCH each other!*
f) *Make sure the transaxle is in Neutral (manual) or Park (automatic).*
g) *If the booster battery is not a maintenance-free type, remove the vent caps and lay a cloth over the vent holes.*

The battery on these vehicles is located in the center of the cowl chamber, just below the windshield. On some models a cover may have to be removed.

Connect the red-colored jumper cable to the positive (+) terminal of the booster battery and the other end to the positive (+) terminal of the dead battery. Then connect one end of the black jumper cable to the negative (-) terminal of the booster battery, and the other end of that cable to a good ground point on the engine of the disabled vehicle, preferably not too near the battery.

Start the engine using the booster battery and let the booster vehicle run at 2000 rpm for a few minutes to put some charge into the weak battery, then, with the engine running at idle speed, disconnect the jumper cables in the reverse order of connection.

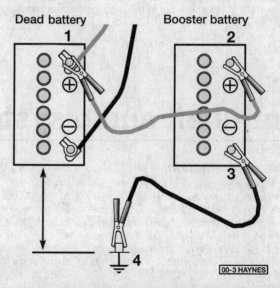

Make the booster battery cable connections in the numerical order shown (note that the negative cable of the booster battery is NOT attached to the negative terminal of the dead battery)

Automotive chemicals and lubricants

A number of automotive chemicals and lubricants are available for use during vehicle maintenance and repair. They include a wide variety of products ranging from cleaning solvents and degreasers to lubricants and protective sprays for rubber, plastic and vinyl.

Cleaners

Carburetor cleaner and choke cleaner is a strong solvent for gum, varnish and carbon. Most carburetor cleaners leave a dry-type lubricant film which will not harden or gum up. Because of this film it is not recommended for use on electrical components.

Brake system cleaner is used to remove brake dust, grease and brake fluid from the brake system, where clean surfaces are absolutely necessary. It leaves no residue and often eliminates brake squeal caused by contaminants.

Electrical cleaner removes oxidation, corrosion and carbon deposits from electrical contacts, restoring full current flow. It can also be used to clean spark plugs, carburetor jets, voltage regulators and other parts where an oil-free surface is desired.

Demoisturants remove water and moisture from electrical components such as alternators, voltage regulators, electrical connectors and fuse blocks. They are non-conductive and non-corrosive.

Degreasers are heavy-duty solvents used to remove grease from the outside of the engine and from chassis components. They can be sprayed or brushed on and, depending on the type, are rinsed off either with water or solvent.

Lubricants

Motor oil is the lubricant formulated for use in engines. It normally contains a wide variety of additives to prevent corrosion and reduce foaming and wear. Motor oil comes in various weights (viscosity ratings) from 0 to 50. The recommended weight of the oil depends on the season, temperature and the demands on the engine. Light oil is used in cold climates and under light load conditions. Heavy oil is used in hot climates and where high loads are encountered. Multi-viscosity oils are designed to have characteristics of both light and heavy oils and are available in a number of weights from 0W-20 to 20W-50.

Gear oil is designed to be used in differentials, manual transmissions and other areas where high-temperature lubrication is required.

Chassis and wheel bearing grease is a heavy grease used where increased loads and friction are encountered, such as for wheel bearings, balljoints, tie-rod ends and universal joints.

High-temperature wheel bearing grease is designed to withstand the extreme temperatures encountered by wheel bearings in disc brake equipped vehicles. It usually contains molybdenum disulfide (moly), which is a dry-type lubricant.

White grease is a heavy grease for metal-to-metal applications where water is a problem. White grease stays soft under both low and high temperatures (usually from -100 to +190-degrees F), and will not wash off or dilute in the presence of water.

Assembly lube is a special extreme pressure lubricant, usually containing moly, used to lubricate high-load parts (such as main and rod bearings and cam lobes) for initial start-up of a new engine. The assembly lube lubricates the parts without being squeezed out or washed away until the engine oiling system begins to function.

Silicone lubricants are used to protect rubber, plastic, vinyl and nylon parts.

Graphite lubricants are used where oils cannot be used due to contamination problems, such as in locks. The dry graphite will lubricate metal parts while remaining uncontaminated by dirt, water, oil or acids. It is electrically conductive and will not foul electrical contacts in locks such as the ignition switch.

Moly penetrants loosen and lubricate frozen, rusted and corroded fasteners and prevent future rusting or freezing.

Heat-sink grease is a special electrically non-conductive grease that is used for mounting electronic ignition modules where it is essential that heat is transferred away from the module.

Sealants

RTV sealant is one of the most widely used gasket compounds. Made from silicone, RTV is air curing, it seals, bonds, waterproofs, fills surface irregularities, remains flexible, doesn't shrink, is relatively easy to remove, and is used as a supplementary sealer with almost all low and medium temperature gaskets.

Anaerobic sealant is much like RTV in that it can be used either to seal gaskets or to form gaskets by itself. It remains flexible, is solvent resistant and fills surface imperfections. The difference between an anaerobic sealant and an RTV-type sealant is in the curing. RTV cures when exposed to air, while an anaerobic sealant cures only in the absence of air. This means that an anaerobic sealant cures only after the assembly of parts, sealing them together.

Thread and pipe sealant is used for sealing hydraulic and pneumatic fittings and vacuum lines. It is usually made from a Teflon compound, and comes in a spray, a paint-on liquid and as a wrap-around tape.

Chemicals

Anti-seize compound prevents seizing, galling, cold welding, rust and corrosion in fasteners. High-temperature ant-seize, usually made with copper and graphite lubricants, is used for exhaust system and exhaust manifold bolts.

Anaerobic locking compounds are used to keep fasteners from vibrating or working loose and cure only after installation, in the absence of air. Medium strength locking compound is used for small nuts, bolts and screws that may be removed later. High-strength locking compound is for large nuts, bolts and studs which aren't removed on a regular basis.

Oil additives range from viscosity index improvers to chemical treatments that claim to reduce internal engine friction. It should be noted that most oil manufacturers caution against using additives with their oils.

Gas additives perform several functions, depending on their chemical makeup. They usually contain solvents that help dissolve gum and varnish that build up on carburetor, fuel injection and intake parts. They also serve to break down carbon deposits that form on the inside surfaces of the combustion chambers. Some additives contain upper cylinder lubricants for valves and piston rings, and others contain chemicals to remove condensation from the gas tank.

Miscellaneous

Brake fluid is specially formulated hydraulic fluid that can withstand the heat and pressure encountered in brake systems. Care must be taken so this fluid does not come in contact with painted surfaces or plastics. An opened container should always be resealed to prevent contamination by water or dirt.

Weatherstrip adhesive is used to bond weatherstripping around doors, windows and trunk lids. It is sometimes used to attach trim pieces.

Undercoating is a petroleum-based, tar-like substance that is designed to protect metal surfaces on the underside of the vehicle from corrosion. It also acts as a sound-deadening agent by insulating the bottom of the vehicle.

Waxes and polishes are used to help protect painted and plated surfaces from the weather. Different types of paint may require the use of different types of wax and polish. Some polishes utilize a chemical or abrasive cleaner to help remove the top layer of oxidized (dull) paint on older vehicles. In recent years many non-wax polishes that contain a wide variety of chemicals such as polymers and silicones have been introduced. These non-wax polishes are usually easier to apply and last longer than conventional waxes and polishes.

Conversion factors

Length (distance)

Inches (in)	X 25.4	= Millimeters (mm)	X 0.0394	= Inches (in)
Feet (ft)	X 0.305	= Meters (m)	X 3.281	= Feet (ft)
Miles	X 1.609	= Kilometers (km)	X 0.621	= Miles

Volume (capacity)

Cubic inches (cu in; in^3)	X 16.387	= Cubic centimeters (cc; cm^3)	X 0.061	= Cubic inches (cu in; in^3)
Imperial pints (Imp pt)	X 0.568	= Liters (l)	X 1.76	= Imperial pints (Imp pt)
Imperial quarts (Imp qt)	X 1.137	= Liters (l)	X 0.88	= Imperial quarts (Imp qt)
Imperial quarts (Imp qt)	X 1.201	= US quarts (US qt)	X 0.833	= Imperial quarts (Imp qt)
US quarts (US qt)	X 0.946	= Liters (l)	X 1.057	= US quarts (US qt)
Imperial gallons (Imp gal)	X 4.546	= Liters (l)	X 0.22	= Imperial gallons (Imp gal)
Imperial gallons (Imp gal)	X 1.201	= US gallons (US gal)	X 0.833	= Imperial gallons (Imp gal)
US gallons (US gal)	X 3.785	= Liters (l)	X 0.264	= US gallons (US gal)

Mass (weight)

Ounces (oz)	X 28.35	= Grams (g)	X 0.035	= Ounces (oz)
Pounds (lb)	X 0.454	= Kilograms (kg)	X 2.205	= Pounds (lb)

Force

Ounces-force (ozf; oz)	X 0.278	= Newtons (N)	X 3.6	= Ounces-force (ozf; oz)
Pounds-force (lbf; lb)	X 4.448	= Newtons (N)	X 0.225	= Pounds-force (lbf; lb)
Newtons (N)	X 0.1	= Kilograms-force (kgf; kg)	X 9.81	= Newtons (N)

Pressure

Pounds-force per square inch (psi; lbf/in^2; lb/in^2)	X 0.070	= Kilograms-force per square centimeter (kgf/cm^2; kg/cm^2)	X 14.223	= Pounds-force per square inch (psi; lbf/in^2; lb/in^2)
Pounds-force per square inch (psi; lbf/in^2; lb/in^2)	X 0.068	= Atmospheres (atm)	X 14.696	= Pounds-force per square inch (psi; lbf/in^2; lb/in^2)
Pounds-force per square inch (psi; lbf/in^2; lb/in^2)	X 0.069	= Bars	X 14.5	= Pounds-force per square inch (psi; lbf/in^2; lb/in^2)
Pounds-force per square inch (psi; lbf/in^2; lb/in^2)	X 6.895	= Kilopascals (kPa)	X 0.145	= Pounds-force per square inch (psi; lbf/in^2; lb/in^2)
Kilopascals (kPa)	X 0.01	= Kilograms-force per square centimeter (kgf/cm^2; kg/cm^2)	X 98.1	= Kilopascals (kPa)

Torque (moment of force)

Pounds-force inches (lbf in; lb in)	X 1.152	= Kilograms-force centimeter (kgf cm; kg cm)	X 0.868	= Pounds-force inches (lbf in; lb in)
Pounds-force inches (lbf in; lb in)	X 0.113	= Newton meters (Nm)	X 8.85	= Pounds-force inches (lbf in; lb in)
Pounds-force inches (lbf in; lb in)	X 0.083	= Pounds-force feet (lbf ft; lb ft)	X 12	= Pounds-force inches (lbf in; lb in)
Pounds-force feet (lbf ft; lb ft)	X 0.138	= Kilograms-force meters (kgf m; kg m)	X 7.233	= Pounds-force feet (lbf ft; lb ft)
Pounds-force feet (lbf ft; lb ft)	X 1.356	= Newton meters (Nm)	X 0.738	= Pounds-force feet (lbf ft; lb ft)
Newton meters (Nm)	X 0.102	= Kilograms-force meters (kgf m; kg m)	X 9.804	= Newton meters (Nm)

Vacuum

Inches mercury (in. Hg)	X 3.377	= Kilopascals (kPa)	X 0.2961	= Inches mercury
Inches mercury (in. Hg)	X 25.4	= Millimeters mercury (mm Hg)	X 0.0394	= Inches mercury

Power

Horsepower (hp)	X 745.7	= Watts (W)	X 0.0013	= Horsepower (hp)

Velocity (speed)

Miles per hour (miles/hr; mph)	X 1.609	= Kilometers per hour (km/hr; kph)	X 0.621	= Miles per hour (miles/hr; mph)

Fuel consumption*

Miles per gallon, Imperial (mpg)	X 0.354	= Kilometers per liter (km/l)	X 2.825	= Miles per gallon, Imperial (mpg)
Miles per gallon, US (mpg)	X 0.425	= Kilometers per liter (km/l)	X 2.352	= Miles per gallon, US (mpg)

Temperature

Degrees Fahrenheit = (°C x 1.8) + 32   Degrees Celsius (Degrees Centigrade; °C) = (°F - 32) x 0.56

*It is common practice to convert from miles per gallon (mpg) to liters/100 kilometers (l/100km), where mpg (Imperial) x l/100 km = 282 and mpg (US) x l/100 km = 235

DECIMALS to MILLIMETERS

Decimal	mm	Decimal	mm
0.001	0.0254	0.500	12.7000
0.002	0.0508	0.510	12.9540
0.003	0.0762	0.520	13.2080
0.004	0.1016	0.530	13.4620
0.005	0.1270	0.540	13.7160
0.006	0.1524	0.550	13.9700
0.007	0.1778	0.560	14.2240
0.008	0.2032	0.570	14.4780
0.009	0.2286	0.580	14.7320
		0.590	14.9860
0.010	0.2540		
0.020	0.5080		
0.030	0.7620		
0.040	1.0160	0.600	15.2400
0.050	1.2700	0.610	15.4940
0.060	1.5240	0.620	15.7480
0.070	1.7780	0.630	16.0020
0.080	2.0320	0.640	16.2560
0.090	2.2860	0.650	16.5100
		0.660	16.7640
0.100	2.5400	0.670	17.0180
0.110	2.7940	0.680	17.2720
0.120	3.0480	0.690	17.5260
0.130	3.3020		
0.140	3.5560		
0.150	3.8100		
0.160	4.0640	0.700	17.7800
0.170	4.3180	0.710	18.0340
0.180	4.5720	0.720	18.2880
0.190	4.8260	0.730	18.5420
		0.740	18.7960
0.200	5.0800	0.750	19.0500
0.210	5.3340	0.760	19.3040
0.220	5.5880	0.770	19.5580
0.230	5.8420	0.780	19.8120
0.240	6.0960	0.790	20.0660
0.250	6.3500		
0.260	6.6040		
0.270	6.8580	0.800	20.3200
0.280	7.1120	0.810	20.5740
0.290	7.3660	0.820	20.8280
		0.830	21.0820
0.300	7.6200	0.840	21.3360
0.310	7.8740	0.850	21.5900
0.320	8.1280	0.860	21.8440
0.330	8.3820	0.870	22.0980
0.340	8.6360	0.880	22.3520
0.350	8.8900	0.890	22.6060
0.360	9.1440		
0.370	9.3980		
0.380	9.6520		
0.390	9.9060	0.900	22.8600
0.400	10.1600	0.910	23.1140
0.410	10.4140	0.920	23.3680
0.420	10.6680	0.930	23.6220
0.430	10.9220	0.940	23.8760
0.440	11.1760	0.950	24.1300
0.450	11.4300	0.960	24.3840
0.460	11.6840	0.970	24.6380
0.470	11.9380	0.980	24.8920
0.480	12.1920	0.990	25.1460
0.490	12.4460	1.000	25.4000

FRACTIONS to DECIMALS to MILLIMETERS

Fraction	Decimal	mm	Fraction	Decimal	mm
1/64	0.0156	0.3969	33/64	0.5156	13.0969
1/32	0.0312	0.7938	17/32	0.5312	13.4938
3/64	0.0469	1.1906	35/64	0.5469	13.8906
1/16	0.0625	1.5875	9/16	0.5625	14.2875
5/64	0.0781	1.9844	37/64	0.5781	14.6844
3/32	0.0938	2.3812	19/32	0.5938	15.0812
7/64	0.1094	2.7781	39/64	0.6094	15.4781
1/8	0.1250	3.1750	5/8	0.6250	15.8750
9/64	0.1406	3.5719	41/64	0.6406	16.2719
5/32	0.1562	3.9688	21/32	0.6562	16.6688
11/64	0.1719	4.3656	43/64	0.6719	17.0656
3/16	0.1875	4.7625	11/16	0.6875	17.4625
13/64	0.2031	5.1594	45/64	0.7031	17.8594
7/32	0.2188	5.5562	23/32	0.7188	18.2562
15/64	0.2344	5.9531	47/64	0.7344	18.6531
1/4	0.2500	6.3500	3/4	0.7500	19.0500
17/64	0.2656	6.7469	49/64	0.7656	19.4469
9/32	0.2812	7.1438	25/32	0.7812	19.8438
19/64	0.2969	7.5406	51/64	0.7969	20.2406
5/16	0.3125	7.9375	13/16	0.8125	20.6375
21/64	0.3281	8.3344	53/64	0.8281	21.0344
11/32	0.3438	8.7312	27/32	0.8438	21.4312
23/64	0.3594	9.1281	55/64	0.8594	21.8281
3/8	0.3750	9.5250	7/8	0.8750	22.2250
25/64	0.3906	9.9219	57/64	0.8906	22.6219
13/32	0.4062	10.3188	29/32	0.9062	23.0188
27/64	0.4219	10.7156	59/64	0.9219	23.4156
7/16	0.4375	11.1125	15/16	0.9375	23.8125
29/64	0.4531	11.5094	61/64	0.9531	24.2094
15/32	0.4688	11.9062	31/32	0.9688	24.6062
31/64	0.4844	12.3031	63/64	0.9844	25.0031
1/2	0.5000	12.7000	1	1.0000	25.4000

Safety first!

Regardless of how enthusiastic you may be about getting on with the job at hand, take the time to ensure that your safety is not jeopardized. A moment's lack of attention can result in an accident, as can failure to observe certain simple safety precautions. The possibility of an accident will always exist, and the following points should not be considered a comprehensive list of all dangers. Rather, they are intended to make you aware of the risks and to encourage a safety conscious approach to all work you carry out on your vehicle.

Essential DOs and DON'Ts

DON'T rely on a jack when working under the vehicle. Always use approved jackstands to support the weight of the vehicle and place them under the recommended lift or support points.

DON'T attempt to loosen extremely tight fasteners (i.e. wheel lug nuts) while the vehicle is on a jack - it may fall.

DON'T start the engine without first making sure that the transmission is in Neutral (or Park where applicable) and the parking brake is set.

DON'T remove the radiator cap from a hot cooling system - let it cool or cover it with a cloth and release the pressure gradually.

DON'T attempt to drain the engine oil until you are sure it has cooled to the point that it will not burn you.

DON'T touch any part of the engine or exhaust system until it has cooled sufficiently to avoid burns.

DON'T siphon toxic liquids such as gasoline, antifreeze and brake fluid by mouth, or allow them to remain on your skin.

DON'T inhale brake lining dust - it is potentially hazardous (see *Asbestos* below).

DON'T allow spilled oil or grease to remain on the floor - wipe it up before someone slips on it.

DON'T use loose fitting wrenches or other tools which may slip and cause injury.

DON'T push on wrenches when loosening or tightening nuts or bolts. Always try to pull the wrench toward you. If the situation calls for pushing the wrench away, push with an open hand to avoid scraped knuckles if the wrench should slip.

DON'T attempt to lift a heavy component alone - get someone to help you.

DON'T *rush or take unsafe shortcuts to finish a job.*

DON'T allow children or animals in or around the vehicle while you are working on it.

DO wear eye protection when using power tools such as a drill, sander, bench grinder, etc. and when working under a vehicle.

DO keep loose clothing and long hair well out of the way of moving parts.

DO make sure that any hoist used has a safe working load rating adequate for the job.

DO get someone to check on you periodically when working alone on a vehicle.

DO carry out work in a logical sequence and make sure that everything is correctly assembled and tightened.

DO keep chemicals and fluids tightly capped and out of the reach of children and pets.

DO remember that your vehicle's safety affects that of yourself and others. If in doubt on any point, get professional advice.

Steering, suspension and brakes

These systems are essential to driving safety, so make sure you have a qualified shop or individual check your work. Also, compressed suspension springs can cause injury if released suddenly - be sure to use a spring compressor.

Airbags

Airbags are explosive devices that can **CAUSE** injury if they deploy while you're working on the vehicle. Follow the manufacturer's instructions to disable the airbag whenever you're working in the vicinity of airbag components.

Asbestos

Certain friction, insulating, sealing, and other products - such as brake linings, brake bands, clutch linings, torque converters, gaskets, etc. - may contain asbestos or other hazardous friction material. Extreme care must be taken to avoid inhalation of dust from such products, since it is hazardous to health. If in doubt, assume that they do contain asbestos.

Fire

Remember at all times that gasoline is highly flammable. Never smoke or have any kind of open flame around when working on a vehicle. But the risk does not end there. A spark caused by an electrical short circuit, by two metal surfaces contacting each other, or even by static electricity built up in your body under certain conditions, can ignite gasoline vapors, which in a confined space are highly explosive. Do not, under any circumstances, use gasoline for cleaning parts. Use an approved safety solvent.

Always disconnect the battery ground (-) cable at the battery before working on any part of the fuel system or electrical system. Never risk spilling fuel on a hot engine or exhaust component. It is strongly recommended that a fire extinguisher suitable for use on fuel and electrical fires be kept handy in the garage or workshop at all times. Never try to extinguish a fuel or electrical fire with water.

Fumes

Certain fumes are highly toxic and can quickly cause unconsciousness and even death if inhaled to any extent. Gasoline vapor falls into this category, as do the vapors from some cleaning solvents. Any draining or pouring of such volatile fluids should be done in a well ventilated area.

When using cleaning fluids and solvents, read the instructions on the container carefully. Never use materials from unmarked containers.

Never run the engine in an enclosed space, such as a garage. Exhaust fumes contain carbon monoxide, which is extremely poisonous. If you need to run the engine, always do so in the open air, or at least have the rear of the vehicle outside the work area.

The battery

Never create a spark or allow a bare light bulb near a battery. They normally give off a certain amount of hydrogen gas, which is highly explosive.

Always disconnect the battery ground (-) cable at the battery before working on the fuel or electrical systems.

If possible, loosen the filler caps or cover when charging the battery from an external source (this does not apply to sealed or maintenance-free batteries). Do not charge at an excessive rate or the battery may burst.

Take care when adding water to a non maintenance-free battery and when carrying a battery. The electrolyte, even when diluted, is very corrosive and should not be allowed to contact clothing or skin.

Always wear eye protection when cleaning the battery to prevent the caustic deposits from entering your eyes.

Household current

When using an electric power tool, inspection light, etc., which operates on household current, always make sure that the tool is correctly connected to its plug and that, where necessary, it is properly grounded. Do not use such items in damp conditions and, again, do not create a spark or apply excessive heat in the vicinity of fuel or fuel vapor.

Secondary ignition system voltage

A severe electric shock can result from touching certain parts of the ignition system (such as the spark plug wires) when the engine is running or being cranked, particularly if components are damp or the insulation is defective. In the case of an electronic ignition system, the secondary system voltage is much higher and could prove fatal.

Hydrofluoric acid

This extremely corrosive acid is formed when certain types of synthetic rubber, found in some O-rings, oil seals, fuel hoses, etc. are exposed to temperatures above 750-degrees F (400-degrees C). The rubber changes into a charred or sticky substance containing the acid. *Once formed, the acid remains dangerous for years. If it gets onto the skin, it may be necessary to amputate the limb concerned.*

When dealing with a vehicle which has suffered a fire, or with components salvaged from such a vehicle, wear protective gloves and discard them after use.

Troubleshooting

Contents

Symptom	Section

Engine
Alternator light fails to come on when key is turned on 13
Alternator light stays on 12
Battery will not hold a charge 11
CHECK ENGINE light on........................ See Chapter 6
Engine backfires... 18
Engine continues to run after being turned off.................. 21
Engine hard to start when cold.................................. 4
Engine hard to start when hot................................... 5
Engine lacks power... 17
Engine 'lopes' while idling or idles erratically................ 8
Engine misses at idle speed..................................... 9
Engine misses throughout driving speed range 14
Engine rotates but will not start 2
Engine stalls 16
Engine starts but stops immediately............................ 7
Engine surges while holding accelerator steady 19
Engine will not rotate when attempting to start................ 1
Excessive fuel consumption 24
Excessive oil consumption 23
Excessively high idle speed..................................... 10
Fuel odor 25
Hesitation or stumble during acceleration 15
Low oil pressure 22
Miscellaneous engine noises..................................... 26
Pinging or knocking engine sounds when engine
  is under load... 20
Starter motor noisy or engages roughly 6
Starter motor operates without turning engine 3

Cooling system
Abnormal coolant loss 31
Corrosion 33
External coolant leakage 29
Internal coolant leakage 30
Overcooling 28
Overheating 27
Poor coolant circulation 32

Clutch
Clutch pedal stays on floor when disengaged.................... 39
Clutch slips (engine speed increases with no increase
  in vehicle speed) 35
Fails to release (pedal pressed to the floor - shift lever
  does not move freely in and out of Reverse) 34
Grabbing (chattering) as clutch is engaged..................... 36
Squeal or rumble with clutch disengaged (pedal depressed)...... 38
Squeal or rumble with clutch engaged (pedal released) 37

Manual transaxle
Difficulty engaging gears 45
Noise occurs while shifting gears 46
Noisy in all gears 41
Noisy in Neutral with engine running 40
Noisy in one particular gear 42
Oil leaks... 44
Slips out of gear... 43

Symptom	Section

Automatic transaxle
Engine will start in gears other than Park or without brake
  pedal being depressed....................................... 50
Fluid leakage 47
General shift mechanism problems............................... 48
Transaxle slips, shifts rough, is noisy or has no
  drive in forward or Reverse gears 51
Transaxle will not downshift with the accelerator
  pedal pressed to the floor.................................. 49

Driveshaft
Knock or clunk when transmission is under initial load
  (just after transmission is put into gear) 53
Leaks at front of driveshaft 52
Metallic grating sound consistent with vehicle speed 54
Scraping noise.. 56
Vibration 55

Rear axle and differential
Knocking sound when starting or shifting gears................. 58
Noise - same when in drive as when vehicle is coasting......... 57
Noise when turning.. 59
Oil leaks... 61
Vibration 60

Brakes
Brake pedal feels spongy when depressed........................ 65
Brake pedal pulsates during brake application.................. 68
Brakes drag (indicated by sluggish engine performance or
  wheels being very hot after driving) 69
Excessive brake pedal travel................................... 64
Excessive effort required to stop vehicle...................... 66
Noise (high-pitched squeal or scraping sound) 63
Pedal travels to the floor with little resistance.............. 67
Rear brakes lock up under heavy brake application.............. 71
Rear brakes lock up under light brake application.............. 70
Vehicle pulls to one side during braking 62

Suspension and steering
Excessive pitching and/or rolling around
  corners or during braking 74
Excessive play in steering 77
Excessive tire wear (not specific to one area) 83
Excessive tire wear on inside edge 85
Excessive tire wear on outside edge 84
Excessively stiff steering 76
Lack of power assistance 78
Miscellaneous noises 82
Noisy power steering pump 81
Shimmy, shake or vibration 73
Steering effort not the same in both directions 80
Steering wheel fails to return to straight-ahead position...... 79
Tire tread worn in one place 86
Vehicle pulls to one side 72
Wandering or general instability 75

Engine

1 Engine will not rotate when attempting to start

1   Battery terminal connections loose or corroded. Check the cable terminals at the battery; tighten cable clamp and/or clean off corrosion as necessary (see Chapter 1).
2   Battery discharged or faulty. If the cable ends are clean and tight on the battery posts, turn the key to the On position and switch on the headlights or windshield wipers. If they won't run, the battery is discharged.
3   Automatic transmission not engaged in Park (P) or Neutral (N).
4   Broken, loose or disconnected wires in the starting circuit. Inspect all wires and connectors at the battery, starter solenoid and ignition switch (on steering column).
5   Starter motor pinion jammed in flywheel/driveplate ring gear. Remove the starter (Chapter 5) and inspect the pinion and ring gear (Chapter 2).
6   Starter solenoid faulty (Chapter 5).
7   Starter motor faulty (Chapter 5).
8   Ignition switch faulty (Chapter 12).
9   Engine seized. Try to turn the crankshaft with a large socket and breaker bar on the pulley bolt.
10   Starter relay faulty (Chapter 4).

2 Engine rotates but will not start

1   Fuel tank empty.
2   Battery discharged (engine rotates slowly).
3   Battery terminal connections loose or corroded.
4   Fuel not reaching fuel injectors. Check for clogged fuel filter or lines and defective fuel pump. Also make sure the tank vent lines aren't clogged (Chapter 4).
5   Low cylinder compression. Check as described in Chapter 2.
6   Water in fuel. Drain tank and fill with new fuel.
7   Defective ignition coil(s) (Chapter 5).
8   Dirty or clogged fuel injector(s) (Chapter 4).
9   Worn, faulty or incorrectly gapped spark plugs (Chapter 1).
10   Timing chain or belt failure or wear affecting valve timing (Chapter 2).
11   Fuel injection or engine control systems failure (Chapters 4 and 6).
12   Defective MAF sensor (Chapter 6).

3 Starter motor operates without turning engine

1   Starter pinion sticking. Remove the starter (Chapter 5) and inspect.
2   Starter pinion or flywheel/driveplate teeth worn or broken. Remove the starter and inspect (Chapter 5).

4 Engine hard to start when cold

1   Battery discharged or low. Check as described in Chapter 1.
2   Fuel not reaching the fuel injectors. Check the fuel filter, lines and fuel pump (Chapters 1 and 4).
3   Defective spark plugs (Chapter 1).
4   Defective engine coolant temperature sensor (Chapter 6).
5   Fuel injection or engine control systems malfunction (Chapters 4 and 6).

5 Engine hard to start when hot

1   Air filter dirty (Chapter 1).
2   Fuel injection or engine control systems malfunction (Chapters 4 and 6).

6 Starter motor noisy or engages roughly

1   Pinion or driveplate teeth worn or broken. Remove the starter and inspect (Chapter 5).
2   Starter motor mounting bolts loose or missing.

7 Engine starts but stops immediately

1   Intake manifold vacuum leaks. Make sure all mounting bolts/nuts are tight and all vacuum hoses connected to the manifold are attached properly and in good condition.
2   Insufficient fuel pressure (see Chapter 4).
3   Fuel injection or engine control systems malfunction (Chapters 4 and 6).

8 Engine 'lopes' while idling or idles erratically

1   Vacuum leaks. Check mounting bolts at the intake manifold for tightness. Make sure that all vacuum hoses are connected and in good condition. Use a stethoscope or a length of fuel hose held against your ear to listen for vacuum leaks while the engine is running. A hissing sound will be heard. A soapy water solution will also detect leaks. Check the intake manifold gasket surfaces.
2   Air filter clogged (Chapter 1).
3   Fuel pump not delivering sufficient fuel (Chapter 4).
4   Leaking head gasket. Perform a cylinder compression check (Chapter 2).
5   Timing chain or belt worn (Chapter 2).

6   Camshaft lobes worn (Chapter 2).
7   Valves burned or otherwise leaking (Chapter 2).
8   Ignition system not operating properly (Chapters 1 and 5).
9   Fuel injection or engine control systems malfunction (Chapters 4 and 6).

9 Engine misses at idle speed

1   Spark plugs faulty or not gapped properly (Chapter 1).
2   Ignition system problem (Chapter 5).
3   Clogged fuel filter and/or foreign matter in fuel.
4   Vacuum leaks at intake manifold or hose connections. Check as described in Section 8.
5   Low or uneven cylinder compression. Check as described in Chapter 2.
6   Fuel injection or engine control systems malfunction (Chapters 4 and 6).

10 Excessively high idle speed

1   Vacuum leaks at intake manifold or hose connections. Check as described in Section 8.
2   Fuel injection or engine control systems malfunction (Chapters 4 and 6).

11 Battery will not hold a charge

1   Drivebelt defective or not adjusted properly (Chapter 1).
2   Battery cables loose or corroded (Chapter 1).
3   Alternator not charging properly (Chapter 5).
4   Loose, broken or faulty wires in the charging circuit (Chapter 5).
5   Short circuit causing a continuous drain on the battery.
6   Battery defective internally.

12 Alternator light stays on

1   Fault in alternator or charging circuit (Chapter 5).
2   Drivebelt defective or not properly adjusted (Chapter 1).

13 Alternator light fails to come on when key is turned on

1   Faulty bulb (Chapter 12).
2   Defective alternator (Chapter 5).
3   Instrument cluster defective (Chapter 12).

14 Engine misses throughout driving speed range

1 Fuel filter clogged and/or impurities in the fuel system.
2 Faulty or incorrectly gapped spark plugs (Chapter 1).
3 Emissions system components faulty (Chapter 6).
4 Low or uneven cylinder compression pressures. Check as described in Chapter 2.
5 Weak or faulty ignition coil(s) (Chapter 5).
6 Vacuum leaks at intake manifold or vacuum hoses (see Section 8).
7 Dirty or clogged fuel injector(s) (Chapter 4).
8 Fuel injection or engine control systems malfunction (Chapters 4 and 6).

15 Hesitation or stumble during acceleration

1 Ignition system not operating properly (Chapter 5).
2 Dirty or clogged fuel injector(s) (Chapter 4).
3 Low fuel pressure. Check for proper operation of the fuel pump and for restrictions in the fuel filter and lines (Chapter 4).
4 Fuel injection or engine control systems malfunction (Chapters 4 and 6).

16 Engine stalls

1 Fuel filter clogged and/or water and impurities in the fuel system (Chapter 1).
2 Emissions system components faulty (Chapter 6).
3 Faulty or incorrectly gapped spark plugs (Chapter 1).
4 Vacuum leak at the intake manifold or vacuum hoses. Check as described in Section 8.
5 Fuel injection or engine control systems malfunction (Chapters 4 and 6).

17 Engine lacks power

1 Faulty or incorrectly gapped spark plugs (Chapter 1).
2 Air filter dirty (Chapter 1).
3 Faulty ignition coil(s) (Chapter 5).
4 Brakes binding (Chapters 1 and 9).
5 Automatic transmission fluid level incorrect, causing slippage (Chapter 1).
6 Fuel filter clogged and/or impurities in the fuel system (Chapter 4).
7 Use of sub-standard fuel. Fill tank with proper octane fuel.
8 Low or uneven cylinder compression pressures. Check as described in Chapter 2.
9 Vacuum leak at intake manifold or vacuum hoses (check as described in Section 8).
10 Dirty or clogged fuel injector(s) (Chapters 1 and 4).
11 Fuel injection or engine control systems malfunction (Chapters 4 and 6).
12 Restricted exhaust system (Chapter 4).

18 Engine backfires

1 Vacuum leak (refer to Section 8).
2 Damaged valve springs or sticking valves (Chapter 2).
3 Vacuum leak at the intake manifold or vacuum hoses (see Section 8).

19 Engine surges while holding accelerator steady

1 Vacuum leak at the intake manifold or vacuum hoses (see Section 8).
2 Restricted air filter (Chapter 1).
3 Fuel pump or pressure regulator defective (Chapter 4).
4 Fuel injection or engine control systems malfunction (Chapters 4 and 6).

20 Pinging or knocking engine sounds when engine is under load

1 Incorrect grade of fuel. Fill tank with fuel of the proper octane rating.
2 Carbon build-up in combustion chambers. Remove cylinder head(s) and clean combustion chambers (Chapter 2).
3 Incorrect spark plugs (Chapter 1).
4 Fuel injection or engine control systems malfunction (Chapters 4 and 6).
5 Restricted exhaust system (Chapter 4).

21 Engine continues to run after being turned off

Defective ignition switch (Chapter 12).

22 Low oil pressure

1 Improper grade of oil.
2 Oil pump worn or damaged (Chapter 2).
3 Engine overheating (refer to Section 27).
4 Clogged oil filter (Chapter 1).
5 Clogged oil strainer (Chapter 2).
6 Oil pressure gauge not working properly (Chapter 2).

23 Excessive oil consumption

1 Pistons and cylinders excessively worn (Chapter 2).
2 Piston rings not installed correctly on pistons (Chapter 2).
3 Worn or damaged piston rings (Chapter 2).
4 Intake and/or exhaust valve oil seals worn or damaged.
5 Worn valve stems or guides.
6 Worn or damaged valves/guides.
7 Faulty or incorrect PCV valve allowing too much crankcase airflow.

24 Excessive fuel consumption

1 Dirty or clogged air filter element (Chapter 1).
2 Low tire pressure or incorrect tire size (Chapter 10).
3 Inspect for binding brakes (Chapters 1 and 9).
4 Fuel leakage. Check all connections, lines and components in the fuel system (Chapter 4).
5 Dirty or clogged fuel injectors (Chapter 4).
6 Fuel injection or engine control systems malfunction (Chapters 4 and 6).
7 Thermostat stuck open (Chapter 3).
8 Improperly operating transmission.

25 Fuel odor

1 Fuel leakage. Check all connections, lines and components in the fuel system (Chapter 4).
2 Fuel tank overfilled. Fill only to automatic shut-off.
3 Evaporative Emissions Control system problem (Chapter 6).

26 Miscellaneous engine noises

1 A strong dull noise that becomes more rapid as the engine accelerates indicates worn or damaged crankshaft bearings or an unevenly worn crankshaft. To pinpoint the trouble spot, disconnect the electrical connector from one coil at a time and crank the engine over. If the noise stops, the cylinder with the removed plug wire or disconnected coil indicates the problem area. Replace the bearing and/or service or replace the crankshaft (Chapter 2).
2 A similar (yet slightly higher pitched) noise to the crankshaft knocking described in the previous paragraph, that becomes more rapid as the engine accelerates, indicates worn or damaged connecting rod bearings (Chapter 2). The procedure for locating the problem cylinder is the same as described in Paragraph 1.
3 An overlapping metallic noise that increases in intensity as the engine speed increases, yet diminishes as the engine warms up indicates abnormal piston and cylinder wear (Chapter 2). To locate the problem cylinder, use the procedure described in Paragraph 1.

4   A rapid clicking noise that becomes faster as the engine accelerates indicates a worn piston pin or piston pin hole. This sound will happen each time the piston hits the highest and lowest points in the stroke (Chapter 2). The procedure for locating the problem piston is described in Paragraph 1.

5   A metallic clicking noise coming from the water pump indicates worn or damaged water pump bearings or pump. Replace the water pump with a new one (Chapter 3).

6   A rapid tapping sound or clicking sound that becomes faster as the engine speed increases indicates "valve tapping." This can be identified by holding one end of a section of hose to your ear and placing the other end at different spots along the valve cover. The point where the sound is loudest indicates the problem valve. If the pushrod and rocker arm components are in good shape, you likely have a collapsed valve lifter. Changing the engine oil and adding a high viscosity oil treatment will sometimes cure a stuck lifter problem. If the problem persists, the lifters, pushrods and rocker arms must be removed for inspection (see Chapter 2).

7   A steady metallic rattling or rapping sound coming from the area of the timing chain cover indicates a worn, damaged or out-of-adjustment timing chain. Service or replace the chain and related components (Chapter 2).

Cooling system

27   Overheating

1   Insufficient coolant in system (Chapter 1).
2   Drivebelt defective or not adjusted properly (Chapter 1).
3   Radiator core blocked or dirty and restricted (Chapter 3).
4   Thermostat faulty (Chapter 3).
5   Cooling fan not functioning properly (Chapter 3).
6   Expansion tank cap not maintaining proper pressure. Have cap pressure tested by gas station or repair shop.
7   Defective water pump (Chapter 3).
8   Improper grade of engine oil.
9   Inaccurate temperature gauge (Chapter 12).

28   Overcooling

1   Thermostat faulty (Chapter 3).
2   Inaccurate temperature gauge (Chapter 12).

29   External coolant leakage

1   Deteriorated or damaged hoses. Loose clamps at hose connections (Chapter 1).
2   Water pump seals defective. If this is the case, water will drip from the weep hole in the water pump body (Chapter 3).
3   Leakage from radiator core or side tanks. This will require the radiator to be professionally repaired (see Chapter 3 for removal procedures).
4   Leakage from the expansion tank or cap.
5   Engine drain plugs or water jacket freeze plugs leaking (see Chapters 1 and 2).
6   Leak from coolant temperature switch (Chapter 3).
7   Leak from damaged gaskets or small cracks (Chapter 2).

30   Internal coolant leakage

Note: *Internal coolant leaks can usually be detected by examining the oil. Check the dipstick and the underside of the engine oil filler cap for water deposits and an oil consistency like that of a milkshake.*

1   Leaking cylinder head gasket. Have the system pressure tested or remove the cylinder head (Chapter 2) and inspect.
2   Cracked cylinder bore or cylinder head. Dismantle engine and inspect (Chapter 2).

31   Abnormal coolant loss

1   Overfilled cooling system (Chapter 1).
2   Coolant boiling away due to overheating (see causes in Section 27).
3   Internal or external leakage (see Sections 29 and 30).
4   Faulty expansion tank cap. Have the cap pressure tested.
5   Cooling system being pressurized by engine compression. This could be due to a cracked head or block or leaking head gasket(s). Have the system tested for the presence of combustion gas in the coolant at a shop. (Combustion leak detectors are also available at some auto parts stores.)

32   Poor coolant circulation

1   Inoperative water pump (Chapter 3).
2   Restriction in cooling system. Drain, flush and refill the system (Chapter 1). If necessary, remove the radiator (Chapter 3) and have it reverse flushed or professionally cleaned.
3   Loose water pump drivebelt (Chapter 1).
4   Thermostat sticking (Chapter 3).
5   Insufficient coolant (Chapter 1).

33   Corrosion

1   Excessive impurities in the water. Soft, clean water is recommended. Distilled or rainwater is satisfactory.
2   Insufficient antifreeze solution (refer to Chapter 1 for the proper ratio of water to antifreeze).
3   Infrequent flushing and draining of system. Regular flushing of the cooling system should be carried out at the specified intervals as described in (Chapter 1).

Clutch

Note: *All clutch service information is located in Chapter 8, unless otherwise noted.*

34   Fails to release (pedal pressed to the floor - shift lever does not move freely in and out of Reverse)

1   Clutch plate warped, distorted or otherwise damaged.
2   Diaphragm spring fatigued. Remove clutch cover/pressure plate assembly and inspect.
3   Seized pilot bearing.

35   Clutch slips (engine speed increases with no increase in vehicle speed)

1   Worn or oil-soaked clutch plate.
2   Clutch plate not broken in. It may take 30 or 40 normal starts for a new clutch to seat.

36   Grabbing (chattering) as clutch is engaged

1   Oil on clutch plate. Remove and inspect. Repair any leaks.
2   Worn or loose engine or transmission mounts. They may move slightly when clutch is released. Inspect mounts and bolts.
3   Worn splines on transmission input shaft. Remove clutch components and inspect.
4   Warped pressure plate or flywheel. Remove clutch components and inspect.
5   Diaphragm spring fatigued. Remove clutch cover/pressure plate assembly and inspect.
6   Clutch linings hardened or warped.
7   Clutch lining rivets loose.

37   Squeal or rumble with clutch engaged (pedal released)

1   Release bearing binding on transmission shaft. Remove clutch components and check bearing. Remove any burrs or nicks, clean and relubricate before reinstallation.
2   Clutch plate cracked.
3   Fatigued clutch plate torsion springs. Replace clutch plate.

38 Squeal or rumble with clutch disengaged (pedal depressed)

1 Worn or damaged release bearing.
2 Worn or broken pressure plate diaphragm fingers.
3 Defective pilot bearing.

39 Clutch pedal stays on floor when disengaged

Defective release system.

Manual transaxle

Note: *All manual transaxle service information is located in Chapter 7A, unless otherwise noted.*

40 Noisy in Neutral with engine running

1 Input shaft bearing worn.
2 Damaged main drive gear bearing.
3 Insufficient transaxle oil (Chapter 1).
4 Transaxle oil in poor condition. Drain and fill with proper grade oil. Check old oil for water and debris (Chapter 1).

41 Noisy in all gears

1 Any of the above causes, and/or:
2 Worn or damaged output gear bearings or shaft.

42 Noisy in one particular gear

1 Worn, damaged or chipped gear teeth.
2 Worn or damaged synchronizer.

43 Slips out of gear

1 Shift linkage binding.
2 Broken or loose input gear bearing retainer.
3 Worn linkage.
4 Damaged or worn check balls, fork rod ball grooves or check springs.
5 Worn mainshaft or countershaft bearings.
6 Excessive gear end play.
7 Worn synchronizers.
8 Chipped or worn gear teeth.

44 Oil leaks

1 Excessive amount of lubricant in transaxle (see Chapter 1 for correct checking procedures). Drain lubricant as required.

2 Oil seal damaged.
3 To pinpoint a leak, first remove all built-up dirt and grime from the transaxle. Degreasing agents and/or steam cleaning will achieve this. With the underside clean, drive the vehicle at low speeds so the air flow will not blow the leak far from its source. Raise the vehicle and determine where the leak is located.

45 Difficulty engaging gears

1 Clutch not releasing completely.
2 Insufficient transaxle oil (Chapter 1).
3 Transaxle oil in poor condition. Drain and fill with proper grade oil. Check oil for water and debris (Chapter 1).
4 Damaged shift fork.
5 Worn or damaged synchronizer.

46 Noise occurs while shifting gears

1 Check for proper operation of the clutch (Chapter 8).
2 Faulty synchronizer assemblies.

Automatic transaxle

Note: *Due to the complexity of the automatic transaxle, it's difficult for the home mechanic to properly diagnose and service. For problems other than the following, the vehicle should be taken to a reputable mechanic.*

47 Fluid leakage

1 Automatic transmission fluid is a transparent yellow color, and fluid leaks should not be confused with engine oil which can easily be blown by air flow to the transaxle.
2 To pinpoint a leak, first remove all built-up dirt and grime from the transaxle. Degreasing agents and/or steam cleaning will achieve this. With the underside clean, drive the vehicle at low speeds so the air flow will not blow the leak far from its source. Raise the vehicle and determine where the leak is located. Common areas of leakage are:

a) **Fluid pan:** *tighten mounting bolts and/or replace pan gasket as necessary (Chapter 1).*
b) **Rear extension:** *tighten bolts and/or replace oil seal as necessary.*
c) **Filler pipe:** *replace the rubber oil seal where pipe enters transmission case.*
d) **Transmission oil lines:** *tighten fittings where lines enter transmission case and/or replace lines.*
e) **Vent pipe:** *transmission overfilled and/or water in fluid (see checking procedures, Chapter 1).*
f) **Vehicle speed sensor:** *replace the O-ring where speed sensor enters transmission case.*

48 General shift mechanism problems

Chapter 7B deals with checking and adjusting the shift linkage on automatic transaxles. Common problems which may be caused by out of adjustment linkage are:

a) *Engine starting in gears other than P (park) or N (Neutral).*
b) *Indicator pointing to a gear other than the one actually engaged.*
c) *Vehicle moves with shift lever in P (Park) position.*

49 Transaxle will not downshift with the accelerator pedal pressed to the floor

Since these transaxles are electronically controlled, check for any diagnostic trouble codes stored in the PCM. The actual repair will most likely have to be performed by a qualified repair shop with the proper equipment.

50 Engine will start in gears other than Park or without brake pedal being depressed

Shift interlock system out of adjustment (Chapter 7B).

51 Transaxle slips, shifts rough, is noisy or has no drive in forward or Reverse gears

1 There are many probable causes for the above problems, but the home mechanic should concern himself only with one possibility: fluid level.
2 Before taking the vehicle to a shop, check the fluid level and condition as described in Chapter 1. Add fluid, if necessary, or change the fluid and filter if needed. If problems persist, have a professional diagnose the transaxle.
3 Transmission fluid break down after 30,000 miles.

Driveshaft

Note: *Refer to Chapter 8, unless otherwise specified, for service information.*

52 Leaks at front of driveshaft

Defective transmission or transfer case seal. See Chapter 7 for replacement procedure. As this is done, check the splined yoke for burrs or roughness that could damage the new seal. Remove burrs with a fine file or whetstone.

53 Knock or clunk when transmission is under initial load (just after transmission is put into gear)

1 Loose or disconnected rear suspension components. Check all mounting bolts and bushings (Chapters 7 and 10).
2 Loose driveshaft bolts. Inspect all bolts and nuts and tighten them securely.
3 Worn or damaged universal joint bearings (Chapter 8).
4 Worn sleeve yoke and mainshaft spline.

54 Metallic grating sound consistent with vehicle speed

Pronounced wear in the universal joints or driveshaft center support bearing. Replace driveshaft or center support bearing, as necessary.

55 Vibration

Note: *Before blaming the driveshaft, make sure the tires are perfectly balanced and perform the following test.*
1 Install a tachometer inside the vehicle to monitor engine speed as the vehicle is driven. Drive the vehicle and note the engine speed at which the vibration (roughness) is most pronounced. Now shift the transaxle to a different gear and bring the engine speed to the same point.
2 If the vibration occurs at the same engine speed (rpm) regardless of which gear the transaxle is in, the driveshaft is NOT at fault since the driveshaft speed varies.
3 If the vibration decreases or is eliminated when the transaxle is in a different gear at the same engine speed, refer to the following probable causes:
a) *Bent or dented driveshaft. Inspect and replace as necessary.*
b) *Undercoating or built-up dirt, etc. on the driveshaft. Clean the shaft thoroughly.*
c) *Worn universal joint bearings. Replace the U-joints or driveshaft as necessary.*
d) *Driveshaft and/or companion flange out of balance. Check for missing weights on the shaft. Have the driveshaft balanced if problem persists.*
e) *Loose driveshaft mounting bolts/nuts.*
f) *Center support bearing is worn or damaged (Chapter 10).*

56 Scraping noise

Make sure there is nothing, such as an exhaust heat shield, rubbing on the driveshaft.

Axle(s) and differential

Note: *For differential servicing information, refer to Chapter 8, unless otherwise specified.*

57 Noise - same when in drive as when vehicle is coasting

1 Road noise. No corrective action available.
2 Tire noise. Inspect tires and check tire pressures (Chapter 1).
3 Front wheel bearings loose, worn or damaged (Chapter 1).
4 Insufficient differential oil (Chapter 1).
5 Defective differential.

58 Knocking sound when starting or shifting gears

Defective or incorrectly adjusted differential.

59 Noise when turning

Defective differential.

60 Vibration

See probable causes under *Driveshaft.* Proceed under the guidelines listed for the driveshaft. If the problem persists, check the rear wheel bearings by raising the rear of the vehicle and spinning the wheels by hand. Listen for evidence of rough (noisy) bearings. Remove and inspect (Chapter 8).

61 Oil leaks

1 Pinion oil seal damaged (Chapter 8).
2 Driveaxle oil seals damaged (Chapter 8).
3 Differential cover leaking. Tighten mounting bolts or replace the gasket as required.
4 Loose filler plug on differential (Chapter 1).
5 Clogged or damaged breather on differential.

Brakes

Note: *Before assuming a brake problem exists, make sure the tires are in good condition and inflated properly, the front end alignment is correct and the vehicle is not loaded with weight in an unequal manner. All service procedures for the brakes are included in Chapter 9, unless otherwise noted.*

62 Vehicle pulls to one side during braking

1 Defective, damaged or contaminated brake pad on one side. Inspect as described in Chapter 1. Refer to Chapter 9 if replacement is required.
2 Excessive wear of brake pad material or disc on one side. Inspect and repair as necessary.
3 Loose front suspension components. Inspect and tighten all bolts securely (Chapters 1 and 10).
4 Defective front brake caliper assembly. Remove caliper and inspect for stuck piston or damage.
5 Scored or out-of-round disc.
6 Loose brake caliper mounting bolts.

63 Noise (high-pitched squeal or scraping sound)

1 Brake pads worn out. Replace pads with new ones immediately!
2 Glazed or contaminated pads.
3 Dirty or scored disc.

64 Excessive brake pedal travel

1 Partial brake system failure. Inspect entire system (Chapter 1) and correct as required.
2 Insufficient fluid in master cylinder. Check (Chapter 1) and add fluid - bleed system if necessary.
3 Air in system. Bleed system.
4 Defective master cylinder.

65 Brake pedal feels spongy when depressed

1 Air in brake lines. Bleed the brake system.
2 Deteriorated rubber brake hoses. Inspect all system hoses and lines. Replace parts as necessary.
3 Master cylinder mounting nuts loose.
4 Master cylinder faulty.
5 Incorrect brake pad clearance.
6 Clogged reservoir cap vent hole.
7 Deformed rubber brake lines.
8 Soft or swollen caliper seals.
9 Poor quality brake fluid. Bleed entire system and fill with new approved fluid.

66 Excessive effort required to stop vehicle

1 Power brake booster not operating properly.

2   Excessively worn brake pads. Check and replace if necessary.
3   One or more caliper pistons seized or sticking. Inspect and rebuild as required.
4   Brake pads contaminated with oil or grease. Inspect and replace as required.
5   Worn or damaged master cylinder or caliper assemblies. Check particularly for frozen pistons.

67   Pedal travels to the floor with little resistance

Little or no fluid in the master cylinder reservoir caused by leaking caliper piston(s) or loose, damaged or disconnected brake lines. Inspect entire system and repair as necessary.

68   Brake pedal pulsates during brake application

1   Wheel bearings damaged or worn (Chapter 10)
2   Caliper not sliding properly due to improper installation or obstructions. Remove and inspect.
3   Disc not within specifications. Check for excessive lateral runout and parallelism. Have the discs resurfaced or replace them with new ones. Also make sure that all discs are the same thickness.

69   Brakes drag (indicated by sluggish engine performance or wheels being very hot after driving)

1   Master cylinder piston seized in bore. Replace master cylinder.
2   Caliper piston seized in bore.
3   Parking brake assembly will not release.
4   Clogged or internally split brake lines.
5   Brake pedal height improperly adjusted.

70   Rear brakes lock up under light brake application

1   Tire pressures too high.
2   Tires excessively worn (Chapter 1).

71   Rear brakes lock up under heavy brake application

1   Tire pressures too high.
2   Tires excessively worn (Chapter 1).
3   Front brake pads contaminated with oil, mud or water. Clean or replace the pads.
4   Front brake pads excessively worn.

Suspension and steering

Note: *All service procedures for the suspension and steering systems are included in Chapter 10, unless otherwise noted.*

72   Vehicle pulls to one side

1   Tire pressures uneven (Chapter 1).
2   Defective tire (Chapter 1).
3   Excessive wear in suspension or steering components (Chapter 1).
4   Front end alignment incorrect.
5   Front brakes dragging. Inspect as described in Section 69.
6   Wheel bearings improperly adjusted (Chapter 1).
7   Wheel bolts loose.

73   Shimmy, shake or vibration

1   Tire or wheel out of balance or out of round.
2   Loose, worn or out of adjustment wheel bearings (Chapter 1).
3   Shock absorbers and/or suspension components worn or damaged (see Chapter 10).

74   Excessive pitching and/or rolling around corners or during braking

1   Defective shock absorbers. Replace as a set.
2   Sagging springs.
3   Worn or damaged stabilizer bar or bushings.

75   Wandering or general instability

1   Improper tire pressures.
2   Incorrect front end alignment.
3   Worn or damaged steering linkage or suspension components.
4   Improperly adjusted steering gear.
5   Out-of-balance wheels.
6   Loose wheel bolts.
7   Worn rear shock absorbers.

76   Excessively stiff steering

1   Lack of fluid in the power steering fluid reservoir, where appropriate (Chapter 1).
2   Incorrect tire pressures (Chapter 1).
3   Front end out of alignment.
4   Steering gear out of adjustment or lacking lubrication.
5   Worn or damaged steering gear.
6   Low tire pressures.
7   Worn or damaged balljoints.
8   Worn or damaged tie-rod ends.

77   Excessive play in steering

1   Worn wheel bearings (Chapter 1).
2   Excessive wear in suspension bushings (Chapter 1).
3   Steering gear worn.
4   Incorrect front end alignment.
5   Steering gear mounting bolts loose.
6   Worn or damaged tie-rod ends.

78   Lack of power assistance

1   Drivebelt faulty or tensioner defective (Chapter 1).
2   Fluid level low (Chapter 1).
3   Hoses or pipes restricting the flow. Inspect and replace parts as necessary.
4   Air in power steering system. Bleed system.
5   Defective power steering pump.

79   Steering wheel fails to return to straight-ahead position

1   Incorrect front end alignment.
2   Tire pressures low.
3   Worn or damaged balljoint.
4   Worn or damaged tie-rod end.
5   Lack of fluid in power steering pump.

80   Steering effort not the same in both directions

1   Leaks in steering gear.
2   Clogged fluid passage in steering gear.

81   Noisy power steering pump

1   Insufficient fluid in pump.
2   Clogged hoses or oil filter in pump.
3   Loose pulley.
4   Drivebelt faulty or tensioner defective (Chapter 1).
5   Defective pump.

82   Miscellaneous noises

1   Improper tire pressures.
2   Defective balljoint or tie-rod end.
3   Loose or worn steering gear or suspension components.
4   Defective shock absorber.
5   Defective wheel bearing.
6   Worn or damaged suspension bushings.
7   Loose wheel lug nuts.
8   Worn or damaged shock absorber mounting bushing.
9   Worn stabilizer bar bushings.
10   Incorrect rear axle endplay.
11   See also causes of noises at the rear axle and driveshaft.

83 Excessive tire wear (not specific to one area)

1   Incorrect tire pressures.
2   Tires out of balance.
3   Wheels damaged. Inspect and replace as necessary.
4   Suspension or steering components worn (Chapter 1).
5   Front end alignment incorrect.
6   Lack of proper tire rotation routine. See *Routine maintenance schedule*, Chapter 1.

84 Excessive tire wear on outside edge

1   Incorrect tire pressure.
2   Excessive speed in turns.
3   Front end alignment incorrect.

85 Excessive tire wear on inside edge

1   Incorrect tire pressure.
2   Front end alignment incorrect.

86 Tire tread worn in one place

1   Tires out of balance.
2   Damaged or buckled wheel. Inspect and replace if necessary.
3   Defective tire.

Chapter 1
Tune-up and routine maintenance

Contents

	Section
Air filter replacement	7
Automatic transaxle fluid change	22
Battery check, maintenance and charging	9
Brake fluid change	20
Brake system check	16
Center differential lubricant level check (all-wheel drive models with automatic transaxles)	25
Cooling system check	13
Cooling system servicing (draining, flushing and refilling)	28
Drivebelt check and replacement	19
Engine oil and filter change	6
Exhaust system check	14
Fluid level checks	4
Front differential lubricant level check (automatic transaxles)	26
Fuel filter replacement	27
Fuel system check	18
Interior ventilation filter replacement	15
Introduction	2
Maintenance schedule	1
Manual transaxle lubricant change	24
Rear differential lubricant change	23
Seat belt check	11
Service indicator resetting	See Section 6
Spark plug check and replacement	21
Suspension, steering and driveaxle boot check	17
Tire and tire pressure checks	5
Tire rotation	10
Tune-up general information	3
Underhood hose check and replacement	12
Windshield wiper blade inspection and replacement	8

Specifications

Recommended lubricants and fluids

Note: *Listed here are manufacturer recommendations at the time this manual was written. Manufacturers occasionally upgrade their fluid and lubricant specifications, so check with your local auto parts store for current recommendations.*

Engine oil	API "certified for gasoline engines" synthetic
Viscosity	5W-30 (see accompanying chart)
Fuel	Unleaded gasoline, 91 octane minimum
Automatic transaxle fluid	
09L transaxle	G 055 005 A2 or equivalent
01V transaxle	G 052 162 (-A2), Esso type LT 71141, or equivalent
01J (CVT) transaxle	G 052 180 (-A2) or equivalent
Manual transaxle lubricant	SAE 75W90 synthetic gear oil
Differential	
Front (automatic transaxles)	
09L and 01V transaxles	SAE 75W-90 synthetic gear oil
01J transaxle	G 052 190 (-A2) or equivalent
Rear (all-wheel drive models)	SAE 90 synthetic gear oil
Center (all-wheel drive models with automatic transaxle)	SAE 75W-90 synthetic gear oil
Power steering fluid	Hydraulic mineral fluid
Brake and clutch fluid	DOT 4 brake fluid
Engine coolant	Phosphate-free coolant 50/50 mixture of G 012 (purple) antifreeze and demineralized water
Hood and trunk hinge lubricant	Lubriplate, lubricant aerosol spray
Door hinge and check spring grease	NLGI no. 2 multi-purpose grease
Key lock cylinder lubricant	Graphite spray
Hood latch assembly lubricant	NLGI no. 2 multi-purpose grease
Door latch lubricant	NLGI no. 2 multi-purpose grease or equivalent

Capacities*

Engine oil (including filter)
1.8L four-cylinder engine
2002 and 2003... 3.7 quarts (3.5 liters)
2004 through 2006... 4.3 quarts (4.1 liters)
2.0L four-cylinder engine.. 4.8 quarts (4.5 liters)
3.0L V6 engine .... 6.8 quarts (6.4 liters)
3.2L V6 engine
2005 .... 8.6 quarts (8.1 liters)
2006 and later.. 6.9 quarts (6.5 liters)
Manual transaxle
01X 6 speed (FWD) .... 2.4 quarts (2.25 liters)
012/01W 5 speed (FWD) .... 2.4 quarts (2.25 liters)
01A 5 speed (AWD) .... 2.9 quarts (2.75 liters)
0A3 6 speed (AWD) .... 3.5 quarts (3.2 liters)
01E 6 speed (AWD) .... 2.6 quarts (2.5 liters)
02X 6 speed (AWD) .... 3.7 quarts (3.5 liters)
Automatic transaxle
09L transaxle (AWD)
Drain and refill... 8.45 quarts (8.0 liters)
From dry .... 10.36 quarts (9.8 liters)
Front differential... 1.4 quart (1.3 liter)
01J transaxle (CVT)
Drain and refill... 5.28 quarts (5.0 liters)
From dry .... 7.93 quarts (7.5 liters)
Front differential... 1.37 quarts (1.3 liters)
01V transaxle (FWD/AWD)
Drain and refill... 2.7 to 3.2 quarts (2.6 to 3.0 liters)
From dry .... 9.5 quarts (9.0 liters)
Front differential... 0.85 quart (0.80 liter)
Differential
Center (AWD)
01V transaxle... 0.85 quart (0.80 liter)
09L transaxle .... 0.58 quart (0.55 liter)
Front
01V transaxle (FWD, AWD)... 9.5 quarts (9.0 liters)
01J transaxle (CVT).. 1.37 quarts (1.3 liters)
Rear (AWD).. 1.58 quarts (1.5 liters)
Cooling system
1.8L four-cylinder engine.. 7.4 quarts (7.0 liters)
2.0L four-cylinder engine.. 9.5 quarts (9.0 liters)
3.0L V6 engine .... 8.5 quarts (8.0 liters)
3.2L V6 engine .... 9.5 quarts (9.0 liters)

All capacities approximate. Add as necessary to bring to appropriate level.

FRONT
OF
VEHICLE

72031-1-SPECS HAYNES

Cylinder locations - four-cylinder engine

Brakes

Disc brake pad wear limit (lining only).. 1/8 inch (3.2 mm)

Ignition system

Spark plug type
1.8L four-cylinder engine.. NGK PFR6Q
2.0L four-cylinder engine.. Denso PK20PR11
3.0L V6 engine .... NGK BCPR6EP-11
3.2L V6 engine
2005 .... Denso PK20PR11
2006 .... Autolite XP3032
2007 .... NGK PFR7W-TG
2008 .... Bosch FR6KPP3325
Spark plug gap
1.8L four-cylinder engine.. 0.032 inch (0.8 to 0.9 mm)
2.0L four-cylinder engine.. 0.035 inch (0.9 to 1.0 mm)
3.0L V6 engine .... 0.044 inch (1.1 to 1.2 mm)
3.2L V6 engine
2005 Denso .... 0.035 inch (0.9 to 1.0 mm)
2006 Autolite.. 0.040 inch (1.0 to 1.1 mm)
2007 NGK .... 0.036 inch (0.9 to 1.0 mm)
2008 Bosch.. 0.028 inch (0.7 to 0.8 mm)

FRONT
OF
VEHICLE

96023-2B-SPECS HAYNES

Cylinder locations - V6 engines

Firing order

Four-cylinder engines	1-3-4-2
3.0L V6 engine	1-4-3-6-2-5
3.2L V6 engine	1-5-3-6-2-4

Torque specifications

	Ft-lbs (unless otherwise indicated)	Nm

Note: *One foot-pound (ft-lb) of torque is equivalent to 12 inch-pounds (in-lbs) of torque. Torque values below approximately 15 ft-lbs are expressed in inch-pounds, because most foot-pound torque wrenches are not accurate at these smaller values.*

	Ft-lbs	Nm
Engine oil drain plug	22	30
Automatic transaxle		
Check/fill plug		
01V, 09L transaxles	59	80
01J (CVT) transaxle	22	30
Drain plug		
09L transaxle	106 in-lbs	12
01V transaxle	29	40
01J (CVT) transaxle	18	24
Front differential check/fill plug	18	24
Center differential (all-wheel drive models)		
Check/fill plug	26	35
Drain plug	15	20
Manual transaxle		
Check/fill plug	15	20
Drain plug	26	35
Rear differential		
Check/fill plug	26	35
Drain plug	26	35
Spark plugs		
1.8L four-cylinder engine	18	24
2.0L four-cylinder engine	22	30
3.0L V6 engine	22	30
3.2L V6 engine	22	30
Drivebelt tensioner mounting bolt(s)		
1.8L four-cylinder engine	18	24
2.0L four-cylinder engine	17	23
3.0L V6 engine		
Lower mounting bolt	17	23
Upper mounting bolt	30	40
3.2L V6 engine	30	40
Coolant pipe bleeder screws		
2.0L four-cylinder engine	70 in-lbs	8
3.0L V6 engine	135 in-lbs	15
Wheel bolts	89	121

Service record

Date	Mileage	Work performed

1 Audi A4 maintenance schedule

The maintenance intervals in this manual are provided with the assumption that you, not the dealer, will be doing the work. These are the minimum maintenance intervals recommended by the factory for vehicles that are driven daily. If you wish to keep your vehicle in peak condition at all times, you may wish to perform some of these procedures even more often. Because frequent maintenance enhances the efficiency, performance and resale value of your car, we encourage you to do so. If you drive in dusty areas, tow a trailer, idle or drive at low speeds for extended periods or drive for short distances (less than four miles) in below freezing temperatures, shorter intervals are also recommended.

When your vehicle is new, it should be serviced by a factory authorized dealer service department to protect the factory warranty. In many cases, the initial maintenance check is done at no cost to the owner.

Every 250 miles (400 km) or weekly, whichever comes first

Check the engine oil level (see Section 4)
Check the engine coolant level (see Section 4)
Check the brake and clutch fluid level (see Section 4)
Check the power steering fluid level (see Section 4)
Check the windshield washer fluid level (see Section 4)
Check the tires and tire pressures (see Section 5)
Check the operation of all lights
Check the horn operation

Every 5,000 miles (8000 km) or 3 months, whichever comes first

All items listed above, plus:
Change the engine oil and filter (see Section 6)
Check and replace, if necessary, the air filter element (see Section 7)

Every 6,000 miles (9600 km) or 6 months, whichever comes first

All items listed above, plus:
Check the wiper blade condition (see Section 8)
Check and clean the battery and terminals (see Section 9)
Rotate the tires (see Section 10)
Check the seatbelts (see Section 11)
Inspect underhood hoses (see Section 12)
Check the cooling system hoses and connections for leaks and damage (see Section 13)
Check the exhaust pipes and hangers (see Section 14)

Every 15,000 miles (24,000 km) or 12 months, whichever comes first

All items listed above, plus:
Replace the interior ventilation filter (see Section 15)
Check the brake system (see Section 16)

Check the suspension/steering components and driveaxle boots (see Section 17)
Check the fuel system hoses and connections for leaks and damage (see Section 18)
Check the drivebelts and replace if necessary (see Section 19)

Every 30,000 miles (48,000 km) or 24 months, whichever comes first

All items listed above, plus:
Replace the air filter element (see Section 7)
Change the brake fluid (see Section 20)
Replace the spark plugs (see Section 21)
Check the ignition coil(s) (see Chapter 5)
Change the automatic transaxle fluid and filter (see Section 22)

Every 60,000 miles (96,000 km) or 48 months, whichever comes first

All items listed above, plus:
Change the rear differential lubricant (see Section 23)
Change the manual transaxle fluid (see Section 24)
Check the center differential lubricant level (see Section 25)
Check the front differential lubricant level (automatic transaxle-equipped models) (see Section 26)
Replace the fuel filter (see Section 27)

Every 60 months (regardless of mileage)

Service the cooling system (drain, flush and refill) (see Section 28)

Every 75,000 miles (120,000 km)

Replace the timing belt (four-cylinder engines, see Chapter 2A; 3.0L V6 engine, see Chapter 2B)

Engine compartment layout (1.8L four-cylinder model)

1	Brake fluid reservoir	5	Power steering fluid reservoir	9	Air filter housing
2	Coolant expansion tank	6	Radiator hose	10	Interior ventilation filter housing (under
3	Engine oil dipstick	7	Drivebelt		cowl cover)
4	Windshield washer fluid reservoir	8	Engine oil filler cap	11	Battery (under cowl cover)

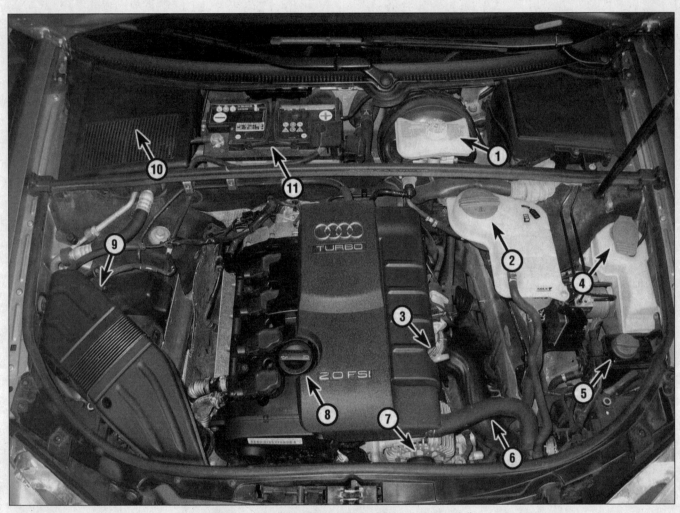

Engine compartment layout (2.0L four-cylinder model)

1	Brake fluid reservoir	5	Power steering fluid reservoir
2	Coolant expansion tank	6	Radiator hose
3	Engine oil dipstick	7	Drivebelt
4	Windshield washer fluid reservoir	8	Engine oil filler cap

9	Air filter housing
10	Interior ventilation filter housing (under cowl cover)
11	Battery

Typical front underside components (2.0L four-cylinder shown, others similar)

1	Engine oil drain plug	5	Exhaust pipe	7	Automatic transaxle (01J) fluid
2	Oil filter housing	6	Automatic transaxle (01J) fluid level		drain plug
3	Radiator drain plug		check/fill plug	8	Front disc brake caliper
4	Drivebelt				

Typical rear underside components

1	Muffler	3	Rear disc brake caliper
2	Fuel tank	4	Rear shock absorber

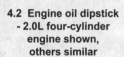

4.2 Engine oil dipstick - 2.0L four-cylinder engine shown, others similar

2   Introduction

This Chapter is designed to help the home mechanic maintain the Audi A4 with the goals of maximum performance, economy, safety and reliability in mind.

Included is a master maintenance schedule, followed by procedures dealing specifically with each item on the schedule. Visual checks, adjustments, component replacement and other helpful items are included. Refer to the accompanying illustrations of the engine compartment and the underside of the vehicle for the locations of various components.

Servicing your vehicle in accordance with the mileage/time maintenance schedule and the step-by-step procedures will result in a planned maintenance program that should produce a long and reliable service life. Keep in mind that it's a comprehensive plan, so maintaining some items but not others at the specified intervals will not produce the same results.

As you service your vehicle, you will discover that many of the procedures can - and should - be grouped together because of the nature of the particular procedure you're performing or because of the close proximity of two otherwise unrelated components to one another.

For example, if the vehicle is raised for chassis lubrication, you should inspect the exhaust, suspension, steering and fuel systems while you're under the vehicle. When you're rotating the tires, it makes good sense to check the brakes since the wheels are already removed. Finally, let's suppose you have to borrow or rent a torque wrench. Even if you only need it to tighten the spark plugs, you might as well check the torque of as many critical fasteners as time allows.

The first step in this maintenance program is to prepare yourself before the actual work begins. Read through all the procedures you're planning to do, then gather up all the parts and tools needed. If it looks like you might run into problems during a particular job, seek advice from a mechanic or an experienced do-it-yourselfer.

Owner's Manual and VECI label information

Your vehicle owner's manual was written for your year and model and contains very specific information on component locations, specifications, fuse ratings, part numbers, etc. The Owner's Manual is an important resource for the do-it-yourselfer to have; if one was not supplied with your vehicle, it can generally be ordered from a dealer parts department.

Among other important information, the Vehicle Emissions Control Information (VECI) label contains specifications and procedures for applicable tune-up adjustments and, in some instances, spark plugs. The information on this label is the exact maintenance data recommended by the manufacturer. This data often varies by intended operating altitude, local emissions regulations, month of manufacture, etc.

This Chapter contains procedural details, safety information and more ambitious maintenance intervals than you might find in manufacturer's literature. However, you may also find procedures or specifications in your Owner's Manual or VECI label that differ with what's printed here. In these cases, the Owner's Manual or VECI label can be considered correct, since it is specific to your particular vehicle.

3   Tune-up general information

The term tune-up is used in this manual to represent a combination of individual operations rather than one specific procedure.

If, from the time the vehicle is new, the routine maintenance schedule is followed closely and frequent checks are made of fluid levels and high wear items, as suggested throughout this manual, the engine will be kept in relatively good running condition and the need for additional work will be minimized.

More likely than not, however, there will be times when the engine is running poorly due to lack of regular maintenance. This is even more likely if a used vehicle, which has not received regular and frequent

maintenance checks, is purchased. In such cases, an engine tune-up will be needed outside of the regular routine maintenance intervals.

The first step in any tune-up or diagnostic procedure to help correct a poor running engine is a cylinder compression check. A compression check (see Chapter 2C) will help determine the condition of internal engine components and should be used as a guide for tune-up and repair procedures. If, for instance, a compression check indicates serious internal engine wear, a conventional tune-up will not improve the performance of the engine and would be a waste of time and money. Because of its importance, the compression check should be done by someone with the right equipment and the knowledge to use it properly.

Minor tune-up

Check all engine-related fluids (Section 4)
Check the air filter (Section 7)
Clean, inspect and test the battery (Section 9)
Check all underhood hoses (Section 12)
Check the cooling system (Section 13)

Major tune-up

All items listed under Minor tune-up, plus . . .

Replace the air filter (Section 7)
Check the drivebelt (Section 19)
Replace the spark plugs (Section 21)
Check the charging system (Chapter 5)

4   Fluid level checks (every 250 miles [400 km] or weekly)

1   Fluids are an essential part of the lubrication, cooling, brake and windshield washer systems. Because the fluids gradually become depleted and/or contaminated during normal operation of the vehicle, they must be periodically replenished. See *Recommended lubricants and fluids* in this Chapter's Specifications before adding fluid to any of the following components. **Note:** *The vehicle must be on level ground when fluid levels are checked.*

Engine oil

Refer to illustrations 4.2, 4.4 and 4.6

2   The oil level is checked with a dipstick, which is located on the side of the engine **(see illustration)**. The dipstick extends through a metal tube down into the oil pan.

3   The oil level should be checked before the vehicle has been driven, or about 5 minutes after the engine has been shut off. If the oil is checked immediately after driving the vehicle, some of the oil will remain in the upper part of the engine, resulting in an inaccurate reading on the dipstick.

4   Pull the dipstick out of the tube and wipe all the oil from the end with a clean rag or paper towel. Insert the clean dipstick all the way back into the tube and pull it out again. Note the oil at the end of the dipstick; the level should be between the MIN and MAX marks

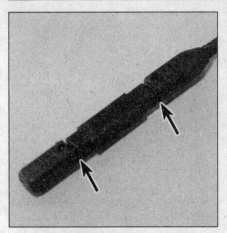

4.4 The oil level must be maintained between the MIN and MAX marks on the dipstick

4.6 Engine oil filler cap - four-cylinder engine shown, others similar

(see illustration).

5   Do not allow the level to drop below the minimum mark, or oil starvation may cause engine damage. Conversely, overfilling the engine (adding oil above the MAX mark) may cause oil fouled spark plugs, oil leaks or oil seal failures. The oil could also be whipped by the crankshaft, causing it to foam, which could cause accelerated wear of the friction surfaces in the engine due to lack of proper lubrication.

6   To add oil, remove the filler cap from the valve cover **(see illustration)**. After adding oil, wait a few minutes to allow the level to stabilize, then pull out the dipstick and check the level again. Add more oil if required. Install the filler cap and tighten it by hand only.

7   Checking the oil level is an important preventive maintenance step. A consistently low oil level indicates oil leakage through damaged seals, defective gaskets or past worn rings or valve guides. If the oil looks milky in color or has water droplets in it, the cylinder head gasket(s) may be blown or the head(s) or block may be cracked. The engine should be checked immediately. The condition of the oil should also be checked. Whenever you check the oil level, slide your thumb and index finger up the dipstick before wiping off the oil. If you see small dirt or metal particles clinging to the dipstick, the oil should be changed (see Section 6).

Engine coolant

Refer to illustration 4.9

Warning: *Do not allow antifreeze to come in contact with your skin or painted surfaces of the vehicle. Flush contaminated areas immediately with plenty of water. Don't store new coolant or leave old coolant lying around where it's accessible to children or pets - they're attracted by its sweet smell. Ingestion of even a small amount of coolant can be fatal! Wipe up garage floor and drip pan spills immediately. Keep antifreeze containers covered and repair cooling system leaks as soon as they're noticed.*

8   All vehicles covered by this manual are equipped with a coolant expansion tank, located in the left side of the engine compartment, and connected by hoses to the cooling system.

9   The coolant level in the tank should be checked regularly. **Warning:** *Never remove the pressure cap when the engine is warm!* The level in the tank varies with the temperature of the engine. When the engine is cold, the coolant level should be between the MIN and MAX marks on the tank **(see illustration)**. If it isn't, remove the cap from the tank and add coolant to the tank. **Warning:** *Remove the cap slowly. If you hear a hissing sound when unscrewing the cap, wait until it stops, then proceed.*

10   Drive the vehicle and recheck the coolant level. If only a small amount of coolant is required to bring the system up to the proper level, water can be used. However, repeated additions of water will dilute the antifreeze and water solution. In order to maintain the proper ratio of antifreeze and water, always top up the coolant level with the correct mixture. Don't use rust inhibitors or additives. An empty plastic milk jug or bleach bottle makes an excellent container for mixing coolant.

11   If the coolant level drops consistently, there may be a leak in the system. Inspect

the radiator, hoses, filler cap, drain plugs and water pump (see Section 13). If no leaks are noted, have the expansion tank cap pressure tested by a service station.

12   If you have to remove the pressure cap, wait until the engine has cooled completely, then wrap a thick cloth around the cap and turn it to the first stop. If coolant or steam escapes, or if you hear a hissing noise, let the engine cool down longer, then remove the cap.

13   Check the condition of the coolant as well. It should be relatively clear. If it's brown or rust colored, the system should be drained, flushed and refilled. Even if the coolant appears to be normal, the corrosion inhibitors wear out, so it must be replaced at the specified intervals.

Brake and clutch fluid

Refer to illustration 4.15

14   The brake master cylinder is located in the driver's side of the engine compartment, under the cowl cover near the firewall. On vehicles with manual transaxles, the clutch master cylinder is connected by a hose to the brake master cylinder resrvoir.

15   To check the fluid level, remove the access cover from the left cowl cover, then look at the MAX and MIN marks on the reservoir **(see illustration)**. The level should be within the specified distance from the maximum fill line.

16   If the level is low, wipe the top of the reservoir cover with a clean rag to prevent contamination of the brake or clutch system before lifting the cover.

17   Add only the specified brake fluid to the brake reservoir (refer to *Recommended lubricants and fluids* in this Chapter's Specifications, or to your owner's manual). Mixing different types of brake fluid can damage the system. Fill the brake master cylinder reservoir only to the MAX line. **Warning:** *Use caution when filling either reservoir - brake fluid can harm your eyes and damage painted surfaces. Do not use brake fluid that is more than one year old or has been left open. Brake fluid absorbs moisture from the air. Excess mois-*

4.9 When the engine is cold, the coolant level should be between the MIN and MAX marks

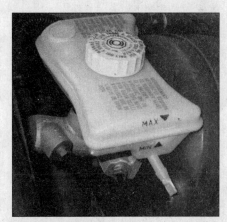

4.15 Never let the brake fluid level drop below the MIN mark

4.23 Power steering fluid reservoir

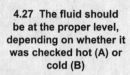
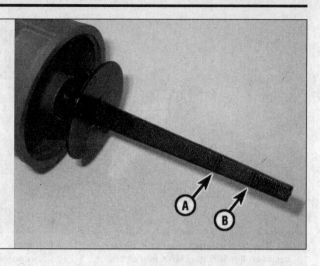

4.27 The fluid should be at the proper level, depending on whether it was checked hot (A) or cold (B)

ture can cause a dangerous loss of braking.

18 While the reservoir cap is removed, inspect the master cylinder reservoir for contamination. If deposits, dirt particles or water droplets are present, the fluid should be changed (see Section 20 for the brake fluid replacement procedure, or Chapter 8 for the clutch hydraulic system bleeding procedure).

19 After filling the reservoir to the proper level, make sure the lid is properly seated to prevent fluid leakage and/or system pressure loss.

20 The fluid in the brake master cylinder will drop slightly as the brake pads at each wheel wear down during normal operation. If the master cylinder requires repeated replenishing to keep it at the proper level, this is an indication of leakage in the brake system, which should be corrected immediately. If the brake system shows an indication of leakage, check all brake lines and connections, along with the calipers and master cylinder (see Section 16 for more information).

21 If, upon checking the brake master cylinder fluid level, you discover the reservoir empty or nearly empty, the brake and clutch systems should be thoroughly inspected (see Chapters 8 and 9).

Power steering fluid

Refer to illustrations 4.23 and 4.27

22 Check the power steering fluid level periodically to avoid steering system problems, such as damage to the pump. **Caution:** *DO NOT hold the steering wheel against either stop (extreme left or right turn) for more than five seconds. If you do, the power steering pump could be damaged.*

23 The power steering fluid reservoir is located at the left side of the engine compartment **(see illustration)**.

24 For the check, the front wheels should be pointed straight ahead and the engine should be off.

25 Use a clean rag to wipe off the reservoir cap and the area around the cap. This will help prevent any foreign matter from entering the reservoir during the check.

26 Twist off the cap and check the temperature of the fluid at the end of the dipstick with

your finger.

27 Wipe off the fluid with a clean rag, reinsert the dipstick, then withdraw it and read the fluid level. The fluid should be at the proper level, depending on whether it was checked hot or cold **(see illustration)**. Never allow the fluid level to drop below the lower mark on the dipstick.

28 If additional fluid is required, pour the specified type directly into the reservoir, using a funnel to prevent spills.

29 If the reservoir requires frequent fluid additions, all power steering hoses, hose connections, steering gear and the power steering pump should be carefully checked for leaks.

Windshield washer fluid

Refer to illustration 4.30

30 Fluid for the windshield washer system is stored in a plastic reservoir located at the left rear of the engine compartment **(see illustration)**.

31 In milder climates, plain water can be used in the reservoir, but it should be kept no more than 2/3 full to allow for expansion if the water freezes. In colder climates, use windshield washer system antifreeze, available

at any auto parts store, to lower the freezing point of the fluid. Mix the antifreeze with water in accordance with the manufacturer's directions on the container. **Caution:** *Do not use cooling system antifreeze - it will damage the vehicle's paint.*

5 Tire and tire pressure checks (every 250 miles [400 km] or weekly)

Refer to illustrations 5.2, 5.3, 5.4a, 5.4b and 5.8

1 Periodic inspection of the tires may spare you the inconvenience of being stranded with a flat tire. It can also provide you with vital information regarding possible problems in the steering and suspension systems before major damage occurs.

2 The original tires on this vehicle are equipped with 1/2-inch wide bands that will appear when tread depth reaches 1/16-inch, at which point they can be considered worn out. Tread wear can be monitored with a simple, inexpensive device known as a tread depth indicator **(see illustration)**.

4.30 The windshield washer fluid reservoir is located in the left side of the engine compartment

5.2 A tire tread depth indicator should be used to monitor tire wear - they are available at auto parts stores and service stations and cost very little

UNDERINFLATION

CUPPING

Cupping may be caused by:
- Underinflation and/or mechanical irregularities such as out-of-balance condition of wheel and/or tire, and bent or damaged wheel.
- Loose or worn steering tie-rod or steering idler arm.
- Loose, damaged or worn front suspension parts.

OVERINFLATION

**INCORRECT TOE-IN
OR EXTREME CAMBER**

**FEATHERING DUE
TO MISALIGNMENT**

5.3 This chart will help you determine the condition of your tires, the probable cause(s) of abnormal wear and the corrective action necessary

3   Note any abnormal tread wear **(see illustration)**. Tread pattern irregularities such as cupping, flat spots and more wear on one side than the other are indications of front end alignment and/or balance problems. If any of these conditions are noted, take the vehicle to a tire shop or service station to correct the problem.

4   Look closely for cuts, punctures and embedded nails or tacks. Sometimes a tire will hold air pressure for a short time or leak down very slowly after a nail has embedded itself in the tread. If a slow leak persists, check the valve stem core to make sure it is tight **(see illustration)**. Examine the tread for an object that may have embedded itself in the tire or for a plug that may have begun to leak (radial tire punctures are repaired with a plug that is installed in a puncture). If a puncture is suspected, it can be easily verified by spraying a solution of soapy water onto the puncture area **(see illustration)**. The soapy solution will bubble if there is a leak. Unless the puncture is unusually large, a tire shop or service station can usually repair the tire.

5   Carefully inspect the inner sidewall of each tire for evidence of brake fluid leakage. If you see any, inspect the brakes immediately.

6   Correct air pressure adds miles to the life span of the tires, improves mileage and enhances overall ride quality. Tire pressure cannot be accurately estimated by looking at a tire, especially if it's a radial. A tire pressure gauge is essential. Keep an accurate gauge in the glove compartment. The pressure gauges attached to the nozzles of air hoses at gas stations are often inaccurate.

7   Always check tire pressure when the tires are cold. Cold, in this case, means the vehicle has not been driven over a mile in the three hours preceding a tire pressure check. A pressure rise of four to eight pounds is not

5.4a If a tire loses air on a steady basis, check the valve core first to make sure it's snug (special inexpensive wrenches are commonly available at auto parts stores)

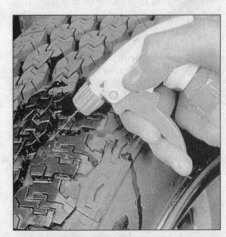

5.4b If the valve core is tight, raise the corner of the vehicle with the low tire and spray a soapy water solution onto the tread as the tire is turned slowly - slow leaks will cause small bubbles to appear

5.8 To extend the life of your tires, check the air pressure at least once a week with an accurate gauge (don't forget the spare!)

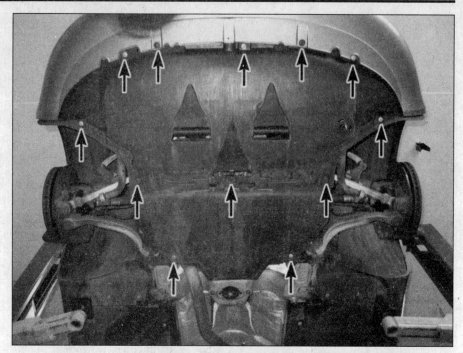

6.7 Splash shield mounting fasteners

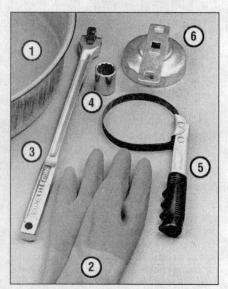

6.2 These tools are required when changing the engine oil and filter

1   *Drain pan - It should be fairly shallow in depth, but wide in order to prevent spills*
2   *Rubber gloves - When removing the drain plug and filter, it is inevitable that you will get oil on your hands (the gloves will prevent burns)*
3   *Breaker bar - Sometimes the oil drain plug is pretty tight and a long breaker bar is needed to loosen it*
4   *Socket - To be used with the breaker bar or a ratchet (must be the correct size to fit the drain plug)*
5   *Filter wrench - This is a metal band-type wrench, which requires clearance around the filter to be effective*
6   *Filter wrench - This type fits on the bottom of the filter and can be turned with a ratchet or breaker bar (different size wrenches are available for different types of filters) (only necessary for 1.8L and 3.0L engines)*

uncommon once the tires are warm.

8   Unscrew the valve cap protruding from the wheel or hubcap and push the gauge firmly onto the valve stem **(see illustration)**. Note the reading on the gauge and compare the figure to the recommended tire pressure shown on the tire placard on the driver's side door. Be sure to reinstall the valve cap to keep dirt and moisture out of the valve stem mechanism. Check all four tires and, if necessary, add enough air to bring them up to the recommended pressure.

9   Don't forget to keep the spare tire inflated to the specified pressure (refer to the pressure molded into the tire sidewall).

6   Engine oil and filter change (every 3000 miles [5000 km] or 3 months)

Refer to illustrations 6.2, 6.7 and 6.8

1   Frequent oil changes are the best preventive maintenance the home mechanic can give the engine, because aging oil becomes diluted and contaminated, which leads to premature engine wear.

2   Make sure you have all the necessary tools before you begin this procedure **(see illustration)**.

3   You should also have plenty of rags or newspapers handy for mopping up any spills.

4   The engine and exhaust components will be warm during the actual work, so try to anticipate any potential problems before the engine and accessories are hot.

5   Park the vehicle on a level spot. Start the engine and allow it to reach its normal operating temperature. Warm oil and sludge will flow

out more easily. Turn off the engine when it's warmed up. Remove the filler cap from the valve cover. If you're working on a model with a 3.2L V6 engine, loosen the oil filter housing (which is located at the rear of the engine on the driver's side) so the oil in the housing can drain into the oil pan. **Note:** *Place rags around the filter housing to catch any oil that might spill out.*

6   Raise the vehicle and support it securely on jackstands. **Warning:** *Never get beneath the vehicle when it is supported only by a jack. The jack provided with your vehicle is designed solely for raising the vehicle to remove and replace the wheels. Always use jackstands to support the vehicle when it becomes necessary to place your body underneath the vehicle.*

7   Remove the splash shield under the engine **(see illustration)**.

8   Being careful not to touch the hot exhaust components, place the drain pan under the drain plug in the bottom of the pan and remove the plug **(see illustration)**. You may want to wear gloves while unscrewing the plug the final few turns if the engine is hot.

9   Allow the old oil to drain into the pan. It may be necessary to move the pan farther under the engine as the oil flow slows to a trickle.

10   Inspect the old oil for the presence of metal shavings and chips.

11   After all the oil has drained, wipe off the drain plug with a clean rag. Even minute metal particles clinging to the plug would immediately contaminate the new oil.

12   Clean the area around the drain plug opening, reinstall the plug and tighten it to the torque listed in this Chapter's Specifications.

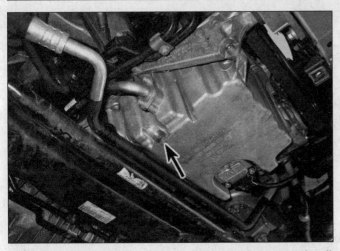

6.8 Use a proper size box-end wrench or socket to remove the oil drain plug and avoid rounding it off

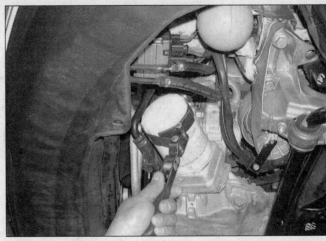

6.14 Since the oil filter is on very tight, you will need a special wrench for removal - DO NOT use the wrench to tighten the new filter

1.8L and 3.0L engine models

Refer to illustrations 6.14 and 6.16

13   Move the drain pan into position under the oil filter.

14   Use the oil filter wrench to loosen the oil filter (**see illustration**).

15   Unscrew the old filter. Be careful; its full of oil. Empty the oil inside the filter into the drain pan. **Note:** *Compare the old filter to the new one to make sure it's the same type.*

16   Wipe off the oil filter housing sealing surface using a clean rag. Make sure the rubber gasket from the old filter is not stuck to the housing. Apply a thin coat of clean oil to the rubber gasket on the new filter (**see illustration**).

17   Install the filter and tighten it securely, following the directions on the filter or filter box. Install the splash shield, lower the vehicle, then proceed to Step 27.

2.0L and 3.2L engine models

Refer to illustrations 6.20, 6.21a, 6.21b, 6.22, 6.23 and 6.24

18   Install the splash shield, then lower the vehicle.

19   Working in the engine compartment, locate the oil filter/housing. On 2.0L engines, the filter is accessed from under the vehicle on the driver's side; on 3.2L engines, the filter is accessed from above on the driver's side rear of the engine. **Note:** *On 3.2L engines, it may be necessary to remove the coolant reservoir mounting fasteners and move the reservoir to gain access to the filter.*

20   On 2.0L engines, remove the valve cap from the bottom of the filter housing (**see illustration**).

21   On 2.0L engines, use a screwdriver to depress the valve at the bottom of the housing, allowing the oil in the filter housing to drain (**see illustrations**).

6.16 Lubricate the oil filter gasket with clean engine oil before installing the filter on the engine

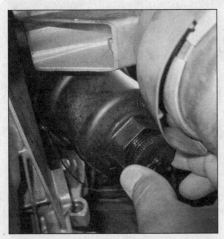

6.20 On four-cylinder models, unscrew the valve cap from the bottom of the filter housing . . .

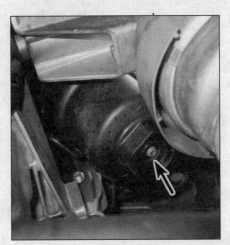

6.21a . . . locate the drain valve in the filter housing . . .

6.21b . . . then use a screwdriver to depress the valve and drain the oil from the housing

6.22 Use a socket and long extension to unscrew the filter housing (2.0L four-cylinder engine shown)

6.23 Pull the used element off of the filter housing stem and install a new O-ring in the housing

22   Unscrew the oil housing **(see illustration)**. The element is withdrawn with the oil filter housing, and can then be separated and discarded.

23   Wipe out the oil filter housing and cap using a clean rag, then install a new O-ring on the housing **(see illustration)**. On 3.2L engines, replace the O-ring in the groove near the end of the filter housing threads.

24   Lubricate the O-ring(s) with clean engine oil, then install the filter element into the housing **(see illustration)**.

25   Screw the filter housing onto the engine and tighten the housing securely.

26   On 2.0L engines, screw the valve cap into the bottom of the housing and tighten the cap securely.

All models

27   Add new oil to the engine through the oil filler cap in the valve cover. Use a funnel, if necessary, to prevent oil from spilling onto the top of the engine. Pour the specified type and

amount of oil into the engine (refer to *Recommended lubricants and fluids* and *Capacities* in this Chapter's Specifications). Wait a few minutes to allow the oil to drain into the pan, then check the level (see Section 4). If the oil level is correct, install the filler cap hand tight, start the engine and allow the new oil to circulate. **Caution:** *Do not rev-up the engine.*

28   Allow the engine to run for about a minute.

29   Wait a few minutes to allow the oil to trickle down into the pan, then recheck the level on the dipstick and, if necessary, add enough oil to bring it to the correct level.

30   During the first few trips after an oil change, make it a point to check frequently for leaks and proper oil level.

31   The old oil drained from the engine cannot be reused in its present state and should be disposed of. Check with your local auto parts store, disposal facility or environmental agency to see if they will accept the oil for recycling. After the oil has cooled, it can be

drained into a container (capped plastic jugs, topped bottles, milk cartons, etc.) for transport to one of these disposal sites. Don't dispose of the oil by pouring it on the ground or down a drain!

Service indicator resetting

Refer to illustrations 6.32 and 6.36

Note: *After changing the engine oil, it's important to reset the service indicator so it can keep an accurate record of engine operating time/vehicle mileage.*

32   Two buttons on the instrument cluster are used to reset the service indicator **(see illustration)**.

33   Begin the process by turning the ignition key to the OFF position.

34   Press the Service button (A) and hold it there, then turn the ignition key to the ON position. Release the button.

35   Look at the multi-function display; "SERVICE IN _____ MILES" or "SERVICE!" should appear on the display.

36   Press and hold down the reset button (B) until the "SERVICE IN ____ MILES ____ DAYS" or "SERVICE!" appears in the multi-function display **(see illustration)**, then turn the ignition key to the OFF position.

---

7   Air filter replacement (every 3000 miles [5000 km] or 3 months)

Refer to illustrations 7.1a, 7.1b and 7.2

1   Remove the fresh air intake ducts **(see illustrations)**. **Note:** *On 3.0L engines, disconnect the EVAP canister purge valve from the intake duct.*

2   Release the clamp and detach the hose from the air filter housing **(see illustration)**. On models so equipped, also detach the smaller hose from the front of the filter housing.

3   Disconnect the Mass Air Flow (MAF) sen-

6.24 Install the new filter element

6.32 Buttons and instrument cluster display used for resetting the service indicator

A Service button
B Reset button

C Multi-function display

6.36 The "SERVICE IN _____ MILES _____ DAYS" or "SERVICE!" will appear in the multi-function display when complete

7.1a Pull up and detach the duct from the air filter housing. Note: *Some models are equipped with a snow screen in this duct. Make sure the screen is clean*

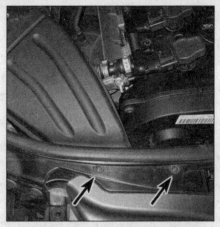

7.1b Remove the fasteners and detach the other half of the air duct

sor electrical connector (on models equipped with a MAF sensor on the air filter housing).
4   On 3.2L V6 models, unclip the fuel line from the air filter housing.
5   Remove the fasteners that secure the upper part of the filter housing. Lift upwards on the housing and remove the air filter element.
6   Clean the inside of the air filter housing with a damp cloth.
7   Installation is the reverse of removal.

8   Windshield wiper blade inspection and replacement (every 6000 miles [9600 km] or 6 months)

Refer to illustration 8.5

1   The windshield wiper and blade assembly should be inspected periodically for dam-

age, loose components and cracked or worn blade elements.
2   Road film can build up on the wiper blades and affect their efficiency, so they should be washed regularly with a mild detergent solution.
3   The action of the wiping mechanism can loosen bolts, nuts and fasteners, so they should be checked and tightened, as necessary, at the same time the wiper blades are checked.
4   If the wiper blade elements are cracked, worn or warped, or no longer clean adequately, they should be replaced with new ones.
5   Lift the arm assembly away from the glass for clearance, pull the blade retainer clip, then disengage the wiper blade assembly from the pivot at the end of the arm **(see illustration)**.

6   Position the new wiper blade on the arm, then slide the retainer clip into place. Connection can be confirmed by an audible click.

9   Battery check, maintenance and charging (every 6000 miles [9600 km] or 6 months)

Refer to illustrations 9.1, 9.6a, 9.6b, 9.7a and 9.7b

Warning: *Certain precautions must be followed when checking and servicing the battery. Hydrogen gas, which is highly flammable, is always present in the battery cells, so keep lighted tobacco and all other open flames and sparks away from the battery. The electrolyte inside the battery is actually diluted sulfuric acid, which will cause injury if splashed*

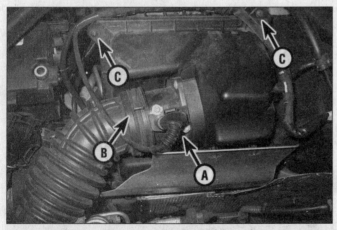

7.2 Air filter housing components (2.0L four-cylinder model shown, others similar)

A   Mass Air Flow (MAF) sensor electrical connector (some models)
B   Air filter outlet hose and clamp
C   Air filter housing fasteners

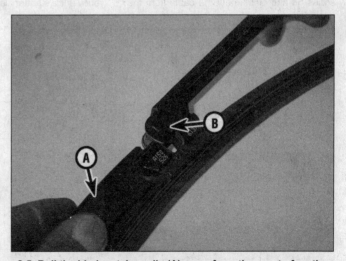

8.5 Pull the blade retainer clip (A) away from the arm to free the wiper blade from the pivot (B)

9.1 Tools and materials required for battery maintenance

1   **Face shield/safety goggles** - *When removing corrosion with a brush, the acidic particles can easily fly up into your eyes*
2   **Baking soda** - *A solution of baking soda and water can be used to neutralize corrosion*
3   **Petroleum jelly** - *A layer of this on the battery posts will help prevent corrosion*
4   **Battery post/cable cleaner** - *This wire brush cleaning tool will remove all traces of corrosion from the battery posts and cable clamps*
5   **Treated felt washers** - *Placing one of these on each post, directly under the cable clamps, will help prevent corrosion*
6   **Puller** - *Sometimes the cable clamps are very difficult to pull off the posts, even after the nut/bolt has been completely loosened. This tool pulls the clamp straight up and off the post without damage*
7   **Battery post/cable cleaner** - *Here is another cleaning tool which is a slightly different version of number 4 above, but it does the same thing*
8   **Rubber gloves** - *Another safety item to consider when servicing the battery; remember that's acid inside the battery!*

on your skin or in your eyes. It will also ruin clothes and painted surfaces. When removing the battery cables, always detach the negative cable first and hook it up last!

1   A routine preventive maintenance program for the battery in your vehicle is the only way to ensure quick and reliable starts. But before performing any battery maintenance, make sure that you have the proper equipment necessary to work safely around the battery **(see illustration)**.

2   There are also several precautions that should be taken whenever battery maintenance is performed. Before servicing the battery, always turn the engine and all accessories off and disconnect the cable from the negative terminal of the battery (see Chapter 5, Section 1).

3   The battery produces hydrogen gas, which is both flammable and explosive. Never create a spark, smoke or light a match around the battery. Always charge the battery in a ventilated area.

4   Electrolyte contains poisonous and corrosive sulfuric acid. Do not allow it to get in your eyes, on your skin or on your clothes. Never ingest it. Wear protective safety glasses when working near the battery. Keep children away from the battery.

5   Note the external condition of the battery. If the positive terminal and cable clamp on your vehicle's battery is equipped with a rubber protector, make sure that it's not torn or damaged. It should completely cover the terminal. Look for any corroded or loose connections, cracks in the case or cover or loose hold-down clamps. Also check the entire length of each cable for cracks and frayed conductors.

6   If corrosion, which looks like white, fluffy deposits **(see illustration)** is evident, particularly around the terminals, the battery should be removed for cleaning. Loosen the cable clamp bolts with a wrench, being careful to remove the ground cable first, and slide them off the terminals **(see illustration)**. Then disconnect the hold-down clamp bolt and nut, remove the clamp and lift the battery from the engine compartment.

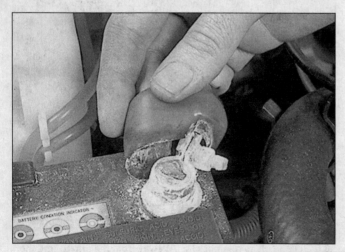

9.6a Battery terminal corrosion usually appears as light, fluffy powder

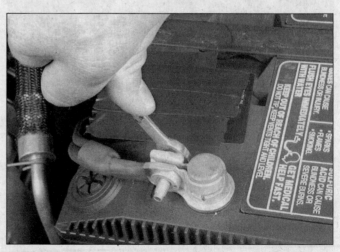

9.6b Removing a cable from the battery post with a wrench - sometimes a pair of special battery pliers are required for this procedure if corrosion has caused deterioration of the nut hex (always remove the ground (-) cable first and hook it up last!)

9.7a When cleaning the cable clamps, all corrosion must be removed

9.7b Regardless of the type of tool used to clean the battery posts, a clean, shiny surface should be the result

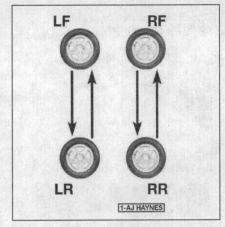

10.2 The recommended four-tire rotation pattern for these vehicles

7   Clean the cable clamps thoroughly with a battery brush or a terminal cleaner and a solution of warm water and baking soda **(see illustration)**. Wash the terminals and the top of the battery case with the same solution but make sure that the solution doesn't get into the battery. When cleaning the cables, terminals and battery top, wear safety goggles and rubber gloves to prevent any solution from coming in contact with your eyes or hands. Wear old clothes too - even diluted, sulfuric acid splashed onto clothes will burn holes in them. If the terminals have been extensively corroded, clean them up with a terminal cleaner **(see illustration)**. Thoroughly wash all cleaned areas with plain water.

8   Make sure that the battery tray is in good condition and the hold-down clamp fasteners are tight. If the battery is removed from the tray, make sure no parts remain in the bottom of the tray when the battery is reinstalled. When reinstalling the hold-down clamp bolts, do not overtighten them.

9   Information on removing and installing the battery can be found in Chapter 5. If you disconnected the cable(s) from the negative and/or positive battery terminals, see Chapter 5, Section 1. Information on jump starting can be found at the front of this manual. For more detailed battery checking procedures, refer to the *Haynes Automotive Electrical Manual*.

Cleaning

10   Corrosion on the hold-down components, battery case and surrounding areas can be removed with a solution of water and baking soda. Thoroughly rinse all cleaned areas with plain water.

11   Any metal parts of the vehicle damaged by corrosion should be covered with a zinc-based primer, then painted.

Charging

Warning: *When batteries are being charged, hydrogen gas, which is very explosive and flammable, is produced. Do not smoke or allow open flames near a charging or a recently charged battery. Wear eye protection when near the battery during charging. Also, make sure the charger is unplugged before connecting or disconnecting the battery from the charger.*

12   Slow-rate charging is the best way to restore a battery that's discharged to the point where it will not start the engine. It's also a good way to maintain the battery charge in a vehicle that's only driven a few miles between starts. Maintaining the battery charge is particularly important in the winter when the battery must work harder to start the engine and electrical accessories that drain the battery are in greater use.

13   It's best to use a one or two-amp battery charger (sometimes called a "trickle" charger). They are the safest and put the least strain on the battery. They are also the least expensive. For a faster charge, you can use a higher amperage charger, but don't use one rated more than 1/10th the amp/hour rating of the battery. Rapid boost charges that claim to restore the power of the battery in one to two hours are hardest on the battery and can damage batteries not in good condition. This type of charging should only be used in emergency situations.

14   The average time necessary to charge a battery should be listed in the instructions that come with the charger. As a general rule, a trickle charger will charge a battery in 12 to 16 hours.

---

10   Tire rotation (every 6000 miles [9600 km] or 6 months)

Refer to illustration 10.2

1   The tires should be rotated at the specified intervals and whenever uneven wear is noticed.

2   Refer to the accompanying **illustration** for the preferred tire rotation pattern.

3   Loosen the wheel bolts. Refer to the information in *Jacking and towing* at the front of this manual for the proper procedures to follow when raising the vehicle and changing a tire. If the brakes are to be checked, don't apply the parking brake as stated. Make sure the tires are blocked to prevent the vehicle from rolling as it's raised.

4   Preferably, the entire vehicle should be raised at the same time. This can be done on a hoist or by jacking up each corner, then lowering the vehicle onto jackstands placed under the frame rails. Always use four jackstands and make sure the vehicle is safely supported.

5   After rotation, check and adjust the tire pressures as necessary. Tighten the wheel bolts to the torque listed in this Chapter's Specifications.

---

11   Seat belt check (every 6000 miles [9600 km] or 6 months)

1   Check seat belts, buckles, latch plates and guide loops for obvious damage and signs of wear.

2   Where the seat belt receptacle bolts to the floor of the vehicle, check that the bolts are secure.

3   See if the seat belt reminder light comes on when the key is turned to the Run or Start position.

---

12   Underhood hose check and replacement (every 6000 miles [9600 km] or 6 months)

General

Caution: *Replacement of air conditioning hoses must be left to a dealer service department or air conditioning shop that has the equipment to depressurize the system safely and recover the refrigerant. Never remove air*

Check for a chafed area that could fail prematurely.

Check for a soft area indicating the hose has deteriorated inside.

Overtightening the clamp on a hardened hose will damage the hose and cause a leak.

Check each hose for swelling and oil-soaked ends. Cracks and breaks can be located by squeezing the hose.

13.4 Hoses, like drivebelts, have a habit of failing at the worst possible time - to prevent the inconvenience of a blown radiator or heater hose, inspect them carefully as shown here

conditioning components or hoses until the system has been depressurized.

1   High temperatures in the engine compartment can cause the deterioration of the rubber and plastic hoses used for engine, accessory and emission systems operation. Periodic inspection should be made for cracks, loose clamps, material hardening and leaks. Information specific to the cooling system hoses can be found in Section 13.

2   Some, but not all, hoses are secured to their fittings with clamps. Where clamps are used, check to be sure they haven't lost their tension, allowing the hose to leak. If clamps aren't used, make sure the hose has not expanded and/or hardened where it slips over the fitting, allowing it to leak.

Vacuum hoses

3   It's quite common for vacuum hoses, especially those in the emissions system, to be color-coded or identified by colored stripes

molded into them. Various systems require hoses with different wall thickness, collapse resistance and temperature resistance. When replacing hoses, be sure the new ones are made of the same material.

4   Often the only effective way to check a hose is to remove it completely from the vehicle. If more than one hose is removed, be sure to label the hoses and fittings to ensure correct installation.

5   When checking vacuum hoses, be sure to include any plastic T-fittings in the check. Inspect the fittings for cracks and the hose where it fits over the fitting for distortion, which could cause leakage.

6   A small piece of vacuum hose (1/4-inch inside diameter) can be used as a stethoscope to detect vacuum leaks. Hold one end of the hose to your ear and probe around vacuum hoses and fittings, listening for the hissing sound characteristic of a vacuum leak. **Warning:** *When probing with the vacuum hose stethoscope, be very careful not to come into contact with moving engine components such as the drivebelt, cooling fan, etc.*

Fuel hose

Warning: *There are certain precautions that must be taken when inspecting or servicing fuel system components. Work in a well-ventilated area and do not allow open flames (cigarettes, appliances, etc.) or bare light bulbs near the work area. Mop up any spills immediately and do not store fuel soaked rags where they could ignite. The fuel system is under high pressure, so if any fuel lines are to be disconnected, the pressure in the system must be relieved first (see Chapter 4 for more information).*

7   Check all rubber fuel lines for deterioration and chafing. Check especially for cracks in areas where the hose bends and just before fittings, such as where a hose attaches to the fuel filter.

8   High quality fuel line, made specifically for high-pressure fuel injection systems, must be used for fuel line replacement. Never, under any circumstances, use unreinforced vacuum line, clear plastic tubing or water hose for fuel lines.

9   Spring-type clamps are commonly used on fuel lines. These clamps often lose their tension over a period of time, and can be sprung during removal. Replace all spring-type clamps with screw clamps whenever a hose is replaced.

Metal lines

10   Sections of metal line are routed along the frame, between the fuel tank and the engine. Check carefully to be sure the line has not been bent or crimped and that cracks have not started in the line.

11   If a section of metal fuel line must be replaced, only seamless steel tubing should be used, since copper and aluminum tubing don't have the strength necessary to withstand normal engine vibration.

12   Check the metal brake lines where they enter the master cylinder and brake propor-

tioning unit for cracks in the lines or loose fittings. Any sign of brake fluid leakage calls for an immediate and thorough inspection of the brake system.

13   Cooling system check (every 6000 miles [9600 km] or 6 months)

Refer to illustration 13.4

Warning: *Wait until the engine is completely cool before performing this procedure.*

1   Many major engine failures can be attributed to a faulty cooling system. If the vehicle is equipped with an automatic transmission, the cooling system also cools the transmission fluid and thus plays an important role in prolonging transmission life.

2   The cooling system should be checked with the engine cold. Do this before the vehicle is driven for the day or after it has been shut off for at least three hours.

3   Remove the cooling system pressure cap and thoroughly clean the cap, inside and out, with clean water. Also clean the opening in the expansion tank. All traces of corrosion should be removed. The coolant inside the expansion tank should be relatively transparent. If it is rust-colored, the system should be drained, flushed and refilled (see Section 28). If the coolant level is not up to the MIN mark, add additional antifreeze/coolant mixture (see Section 4).

4   Carefully check the large upper and lower radiator hoses along with the smaller diameter heater hoses that run from the engine to the firewall. Inspect each hose along its entire length, replacing any hose that is cracked, swollen or shows signs of deterioration. Cracks may become more apparent if the hose is squeezed **(see illustration)**.

5   Make sure all hose connections are tight. A leak in the cooling system will usually show up as white or rust-colored deposits on the areas adjoining the leak. If spring-type clamps are used at the ends of the hoses, it may be a good idea to replace them with more secure screw-type clamps.

6   Use compressed air or a soft brush to remove bugs, leaves, etc. from the front of the radiator or air conditioning condenser. Be careful not to damage the delicate cooling fins or cut yourself on them.

7   Every other inspection, or at the first indication of cooling system problems, have the cap and system pressure tested. If you don't have a pressure tester, most repair shops will do this for a minimal charge.

14   Exhaust system check (every 6000 miles [9600 km] or 6 months)

Refer to illustration 14.2

1   With the engine cold (at least three hours after the vehicle has been driven), check the

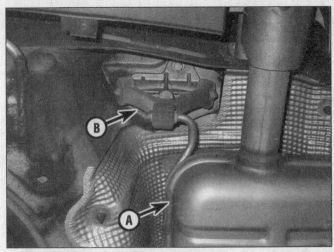

14.2 Inspect the muffler (A) and all hangers (B) for signs of deterioration

15.2 Remove the cowl cover

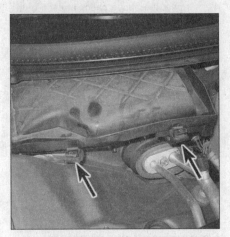

15.3a Release the clips to open the air inlet cover

15.3b Remove the filter element

16 Brake system check (every 15,000 miles [24,000 km] or 12 months)

Warning: *The dust created by the brake system is harmful to your health. Never blow it out with compressed air and don't inhale any of it. An approved filtering mask should be worn when working on the brakes. Do not, under any circumstances, use petroleum-based solvents to clean brake parts. Use brake system cleaner only!*
Note: *For detailed photographs of the brake system, refer to Chapter 9.*

1   In addition to the specified intervals, the brakes should be inspected every time the wheels are removed or whenever a defect is suspected.

2   Any of the following symptoms could indicate a potential brake system defect: The vehicle pulls to one side when the brake pedal is depressed; the brakes make squealing or dragging noises when applied; brake pedal travel is excessive; the pedal pulsates; or brake fluid leaks, usually onto the inside of the tire or wheel. A brake pedal that sinks slowly to the floor, with no apparent external fluid leakage, indicates a faulty master cylinder.
Note: *A faulty master cylinder can leak fluid into the power brake booster.*

3   Loosen the wheel bolts.

4   Raise the vehicle and place it securely on jackstands.

5   Remove the wheels (see *Jacking and towing* at the front of this book, or your owner's manual, if necessary).

Disc brakes

Refer to illustrations 16.7 and 16.9

6   There are two pads (an outer and an inner) in each caliper. The pads are visible with the wheels removed.

7   Check the pad thickness by looking at each end of the caliper and through the

complete exhaust system from the manifold to the end of the tailpipe. Be careful around the catalytic converter, which may be hot even after three hours. The inspection should be done with the vehicle on a hoist to permit unrestricted access. If a hoist isn't available, raise the vehicle and support it securely on jackstands.

2   Check the exhaust pipes and connections for signs of leakage and/or corrosion indicating a potential failure. Make sure that all brackets and hangers are in good condition and tight **(see illustration)**.

3   Inspect the underside of the body for holes, corrosion, open seams, etc. which may allow exhaust gasses to enter the passenger compartment. Seal all body openings with silicone sealant or body putty.

4   Rattles and other noises can often be traced to the exhaust system, especially the hangers, mounts and heat shields. Try to move the pipes, mufflers and catalytic converter. If the components can come in contact

with the body or suspension parts, secure the exhaust system with new brackets and hangers.

15 Interior ventilation filter replacement (every 15,000 miles [24,000 km] or 12 months)

Refer to illustrations 15.2, 15.3a and 15.3b

1   The interior ventilation filter is located inside a housing at the right (passenger's) side of the engine compartment.

2   Remove the corner cowl cover **(see illustration)**.

3   To remove the ventilation filter, release the clips that secure the cover, then lift the cover off and remove the ventilation filter element **(see illustrations)**.

4   Install the new filter with the arrows indicating air flow pointing down.

5   Installation is the reverse of the removal procedure.

16.7 With the wheel off, check the thickness of the inner brake pad through the inspection hole (front brake shown, rear brake similar)

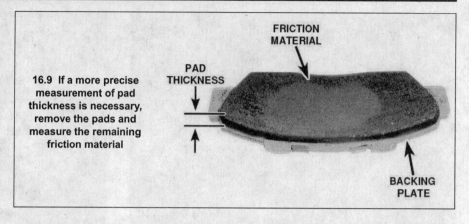

16.9 If a more precise measurement of pad thickness is necessary, remove the pads and measure the remaining friction material

PAD THICKNESS

FRICTION MATERIAL

BACKING PLATE

inspection window in the caliper body **(see illustration)**. If the lining material is less than the thickness listed in this Chapter's Specifications, replace the pads. **Note:** *Keep in mind that the lining material is riveted or bonded to a metal backing plate and the metal portion is not included in this measurement.*

8   If it is difficult to determine the exact thickness of the remaining pad material by the above method, or if you are at all concerned about the condition of the pads, remove the caliper(s), then remove the pads from the calipers for further inspection (see Chapter 9).

9   Once the pads are removed from the calipers, clean them with brake cleaner and re-measure them with a ruler or a vernier caliper **(see illustration)**.

10   Measure the disc thickness with a micrometer to make sure that it still has service life remaining. If any disc is thinner than the specified minimum thickness, replace it (see Chapter 9). Even if the disc has service life remaining, check its condition. Look for scoring, gouging and burned spots. If these conditions exist, remove the disc and have it resurfaced (see Chapter 9).

11   Before installing the wheels, check all brake lines and hoses for damage, wear, deformation, cracks, corrosion, leakage, bends and twists, particularly in the vicinity of the rubber hoses at the calipers. Check the clamps for tightness and the connections for leakage. Make sure that all hoses and lines are clear of sharp edges, moving parts and the exhaust system. If any of the above conditions are noted, repair, reroute or replace the lines and/or fittings as necessary (see Chapter 9).

Brake booster check

12   Sit in the driver's seat and perform the following sequence of tests.

13   With the brake fully depressed, start the engine - the pedal should move down a little when the engine starts.

14   With the engine running, depress the

brake pedal several times - the travel distance should not change.

15   Depress the brake, stop the engine and hold the pedal in for about 30 seconds - the pedal should neither sink nor rise.

16   Restart the engine, run it for about a minute and turn it off. Then firmly depress the brake several times - the pedal travel should decrease with each application.

17   If your brakes do not operate as described, the brake booster has failed. Refer to Chapter 9 for the replacement procedure.

Parking brake

Note: *The rear brakes are self-adjusting, and do not require normal maintenance adjustments. Adjustment is only required after replacing brake discs, brake pads, brake calipers or parking brake cables.*

18   One method of checking the parking brake is to park the vehicle on a steep hill with the parking brake set and the transmission in Neutral (be sure to stay in the vehicle for this check!). If the parking brake cannot prevent the vehicle from rolling, it's in need of adjustment (see Chapter 9).

---

17   Suspension, steering and driveaxle boot check (every 15,000 miles [24,000 km] or 12 months)

Note: *The steering linkage and suspension components should be checked periodically. Worn or damaged suspension and steering linkage components can result in excessive and abnormal tire wear, poor ride quality and vehicle handling and reduced fuel economy. For more information on the steering and suspension components, refer to Chapter 10.*

Shock absorber check

Refer to illustration 17.6

1   Park the vehicle on level ground, turn the engine off and set the parking brake. Check the tire pressures.

2   Push down at one corner of the vehicle, then release it while noting the movement of the body. It should stop moving and come

to rest in a level position within one or two bounces.

3   If the vehicle continues to move up-and-down or if it fails to return to its original position, a worn or weak shock absorber is probably the reason.

4   Repeat the above check at each of the three remaining corners of the vehicle.

5   Raise the vehicle and support it securely on jackstands.

6   Check the shock absorbers for evidence of fluid leakage **(see illustration)**. A light film of fluid is no cause for concern. Make sure that any fluid noted is from the shocks and not from some other source. If leakage is noted, replace the shocks as a set.

7   Check the shocks to be sure that they are securely mounted and undamaged. Check the upper mounts for damage and wear. If damage or wear is noted, replace the shocks as a set (front or rear).

8   If the shocks must be replaced, refer to Chapter 10 for the procedure.

Steering and suspension check

Refer to illustrations 17.9 and 17.11

9   Visually inspect the steering and suspension components (front and rear) for damage and distortion. Look for damaged seals, boots and bushings and leaks of any kind. Examine

17.6 Check the shocks for leakage at the indicated area

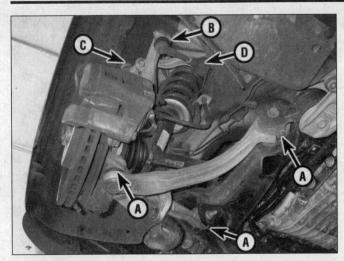

17.9 Examine the mounting points for the lower control arm (A), the tie-rod ends (B), the upper control arms (links) (C), and the steering gear boots (D)

17.11 With the steering wheel in the locked position and the vehicle raised, grasp the front tire as shown and try to move it back-and-forth - if any play is noted, check the steering gear mounts and tie-rod ends for looseness

the bushings where the control arms meet the chassis **(see illustration)**.

10   Clean the lower end of the steering knuckle. Have an assistant grasp the lower edge of the tire and move the wheel in-and-out while you look for movement at the steering knuckle-to-control arm balljoint. If there is any movement the suspension balljoint(s) must be replaced.

11   Grasp each front tire at the front and rear edges, push in at the front, pull out at the rear and feel for play in the steering system components. If any freeplay is noted, check the steering gear mounts and the tie-rod ends for looseness **(see illustration)**.

12   Additional steering and suspension system information and illustrations can be found in Chapter 10.

Driveaxle boot check

Refer to illustration 17.14

13   The driveaxle boots are very important because they prevent dirt, water and for-

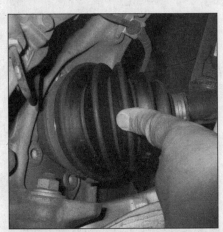

17.14 Inspect the inner and outer driveaxle boots for loose clamps, cracks or signs of leaking lubricant

eign material from entering and damaging the constant velocity (CV) joints. Because it constantly pivots back and forth following the steering action of the front hub, the outer CV boot wears out sooner and should be inspected regularly.

14   Inspect the boots for tears and cracks as well as loose clamps **(see illustration)**. If there is any evidence of cracks or leaking lubricant, they must be replaced as described in Chapter 8.

18   Fuel system check (every 15,000 miles [24,000 km] or 12 months)

Warning: *Gasoline is flammable, so take extra precautions when you work on any part of the fuel system. Don't smoke or allow open flames or bare light bulbs near the work area, and don't work in a garage where a gas-type appliance (such as a water heater or clothes dryer) is present. Since fuel is carcinogenic, wear fuel-resistant gloves when there's a possibility of being exposed to fuel, and, if you spill any fuel on your skin, rinse it off immediately with soap and water. Mop up any spills immediately and do not store fuel-soaked rags where they could ignite. When you perform any kind of work on the fuel system, wear safety glasses and have a Class B type fire extinguisher on hand. The fuel system is under constant pressure, so, before any lines are disconnected, the fuel system pressure must be relieved (see Chapter 4).*

1   If you smell fuel while driving or after the vehicle has been sitting in the sun, inspect the fuel system immediately.

2   Remove the fuel filler cap and inspect it for damage and corrosion. The gasket should have an unbroken sealing imprint. If the gasket is damaged or corroded, install a new cap.

3   Inspect the fuel feed line for cracks. Make sure that the connections in the fuel line are free of leaks. **Warning:** *Your vehicle is fuel injected, so you must relieve the fuel system pressure before servicing fuel system components. The fuel system pressure relief procedure is outlined in Chapter 4.*

4   Since some components of the fuel system - the fuel tank and part of the fuel feed and return lines, for example - are underneath the vehicle, they can be inspected more easily with the vehicle raised on a hoist. If that's not possible, raise the vehicle and support it on jackstands.

5   With the vehicle raised and safely supported, inspect the fuel tank and filler neck for punctures, cracks and other damage. The connection between the filler neck and the tank is particularly critical. Sometimes a rubber filler neck will leak because of loose clamps or deteriorated rubber. Inspect all fuel tank mounting brackets and straps to be sure that the tank is securely attached to the vehicle.

6   Carefully check all rubber hoses and metal lines leading away from the fuel tank. Check for loose connections, deteriorated hoses, crimped lines and other damage. Replace damaged sections as necessary (see Chapter 4).

19   Drivebelt check and replacement (every 15,000 miles [24,000 km] or 12 months)

1   The drivebelt is located at the front of the engine and plays an important role in the overall operation of the vehicle and its components. Due to its function and material make-up, the drivebelt is prone to failure after a period of time and should be inspected and adjusted periodically to prevent major engine damage.

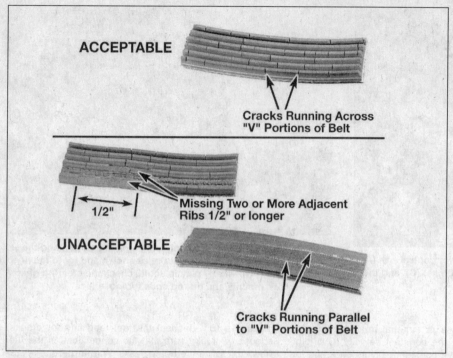

ACCEPTABLE

Cracks Running Across
"V" Portions of Belt

1/2"

Missing Two or More Adjacent
Ribs 1/2" or longer

UNACCEPTABLE

Cracks Running Parallel
to "V" Portions of Belt

19.4 Here are some of the more common problems associated with drivebelts (check the belts very carefully to prevent an untimely breakdown)

19.6 Rotate the tensioner arm to relieve belt tension

2   The vehicles covered by this manual are equipped with a single self-adjusting serpentine drivebelt, which is used to drive all of the accessory components such as the alternator, power steering pump, water pump and air conditioning compressor.

Inspection

Refer to illustration 19.4

3   With the engine off, open the hood and locate the drivebelt at the front of the engine. Using your fingers (and a flashlight, if necessary), move along the belt checking for cracks and separation of the belt plies. Also check for fraying and glazing, which gives the belt a shiny appearance. Both sides of the belt should be inspected, which means you will have to twist the belt to check the underside.

4   Check the ribs on the underside of the belt. They should all be the same depth, with none of the surface uneven **(see illustration)**.

5   The tension of the belt is automatically adjusted by the belt tensioner and does not require any adjustments.

Replacement

Four-cylinder engines

Refer to illustration 19.6

6   To replace the belt, rotate the tensioner to relieve the tension on the belt **(see illustration)**.

7   Remove the belt from the auxiliary components and carefully release the tensioner.

8   Route the new belt over the various pulleys, again rotating the tensioner to allow the belt to be installed, then release the belt

tensioner. Make sure the belt fits properly into the pulley grooves - it must be completely engaged.

3.0L V6 engines

9   Remove the front engine cover.

10   To replace the belt, rotate the tensioner using the cast square to relieve the tension on the belt.

11   Remove the belt from the auxiliary components and carefully release the tensioner.

12   Route the new belt over the various pulleys, again rotating the tensioner to allow the belt to be installed, then release the belt tensioner. Make sure the belt fits properly into the pulley grooves - it must be completely engaged.

3.2L V6 engines

13   Disconnect and remove the front engine cover.

14   Remove the fresh air intake ducts (see Section 7).

15   Place the radiator support panel in the service position (see Chapter 11).

16   To replace the belt, rotate the tensioner using a box end wrench to relieve the tension on the belt.

17   Remove the belt from the auxiliary components and carefully release the tensioner.

18   Route the new belt over the various pulleys, again rotating the tensioner to allow the belt to be installed, then release the belt tensioner. Make sure the belt fits properly into the pulley grooves - it must be completely engaged.

19   The remainder of installation is the reverse of removal.

Tensioner replacement

Refer to illustration 19.21

20   Remove the drivebelt.

21   Remove the fasteners that secure the tensioner to the engine **(see illustration)**, then remove the tensioner. **Note:** *On 3.2L engines, the mounting fastener is located under the tensioner center cap in the middle of the tensioner.*

22   Installation is the reverse of removal. Tighten the mounting bolt(s) to the torque listed in this Chapter's Specifications.

20   Brake fluid change (every 30,000 miles [48,000 km] or 24 months)

Refer to illustration 20.3

Warning: *Brake fluid can harm your eyes and damage painted surfaces, so use extreme caution when handling or pouring it. Do not use brake fluid that has been standing open or is more than one year old. Brake fluid absorbs moisture from the air. Excess moisture can cause a dangerous loss of braking effectiveness.*

19.21 Tensioner assembly mounting fasteners - 2.0L engine shown

20.3 Brake fluid reservoir siphon plug

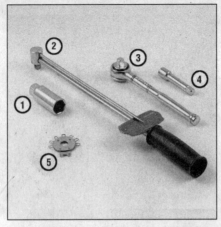

21.2 Tools required for changing spark plugs

1   **Spark plug socket** - *This will have special padding inside to protect the spark plug porcelain insulator*
2   **Torque wrench** - *Although not mandatory, use of this tool is the best way to ensure that the plugs are tightened properly*
3   **Ratchet** - *Standard hand tool to fit the plug socket*
4   **Extension** - *Depending on model and accessories, you may need special extensions and universal joints to reach one or more of the plugs*
5   **Spark plug gap gauge** - *This gauge for checking the gap comes in a variety of styles. Make sure the gap for your engine is included*

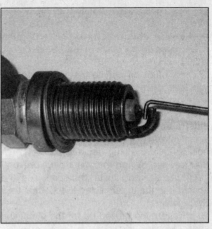

21.5 When checking the spark plug gap, the wire should slide between the electrodes with a slight drag

Note: *Used brake fluid is considered a hazardous waste and it must be disposed of in accordance with federal, state and local laws.* **DO NOT pour it down the sink, into septic tanks or storm drains, or on the ground.**

1   At the specified intervals, the brake fluid should be replaced. Since the brake fluid may drip or splash when pouring it, place plenty of rags around the master cylinder to protect any surrounding painted surfaces.

2   Before beginning work, purchase the specified brake fluid (see *Recommended lubricants and fluids* in this Chapter's Specifications).

3   Using a flat-blade screwdriver, remove the plug from the master cylinder reservoir **(see illustration)**.

4   Using a hand-held suction pump or similar device, withdraw the fluid from the master cylinder reservoir, then reinstall the plug.

5   Add new fluid to the master cylinder until the level of the fluid rises to the base of the filler neck.

6   Bleed the brake system as described in Chapter 9 at all four brakes until new and uncontaminated fluid is expelled from the bleeder screw. Be sure to maintain the fluid level in the master cylinder as you perform the bleeding process. If you allow the master cylinder to run dry, air will enter the system.

7   Refill the master cylinder with fluid and check the operation of the brakes. The pedal should feel solid when depressed, with no sponginess. **Warning:** *Do not operate the vehicle if you are in doubt about the effectiveness of the brake system.*

21 Spark plug check and replacement (every 30,000 miles [48,000 km] or 24 months)

Refer to illustrations 21.2, 21.5, 21.9, 21.11 and 21.12

1   The spark plugs are located in the cylinder head(s).

2   In most cases, the tools necessary for spark plug replacement include a spark plug socket which fits onto a ratchet (this special socket is padded inside to protect the porcelain insulators on the new plugs and hold them in place), various extensions and a feeler gauge to check and adjust the spark plug gap **(see illustration)**. Since these engines are equipped with an aluminum cylinder head, a torque wrench should be used when tightening the spark plugs.

3   The best approach when replacing the spark plugs is to purchase the new spark plugs beforehand, adjust them to the proper gap, then replace each plug one at a time. When buying the new spark plugs, be sure to obtain the correct plug for your specific engine. This information can be found in this Chapter's Specifications.

4   Allow the engine to cool completely before attempting to remove any of the plugs. During this cooling off time, each of the new spark plugs can be inspected for defects and the gaps can be checked.

5   The gap is checked by inserting the proper thickness gauge between the electrodes at the tip of the plug **(see illustration)**. The gap between the electrodes should be as listed in this Chapter's Specifications or in your owner's manual. Also check for cracks in

the spark plug body (if any are found, the plug must not be used).

6   Cover the fender to prevent damage to the paint. Fender covers are available from auto parts stores but an old blanket will work just fine.

7   There is one centrally mounted spark plug per cylinder. The ignition coils are mounted directly over the plugs. Remove each ignition coil from the spark plug (see Chapter 5).

8   If compressed air is available, use it to blow any dirt or foreign material away from the spark plug area. **Warning:** *Wear eye protection!* The idea here is to eliminate the possibility of material falling into the cylinder through the spark plug hole as the spark plug is removed.

9   Place the spark plug socket over the plug and remove it from the engine by turning it in a counterclockwise direction **(see illustration)**.

10   Compare the spark plug with the chart on the inside back cover of this manual to get an indication of the overall running condition of the engine.

21.9 Use a socket and extension to unscrew the spark plugs

11   It's a good idea to lightly coat the threads of the spark plugs with an anti-seize compound **(see illustration)** to insure that the spark plugs do not seize in the aluminum cylinder head.

12   It's often difficult to insert spark plugs into their holes without cross-threading them. To avoid this possibility, fit a piece of rubber hose over the end of the spark plug **(see illustration)**. The flexible hose acts as a universal joint to help align the plug with the plug hole. Should the plug begin to cross-thread, the hose will slip on the spark plug, preventing thread damage. Install the spark plug and tighten it to the torque listed in this Chapter's Specifications.

13   Repeat the procedure for the remaining spark plugs.

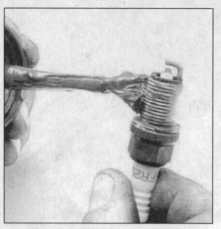

21.11 Apply a thin film of anti-seize compound to the spark plug threads to prevent damage to the cylinder head

21.12 A length of snug-fitting rubber hose will save time and prevent damaged threads when installing the spark plugs

22   Automatic transaxle fluid change (every 30,000 miles [48,000 km] or 24 months)

Refer to illustrations 22.5a, 22.5b and 22.7

Warning: *This procedure is potentially dangerous and is best left to a professional shop. The vehicle must be kept level while being safely raised high enough for access to the plugs on the transmission.*

Note: *When the vehicle is serviced by a dealer or other qualified repair shop, a scan tool is used to read the transaxle fluid temperature. To perform the job at home, you will have to estimate the temperature of the fluid.*

Note: *The engine must be running when checking the fluid level and when adding fluid.*

1   At the specified intervals, the transmission fluid should be drained and replaced. Since the fluid will remain hot long after driving, perform this procedure only after everything has cooled down completely.

2   Before beginning work, purchase the specified transmission fluid (see *Recom-*

mended lubricants and fluids in this Chapter's Specifications).

3   Other tools necessary for this job include jackstands to support the vehicle in a raised position, a drain pan capable of holding several quarts, newspapers and clean rags.

4   Raise and support the vehicle on jackstands. Remove the under-vehicle splash shield **(see illustration 6.7)**.

5   Place the drain pan underneath the transmission. Remove the drain plug **(see illustrations)** and allow the fluid to drain.

6   Install a new seal on the drain plug, then reinsert the plug and tighten it to the torque listed in this Chapter's Specifications. Measure the amount of fluid drained (the same amount will be added to the transmission later).

7   On these transaxles, the fluid is added through the check/fill plug hole. A special tool is available for this purpose, but a suction gun equipped with an angled nozzle can be used to pump the fluid up into the transaxle. The nozzle must pass through the opening in the

deflector cap. Remove the check/fill plug **(see illustration 22.5a or 22.5b)** and slowly add fluid through the check/fill hole until it runs out **(see illustration)**. Temporarily reinstall the check/fill plug.

8   With the transmission in Park and the parking brake set, run the engine at a fast idle.

9   Move the gear selector through each range, pausing for about two seconds in each range, then back to Park. Let the engine idle for a few minutes, then remove the check/fill plug. If fluid runs out of the hole, allow it to run out until it just drips. If no fluid runs out, add fluid through the hole until it does run out, allowing it to flow out until it just drips. **Note:** *The ideal temperature of the fluid when adjusting the level should be 95 to 113-degrees F.*

10   Install a new seal on the check/fill plug, then reinsert the plug and tighten it to the torque listed in this Chapter's Specifications.

11   Reinstall the under-vehicle splash shield.

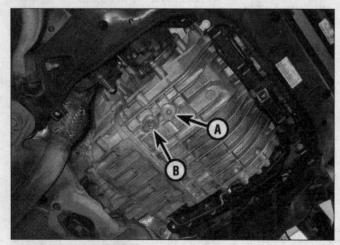

22.5a Automatic transmission level check/fill plug (A) and drain plug (B) - 01J transaxle

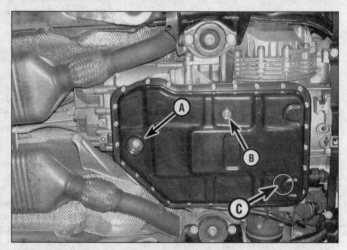

22.5b Automatic transmission level check/fill plug (A) and drain plug (B) - 01V transaxle. (C) is the vicinity of the drain plug on the 09L transaxle

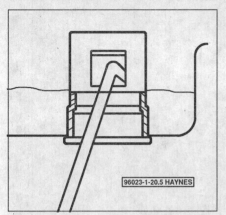

96023-1-20.5 HAYNES

22.7 The nozzle of the tool being used to add fluid to the transmission must pass through the window in the deflector cap

23.2 Differential check/fill plug (A) and drain plug (B) - 01R differential shown, 0AR differential similar

---

23 Rear differential lubricant change (every 60,000 miles [96,000 km] or 48 months)

Refer to illustration 23.2

1   This procedure should be performed after the vehicle has been driven so the lubricant will be warm and therefore will flow out of the differential more easily. Raise the vehicle and support it securely on jackstands.

2   Remove the check/fill plug, then remove the drain plug and drain the lubricant **(see illustration)**.

3   Reinstall the drain plug and tighten it securely.

4   Use a hand pump, syringe or funnel to fill the differential housing with the specified lubricant until the lubricant level is up to the bottom of the hole.

5   Install the filler plug and tighten it securely.

---

24 Manual transaxle lubricant change (every 60,000 miles [96,000 km] or 48 months)

Refer to illustration 24.3

1   This procedure should be performed after the vehicle has been driven so the lubricant will be warm and therefore will flow out of the transmission more easily. Raise the vehicle and support it securely on jackstands.

2   Move a drain pan, rags, newspapers and wrenches under the transmission.

3   Remove the fill plug from the side of the transmission case **(see illustration)**. Remove the transmission drain plug and allow the lubricant to drain into the pan.

4   After the lubricant has drained completely, reinstall the drain plug and tighten it securely.

5   Using a hand pump, syringe or squeeze bottle, fill the transmission with the specified lubricant until it just reaches the bottom edge

of the hole. Reinstall the fill plug and tighten it securely.

6   Lower the vehicle.

7   Drive the vehicle for a short distance, then check the drain and fill plugs for leakage.

---

25 Center differential lubricant level check (all-wheel drive models with automatic transaxles) (every 60,000 miles [96,000 km] or 48 months)

Note: *On manual transaxle models, the center differential lubricant is not separated from the transmission lubricant; filling the transmission fills the center differential, too (see Section 19).*

1   Raise the vehicle and support it securely on jackstands.

2   Using the appropriate wrench, unscrew the plug from the center differential, located on the right side of the center differential case.

3   Use your little finger to reach inside the housing to feel the lubricant level. The level

should be at or near the bottom of the plug hole. If it isn't, add the recommended lubricant through the plug hole with a syringe or squeeze bottle. Wait five minutes, then recheck the lubricant level, adding if necessary.

4   Install and tighten the plug. Check for leaks after the first few miles of driving.

---

26 Front differential lubricant level check (automatic transaxles) (every 60,000 miles [96,000 km] or 48 months)

Refer to illustration 26.2

Note: *On manual transaxle models, the differential lubricant is not separated from the transmission lubricant; filling the transmission fills the differential, too. The differential has a separate filler, and a different lubricant, on automatic transaxle models.*

1   Loosen the right front wheel lug bolts. Raise the vehicle and support it securely on jackstands. Remove the right front wheel.

2   Using the appropriate wrench, unscrew the plug from the transaxle **(see illustration)**.

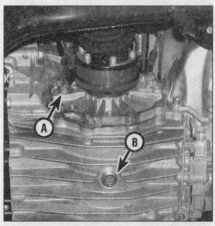

24.3 Location of the manual transmission check/fill plug (A) and drain plug (B; on some models the drain plug is on the lower side of the case)

26.2 Location of the check/fill plug for the automatic transaxle differential

27.1 Fuel filter details

A   *Fuel line fittings (one not visible)*
B   *Clamp screw*

28.4 On some models, the cooling system drain valve is located at the lower radiator hose connection

3   Use your little finger to reach inside the housing to feel the lubricant level. The level should be at or near the bottom of the plug hole. If it isn't, add the recommended lubricant through the plug hole with a syringe or squeeze bottle.
4   Install and tighten the plug. Check for leaks after the first few miles of driving.

27   Fuel filter replacement (every 60,000 miles [96,000 km] or 48 months)

Refer to illustration 27.1
Warning: *Gasoline is extremely flammable, so take extra precautions when you work on any part of the fuel system. Don't smoke or allow open flames or bare light bulbs near the work area, and don't work in a garage where a gas-type appliance (such as a water heater or clothes dryer) is present. Since gasoline is carcinogenic, wear fuel-resistant gloves when there's a possibility of being exposed to fuel, and, if you spill any fuel on your skin, rinse it off immediately with soap and water. Mop up any spills immediately and do not store fuel-soaked rags where they could ignite. When you perform any kind of work on the fuel system, wear safety glasses and have a Class B type fire extinguisher on hand. The fuel system is under pressure, so if any lines must be disconnected, the pressure in the system must be relieved first* (see Chapter 4 for more information).
1   The fuel filter is located under the rear of the vehicle, ahead of the right-rear wheel, adjacent to the fuel tank **(see illustration)**.
2   The manufacturer does not give a replacement interval, but our suggested interval is based on experience with many other vehicles; replacing it is like inexpensive insurance and may prevent an untimely breakdown.

3   Depressurize the fuel system (see Chapter 4), then disconnect the cable from the negative terminal of the battery. Raise the vehicle and support it securely on jackstands.
4   Use compressed air or brake system cleaner to clean any dirt surrounding the fuel inlet and outlet line fittings. **Note:** *On some models, it is necessary to remove a plastic splash shield for access.*
5   Disconnect the fuel lines from the filter; refer to Chapter 4 for information on how to disconnect quick-connect fittings. **Note:** *Have rags ready to catch or wipe up gasoline that will spill from the filter.*
6   Remove the clamp screw and detach the filter.
7   Installation is the reverse of removal. Make sure the arrow on the side of the new filter is pointing toward the engine side of the fuel system, and check for leaks after running the vehicle.

28   Cooling system servicing (draining, flushing and refilling) (every 60 months)

Warning: *Do not allow antifreeze to come in contact with your skin or painted surfaces of the vehicle. Rinse off spills immediately with plenty of water. Antifreeze is highly toxic if ingested. Never leave antifreeze lying around in an open container or in puddles on the floor; children and pets are attracted by it's sweet smell and may drink it. Check with local authorities about disposing of used antifreeze. Many communities have collection centers which will see that antifreeze is disposed of safely.*
Warning: *Wait until the engine is completely cool before beginning this procedure.*
1   Periodically, the cooling system should be drained, flushed and refilled to replenish the antifreeze mixture and prevent formation

of rust and corrosion, which can impair the performance of the cooling system and cause engine damage. When the cooling system is serviced, all hoses and the expansion tank cap should be checked and replaced if necessary.

Draining
Refer to illustration 28.4
2   Apply the parking brake and block the wheels. If the vehicle has just been driven, wait several hours to allow the engine to cool down before beginning this procedure.
3   Once the engine is completely cool, remove the expansion tank cap.

Models equipped with a drain valve
4   Move a large container under the cooling system drain valve to catch the coolant. Attach a length of hose to the drain fitting to direct the coolant into the container, then open the drain fitting (a pair of pliers may be required to turn it) **(see illustration)**.

Models not equipped with a drain valve
5   **1.8L four-cylinder and 3.0L V6 engines:** Remove the clip for the temperature sensor, either at the lower radiator hose or the radiator, and take out the sensor, allowing the coolant to drain.
6   **3.2L V6 engine:** Detach the rear coolant hose from the engine oil cooler and allow the coolant to drain, then disconnect the lower right radiator hose from the radiator and let the remaining coolant drain.

1.8L four-cylinder and 3.0L V6 engines
7   On the 1.8L four-cylinder engine, detach the rear coolant hose from the engine oil cooler and allow the remaining coolant to drain.
8   On the 3.0L V6 engine, detach the coolant hose from the top of the engine oil cooler and allow the remaining coolant to drain.

28.15 Loosen the clamp and slide the upper heater hose off the heater core pipe until this small hole is just forward of the pipe (all except 1.8L four-cylinder models)

All models

9 While the coolant is draining, check the condition of the radiator hoses, heater hoses and clamps (refer to Section 13 if necessary). Replace any damaged clamps or hoses.

10 Fill the cooling system at the expansion tank with clean water from a garden hose until it runs clear from all drains/disconnected hoses.

11 Reconnect all hoses that were detached. Also reinstall the temperature sensor, if removed. Close the drain valve on models so equipped.

12 When the coolant is regularly drained and the system refilled with the correct coolant mixture, there should be no need to employ chemical cleaners or descalers.

Refilling

Refer to illustration 28.15

13 Place the heater temperature control in the maximum heat position.

Models with a 3.0L V6 engine

14 Remove the bleeder screw from the coolant pipe at the front of the engine, between the right (passenger's side) cylinder head and the power steering pump. Slowly fill the cooling system at the expansion tank with the recommended mixture of antifreeze and water until coolant flows out of the bleeder screw hole, then install the bleeder screw and tighten it securely.

All except models with a 1.8L four-cylinder engine

15 Remove the cowl cover (see Chapter 11). Loosen the hose clamp and slide the upper heater hose off the heater core pipe just until the small hole in the hose is no longer blocked by the pipe **(see illustration)**.

16 Slowly add coolant to the expansion tank until coolant flows out of the hole in the hose, then push the hose onto the pipe and reinstall the hose clamp in the proper position.

All models

17 Add coolant to the expansion tank until the level is between the MIN and MAX marks on the expansion tank. Wait five minutes and recheck the coolant level, adding if necessary.

18 Install the expansion tank cap and run the engine in a well-ventilated area at 2000 rpm for three minutes.

19 Allow the engine to idle until both radiator hoses are warm (indicating that the thermostat has opened).

20 Raise the engine speed to 2000 rpm for one minute.

21 Turn the engine off and let it cool. Check the coolant level; add more coolant mixture, if necessary, to bring it up to the MAX mark on the expansion tank. Install the expansion tank cap.

22 Start the engine, allow it to reach normal operating temperature and check for leaks. Also, set the heater and blower controls to the maximum setting and check to see that the heater output from the air ducts is warm. This is a good indication that all air has been purged from the cooling system.

Service record

Date　　Mileage　　　　　　Work performed

Service record

Date	Mileage	Work performed

Notes

Chapter 2   Part A
Four-cylinder engines

Contents

	Section		Section
Camshafts and lifters - removal, inspection and installation	6	General information	1
CHECK ENGINE light on	See Chapter 6	Intake manifold - removal and installation	8
Crankshaft front oil seal and housing - replacement	12	Intermediate shaft oil seal - replacement	17
Crankshaft pulley - removal and installation	11	Oil pan - removal and installation	13
Cylinder compression check	See Chapter 2C	Oil pump - removal, inspection and installation	14
Cylinder head - removal and installation	10	Rear main oil seal - replacement	16
Drivebelt check, adjustment and replacement	See Chapter 1	Repair operations possible with the engine in the vehicle	2
Engine - removal and installation	See Chapter 2C	Spark plug replacement	See Chapter 1
Engine mounts - check and replacement	18	Timing belt and sprockets - removal, inspection and installation	5
Engine oil and filter change	See Chapter 1	Top Dead Center (TDC) for number one piston - locating	3
Engine overhaul - general information	See Chapter 2C	Valve cover - removal and installation	4
Exhaust manifold - removal and installation	9	Valve springs, retainers and seals - replacement	7
Flywheel/driveplate - removal and installation	15	Water pump - removal and installation	See Chapter 3

Specifications

General

1.8L four-cylinder engine designation	AMB
2.0L four-cylinder engine designations	BPG, BWT
Firing order	1-3-4-2
Cylinder numbering (front to rear)	1-2-3-4
Cylinder compression	
Minimum/maximum	130 to 203 psi
Variation between cylinders	44 psi
Oil pressure	
Idle	15 psi
300 rpm	51 to 65

FRONT
OF
VEHICLE

④
③
②
❶

72031-1-SPECS HAYNES

Cylinder numbering

Driveplate

Driveplate installed height	0.76 to 0.83 inch (19.5 to 21.1 mm)

Camshafts

Endplay (maximum)	0.008 inch (0.20 mm)
Bearing journal oil clearance (maximum)	0.004 inch (0.10 mm)
Runout (maximum)	0.001 inch (0.035 mm)

Torque specifications

	Ft-lbs (unless otherwise specified)	Nm

Note: *One foot-pound (ft-lb) of torque is equivalent to 12 inch-pounds (in-lbs) of torque. Torque values below approximately 15 foot-pounds are expressed in inch-pounds, because most foot-pound torque wrenches are not accurate at these smaller values.*

1.8L engines

	Ft-lbs (unless otherwise specified)	Nm
Camshaft bearing cap bolts (in sequence - **see illustration 6.7**)		
Step 1	Hand tighten	
Step 2	88 in-lbs	10
Cam adjuster solenoid housing bolts	88 in-lbs	10
Camshaft position sensor housing bolts	88 in-lbs	10
Camshaft position sensor rotor ring bolt	18.5	25
Camshaft sprocket bolts (new)	48	65
Crankshaft pulley (new)		
Step 1	88 in-lbs	10
Step 2	Tighten an additional 90-degrees	
Crankshaft sprocket		
Step 1	66	89
Step 2	Tighten an additional 90-degrees	
Crankshaft seal retainer flange		
Front	133 in-lbs	15
Rear	88 in-lbs	10
Cylinder head bolts (in sequence - **see illustration 10.23a**)		
Step 1	29.5	40
Step 2	Tighten an additional 180-degrees	
Drivebelt tensioner	18.5	25
Exhaust manifold bolts/nuts	18.5	25
Flywheel bolts (dual-mass flywheel)		
22.5 mm bolts		
Step 1	44	60
Step 2	Tighten an additional 90-degrees	
35 mm and 43 mm bolts		
Step 1	44	60
Step 2	Tighten an additional 180-degrees	
Driveplate		
Step 1	44	60
Step 2	Tighten an additional 90-degrees	
Intake manifold	88 in-lbs	10
Valve cover nuts	88 in-lbs	10
Oil pan bolts (new)		
Step 1, pan-to-engine block bolts	44 in-lbs	5
Step 2, pan-to-transmission bolts	33	45
Step 3, M10 bolts	29.5	40
Step 4, pan-to-engine block bolts	132 in-lbs	15
Baffle plate	142 in-lbs	16
Oil pump-to-block	142 in-lbs	16
Oil pump sprocket bolt	16.5	22
Oil pump chain tensioner	142 in-lbs	16
Timing belt cover bolts	88 in-lbs	10
Tensioner bolts	133 in-lbs	15
Tensioner pulley nut	20	27
Tensioner idler wheel bolt	18.5	25
Idler bracket bolt	88 in-lbs	10
Crankshaft TDC locking tool	18.5	25
Rear timing belt cover bolts	88 in-lbs	10
Camshaft sprocket bolts	74	100
Crankshaft sprocket bolt		
Step 1	147	199
Step 2	Tighten an additional 180-degrees	

2.0L engines

	Ft-lbs (unless otherwise specified)	Nm
Camshaft bearing guide bolts (in sequence - **see illustration 6.41**)		
Step 1	71 in-lbs	8
Step 2	Tighten an additional 90 degrees	
Cam adjuster sprocket bolts		
Step 1	177 in-lbs	20
Step 2	Tighten an additional 90 degrees	
Camshaft adjuster housing	88 in-lbs	10
Camshaft chain tensioner bolt	88 in-lbs	10

Torque specifications

	Ft-lbs (unless otherwise specified)	Nm
Camshaft sprocket bolts (new)		
Step 1	37	50
Step 2	Tighten an additional 180 degrees	
Valve cover bolts	88 in-lbs	10
Crankshaft damper/pulley (new bolts)		
Step 1	88 in-lbs	10
Step 2	Tighten an additional 90 degrees	
Crankshaft sprocket		
Step 1	66	89
Step 2	Tighten an additional 90 degrees	
Crankshaft seal retainer flange		
Front		
Step 1, bolts 1 through 6	132 in-lbs	15
Step 2, bolts 7 through 10	132 in-lbs	15
Rear	132 in-lbs	15
Cylinder head bolts (in sequence - **see illustration 10.23b**)		
Step 1	29.5	40
Step 2	Tighten an additional 180 degrees	
Drivebelt tensioner pulley	17	23
Drivebelt idler pulley		
Step 1	15	20
Step 2	Tighten an additional 90 degrees	
Exhaust manifold bolts/nuts	18.5	25
Flywheel bolts		
22.5 mm bolts		
Step 1	44	60
Step 2	Tighten an additional 90 degrees	
35 mm and 43 mm bolts		
Step 1	44	60
Step 2	Tighten an additional 180 degrees	
Driveplate		
Step 1	44	60
Step 2	Tighten an additional 90 degrees	
Intake manifold	80 in-lbs	9
Oil pan bolts (new)		
Step 1, pan-to-engine block bolts	44 in-lbs	5
Step 2, pan-to-transmission bolts	33	45
Step 3, M10 bolts	29.5	40
Step 4, pan-to-engine block bolts	132 in-lbs	15
Oil baffle		
Bolt 1	16	22
Bolt 2	80 in-lbs	9
Oil pump/balance shaft assembly-to-block		
Step 1	Hand tight	
Step 2	132 in-lbs	15
Step 3	Tighten an additional 90 degrees	
Oil pump sprocket bolt		
Step 1	15	20
Step 2	Tighten an additional 90 degrees	
Oil pump chain tensioner	142 in-lbs	16
Oil filter housing	132 in-lbs	15
Timing belt cover bolts (upper and lower)	88 in-lbs	10
Tensioner nut	18.5	25
Tensioner pulley nut	20	27
Damper roller bolt	17	23
Idler bracket bolt	88 in-lbs	10
Crankshaft TDC locking tool	18.5	25
Camshaft sprocket bolts		
Step 1	37	50
Step 2	Tighten an additional 180 degrees	
Crankshaft sprocket bolt		
Step 1	66	89
Step 2	Tighten an additional 90 degrees	

1.3a Engine cover mounting fasteners - 1.8L engine

1.3b On 2.0L engines, pull upward to release the cover grommets from the ballstuds

1   General information

Refer to illustrations 1.3a and 1.3b

This Part of Chapter 2 is devoted to in-vehicle repair procedures for the 1.8L and 2.0L four-cylinder gasoline engines. These engines utilize a cast-iron engine block with an aluminum cylinder head. Both engines are turbocharged and utilize dual overhead camshafts. Hydraulic lifters are used to actuate the valves. The aluminum cylinder head is equipped with pressed-in valve guides and hardened valve seats. The oil pump is mounted below the front of the engine and is chain driven from the crankshaft. The three-letter engine identification is stamped on top of the left front corner of the engine.

Information concerning engine removal and installation and engine overhaul can be found in Part C of this Chapter.

The following repair procedures are based on the assumption that the engine is installed in the vehicle. If the engine has been removed from the vehicle and mounted on a stand, many of the steps outlined in this Part of Chapter 2 will not apply. **Note:** *The engine cover must be removed before performing many of the procedures in this Chapter* **(see illustrations).**

2   Repair operations possible with the engine in the vehicle

Many major repair operations can be accomplished without removing the engine from the vehicle.

Clean the engine compartment and the exterior of the engine with some type of degreaser before any work is done. It will make the job easier and help keep dirt out of the internal areas of the engine.

Depending on the components involved, it may be helpful to remove the hood to improve access to the engine as repairs are performed (refer to Chapter 11 if necessary). Cover the fenders to prevent damage to the paint. Special pads are available, but an old bedspread or blanket will also work.

If vacuum, exhaust, oil or coolant leaks develop, indicating a need for gasket or seal replacement, the repairs can generally be made with the engine in the vehicle. The intake and exhaust manifold gaskets, oil pan gasket, crankshaft oil seals and cylinder head gasket are all accessible with the engine in place.

Exterior engine components, such as the intake and exhaust manifolds, the oil pan, the oil pump, the water pump, the starter motor, the alternator and the fuel system components can be removed for repair with the engine in place.

Since the cylinder head can be removed without pulling the engine, camshaft and valve component servicing can also be accomplished with the engine in the vehicle. Replacement of the timing belt and pulleys is also possible with the engine in the vehicle.

In extreme cases caused by a lack of necessary equipment, repair or replacement of piston rings, pistons, connecting rods and rod bearings is possible with the engine in the vehicle. However, this practice is not recommended because of the cleaning and preparation work that must be done to the components involved.

3   Top Dead Center (TDC) for number one piston - locating

Refer to illustration 3.6

1   Top Dead Center (TDC) is the highest point in the cylinder that each piston reaches as it travels up-and-down when the crankshaft turns. Each piston reaches TDC on the compression stroke and again on the exhaust stroke, but TDC generally refers to piston position on the compression stroke. The timing marks on the vibration damper/crankshaft pulley installed on the front of the crankshaft are referenced to the number one piston at TDC.

2   Positioning the piston(s) at TDC is an essential part of procedures such as timing belt and sprocket replacement.

3   In order to bring any piston to TDC, the crankshaft must be turned using one of the methods outlined below. When looking at the timing belt end of the engine, normal crankshaft rotation is clockwise. **Warning:** *Before beginning this procedure, be sure to place the transmission in Park or Neutral, set the parking brake and remove the ignition key.*

   a) *The preferred method is to turn the crankshaft with a large socket and breaker bar attached to the large bolt threaded into the center of the crankshaft pulley.*

   b) *A remote starter switch, which may save some time, can also be used. Attach the switch leads to the S (switch) and B (battery) terminals on the starter motor. Once the piston is close to TDC, use a socket and breaker bar as described in the previous paragraph.*

3.6 Align the notch on the crankshaft drivebelt pulley with the arrow on the timing belt cover

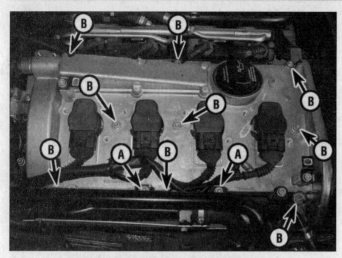

4.7a Valve cover mounting details - 1.8L engine

A   Coolant pipe bolts
B   Valve cover nuts

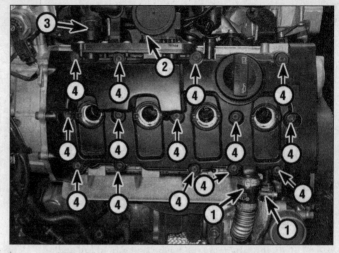

4.7b Valve cover mounting details - 2.0L engine

1   Disconnect the two hoses (unbolt the large one down at
      the turbocharger)
2   Unbolt and set aside the valve housing
3   Disconnect the EVAP line
4   Valve cover bolts

c)   If an assistant is available to turn the igni-
     tion switch to the Start position in short
     bursts, you can get the piston close to
     TDC without a remote starter switch. Use
     a socket and breaker bar as described in
     Paragraph a) to complete the procedure.

4   If method b) or c) described in the above
step will be used to rotate the engine, disable
the fuel system by removing the fuel pump
fuse (see Chapter 4).
5   Remove the all of the spark plugs (see
Chapter 1) and install a compression gauge in
the number one cylinder.
6   Rotate the crankshaft while observing
for pressure on the gauge. When the piston
approaches TDC, compression will be noted
on the compression gauge. Continue turning
the crankshaft until the notch in the crankshaft damper is aligned with the TDC mark
on the front cover (see illustration). At this
point number one cylinder is at TDC on the
compression stroke. If the marks aligned but
there was no compression, the piston was
on the exhaust stroke; continue rotating the
crankshaft 360-degrees (1-turn) and line-up
the marks. **Note:** *If a compression gauge is
not available, TDC for the No. 1 piston can
be obtained by simultaneously aligning the
marks on the camshaft (timing belt) sprocket
with the marks on the rear timing belt cover
and the marks on the crankshaft damper with
the TDC mark on the front cover* (see illustrations 5.10a and 5.10b).
7   After the number one piston has been
positioned at TDC on the compression stroke,
TDC for any of the remaining cylinders can be
located by turning the crankshaft 180-degrees
at a time, clockwise, and following the firing
order (refer to the Specifications). Rotating
the engine 180-degrees past TDC no. 1 will
put the engine at TDC compression for cylinder no. 3.

4   Valve cover - removal and installation

Removal

Refer to illustrations 4.7a and 4.7b

1   Remove the engine cover **(see illustration 1.3a or 1.3b)**. Remove the piping for the
PCV system and the secondary air combination valve, if so equipped.
2   If equipped, loosen the clip securing
the crankcase breather hose to the breather
pipe, then loosen the bolts securing the pipe
to the engine and remove the breather pipe.
On 2.0L engines, disconnect the EVAP hoses
at the right front corner of the valve cover and
on the left side of the valve cover, and unbolt
the crankcase ventilation pipe from the turbocharger.
3   Remove the ignition coils (see Chapter 5).
4   Remove the heat shield from the valve
cover, if equipped.
5   Remove the upper timing belt cover
from the engine **(see illustrations 5.12a,
5.12b, and 5.12c)**. Clips secure the cover
on 1.8L engines, but bolts are used on 2.0L
engines.
6   Remove the ground strap from the valve
cover.
7   Remove the retaining fasteners and
detach the valve cover from the cylinder head
(see illustrations).
8   If the cover is stuck to the head, bump
the end with a block of wood and a hammer
to jar it loose. If that doesn't work, try to slip
a flexible putty knife between the head and
cover to break the seal. **Caution:** *Don't pry at
the cover-to-head joint or damage to the sealing surfaces may occur, leading to oil leaks
after the cover is reinstalled.*

Installation

Refer to illustrations 4.10, 4.11a and 4.11b

9   The mating surfaces of the cylinder head
and cover must be clean when the cover is
installed. Remove all traces of sealant and
old gasket material including the spark plug
tube seal gaskets, then clean the mating surfaces with brake system cleaner. If there's
residue or oil on the mating surfaces when the
cover is installed, oil leaks may develop. Also
inspect the rubber end plug at the rear of the
cylinder head for cracks and damage. Now
would be a good time to replace it, if damage
has occurred.
10   On 1.8L engines, apply RTV sealant to
the corners of the camshaft front bearing cap
and to the camshaft drive chain tensioner
where they meet the cylinder head **(see illustration)**.

**4.10 Apply sealant to the corners of the
camshaft drive chain tensioner and to the
two points at the front camshaft bearing
cap where they meet the cylinder head**

4.11a On 1.8L engines, install the spark plug tube seal gasket with the tab facing the timing belt end of the engine

4.11b On 2.0L engines, the gasket is reusable - clean it and press it into the groove in the valve cover

11   On 1.8L engines, position a new valve cover gasket over the studs on the cylinder head, and install the spark plug tube grommet gasket over the studs on the cylinder head with the index marks facing the timing belt end of the engine **(see illustration)**. On 2.0L engines, the rubber gasket can be reused if not damaged **(see illustration)**. Tighten the inner nuts first, then the outer nuts in a criss-cross pattern.

12   Install the valve cover and any brackets removed, then tighten the retaining nuts or bolts to the torque listed in this Chapter's Specifications in several steps.

13   Reinstall the remaining parts, run the engine and check for oil leaks.

5   Timing belt and sprockets - removal, inspection and installation

Warning: *Wait until the engine is completely cool before beginning this procedure.*
Caution: *Do not rotate the crankshaft or the camshaft separately during this procedure with the timing belt removed as damage to valves may occur. Only rotate the camshaft a few degrees as necessary to align the camshaft sprocket marks with the marks on the rear timing belt cover.*

Removal

Refer to illustrations 5.9, 5.10a, 5.10b, 5.12a, 5.12b, 5.12c, 5.13, 5.18a, 5.18b and 5.19

Caution: *The timing system is complex. Severe engine damage will occur if you make any mistakes. Do not attempt this procedure unless you are highly experienced with this type of repair. If you are at all unsure of your abilities, consult an expert. Double-check all your work and be sure everything is correct before you attempt to start the engine.*

1   Disconnect the cable from the negative terminal of the battery (see Chapter 5).

2   Raise the front of the vehicle and support it securely on jackstands.

3   Working under the vehicle, remove the lower splash shield below the engine.

4   Place the radiator support panel in the service position (see Chapter 11). **Note:** *Access to the front of the engine is limited, therefore it will be necessary to remove the front bumper and position the radiator support panel forward enough to allow removal of the timing belt and the surrounding components.*

5   Working from above in the engine compartment, remove the engine cover **(see illustration 1.3a or 1.3b)**.

6   Remove the cooling fan (see Chapter 3).

7   Remove the spark plugs and the drivebelt (see Chapter 1).

8   Remove the drivebelt tensioner and drivebelt from the front of the engine (see Chapter 1).

9   Remove the bolts and the upper timing belt cover from the engine **(see illustration)**.

10   Rotate the engine in the normal direction of rotation (clockwise) until the No. 1 cylinder is located at TDC (see Section 3). Verify that the camshaft sprocket mark is aligned with the mark on the rear timing belt cover **(see illustrations)**.

11   Use an offset box wrench on the crankshaft center bolt to keep the crankshaft from rotating while removing the pulley mounting bolts. Loosen the crankshaft drive sprocket retaining bolt (only if the sprocket is to be removed) and the crankshaft pulley bolts, then remove the pulley (see Section 11). After the bolts are loosened, verify that the crankshaft has not moved from TDC. **Note:** *Loosening the drive sprocket bolt is only required if the crankshaft drive sprocket is expected to be removed. It is not typically necessary to remove the drive sprocket when you're simply replacing a timing belt, but it will have to be removed if you are replacing the crankshaft front oil seal or housing. If you do remove the drive sprocket, obtain a new bolt (the manufacturer doesn't recommend re-using it).*

12   Unscrew the retaining fasteners from the lower timing belt cover and remove the cover **(see illustrations)**.

13   If you plan to re-use the timing belt, apply match marks on the sprocket and belt, and make an arrow indicating direction of travel on the belt **(see illustration)**.

1.8L engine

14   Insert a hex tool into the tensioner pulley and slowly rotate the pulley counterclockwise to compress the tensioner piston until Audi tool no. T10008 (or equivalent) can be inserted to lock the piston into place. **Caution:** *Don't apply excessive force - it can take up to five minutes for the tensioner piston to be compressed.*

5.9 Upper timing belt cover bolts - 2.0L engines

5.10a When the engine is positioned at TDC for the No. 1 cylinder on the compression stroke, the camshaft sprocket mark will be aligned with the mark on the rear timing belt cover - 1.8L engines

5.10b Camshaft sprocket timing mark alignment - 2.0L engines

5.12a Remove the bolts . . .

5.12b . . . and detach the lower timing belt cover from the engine - 1.8L engines

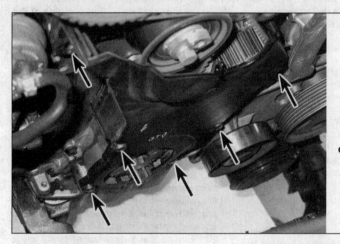

5.12c Screw locations on the lower timing belt cover - 2.0L engines

15 Loosen the tensioner pulley nut, then turn the eccentric bolt clockwise using Audi tool no. 3387, or equivalent.

2.0L engine

16 Loosen the tensioner pulley nut, then insert a hex tool into the tensioner pulley and turn the tensioner counterclockwise until the timing belt can be removed from the sprockets.

1.8L and 2.0L engines

17 Remove the timing belt from the engine, taking care to avoid twisting or kinking it excessively. **Note:** *If you're removing the upper part of the belt only, for camshaft seal replacement or cylinder head removal, it isn't necessary to detach the belt from the crankshaft sprocket.*

18 If the crankshaft sprocket is worn or damaged, or if you need to replace the crankshaft front oil seal, remove the drive sprocket retaining bolt which was loosened in Step 11 and detach the crankshaft sprocket from the crankshaft **(see illustrations)**.

19 If the camshaft sprocket is damaged or needs to be removed for other procedures

5.13 If you intend to re-use the timing belt, apply directional marks on the belt

5.18a With the crankshaft drive sprocket retaining bolt removed . . .

5.18b . . . the crankshaft sprocket is easily detached from the engine

5.19 If necessary, the camshaft sprocket bolt and the intermediate shaft sprocket bolt can be loosened while holding the sprocket in place with a pin spanner wrench

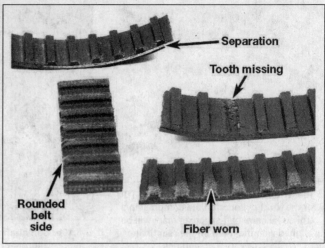

5.21 Check the timing belt for cracked and missing teeth - wear on one side of the belt indicates sprocket misalignment problems

such as cylinder head removal, use a pin spanner wrench or similar tool to hold the sprocket in place as the sprocket retaining bolt is loosened, then remove the camshaft sprocket from the end of the camshaft (**see illustration**). On 2.0L engines, use a two-jaw puller to remove the camshaft sprocket. **Note:** *The intermediate shaft sprocket may also be removed in the same manner as the camshaft sprocket if necessary.*

Inspection

Refer to illustration 5.21

Caution: *Do not bend, twist or turn the timing belt inside out. Do not allow it to come in contact with oil, coolant or fuel. Do not turn the crankshaft or camshaft more than a few degrees (if necessary for tooth alignment) while the timing belt is removed.*

20   Spin the timing belt tensioner pulley (which is the large pulley bolted to the engine block) and the idler wheel (which is the small roller mounted on the tensioner body) and check the bearings for smooth operation and excessive play. Also inspect the remaining timing belt sprockets for any obvious damage. Replace all worn parts as necessary.
21   Examine the belt for evidence of contamination by coolant or lubricant. If this is the case, find the source of the contamination before progressing any further. Check the belt for signs of wear or damage, particularly around the leading edges of the belt teeth (**see illustration**). **Caution:** *If the belt appears to be in good condition and can be re-used, it is essential that it is reinstalled the same way around, otherwise accelerated wear will result, leading to premature failure.*
22   Replace the belt if its condition is in doubt; the cost of belt replacement is negligible compared with potential cost of the engine repairs, should the belt fail in service. Similarly, if the belt is known to have covered more than 60,000 miles, it is prudent to replace it

regardless of condition, as a precautionary measure.

Installation

Caution: *Before starting the engine, carefully rotate the crankshaft by hand through at least two full revolutions (use a socket and breaker bar on the crankshaft pulley center bolt). If you feel any resistance, STOP! There is something wrong - most likely, valves are contacting the pistons. You must find the problem before proceeding. Check your work and see if any updated repair information is available.*

23   Ensure that the crankshaft is still set to TDC on No. 1 cylinder, as described in Section 3. If any of the timing sprockets or the tensioner pulley were removed for inspection or needed replacement, install them back onto the engine now. If the timing belt tensioner was removed, reinstall it now and tighten the bolts to the torque listed in this Chapter's Specifications, then install the tensioner pulley adjustment bolt loosely.
24   Make sure the camshaft sprocket mark is still in alignment with the mark on the rear timing belt cover (**see illustrations 5.10a and 5.10b**).

1.8L engines

25   Loop the timing belt loosely under the crankshaft sprocket. **Caution:** *Observe the direction of rotation markings on the belt.*
26   Engage the timing belt teeth with the crankshaft sprocket, then maneuver it into position over the water pump sprocket, tensioner pulley and the camshaft sprocket. **Note:** *Slight adjustments to the position of the camshaft sprocket may be necessary to achieve this.*
27   Ensure that the front run of the belt is taut and all the slack is in the section of the belt that passes over the tensioner pulley.
28   On 1.8L engines, use Audi tool #3387 to rotate the tensioner counterclockwise enough to remove the locking tool T10008 (or equiv-

alent). Use tool no. 3387 to turn the eccentric bolt clockwise until you can insert an 8 mm drill bit between the top of the tensioner body and the tensioner pulley lever. Hold the eccentric bolt in this position and tighten the tensioner pulley nut to the torque listed in this Chapter's Specifications.
29   Rotate the crankshaft two turns (clockwise) and bring it back to TDC on the compression stroke.
30   Make sure the gap between the top of the tensioner body and the tensioner pulley lever is between 6 to 10 mm. If it isn't, repeat Steps 14, 28 and 29 and check the dimension again.
31   The remainder of installation is the reverse of the removal procedure.

2.0L engines

Refer to illustration 5.34

32   Loop the timing belt loosely under the crankshaft sprocket. **Caution:** *Observe the direction of rotation markings on the belt.*

5.34 Timing belt tensioner details - 2.0L engine

A Tab   B Notch

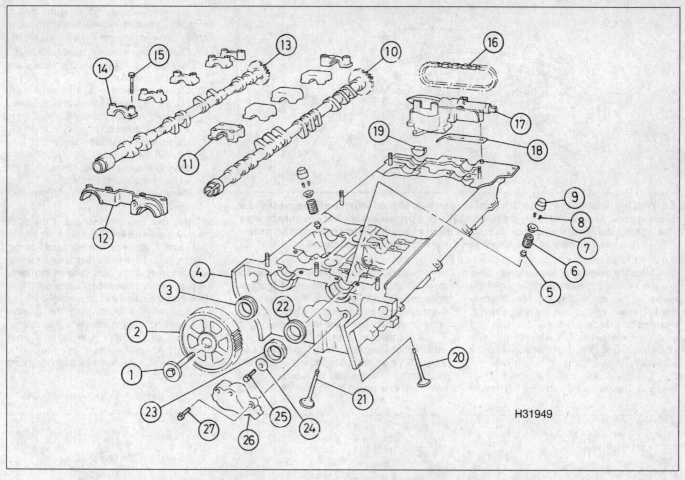

6.4 Exploded view of the camshafts and related components - 1.8L engine

1	Camshaft sprocket bolt	9	Hydraulic lifter
2	Camshaft sprocket	10	Intake camshaft
3	Oil seal	11	Intake camshaft bearing cap
4	Cylinder head	12	No. 1 bearing cap
5	Valve stem seal	13	Exhaust camshaft
6	Valve spring	14	Exhaust camshaft
7	Valve spring retainer		bearing cap
8	Valve keepers	15	Bolt

16	Camshaft drive chain	23	Reluctor ring
17	Camshaft drive chain	24	Washer
	tensioner	25	Bolt
18	Gasket	26	Camshaft position
19	End plug		sensor
20	Exhaust valve	27	Bolt
21	Intake valve		
22	Oil seal		

33   Route the belt clockwise in this order: around the lower guide pulley, the tensioning roller, the camshaft sprocket, water pump sprocket, then the relay pulley (the small roller). Ensure the belt teeth seat correctly on the sprockets. **Note:** *Slight adjustments to the position of the camshaft sprocket may be necessary to achieve this.*

34   Using a hex wrench, rotate the tensioner clockwise until the notch is positioned above the tab **(see illustration)**; this applies tension to the belt. Loosen the tensioner again, then rotate the tensioner until the notch is aligned with the tab, then tighten the nut to the torque listed in this Chapter's Specifications.

35   Install the lower timing belt cover and the crankshaft pulley.

36   Rotate the crankshaft two complete revolutions, bringing it back to TDC on the compression stroke. Check the alignment marks

again. Also re-check that the tensioner tab is positioned by the middle of the notch **(see illustration 5.34)**.

37   The remainder of installation is the reverse of removal.

6   Camshafts and lifters - removal, inspection and installation

Caution: *Performing this procedure may cause a trouble code to be set, which will require taking the vehicle to a dealer service department (or other repair shop equipped with the necessary scan tool) to have the cam sensor synchronized and the trouble code cleared.*

Note: *The camshafts and lifters should always be thoroughly inspected before installation and camshaft endplay should always be checked*

prior to camshaft removal. Although the hydraulic lifters are self adjusting and require no periodic service, there is an in-vehicle procedure for checking excessively noisy hydraulic lifters.

Removal

1.8L engine

Refer to illustrations 6.4, 6.5, 6.6a, 6.6b, 6.7, 6.9a and 6.9b

1   Remove the engine cover **(see illustration 1.3a)**.

2   Remove the valve cover (see Section 4).

3   Remove the timing belt and camshaft sprocket (see Section 5). Remove the secondary air combination valve (see Chapter 6).

4   Remove the camshaft position sensor (see Chapter 6). Remove the camshaft sensor reluctor ring from the end of the intake camshaft **(see illustration)**.

6.5 With the notches in the rear drive chain sprockets aligned with the arrows on the rear bearing caps, apply match marks on the chain with a permanent marker - be sure to wipe the oil from the chain and sprockets first, so the marker will adhere to the components - the number of rollers between the marks should be exactly 16

5   Mark the position of the camshaft drive chain in relationship to the sprockets and the marks on the rear bearing cap **(see illustration)**. This will ensure that the drive chain is installed in exactly the same direction and position from which it was removed. The chain has two colored links that align with the camshaft sprocket marks

6   Compress the camshaft drive chain tensioner. This can be accomplished by purchasing a special tool from the dealer service department which is specifically made for this purpose or by fabricating a home made tool using a threaded rod, several nuts, a plastic cable tie and a small metal plate **(see illustrations)**.

7   If not marked, mark the location of the camshaft bearing caps from 1 to 5 (and **I** for intake, **E** for exhaust), starting with the double bearing cap (which needs no number, since it only fits in one place) at the front (timing belt)

end. Also mark arrows indicating the front of the engine **(see illustration)**. Loosen the bearing cap nuts alternately in the following order:

1) *Loosen and remove the No. 3 and 5 bearing cap bolts from the intake and exhaust camshafts*
2) *Loosen and remove the front bearing cap*
3) *Loosen and remove the rearmost bearing cap bolts at each camshaft (No. E1 and I1 in* **illustration 6.7**)
4) *Remove the camshaft adjuster*
5) *Loosen and remove the No. 2 and 4 bearing caps, a little at a time, from the intake and exhaust camshafts*
6) *Remove both camshafts with the camshaft adjuster*

8   Remove the camshafts and the drive chain tensioner as an assembly from the cylinder head. **Caution:** *Keep the caps in order. They must go back in the same location they were removed from (and face in the same direction). Separate the tensioner and the drive chain from the camshafts on a workbench.*

9   Remove the lifters from the cylinder head, keeping them in order with their respective valve and cylinder **(see illustrations)**. **Caution:** *Keep the lifters in order. They must go back in the same location they were removed from.*

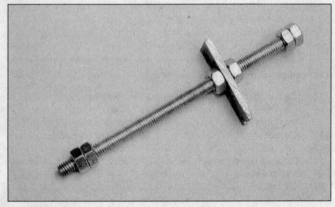

6.6a A homemade tool can be fabricated to compress the camshaft drive chain tensioner

6.6b The plastic cable tie is used to help secure the homemade tool in position as the tensioner is compressed

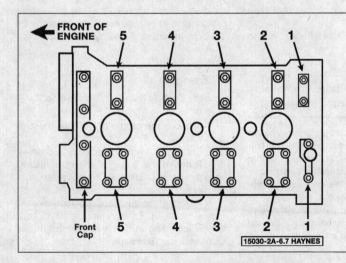

6.7 Camshaft cap numbering - 1.8L engine

6.9a The lifters can be removed from the cylinder head by hand or with a magnet . . .

6.9b . . . and stored in individually marked plastic bags or a divided box as shown - be sure to keep them in order with their respective valves

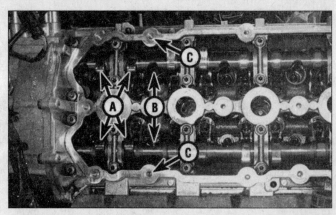

6.13 At TDC, the camshaft lobes for cylinder No. 4 should be pointed like this (A) - install a camshaft holding tool to engage the notches (B) and lock the cams in this position. The tool bolts to the cylinder head at holes (C)

2.0L engine

Refer to illustration 6.13

Warning: *Wait until the engine is completely cool before beginning this procedure.*

10   Remove the cylinder head (see Section 10). Place the cylinder head on blocks of wood positioned at each end to prevent damage to the valves.

11   Remove the camshaft position sensor (see Chapter 6).

12   Remove the bolts securing the cover over the camshaft adjuster at the rear of the cylinder head.

13   With the camshafts and crankshaft at TDC, use a locking tool (Audi # T10252 or similar homemade tool) to fit into the facing notches on both camshafts, then bolt the tool to the cylinder head so the camshafts cannot rotate **(see illustration)**.

14   Compress the camshaft drive chain tensioner and insert a drill bit or thick wire to retain the tensioner in the retracted position.

15   Remove the bolt securing the camshaft adjuster, then remove the chain and adjuster together.

16   The 2.0L engines do not have individual camshaft bearing caps. The front of each camshaft is secured by one cap over both camshafts. All of the remaining caps are part of one assembly called a guide frame. Remove the camshaft guide frame bolts in the reverse of the tightening sequence **(see illustration 6.41)**.

17   Remove the guide frame, then remove the camshafts and set them aside in a clean space. Remove all traces of gasket sealing material from the guide frame and cylinder head mating surfaces.

18   Do not reinstall camshaft and valvetrain components unless a thorough inspection proves they are in perfect condition.

Inspection

Refer to illustrations 6.20, 6.22, 6.23, 6.24a and 6.24b

19   Visually check the camshaft bearing surfaces for pitting, score marks, galling and abnormal wear. If the bearing surfaces are damaged, the cylinder head will have to be replaced. **Note:** *On 2.0L engines, if there is scoring on either the guide frame or the camshaft saddles in the cylinder head, both the cylinder head **and** the guide frame must be replaced.*

20   Measure the outside diameter of each camshaft bearing journal and record your measurements **(see illustration)**. Then measure the inside diameter of each corresponding camshaft bearing and record the measurements. Subtract each cam journal outside diameter from its respective cam bearing bore inside diameter to determine the oil clearance for each bearing. Compare the results to the specified journal-to-bearing clearance. If any of the measurements fall outside the standard specified wear limits in this Chapter, either the camshaft or the cylinder head, or both, must be replaced.

21   Check camshaft runout by placing the camshaft back into the cylinder head and set up a dial indicator on the center journal. Zero the dial indicator. Turn the camshaft slowly and note the dial indicator readings. Record your readings and compare them with the specified runout in this Chapter. If the measured runout exceeds the runout specified in this Chapter, replace the camshaft.

22   Place the camshafts back into the cylinder head and temporarily install the bearing caps/guide frame. Check the camshaft endplay by placing a dial indicator with the stem in line with the camshaft and touching the snout **(see illustration)**. Push the camshaft

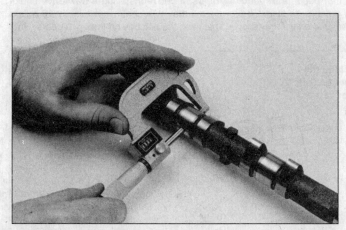

6.20 Measure the outside diameter of each camshaft journal and the inside diameter of each bearing surface on the cylinder head to determine the oil clearance measurement

6.22 Checking camshaft endplay with a dial indicator

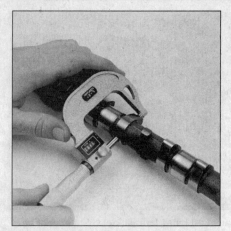

6.23 Measuring the camshaft lobe height with a micrometer - make sure you move the micrometer to get the highest reading (top of cam lobe)

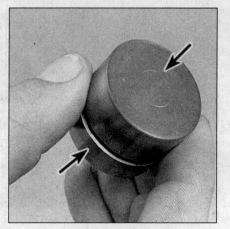

6.24a Inspect the valve lifters at the area shown

6.24b Also check the valve stem contact area of the lifter

all the way to the rear and zero the dial indicator. Next, pry the camshaft to the front as far as possible and check the reading on the dial indicator. The distance it moves is the end-

6.26 Lubricate the lifters with clean engine oil before installing them into the cylinder head

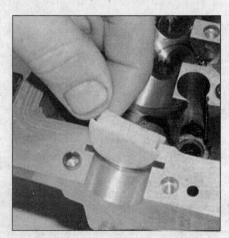

6.27a Install the rubber end plugs at the rear of the cylinder head

play. If it's greater than the value listed in this Chapter's Specifications, check the bearing caps/guide frame for wear. If the bearing caps or guide frame are worn, the cylinder head must be replaced.

23   Compare the camshaft lobe height by measuring each lobe with a micrometer **(see illustration)**. Measure each of the intake lobes and record the measurements and relative positions. Then measure each of the exhaust lobes and record the measurements and relative positions also. This will let you compare all of the intake lobes to one another and all of the exhaust lobes to one another. If the difference between the lobes exceeds 0.005 inch, the camshaft should be replaced. Do not compare intake lobe heights to exhaust lobe heights as lobe lift may be different. Only compare intake lobes-to-intake lobes and exhaust lobes-to exhaust lobes for this comparison.

24   Inspect the contact and sliding surfaces of each lifter for wear and scratches **(see illustrations)**. **Note:** *If the lifter pad is worn, it's a good idea to check the corresponding camshaft. Do not lay the lifters on their side or upside down, or air can become trapped inside and the lifter will have to be bled. The lifters can be laid on their side only if they are*

submerged in a pan of clean engine oil until reassembly.
25   Check that each lifter moves up and down freely in its bore on the cylinder head. If it doesn't the valve may stick open and cause internal engine damage.

Installation
1.8L engine
Refer to illustrations 6.26, 6.27a, 6.27b, 6.31, 6.32 and 6.34

26   Apply clean engine oil onto the sides and underside of the hydraulic lifters, and install them into position in their bores in the cylinder head **(see illustration)**. Push them down until they contact the valves, then lubricate the camshaft lobe contact surfaces.

27   Clean the mating surfaces of the drive chain tensioner and the cylinder head, then install the half-round end plugs at the rear of the cylinder head and a new drive chain tensioner gasket **(see illustrations)**.

28   Align the marks on the drive chain (made previously) with the notches on the camshaft drive gears and install the chain over the drive gears. If you're installing a new drive chain, install the drive chain with exactly 16 rollers between the notches on the drive gears. Note

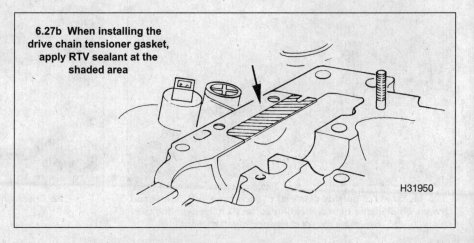

6.27b When installing the drive chain tensioner gasket, apply RTV sealant at the shaded area

H31950

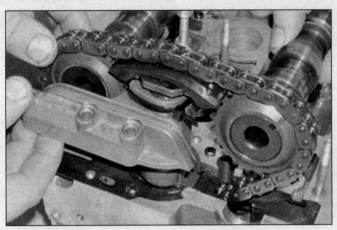

6.31 Align the drive chain tensioner over the dowels on the cylinder head

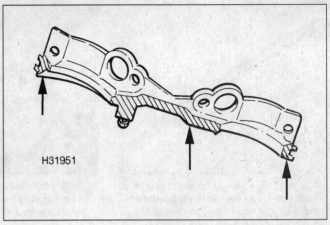

6.32 Apply a small amount of RTV sealant to the front bearing cap at the shaded areas

that the exhaust camshaft notch is slightly off center. In either case verify that there are 16 rollers between the notches of the intake and exhaust camshaft.

29   Compress the camshaft drive chain tensioner with the special tool and insert it between the drive chain and the camshafts.

30   Lubricate the camshaft and cylinder head bearing journals with clean engine oil. Carefully lower the camshafts, drive chain and tensioner as an assembly into position on the cylinder head with the No. 1 camshaft lobes facing up. Support the ends of the shaft as it is inserted, to avoid damaging the lobes and journals.

31   Install the drive chain tensioner over the dowels on the cylinder head and tighten the bolts to the torque listed in this Chapter's Specifications **(see illustration)**.

32   Install the camshaft bearing caps in the reverse order of removal (see Step 7). Be sure to apply a small amount of RTV sealant to the mating surface of the front bearing cap before installing it **(see illustration)**. After the bearing caps have been tightened, remove the drive chain tensioning tool from the tensioner.

Reconfirm that there are 16 rollers between the notches of the intake and exhaust camshaft, that the notches align with the arrows on the caps and that the No. 1 camshaft lobes face up.

33   Clean the oil seal housing bores, lubricate the lip of new camshaft oil seals with clean engine oil and locate them over the end of the camshafts. Slide the seals along the camshaft until they locate squarely in the housing bores.

34   Using a socket with an outside diameter slightly smaller than the outside diameter of the seal, carefully drive the new seals into place with a hammer **(see illustration)**. Make sure they're installed squarely and driven into the same depth as the original. If a socket isn't available, a short section of pipe will also work. **Note:** *Be sure to install both camshaft oil seals, one for the intake camshaft and one for the exhaust camshaft.*

35   Install the camshaft sprocket on the exhaust camshaft and the camshaft position sensor reluctor ring, conical washer and retaining bolt on the intake camshaft. Tighten the bolts to the torque listed in this

Chapter's Specifications.

36   Install the timing belt (see Section 5). When installing the timing belt, make sure the crankshaft is at TDC for the No. 1 cylinder and the camshaft sprocket mark is aligned with the rear timing cover.

37   The remainder of installation is the reverse of removal. **Caution:** *If new lifters were used, wait at least 30 minutes before starting the vehicle to allow the lifters to bleed down. Failure to do so will result in serious engine damage.*

2.0L engine

Refer to illustration 6.41

38   Clean and lubricate the camshafts, bearing saddles and the guide frame bearing surfaces with clean engine oil.

39   Install the camshafts in their original locations.

40   Before installing the guide frame, reinstall the exhaust camshaft seal, if necessary, then the exhaust camshaft timing belt sprocket.

41   Install the guide frame and tighten the bolts to this Chapter's Specifications, in the order shown **(see illustration)**.

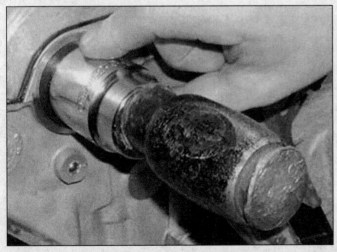

6.34 Gently drive the new camshaft oil seals into place with the spring side facing the engine

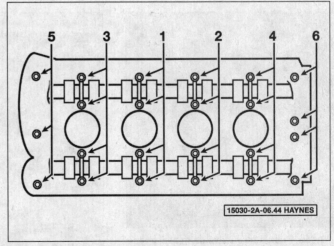

6.41 Camshaft bearing guide frame bolts - TIGHTENING sequence (2.0L engines)

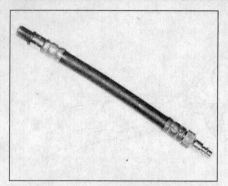

7.4 You'll need an air hose adapter to reach down into the spark plug wells on the cylinder head - they're commonly available at auto parts stores

7.8 While the valve spring tool is compressing the spring, remove the keepers with a small magnet or pliers

7.10 The old valve stem seals can be removed with a pair of needle-nose pliers

42   Position the camshafts as shown in **illustration 6.13**, then install the camshaft holding tool.

43   Reinstall the camshaft adjuster and the chain at the rear of the cylinder head, aligning the notch in the adjuster with the tab on the exhaust camshaft. Tighten the fasteners

7.15a Install the protective plastic sleeve over the valve end face to avoid damage to the valve seal as the seal is installed

to the torque listed in this Chapter's Specifications. **Note:** *When engaging the chain with the intake camshaft, place it over the top of the sprocket first.*

44   Remove the locking pin from the chain tensioner.

45   Install the camshaft adjuster housing, using a new gasket, and tighten the bolts to the torque listed in this Chapter's Specifications.

46   Install the cylinder head (see Section 10) and the timing belt (see Section 5).

47   The remainder of installation is the reverse of removal. **Note:** *Rotate the engine through two complete revolutions and ensure that both TDC marks still align.*

7   Valve springs, retainers and seals - replacement

Refer to illustrations 7.4, 7.8, 7.10, 7.15a, 7.15b, 7.15c, 7.16 and 7.17

Note: *Broken valve springs and defective valve stem seals can be replaced without removing the cylinder heads. Two special tools and a compressed air source are normally required to perform this operation, so*

read through this Section carefully and rent or buy the tools before beginning the job.

1   Remove the valve cover (see Section 4). Remove the camshaft and lifters (see Section 6). **Note:** *On the 2.0L four-cylinder engine, the cylinder head will have to be removed to remove the camshafts.*

2   Remove the spark plug from the cylinder which has the defective component. If all of the valve stem seals are being replaced, all of the spark plugs should be removed.

3   Turn the crankshaft until the piston in the affected cylinder is at Top Dead Center (TDC) on the compression stroke (see Section 3). If you're replacing all of the valve stem seals, begin with cylinder number one and work on the valves for one cylinder at a time. Move from cylinder-to-cylinder following the firing order sequence (see this Chapter's Specifications).

4   Thread an adapter into the spark plug hole **(see illustration)** and connect an air hose from a compressed air source to it. Most auto parts stores can supply the air hose adapter. **Note:** *Many cylinder compression gauges utilize a screw-in fitting that may work with your air hose quick-disconnect fitting.*

5   Apply compressed air to the cylinder. The valves should be held in place by the air

7.15b Push a new valve stem seal over the valve and down to the top of the guide, then remove the plastic installation tool

7.15c Gently tap the new seal in place on the guide with a socket

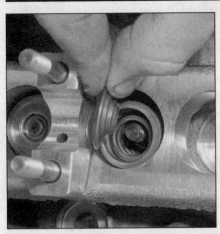

7.16 Install the valve spring and the retainer over the valve

7.17 Apply a small dab of grease to each keeper as shown here before installation - it'll hold them in place on the valve stem as the spring is released

pressure. **Warning:** *If the cylinder isn't exactly at TDC, air pressure may force the piston down, causing the engine to quickly rotate. DO NOT leave a wrench on the crankshaft drive sprocket bolt or you may be injured by the tool.*

6   Stuff shop rags into the cylinder head holes around the valves to prevent parts and tools from falling into the engine.

7   Using a socket and a hammer, gently tap on the top of the each valve spring retainer several times. This will break the bond between the valve keeper and the spring retainer and allow the keeper to separate from the valve spring retainer as the valve spring is compressed.

8   Use a valve spring compressor to compress the spring. Remove the keepers with small needle-nose pliers or a magnet **(see illustration)**. **Note:** *Several different types of tools are available for compressing the valve springs with the head in place. Be sure to purchase or rent the Import type that bolts to the top of the cylinder head. This type uses a support bar across the cylinder head for leverage as the valve spring is compressed. The lack of clearance surrounding the valve springs on these engines prohibits other types of valve spring compressors from being used.*

9   Remove the valve spring and retainer. **Note:** *If air pressure fails to retain the valve in the closed position during this operation, the valve face or seat may be damaged. If so, the cylinder head will have to be removed for repair.*

10   Remove the old valve stem seals, noting differences between the intake and exhaust seals **(see illustration)**.

11   Wrap a rubber band or tape around the top of the valve stem so the valve won't fall into the combustion chamber, then release the air pressure.

12   Inspect the valve stem for damage. Rotate the valve in the guide and check the end for eccentric movement, which would indicate that the valve is bent.

13   Move the valve up-and-down in the guide and make sure it doesn't bind. If the valve stem binds, either the valve is bent or the guide is damaged. In either case, the head will have to be removed for repair.

14   Reapply air pressure to the cylinder to retain the valve in the closed position, then remove the tape or rubber band from the valve stem.

15   Lubricate the valve stem with engine oil and install a new seal on the valve guide **(see illustrations)**.

16   Install the valve spring and the spring retainer in position over the valve **(see illustration)**.

17   Compress the valve spring and carefully position the keepers in the groove. Apply a small dab of grease to the inside of each keeper to hold it in place **(see illustration)**.

18   Remove the pressure from the spring tool and make sure the keepers are seated.

19   Disconnect the air hose and remove the adapter from the spark plug hole.

20   Install the camshaft, lifters, timing belt and the valve cover by referring to the appropriate Sections.

21   Install the spark plug(s) and ignition coil(s).

22   Start and run the engine, then check for oil leaks and unusual sounds coming from the valve cover area.

8   Intake manifold - removal and installation

Warning: *Wait until the engine is completely cool before beginning this procedure.*
Note: *This procedure applies to the 1.8L engine only. For intake manifold removal/ installation on 2.0L engines, see Chapter 4, Section 12.*

1   Remove the engine cover **(see illustration 1.3a or 1.3b)**.

2   Partially drain the engine coolant and remove the coolant expansion tank (see Chapter 3).

3   Disconnect the electrical connector at the throttle body.

4   Label and detach the electrical connectors from the throttle valve control module and the intake air temperature sensor (see Chapter 6).

5   Remove the upper intercooler hose from the throttle body.

6   Relieve the fuel system pressure and remove the fuel rail and injectors (see Chapter 4).

7   Remove the upper coolant pipe from the engine (see Chapter 3) and the coolant hoses from the throttle body (see Chapter 4). Also remove the oil dipstick and dipstick tube.

8   Label and detach any remaining vacuum lines (such as the brake booster vacuum hose) or electrical wiring that would interfere with removal of the intake manifold.

9   Remove the intake manifold lower support brace.

10   Remove the mounting nuts/bolts then detach the manifold and the throttle body as an assembly from the engine.

11   Use a scraper to remove all traces of old gasket material and sealant from the manifold and cylinder head, then clean the mating surfaces with brake system cleaner. If the gasket was leaking, have the manifold checked for warpage at an automotive machine shop and resurfaced if necessary.

12   Install a new gasket, then position the manifold on the head and install the nuts/ bolts.

13   Tighten the nuts/bolts in three or four equal steps to the torque listed in this Chapter's Specifications. Work from the center out towards the ends to avoid warping the manifold.

14   Install the remaining parts in the reverse order of removal.

15   Check the coolant and add some, if necessary, to bring it to the appropriate level. Run the engine and check for coolant and vacuum leaks.

16   Road test the vehicle and check for proper operation of all accessories, including the cruise control system.

9   Exhaust manifold - removal and installation

Warning: *The engine must be completely cool before beginning this procedure.*
Note: *This procedure applies to the 1.8L engine only. For exhaust manifold removal/ installation on 2.0L engines, see Chapter 4, Section 13.*

Removal

Refer to illustration 9.8

1   Remove the engine cover **(see illustration 1.3a or 1.3b)**.

2   Remove the air intake duct and the air cleaner housing (see Chapter 4).

3   Raise the front of the vehicle and support it securely on jackstands.

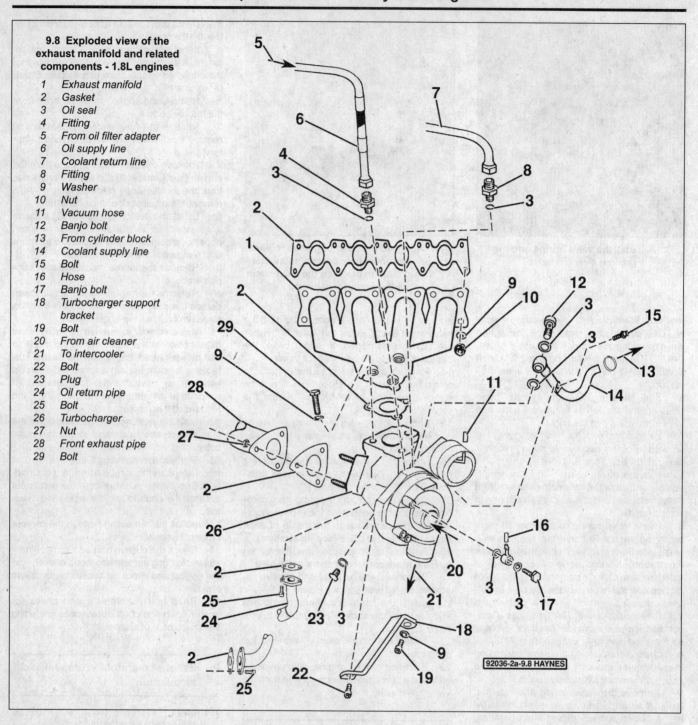

9.8 Exploded view of the exhaust manifold and related components - 1.8L engines

1   Exhaust manifold
2   Gasket
3   Oil seal
4   Fitting
5   From oil filter adapter
6   Oil supply line
7   Coolant return line
8   Fitting
9   Washer
10 Nut
11 Vacuum hose
12 Banjo bolt
13 From cylinder block
14 Coolant supply line
15 Bolt
16 Hose
17 Banjo bolt
18 Turbocharger support bracket
19 Bolt
20 From air cleaner
21 To intercooler
22 Bolt
23 Plug
24 Oil return pipe
25 Bolt
26 Turbocharger
27 Nut
28 Front exhaust pipe
29 Bolt

92036-2a-9.8 HAYNES

4   Remove the splash guard from below the engine compartment.
5   Refer to Chapter 4 and loosen the turbocharger support bracket bolts several turns, then detach the turbocharger oil supply line from the exhaust manifold heat shield if equipped.
6   Remove the exhaust manifold heat shield.
7   Remove the three bolts securing the turbocharger to the exhaust manifold and lower the turbocharger slightly. Remove the turbocharger to exhaust manifold gasket and cover the opening of the turbocharger with a rag to

prevent dirt particles and foreign objects from entering the turbocharger.
8   Remove the nuts/bolts and detach the exhaust manifold and gasket **(see illustration)**. If necessary, apply penetrating oil to the manifold mounting nuts/bolts to help facilitate removal.

Installation

9   Use a scraper to remove all traces of old gasket material and carbon deposits from the manifold and cylinder head mating surfaces. If the gasket was leaking, have the manifold checked for warpage at an automotive

machine shop and resurfaced if necessary.
10   Position a new gasket over the cylinder head studs.
11   Install the manifold and thread the mounting nuts/bolts into place. Make sure to use hi-temp anti-seize compound on the exhaust manifold fasteners.
12   Working from the center out, tighten the nuts/bolts to the torque listed in this Chapter's Specifications in three or four equal steps.
13   Reinstall the remaining parts in the reverse order of removal.
14   Run the engine and check for exhaust leaks.

10.9a Lift the cylinder head off the engine with the exhaust manifold attached (1.8L engines)

10 Cylinder head - removal and installation

Warning: *The engine must be completely cool before beginning this procedure.*
Caution: *Performing this procedure may cause a trouble code to be set, which will require taking the vehicle to a dealer service department (or other repair shop equipped with the necessary scan tool) to have the cam sensor synchronized and the trouble code cleared.*
Note: *On 1.8L engines only, the cylinder head can be removed with the exhaust manifold attached.*

Removal

Refer to illustrations 10.9a and 10.9b

1   Disconnect the cable from the negative terminal of the battery (see Chapter 5).
2   Drain the engine coolant (see Chapter 1). Refer to Section 3 and set the engine to TDC.
3   Remove the intake manifold (see Section 8).
4   Refer to Section 5 and remove the timing belt, following Steps 1 through 15. Also remove the rear timing belt cover.
5   On 1.8L engines, refer to Steps 1 through 7 in Section 9 and detach the turbocharger from the exhaust manifold. On 2.0L engines, remove the exhaust manifold/turbocharger assembly (see Chapter 4, Section 13).
6   Remove the valve cover (see Section 4).
7   Unplug all electrical connectors and the heater hose from the elbow at the rear of the cylinder head, labeling each wiring connector or hose to aid the installation process.
8   Working in the reverse of the sequence shown in **illustration 10.23a**, progressively loosen the cylinder head bolts, by half a turn at a time, until all bolts can be unscrewed by hand. Discard the bolts - new ones must be installed on reassembly.
9   Check that nothing remains connected to the cylinder head, then lift the head away from the cylinder block; seek assistance if possible, as it is very heavy, especially when being

10.9b If the cylinder head is stuck, it may be necessary to pry upward on the casting protrusion to dislodge the head from the block

removed with the exhaust manifold **(see illustration)**. If resistance is felt, carefully pry the cylinder head upward, beyond the gasket surface, at a casting protrusion **(see illustration)**.
10   Remove the gasket from the top of the block. Do not discard the gasket - it will be needed for identification purposes.
11   Before the cylinder head is reinstalled, your engine machine shop will have to inspect the cylinder head, valves, valve guides and other critical dimensions with precision measuring tools.

Installation

Refer to illustrations 10.19a, 10.19b, 10.23a and 10.23b

12   The mating faces of the cylinder head and cylinder block must be perfectly clean before installing the head. Use a hard plastic or wood scraper to remove all traces of gasket and carbon; also clean the piston crowns. Take particular care during the cleaning operations, as aluminum alloy is easily damaged. Also, make sure that the carbon is not allowed to enter the oil and water passages - this is particularly important for the lubrication system, as carbon could

block the oil supply to the engine's components. Using adhesive tape and paper, seal the water, oil and bolt holes in the cylinder block.
13   Check the mating surfaces of the cylinder block and the cylinder head for nicks, deep scratches and other damage. If slight, they may be removed carefully with abrasive paper.
14   If warpage of the cylinder head gasket surface is suspected, use a straight-edge to check it for distortion. At no point should a 0.004-inch feeler gauge fit between the straightedge and the head's gasket surface. This is only a rough test, your machinist will tell you if the head can be used again.
15   Clean out the cylinder head bolt holes using a suitable tap. Be sure they're clean and dry before installation of the head bolts.
16   It is possible for the piston crowns to strike and damage the valve heads if the camshaft is rotated with the timing belt removed and the crankshaft set to TDC. For this reason, the crankshaft must be set to a position other than TDC on No. 1 cylinder before the cylinder head is reinstalled. Use a wrench and socket on the crankshaft pulley center bolt to turn the crankshaft in the opposite direction of rotation (counterclockwise), until all four pistons are positioned halfway down their bores - approximately 90-degrees before TDC.
17   If the cylinder head has been resurfaced, make sure the machine shop also reworked the valve seats by the same amount to allow the correct piston to valve clearance before installing the cylinder head.
18   Cut off the heads from two of the old cylinder head bolts to use as alignment dowels during cylinder head installation. Also cut a slot in the end of these two bolts, big enough for a screwdriver blade, so that the alignment dowels can be removed after the cylinder head is installed.
19   Install the alignment dowels in the cylinder block and position the new head gasket on the cylinder block, engaging it with the locating dowels. Ensure that the manufacturer's "TOP" and part number markings are facing up **(see illustrations)**.

10.19a Two of the old head bolts can be used as cylinder head alignment dowels (typical)

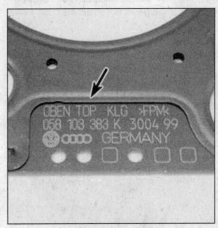

10.19b Be sure the "TOP" mark faces upward

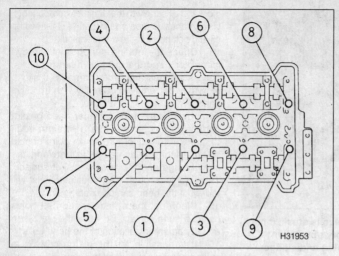

10.23a Cylinder head bolt TIGHTENING sequence

10.23b Using an angle measurement gauge during the final stages of tightening

20   With the help of an assistant, place the cylinder head centrally on the cylinder block, ensuring that the locating dowels engage with the recesses in the cylinder head. Check that the head gasket is correctly seated before allowing the full weight of the cylinder head to rest upon it. **Note:** *If the cylinder head had been disassembled for repair, be sure the camshaft(s) are reinstalled on the cylinder head with the No. 1 cylinder camshaft lobes pointing upward.*

21   Install the cylinder head bolts and screw them in hand tight. Be sure to use NEW cylinder head bolts, as the old bolts are stretch-type fasteners that will not provide the correct torque readings if reused.

22   Unscrew the homemade alignment dowels, using a flat-bladed screwdriver and install the remaining two bolts hand tight.

23   Working in the sequence shown **(see illustration)**, tighten the cylinder head bolts in four steps to the torque and angle of rotation listed in this Chapter's Specifications. **Note:** *It is recommended that an angle-measuring gauge be used during the final stages of the tightening, to ensure accuracy* **(see illustration)**. *If a gauge is not available, use white*

paint to make alignment marks between the bolt head and cylinder head prior to tightening; the marks can then be used to check that the bolt has been rotated through the correct angle during tightening.

24   Rotate the crankshaft clockwise 90-degrees to set the engine back at TDC. Be sure the alignment mark on the crankshaft pulley aligns with the mark on the front cover. Refer to Section 3, if necessary.

25   Install the timing belt tensioner and the camshaft sprocket on the engine if removed.

26   Install and adjust the timing belt as described in Section 5.

27   The remainder of the installation is the reverse of removal.

28   Change the engine oil and filter, and refill the cooling system (see Chapter 1). Run the engine and check for leaks.

11 Crankshaft pulley - removal and installation

Refer to illustration 11.5

1   Raise the front of the vehicle and support it securely on jackstands.

2   Working under the vehicle, remove the lower splash shield below the engine.

3   Place the radiator support panel in the service position (see Chapter 11). **Note:** *Access to the front of the engine is limited, therefore it will be necessary to remove the front bumper and position the radiator support panel forward enough to allow removal of the surrounding components.*

4   Remove the serpentine drivebelts (see Chapter 1).

5   Remove the bolts from the front of the crankshaft pulley and detach it from the engine **(see illustration)**.

6   If you're removing the crankshaft pulley for other procedures in this manual, such as crankshaft front oil seal removal, loosen the

drive sprocket retaining bolt by holding the engine from rotating with a locking tool on the sprocket, or remove the starter motor (see Chapter 5) and use a flywheel holding tool on the ring gear. **Note:** *If you remove this bolt, obtain a new one (the manufacturer doesn't recommend re-using it).* Upon installation, be sure to tighten the crankshaft drive sprocket bolt to the torque and angle of rotation listed in this Chapter's Specifications.

7   Position the crankshaft pulley on the crankshaft drive sprocket and align the mounting holes. Note that the pulley can only go on one way.

8   Install the pulley mounting bolts and tighten them to the torque listed in this Chapter's Specifications.

9   The remaining installation steps are the reverse of removal.

12 Crankshaft front oil seal and housing - replacement

Refer to illustrations 12.2 and 12.4

1   Remove the timing belt and crankshaft sprocket (see Section 5).

2   Note how far the seal is recessed in the bore, then carefully pry it out of the front cover with a screwdriver or seal removal tool. Don't scratch the housing bore or damage the crankshaft in the process (if the crankshaft is damaged, the new seal will end up leaking). **Note:** *If a seal removal tool is unavailable, you can thread two self-tapping screws (180-degrees apart from one another) into the front seal to pry the seal out* **(see illustration)**.

3   Clean the bore in the housing and coat the outer edge of the new seal with engine oil or multi-purpose grease. Apply multi-purpose grease to the seal lip.

4   Using a seal driver or a socket with an outside diameter slightly smaller than the out-

11.5 Crankshaft pulley retaining bolts

12.2 If a seal removal tool is unavailable, the front seal can also be removed with self-tapping screws to pry the seal out

12.4 Lubricate the seal lip and drive the new crankshaft seal into place with a seal driver or a large socket and a hammer

5   Drain the engine oil (see Chapter 1).
6   Remove the oil dipstick.
7   Remove the drivebelt (see Chapter 1).
8   Remove the engine cooling fan (see Chapter 3).
9   Unbolt the air conditioning compressor and secure it out of the way with rope or wire. **Warning:** *Do not disconnect the refrigerant lines.*
10   Remove the front torque rod (see Section 18).
11   Detach the starter motor cables from under the engine mount by cutting the plastic cable ties.
12   Disconnect the electrical connector from the oil temperature sending unit at the bottom of the oil pan.
13   1.8L models: Loosen the rear bolt on the right-hand transmission mount a few turns, then unscrew and remove the front bolt. On automatic transmission models, repeat this procedure on the left-hand transmission mount as well.
14   1.8L models: On manual transmission models, unscrew the left-hand transmission mount nut until it is flush with the end of the bolt (approximately four turns).
15   Connect an engine support fixture to the top of the engine, then raise it as far as possible without damaging or stretching the coolant hoses and wiring **(see illustration)**. Support the front of the suspension subframe with a floor jack. Remove the front stabilizer bar bracket bolts (see Chapter 10). On models with suspension level control, disconnect the front suspension level control link at the lower A-arm.
16   Remove the left engine mount and the bracket from the engine block (see Section 18).
17   Unscrew the flange bolts and disconnect the turbocharger oil return line from the side of the oil pan (see Chapter 4). Position the oil return line aside and remove the gasket. Be sure to replace the gasket with a new one upon installation.
18   Remove the front subframe bolts and lower the front of the subframe enough to

side diameter of the seal, carefully drive the new seal into place with a hammer **(see illustration)**. Make sure it's installed squarely and driven in to the same depth as the original. If a socket isn't available, a short section of large diameter pipe will also work. Check the seal after installation to make sure the spring didn't pop out of place.
5   If the front oil seal housing needs to be removed for access to other components, remove the housing mounting bolts and remove the housing from the engine while noting the installed position of the fasteners. In some instances the front oil seal removal and installation is easier with the front housing removed, since the seal can be placed on a workbench and driven straight in and out of the bore with no special tools or adapters.
6   If the front of the oil pan gasket was damaged while removing the housing, use a razor blade or utility knife to cut the pan gasket off flush with front edge of the cylinder block. This part of the oil pan gasket will be replaced with RTV sealant upon installation of the cover.
7   Before installing the front cover, make sure the mating surfaces of the cover, the cylinder block and the oil pan rail are perfectly clean. Use a hard plastic or wood scraper to remove all traces of gasket material. Take particular care when cleaning the front cover, as aluminum alloy is easily damaged.
8   Apply a 3/16-inch (5 mm) bead of RTV sealant to the oil pan flange.
9   Locate the oil seal housing gasket over the dowels on the engine block and install the oil seal housing. **Note:** *Be sure to lubricate the oil seal lip before installing the front cover onto the engine. This will aid the installation process and prevent dry start ups, which may damage the seal and lead to future oil leaks.*
10   Tighten the front oil seal housing bolts a little at a time to the torque listed in this Chapter's Specifications.

11   Reinstall the crankshaft sprocket and timing belt (see Section 5).
12   Run the engine and check for oil leaks at the front seal.

13   Oil pan - removal and installation

Removal

Refer to illustrations 13.15, 13.18 and 13.19
1   Set the parking brake and block the rear wheels.
2   Raise the front of the vehicle and support it securely on jackstands.
3   Remove the splash shield under the engine.
4   Place the radiator support panel in the service position (see Chapter 11). **Note:** *Access to the front of the engine is limited, therefore it will be necessary to remove the front bumper and position the radiator support panel forward enough to allow removal of the surrounding components.*

13.15 Raise the engine from above with a support fixture

13.18 Subframe mounting details

A   *Rear subframe crossmember and bolts*
B   *Stabilizer bar mounting bracket bolts*
C   *Front subframe bolts*

13.19 On models with a manual transmission, it will be necessary to align the cut-outs in the flywheel with the cut-outs on the oil pan to access the rear bolts

allow oil pan removal **(see illustration)**. **Note:** *Loosen but do not remove the rear subframe bolts, as a front end alignment will have to be performed after the oil pan procedure.*

19   Unscrew and remove the oil pan bolts. Note that on manual transmission models, the two rear oil pan bolts are accessed through a cut-out in the flywheel - turn the flywheel as necessary to align the cut-out **(see illustration)**.

20   Remove the oil pan and the gasket if equipped. If it is stuck, tap it gently with a mallet to free it.

Installation

Refer to illustrations 13.25 and 13.26

21   Use a scraper to remove all traces of old sealant from the block and oil pan. Clean the mating surfaces with brake system cleaner.

Note: *Some models use RTV sealant to seal the oil pan-to-cylinder block mating surface while others use a solid gasket material to seal the oil pan-to-cylinder block mating surface. Always reseal the oil pan-to-cylinder block mating surface with the same type of sealing material that it was originally equipped.*

22   Make sure the threaded bolt holes in the block are clean.

23   Check the oil pan flange for distortion, particularly around the bolt holes. Remove any nicks or burs as necessary.

24   Inspect the oil pump pick-up tube assembly for cracks and a blocked strainer. If the pick-up was removed, clean it thoroughly and install it now, using a new O-ring or gasket. Tighten the nuts/bolts to the torque listed in this Chapter's Specifications.

25   Apply a 1/8-inch (3 mm) bead of RTV sealant to the oil pan flange **(see illustration)**. **Note:** *The oil pan must be installed within 5*

minutes once the sealant has been applied.

26   Carefully position the oil pan on the engine block and install the oil pan-to-engine block bolts. **Note:** *If the engine or transmission is not installed in the vehicle, use a straightedge to align the rear surface of the oil pan with the rear face of the intermediate plate* **(see illustration)**. Tighten the bolts to the Step 1 torque listed in this Chapter's Specifications.

27   Install the oil pan-to-transmission bolts and tighten them to the Step 2 torque listed in this Chapter's Specifications.

28   Tighten the M10 bolts at the rear corners of the pan to the Step 3 torque listed in this Chapter's Specifications.

29   Working from the center out, tighten the oil pan-to-engine block bolts to the Step 4 torque listed in this Chapter's Specifications.

30   The remainder of installation is the reverse of removal. **Note:** *Be sure to follow*

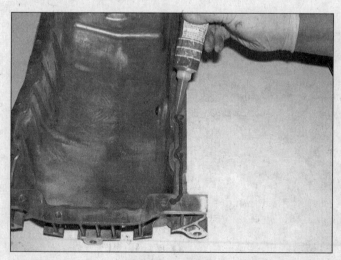

13.25 Apply a 3 mm bead of RTV sealant as shown to the oil pan sealing flange

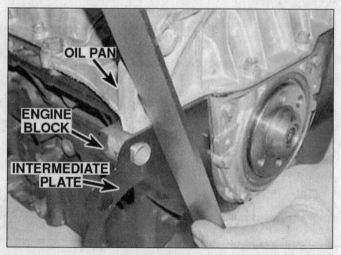

13.26 Use a straightedge to align the rear of the oil pan with the intermediate plate

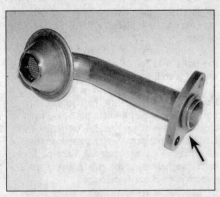

14.11 Always replace the pick-up tube O-ring

the sealant manufacturer's recommendations on curing times and allow the sealant to properly cure before adding oil.
31   Run the engine and check for oil pressure and leaks.

---

14   Oil pump - removal, inspection and installation

1.8L engine

Removal

1   Remove the oil pan (see Section 13).
2   Release and remove the baffle plate from the bottom of the crankcase.
3   Remove the bolt securing the drive sprocket to the oil pump and move the chain and sprocket aside.
4   Unscrew and remove the oil pump mounting bolts, then withdraw the pump from the block.

Inspection

5   Unscrew the two bolts and lift off the cover. Note that the cover incorporates the pressure relief valve.
6   Clean all components with solvent, then inspect them for wear and damage.
7   If damage or wear is noted, replacement of the entire oil pump assembly is recommended.

Installation

Refer to illustration 14.11

8   Clean the contact faces, then install the cover to the oil pump and tighten the bolts to the specified torque.
9   Prime the pump with oil by pouring oil into the pick-up tube aperture while turning the driveshaft.
10   Clean the oil pump and block, then install the oil pump, insert the mounting bolts, and tighten them to the specified torque. **Caution:** *Make sure the two dowel pins are in place and not cocked.*
11   Locate a new O-ring seal on the end of the pick-up tube **(see illustration)**. Insert the tube into the oil pump, then install the bolts and tighten them to the specified torque.

12   Reinstall the remaining parts in the reverse order of removal.
13   Add oil, start the engine and check for oil pressure and leaks.
14   Recheck the engine oil level.

2.0L engine

Removal

15   Rotate the engine to TDC compression for cylinder no. 1 (see Section 3).
16   Remove the fasteners securing the chain guard, and remove the guard.
17   While securing the crankshaft from moving, loosen the pump assembly sprocket bolt.
18   Depress the chain tensioner with a taped screwdriver until a small Allen wrench or drill bit can be inserted in the hole to hold the tensioner in this position.
19   Remove the chain from the oil pump sprocket.
20   Remove the oil baffle from the assembly, and remove the assembly mounting bolts, working from the ends toward the middle.

Inspection

21   The oil pump/balance shaft assembly must be replaced as a unit if wear is noted.

Installation

22   Installation is the reverse of the removal procedure, with the following exceptions.

   a)   *The balance shaft assembly mounting bolts should be replaced with new ones.*
   b)   *The assembly must be installed with a new gasket and O-ring seal.*

23   Add oil, start the engine and check for oil pressure and leaks.
24   Recheck the engine oil level.

---

15   Flywheel/driveplate - removal and installation

Caution: *The manufacturer recommends replacing the flywheel/driveplate bolts with new ones whenever they are removed.*

15.3 Mark the flywheel/driveplate and the crankshaft so they can be reassembled in the same relative positions

Removal

Standard flywheel/driveplate

Refer to illustrations 15.3 and 15.5

1   Raise the vehicle and support it securely on jackstands, then refer to Chapter 7 and remove the transaxle. If it's leaking, now would be a very good time to replace the front pump seal/O-ring (automatic transaxle) or input shaft seal (manual transaxle).
2   On manual transaxle equipped vehicles, remove the pressure plate and clutch disc (see Chapter 8). Now is a good time to check/replace the clutch components.
3   Use a center punch or paint to make alignment marks on the flywheel/driveplate and crankshaft to ensure correct alignment during reinstallation **(see illustration)**.
4   Remove the bolts that secure the flywheel/driveplate to the crankshaft. If the crankshaft turns, wedge a screwdriver in the ring gear teeth to jam the flywheel.
5   Remove the flywheel/driveplate from the crankshaft. Since the flywheel is fairly heavy, be sure to support it while removing the last bolt. Automatic transaxle equipped vehicles have spacers on both sides of the driveplate **(see illustration)**. Keep them with the driveplate.

Dual-Mass and Multitronic

6   On engines with the dual-mass flywheel, rotate the engine to TDC (see Section 3) and install the TDC timing stop in the front of the block. Use a flywheel-holding tool on the ring-gear to secure the flywheel.
7   Remove the clutch (see Chapter 8). Mark the relationship of the flywheel to the block.
8   Turn the rearmost section of the dual-mass flywheel by hand until the flywheel mounting bolts are centered in their openings. Remove the bolts using only hand tools, not impact tools. **Caution:** *The bolts should not touch the opening during removal or they could be damaged.*

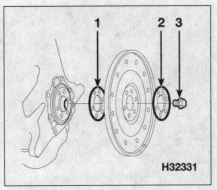

H32331

15.5 On vehicles with an automatic transaxle, there is a spacer plate on each side of the driveplate - mark each plate as it is removed so it can be installed back in the same position

   1   *Backing plate*
   2   *Shim*
   3   *Bolt*

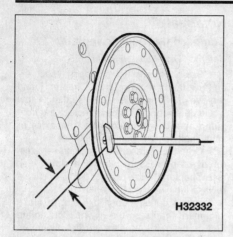

15.15 The driveplate installed height can be measured with a machinist's ruler or depth gauge, from the surface of the driveplate, through one of the holes to the engine block

9   The dual-mass flywheel has a needle-bearing insert that can be removed with a puller and installed with a driver.

10   On models with Multitronic transmission, the flywheel is fitted with a damper similar to a clutch plate on a manual-transmission application. Refer to Chapter 8 for basic removal and installation. The damper must be removed to access the flywheel bolts.

Installation

Refer to illustration 15.15

11   Use brake system cleaner on the flywheel to remove any dust, grease and oil. Inspect the surface for cracks, rivet grooves, burned areas and score marks. Light scoring can be removed with emery cloth. Check for cracked and broken ring gear teeth. Lay the flywheel on a flat surface and use a straight-

edge to check for warpage.

12   Clean and inspect the mating surfaces of the flywheel/driveplate and the crankshaft. If the crankshaft rear seal is leaking, replace it before reinstalling the flywheel/driveplate.

13   Position the flywheel/driveplate and spacer (if used) against the crankshaft. Be sure to align the marks made during removal. Note that some engines have an alignment dowel or staggered bolt holes to ensure correct installation. Before installing the bolts, apply thread locking compound to the threads.

14   Wedge a screwdriver in the ring gear teeth to keep the flywheel/driveplate from turning and tighten the bolts to the torque listed in this Chapter's Specifications. Follow a criss-cross pattern and work up to the final torque in three or four steps.

15   On vehicles equipped with an automatic transaxle, measure the installed height at three equal places around the driveplate and compare the average measurement to this Chapter's Specifications **(see illustration)**. If the measurement is incorrect, the driveplate must be removed and shimmed to the proper height.

16   The remainder of installation is the reverse of the removal procedure.

---

16   Rear main oil seal - replacement

Refer to illustrations 16.3, 16.7, 16.8a and 16.8b

1   The transaxle and the flywheel/driveplate must be removed from the vehicle for this procedure (see Chapter 7 and Section 15). Remove the sheetmetal intermediate plate that is between the block and the flywheel.

2   The rear oil seal and housing are an integral part which must be removed and replaced

together as a unit, however the rear seal and housing can be replaced without removing the oil pan.

3   Remove the rear oil seal housing mounting bolts and remove the housing from the engine **(see illustration)**.

4   Before installing a new rear seal and housing, make sure the mating surfaces of the cover, the intermediate plate, the cylinder block and the oil pan rail are perfectly clean. Use a hard plastic or wood scraper to remove all traces of gasket material. Take particular care when cleaning the rear housing, as aluminum alloy is easily damaged.

5   Install a new gasket on the cylinder block.

6   If the vehicle was originally equipped with a solid oil pan gasket material and it was not damaged during removal, apply a 1/8-inch (3 mm) bead of RTV sealant to the corners where the oil pan gasket meets the engine block.

7   Apply a 1/8-inch (3 mm) bead of RTV sealant to the oil pan sealing surface on the rear oil seal housing flange **(see illustration)**. **Note:** *Do not apply sealant to the oil pan, as this will cause the sealant to be pushed inward into the oil pan as the rear oil seal housing is positioned on the block.*

8   Install the rear oil seal housing over the dowels onto the engine. **Note:** *Be sure to lubricate the oil seal lip before installing the housing onto the engine. This will aid the installation process and prevent dry start ups, which may damage the seal and to lead to future oil leaks.* **(see illustrations)**.

9   Tighten the rear oil seal housing bolts evenly, in several steps to the torque listed in this Chapter's Specifications. Be sure to follow the sealant manufacturer's recommendations on curing times and allow the sealant to properly cure before adding oil.

10   The remaining steps are the reverse of removal.

16.3 Crankshaft rear oil seal housing mounting bolts

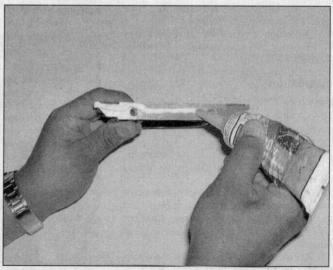

16.7 Apply a 1/8-inch (3 mm) bead of RTV sealant to the oil pan sealing surface on the rear oil seal housing

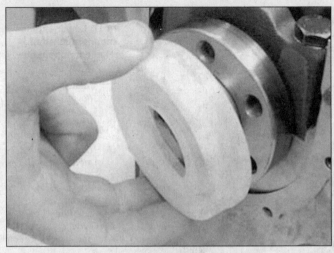

16.8a Install the seal installation tool over the end of the crankshaft . . .

16.8b . . . and slide the oil seal and housing over the tool

17 Intermediate shaft oil seal - replacement

1   Remove the timing belt and intermediate shaft sprocket as described in Section 5.
2   Drill two small holes into the existing oil seal, diagonally opposite each other. Thread two self-tapping screws into the holes, and using two pairs of pliers, pull on the heads of the screws to extract the oil seal **(see illustration 12.2)**. Take great care to avoid drilling through into the seal flange. An alternative method is to unbolt the flange, remove the inner O-ring from the inner groove, and press out the seal.
3   Clean out the seal flange and sealing surface of the camshaft by wiping it with a lint-free cloth. Remove any chips or burrs that may cause the seal to leak.
4   Lubricate the lip and outer edge of the new oil seal with clean engine oil, and start it in its housing by hand initially making sure that the closed end of the seal is facing outwards.
5   Using a seal driver or a hammer and a socket of suitable diameter, drive the seal squarely into its housing **(see illustration 12.4)**. **Note:** *Select a socket that bears only on the hard outer surface of the seal, not the inner lip which can easily be damaged.*
6   If the flange has been removed, replace the O-ring, then reinstall the flange and tighten the bolts to the torque listed in this Chapter's Specifications.
7   Reinstall the intermediate shaft sprocket and timing belt (see Section 5).

18 Engine mounts - check and replacement

1   Engine mounts seldom require attention, but broken or deteriorated mounts should be replaced immediately or the added strain placed on the driveline components may cause damage or wear.

Check

2   During the check, the engine must be raised slightly to remove the weight from the mounts.
3   Raise the vehicle and support it securely on jackstands, then position a jack under the engine oil pan. Place a large block of wood between the jack head and the oil pan, then carefully raise the engine just enough to take the weight off the mounts. Do not position the wood block under the drain plug. **Warning:** *DO NOT place any part of your body under the engine when it's supported only by a jack!*
4   Remove the splash shield under the engine, if equipped. Check the mounts to see if the rubber is cracked, hardened or separated from the metal plates. Sometimes the rubber will split right down the center.
5   Check for relative movement between the mount plates and the engine or frame (use a large screwdriver or pry bar to attempt to move the mounts). If movement is noted, lower the engine and tighten the mount fasteners.

Replacement

6   Raise the vehicle and support it securely on jackstands (if not already done). Support the engine as described in Step 3.
7   Remove the splash shield under the engine, if equipped.

Front torque rod

Refer to illustration 18.8

8   Unbolt the bracket from the bottom of the radiator support **(see illustration)**.
9   Unbolting the torque rod from the front of the cylinder block.
10   Pull the rubber stopper off the torque rod and replace it with a new one if it's damaged.
11   Installation is the reverse of the removal procedure.

Driver and passenger side engine mounts

Refer to illustration 18.17

Warning: *The weight of the entire engine will*

18.8 Torque rod mounting and bracket mounting fasteners

be supported by the transaxle mounts and the front torque rod during this procedure. Never place any part of your body directly under the engine when performing this procedure.

12   Set the parking brake and block the rear wheels. Support the engine from above with an engine support fixture or an engine hoist.

13   Raise the front of the vehicle and support it securely on jackstands.

14   Remove the splash shield under the engine, if equipped. **Caution:** *Remove the heat shield over the inboard joint of the right driveaxle before raising the engine.*

15   Detach the starter motor cables from the lower engine mount brackets by cutting the plastic cable ties and maneuvering the wires out of the plastic retainers.

16   Mark the relationship of the engine mount locating dowel to the bottom of the aluminum engine mount bracket for installation purposes, then unscrew and remove the nuts from the bottom of left and right engine mounts.

17   Support the front suspension subframe with a floor jack, then unscrew and remove the engine mount bracket bolts. The front two

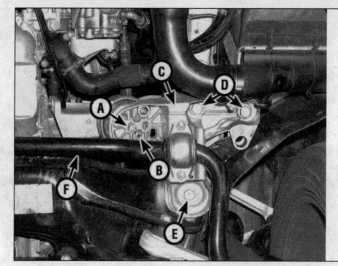

18.17 Lower engine mount bracket and related components

A   *Engine mount retaining nut (lower)*
B   *Locating dowel*
C   *Lower engine mount bracket*
D   *Lower engine mount bracket bolts (front)*
E   *Lower engine mount bracket bolt (rear)*
F   *Front stabilizer bar*

bolts must be unscrewed first, then the rear bolts **(see illustration)**. Lower the aluminum engine mount brackets together with the stabilizer bar.

18   Remove the upper engine mount nut.

19   If necessary, unbolt the mounting bracket from the side of the cylinder block.

20   Installation is the reverse of the removal procedure.

Chapter 2 Part B
3.0L and 3.2L V6 engines

Contents

	Section
Balance shaft - removal and installation	See Chapter 2C
Camshafts and lifters - removal and installation	7
CHECK ENGINE light on	See Chapter 6
Crankshaft front oil seal and housing - replacement	12
Crankshaft pulley - removal and installation	11
Cylinder compression check	See Chapter 2C
Cylinder head - removal and installation	10
Drivebelt check, adjustment and replacement	See Chapter 1
Engine - removal and installation	See Chapter 2C
Engine mounts - check and replacement	17
Engine oil and filter change	See Chapter 1
Engine overhaul - general information	See Chapter 2C
Exhaust manifold - removal and installation	9
Flywheel/driveplate - removal and installation	15

	Section
General information	1
Intake manifold - removal and installation	8
Oil pan - removal and installation	13
Oil pump - removal, inspection and installation	14
Rear main oil seal - replacement	16
Repair operations possible with the engine in the vehicle	2
Spark plug replacement	See Chapter 1
Timing belt and sprockets (3.0L engines) - removal, inspection and installation	5
Timing chain and sprockets (3.2L engines) - removal, inspection and installation	6
Top Dead Center (TDC) - locating	3
Valve covers - removal and installation	4
Water pump - removal and installation	See Chapter 3

Specifications

General

3.0L V6 engine designations	AVK, BGN
3.2L V6 engine designation	BKH
Firing order	
3.0L V6 engine	1-4-3-6-2-5
3.2L V6 engine	1-5-3-6-2-4
Cylinder numbering (front to rear)	
Left bank	4-5-6
Right bank	1-2-3

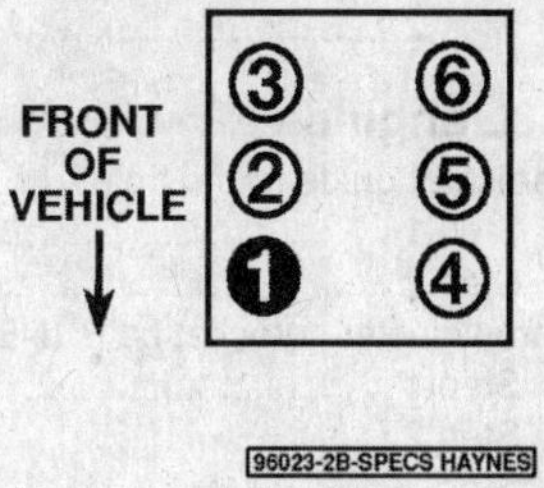

FRONT OF VEHICLE

③ ⑥
② ⑤
❶ ④

96023-2B-SPECS HAYNES

Cylinder locations

Camshaft

Endplay	
3.0L V6 engines	
New	0.003 to 0.006 inch (0.08 to 0.16 mm)
Wear limit	0.008 inch (0.20 mm)
3.2L engines	0.004 to 0.0075 inch (0.100 to 0.191 mm)

Torque specifications

	Ft-lbs (unless otherwise indicated)	**Nm**

Note: One foot-pound (ft-lb) of torque is equivalent to 12 inch-pounds (in-lbs) of torque. Torque values below approximately 15 foot-pounds are expressed in inch-pounds, because most foot-pound torque wrenches are not accurate at these smaller values.

3.0L engine

	Ft-lbs	**Nm**
Camshaft guide frame bolts		
Step 1	Hand tighten	
Step 2	88 in-lbs	10
Cam adjuster solenoid housing bolts	88 in-lbs	10
Camshaft position sensor housing bolts	88 in-lbs	10
Camshaft position sensor wheel	17	23
Cylinder head bolts **(see illustration 10.21a)**		
Step 1	29.5	40
Step 2	Tighten an additional 90 degrees	
Step 3	Tighten an additional 90 degrees	
Drivebelt tensioner		
To cylinder block	29.5	40
To alternator bracket	17	23
Exhaust manifold bolts/nuts (replace nuts)	18.5	25
Flywheel/driveplate bolts		
22.5 mm bolts		
Step 1	44	60
Step 2	Tighten an additional 90 degrees	
35 mm and 43 mm bolts		
Step 1	44	60
Step 2	Tighten an additional 180 degrees	
Intake manifold	88 in-lbs	10
Lower oil pan bolts	88 in-lbs	10
Upper oil pan		
M7 bolts	144 in-lbs	16
M8 bolts	16.5	22
Pan-to-transmission bolts	33	45
Front baffle fasteners	88 in-lbs	10
Rear baffle fasteners		
Step 1	15	20
Step 2	Tighten an additional 120 degrees	
Oil pump/balance shaft housing		
Bolts	16.5	22
Stud nuts		
Step 1	15	20
Step 2	Tighten an additional 120 degrees	
Balance shaft drive gear bolt		
Step 1	15	20
Step 2	Tighten an additional 90 degrees	
Tensioner bolts	88 in-lbs	10
Tensioner lever pivot bolt		
Step 1	22	30
Step 2	Tighten an additional 90 degrees	
Eccentric roller bolt	33	45
Idler bracket bolt	88 in-lbs	10
Crankshaft TDC locking tool	18.5	25
Camshaft sprocket bolts	74	100
Crankshaft sprocket bolt (new)		
Step 1	147	200
Step 2	Tighten an additional 180 degrees	

3.2L engines

	Ft-lbs	**Nm**
Camshaft guide frame bolts		
Step 1	71 in-lbs	8
Step 2	Tighten an additional 90 degrees	
Cam adjuster sprocket bolts (NEW)		
Step 1	29.5	40
Step 2	59	80
Step 3	Tighten an additional 90 degrees	
Camshaft position sensor housing bolts	88 in-lbs	10
Camshaft chain tensioner bolts	80 in-lbs	9
Drive sprocket mounting bracket bolts		
Step 1	71 in-lbs	8
Step 2	Tighten an additional 45 degrees	

Torque specifications

	Ft-lbs (unless otherwise indicated)	Nm
Timing chain upper cover bolts		
Step 1	44 in-lbs	5
Step 2	Tighten an additional 90 degrees	
Timing chain lower cover bolts		
M6 bolts	80 in-lbs	9
M8 bolts	15	20
Chain tensioner mounting bolts		
Step 1	53 in-lbs	6
Step 2	Tighten an additional 45 degrees	
Drive sprocket bracket		
Step 1	53 in-lbs	6
Step 2	Tighten an additional 45 degrees	
Drive sprocket bolts		
Left side		
Step 1	53 in-lbs	6
Step 2	Tighten an additional 60 degrees	
Right side		
Step 1	22	30
Step 2	Tighten an additional 90 degrees	
Chain guides		
Bolts with shaft		
Step 1	53 in-lbs	6
Step 2	Tighten an additional 60 degrees	
Convex bolts with collars, bolts with washers		
Step 1	22	30
Step 2	Tighten an additional 90 degrees	
Cylinder head bolts		
Step 1	29.5	40
Step 2	Tighten an additional 90 degrees	
Step 3	Tighten an additional 90 degrees	
Crankshaft TDC locking tool	120 in-lbs	13.5
Drivebelt tensioner		
To cylinder block	29.5	40
To alternator bracket	17	23
Exhaust manifold fasteners (new)	18.5	25
Flywheel/driveplate bolts		
22.5 mm bolts		
Step 1	44	60
Step 2	Tighten an additional 90 degrees	
35 mm and 43 mm bolts		
Step 1	44	60
Step 2	Tighten an additional 180 degrees	
Intake manifold bolts		
Upper	88 in-lbs	10
Lower (see Chapter 4)	88 in-lbs	10
Lower oil pan bolts	88 in-lbs	10
Upper oil pan		
M7 bolts	144 in-lbs	16
M8 bolts	16.5	22
Pan-to-transmission bolts	33	45
Front baffle fasteners	88 in-lbs	10
Rear baffle fasteners		
Step 1	15	20
Step 2	Tighten an additional 120 degrees	
Oil pump/balance shaft housing		
Bolts	16.5	22
Stud nuts		
Step 1	15	20
Step 2	Tighten an additional 120 degrees	
Balance shaft drive gear bolt		
Step 1	15	20
Step 2	Tighten an additional 90 degrees	

1   General information

Note: *The engine cover must be removed before performing many of the procedures in this Chapter.*

This Part of Chapter 2 is devoted to in-vehicle repair procedures for the 3.0L and 3.2L Dual Overhead Camshaft (DOHC) V6 engines. Both engines utilize a cast-iron engine block with aluminum cylinder heads. The 3.0L engines use five valves per cylinder (three intake and two exhaust), while the 3.2L engines use four valves per cylinder (two intake and two exhaust). Hydraulic lifters that ride directly below the camshafts are used to actuate the valves on both engines. The aluminum cylinder heads are equipped with pressed-in valve guides and hardened valve seats. The oil pump on both V6 engines is mounted below the front of the engine and is chain driven from the crankshaft.

Information concerning engine removal and installation and engine overhaul can be found in Part C of this Chapter.

The following repair procedures are based on the assumption that the engine is installed in the vehicle. If the engine has been removed from the vehicle and mounted on a stand, many of the steps outlined in this Part of Chapter 2 will not apply.

2   Repair operations possible with the engine in the vehicle

Many smaller repair operations can be accomplished without removing the engine from the vehicle, but some repair procedures require the engine be removed from the vehicle, as is noted in the beginning of those Sections. Clean the engine compartment and the exterior of the engine with some type of degreaser before any work is done. It will make the job easier and help keep dirt out of the internal areas of the engine.

Depending on the components involved, it may be helpful to remove the hood to improve access to the engine as repairs are performed (refer to Chapter 11 if necessary). Cover the fenders to prevent damage to the paint. Special pads are available, but an old bedspread or blanket will also work.

If vacuum, exhaust, oil or coolant leaks develop, indicating a need for gasket or seal replacement, the repairs can generally be made with the engine in the vehicle. The intake and exhaust manifold gaskets, oil pan gasket, crankshaft oil seals and cylinder head gasket are all accessible with the engine in place.

Exterior engine components, such as the intake and exhaust manifolds, the oil pan, the oil pump, the water pump, the starter motor, the alternator and the fuel system components can be removed for repair with the engine in place.

Since the cylinder head can be removed without pulling the engine, camshaft and valve component servicing can also be accomplished with the engine in the vehicle.

3   Top Dead Center (TDC) - locating

1   Top Dead Center (TDC) is the highest point in the cylinder that each piston reaches as it travels up the cylinder bore. Each piston reaches TDC on the compression stroke and again on the exhaust stroke, but TDC generally refers to piston position on the compression stroke.

2   Before beginning this procedure, be sure to place the transmission in Neutral and apply the parking brake or block the rear wheels. Remove the spark plugs (see Chapter 1). If method *b)* or *c)* will be used to rotate the engine in the next Step, also disable the fuel system (see Chapter 4, Section 2).

3   In order to bring any piston to TDC, the crankshaft must be turned using one of the methods outlined below. When looking at the front of the engine, normal crankshaft rotation is clockwise.

a) *The preferred method is to turn the crankshaft with a socket and ratchet attached to the bolt threaded into the front of the crankshaft. Turn the bolt in a clockwise direction.* **Note:** *On 3.2L V6 engines, a special socket adapter (Audi tool no. T40058) is necessary to rotate the crankshaft by the center bolt.*

b) *A remote starter switch, which may save some time, can also be used. Follow the instructions included with the switch. Once the piston is close to TDC, use a socket and ratchet as described in the previous paragraph.*

c) *If an assistant is available to turn the ignition switch to the Start position in short bursts, you can get the piston close to TDC without a remote starter switch. Make sure your assistant is out of the vehicle, away from the ignition switch, then use a socket and ratchet as described in Paragraph (a) to complete the procedure.*

4   Install a compression gauge in the spark plug hole for the cylinder in which you want to find TDC and rotate the crankshaft using one of the methods described above until pressure registers on the gauge, which indicates the cylinder has started the compression stroke. Once the compression stroke has begun, TDC for that cylinder is obtained when the piston reaches the top of the cylinder on the compression stroke.

5   To bring the piston to the top of the cylinder, remove the compression gauge and insert a long wooden or plastic dowel into the spark plug hole until it touches the top of the piston. Use the dowel (as a feeler gauge) to tell where the top of the piston is located in the cylinder while slowly rotating the crankshaft. As the piston rises, the dowel will be pushed out. The point at which the dowel stops moving outward is TDC.

6   If you go past TDC, rotate the crankshaft counterclockwise until the piston is approximately 1 inch below TDC, then slowly rotate the crankshaft clockwise again until TDC is reached.

7   After the piston has been positioned at TDC on the compression stroke, TDC for any of the remaining pistons can be rotating the engine clockwise, 120-degrees at a time, and following the firing order.

8   Section 5 describes how to precisely position the engine at TDC compression for cylinder no. 3 on the 3.0L engine, which is necessary for timing belt removal and installation.

4   Valve covers - removal and installation

Removal

1   Remove the engine cover(s). Early models have screws, while later covers can be removed by hand (they are retained by grommets).

2   Remove the ignition coils (see Chapter 5).

3   If equipped, loosen the clip securing the crankcase breather hose to the valve cover, then position the breather hose aside.

4   For access to the right valve cover, remove the right front engine cover, then the air intake tube and air filter housing (see Chapter 4). Remove the engine oil dipstick, then remove the bolt securing the dipstick tube to the engine and remove the tube.

5   For access to the left valve cover, remove the left front engine cover, then remove the coolant recovery tank (see Chapter 3).

6   Remove any electrical wiring, ground straps or hoses attached to the valve cover. Disconnect only those connectors and wiring that interferes with valve cover removal, which may include: engine coolant temperature sensor, low fuel pressure sensor, camshaft adjuster valve, intake runner position sensor, and the camshaft position sensor. Refer to Chapter 6 for sensor connector locations.

7   Remove the ignition coils and set the ignition coil harness aside. Remove the retaining bolts and detach the valve cover from the cylinder head.

8   If the cover is stuck to the head, bump the end with a block of wood and a hammer to jar it loose. If that doesn't work, try to slip a flexible putty knife between the head and cover to break the seal. **Caution:** *Don't pry at the cover-to-head joint or damage to the sealing surfaces may occur, leading to oil leaks after the cover is reinstalled.*

Installation

Refer to illustration 4.11

9   The mating surfaces of the housing or cylinder head and cover must be clean when the cover is installed. Use a gasket scraper to remove all traces of sealant and old gasket material including the spark plug tube seal

gasket, then clean the mating surfaces with brake system cleaner. If there's residue or oil on the mating surfaces when the cover is installed, oil leaks may develop.

10 The rubber gasket may be reused if it is not damaged. Clean the gasket and its groove before installation.

11 Install the valve cover and tighten the retaining bolts to the torque listed in this Chapter's Specifications in sequence (see illustration).

12 Reinstall the remaining parts, run the engine and check for oil leaks.

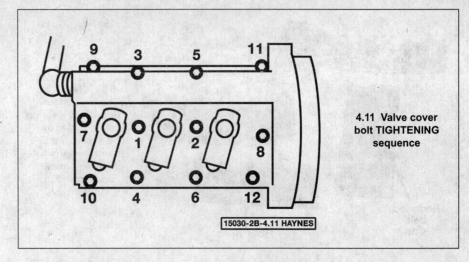

4.11 Valve cover bolt TIGHTENING sequence

5 Timing belt and sprockets (3.0L engines) - removal, inspection and installation

Warning: *Wait until the engine is completely cool before beginning this procedure.*

Caution: *The timing system is complex. Severe engine damage will occur if you make any mistakes. Do not attempt this procedure unless you are highly experienced with this type of repair and have access to the special tools. If you are at all unsure of your abilities, consult an expert. Double-check all your work and be sure everything is correct before you attempt to start the engine.*

Caution: *Do not rotate the crankshaft or the camshaft separately during this procedure with the timing belt removed as damage to valves may occur. Only rotate the camshaft a few degrees as necessary to align the camshaft alignment tool with the holes in the camshaft retainer plate.*

Note: *Special tools are required to complete this procedure, so read through the entire Section and obtain the special tools before beginning work.*

Removal

Refer to illustration 5.14

1 Disconnect the cable from the negative terminal of the battery (see Chapter 5).

2 Raise the front of the vehicle and support it securely on jackstands. Remove the drivebelt and the drivebelt tensioner (see Chapter 1).

3 Remove the under-vehicle splash shields. Working from above in the engine compartment, remove the engine covers.

4 Place the radiator support panel in the service position (see Chapter 11). **Note:** *Access to the front of the engine is limited, therefore it will be necessary to remove the front bumper and position the radiator support panel forward enough to allow removal of the timing belt and the surrounding components. In some instances, from the lack of sufficient working room and from a procedural standpoint, it may be easier to remove the entire support panel to gain full access to the components at the front of the engine. The extra time spent removing the panel will expedite* some procedures significantly.

5 Remove the spark plugs (see Chapter 1).

6 Remove the valve covers (see Section 4).

7 Remove the power steering pump pulley (see Chapter 10). Remove the bolts securing the crankshaft damper to the crankshaft, keeping note of the thrust washer behind the damper (if equipped) and which side faces the damper.

8 Remove the left, right and center timing belt covers.

9 Using a breaker bar and socket placed on the crankshaft sprocket bolt, rotate the engine until the mark on the crankshaft pulley is aligned with the pointer on the timing belt cover and the lobes of the intake and exhaust camshafts for cylinder number 3 are pointing upward at about a 45-degree angle towards each other. The crankshaft should be secured at the TDC position by removing the sealing plug at the lower-front of the block on the right side and inserting a TDC holding pin (Audi tool no. T40026) in the hole. You may have to rotate the crankshaft slightly to allow the TDC tool to align with the crankshaft.

10 Install a camshaft locking tool (Audi tool no. T40030) on each cylinder head. The tool should fit against the notches in each camshaft. **Caution:** *Tighten the tool to no more than 88 in-lbs (10 Nm) to secure the camshafts.*

11 Use a small screwdriver to pry out the circlips retaining the camshaft sprocket covers. **Note:** *Hold a rag under the camshaft covers to catch oil when removing the covers.*

12 Loosen the four camshaft sprocket bolts, but do not remove them.

13 Use a male hex socket to rotate the timing belt tensioner slowly counterclockwise until a drill bit or pin can be inserted through the hole in the tensioner body to secure the tensioner in the retracted position. **Caution:** *Don't apply excessive force to the tensioner, as it could be damaged.*

14 Remove the bolt securing the eccentric pulley at the lower left-front of the engine **(see illustration)**. If the belt is to be reused, mark the rotational direction of the belt with a marker. Remove the timing belt. If the timing belt sprockets show signs of wear or are to be removed for access in a different procedure, they can be removed now.

Inspection

Refer to illustration 5.16

Caution: *Do not bend, twist or turn the timing belt inside out. Do not allow it to come in*

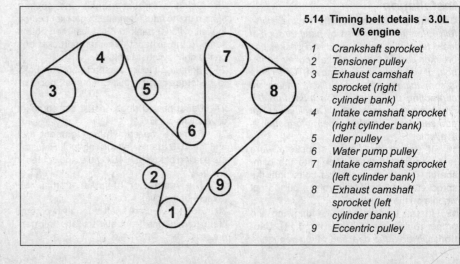

5.14 Timing belt details - 3.0L V6 engine

1 Crankshaft sprocket
2 Tensioner pulley
3 Exhaust camshaft sprocket (right cylinder bank)
4 Intake camshaft sprocket (right cylinder bank)
5 Idler pulley
6 Water pump pulley
7 Intake camshaft sprocket (left cylinder bank)
8 Exhaust camshaft sprocket (left cylinder bank)
9 Eccentric pulley

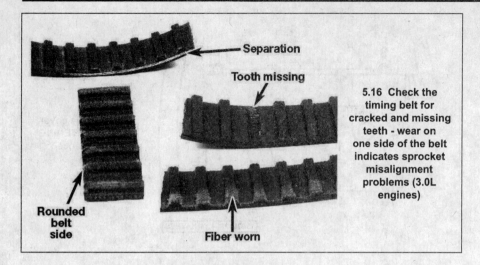

5.16 Check the timing belt for cracked and missing teeth - wear on one side of the belt indicates sprocket misalignment problems (3.0L engines)

contact with oil, coolant or fuel. Do not turn the crankshaft or camshaft more than a few degrees (if necessary for tooth alignment) while the timing belt is removed.

15   Inspect the remaining timing belt sprockets, pulleys, the tensioner(s) and the tensioner lever (if equipped) for any obvious damage. Replace all worn parts as necessary.

16   Examine the belt for evidence of contamination by coolant or lubricant. If this is the case, find the source of the contamination before progressing any further. Check the belt for signs of wear or damage, particularly around the leading edges of the belt teeth **(see illustration)**. **Caution:** If the belt appears to be in good condition and can be re-used, it is essential that it is reinstalled the same way around, otherwise accelerated wear will result, leading to premature failure.

17   Replace the belt if its condition is in doubt; the cost of belt replacement is negligible compared with potential cost of the engine repairs, should the belt fail in service. Similarly, if the belt is known to have covered more than 60,000 miles, it is prudent to replace it regardless of condition, as a precautionary measure.

Installation

Caution: Before starting the engine, carefully rotate the crankshaft by hand through at least two full revolutions (use a socket and breaker bar on the crankshaft pulley center bolt). If you feel any resistance, STOP! There is something wrong - most likely, valves are contacting the pistons. You must find the problem before proceeding. Check your work and see if any updated repair information is available.

18   If any of the timing sprockets were removed, install them back onto the camshafts. Tighten the sprocket bolts until the sprockets are just able to rotate, but do not wobble on the camshaft.

19   Install the timing belt, following the proper routing **(see illustration 5.14)**. **Caution:** Observe the direction of rotation markings on the belt if the old belt is being reinstalled.

20   On each sprocket, the front edge of the belt must be aligned exactly with the edge of the sprocket.

21   Using a two-pin spanner, rotate the eccentric pulley until the handle of the spanner is centered over the water pump pulley. While holding the spanner in this position, use a socket and ratchet to tighten the eccentric bolt to the torque listed in this Chapter's Specifications.

22   Using the hex tool on a torque wrench, rotate the tensioner slowly clockwise to approximately 33 ft-lbs (45 Nm) to pre-tension the belt. **Note:** The torque wrench must be in a horizontal position, with the handle of the wrench pointing towards the right side of the vehicle.

23   Using a male hex socket, rotate the timing belt tensioner counterclockwise slightly, until the holding pin can be removed. Release the tensioner slowly.

24   Using the hex tool on a torque wrench, rotate the tensioner slowly clockwise to approximately 19 ft-lbs (25 Nm) to tension the belt. **Note:** The torque wrench must be in a horizontal position, with the handle of the wrench pointing towards the right side of the vehicle.

25   Using a torque wrench and socket, tighten the exhaust camshaft sprocket bolt on the left cylinder bank to 89 in-lbs, then do the same to the exhaust camshaft sprocket bolt on the right cylinder bank.

26   Tighten all four camshaft sprocket bolts to the torque listed in this Chapter's Specifications.

27   Using new O-rings, install the sprocket covers with circlips.

28   Remove the camshaft alignment tool and the TDC crankshaft locking tool. Reinstall the sealing plug in the TDC hole and tighten it securely.

29   The remainder of installation is the reverse of removal.

30   Rotate the crankshaft through two complete revolutions to check for any interference.

6   Timing chain and sprockets (3.2L engines) - removal, inspection and installation

This repair procedure requires several expensive special tools. Because of the difficulty of this repair procedure and the necessary special tools, it is recommended to have the timing chain replaced by a dealer service department or other qualified automotive repair facility.

7   Camshafts and lifters - removal, inspection and installation

Caution: Performing this procedure may cause a trouble code to be set, which will require taking the vehicle to a dealer service department (or other repair shop equipped with the necessary scan tool) to have the cam sensor(s) synchronized and the trouble code cleared.

Note: The camshafts and lifters should always be thoroughly inspected before installation and camshaft endplay should always be checked prior to camshaft removal. Although the hydraulic lifters are self adjusting and require no periodic service, there is an in-vehicle procedure for checking excessively noisy hydraulic lifters.

Note: All V6 models covered in this manual make some valvetrain noise upon cold startup. This is normal. If there is noise regularly after the engine is warmed up, the intake manifold should be removed (see Section 8) and the oil check valves in the engine valley should be replaced. Remove the oil baffle for access to the valves (one at the front and one at the center of the valley).

3.0L V6 engine

Removal

Refer to illustrations 7.10a and 7.10b

1   Remove the engine covers.

2   Remove the valve covers (see Section 4). To check the lifters, rotate the camshaft lobes for the cylinder you are checking to straight up. Depress the lifter with a plastic tool and insert a feeler gauge between the camshaft lobe and the lifter. If a 0.20 mm feeler gauge can be inserted, the lifter is worn. All lifters should be replaced.

3   Remove the timing belt and camshaft adjusters (see Section 5).

4   Remove the rear timing belt cover on the cylinder head from which the camshafts are to be removed.

5   Disconnect the harness from the left end of the camshaft adjuster solenoid housing, then remove the solenoid housing mounting bolts.

6   At the rear of the cylinder head, remove the bolts securing the camshaft position sensor housing (see Chapter 6).

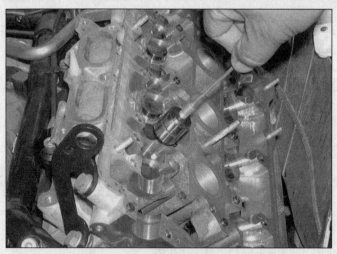

7.10a The lifters can be removed from the cylinder head by hand or with a magnet . . .

7.10b . . . and stored in individually marked plastic bags or a divided box

7   The camshafts mount to the cylinder head with a guide frame, rather than individual bearing caps. Loosen the guide frame bolts a little at a time, starting with the bolts at the ends of the guide frame and working your way inwards.

8   There are two threaded holes in the guide frame; one at the front and one at the rear. Insert two M6 bolts and tighten them evenly to push the guide frame up from the cylinder head.

9   Mark the camshafts for identification. Remove the guide frame, then the camshafts. **Note:** *Do not mix the camshafts for the left and right cylinder heads - they are specific to each cylinder head and will not interchange.*

10   Remove the lifters from the cylinder head, keeping the them in order with their respective valve and cylinder **(see illustrations). Caution:** *Keep the lifters in order.*

They must go back in the same location from which they were removed.

Inspection

Refer to illustrations 7.12 and 7.13

11   After the camshaft has been removed from the engine, cleaned with solvent and dried, inspect the bearing journals for uneven wear, pitting and evidence of seizure. If the camshaft journals are damaged, inspect the cylinder head also.

12   Measure the lobe height of each cam lobe on the intake camshaft and record your measurements **(see illustration)**. Compare the measurements for excessive variations. Standard measurements should be within 0.001 inch (0.025 mm). If the lobe heights vary more than 0.010 inch (0.254 mm), replace the camshaft. Compare the lobe height measurements on the exhaust camshaft and follow the same procedure. Do not

compare intake camshaft lobe heights with exhaust camshaft lobe heights, as they are different. Only compare intake lobes with intake lobes and exhaust lobes with other exhaust lobes.

13   Place the camshafts back into the cylinder head and temporarily install the guide frame. Check the camshaft endplay by placing a dial indicator with the stem in line with the camshaft and touching the snout **(see illustration)**. Push the camshaft all the way to the rear and zero the dial indicator. Next, pry the camshaft to the front as far as possible and check the reading on the dial indicator. The distance it moves is the endplay. If it's greater than the value listed in this Chapter's Specifications, check the guide frame for wear. If the guide frame is worn, the cylinder head must be replaced.

14   Check the camshaft lobes for heat discoloration, score marks, chipped areas, pit-

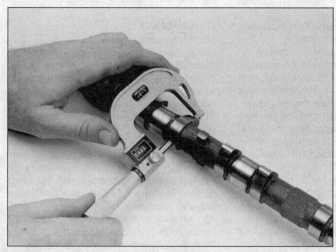

7.12 Measuring the camshaft lobe height with a micrometer - make sure you move the micrometer to get the highest reading (top of cam lobe)

7.13 Checking camshaft endplay with a dial indicator

ting and uneven wear. If the lobes are in good condition and if the lobe lift variation measurements recorded earlier are within the limits, the camshaft can be reused.

Installation

15   Apply clean engine oil onto the sides of the lifters/hydraulic adjusters, then install them into position in their original bores in the cylinder head. Push them down until they contact the valves, then lubricate the camshaft lobe contact surfaces.

16   Lubricate the camshaft and cylinder head bearing journals with clean engine oil. Carefully lower the camshafts into position on the cylinder head. Support the ends of the shaft as it is inserted, to avoid damaging the lobes and journals.

17   On the left cylinder head, position both camshafts so that the lobes of cylinder No. 5 point downward, towards the middle of the head, so the lobes are just below the top of the cylinder head surface.

18   On the right cylinder head, position both camshafts so that the lobes of cylinder No. 3 point upward, and slightly away from each other, at the same angle.

19   Clean the guide frame and cylinder head mating surfaces thoroughly to remove any traces of old sealant. Apply a 1.2 mm bead of sealant to the perimeter mating surfaces of the guide frame, and the mating surfaces around the spark plug access holes of the guide frame. The guide frame must be installed within five minutes of applying the sealant.

20   Install the guide frame over the camshafts and install the bolts. A special tool (Audi tool no. T40029) is used to precisely align the guide frame to the head; this tool fits through the front-most spark plug hole. Tighten the bolts to the Specifications listed in this Chapter, in the proper sequence. Immediately use clean paper towels or cloth to remove any excess sealant that squeezes out.

21   Turn the camshafts so that the camshaft locking tools (Audi tool no. T40030) properly position the camshafts on each cylinder head. The tool should fit against the notches in each camshaft. **Caution:** *Tighten the tool to no more than 88 in-lbs (10 Nm) to secure the camshafts.*

22   The remainder of installation is the reverse of removal (see Section 5). When installing the camshaft adjuster solenoid housing, use new O-rings. Before installing the camshaft adjuster valve housing, remove the camshaft oil seals from the housing.

23   Install new camshaft oil seals, driving them in carefully with a seal driver.

24   Remove the crankshaft locking tool and rotate the crankshaft through two complete revolutions to check for any interference.

25   The remainder of installation is the reverse of removal. **Caution:** *If new lifters were installed, wait at least 30 minutes before starting the vehicle to allow the lifters to bleed down. Failure to do so will result in serious engine damage.*

3.2L engine

26   This repair procedure requires several expensive special tools. Because of the difficulty of this repair procedure and the necessary special tools, it is recommended to have this procedure performed by a dealer service department or other qualified automotive repair facility.

---

8   Intake manifold - removal and installation

Warning: *Wait until the engine is completely cool before beginning this procedure.*
Note: *The following procedure applies to 3.0L engines, and the upper intake manifold on 3.2L engines. For lower intake manifold removal and installation on the 3.2L V6, see Chapter 4, Section 12.*

1   Relieve the fuel system pressure (see Chapter 4) and disconnect the cable from the negative terminal of the battery (see Chapter 5).

2   Partially drain the engine coolant (see Chapter 3).

3   Disconnect the electrical connector from the throttle body.

4   Remove the engine covers. Remove the air intake tube and air filter housing (see Chapter 4), and the coolant expansion tank (see Chapter 3).

5   Detach the crankcase breather tube from the valve covers and the rear of the intake manifold. Tag and disconnect any hoses or electrical connectors at the intake manifold.

6   Remove the oil dipstick, then remove the bolt securing the dipstick tube to the valve cover. Rotate the tube to position it out of the way.

7   Remove the ignition coils and set the harnesses aside.

8   Remove the bolts securing the AIR pipe to the heads or valve covers.

9   If you're working on a 3.0L engine, remove the fuel rail and injectors (see Chapter 4).

10   Remove the mounting fasteners and detach the manifold from the engine.

11   Use a plastic scraper to remove all traces of gasket material from the manifold and the cylinder head. Where equipped, peel the O-ring gaskets from the receiver grooves on the intake manifold. Clean the mating surfaces on the cylinder head and the manifold with brake system cleaner. Check the manifold for warpage with a straightedge. If the manifold is warped, replacement is the only alternative.

12   Install new gaskets and O-rings in the receiver grooves on the manifold, then position the manifold on the engine and install the bolts.

13   Tighten the fasteners in three or four equal steps to the torque listed in this Chapter's Specifications. Work from the center out towards the ends to avoid warping the manifold.

14   Install the remaining parts in the reverse order of removal. If the dipstick tube was removed completely, use a new O-ring on the bottom, lubricated with clean engine oil.

15   Before starting the engine, check the throttle linkage for smooth operation.

16   Refill and bleed the cooling system (see Chapter 1). Run the engine and check for coolant and vacuum leaks.

---

9   Exhaust manifold - removal and installation

Warning: *The engine must be completely cool before beginning this procedure.*

Removal

1   Remove the engine covers.

2   Remove the air intake duct and the air cleaner housing for access to the right exhaust manifold (see Chapter 4). Unbolt and reposition the coolant expansion tank for access to the left exhaust manifold (see Chapter 3).

3   Raise the front of the vehicle and support it securely on jackstands.

4   Remove the splash guard from below the engine compartment.

5   Detach the exhaust pipe from the exhaust manifold.

6   If you're removing the right exhaust manifold on a 3.2L engine, partially drain the cooling system and disconnect the upper radiator hose.

7   Disconnect the electrical connector for the oxygen sensor and remove the sensor (see Chapter 6).

8   Remove the exhaust manifold heat shields. If you're removing the right manifold, detach the oil level dipstick tube.

9   Unscrew the fasteners and remove the exhaust manifold and gasket. If necessary, apply penetrating oil to the manifold mounting nuts/bolts to help facilitate removal. **Note:** *Removing the wheel and inner fender liner improves access to the fasteners.*

Installation

10   Use a scraper to remove all traces of old gasket material and carbon deposits from the manifold and cylinder head mating surfaces. If the gasket was leaking, have the manifold checked for warpage at an automotive machine shop and resurfaced if necessary.

11   Position a new gasket over the cylinder head studs.

12   Install the manifold and thread the mounting fasteners into place. Make sure to use hi-temp anti-seize compound on the exhaust manifold fasteners. **Note:** *The manufacturer recommends replacing self-locking nuts with new ones.*

13   Working from the center out, tighten the nuts/bolts to the torque listed in this Chapter's Specifications in three or four equal steps.

14   Reinstall the remaining parts in the reverse order of removal. On 3.2L engines, lubricate a new O-ring with coolant and install

10.10 If the cylinder head is stuck, it may be necessary to pry upward on the casting protrusion to dislodge the head from the block

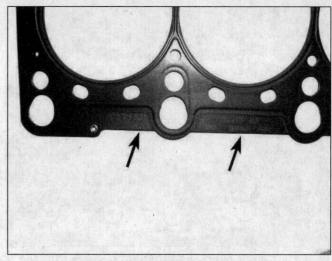

10.18 Be sure the "TOP" or "OBEN" mark and part number face upward

it in the upper radiator hose. Push the hose onto the pipe until you hear it click into place.
15 Refill and bleed the cooling system (see Chapter 1).
16 Run the engine and check for exhaust leaks.

10 Cylinder head - removal and installation

Warning: *The engine must be completely cool before beginning this procedure.*
Caution: *Performing this procedure may cause a trouble code to be set, which will require taking the vehicle to a dealer service department (or other repair shop equipped with the necessary scan tool) to have the cam sensor(s) synchronized and the trouble code cleared.*
Note: *The cylinder head can be removed with the exhaust manifold attached.*
Note: *This is a difficult procedure for the home mechanic, requiring some special tools and equipment.*

3.0L engine

Removal

Refer to illustration 10.10

1 Relieve the fuel system pressure (see Chapter 4) and disconnect the cable from the negative terminal of the battery (see Chapter 5).
2 Drain the engine coolant (see Chapter 1).
3 Detach the front exhaust pipe from the exhaust manifold.
4 Remove the valve cover(s) (see Section 4).
5 Remove the intake manifold (see Section 8).

6 Refer to Section 5 and remove the timing belt and the rear timing belt covers. **Caution:** *Do not overlook removing the bolts securing the bottom of the camshaft adjuster housing to the lower timing chain cover.*
7 Remove the coolant pipe from the front of the cylinder heads. If you're removing the left cylinder head, remove the secondary air injection pipes and remove the secondary air combination valve.
8 Unplug all electrical connectors and coolant hoses, labeling each wiring connector or hose to aid the installation process.
9 Working in the reverse of the sequence shown in **illustration 10.21a**, progressively loosen the cylinder head bolts, by half a turn at a time, until all bolts can be unscrewed by hand. Discard the bolts - new ones must be installed on reassembly.
10 Check that nothing remains connected to the cylinder head, then lift the head away from the cylinder block; seek assistance if possible, as it is very heavy, especially when being removed with the exhaust manifold. If the head is stuck to the block, carefully pry the cylinder head upward, at a casting protrusion beyond the gasket surface **(see illustration)**.
11 Remove the gasket from the top of the block. Do not discard the gasket - it will be needed for identification purposes.
12 Bring the cylinder heads to an automotive machine shop for inspection and/or overhaul.

Installation

Refer to illustrations 10.18, 10.21a and 10.21b

13 The mating faces of the cylinder head and cylinder block must be perfectly clean before installing the head. Use a hard plastic or wood scraper to remove all traces of gasket and carbon; also clean the piston crowns. Take particular care during the cleaning oper-

ations, as aluminum alloy is easily damaged. Also, make sure that the carbon is not allowed to enter the oil and water passages - this is particularly important for the lubrication system, as carbon could block the oil supply to the engine's components. Using adhesive tape and paper, seal the water, oil and bolt holes in the cylinder block.
14 Check the mating surfaces of the cylinder block and the cylinder head for nicks, deep scratches and other damage. If slight, they may be removed carefully with abrasive paper.
15 If warpage of the cylinder head gasket surface is suspected, use a straight-edge to check it for distortion. If it's distorted beyond the amount listed in this Chapter's Specifications it must be resurfaced. The specific resurfacing dimension is listed in the Chapter 2C Specifications.
16 Clean out the cylinder head bolt holes using a suitable tap. Be sure they're clean and dry before installation of the head bolts.
17 Double-check to make sure that the crankshaft is still locked in the TDC position, and the camshafts are properly positioned with the holding tools that were installed prior to timing belt removal.
18 Position the new head gasket on the cylinder block, engaging it with the locating dowels. Ensure that the manufacturer's "TOP" or "OBEN" and part number markings are face up, toward the cylinder head **(see illustration)**.
19 With the help of an assistant, place the cylinder head on the cylinder block, ensuring that the locating dowels engage with the recesses in the cylinder head. Check that the head gasket is correctly seated before allowing the full weight of the cylinder head to rest upon it.
20 Install the cylinder head bolts and screw them in hand tight. Be sure to use NEW cylinder head bolts.
21 Working progressively and in the

10.21a Cylinder head bolt TIGHTENING sequence - 3.0L and 3.2L engines

10.21b Using an angle measurement gauge during the final stages of tightening

sequence shown **(see illustration)**, tighten the cylinder head bolts in three steps to the torque and angle of rotation listed in this Chapter's Specifications. **Note:** *It is recommended that an angle-measuring gauge be used during the final stages of the tightening, to ensure accuracy* **(see illustration)**. *If a gauge is not available, use white paint to make alignment marks between the bolt head and cylinder head prior to tightening; the marks can then be used to check the bolt has been rotated through the correct angle during tightening.*

22   Install the timing belt tensioner and the camshaft sprockets on the engine if removed.

23   Install and adjust the timing belt as described in Section 5 or 6.

25   The remainder of the installation is the reverse of removal.

26   Change the engine oil and filter, and refill and bleed the cooling system (see Chapter 1). Run the engine and check for leaks.

3.2L engine

27   This repair procedure requires several expensive special tools. Because of the difficulty of this repair procedure and the necessary special tools, it is recommended to have this procedure performed by a dealer service department or other qualified automotive repair facility.

11   Crankshaft pulley - removal and installation

The procedure for removal and installation of the crankshaft pulley on V6 engines is essentially the same as it is on the four cylinder engine, except for the fact that the V6 pulley uses eight retaining bolts instead of four retaining bolts. Refer to Chapter 2A for this procedure. When tightening the bolts, use the torque specification listed in this Chapter's Specifications. **Note:** *On some 3.0L engines, a thrust washer is between the damper and the crankshaft. It should only be used with*

timing belt gear part number 06C-105-063A. **Note:** *On 3.2L engines, a special socket adapter (Audi tool no. T40058) is necessary to rotate the crankshaft pulley center bolt.*

12   Crankshaft front oil seal and housing - replacement

Refer to illustrations 12.3 and 12.5

1   If you're working on a 3.0L engine, remove the timing belt and crankshaft sprocket (see Section 5). If only the seal is being replaced, there is no further disassembly on 3.0L engines; the upper oil pan will have to be removed and the oil pump drive chain tensioner will have to be retracted if the sealing flange is to be removed from the engine.

2   On 3.2L engines, remove the crankshaft pulley (see Section 11) and the water pump pulley (see Chapter 3). The seal can be replaced with the sealing flange in place, or

with the sealing flange removed.

3   Note how far the seal is recessed in the bore, then carefully pry it out of the front cover with a screwdriver or seal removal tool **(see illustration)**. Don't scratch the housing bore or damage the crankshaft in the process (if the crankshaft is damaged, the new seal will end up leaking). **Note:** *If a seal removal tool is unavailable, you can thread two self-tapping screws (180 degrees apart from one another) into the front seal to pry the seal out.*

4   Clean the bore in the housing. **Note:** *Do not apply oil to the outer diameter of the seal.*

5   Using a seal driver or a socket with an outside diameter slightly smaller than the outside diameter of the seal, carefully drive the new seal into place with a hammer **(see illustration)**. Make sure it's installed squarely and driven in to the same depth as the original. If a socket isn't available, a short section of large diameter pipe will also work. Check the seal after installation to make sure the spring didn't pop out of place.

12.3 If a seal removal tool is unavailable, the front seal can also be pried out with a screwdriver

12.5 Lubricate the seal lip and drive the new crankshaft seal into place with a seal driver or a large socket and a hammer

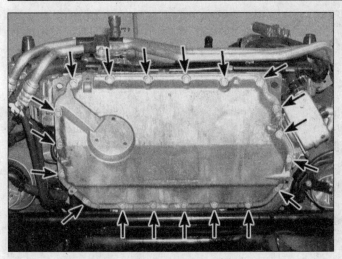

13.9 Lower oil pan mounting bolts (typical)

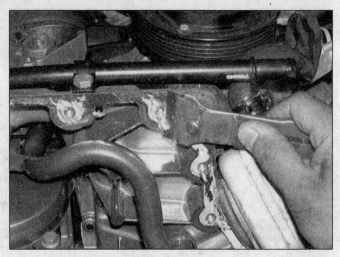

13.11 Use a scraper to remove all traces of old sealant from the upper and lower oil pan

6   If the sealing flange was removed, make sure the mating surfaces of the flange, the cylinder block and the oil pan rail are perfectly clean. Use a hard plastic or wood scraper to remove all traces of gasket material.

7   If the sealing flange was removed, use a new gasket and apply a 3/16-inch (5 mm) bead of RTV sealant to the front of the block where the oil pan and the engine block meet. On 3.2L engines, apply a 1/16-inch (1.5 mm) RTV bead on the engine side of the front sealing flange and install the flange within five minutes of applying the sealant. **Note:** *On 3.2L engines, use Audi tools T40048/1 and T40048/2 to align and install the new seal.*

8   Tighten the bolts in several steps to the torque listed in this Chapter's Specifications.

9   On 3.0L engines, reinstall the crankshaft sprocket and timing belt (see Section 5).

10   Run the engine and check for oil leaks at the front seal.

13   Oil pan - removal and installation

Note: *V6 engines are equipped with a two-piece oil pan. The upper half of the oil pan can only be removed with the engine raised and the front suspension subframe lowered. Refer to Chapter 2A, Section 13, as the procedure is similar to that on the 2.0L four-cylinder engine. The following Steps apply to the lower oil pan.*

Removal

Refer to illustration 13.9

1   Set the parking brake and block the rear wheels.

2   Raise the front of the vehicle and support it securely on jackstands.

3   Remove the splash shield under the engine.

4   Drain the engine oil (see Chapter 1).

Remove the oil dipstick.

5   Disconnect the clamps securing the refrigerant lines to the oil pan. **Caution:** *Set the lines aside without bending the metal portion of the lines.*

6   On 3.0L engines, remove the bolts securing the automatic transmission fluid lines to the oil pan.

7   On 3.2L engines, remove the stabilizer bar bushing bolts and lower the stabilizer bar (see Chapter 10).

8   On 3.2L engines, unbolt and set aside the engine oil cooler from the oil pan, leaving the coolant lines attached.

9   Remove the oil pan bolts **(see illustration)**.

10   Remove the oil pan. If it is stuck, tap it gently with a mallet to free it.

Installation

Refer to illustration 13.11

11   Use a scraper to remove all traces of old sealant or gasket material from the upper and lower oil pan **(see illustration)**. Clean the mating surfaces with brake system cleaner.

12   Make sure the threaded bolt holes in the upper oil pan are clean.

13   Check the oil pan flange for distortion, particularly around the bolt holes. Remove any nicks or burrs as necessary.

14   Apply a 1/16-inch (1.5 mm) bead of RTV sealant to the oil pan flange. **Note:** *The oil pan must be installed within five minutes once the sealant has been applied.*

15   Carefully position the oil pan on the upper oil pan and install the oil pan bolts loosely. Tighten the bolts, a little at a time in a criss-cross pattern, working from the center bolts outward, to the torque listed in this Chapter's Specifications.

16   The remainder of installation is the reverse of removal. On 3.2L engines, reinstall the oil cooler with new gaskets and O-rings, if equipped. **Note:** *Be sure to follow the sealant manufacturer's recommendations on curing*

times and allow the sealant to properly cure before adding oil.

17   Run the engine and check for oil pressure and leaks.

14   Oil pump - removal, inspection and installation

3.0L engine

Removal

1   Remove the oil pan (see Section 13).

2   Rotate the engine to TDC for the camshafts and the crankshaft (see Section 5). The crankshaft should be positioned with a TDC holding pin (Audi tool no. T40026); it isn't necessary to use the camshaft positioning tools for this procedure, as long as the lobes of the no. 3 camshafts are pointing up when the crankshaft is in proper alignment.

3   Remove the bolts securing the oil tubes, then remove the baffle mounting bolts.

4   Remove the bolt from the drive gear and detach the gear, remove the "diamond disc" washer, disengage the sprocket from the pump, then remove the two pump mounting bolts and two nuts.

5   To remove the assembly, insert bolts into two threaded holes in the assembly, and using a slide-hammer, pull the assembly downward, off the studs.

Inspection

6   If damage or wear is noted, replacement of the entire oil pump assembly (and the drive chain and sprockets) is recommended.

Installation

7   Installation is the reverse of the removal procedure, with the following exceptions.

a)   *The assembly must be installed with a new gasket and O-ring seal.*

b)   *A new "diamond disc" washer and a new drive gear bolt must be used.*

c) Rotate the balance shaft until a pin can be inserted to hold it, then reinstall the "diamond disc" and the drive gear onto the hub of the oil pump sprocket, meshing it with the balance shaft gear. Install the bolt through the gear and tighten the bolt to the torque listed in this Chapter's Specifications. Remove the pin.

d) Don't forget to remove the crankshaft holding pin.

e) Proceed to Step 14.

3.2L engine

Removal

8   Remove the lower oil pan (see Section 13).

9   The oil pump on this engine is driven by an oil pump driveshaft. Remove the oil pump mounting bolts. To remove the pump, you must pull the pump away from the oil pump driveshaft, while pushing the driveshaft away from the pump.

Inspection

10   If damage or wear is noted, replacement of the entire oil pump assembly is recommended.

Installation

11   Before installing the assembly, make sure the mating surfaces of the pump, the cylinder block and the upper oil pan rail are perfectly clean. Take particular care when cleaning the oil pump housing and the section of the upper oil pan, as aluminum alloy is easily damaged.

12   With new O-rings on the oil pump, install the oil pump onto the driveshaft, then install and tighten the mounting bolts.

13   Reinstall the remaining parts in the reverse order of removal.

All engines

14   Add oil (and coolant, if hoses were disconnected) (see Chapter 1), start the engine and check for oil pressure and leaks.

15   Recheck the engine oil level.

---

15   Flywheel/driveplate - removal and installation

1   The procedure for removal and installation of the flywheel/driveplate on V6 engines is essentially the same as it is on the four-cylinder engine. Refer to Chapter 2A for this procedure (but use the torque specification listed in this Chapter's Specifications).

2   On engines with the dual-mass flywheel, rotate the engine to TDC (see Section 3) and install the TDC timing stop in the front of the block. Use a flywheel-holding tool on the ring-gear to secure the flywheel.

3   Turn the rearmost section of the dual-mass flywheel by hand until the flywheel mounting bolts are centered in their openings. Remove the bolts using only hand tools,

17.11 Front torque rod mounting bolts (typical)

not impact tools. **Caution:** *The bolts should not touch the opening during removal or they could be damaged.*

4   The dual-mass flywheel has a needle-bearing insert that can be removed with a puller and installed with a driver.

5   On models with Multitronic transmission, the flywheel is fitted with a damper similar to a clutch plate on a manual transmission application. Refer to Chapter 8 for basic removal and installation. The damper must be removed to access the flywheel bolts.

---

16   Rear main oil seal - replacement

The procedure for removal and installation of the rear main oil seal on V6 engines is essentially the same as it is on the four cylinder engine. Refer to Chapter 2A for this procedure (but use the torque specification listed in this Chapter's Specifications). **Note:** *On 3.2L engines, the crankshaft rear seal is mounted in the lower timing chain cover, and can be replaced without removing the chain cover.*

---

17   Engine mounts - check and replacement

1   Engine mounts seldom require attention, but broken or deteriorated mounts should be replaced immediately or the added strain placed on the driveline components may cause damage or wear.

Check

2   During the check, the engine must be raised slightly to remove the weight from the mounts.

3   Raise the vehicle and support it securely on jackstands, then position a jack under the engine oil pan. Place a large block of wood between the jack head and the oil pan, then carefully raise the engine just enough to take

the weight off the mounts. Do not position the wood block under the drain plug. **Warning:** *DO NOT place any part of your body under the engine when it's supported only by a jack!*

4   Check the mounts to see if the rubber is cracked, hardened or separated from the metal plates. Sometimes the rubber will split right down the center.

5   Check for relative movement between the mount plates and the engine or frame (use a large screwdriver or pry bar to attempt to move the mounts). If movement is noted, lower the engine and tighten the mount fasteners.

6   Rubber preservative should be applied to the mounts to slow deterioration.

Replacement

7   Raise the vehicle and support it securely on jackstands (if not already done). Support the engine as described in Step 3.

8   Remove the splash shield under the engine, if equipped.

Front torque rod

Refer to illustration 17.11

9   Place the radiator support panel in the service position (see Chapter 11).

10   Pull the rubber stopper off the torque rod and replace it with a new one if it's damaged.

11   If necessary, the torque rod can be removed or replaced by unbolting it from the front of the engine **(see illustration)**.

12   Installation is the reverse of the removal procedure.

Driver and passenger side engine mounts

Refer to illustrations 17.15 and 17.16

Warning: *The weight of the entire engine will be supported by the transaxle mounts and the front torque rod during this procedure. Never place any part of your body directly under the engine when performing this procedure.*

13   Detach the starter motor cables from the lower engine mount brackets by cutting the plastic cable ties and maneuvering the wires out of the plastic retainers.

14   Mark the relationship of the engine

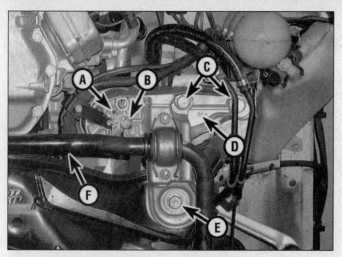

17.15 Lower engine mount bracket and related components (typical)

17.16 Engine mount upper retaining nut

A   Locating dowel
B   Engine mount retaining nut (lower)
C   Lower engine mount bracket bolts (front)
D   Lower engine mount bracket
E   Lower engine mount bracket bolt (rear)
F   Front stabilizer bar

mount locating dowel to the bottom of the aluminum engine mount bracket for installation purposes, then unscrew and remove the nuts from the bottom of left and right engine mounts.

15   Support the front stabilizer bar with a floor jack, then unscrew and remove the engine mount bracket bolts. The front two bolts must be unscrewed first, then the rear bolts **(see illustration)**. Lower the aluminum engine mount brackets together with the stabilizer bar to the ground. **Note:** *Lowering the stabilizer bar and the lower engine mount brackets will allow the front half of the subframe to be lowered slightly. Never loosen the rear subframe bolts as front wheel align-*

ment will be changed.

16   Remove the engine mount from the bracket on the engine block **(see illustration)**.

17   If necessary, unbolt the mounting bracket from the side of the cylinder block.

18   Installation is the reverse removal procedure.

Notes

Chapter 2 Part C
General engine overhaul procedures

Contents

	Section
CHECK ENGINE/MIL light on	See Chapter 6
Crankshaft - removal and installation	10
Cylinder compression check	3
Engine - removal and installation	7
Engine overhaul - disassembly sequence	8
Engine overhaul - reassembly sequence	11
Engine rebuilding alternatives	5

	Section
Engine removal - methods and precautions	6
General information - engine overhaul	1
Initial start-up and break-in after overhaul	12
Oil pressure check	2
Pistons and connecting rods - removal and installation	9
Vacuum gauge diagnostic checks	4

Specifications

General

Four-cylinder engines

1.8L four-cylinder engine designation	AMB
2.0L four-cylinder engine designations	BPG, BWT
Firing order	1-3-4-2
Cylinder numbering (front to rear)	1-2-3-4
Cylinder compression (min/max)	
1.8L engines	130-203 psi
2.0L engines	160-203 psi
Variation between cylinders	44 psi
Oil pressure	
1.8L engines	
Idle	15 psi
3000 rpm	51-65 psi
2.0L engines	
Idle	15 psi
3000 rpm	51-65 psi

V6 engines

3.0L V6 engine designations	AVK, BGN
3.2L V6 engine designation	BKH
Firing order	
3.0L V6..	1-4-3-6-2-5
3.2L V6..	1-5-3-6-2-4
Cylinder numbering (front to rear)	
Left bank	4-5-6
Right bank	1-2-3
Cylinder compression (min/max)...............................	160-203 psi
Variation between cylinders......................................	44 psi
Oil pressure	
Idle	17 psi
2000 rpm..	44 psi

Torque specifications*

Note: *One foot-pound (ft-lb) of torque is equivalent to 12 inch-pounds (in-lbs) of torque. Torque values below approximately 15 foot-pounds are expressed in inch-pounds, because most foot-pound torque wrenches are not accurate at these smaller values.*

	Ft-lbs (unless otherwise indicated)	**Nm**
1.8L engines		
Connecting rod bolts/nuts (new)		
Step 1	22	30
Step 2	Tighten an additional 90 degrees	
Crankshaft bearing cap bolts (new)		
Step 1	48	65
Step 2	Tighten an additional 90 degrees	
Oil baffle		
Bolt 1	16	21
Bolt 2	80 in-lbs	9
Oil pump sprocket bolt		
Step 1	15	20
Step 2	Tighten an additional 90 degrees	
Oil pump chain tensioner..	142 in-lbs	16
Oil filter housing..	132 in-lbs	15
2.0L engines		
Connecting rod bolts/nuts (new)		
Step 1	22	30
Step 2	Tighten an additional 90 degrees	
Crankshaft bearing cap bolts (new)		
Step 1	48	65
Step 2	Tighten an additional 90 degrees	
Toothed wheel-to-crankshaft		
Step 1	88 in-lbs	10
Step 2	Tighten an additional 90 degrees	
Oil pump/balance shaft assembly-to-block		
Step 1	Hand tight	
Step 2	132 in-lbs	15
Step 3	Tighten an additional 90 degrees	
3.0L engines		
Connecting rod bolts/nuts (new)		
Step 1	22	30
Step 2	Tighten an additional 90 degrees	
Crankshaft bearing cap bolts (new)		
Step 1	Hand-tighten all	
Step 2, 1 through 8 (inner).......................................	26	35
Step 3, 1 through 8 (inner).......................................	Tighten an additional 90 degrees	
Step 4, side bolts...	15	20
Step 5, side bolts...	Tighten an additional 90 degrees	
3.2L engines		
Connecting rod bolts/nuts (new)		
Step 1	22	30
Step 2	Tighten an additional 90 degrees	
Crankshaft bearing cap bolts (new)............................	Specifications not available	

*****Note:** *Refer to Chapter 2A or 2B for additional torque specifications.*

1   General information - engine overhaul

Refer to illustrations 1.1, 1.2, 1.3, 1.4, 1.5 and 1.6

Included in this portion of Chapter 2 are general information and diagnostic testing procedures for determining the overall mechanical condition of your engine.

The information ranges from advice concerning preparation for an overhaul and the purchase of replacement parts and/or components to detailed, step-by-step procedures covering removal and installation.

The following Sections have been written to help you determine whether your engine needs to be overhauled and how to remove and install it once you've determined it needs to be rebuilt. For information concerning in-vehicle engine repair, see Chapter 2A or 2B.

The Specifications included in this Part are general in nature and include only those necessary for testing the oil pressure and engine compression, and bottom-end torque specifications. Refer to Chapter 2A (four-cylinder engines) or 2B (V6 engines) for additional engine Specifications.

It's not always easy to determine when, or if, an engine should be completely overhauled, because a number of factors must be considered.

High mileage is not necessarily an indication that an overhaul is needed, while low mileage doesn't preclude the need for an overhaul. Frequency of servicing is probably the most important consideration. An engine that's had regular and frequent oil and filter changes, as well as other required maintenance, will most likely give many thousands of miles of reliable service. Conversely, a neglected engine may require an overhaul very early in its service life.

Excessive oil consumption is an indication that piston rings, valve seals and/or valve guides are in need of attention. Make sure that oil leaks aren't responsible before deciding that the rings and/or guides are bad. Per-form a cylinder compression check to determine the extent of the work required (see Section 3). Also, check the vacuum readings under various conditions (see Section 4).

Check the oil pressure with a gauge installed in place of the oil pressure sending unit and compare it to this Chapter's Specifications (see Section 2). If it's extremely low, the bearings and/or oil pump are probably worn out.

Loss of power, rough running, knocking or metallic engine noises, excessive valve train noise and high fuel consumption rates may also point to the need for an overhaul, especially if they're all present at the same time. If a complete tune-up doesn't remedy the situation, major mechanical work is the only solution.

An engine overhaul involves restoring the internal parts to the specifications of a new engine. During an overhaul, the piston rings are replaced and the cylinder walls are reconditioned (rebored and/or honed) **(see illustrations 1.1 and 1.2)**. If a rebore is done

1.1 An engine block being bored. An engine rebuilder will use special machinery to recondition the cylinder bores

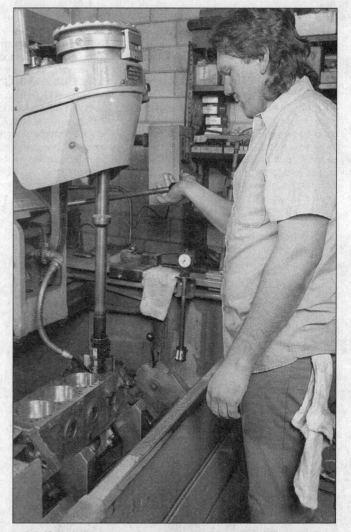

1.2 If the cylinders are bored, the machine shop will normally hone the engine on a machine like this

1.3 A crankshaft having a main bearing journal ground

1.4 A machinist checks for a bent connecting rod, using specialized equipment

by an automotive machine shop, new oversize pistons will also be installed. The main bearings, connecting rod bearings and camshaft bearings are generally replaced with new ones and, if necessary, the crankshaft may be reground to restore the journals **(see illustration 1.3)**. Generally, the valves are serviced as well, since they're usually in less-than-perfect condition at this point. While the engine is being overhauled, other components, such as the distributor, starter and alternator, can be rebuilt as well. The end result should be similar to a new engine that will give many trouble free miles. **Note:** *Critical cooling system components such as the hoses, drivebelts, thermostat and water pump should be replaced with new parts when an engine is overhauled. The radiator should be checked carefully to ensure that it isn't clogged or leaking (see Chapter 3). If you purchase a rebuilt engine or short block, some rebuilders will not warranty their engines unless the radiator has*

been professionally flushed. Also, we don't recommend overhauling the oil pump - always install a new one when an engine is rebuilt.

Overhauling the internal components on today's engines is a difficult and time-consuming task which requires a significant amount of specialty tools and is best left to a professional engine rebuilder **(see illustrations 1.4, 1.5 and 1.6)**. A competent engine rebuilder will handle the inspection of your old parts and offer advice concerning the reconditioning or replacement of the original engine, never purchase parts or have machine work done on other components until the block has been thoroughly inspected by a professional machine shop. As a general rule, time is the primary cost of an overhaul, especially since the vehicle may be tied up for a minimum of two weeks or more. Be aware that some engine builders only have the capability to rebuild the engine you bring them while other rebuilders have a large inventory of rebuilt

exchange engines in stock. Also be aware that many machine shops could take as much as two weeks time to completely rebuild your engine depending on shop workload. Sometimes it makes more sense to simply exchange your engine for another engine that's already rebuilt to save time.

2   Oil pressure check

1   Low engine oil pressure can be a sign of an engine in need of rebuilding. A low oil pressure indicator (often called an "idiot light") is not a test of the oiling system. Such indicators only come on when the oil pressure is dangerously low. Even a factory oil pressure gauge in the instrument panel is only a relative indication, although much better for driver information than a warning light. A better test is with a mechanical (not electrical) oil pressure gauge.

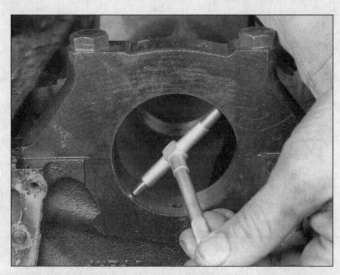

1.5 A bore gauge being used to check the main bearing bore

1.6 Uneven piston wear like this indicates a bent connecting rod

3.4 The 8-pin electrical connector for the fuel injector harness on the 2.0L four-cylinder engine is located to the rear of and below the throttle body

3.6 Use a compression gauge with a threaded fitting for the spark plug hole, not the type that requires hand pressure to maintain the seal

2   Locate the oil pressure switch, remove it, then screw in the hose for your oil pressure gauge. If necessary, install an adapter fitting. Use Teflon tape or thread sealant on the threads of the adapter and/or the fitting on the end of your gauge's hose.

3   Check the oil pressure with the engine running (normal operating temperature) at the specified engine speed, and compare it to this Chapter's Specifications. If it's extremely low, the bearings and/or oil pump are probably worn out.

3   Cylinder compression check

Refer to illustrations 3.4 and 3.6

1   A compression check will tell you what mechanical condition the upper end of your engine (pistons, rings, valves, head gaskets) is in. Specifically, it can tell you if the compression is down due to leakage caused by worn piston rings, defective valves and seats or a blown head gasket. **Note:** *The engine must be at normal operating temperature and the battery must be fully charged for this check.*

2   Begin by cleaning the area around the spark plugs before you remove them (compressed air should be used, if available). The idea is to prevent dirt from getting into the cylinders as the compression check is being done.

3   Remove the ignition coil assemblies (see Chapter 5). Remove the spark plugs (see Chapter 1).

4   If you're working on a 1.8L four-cylinder engine or a 3.0L V6 engine, disconnect the electrical connectors from all of the fuel injectors. If you're working on a 2.0L four-cylinder engine, disconnect the 8-pin electrical connector in the fuel injector harness **(see illustration)**. If you're working on a 3.2L V6

engine, disconnect the electrical connectors in the harness to the fuel injectors - they're at the rear end of each cylinder head.

5   Remove the air intake duct from the throttle body (see Chapter 4), then block the throttle wide open.

6   Install a compression gauge in the spark plug hole **(see illustration)**.

7   Crank the engine over at least seven compression strokes and watch the gauge. The compression should build up quickly in a healthy engine. Low compression on the first stroke, followed by gradually increasing pressure on successive strokes, indicates worn piston rings. A low compression reading on the first stroke, which doesn't build up during successive strokes, indicates leaking valves or a blown head gasket (a cracked head could also be the cause). Deposits on the undersides of the valve heads can also cause low compression. Record the highest gauge reading obtained.

8   Repeat the procedure for the remaining cylinders and compare the results to this Chapter's Specifications.

9   Add some engine oil (about three squirts from a plunger-type oil can) to each cylinder, through the spark plug hole, and repeat the test.

10   If the compression increases after the oil is added, the piston rings are definitely worn. If the compression doesn't increase significantly, the leakage is occurring at the valves or head gasket. Leakage past the valves may be caused by burned valve seats and/or faces or warped, cracked or bent valves.

11   If two adjacent cylinders have equally low compression, there's a strong possibility that the head gasket between them is blown. The appearance of coolant in the combustion chambers or the crankcase would verify this condition.

12   If one cylinder is slightly lower than the others, and the engine has a slightly rough

idle, a worn lobe on the camshaft could be the cause.

13   If the compression is unusually high, the combustion chambers are probably coated with carbon deposits. If that's the case, the cylinder head(s) should be removed and decarbonized.

14   If compression is way down or varies greatly between cylinders, it would be a good idea to have a leak-down test performed by an automotive repair shop. This test will pinpoint exactly where the leakage is occurring and how severe it is.

4   Vacuum gauge diagnostic checks

Refer to illustrations 4.4 and 4.6

1   A vacuum gauge provides inexpensive but valuable information about what is going on in the engine. You can check for worn rings or cylinder walls, leaking head or intake manifold gaskets, incorrect carburetor adjustments, restricted exhaust, stuck or burned valves, weak valve springs, improper ignition or valve timing and ignition problems.

2   Unfortunately, vacuum gauge readings are easy to misinterpret, so they should be used in conjunction with other tests to confirm the diagnosis.

3   Both the absolute readings and the rate of needle movement are important for accurate interpretation. Most gauges measure vacuum in inches of mercury (in-Hg). The following references to vacuum assume the diagnosis is being performed at sea level. As elevation increases (or atmospheric pressure decreases), the reading will decrease. For every 1,000 foot increase in elevation above approximately 2,000 feet, the gauge readings will decrease about one inch of mercury.

4   Connect the vacuum gauge directly to

4.4 A simple vacuum gauge can be handy in diagnosing engine condition and performance. Connect it to a manifold vacuum source (not *ported*, or in front of the throttle plate, vacuum source)

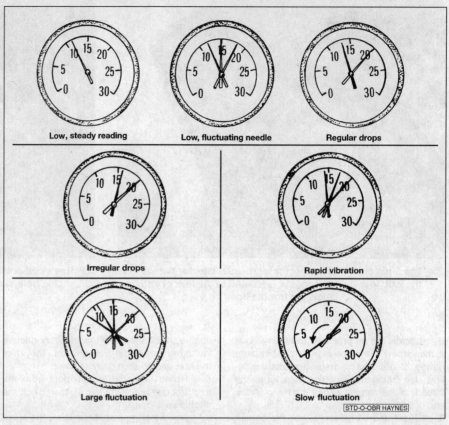

4.6 Typical vacuum gauge readings

the intake manifold vacuum, not to ported (throttle body) vacuum **(see illustration)**. If you have tapped into a manifold vacuum source, the gauge will read 18 to 20 inches with the engine idling. If you have tapped into a ported vacuum source, there will be little or no vacuum reading at idle, but the vacuum reading will go up if you rev the engine. Use only manifold vacuum for engine testing.

5   Before you begin the test, allow the engine to warm up completely. Block the wheels and set the parking brake. With the transmission in Park, start the engine and allow it to run at normal idle speed. **Warning:** *Keep your hands and the vacuum gauge clear of the fans.*

6   Read the vacuum gauge; an average, healthy engine should normally produce about 17 to 22 in-Hg with a fairly steady needle **(see illustration)**. Refer to the following vacuum gauge readings and what they indicate about the engine's condition:

7   A low, steady reading usually indicates a leaking gasket between the intake manifold and cylinder head(s) or throttle body, a leaky vacuum hose, late ignition timing or incorrect camshaft timing. Check ignition timing with a timing light and eliminate all other possible causes, utilizing the tests provided in this Chapter before you remove the timing chain cover to check the timing marks.

8   If the reading is three to eight inches below normal and it fluctuates at that low reading, suspect an intake manifold gasket leak at an intake port or a faulty fuel injector.

9   If the needle has regular drops of about two-to-four inches at a steady rate, the valves are probably leaking. Perform a compression check or leak-down test to confirm this.

10   An irregular drop or down-flick of the needle can be caused by a sticking valve or

an ignition misfire. Perform a compression check or leak-down test and read the spark plugs.

11   A rapid vibration of about four in-Hg vibration at idle combined with exhaust smoke indicates worn valve guides. Perform a leak-down test to confirm this. If the rapid vibration occurs with an increase in engine speed, check for a leaking intake manifold gasket or head gasket, weak valve springs, burned valves or ignition misfire.

12   A slight fluctuation, say one inch up and down, may mean ignition problems. Check all the usual tune-up items and, if necessary, run the engine on an ignition analyzer.

13   If there is a large fluctuation, perform a compression or leak-down test to look for a weak or dead cylinder or a blown head gasket.

14   If the needle moves slowly through a wide range, check for a clogged PCV system, incorrect idle fuel mixture, throttle body or intake manifold gasket leaks.

15   Check for a slow return after revving the engine by quickly snapping the throttle open until the engine reaches about 2,500 rpm and let it shut. Normally the reading should drop to near zero, rise above normal idle reading (about 5 in-Hg over) and then return to the previous idle reading. If the vacuum returns slowly and doesn't peak when the throttle is snapped shut, the rings may be worn. If there is a long delay, look for a restricted exhaust system (often the muffler or catalytic con-

verter). An easy way to check this is to temporarily disconnect the exhaust ahead of the suspected part and redo the test.

5   Engine rebuilding alternatives

The do-it-yourselfer is faced with a number of options when purchasing a rebuilt engine. The major considerations are cost, warranty, parts availability and the time required for the rebuilder to complete the project. The decision to replace the engine block, piston/connecting rod assemblies and crankshaft depends on the final inspection results of your engine. Only then can you make a cost effective decision whether to have your engine overhauled or simply purchase an exchange engine for your vehicle.

Some of the rebuilding alternatives include:

Individual parts - If the inspection procedures reveal that the engine block and most engine components are in reusable condition, purchasing individual parts and having a rebuilder rebuild your engine may be the most economical alternative. The block, crankshaft and piston/connecting rod assemblies should all be inspected carefully by a machine shop first.

Short block - A short block consists of an engine block with a crankshaft and piston/connecting rod assemblies already installed.

6.1 After tightly wrapping water-vulnerable components, use a spray cleaner on everything, with particular concentration on the greasiest areas, usually around the valve cover and lower edges of the block. If one section dries out, apply more cleaner

6.2 Depending on how dirty the engine is, let the cleaner soak in according to the directions and then hose off the grime and cleaner. Get the rinse water down into every area you can get at; then dry important components with a hair dryer or paper towels

All new bearings are incorporated and all clearances will be correct. The existing camshafts, valve train components, cylinder head and external parts can be bolted to the short block with little or no machine shop work necessary.

Long block - A long block consists of a short block plus an oil pump, oil pan, cylinder head, valve cover, camshaft and valve train components, timing sprockets and chain or gears and timing cover. All components are installed with new bearings, seals and gaskets incorporated throughout. The installation of manifolds and external parts is all that's necessary.

Low mileage used engines - Some companies now offer low mileage used engines which is a very cost effective way to get your vehicle up and running again. These engines often come from vehicles which have been in totaled in accidents or come from other countries which have a higher vehicle turn over rate. A low mileage used engine also usually has a warranty similar to the newly remanufactured engines.

Give careful thought to which alternative is best for you and discuss the situation with local automotive machine shops, auto parts dealers and experienced rebuilders before ordering or purchasing replacement parts.

6   Engine removal - methods and precautions

Refer to illustrations 6.1, 6.2, and 6.3

If you've decided that an engine must be removed for overhaul or major repair work, several preliminary steps should be taken. Read all removal and installation procedures carefully prior to committing to this job. Four-cylinder and 3.0L V6 engines are removed from the top of the engine compartment. 3.2L

V6 engines are removed by lowering the engine to the floor, along with the transmission, and then raising the vehicle sufficiently to slide the assembly out; this will require a vehicle hoist as well as an engine hoist.

Locating a suitable place to work is extremely important. Adequate work space, along with storage space for the vehicle, will be needed. If a shop or garage isn't available, at the very least a flat, level, clean work surface made of concrete or asphalt is required.

Cleaning the engine compartment and engine before beginning the removal procedure will help keep tools clean and organized **(see illustrations 6.1 and 6.2).**

An engine hoist will also be necessary and a transmission jack is also very helpful. If you're removing the engine from a model with a 3.2L V6, a vehicle hoist will be necessary; the engine is removed out the bottom

along with the transaxle (with a floor jack and jackstands the vehicle can't be raised high enough and supported safely enough for the engine/transaxle assembly to slide out from underneath). Safety is of primary importance, considering the potential hazards involved in removing the engine from the vehicle.

If you're a novice at engine removal, get at least one helper. One person cannot easily do all the things you need to do to remove a big heavy engine from the engine compartment. Also helpful is to seek advice and assistance from someone who's experienced in engine removal.

Plan the operation ahead of time. Arrange for or obtain all of the tools and equipment you'll need prior to beginning the job **(see illustration 6.3)**. Some of the equipment necessary to perform engine removal and installation safely and with relative ease are

6.3 Get an engine stand sturdy enough to firmly support the engine while you're working on it. Stay away from three-wheeled models; they have a tendency to tip over more easily, so get a four-wheeled unit

... an engine ... ferably fit-... ead adapter), ... and sockets as ... manual, wooden ... cleaning solvent for ... olant and gasoline. ... e to be out of use for ... A machine shop can do the ... the scope of the home ... e shops often have a busy ... efore removing the engine, ... op for an estimate of how long ... ebuild or repair the components ... ed work.

ngine - removal and installation

arning: *The models covered by this manual re equipped with airbags. Always disable the airbag system before working in the vicinity of any airbag system component to avoid the possibility of accidental deployment of the airbag(s), which could cause personal injury (see Chapter 12).*

Warning: *Gasoline is extremely flammable so take extra precautions when you work on any part of the fuel system. Don't smoke or allow open flames or bare light bulbs near the work area, and don't work in a garage where a gas-type appliance (such as a water heater or a clothes dryer) is present. Since gasoline is carcinogenic, wear latex gloves when there's a possibility of being exposed to fuel, and, if you spill any fuel on your skin, rinse it off immediately with soap and water. Mop up any spills immediately and do not store fuel-soaked rags where they could ignite. The fuel system is under constant pressure, so, if any fuel lines are to be disconnected, the fuel pressure in the system must be relieved first (see Chapter 4). When you perform any kind of work on the fuel system, wear safety glasses and have a Class B type fire extinguisher on hand.*

Warning: *The air conditioning system is under high pressure - have a dealer service department or service station evacuate the system and recover the refrigerant before disconnecting any of the hoses or fittings.*

Caution: *When disassembling the air intake system on turbocharged vehicles, ensure that no foreign material can get into the turbo air intake port. Cover the opening with a sheet of plastic and a rubber band. The turbocharger compressor blades could be severely damaged if debris is allowed to enter.*

Note: *Removal and installation of the 3.2L V6 engine is from the bottom of the vehicle, with the subframe. The procedure is complicated and requires a number of specialized tools. It is not recommended for the home mechanic.*

1   If you're working on a model with a 3.2L V6, have the air conditioning system properly discharged by a licensed air conditioning technician.

2   Relieve the fuel system pressure (see Chapter 4).

3   Disconnect the cable from the negative terminal of the battery (see Chapter 5).

4   Remove the engine covers.

5   Remove the air cleaner assembly (see Chapter 4). On four-cylinder models, also disconnect the charge air hoses from the turbocharger and throttle body (see Chapter 4).

All except 3.2L V6 models

Removal

Refer to illustrations 7.17, 7.25a and 7.25b

6   Raise the vehicle and support it securely on jackstands. Drain the cooling system and engine oil and remove the drivebelts (see Chapter 1).

7   Refer to Chapter 3 and unbolt and set aside the air conditioning compressor. **Warning:** *Do not disconnect the refrigerant lines.* Refer to Chapter 5 and remove the alternator and starter.

8   Remove the secondary air injection pump and hoses from the engine, if equipped (see Chapter 6).

9   Remove the front section of the exhaust system (see Chapter 4).

10   On automatic transaxle models, disconnect the fluid lines from the oil pan, and any electrical connectors in the harness between the engine and the transaxle. Disconnect any engine-to-chassis ground wires.

11   Remove the transaxle-to-engine bolts that are accessible from below. If equipped with an automatic transaxle, mark the relationship of the torque converter to the driveplate, remove the torque converter bolts (working through the opening for the starter) and push the torque converter away from the driveplate back towards the transaxle. This will help keep the torque converter engaged in the transaxle while the engine and driveplate are being separated from the transaxle. **Note:** *Rotate the engine using the center bolt of the crankshaft pulley to bring the torque converter bolts into the opening for the starter.*

12   On V6 engines, remove the oil cooler, and on 1.8L engines, remove the oil filter/cooler housing.

13   Remove the lower engine mount retaining nuts (see Chapter 2A or 2B).

14   Lower the vehicle.

15   Place protective covers on the fenders and cowl and remove the hood (see Chapter 11).

16   Remove the cowl cover (see Chapter 11) and the PCM (see Chapter 6). Remove the underhood fuse/relay box (see Chapter 12). It (and the harness) will be removed along with the engine.

17   Clearly label, then disconnect all vacuum lines, coolant and emissions hoses, wiring harness connectors and ground straps that run between the engine and the chassis. Masking tape and/or a touch up paint applicator work well for marking items **(see illustration)**. Take instant photos or sketch the locations of components and brackets.

18   Remove the cooling fan, and disconnect the radiator hoses and heater hoses from the engine. Also remove the coolant expansion tank (see Chapter 3).

19   Refer to Chapter 11 and remove the bumper cover.

20   Unbolt and set aside the power steering oil cooler, then remove the condenser without disconnecting the refrigerant lines (see Chapter 3). Position the condenser out of the way.

21   Remove the radiator support panel, along with the radiator (see Chapter 11, Section 9). Remove the bumper reinforcement and the energy absorbing struts.

22   Unbolt the power steering pump and the steering pump hoses (see Chapter 10).

23   Disconnect the fuel line(s) from the fuel rail (see Chapter 4). Plug or cap all open fittings.

24   Support the transaxle with a floor jack positioned as far forward on the transaxle as possible. Place a block of wood on the jack head to protect the transaxle.

25   Attach a lifting sling or chain to the lifting eyes (if equipped) on the engine **(see illustrations)**. Position a hoist and connect the sling or chain to it. Take up the slack until there is slight tension on the chain.

26   Remove the transaxle-to-engine bolts accessible from above.

27   Loosen the engine mount upper nuts several turns.

28   Recheck to be sure nothing is still connecting the engine/transaxle to the vehicle. Tag and disconnect anything still remaining.

29   Slowly raise the engine while simultaneously raising the transaxle with the floor jack until the lower engine mount studs are clear of the mounting bracket, then pull the engine forward out of the engine compartment. **Warning:** *Do not place any part of your body under the engine when it's supported only by a hoist or other lifting device.*

30   Place the engine on the floor or remove the flywheel/driveplate and mount the engine on an engine stand.

Installation

31   Install the flywheel/driveplate on the engine (see Chapter 2A or 2B). Check the

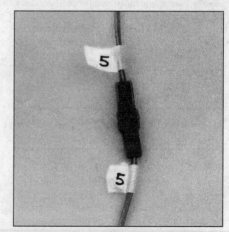

7.17 Label both ends of each wire or vacuum connection before disconnecting them

7.25a Attach the chains of your engine hoist to the lifting brackets at the rear of the engine . . .

7.25b . . . and at the front (2.0L four-cylinder engine shown)

engine mounts. If they're worn or damaged, replace them.

32   If you're working on a vehicle with a manual transaxle, install the clutch and pressure plate (see Chapter 7A). Now is a good time to install a new clutch. Apply a dab of high-temperature grease to the input shaft

33   Carefully guide the engine into place. If you're working on a vehicle with a manual transaxle, guide the input shaft into the splines of the clutch disc and the crankshaft pilot bearing until the bellhousing is flush with the engine block. **Note:** *It may be necessary to turn the crankshaft with a socket and breaker bar until the splines on the input shaft align with the splines on the clutch disc.*

34   Install the transaxle-to-engine bolts and tighten them securely. **Caution:** *DO NOT use the bolts to force the transaxle and engine together!*

35   If you're working on a vehicle with an automatic transaxle, install the torque converter bolts.

36   Reinstall the remaining components in the reverse order of removal.

37   Add coolant, oil, power steering and transaxle fluid as needed. **Caution:** *Be sure to bleed the air from the cooling system as described in Chapter 1.*

38   Run the engine and check for leaks and proper operation of all accessories, then install the hood and test drive the vehicle.

39   Have the air conditioning system recharged and leak tested by the shop that discharged it.

3.2L V6 models

Refer to illustration 7.40

40   The 3.2L V6 engine is removed along with the transaxle and the front suspension subframe from underneath the vehicle. For this reason, a vehicle hoist is necessary, as is a large sturdy workbench on which to set the engine/transaxle assembly **(see illustration).**

41   Essentially, everything described above applies to the removal of this engine, as far as

7.40 On models with a 3.2L V6, the engine and transaxle are removed as a unit from under the vehicle (typical)

disconnecting everything between the engine and the chassis. Exceptions to this, and additions to the above procedure are as follows:

a)   *The air conditioning system must be discharged by a licensed air conditioning technician before work is started.*

b)   *The bumper cover, bumper, condenser, radiator support panel and radiator can remain in place.*

c)   *The refrigerant lines must be detached from the air conditioning compressor.*

d)   *The driveaxles must be removed (see Chapter 8).*

e)   *On all-wheel drive models the driveshaft must be detached from the transfer case. Support it with wire (don't let it hang).*

f)   *The steering knuckles must be supported with straps or wire from the shock absorber/coil spring assembly, and the lower control arms must be unbolted from the suspension subframe, swung out of the way, and supported by wire or rope.*

g)   *Once everything has been disconnected, a large, sturdy workbench is moved under the vehicle, then the vehicle (on*

the vehicle hoist) is carefully lowered onto jackstands placed on the workbench, which must contact the rear of the transaxle and the subframe.

h)   *With the transaxle and engine subframe supported by the jackstands, the subframe-to-chassis bolts are removed, then the vehicle is raised on the hoist until it clears the engine/transaxle assembly.*

8   Engine overhaul - disassembly sequence

1   It's much easier to remove the external components if it's mounted on a portable engine stand. A stand can often be rented quite cheaply from an equipment rental yard. Before the engine is mounted on a stand, the flywheel/driveplate should be removed from the engine.

2   If a stand isn't available, it's possible to remove the external engine components with it blocked up on the floor. Be extra careful not

9.1 Before you try to remove the pistons, use a ridge reamer to remove the raised material (ridge) from the top of the cylinders

to tip or drop the engine when working without a stand.

3   If you're going to obtain a rebuilt engine, all external components must come off first, to be transferred to the replacement engine. These components include:

 Flywheel/driveplate
 Ignition system components
 Emissions-related components
 Engine mounts and mount brackets
 Intake/exhaust manifolds
 Supercharger (four-cylinder models)
 Fuel injection components
 Oil filter and oil cooler
 Spark plug wires and spark plugs
 Thermostat and housing assembly
 Water pump

Note: *When removing the external components from the engine, pay close attention to details that may be helpful or important during installation. Note the installed position of gaskets, seals, spacers, pins, brackets, washers, bolts and other small items.*

4   If you're going to obtain a short block (assembled engine block, crankshaft, pistons and connecting rods), then remove the timing

chain, cylinder head(s), oil pan, oil pump pick-up tube, oil pump and water pump from your engine so that you can turn in your old short block to the rebuilder as a core. See *Engine rebuilding alternatives* for additional information regarding the different possibilities to be considered.

9   Pistons and connecting rods - removal and installation

Removal

Refer to illustrations 9.1, 9.3 and 9.4

Note: *Prior to removing the piston/connecting rod assemblies, remove the cylinder head(s) and oil pan (see Chapter 2A or 2B).*

1   Use your fingernail to feel if a ridge has formed at the upper limit of ring travel (about 1/4-inch down from the top of each cylinder). If carbon deposits or cylinder wear have produced ridges, they must be completely removed with a special tool **(see illustration)**. Follow the manufacturer's instructions provided with the tool. Failure to remove

the ridges before attempting to remove the piston/connecting rod assemblies may result in piston breakage. After the cylinder ridges have been removed, turn the engine so the crankshaft is facing up.

2   On four-cylinder and 3.0L V6 engines, remove the oil pump/balance shaft assembly for access to the rod and main bearing caps.

3   Before the main bearing cap assembly and connecting rods are removed, check the connecting rod endplay with feeler gauges. Slide them between the first connecting rod and the crankshaft throw until the play is removed **(see illustration)**. Repeat this procedure for each connecting rod. The endplay is equal to the thickness of the feeler gauge(s). Check with an automotive machine shop for the endplay service limit (a typical endplay should measure from 0.005 to 0.015 inch [0.127 to 0.381 mm]). If the play exceeds the service limit, new connecting rods will be required. If new rods (or a new crankshaft) are installed, the endplay may fall under the minimum allowable. If it does, the rods will have to be machined to restore it. If necessary, consult an automotive machine shop for advice.

4   Check the connecting rods and caps for identification marks. If they aren't plainly marked, use paint or marker **(see illustration)** to clearly identify each rod and cap (1, 2, 3, etc., depending on the cylinder they're associated with). Do not interchange the rod caps. Install the exact same rod cap onto the same connecting rod. **Caution:** *Do not use a punch and hammer to mark the connecting rods or they may be damaged.*

5   Loosen each of the connecting rod cap bolts or nuts 1/2-turn at a time until they can be removed by hand.

6   Remove the number one connecting rod cap and bearing insert. Don't drop the bearing insert out of the cap.

7   Remove the bearing insert and push the connecting rod/piston assembly out through the top of the engine. Use a wooden or plastic hammer handle to push on the upper bearing

9.3 Checking the connecting rod endplay (side clearance)

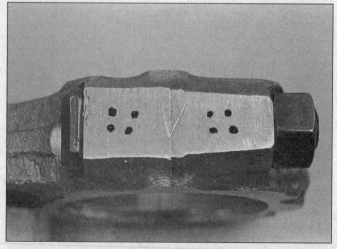

9.4 If the connecting rods or caps are not marked, use permanent ink or paint to mark the caps to the rods by cylinder number (for example, this would be number 4 cylinder connecting rod)

surface in the connecting rod. If resistance is felt, double-check to make sure that all of the ridge was removed from the cylinder.

8   Repeat the procedure for the remaining cylinders.

9   After removal, measure the length of the rod bolts, from the underside of the bolt head to the end, and compare your measurements with the values listed in this Chapter's Specifications. Replace any bolts that have stretched excessively. Reassemble the connecting rod caps and bearing inserts in their respective connecting rods and install the cap bolts finger tight. Leaving the old bearing inserts in place until reassembly will help prevent the connecting rod bearing surfaces from being accidentally nicked or gouged.

10   The pistons and connecting rods are now ready for inspection and overhaul at an automotive machine shop.

Piston ring installation

Refer to illustrations 9.13, 9.14, 9.15, 9.19a, 9.19b and 9.22

11   Before installing the new piston rings, the ring end gaps must be checked. It's assumed that the piston ring side clearance has been checked and verified correct.

12   Lay out the piston/connecting rod assemblies and the new ring sets so the ring sets will be matched with the same piston and cylinder during the end gap measurement and engine assembly.

13   Insert the top (number one) ring into the first cylinder and square it up with the cylinder walls by pushing it in with the top of the piston (see illustration). The ring should be near the bottom of the cylinder, at the lower limit of ring travel.

14   To measure the end gap, slip feeler gauges between the ends of the ring until a gauge equal to the gap width is found (see illustration). The feeler gauge should slide between the ring ends with a slight amount of drag. A typical ring gap should fall between 0.010 and 0.020 inch (0.25 to 0.50 mm) for compression rings and up to 0.030 inch (0.76 mm) for the oil ring steel rails. If the gap is larger or smaller than specified, double-check to make sure you have the correct rings before proceeding.

15   If the gap is too small, it must be enlarged or the ring ends may come in contact with each other during engine operation, which can cause serious damage to the engine. If necessary, increase the end gaps by filing the ring ends very carefully with a fine file. Mount the file in a vise equipped with soft jaws, slip the ring over the file with the ends contacting the file face and slowly move the ring to remove material from the ends. When performing this operation, file only by pushing the ring from the outside end of the file towards the vise (see illustration).

16   Excess end gap isn't critical unless it's greater than 0.040 inch (1.01 mm). Again, double-check to make sure you have the correct ring type.

17   Repeat the procedure for each ring that will be installed in the first cylinder and for each ring in the remaining cylinders. Remember to keep rings, pistons and cylinders matched up.

18   Once the ring end gaps have been checked/corrected, the rings can be installed on the pistons.

19   The oil control ring (lowest one on the piston) is usually installed first. It's composed of three separate components. Slip the spacer/expander into the groove (see illustration). If an anti-rotation tang is used, make sure it's inserted into the drilled hole in the ring groove. Next, install the lower side rail in the same manner (see illustration). Don't use a piston ring installation tool on the

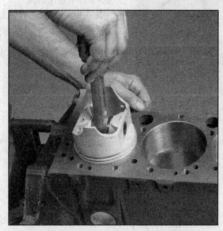

9.13 Install the piston ring into the cylinder then push it down into position using a piston so the ring will be square in the cylinder

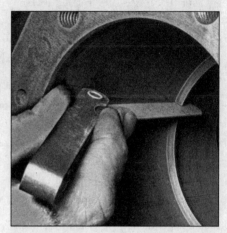

9.14 With the ring square in the cylinder, measure the ring end gap with a feeler gauge

9.15 If the ring end gap is too small, clamp a file in a vise as shown and file the piston ring ends - be sure to remove all raised material

9.19a Installing the spacer/expander in the oil ring groove

9.19b DO NOT use a piston ring installation tool when installing the oil control side rails

9.22 Use a piston ring installation tool to install the compression rings - on some engines the number two compression ring has a directional mark that must face toward the top of the piston

oil ring side rails, as they may be damaged. Instead, place one end of the side rail into the groove between the spacer/expander and the piston land, hold it firmly in place and slide a finger around the piston while pushing the rail into the groove. Finally, install the upper side rail.

20 After the three oil ring components have been installed, check to make sure that both the upper and lower side rails can be rotated smoothly inside the ring grooves.

21 The number two (middle) ring is installed next. It's usually stamped with a mark which must face up, toward the top of the piston. Do not mix up the top and middle rings, as they have different cross-sections. **Note:** *Always follow the instructions printed on the ring package or box - different manufacturers may require different approaches.*

22 Use a piston ring installation tool and make sure the identification mark is facing the top of the piston, then slip the ring into the middle groove on the piston **(see illustration)**. Don't expand the ring any more than necessary to slide it over the piston. **Note:** *Be careful not to confuse the number one and number two rings.*

23 Install the number one (top) ring in the same manner.

24 Repeat the procedure for the remaining pistons and rings.

Installation

25 Before installing the piston/connecting rod assemblies, the cylinder walls must be perfectly clean, the top edge of each cylinder bore must be chamfered, and the crankshaft must be in place.

26 Remove the cap from the end of the number one connecting rod (refer to the marks made during removal). Remove the original bearing inserts and wipe the bearing surfaces of the connecting rod and cap with a clean, lint-free cloth. They must be kept spotlessly clean.

Connecting rod bearing oil clearance check

Refer to illustrations 9.30, 9.35, 9.37 and 9.41

27 Clean the back side of the new upper bearing insert, then lay it in place in the connecting rod.

28 Make sure the tab on the bearing fits into the recess in the rod. Don't hammer the bearing insert into place and be very careful not to nick or gouge the bearing face. Don't lubricate the bearing at this time.

29 Clean the back side of the other bearing insert and install it in the rod cap. Again, make sure the tab on the bearing fits into the recess in the cap, and don't apply any lubricant. It's critically important that the mating surfaces of the bearing and connecting rod are perfectly clean and oil free when they're assembled.

30 Position the piston ring gaps at the intervals around the piston as shown **(see illustration)**.

31 Lubricate the piston and rings with clean engine oil and attach a piston ring compressor to the piston. Leave the skirt protruding about 1/4-inch to guide the piston into the cylinder. The rings must be compressed until they're flush with the piston.

32 Rotate the crankshaft until the number one connecting rod journal is at BDC (bottom dead center) and apply a liberal coat of engine oil to the cylinder walls. Refer to the TDC locating procedure in Chapter 2A for additional information.

33 With the "front" mark (letter F or arrow) on the piston facing the front (timing chain end) of the engine, gently insert the piston/connecting rod assembly into the number one cylinder bore and rest the bottom edge of the ring compressor on the engine block.

34 Tap the top edge of the ring compressor to make sure it's contacting the block around its entire circumference.

35 Gently tap on the top of the piston with the end of a wooden or plastic hammer handle **(see illustration)** while guiding the end of the

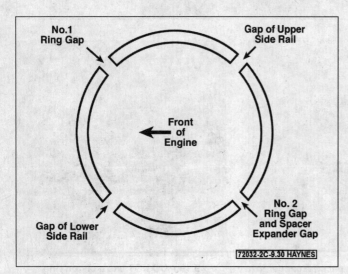

9.30 Position the piston ring end gaps as shown

9.35 Use a plastic or wooden hammer handle to push the piston into the cylinder

9.37 Place Plastigage on each connecting rod bearing journal parallel to the crankshaft centerline

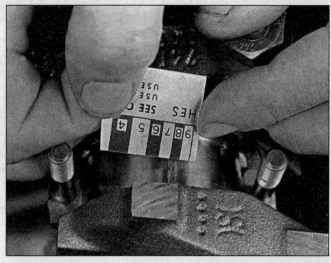

9.41 Use the scale on the Plastigage package to determine the bearing oil clearance - be sure to measure the widest part of the Plastigage and use the correct scale; it comes with both standard and metric scales

connecting rod into place on the crankshaft journal. The piston rings may try to pop out of the ring compressor just before entering the cylinder bore, so keep some downward pressure on the ring compressor. Work slowly, and if any resistance is felt as the piston enters the cylinder, stop immediately. Find out what's hanging up and fix it before proceeding. Do not, for any reason, force the piston into the cylinder - you might break a ring and/or the piston.

36   Once the piston/connecting rod assembly is installed, the connecting rod bearing oil clearance must be checked before the rod cap is permanently installed.

37   Cut a piece of the appropriate size Plastigage slightly shorter than the width of the connecting rod bearing and lay it in place on the number one connecting rod journal, parallel with the journal axis **(see illustration)**.

38   Clean the connecting rod cap bearing face and install the rod cap. Make sure the mating mark on the cap is on the same side as the mark on the connecting rod **(see illustration 9.4)**.

39   Install the rod bolts and tighten them to the torque listed in this Chapter's Specifications. **Note:** *Use a thin-wall socket to avoid erroneous torque readings that can result if the socket is wedged between the rod cap and the bolt or nut. If the socket tends to wedge itself between the fastener and the cap, lift up on it slightly until it no longer contacts the cap. DO NOT rotate the crankshaft at any time during this operation.*

40   Remove the fasteners and detach the rod cap, being very careful not to disturb the Plastigage.

41   Compare the width of the crushed Plastigage to the scale printed on the Plastigage envelope to obtain the oil clearance **(see illustration)**. The connecting rod bearing oil clearance is usually about 0.001 to 0.002 inch. Consult an automotive machine shop for

the clearance specified for the rod bearings on your engine.

42   If the clearance is not as specified, the bearing inserts may be the wrong size (which means different ones will be required). Before deciding that different inserts are needed, make sure that no dirt or oil was between the bearing inserts and the connecting rod or cap when the clearance was measured. Also, recheck the journal diameter. If the Plastigage was wider at one end than the other, the journal may be tapered. If the clearance still exceeds the limit specified, the bearing will have to be replaced with an undersize bearing. **Caution:** *When installing a new crankshaft always use a standard size bearing.*

Final installation

43   Carefully scrape all traces of the Plastigage material off the rod journal and/or bearing face. Be very careful not to scratch the bearing - use your fingernail or the edge of a plastic card.

44   Make sure the bearing faces are perfectly clean, then apply a uniform layer of clean moly-base grease or engine assembly lube to both of them. You'll have to push the piston into the cylinder to expose the face of the bearing insert in the connecting rod.

45   Slide the connecting rod back into place on the journal, install the rod cap, install the bolts and tighten them to the torque listed in this Chapter's Specifications.

46   Repeat the entire procedure for the remaining pistons/connecting rods.

47   The important points to remember are:

a) *Keep the back sides of the bearing inserts and the insides of the connecting rods and caps perfectly clean when assembling them.*

b) *Make sure you have the correct piston/rod assembly for each cylinder.*

c) *The mark on the piston must face the front (timing chain end) of the engine.*

d) *Lubricate the cylinder walls liberally with clean oil.*

e) *Lubricate the bearing faces when installing the rod caps after the oil clearance has been checked.*

48   After all the piston/connecting rod assemblies have been correctly installed, rotate the crankshaft a number of times by hand to check for any obvious binding.

49   As a final step, check the connecting rod endplay again. If it was correct before disassembly and the original crankshaft and rods were reinstalled, it should still be correct. If new rods or a new crankshaft were installed, the endplay may be inadequate. If so, the rods will have to be removed and taken to an automotive machine shop for resizing.

10   Crankshaft - removal and installation

Removal

Refer to illustrations 10.1 and 10.3

Note: *The crankshaft can be removed only after the engine has been removed from the vehicle. It's assumed that the flywheel or driveplate, crankshaft pulley, timing chain, oil pan, oil pump, oil filter, balance shaft assembly (four-cylinder and 3.0L V6 models) and piston/connecting rod assemblies have already been removed. The rear main oil seal retainer must be unbolted and separated from the block before proceeding with crankshaft removal.*

1   Before the crankshaft is removed, measure the endplay. Mount a dial indicator with the indicator in line with the crankshaft and

ENGINE BEARING ANALYSIS

Debris

Babbitt bearing embedded with debris from machinings

Microscopic detail of debris

Microscopic detail of gouges

Overplated copper alloy bearing gouged by cast iron debris

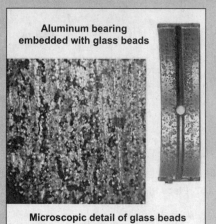

Aluminum bearing embedded with glass beads

Microscopic detail of glass beads

Damaged lining caused by dirt left on the bearing back

Misassembly

Result of a lower half assembled as an upper - blocking the oil flow

Excessive oil clearance is indicated by a short contact arc

Polished and oil-stained backs are a result of a poor fit in the housing bore

Result of a wrong, reversed, or shifted cap

Overloading

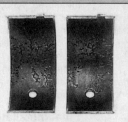

Damage from excessive idling which resulted in an oil film unable to support the load imposed

Damaged upper connecting rod bearings caused by engine lugging; the lower main bearings (not shown) were similarly affected

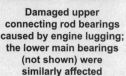

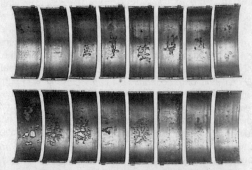

The damage shown in these upper and lower connecting rod bearings was caused by engine operation at a higher-than-rated speed under load

Misalignment

A warped crankshaft caused this pattern of severe wear in the center, diminishing toward the ends

A poorly finished crankshaft caused the equally spaced scoring shown

A tapered housing bore caused the damage along one edge of this pair

A bent connecting rod led to the damage in the "V" pattern

Lubrication

Result of dry start: The bearings on the left, farthest from the oil pump, show more damage

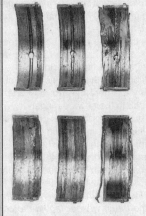

Result of a low oil supply or oil starvation

Severe wear as a result of inadequate oil clearance

Corrosion

Microscopic detail of corrosion

Corrosion is an acid attack on the bearing lining generally caused by inadequate maintenance, extremely hot or cold operation, or inferior oils or fuels

Microscopic detail of cavitation

Example of cavitation - a surface erosion caused by pressure changes in the oil film

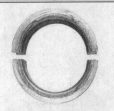

Damage from excessive thrust or insufficient axial clearance

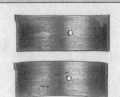

Bearing affected by oil dilution caused by excessive blow-by or a rich mixture

10.1 Checking crankshaft endplay with a dial indicator

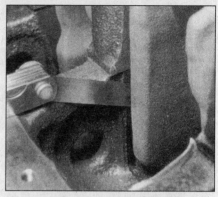

10.3 Checking crankshaft endplay with feeler gauges at the thrust bearing journal

touching the end of the crankshaft **(see illustration)**.

2   Pry the crankshaft all the way to the rear and zero the dial indicator. Next, pry the crankshaft to the front as far as possible and check the reading on the dial indicator. The distance traveled is the endplay. A typical crankshaft endplay will be from 0.003 to 0.010 inch (0.076 to 0.254 mm). If it is greater than that, check the crankshaft thrust washer/bearing assembly surfaces for wear after it's removed. If no wear is evident, new main bearings should correct the endplay.

3   If a dial indicator isn't available, feeler gauges can be used. Gently pry the crankshaft all the way to the front of the engine. Slip feeler gauges between the crankshaft and the front face of the thrust bearing or washer to determine the clearance **(see illustration)**.

4   Loosen the main bearing cap bolts 1/4-turn at a time each, until they can be removed by hand. Crankshaft main bearing caps on 3.0L V6 engines are retained by studs and nuts.

5   Gently tap the main bearing caps assembly with a soft-face hammer to loosen them. Pull the main bearing caps straight up and off the cylinder block. Try not to drop the bear-

ing inserts if they come out with the assembly. **Note:** *V6 engines have side bolts that go through the side of the block into the caps. Do not try to remove the caps until all cap and side bolts are removed.*

6   Carefully lift the crankshaft out of the engine. It may be a good idea to have an assistant available, since the crankshaft is quite heavy and awkward to handle. With the bearing inserts in place inside the engine block and main bearing caps, reinstall the main bearing caps onto the engine block and tighten the bolts finger tight. Make sure you install the main bearing caps with the arrows facing the front of the engine.

Installation

7   Crankshaft installation is the first step in engine reassembly. It's assumed at this point that the engine block and crankshaft have been cleaned, inspected and repaired or reconditioned.

8   Position the engine block with the bottom facing up.

9   Remove the mounting bolts and lift off the main bearing cap.

10   If they're still in place, remove the original bearing inserts from the block and from

the main bearing caps. Wipe the bearing surfaces of the block and main bearing caps with a clean, lint-free cloth. They must be kept spotlessly clean. This is critical for determining the correct bearing oil clearance.

Main bearing oil clearance check

Refer to illustrations 10.14, 10.17 and 10.21

11   Without mixing them up, clean the back sides of the new upper main bearing inserts (with grooves and oil holes) and lay one in each main bearing saddle in the block. Each upper bearing has an oil groove and oil hole in it. **Caution:** *The oil holes in the block must line up with the oil holes in the upper bearing inserts.* Clean the back sides of the lower main bearing inserts and lay them in the corresponding location in the main bearing caps. Make sure the tab on the bearing insert fits into the recess in the block or main bearing cap. The upper bearings with the oil holes are installed into the engine block while the lower bearings without the oil holes are installed in the caps. **Caution:** *Do not hammer the bearing insert into place and don't nick or gouge the bearing faces. DO NOT apply any lubrication at this time.*

12   Clean the faces of the bearing inserts in the block and the crankshaft main bearing journals with a clean, lint-free cloth.

13   Check or clean the oil holes in the crankshaft, as any dirt here can go only one way - straight through the new bearings.

14   Once you're certain the crankshaft is clean, carefully lay it in position in the block. Lube and insert the thrust washers on either side of journal no. 3 on four-cylinder engines, and on journal no. 4 on V6 engines. The thrust washers must be installed in the correct journal. **Note:** *Install the thrust washers with the groove in the thrust washer facing the crankshaft and the smooth sides facing the main bearing saddle.*

15   Before the crankshaft can be permanently installed, the main bearing oil clearance must be checked.

16   Cut several strips of the appropriate size

10.14 Insert the thrust washer into the machined surface between the crankshaft and the upper bearing saddle, then rotate it down into the block until it's flush with the parting line on the main bearing saddle - make sure the oil grooves on the thrust washer face the crankshaft

10.17 Place the Plastigage onto the crankshaft bearing journal as shown

10.21 Use the scale on the Plastigage package to determine the bearing oil clearance - be sure to measure the widest part of the Plastigage and use the correct scale; it comes with both standard and metric scales

of Plastigage. They must be slightly shorter than the width of the main bearing journal.

17   Place one piece on each crankshaft main bearing journal, parallel with the journal axis as shown **(see illustration)**.

18   Clean the faces of the bearing inserts in the main bearing caps. Hold the bearing inserts in place and install the caps onto the crankshaft and cylinder block. DO NOT disturb the Plastigage. Make sure you install the main bearing caps with the arrows facing the front (timing chain end) of the engine.

19   Apply clean engine oil to all bolt threads prior to installation, then install all bolts finger-tight. Tighten the main bearing cap bolts in progressing in steps, working from the center bolts outward, to the torque listed in this Chapter's Specifications. DO NOT rotate the crankshaft at any time during this operation. **Note:** *Use the old bolts at this time, not the new ones.*

20   Remove the bolts in the reverse order of the tightening sequence and carefully lift the main bearing caps straight up and off the block. Do not disturb the Plastigage or rotate the crankshaft. If the main bearing caps are difficult to remove, use the bolts, partially inserted into the caps, as a handle.

21   Compare the width of the crushed Plastigage on each journal to the scale printed on the Plastigage envelope to determine the main bearing oil clearance **(see illustration)**. A typical main bearing oil clearance should fall between 0.0015 and 0.0023-inch. Check with an automotive machine shop for the clearance specified for your engine.

22   If the clearance is not as specified, the bearing inserts may be the wrong size (which means different ones will be required). Before deciding if different inserts are needed, make sure that no dirt or oil was between the bearing inserts and the caps or block when the clearance was measured. If the Plastigage was wider at one end than the other, the crankshaft journal may be tapered. If the

clearance still exceeds the limit specified, the bearing insert(s) will have to be replaced with an undersize bearing insert(s). **Caution:** *When installing a new crankshaft, always install a standard bearing insert set.*

23   Carefully scrape all traces of the Plastigage material off the main bearing journals and/or the bearing insert faces. Be sure to remove all residue from the oil holes. Use your fingernail or the edge of a plastic card - don't nick or scratch the bearing faces.

Final installation

24   Carefully lift the crankshaft out of the cylinder block.

25   Clean the bearing insert faces in the cylinder block, then apply a thin, uniform layer of moly-base grease or engine assembly lube to each of the bearing surfaces. Be sure to coat the thrust faces as well as the journal face of the thrust washers. **Note:** *Install the thrust washers after the crankshaft has been installed.*

26   Make sure the crankshaft journals are clean, then lay the crankshaft back in place in the cylinder block.

27   Clean the bearing insert faces and then apply the same lubricant to them. Clean the engine block thoroughly. The surfaces must be free of oil residue. Install the thrust washers.

28   Install each main bearing cap onto the crankshaft and cylinder block.

29   Prior to installation, apply clean engine oil to all bolt threads and under the bolt heads, wiping off any excess, then install all bolts finger-tight. **Note:** *The manufacturer recommends using only NEW bolts or nuts for the main caps (and side bolts on V6 engines). On V6 engines, install the new side bolts hand-tight, then install and tighten the new main cap nuts in sequence.*

30   Tighten the *new* main bearing cap bolts in progressing in steps, working from the center bolts outward, to the torque listed in this Chapter's Specifications.

31   Recheck crankshaft endplay with a feeler gauge or a dial indicator. The endplay should be correct if the crankshaft thrust faces aren't worn or damaged and if new bearings have been installed.

32   Rotate the crankshaft a number of times by hand to check for any obvious binding. It should rotate with a running torque of 50 in-lbs or less. If the running torque is too high, identify and correct the problem at this time.

33   Install the new rear main oil seal (see Chapter 2A).

11   Engine overhaul - reassembly sequence

1   Before beginning engine reassembly, make sure you have all the necessary new parts, gaskets and seals as well as the following items on hand:

> *Common hand tools*
> *A 1/2-inch drive torque wrench*
> *New engine oil*
> *Gasket sealant*
> *Thread locking compound*

2   If you obtained a short block, it will be necessary to install the cylinder heads, the oil pump and pick-up tube, the oil pans, the water pump, the timing chain and timing cover, and the valve covers (see Chapter 2A). In order to save time and avoid problems, the external components must be installed in the following general order:

> *Thermostat and housing cover*
> *Water pump*
> *Intake and exhaust manifolds*
> *Fuel injection components*
> *Emission control components*
> *Spark plugs*
> *Ignition coils*
> *Oil filter and oil cooler*
> *Engine mounts and mount brackets*
> *Flywheel/driveplate*

12 Initial start-up and break-in after overhaul

Warning: *Have a fire extinguisher handy when starting the engine for the first time.*

1   Once the engine has been installed in the vehicle, double-check the engine oil and coolant levels.

2   With the spark plugs out of the engine and the ignition system and fuel pump disabled, crank the engine until oil pressure registers on the gauge or the light goes out.

3   Install the spark plugs and ignition coils, and reinstall the fuel pump relay.

4   Start the engine. It may take a few moments for the fuel system to build up pressure, but the engine should start without a great deal of effort.

5   After the engine starts, it should be allowed to warm up to normal operating temperature. While the engine is warming up, make a thorough check for fuel, oil and coolant leaks.

6   Shut the engine off and recheck the engine oil and coolant levels.

7   Drive the vehicle to an area with minimum traffic, accelerate from 30 to 50 mph, then allow the vehicle to slow to 30 mph with the throttle closed. Repeat the procedure 10 or 12 times. This will load the piston rings and cause them to seat properly against the cylinder walls. Check again for oil and coolant leaks.

8   Drive the vehicle gently for the first 500 miles (no sustained high speeds) and keep a constant check on the oil level. It is not unusual for an engine to use oil during the break-in period.

9   At approximately 500 to 600 miles, change the oil and filter.

10   For the next few hundred miles, drive the vehicle normally. Do not pamper it or abuse it.

11   After 2000 miles, change the oil and filter again and consider the engine broken in.

COMMON ENGINE OVERHAUL TERMS

B

Backlash - The amount of play between two parts. Usually refers to how much one gear can be moved back and forth without moving the gear with which it's meshed.

Bearing Caps - The caps held in place by nuts or bolts which, in turn, hold the bearing surface. This space is for lubricating oil to enter.

Bearing clearance - The amount of space left between shaft and bearing surface. This space is for lubricating oil to enter.

Bearing crush - The additional height which is purposely manufactured into each bearing half to ensure complete contact of the bearing back with the housing bore when the engine is assembled.

Bearing knock - The noise created by movement of a part in a loose or worn bearing.

Blueprinting - Dismantling an engine and reassembling it to EXACT specifications.

Bore - An engine cylinder, or any cylindrical hole; also used to describe the process of enlarging or accurately refinishing a hole with a cutting tool, as to bore an engine cylinder. The bore size is the diameter of the hole.

Boring - Renewing the cylinders by cutting them out to a specified size. A boring bar is used to make the cut.

Bottom end - A term which refers collectively to the engine block, crankshaft, main bearings and the big ends of the connecting rods.

Break-in - The period of operation between installation of new or rebuilt parts and time in which parts are worn to the correct fit. Driving at reduced and varying speed for a specified mileage to permit parts to wear to the correct fit.

Bushing - A one-piece sleeve placed in a bore to serve as a bearing surface for shaft, piston pin, etc. Usually replaceable.

C

Camshaft - The shaft in the engine, on which a series of lobes are located for operating the valve mechanisms. The camshaft is driven by gears or sprockets and a timing chain. Usually referred to simply as the cam.

Carbon - Hard, or soft, black deposits found in combustion chamber, on plugs, under rings, on and under valve heads.

Cast iron - An alloy of iron and more than two percent carbon, used for engine blocks and heads because it's relatively inexpensive and easy to mold into complex shapes.

Chamfer - To bevel across (or a bevel on) the sharp edge of an object.

Chase - To repair damaged threads with a tap or die.

Combustion chamber - The space between the piston and the cylinder head, with the piston at top dead center, in which air-fuel mixture is burned.

Compression ratio - The relationship between cylinder volume (clearance volume) when the piston is at top dead center and cylinder volume when the piston is at bottom dead center.

Connecting rod - The rod that connects the crank on the crankshaft with the piston. Sometimes called a con rod.

Connecting rod cap - The part of the connecting rod assembly that attaches the rod to the crankpin.

Core plug - Soft metal plug used to plug the casting holes for the coolant passages in the block.

Crankcase - The lower part of the engine in which the crankshaft rotates; includes the lower section of the cylinder block and the oil pan.

Crank kit - A reground or reconditioned crankshaft and new main and connecting rod bearings.

Crankpin - The part of a crankshaft to which a connecting rod is attached.

Crankshaft - The main rotating member, or shaft, running the length of the crankcase, with offset throws to which the connecting rods are attached; changes the reciprocating motion of the pistons into rotating motion.

Cylinder sleeve - A replaceable sleeve, or liner, pressed into the cylinder block to form the cylinder bore.

D

Deburring - Removing the burrs (rough edges or areas) from a bearing.

Deglazer - A tool, rotated by an electric motor, used to remove glaze from cylinder walls so a new set of rings will seat.

COMMON ENGINE OVERHAUL TERMS (continued)

E

Endplay - The amount of lengthwise movement between two parts. As applied to a crankshaft, the distance that the crankshaft can move forward and back in the cylinder block.

F

Face - A machinist's term that refers to removing metal from the end of a shaft or the face of a larger part, such as a flywheel.

Fatigue - A breakdown of material through a large number of loading and unloading cycles. The first signs are cracks followed shortly by breaks.

Feeler gauge - A thin strip of hardened steel, ground to an exact thickness, used to check clearances between parts.

Free height - The unloaded length or height of a spring.

Freeplay - The looseness in a linkage, or an assembly of parts, between the initial application of force and actual movement. Usually perceived as slop or slight delay.

Freeze plug - See Core plug.

G

Gallery - A large passage in the block that forms a reservoir for engine oil pressure.

Glaze - The very smooth, glassy finish that develops on cylinder walls while an engine is in service.

H

Heli-Coil - A rethreading device used when threads are worn or damaged. The device is installed in a retapped hole to reduce the thread size to the original size.

I

Installed height - The spring's measured length or height, as installed on the cylinder head. Installed height is measured from the spring seat to the underside of the spring retainer.

J

Journal - The surface of a rotating shaft which turns in a bearing.

K

Keeper - The split lock that holds the valve spring retainer in position on the valve stem.

Key - A small piece of metal inserted into matching grooves machined into two parts fitted together - such as a gear pressed onto a shaft - which prevents slippage between the two parts.

Knock - The heavy metallic engine sound, produced in the combustion chamber as a result of abnormal combustion - usually detonation. Knock is usually caused by a loose or worn bearing. Also referred to as detonation, pinging and spark knock. Connecting rod or main bearing knocks are created by too much oil clearance or insufficient lubrication.

L

Lands - The portions of metal between the piston ring grooves.

Lapping the valves - Grinding a valve face and its seat together with lapping compound.

Lash - The amount of free motion in a gear train, between gears, or in a mechanical assembly, that occurs before movement can begin. Usually refers to the lash in a valve train.

Lifter - The part that rides against the cam to transfer motion to the rest of the valve train.

M

Machining - The process of using a machine to remove metal from a metal part.

Main bearings - The plain, or babbit, bearings that support the crankshaft.

Main bearing caps - The cast iron caps, bolted to the bottom of the block, that support the main bearings.

COMMON ENGINE OVERHAUL TERMS (continued)

O

O.D. - Outside diameter.

Oil gallery - A pipe or drilled passageway in the engine used to carry engine oil from one area to another.

Oil ring - The lower ring, or rings, of a piston; designed to prevent excessive amounts of oil from working up the cylinder walls and into the combustion chamber. Also called an oil-control ring.

Oil seal - A seal which keeps oil from leaking out of a compartment. Usually refers to a dynamic seal around a rotating shaft or other moving part.

O-ring - A type of sealing ring made of a special rubber-like material; in use, the O-ring is compressed into a groove to provide the sealing action.

Overhaul - To completely disassemble a unit, clean and inspect all parts, reassemble it with the original or new parts and make all adjustments necessary for proper operation.

P

Pilot bearing - A small bearing installed in the center of the flywheel (or the rear end of the crankshaft) to support the front end of the input shaft of the transmission.

Pip mark - A little dot or indentation which indicates the top side of a compression ring.

Piston - The cylindrical part, attached to the connecting rod, that moves up and down in the cylinder as the crankshaft rotates. When the fuel charge is fired, the piston transfers the force of the explosion to the connecting rod, then to the crankshaft.

Piston pin (or wrist pin) - The cylindrical and usually hollow steel pin that passes through the piston. The piston pin fastens the piston to the upper end of the connecting rod.

Piston ring - The split ring fitted to the groove in a piston. The ring contacts the sides of the ring groove and also rubs against the cylinder wall, thus sealing space between piston and wall. There are two types of rings: Compression rings seal the compression pressure in the combustion chamber; oil rings scrape excessive oil off the cylinder wall.

Piston ring groove - The slots or grooves cut in piston heads to hold piston rings in position.

Piston skirt - The portion of the piston below the rings and the piston pin hole.

Plastigage - A thin strip of plastic thread, available in different sizes, used for measuring clearances. For example, a strip of plastigage is laid across a bearing journal and mashed as parts are assembled. Then parts are disassembled and the width of the strip is measured to determine clearance between journal and bearing. Commonly used to measure crankshaft main-bearing and connecting rod bearing clearances.

Press-fit - A tight fit between two parts that requires pressure to force the parts together. Also referred to as drive, or force, fit.

Prussian blue - A blue pigment; in solution, useful in determining the area of contact between two surfaces. Prussian blue is commonly used to determine the width and location of the contact area between the valve face and the valve seat.

R

Race (bearing) - The inner or outer ring that provides a contact surface for balls or rollers in bearing.

Ream - To size, enlarge or smooth a hole by using a round cutting tool with fluted edges.

Ring job - The process of reconditioning the cylinders and installing new rings.

Runout - Wobble. The amount a shaft rotates out-of-true.

S

Saddle - The upper main bearing seat.

Scored - Scratched or grooved, as a cylinder wall may be scored by abrasive particles moved up and down by the piston rings.

Scuffing - A type of wear in which there's a transfer of material between parts moving against each other; shows up as pits or grooves in the mating surfaces.

Seat - The surface upon which another part rests or seats. For example, the valve seat is the matched surface upon which the valve face rests. Also used to refer to wearing into a good fit; for example, piston rings seat after a few miles of driving.

Short block - An engine block complete with crankshaft and piston and, usually, camshaft assemblies.

COMMON ENGINE OVERHAUL TERMS (continued)

Static balance - The balance of an object while it's stationary.

Step - The wear on the lower portion of a ring land caused by excessive side and back-clearance. The height of the step indicates the ring's extra side clearance and the length of the step projecting from the back wall of the groove represents the ring's back clearance.

Stroke - The distance the piston moves when traveling from top dead center to bottom dead center, or from bottom dead center to top dead center.

Stud - A metal rod with threads on both ends.

T

Tang - A lip on the end of a plain bearing used to align the bearing during assembly.

Tap - To cut threads in a hole. Also refers to the fluted tool used to cut threads.

Taper - A gradual reduction in the width of a shaft or hole; in an engine cylinder, taper usually takes the form of uneven wear, more pronounced at the top than at the bottom.

Throws - The offset portions of the crankshaft to which the connecting rods are affixed.

Thrust bearing - The main bearing that has thrust faces to prevent excessive endplay, or forward and backward movement of the crankshaft.

Thrust washer - A bronze or hardened steel washer placed between two moving parts. The washer prevents longitudinal movement and provides a bearing surface for thrust surfaces of parts.

Tolerance - The amount of variation permitted from an exact size of measurement. Actual amount from smallest acceptable dimension to largest acceptable dimension.

U

Umbrella - An oil deflector placed near the valve tip to throw oil from the valve stem area.

Undercut - A machined groove below the normal surface.

Undersize bearings - Smaller diameter bearings used with re-ground crankshaft journals.

V

Valve grinding - Refacing a valve in a valve-refacing machine.

Valve train - The valve-operating mechanism of an engine; includes all components from the camshaft to the valve.

Vibration damper - A cylindrical weight attached to the front of the crankshaft to minimize torsional vibration (the twist-untwist actions of the crankshaft caused by the cylinder firing impulses). Also called a harmonic balancer.

W

Water jacket - The spaces around the cylinders, between the inner and outer shells of the cylinder block or head, through which coolant circulates.

Web - A supporting structure across a cavity.

Woodruff key - A key with a radiused backside (viewed from the side).

Chapter 3
Cooling, heating and air conditioning systems

Contents

	Section
Air conditioning accumulator - removal and installation	14
Air conditioning and heating system - check and maintenance	3
Air conditioning compressor - removal and installation	13
Air conditioning condenser - removal and installation	16
Air conditioning evaporator core - removal and installation	17
Air conditioning expansion (orifice) tube - removal and installation	15
Blower motor - removal and installation	9
CHECK ENGINE light on	See Chapter 6
Coolant level check	See Chapter 1
Coolant temperature gauge sending unit - check and replacement	8

	Section
Drivebelt check and replacement	See Chapter 1
Engine cooling fans - removal and installation	5
General information	1
Heater and air conditioning control assembly - removal and installation	10
Heater and air conditioning housing - removal and installation	12
Heater core - removal and installation	11
Interior ventilation filter replacement	See Chapter 1
Radiator and expansion tank - removal and installation	6
Thermostat - replacement	4
Troubleshooting	2
Water pump and after-run coolant pump - replacement	7

Specifications

General

Coolant capacity	See Chapter 1
Refrigerant type	R-134a

Torque specifications

Note: *One foot-pound (ft-lb) of torque is equivalent to 12 inch-pounds (in-lbs) of torque. Torque values below approximately 15 foot-pounds are expressed in inch-pounds, because most foot-pound torque wrenches are not accurate at these smaller values.*

	Ft-lbs (unless otherwise indicated)	Nm
Accessory bracket fasteners	33	45
Idler pulley-to-block fastener (3.2L V6)	30	40
Thermostat housing fasteners		
Four-cylinder engines	133 in-lbs	15
3.0L V6 engines	88 in-lbs	10
3.2L V6 engines	79 in-lbs	9
Water pump fasteners		
Four-cylinder engines	133 in-lbs	15
3.0L V6 engines	88 in-lbs	10
3.2L V6 engines	79 in-lbs	9
Water pump pulley fasteners (3.2L V6)	15	20

1   General information

Warning: *Do not allow antifreeze to come in contact with your skin or painted surfaces of the vehicle. Rinse off spills immediately with plenty of water. Antifreeze is highly toxic if ingested. Never leave antifreeze lying around in an open container or in puddles on the floor; children and pets are attracted by it's sweet smell and may drink it. Check with local authorities about disposing of used antifreeze. Many communities have collection centers which will see that antifreeze is disposed of safely. Never dump used antifreeze on the ground or pour it into drains.*

Engine cooling system

All modern vehicles employ a pressurized engine cooling system with thermostatically controlled coolant circulation. The cooling system consists of a radiator, an expansion tank or coolant reservoir, a pressure cap (located on the expansion tank or radiator), a thermostat, a cooling fan, and a water pump.

The water pump circulates coolant through the engine. The coolant flows around each cylinder and around the intake and exhaust ports, near the spark plug areas and in close proximity to the exhaust valve guides.

A thermostat controls engine coolant temperature. During warm up, the closed thermostat prevents coolant from circulating through the radiator. As the engine nears normal operating temperature, the thermostat opens and allows hot coolant to travel through the radiator, where it's cooled before returning to the engine.

Heating system

The heating system consists of a blower fan and heater core located in a housing under the dash, the hoses connecting the heater core to the engine cooling system and the heater/air conditioning control head on the dashboard. Hot engine coolant is circulated through the heater core. When the heater mode is activated, a flap door in the housing opens to expose the heater core to the passenger compartment through air ducts. A fan switch on the control head activates the blower motor, which forces air through the core, heating the air.

Air conditioning system

The air conditioning system consists of a condenser mounted in front of the radiator, an evaporator mounted adjacent to the heater core, a compressor mounted on the engine, a receiver-drier or accumulator and the plumbing connecting all of the above components.

A blower fan forces the warmer air of the passenger compartment through the evaporator core (sort of a radiator-in-reverse), transferring the heat from the air to the refrigerant. The liquid refrigerant boils off into low pressure vapor, taking the heat with it when it leaves the evaporator.

2   Troubleshooting

Coolant leaks

Refer to illustration 2.2

1   A coolant leak can develop anywhere in the cooling system, but the most common causes are:

a) A loose or weak hose clamp
b) A defective hose
c) A faulty pressure cap
d) A damaged radiator
e) A bad heater core
f) A faulty water pump
g) A leaking gasket at any joint that carries coolant

2   Coolant leaks aren't always easy to find. Sometimes they can only be detected when the cooling system is under pressure. Here's where a cooling system pressure tester comes in handy. After the engine has cooled completely, the tester is attached in place of the pressure cap, then pumped up to the pressure value equal to that of the pressure cap rating **(see illustration)**. Now, leaks that only exist when the engine is fully warmed up will become apparent. The tester can be left connected to locate a nagging slow leak.

Coolant level drops, but no external leaks

Refer to illustrations 2.5a and 2.5b

3   If you find it necessary to keep adding coolant, but there are no external leaks, the probable causes include:

a) A blown head gasket
b) A leaking intake manifold gasket (only on engines that have coolant passages in the manifold)
c) A cracked cylinder head or cylinder block

4   Any of the above problems will also usually result in contamination of the engine oil, which will cause it to take on a milkshake-like appearance. A bad head gasket or cracked head or block can also result in engine oil contaminating the cooling system.

5   Combustion leak detectors (also known as block testers) are available at most auto parts stores. These work by detecting exhaust gases in the cooling system, which indicates a compression leak from a cylinder into the coolant. The tester consists of a large bulb-type syringe and bottle of test fluid **(see illustration)**. A measured amount of the fluid is added to the syringe. The syringe is placed over the cooling system filler neck and, with the engine running, the bulb is squeezed and a sample of the gases present in the cooling system are drawn up through the test fluid **(see illustration)**. If any combustion gases are present in the sample taken, the test fluid will change color.

6   If the test indicates combustion gas is present in the cooling system, you can be sure that the engine has a blown head gasket or a crack in the cylinder head or block, and will require disassembly to repair.

Pressure cap

Refer to illustration 2.8

Warning: *Wait until the engine is completely cool before beginning this check.*

7   The cooling system is sealed by a spring-loaded cap, which raises the boiling point of the coolant. If the cap's seal or spring are worn out, the coolant can boil and escape past the cap. With the engine completely cool, remove the cap and check the seal; if it's cracked, hardened or deteriorated in any way, replace it with a new one.

8   Even if the seal is good, the spring might not be; this can be checked with a cooling system pressure tester **(see illustration)**. If the cap can't hold a pressure within approximately 1-1/2 lbs of its rated pressure (which is marked on the cap), replace it with a new one.

9   The cap is also equipped with a vacuum relief spring. When the engine cools off, a vacuum is created in the cooling system. The vacuum relief spring allows air back into the system, which will equalize the pressure and prevent damage to the radiator (the radiator tanks could collapse if the vacuum is great enough). If, after turning the engine off and

2.2 The cooling system pressure tester is connected in place of the pressure cap, then pumped up to pressurize the system

2.5a The combustion leak detector consists of a bulb, syringe and test fluid

2.5b Place the tester over the cooling system filler neck and use the bulb to draw a sample into the tester

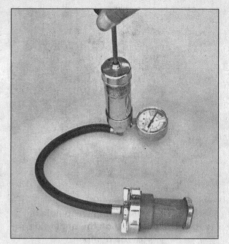

2.8 Checking the cooling system pressure cap with a cooling system pressure tester

allowing it to cool down you notice any of the cooling system hoses collapsing, replace the pressure cap with a new one.

Thermostat

Refer to illustration 2.10

10   Before assuming the thermostat **(see illustration)** is responsible for a cooling system problem, check the coolant level (see Chapter 1), drivebelt tension (see Chapter 1) and temperature gauge (or light) operation.

11   If the engine takes a long time to warm up (as indicated by the temperature gauge or heater operation), the thermostat is probably stuck open. Replace the thermostat with a new one.

12   If the engine runs hot or overheats, a thorough test of the thermostat should be performed.

13   Definitive testing of the thermostat can only be made when it is removed from the vehicle. If the thermostat is stuck in the open position at room temperature, it is faulty and must be replaced. **Caution:** *Do not drive the vehicle without a thermostat. The computer*

may stay in open loop and emissions and fuel economy will suffer.

14   To test a thermostat, suspend the (closed) thermostat on a length of string or wire in a pot of cold water.

15   Heat the water on a stove while observing thermostat. The thermostat should fully open before the water boils.

16   If the thermostat doesn't open and close as specified, or sticks in any position, replace it.

Cooling fan

Electric cooling fan

17   If the engine is overheating and the cooling fan is not coming on when the engine temperature rises to an excessive level, unplug the fan motor electrical connector(s) and connect the motor directly to the battery with fused jumper wires. If the fan motor doesn't come on, replace the motor.

18   If the radiator fan motor is okay, but it isn't coming on when the engine gets hot, the fan relay might be defective. A relay is used to control a circuit by turning it on and off in

response to a control decision by the Powertrain Control Module (PCM). These control circuits are fairly complex, and checking them should be left to a qualified automotive technician. Sometimes, the control system can be fixed by simply identifying and replacing a bad relay.

19   Locate the fan relays in the engine compartment fuse/relay box.

20   Test the relay (see Chapter 12).

21   If the relay is okay, check all wiring and connections to the fan motor. Refer to the wiring diagrams at the end of Chapter 12. If no obvious problems are found, the problem could be the Engine Coolant Temperature (ECT) sensor or the Powertrain Control Module (PCM). Have the cooling fan system and circuit diagnosed by a dealer service department or repair shop with the proper diagnostic equipment. **Note:** *These models are equipped with a cooling fan motor resistor. Have the resistor checked if the fan motor does not respond to the speed variations signaled by the PCM.*

Belt-driven cooling fan

22   Disconnect the cable from the negative terminal of the battery and rock the fan back and forth by hand to check for excessive bearing play.

23   With the engine cold (and not running), turn the fan blades by hand. The fan should turn freely.

24   Visually inspect for substantial fluid leakage from the clutch assembly. If problems are noted, replace the clutch assembly.

25   With the engine completely warmed up, turn off the ignition switch and disconnect the negative battery cable from the battery. Turn the fan by hand. Some drag should be evident. If the fan turns easily, replace the fan clutch.

Water pump

26   A failure in the water pump can cause serious engine damage due to overheating.

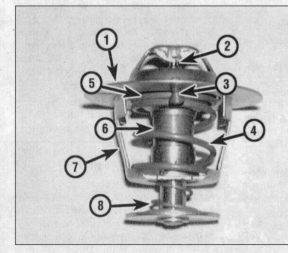

2.10 Typical thermostat:

1   *Flange*
2   *Piston*
3   *Jiggle valve*
4   *Main coil spring*
5   *Valve seat*
6   *Valve*
7   *Frame*
8   *Secondary coil spring*

2.28 The water pump weep hole is generally located on the underside of the pump

Drivebelt-driven water pump

Refer to illustration 2.28

27   There are two ways to check the operation of the water pump while it's installed on the engine. If the pump is found to be defective, it should be replaced with a new or rebuilt unit.

28   Water pumps are equipped with weep (or vent) holes **(see illustration)**. If a failure occurs in the pump seal, coolant will leak from the hole.

29   If the water pump shaft bearings fail, there may be a howling sound at the pump while it's running. Shaft wear can be felt with the drivebelt removed if the water pump pulley is rocked up and down (with the engine off). Don't mistake drivebelt slippage, which causes a squealing sound, for water pump bearing failure.

Timing chain or timing belt-driven water pump

30   Water pumps driven by the timing chain or timing belt are located underneath the timing chain or timing belt cover.

31   Checking the water pump is limited because of where it is located. However, some basic checks can be made before deciding to remove the water pump. If the pump is found to be defective, it should be replaced with a new or rebuilt unit.

32   One sign that the water pump may be failing is that the heater (climate control) may not work well. Warm the engine to normal operating temperature, confirm that the coolant level is correct, then run the heater and check for hot air coming from the ducts.

33   Check for noises coming from the water pump area. If the water pump impeller shaft or bearings are failing, there may be a howling sound at the pump while the engine is running. **Note:** *Be careful not to mistake drivebelt noise (squealing) for water pump bearing or shaft failure.*

34   It you suspect water pump failure due to noise, wear can be confirmed by feeling for play at the pump shaft. This can be done by rocking the drive sprocket on the pump shaft up and down. To do this you will need to

remove the tension on the timing chain or belt as well as access the water pump.

All water pumps

35   In rare cases or on high-mileage vehicles, another sign of water pump failure may be the presence of coolant in the engine oil. This condition will adversely affect the engine in varying degrees. **Note:** *Finding coolant in the engine oil could indicate other serious issues besides a failed water pump, such as a blown head gasket or a cracked cylinder head or block.*

36   Even a pump that exhibits no outward signs of a problem, such as noise or leakage, can still be due for replacement. Removal for close examination is the only sure way to tell. Sometimes the fins on the back of the impeller can corrode to the point that cooling efficiency is diminished significantly.

Heater system

37   Little can go wrong with a heater. If the fan motor will run at all speeds, the electrical part of the system is okay. The three basic heater problems fall into the following general categories:

a) *Not enough heat*
b) *Heat all the time*
c) *No heat*

38   If there's not enough heat, the control valve or door is stuck in a partially open position, the coolant coming from the engine isn't hot enough, or the heater core is restricted. If the coolant isn't hot enough, the thermostat in the engine cooling system is stuck open, allowing coolant to pass through the engine so rapidly that it doesn't heat up quickly enough. If the vehicle is equipped with a temperature gauge instead of a warning light, watch to see if the engine temperature rises to the normal operating range after driving for a reasonable distance.

39   If there's heat all the time, the control valve or the door is stuck wide open.

40   If there's no heat, coolant is probably not reaching the heater core, or the heater core is plugged. The likely cause is a collapsed or plugged hose, core, or a frozen heater control valve. If the heater is the type that flows coolant all the time, the cause is a stuck door or a broken or kinked control cable.

Air conditioning system

41   If the cool air output is inadequate:

a) *Inspect the condenser coils and fins to make sure they're clear*
b) *Check the compressor clutch for slippage.*
c) *Check the blower motor for proper operation.*
d) *Inspect the blower discharge passage for obstructions.*
e) *Check the system air intake filter for clogging.*

42   If the system provides intermittent cooling air:

a) *Check the circuit breaker, blower switch and blower motor for a malfunction.*
b) *Make sure the compressor clutch isn't slipping.*

c) *Inspect the plenum door to make sure it's operating properly.*
d) *Inspect the evaporator to make sure it isn't clogged.*
e) *If the unit is icing up, it may be caused by excessive moisture in the system, incorrect super heat switch adjustment or low thermostat adjustment.*

43   If the system provides no cooling air:

a) *Inspect the compressor drivebelt. Make sure it's not loose or broken.*
b) *Make sure the compressor clutch engages. If it doesn't, check for a blown fuse.*
c) *Inspect the wire harness for broken or disconnected wires.*
d) *If the compressor clutch doesn't engage, bridge the terminals of the A/C pressure switch(es) with a jumper wire; if the clutch now engages, and the system is properly charged, the pressure switch is bad.*
e) *Make sure the blower motor is not disconnected or burned out.*
f) *Make sure the compressor isn't partially or completely seized.*
g) *Inspect the refrigerant lines for leaks.*
h) *Check the components for leaks.*
i) *Inspect the receiver-drier/accumulator or expansion valve/tube for clogged screens.*

44   If the system is noisy:

a) *Look for loose panels in the passenger compartment.*
b) *Inspect the compressor drivebelt. It may be loose or worn.*
c) *Check the compressor mounting bolts. They should be tight.*
d) *Listen carefully to the compressor. It may be worn out.*
e) *Listen to the idler pulley and bearing and the clutch. Either may be defective.*
f) *The winding in the compressor clutch coil or solenoid may be defective.*
g) *The compressor oil level may be low.*
h) *The blower motor fan bushing or the motor itself may be worn out.*
i) *If there is an excessive charge in the system, you'll hear a rumbling noise in the high pressure line, a thumping noise in the compressor, or see bubbles or cloudiness in the sight glass.*
j) *If there's a low charge in the system, you might hear hissing in the evaporator case at the expansion valve, or see bubbles or cloudiness in the sight glass.*

---

3   Air conditioning and heating system - check and maintenance

---

Air conditioning system

Refer to illustration 3.1

Warning: *The air conditioning system is under high pressure. Do not loosen any hose fittings or remove any components until after the system has been discharged. Air conditioning*

3.1 Detach the evaporator drain hose at this location under the right side of the instrument panel and blow through the hose with compressed air

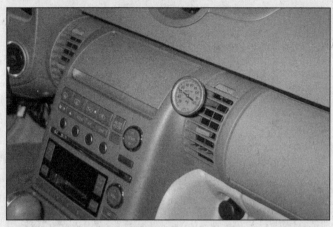

3.9 Insert a thermometer in the center vent, turn on the air conditioning system and wait for it to cool down; depending on the humidity, the output air should be 30 to 40 degrees cooler than the ambient air temperature

refrigerant should be properly discharged into an EPA-approved recovery/recycling unit at a dealer service department or an automotive air conditioning repair facility. Always wear eye protection when disconnecting air conditioning system fittings.

Caution 1: *All models covered by this manual use environmentally friendly R-134a. This refrigerant (and its appropriate refrigerant oils) are not compatible with R-12 refrigerant system components and must never be mixed or the components will be damaged.*

Caution 2: *When replacing entire components, additional refrigerant oil should be added equal to the amount that is removed with the component being replaced. Be sure to read the can before adding any oil to the system, to make sure it is compatible with the R-134a system.*

1 The following maintenance checks should be performed on a regular basis to ensure that the air conditioning continues to operate at peak efficiency.

a) *Inspect the condition of the compressor drivebelt. If it is worn or deteriorated, replace it (see Chapter 1).*

b) *Check the drivebelt tension (see Chapter 1).*

c) *Inspect the system hoses. Look for cracks, bubbles, hardening and deterioration. Inspect the hoses and all fittings for oil bubbles or seepage. If there is any evidence of wear, damage or leakage, replace the hose(s).*

d) *Inspect the condenser fins for leaves, bugs and any other foreign material that may have embedded itself in the fins. Use a fin comb or compressed air to remove debris from the condenser.*

e) *Make sure the system has the correct refrigerant charge.*

f) *If you hear water sloshing around in the dash area or have water dripping on the carpet, check the evaporator housing drain tube (see illustration) for blockage.*

2 It's a good idea to operate the system for about ten minutes at least once a month. This is particularly important during the winter months because long term non-use can cause hardening, and subsequent failure, of the seals. Note that using the Defrost function operates the compressor.

3 If the air conditioning system is not working properly, proceed to Step 6 and perform the general checks outlined below.

4 Because of the complexity of the air conditioning system and the special equipment necessary to service it, in-depth troubleshooting and repairs beyond checking the refrigerant charge and the compressor clutch operation are not included in this manual. However, simple checks and component replacement procedures are provided in this Chapter. For more complete information on the air conditioning system, refer to the *Haynes Automotive Heating and Air Conditioning Manual*.

5 The most common cause of poor cooling is simply a low system refrigerant charge. If a noticeable drop in system cooling ability occurs, one of the following quick checks will help you determine if the refrigerant level is low.

Checking the refrigerant charge

Refer to illustration 3.9

6 Warm the engine up to normal operating temperature.

7 Place the air conditioning temperature selector at the coldest setting and put the blower at the highest setting.

8 After the system reaches operating temperature, feel the larger pipe exiting the evaporator at the firewall. The outlet pipe should be cold (the tubing that leads back to the compressor). If the evaporator outlet pipe is warm, the system probably needs a charge.

9 Insert a thermometer in the center air distribution duct **(see illustration)** while operating the air conditioning system at its maximum setting - the temperature of the output air should be 35 to 40 degrees F below the ambient air temperature (down to approxi-

mately 40 degrees F). If the ambient (outside) air temperature is very high, say 110 degrees F, the duct air temperature may be as high as 60 degrees F, but generally the air conditioning is 35 to 40 degrees F cooler than the ambient air.

10 Further inspection or testing of the system requires special tools and techniques and is beyond the scope of the home mechanic.

Adding refrigerant

Refer to illustrations 3.11 and 3.13

Caution: *Make sure any refrigerant, refrigerant oil or replacement component you purchase is designated as compatible with R-134a systems.*

11 Purchase an R-134a automotive charging kit at an auto parts store **(see illustration)**. A charging kit includes a can of refrigerant, a tap valve and a short section of hose that can be attached between the tap valve and the system low side service valve. **Caution:** *Never add more than one can of refrigerant to the system. If more refrigerant than that is required, the system should be evacuated and leak tested.*

3.11 R-134a automotive air conditioning charging kit

3.13 Location of the low-side charging port

3.24 Remove the interior ventilation filter and spray the disinfectant into the blower housing with the blower on high (be sure to wear safety goggles)

12   Back off the valve handle on the charging kit and screw the kit onto the refrigerant can, making sure first that the O-ring or rubber seal inside the threaded portion of the kit is in place. **Warning:** *Wear protective eyewear when dealing with pressurized refrigerant cans.*

13   Remove the dust cap from the low-side charging port and attach the hose's quick-connect fitting to the port **(see illustration)**. **Warning:** *DO NOT hook the charging kit hose to the system high side! The fittings on the charging kit are designed to fit **only** on the low side of the system.*

14   Warm up the engine and turn On the air conditioning. Keep the charging kit hose away from the fan and other moving parts. **Note:** *The charging process requires the compressor to be running. If the clutch cycles off, you can put the air conditioning switch on High and leave the car doors open to keep the clutch on and compressor working. The compressor can be kept on during the charging by removing the connector from the pressure switch and bridging it with a paper clip or jumper wire during the procedure.*

15   Turn the valve handle on the kit until the stem pierces the can, then back the handle out to release the refrigerant. You should be able to hear the rush of gas. Keep the can upright at all times, but shake it occasionally. Allow stabilization time between each addition. **Note:** *The charging process will go faster if you wrap the can with a hot-water-soaked rag to keep the can from freezing up.*

16   If you have an accurate thermometer, you can place it in the center air conditioning duct inside the vehicle and keep track of the output air temperature. A charged system that is working properly should cool down to approximately 40 degrees F. If the ambient (outside) air temperature is very high, say 110 degrees F, the duct air temperature may be as high as 60 degrees F, but generally the air conditioning is 35 to 40 degrees F cooler than the ambient air.

17   When the can is empty, turn the valve handle to the closed position and release the connection from the low-side port. Reinstall the dust cap.

18   Remove the charging kit from the can and store the kit for future use with the piercing valve in the UP position, to prevent inadvertently piercing the can on the next use.

Heating systems

19   If the carpet under the heater core is damp, or if antifreeze vapor or steam is coming through the vents, the heater core is leaking. Remove it (see Section 11) and install a new unit (most radiator shops will not repair a leaking heater core).

20   If the air coming out of the heater vents isn't hot, the problem could stem from any of the following causes:

a)   *The thermostat is stuck open, preventing the engine coolant from warming up enough to carry heat to the heater core. Replace the thermostat (see Section 4).*

b)   *There is a blockage in the system, preventing the flow of coolant through the heater core. Feel both heater hoses at the firewall. They should be hot. If one of them is cold, there is an obstruction in one of the hoses or in the heater core, or the heater control valve is shut. Detach the hoses and back flush the heater core with a water hose. If the heater core is clear but circulation is impeded, remove the two hoses and flush them out with a water hose.*

c)   *If flushing fails to remove the blockage from the heater core, the core must be replaced (see Section 11).*

Eliminating air conditioning odors

Refer to illustration 3.24

21   Unpleasant odors that often develop in air conditioning systems are caused by the growth of a fungus, usually on the surface of the evaporator core. The warm, humid environment there is a perfect breeding ground for mildew to develop.

22   The evaporator core on most vehicles is difficult to access, and factory dealerships have a lengthy, expensive process for eliminating the fungus by opening up the evaporator case and using a powerful disinfectant and rinse on the core until the fungus is gone. You can service your own system at home, but it takes something much stronger than basic household germ-killers or deodorizers.

23   Aerosol disinfectants for automotive air conditioning systems are available in most auto parts stores, but remember when shopping for them that the most effective treatments are also the most expensive. The basic procedure for using these sprays is to start by running the system in the RECIRC mode for ten minutes with the blower on its highest speed. Use the highest heat mode to dry out the system and keep the compressor from engaging by disconnecting the wiring connector at the compressor.

24   The disinfectant can usually comes with a long spray hose. Remove the interior ventilation filter (see Chapter 1), insert the nozzle into the air intake and spray according to the manufacturer's recommendations **(see illustration)**. **Warning:** *Wear safety goggles.* Follow the manufacturer's recommendations for the length of spray and waiting time between applications.

25   Once the evaporator has been cleaned, the best way to prevent the mildew from coming back again is to make sure your evaporator housing drain tube is clear **(see illustration 3.1)**.

Automatic heating and air conditioning systems

26   Some vehicles are equipped with an optional automatic climate control system. This system has its own computer that receives inputs from various sensors in the heating and air conditioning system. This computer, like the PCM, has self-diagnostic capabilities to help pinpoint problems or

4.20 Remove the drivebelt tensioner and lift bracket mounting fasteners

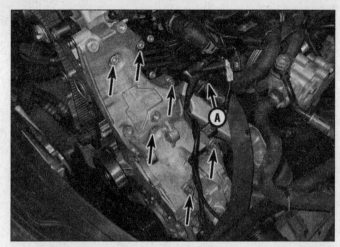

4.23 Remove the lower hose retaining clip (A) and accessory bracket mounting fasteners

faults within the system. Vehicles equipped with automatic heating and air conditioning systems are very complex and considered beyond the scope of the home mechanic. Vehicles equipped with automatic heating and air conditioning systems should be taken to dealer service department or other qualified facility for repair.

4 Thermostat - replacement

Warning: *The engine must be completely cool when this procedure is performed.*
Caution: *Don't drive the vehicle without a thermostat! The computer may stay in open loop mode and emissions and fuel economy will suffer.*
Note: *The thermostats on four-cylinder engines are electronically controlled. The sensor, thermostat and housing are a complete unit and the individual components are not serviceable separately.*
1   Remove the engine covers.

4.24 Remove the coolant hose and clamps (A), then the lower radiator hose mounting clip (B) and the coolant pipe mounting fastener (C)

2   Disconnect the cable from the negative terminal of the battery (see Chapter 5).
3   Raise the front of the vehicle and support it securely on jackstands.
4   Remove the splash shield from below the engine.
5   Drain the coolant from the radiator (see Chapter 1). If the coolant is relatively new or in good condition, save it and reuse it. If it is to be replaced, see Section 1 for cautions about proper handling of used antifreeze.

Four-cylinder engines
1.8L four-cylinder engine
6   Remove the front bumper cover and place the radiator support panel in the service position (see Chapter 11).
7   Remove the drivebelt (see Chapter 1).
8   Remove the hose between the coolant expansion tank and the radiator.
9   Remove the upper radiator hose.
10   Remove the air intake hose between the throttle body and the intercooler. **Note:** *Removing the throttle body will give you better access to the thermostat housing.*

11   Remove the alternator (see Chapter 5).
12   Remove the intake manifold support brace.
13   Remove the bolt securing the lower coolant pipe bracket to the thermostat housing.
14   Remove the bolt securing the lower coolant pipe bracket to the oil filter housing.
15   Detach the hoses and electrical connector from the thermostat housing.
16   Remove the thermostat housing bolts and detach the housing from the engine block. Be prepared for some coolant to spill as the gasket seal is broken. On some models, there are two thermostat fasteners at the base of the distribution housing which can be removed to separate the thermostat assembly **Note:** *The thermostat and housing are one piece and must be replaced as a unit.* Clean the mating surfaces of the engine block and the thermostat, then proceed to Step 26.

2.0L four-cylinder engine
Refer to illustrations 4.20, 4.23, 4.24 and 4.25
17   Disconnect the oil pressure sensor electrical connector.
18   Remove the lower radiator hose (see Chapter 1).
19   Remove the drivebelt (see Chapter 1).
20   Remove the drivebelt tensioner and engine lifting bracket fasteners **(see illustration)**, then remove the assembly.
21   Remove the alternator (see Chapter 5).
22   Disconnect the air conditioning compressor connector and remove the mounting fasteners **(see illustration 13.7)**, then move the compressor to the side. Support the compressor with rope or wire. **Warning:** *Don't disconnect the refrigerant lines.*
23   Remove the accessory bracket fasteners and remove the bracket **(see illustration)**.
24   Remove the upper coolant hose clamps, hose and the coolant tube fastener, then pull the tube and O-ring from the housing **(see illustration)**. Pull the lower hose clip and remove the hose (if not already done).

4.25 Remove the thermostat (coolant distribution) housing fasteners and remove the housing

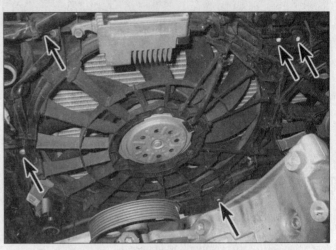

5.6a Cooling fan mounting fasteners

25   Disconnect the electrical connector and remove the coolant distribution housing fasteners, then detach the housing **(see illustration)**. Be prepared for some coolant to spill as the gasket seal is broken. On some models, there are two thermostat fasteners at the base of the distribution housing which can be removed to separate the thermostat assembly **Note:** *The thermostat and housing are one piece and must be replaced as a unit.* Clean the mating surfaces of the engine block and the thermostat.

All four-cylinder engines

26   Install a new O-ring and reattach the thermostat to the engine block. Tighten the bolts to the torque listed in this Chapter's Specifications.

27   The remainder of installation is the reverse of the removal procedure. **Note:** *Coat the accessory bracket fasteners with thread locking compound before installation.*

28   Refer to Chapter 1 and refill and bleed the system, then run the engine and check carefully for leaks.

V6 engines

29   On 3.0L engines, remove the intake manifold (see Chapter 2A).

30   On 3.2L engines, remove the front bumper cover and place the radiator support panel in the service position (see Chapter 11).

31   On 3.2L engines, remove the upper intake manifold (see Chapter 4).

32   Remove the upper radiator hose (see Chapter 1).

33   Remove the thermostat housing fasteners and remove the housing. **Note:** *The thermostat and housing are one piece and must be replaced as a unit.*

34   Clean the mating surfaces of the engine block and the thermostat.

35   Install a new O-ring and reattach the thermostat to the engine block. Tighten the bolts to the torque listed in this Chapter's Specifications.

36   The remainder of the installation procedure is the reverse of removal.

37   Refer to Chapter 1 and refill and bleed the system, then run the engine and check carefully for leaks.

---

5   Engine cooling fans - removal and installation

Refer to illustration 5.6a, 5.6b and 5.7

Warning: *Keep hands, tools and clothing away from the fan. To avoid injury or damage, DO NOT operate the engine with a damaged fan. Do not attempt to repair fan blades - always replace a damaged fan with a new one.*

1   Remove the air intake duct from the radiator support panel and the air cleaner housing.

2   Raise the vehicle and support it securely on jackstands. Remove the splash shield from below the engine.

3   Place the radiator support panel in the service position (see Chapter 11).

4   On 1.8L models, drain the coolant (see Chapter 1) and remove the radiator (see Section 6).

5   Disconnect the electrical connector(s) from the cooling fan(s). **Note:** *The wiring harness is held in place by cable ties and may have to be cut to allow the connectors to be disconnected.*

6   Remove the cooling fan shroud fasteners **(see illustrations)** and remove the assembly.

7   Remove the cooling fan motor fasteners **(see illustration)** and the fan from the shroud.

8   If the fan blades or the fan motor are damaged, they can be replaced by removing the fan blade from the fan motor.

9   The remainder of installation is the reverse of the removal procedure. On 1.8L models, refer to Chapter 1 and refill and bleed the system, then run the engine and check carefully for leaks.

5.6b Auxiliary cooling fan mounting fasteners

5.7 Remove the cooling fan motor mounting fasteners

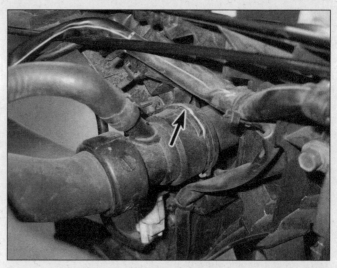

6.5 Separate the hose from the radiator by prying the clip up and remove the hose

6 Radiator and expansion tank - removal and installation

Warning: *The engine must be completely cool when this procedure is performed.*

Radiator

Refer to illustration 6.5

1 Raise the front of the vehicle and support it securely on jackstands.

2 Remove the lower splash shield (see Chapter 11) and drain the cooling system as described in Chapter 1. Refer to the coolant **Warning** in Section 1.

3 Remove the engine covers and front bumper (see Chapter 11). On 2.0L models, place the radiator support panel in the service position (see Chapter 11).

4 Disconnect the upper and lower automatic transaxle cooler lines and cap the lines to prevent further leakage.

5 Pry up the clip on the upper and lower radiator hose couplers and separate the hoses from the radiator **(see illustration)**. **Note:** *It may be necessary to twist the hose back and forth to free the O-ring before the hose will come off.*

6 Remove the air duct fasteners from each side of the radiator and remove the ducts.

7 Disconnect the air conditioning pressure switch and ambient temperature sensor from the driver's side of the radiator **(see illustration 16.7)**. Move the harness out of the way of the radiator.

8 Remove the power steering cooler mounting fasteners and lower the cooler, but do not disconnect the lines (if equipped).

9 Remove the air conditioning condenser mounting fasteners (see Section 16) and rotate the condenser away and down from the radiator. **Caution:** *Make sure not to kink, stretch or bend the air conditioning lines.*

10 Release the two radiator mounting pins and pull up on the pins to remove them and remove the radiator.

11 Prior to installation of the radiator, replace any damaged hose clips and/or radiator hoses and O-rings.

12 Radiator installation is the reverse of removal.

13 After installation, refer to Chapter 1 and refill and bleed the system, then run the engine and check carefully for leaks.

Expansion tank

Refer to illustration 6.15

14 Drain the cooling system as described in Chapter 1 until the expansion tank is empty. Refer to the coolant **Warning** in Section 1.

15 Remove the coolant recovery hoses from the expansion tank **(see illustration)**.

16 Remove the expansion tank mounting screw, then lift the expansion tank up and disconnect the coolant level sensor connector.

17 Remove the expansion tank from the engine compartment.

18 Prior to installation, make sure the reservoir is clean and free of debris which could be drawn into the radiator (wash it with soapy water and a brush if necessary, then rinse thoroughly).

19 Installation is the reverse of removal.

7 Water pump and after-run coolant pump - replacement

Water pump

Warning: *Wait until the engine is completely cool before starting this procedure.*

1 Raise the vehicle and support it securely on jackstands.

2 Drain the coolant (see Chapter 1).

3 Place the radiator support panel in the service position (see Chapter 11).

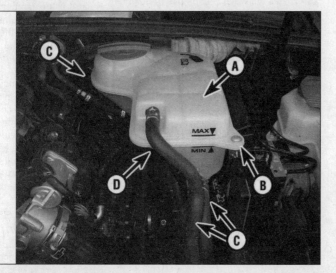

6.15 Expansion tank details

A Expansion tank
B Mounting screw
C Coolant recovery hoses
D Coolant level sensor

7.7 Remove the water pump mounting fasteners (2.0L four-cylinder engine shown)

9.2 Remove the support brace mounting bolts - instrument panel removed for clarity

4   Remove the drivebelt (see Chapter 1).
5   Remove the engine cooling fans as described in Section 4.

Four-cylinder engines

Refer to illustration 7.7

6   Remove the timing belt (see Chapter 2A).
7   Remove the water pump mounting fasteners **(see illustration)** and remove the pump.
8   Remove the O-ring located between the housing and block and discard it; a new one should be used on installation.
9   Installation is the reverse of removal. Be sure to install a new O-ring between the water pump housing and the engine block, and tighten the fasteners to the torque listed in this Chapter's Specifications. Refer to Chapter 2A and install the timing belt.
10   Refill and bleed the cooling system (see Chapter 1). Start the engine and check for the proper coolant level and the water pump and hoses for leaks.

3.0L V6 engines

11   Remove the timing belt (see Chapter 2B).
12   Remove the camshaft sprockets from the camshafts on the right (passenger's side) cylinder head (see Chapter 2B).
13   Remove the timing belt idler pulley fasteners and remove the pulley and bracket. Remove the rear timing belt guard fasteners and remove the guard.
14   Remove the water pump mounting fasteners and the water pump from the engine block.
15   Remove all traces of gasket material from the mating surfaces on the water pump and the engine block. Wipe the mating surfaces clean with brake system cleaner.
16   Apply a small amount of RTV sealant to the water pump gasket surface to help keep the gasket in place as the water pump is being installed. Install the gasket on the water pump, then install the water pump

onto the engine block.
17   Install the water pump bolts and tighten them to the torque listed in this Chapter's Specifications.
18   The remainder of the installation procedure is the reverse of removal. Be sure to properly install the timing belt. Refill and bleed the cooling system (see Chapter 1).
19   Start the engine and check for the proper coolant level and the water pump and hoses for leaks.

3.2L V6 engines

20   Using a pin spanner that engages the water pump pulley holes, hold the water pump pulley from turning and remove the three mounting fasteners and the pulley.
21   Pry the center cap out of the idler pulley and remove the idler mounting nut and pulley.
22   Remove the water pump mounting bolts and the water pump from the engine block.
23   Wipe the mating surfaces clean with brake system cleaner.
24   Apply a small amount of RTV sealant to the water pump gasket surface. Install the water pump onto the engine block.
25   Install the water pump bolts and tighten them to the torque listed in this Chapter's Specifications.
26   The remainder of the installation procedure is the reverse of removal. Refill and bleed the cooling system (see Chapter 1).
27   Start the engine and check for the proper coolant level and the water pump and hoses for leaks.

After-run coolant pump

Warning: *Wait until the engine is completely cool before starting this procedure.*
Note: *Not all models are equipped with this pump; it's available only on models in countries with high-temperature climates.*
28   Raise the vehicle and support it securely on jackstands.
29   Drain the coolant (see Chapter 1).
30   Remove the lower radiator hose.
31   Remove the inlet and outlet hoses from

the after-run coolant pump.
32   Disconnect the electrical connector from the pump, then remove the retaining bracket bolt and detach the after-run coolant pump from the engine.
33   Installation is the reverse of removal. Refill and bleed the cooling system (see Chapter 1).

---

8   Coolant temperature gauge sending unit - check and replacement

Check

Warning: *Wait until the engine is completely cool before beginning this procedure.*
1   The coolant temperature indicator system consists of the temperature gauge, a sensor mounted on the engine and the vehicle's main computer. The Engine Coolant Temperature (ECT) sensor provides a signal to the Powertrain Control Module (PCM) (see Chapter 6). The PCM uses this signal to control the temperature gauge.
2   If the temperature gauge goes above normal and begins to read hot, check the coolant level in the system (see Chapter 1). Also, refer to the *Troubleshooting* Section before assuming that the temperature indicator is faulty.
3   Start the engine and monitor it while it warms up for 10 minutes. If the gauge has not moved from the cold position, check the wiring harness connections going to the instrument cluster and the sensor.
4   If there is a problem with the ECT sensor, it is likely that the CHECK ENGINE light will come on and the sensor will have to be replaced or the circuit will have to be repaired (see Chapter 6).

Replacement

5   Refer to Chapter 6 for the engine coolant temperature sensor replacement procedure.

9.3 Disconnect the electrical connector and harness cable tie

9.4 Blower motor mounting fasteners (housing removed for clarity)

9   Blower motor - removal and installation

Refer to illustrations 9.2, 9.3 and 9.4

Warning: *These models have airbags. Always disable the airbag system before working in the vicinity of any airbag system component to avoid the possibility of accidental deployment of the airbag(s), which could cause personal injury (see Chapter 12).*

Note: *The blower control module is an integral part of the blower motor and can't be replaced separately.*

1   Remove the glove box (see Chapter 11).
2   Remove the kick panels (see Chapter 11, Section 27) and support brace fasteners **(see illustration)** to allow for movement.
3   Disconnect the electrical connector and loosen the cable ties for the wiring harness **(see illustration)**.
4   Remove the blower motor retaining screws and withdraw the blower motor **(see illustration)**.
5   Installation is the reverse of removal; tighten the support brace securely.

10   Heater and air conditioning control assembly - removal and installation

Refer to illustrations 10.2 and 10.3

Warning: *These models have airbags. Always disable the airbag system before working in the vicinity of any airbag system component to avoid the possibility of accidental deployment of the airbag(s), which could cause personal injury (see Chapter 12).*

1   Remove the radio (see Chapter 11).
2   Once the radio is removed, simply pull the control unit outward from the mounting clips **(see illustration)** several inches away from the dash.
3   Disconnect the electrical connectors from the rear of the control head **(see illustration)**.
4   The remainder of the installation is the reverse the removal.

11   Heater core - removal and installation

Refer to illustrations 11.4, 11.7 and 11.8

Warning: *Wait until the engine is completely cool before beginning this procedure.*

Warning: *These models have airbags. Always disable the airbag system before working in the vicinity of any airbag system component to avoid the possibility of accidental deployment of the airbag(s), which could cause personal injury (see Chapter 12).*

1   Remove the engine covers.
2   Disconnect and remove the battery (see Chapter 5).
3   Drain the cooling system (see Chapter 1).

10.2 Pull the control module forward releasing the retaining clips - two of four clips shown

10.3 Unplug all the electrical connectors from the control assembly

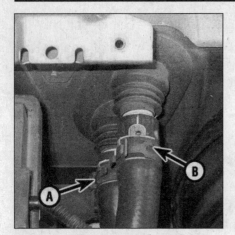

11.7 Remove the heater core cover fasteners

11.4 Heater core hose details

A   Supply side-from-cylinder head
B   Return side-to-water pump

Refer to the coolant **Warning** in Section 1.
4   Mark the heater hoses, then disconnect the hoses at the heater core inlet and outlet on the engine side of the firewall **(see illustration)**. **Note:** *If the hoses are stuck to the pipes, cut them off and replace them with new ones upon installation.*
5   Using a suction gun, remove as much of the coolant as possible from the heater core tubes and plug the open tubes.
6   Remove the knee bolster (see Chapter 11).
7   Remove the heater core cover fasteners and the cover **(see illustration)**. **Note:** *Cover the carpet with plastic sheeting to prevent coolant from getting on the carpet.*
8   Loosen the heater core tube clamp fasteners **(see illustration)**. Place a rag or a small drain pan under the tubes and carefully separate the tubes from the core. Once the remaining coolant has drained, pull the heater core from the housing.
9   Installation is the reverse of removal.

Note: *When reinstalling the heater core, make sure any original insulating/sealing materials are in place around the heater core pipes and around the core.*
10   Refill and bleed the cooling system (see Chapter 1).
11   Start the engine and check for proper operation.

---

12   Heater and air conditioning housing - removal and installation

---

Refer to illustrations 12.6, 12.9a, 12.9b, 12.9c, 12.10, 12.12a and 12.12b
Warning: *Wait until the engine is completely cool before beginning this procedure.*
Warning: *The air conditioning system is under high pressure. DO NOT loosen any fittings or remove any components until after the system has been discharged. Air conditioning refrigerant should be properly discharged into an EPA-approved container at a dealership service department or an automotive air conditioning repair facility. Always wear eye*

protection when disconnecting air conditioning system fittings.
Warning: *These models have airbags. Always disable the airbag system before working in the vicinity of any airbag system component to avoid the possibility of accidental deployment of the airbag(s), which could cause personal injury (see Chapter 12).*
1   Have the air conditioning system discharged (see **Warning** above).
2   Remove the engine covers. Disconnect and remove the battery (see Chapter 5).
3   Drain the cooling system (see Chapter 1) Refer to the coolant **Warning** in Section 1.
4   Mark, then disconnect the hoses at the heater core inlet and outlet on the engine side of the firewall **(see illustration 11.4)**. **Note:** *If the hoses are stuck to the pipes, cut them off and replace them with new ones upon installation.*
5   Disconnect the heater core tubes from the heater core (see Section 11).
6   Remove the air conditioning line fastener from the evaporator core fitting at the firewall **(see illustration)**.
7   Remove the instrument panel (see Chapter 11).

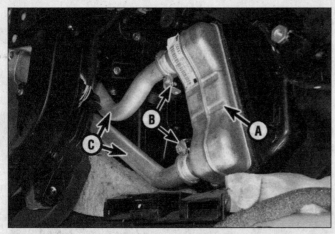

11.8 Heater core details

A   Heater core   C   Heater core tubes
B   Heater core fasteners

12.6 Remove the air conditioning evaporator line fastener and detach the line

12.9a Remove the center support brace fasteners and remove the brace

12.9b Use a screwdriver to unclip the upper dash vents . . .

8   Once the instrument panel is removed from the vehicle, remove the passenger side airbag (see Chapter 12).

9   Remove the center console support brace **(see illustration)**. Remove the upper and lower air ducts from the heating/air conditioning unit **(see illustrations)**.

10   From the engine compartment side, disconnect the electrical connection fasteners and heater A/C housing fastener **(see illustration)**.

11   Disconnect the electrical connectors at the right side of the instrument panel.

12   Remove the fasteners from the right side of the cross beam support **(see illustration)** and unclip the main harness from the back side of the cross beam support, then pull the beam forward **(see illustration)**.

13   Carefully remove the housing from the vehicle.

12.9c . . . and remove the push pin fasteners from the cross beam

12.10 Remove the exterior mounting fasteners for the harness connector and end of the housing

12.12a Remove the cross beam nut and lower support brace fasteners . . .

12.12b . . . separate the harness holder from the cross beam and pull the beam forward

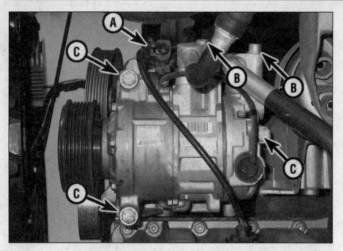

13.7 Air conditioning compressor details

A   Electrical connector
B   Refrigerant lines and fasteners
C   Compressor mounting fasteners

14.5 Air conditioning accumulator details

A   Refrigerant lines and fasteners
B   Bracket mounting fasteners
C   Accumulator mounting fastener

14   Installation is the reverse of removal.
15   Refill and bleed the cooling system (see Chapter 1).
16   Have the system evacuated, recharged and leak tested by the shop that discharged it.
17   Check for proper operation.

13   Air conditioning compressor - removal and installation

Refer to illustration 13.7

Warning: *The air conditioning system is under high pressure. DO NOT loosen any fittings or remove any components until after the system has been discharged. Air conditioning refrigerant should be properly discharged into an EPA-approved container at a dealership service department or an automotive air conditioning repair facility. Always wear eye protection when disconnecting air conditioning system fittings.*

Note: *Whenever the compressor is replaced because of internal damage, the orifice tube should also be replaced (see Section 14).*

Note: *The accumulator (see Section 14) should be replaced whenever the compressor is replaced.*

1   Have the air conditioning system discharged (see **Warning** above).
2   Raise the vehicle and support it securely on jackstands.
3   Remove the splash shield from below the engine (if equipped).
4   Remove the drivebelt (see Chapter 1).
5   Clean the compressor thoroughly around the refrigerant line fittings.
6   Disconnect the electrical connector from the air conditioning compressor.
7   Disconnect the suction and discharge lines from the compressor **(see illustration)**. Plug the open fittings to prevent the entry

of dirt and moisture, and discard the seals between the plates and compressor
8   Remove the compressor mounting bolts. Detach the compressor from the mounting bracket and remove the compressor from the engine compartment.
9   If a new compressor is being installed, pour the oil from the old compressor into a graduated container and add that exact amount of new refrigerant oil to the new compressor. Also follow any directions included with the new compressor. **Note:** *Some replacement compressors come with refrigerant oil in them. Follow the directions with the compressor regarding the draining of excess oil prior to installation.* **Caution:** *The oil used must be labeled as compatible with R-134a refrigerant systems.*
10   Installation is the reverse of removal. When installing the line fitting bolt to the compressor, use new seals lubricated with clean refrigerant oil, and tighten the bolt securely.
11   Have the system evacuated, recharged and leak tested by the shop that discharged it.

14   Air conditioning accumulator - removal and installation

Refer to illustration 14.5

Warning: *The air conditioning system is under high pressure. DO NOT loosen any fittings or remove any components until after the system has been discharged. Air conditioning refrigerant should be properly discharged into an EPA-approved container at a dealership service department or an automotive air conditioning repair facility. Always wear eye protection when disconnecting air conditioning system fittings.*

1   Have the air conditioning system discharged (see **Warning** above).

2   Raise the vehicle and support it securely on jackstands.
3   Place the radiator support panel in the service position (see Chapter 11).
4   If you're working on a 2.0L model, remove the right-side intercooler.
5   Disconnect the refrigerant lines from the accumulator **(see illustration)**. Cap or plug the open lines immediately to prevent the entry of dirt or moisture.
6   Remove the mounting bracket fasteners and lift the accumulator out with the mounting bracket.
7   Remove the accumulator fastener and separate the accumulator from the bracket.
8   If you are replacing the accumulator with a new one, add fresh refrigerant oil to the new unit following the directions included with the accumulator (the oil must be R-134a compatible).
9   Place the new accumulator into the bracket, install the bracket/accumulator and tighten the fasteners securely.
10   Connect the inlet and outlet lines, using clean refrigerant oil on the new O-rings. Tighten the refrigerant line fasteners securely.
11   Have the system evacuated, recharged and leak tested by the shop that discharged it.

15   Air conditioning expansion (orifice) tube - removal and installation

Refer to illustrations 15.2 and 15.3

Warning: *The air conditioning system is under high pressure. DO NOT loosen any fittings or remove any components until after the system has been discharged. Air conditioning refrigerant should be properly discharged into an EPA-approved container at a dealership service department or an automotive air*

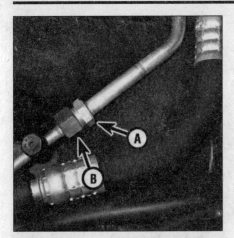

15.2 Hold the stationary fitting (A) with a wrench while loosening the tube nut (B) with another wrench, then pull the orifice tube out from the pipe

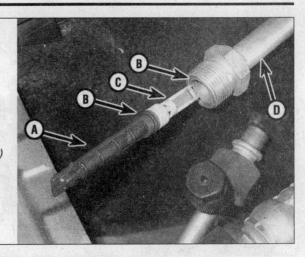

15.3 Orifice tube details

A   Long screen end (inlet)
B   O-ring
C   Short screen end (outlet)
D   Line to evaporator inlet

conditioning repair facility. Always wear eye protection when disconnecting air conditioning system fittings.

1   Have the air conditioning system discharged and the refrigerant recovered (see **Warning** above).

2   Working at the right rear corner of the engine compartment, disconnect the refrigerant line at the orifice tube and remove the orifice tube **(see illustration)**.

3   The expansion tube is a tube with a fixed-diameter orifice and a mesh filter at each end **(see illustration)**. When you separate the pipe at the fitting, you will see one end of the orifice tube inside the pipe leading to the evaporator. Use needle-nose pliers to remove the orifice tube.

4   The orifice tube acts to meter the refrigerant, changing it from high-pressure liquid to low-pressure liquid/vapor. It is possible to reuse the orifice tube if:

a)   *The screens aren't plugged with grit or foreign material*

b)   *Neither screen is torn*
c)   *The plastic housing over the screens is intact*
d)   *The brass orifice inside the plastic housing is unrestricted*

5   Installation is the reverse of removal. Be sure to insert the expansion tube with the shorter end in first, toward the evaporator. **Caution:** *Always use a new O-ring when installing the expansion (orifice) tube.* Retighten the fitting securely.

6   Have the system evacuated, recharged and leak tested by the shop that discharged it.

16   Air conditioning condenser - removal and installation

Refer to illustrations 16.7 and 16.8

Warning: *The air conditioning system is under high pressure. DO NOT loosen any fittings or remove any components until after the system has been discharged. Air conditioning refrigerant should be properly discharged into an EPA-approved container at a dealer-*

ship service department or an automotive air conditioning repair facility. Always wear eye protection when disconnecting air conditioning system fittings.

1   Have the air conditioning system discharged (see **Warning** above).

2   Raise the vehicle and support it securely on jackstands.

3   Remove the splash shield from below the engine (if equipped).

4   Remove the front bumper assembly (see Chapter 11).

5   Detach the power steering oil cooler line from the radiator support panel and set it aside **(see illustration 16.7)**.

6   Remove the cooling fan control module mounting fastener and module (if equipped).

7   Disconnect the air conditioning pressure switch and ambient temperature sensor from the driver's side of the radiator **(see illustration)**. Move the harness out of the way of the radiator.

8   Remove the condenser fasteners and separate the condenser from the radiator **(see illustration)**.

9   Installation is the reverse of removal. Always use new O-rings on air conditioning

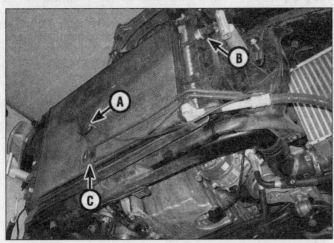

16.7 Remove the air conditioning pressure switch (B), ambient temperature sensor (A) and the power steering cooler line (C)

16.8 Condenser mounting details

A   Condenser lines
B   Condenser mounting fasteners

17.4a Remove the fasteners from the top of the housing . . .

17.4b . . . and the side of the housing

17.4c Separate the housing . . .

17.4d . . . and remove the evaporator core

system fittings. If you are replacing the condenser with a new one, add fresh refrigerant oil to the new unit following the directions included with the new condenser (the oil must be R-134a compatible).

10   Have the system evacuated, recharged and leak tested by the shop that discharged it.

17   Air conditioning evaporator core - removal and installation

Refer to illustrations 17.4a, 17.4b, 17.4c and 17.4d

Warning: *The air conditioning system is under high pressure. DO NOT loosen any fittings or*

remove any components until after the system has been discharged. Air conditioning refrigerant should be properly discharged into an EPA-approved container at a dealership service department or an automotive air conditioning repair facility. Always wear eye protection when disconnecting air conditioning system fittings.

1   Have the air conditioning system discharged by a dealership service department or an automotive air conditioning facility.

2   Remove the heater and air conditioner housing (see Section 12).

3   Set the housing on a clean working surface.

4   Remove the evaporator core fasteners, separate the housing and carefully remove

the evaporator core from the heating A/C housing **(see illustrations)**.

5   Installation is the reverse of removal. **Note:** *When reinstalling the evaporator core, make sure any original insulating/sealing materials are in place around the evaporator core pipes and around the core.*

6   Installation is the reverse of removal. Always use new O-rings on air conditioning system fittings. If you are replacing the evaporator core with a new one, add fresh refrigerant oil to the new unit following the directions included with the new evaporator (the oil must be R-134a compatible).

7   Have the system evacuated, recharged and leak tested by the shop that discharged it.

Chapter 4
Fuel and exhaust systems

Contents

	Section			Section
Air filter housing - removal and installation	8		Fuel rail and injectors - removal and installation	12
Exhaust system servicing - general information	6		General information	1
Fuel lines and fittings - general information	5		High-pressure fuel pump - removal and installation	11
Fuel pump/fuel level sensor module - removal and installation	7		Throttle body - removal and installation	9
Fuel pressure - check	4		Troubleshooting	2
Fuel pressure regulator - replacement	10		Turbocharger and intercooler(s) - check and replacement	13
Fuel pressure relief procedure	3			

Specifications

Fuel system pressure
Four-cylinder models
    1.8L
        At idle .... 58 psi (4.0 bar)
        Holding pressure, after 10 minutes .... 36 psi (2.5 bar) minimum
    2.0L (before high-pressure pump only) .... 87 psi (6.0 bar)
V6 models
    3.0L
        At idle
            Vacuum hose connected .... 46.4 to 55.1 psi (3.2 to 3.8 bar)
            Vacuum hose disconnected .... 55.1 to 60.9 psi (3.8 to 4.2 bar)
        Holding pressure, after 10 minutes
            Cold engine .... Approximately 31.9 psi (2.2 bar)
            Warm engine .... Approximately 43.5 psi (3.0 bar)
    3.2L (before high-pressure pump only) .... 87 psi (6.0 bar)

Torque specifications

Note: *One foot-pound (ft-lb) of torque is equivalent to 12 inch-pounds (in-lbs) of torque. Torque values below approximately 15 foot-pounds are expressed in inch-pounds, because most foot-pound torque wrenches are not accurate at these smaller values.*

	Ft-lbs (unless otherwise indicated)	Nm
High-pressure fuel pump mounting fasteners	88 in-lbs	10
Intake manifold fasteners		
2.0L four-cylinder models	80 in-lbs	9
Lower intake manifold fasteners (3.2L V6 models)	Tighten securely	

Note: *See Chapter 2A or 2B for intake manifold fastener torque on other engines.*

	Ft-lbs (unless otherwise indicated)	Nm
Exhaust manifold/turbocharger assembly (1.8L four-cylinder models)		
Exhaust manifold-to-turbocharger bolts	26	35
Turbocharger-to-catalytic converter fasteners	22	30
Oil supply line fittings		
Banjo bolt (at engine)	22	30
Threaded fitting at turbocharger	17	23
Oil return line flange bolts (both ends)	88 in-lbs	10
Coolant supply line banjo bolts (both ends)	26	35
Exhaust manifold/turbocharger assembly (2.0L four-cylinder models)		
Exhaust manifold-to-cylinder head nuts	15	20
Turbocharger-to-catalytic converter fasteners/nuts	18	24
Oil supply line banjo fasteners (both ends)	22	30
Oil return line flange fasteners (both ends)	80 in-lbs	9
Coolant supply and return line banjo fasteners (both ends)	26	35

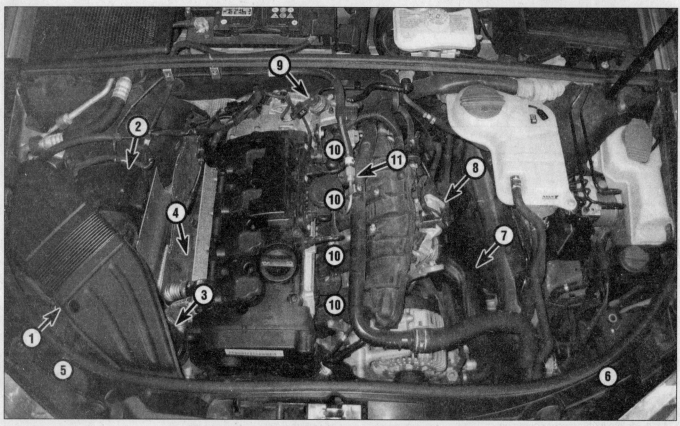

Typical fuel system details (2.0L four-cylinder model shown):

1   Fresh air inlet duct
2   Air filter housing
3   Air intake duct (to inlet side of turbocharger)
4   Turbocharger (lower part of exhaust manifold)
5   Right intercooler (below right headlight housing), connected to left intercooler via intake duct below radiator
6   Left intercooler (below left headlight housing), connected to right intercooler via intake duct below radiator

7   Air intake hose (connects left intercooler to throttle body)
8   Throttle body
9   High-pressure mechanical fuel pump
10 Fuel rail and injectors (located underneath intake manifold)
11 Fuel supply line fitting location (to tee into fuel system to measure fuel pressure)

1   General information

Fuel system warnings

Gasoline is extremely flammable and repairing fuel system components can be dangerous. Consider your automotive repair knowledge and experience before attempting repairs which may be better suited for a professional mechanic.

- Don't smoke or allow open flames or bare light bulbs near the work area
- Don't work in a garage with a gas-type appliance (water heater, clothes dryer)
- Use fuel-resistant gloves. If any fuel spills on your skin, wash it off immediately with soap and water

- Clean up spills immediately
- Do not store fuel-soaked rags where they could ignite
- Prior to disconnecting any fuel line, you must relieve the fuel pressure (see Section 3)
- Wear safety glasses
- Have a proper fire extinguisher on hand

Fuel system

The fuel system consists of the fuel tank, electric fuel pump/fuel level sending unit (located in the fuel tank), fuel rail and fuel injectors. The fuel injection system is a multi-port system; multi-port fuel injection uses timed impulses to inject the fuel directly into the intake port of each cylinder. The Pow-

ertrain Control Module (PCM) controls the injectors. The PCM monitors various engine parameters and delivers the exact amount of fuel required into the intake ports.

Fuel is circulated from the fuel pump to the fuel rail through fuel lines running along the underside of the vehicle. Various sections of the fuel line are either rigid metal or nylon, or flexible fuel hose. The various sections of the fuel hose are connected either by quick-connect fittings or threaded metal fittings.

Exhaust system

The exhaust system consists of the exhaust manifold(s), catalytic converter(s), muffler(s), tailpipe(s) and all connecting pipes, flanges and clamps. A catalytic converter is an emission control device added to the exhaust system to reduce pollutants.

2.2a The fuel pump fuse is located in the fuse box at the left end of the instrument panel (be sure to check the guide on the end panel to locate the fuse for your particular model)

2.2b On 2002 through 2005 models, the fuel pump relay is located at the far left end of the relay panel, which is located inside the left end of the instrument panel, to the left of the steering column (2006 model, which doesn't use a fuel pump relay, shown; but arrow indicates correct location on relay-equipped earlier models)

2   Troubleshooting

Fuel pump

Refer to illustrations 2.2a and 2.2b

1   The fuel pump is located inside the fuel tank. Sit inside the vehicle with the windows closed, turn the ignition key to ON (not START) and listen for the sound of the fuel pump as it's briefly activated. You will only hear the sound for a second or two, but that sound tells you that the pump is working. Alternatively, have an assistant listen at the fuel filler cap.

2   If the pump does not come on, check the fuel pump fuse **(see illustration)** and, on 2002 through 2005 models, the fuel pump relay **(see illustration)**. All models are equipped with a fuel pump fuse, but there is no fuel pump relay on 2006 and later models; the fuel pump circuit on these models is controlled by

2.9 With the engine running, place an automotive stethoscope against each injector, one at a time, and listen for a clicking sound that indicates operation

the Fuel Pump Control Module (FPCM), which cannot be diagnosed at home.

Fuel injection system

Refer to illustration 2.9

Note: *The following procedure is based on the assumption that the fuel pump is working and the fuel pressure is adequate (see Section 4).*

3   Check all electrical connectors that are related to the system. Check the ground wire connections for tightness.

4   Verify that the battery is fully charged (see Chapter 5).

5   Inspect the air filter element (see Chapter 1).

6   Check all fuses related to the fuel system (see Chapter 12).

7   Check the air induction system between the throttle body and the intake manifold for air leaks. Also inspect the condition of all vacuum hoses connected to the intake manifold and to the throttle body.

8   Remove the air intake duct from the throttle body and look for dirt, carbon, varnish, or other residue in the throttle body, particularly around the throttle plate. If it's dirty, clean it with carb cleaner, a toothbrush and a clean shop towel.

9   With the engine running, place an automotive stethoscope against each injector, one at a time, and listen for a clicking sound that indicates operation **(see illustration)**. **Warning:** *Stay clear of the drivebelt and any rotating or hot components.*

10   If you can hear the injectors operating, but the engine is misfiring, the electrical circuits are functioning correctly, but the injectors might be dirty or clogged. Try a commercial injector cleaning product (available at auto parts stores). If cleaning the injectors doesn't help, replace the injectors.

11   If an injector is not operating (it makes no sound), disconnect the injector electri-

cal connector and measure the resistance across the injector terminals with an ohmmeter. Compare this measurement to the other injectors. If the resistance of the non-operational injector is quite different from the other injectors, replace it.

12   If the injector is not operating, but the resistance reading is within the range of resistance of the other injectors, the PCM or the circuit between the PCM and the injector might be faulty.

3   Fuel pressure relief procedure

Warning: *Gasoline is extremely flammable. See **Fuel system warnings** in Section 1.*

1.8L four-cylinder and 3.0L V6 models

1   Remove the fuel filler cap to relieve any pressure built-up in the fuel tank.

2   Disconnect the cable from the negative terminal of the battery (see Chapter 5).

3   Surround the fitting to be disconnected with rags, then slowly loosen the connection and allow the residual fuel pressure to bleed off.

4   The fuel system is now depressurized. Properly dispose of the rags.

2.0L four-cylinder and 3.2L V6 models

Refer to illustration 3.7

5   The fuel delivery systems on 2.0L four-cylinder and 3.2L V6 models are equipped with both a low-pressure system and a second, high-pressure system that operates at extremely high pressure. At idle, the fuel pressure in the fuel rail is about 725 psi; under certain operating conditions such as hard acceleration, the system pressure can reach almost

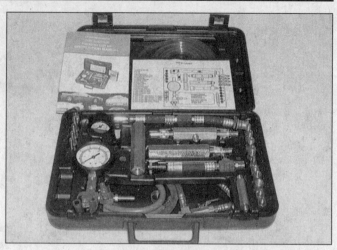

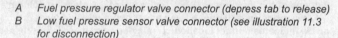

3.7 Electrical connectors on the mechanical high-pressure pump (2.0L model shown):

A   *Fuel pressure regulator valve connector (depress tab to release)*
B   *Low fuel pressure sensor valve connector (see illustration 11.3 for disconnection)*

4.1a This fuel pressure testing kit contains all the necessary fittings and adapters, along with the fuel pressure gauge, to test most automotive fuel systems

1600 psi. So before you remove or replace any component (mechanical high-pressure pump, high-pressure fuel lines, fuel rail and/or fuel injectors) in the high-pressure part of the fuel injection system, be sure to use the following procedure to relieve fuel pressure.

6   Remove the fuel pump fuse **(see illustration 2.2a)**. This opens the circuit to the Fuel Pump Control Module (FPCM) so that the fuel pump inside the fuel tank will not operate.

7   Disconnect the electrical connector from the fuel pressure regulator valve on the mechanical high-pressure pump **(see illustration)**.

8   Start the engine and allow it to idle until it stalls, then turn the ignition key to the Off position and disconnect the cable from the negative terminal of the battery (see Chapter 5). Even though the low-pressure pump inside the fuel tank is already disabled, the engine might run briefly on the residual pressure inside the high-pressure part of the system.

9   At this point, the residual fuel pressure in

the high side of the system might still be about 116 psi (8 bar). So when you crack open the first fitting, make sure that you are wearing safety goggles and that you completely surround the fitting with plenty of shop rags to catch any fuel that might spill out.

---

4   Fuel pressure - check

Refer to illustrations 4.1a, 4.1b, 4.1c and 4.1d

Warning: *Gasoline is extremely flammable. See **Fuel system warnings** in Section 1.*

Warning: *Before performing this check, review the fuel pressure values in this Chapter's Specifications and make sure your gauge is capable of reading the pressures that the system on your vehicle can produce.*

Warning: *This fuel pressure check procedure does not include the high-pressure side of 2.0L four-cylinder and 3.2L V6 models. The*

fuel pressure between the mechanical high-pressure pump and the fuel rail on those models is between 725 psi (idle) to almost 1600 psi. Do not attempt to measure it.

Note: *The following procedure assumes that the fuel pump is receiving voltage and runs.*

1   Relieve the fuel system pressure (see Section 3), then, using the proper adapters, tee into the system at the fuel supply line fitting **(see illustrations)**.

All except 3.0L V6 models manufactured before June of 2003

2   Start the engine and allow it to idle. Note the gauge reading as soon as the pressure stabilizes, and compare it with the pressure listed in this Chapter's Specifications.

3   If the fuel pressure is not within specifications, check the following:

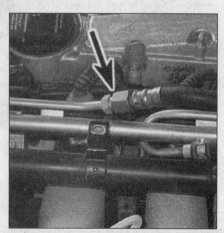

4.1b To measure fuel pressure on 1.8L four-cylinder models, tee into the system at this point

4.1c To measure fuel pressure on 3.0L V6 models, tee into the fuel system at this point

4.1d To measure fuel pressure on 2.0L four-cylinder (shown) and 3.2L V6 models, tee into the fuel system at this point

Disconnecting Fuel Line Fittings

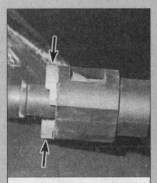

Two-tab type fitting; depress both tabs with your fingers, then pull the fuel line and the fitting apart

On this type of fitting, depress the two buttons on opposite sides of the fitting, then pull it off the fuel line

Threaded fuel line fitting; hold the stationary portion of the line or component (A) while loosening the tube nut (B) with a flare-nut wrench

Plastic collar-type fitting; rotate the outer part of the fitting

Metal collar quick-connect fitting; pull the end of the retainer off the fuel line, and disengage the other end from the female side of the fitting . . .

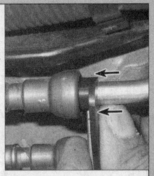

. . . insert a fuel line separator tool into the female side of the fitting, push it into the fitting until it releases the locking tabs inside the fitting, and pull the two halves of the fitting apart

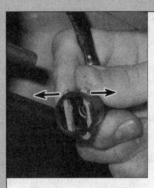

Hairpin-type clip; spread the two legs of the clip apart . . .

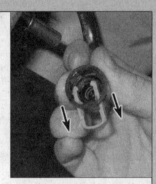

. . . pull the clip out and detach the coupling from the component (fitting detached for clarity)

Spring-lock coupling; remove the safety cover . . .

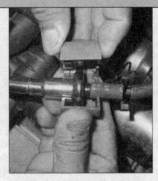

. . . install a coupling release tool and close the clamshell halves of the tool around the coupling . . .

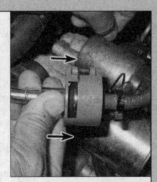

. . . push the tool into the fitting, then pull the two lines apart

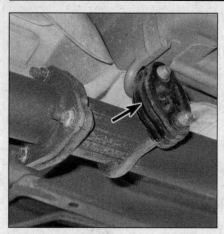

6.1 A typical exhaust system hanger. Inspect regularly and replace at the first sign of damage or deterioration

a) *If the pressure is lower than specified, inspect the fuel lines for any obvious problems, such as a kink or dent). If no problems are found, replace the fuel filter (see Chapter 1) (it might be clogged, or the fuel pressure regulator, which is an integral part of the filter, might be defective). If that doesn't cure the problem, remove the fuel pump module (see Section 7) and check to see if the inlet strainer is clogged. If the strainer isn't clogged, replace the fuel pump module.*

b) *If the fuel pressure is higher than specified, replace the fuel filter (see Chapter 1) (the fuel pressure regulator, which is an integral part of the filter, might be defective).*

4   Turn off the engine. Fuel pressure should not fall below the minimum hold pressure listed in this Chapter's Specifications. If it does, the problem could be a leaky fuel injector, a fuel line leak, a defective fuel pressure regulator (which is an integral part of the fuel filter), or a faulty check valve in the fuel pump.

5   Relieve the fuel system pressure (see Section 3), then disconnect the fuel pressure gauge. Wipe up any spilled gasoline. Turn the ignition key to the On position and check for leaks.

3.0L V6 models manufactured before June of 2003

6   Reconnect the cable to the negative battery terminal, then turn the ignition key to ON (don't start the engine yet). The fuel pump should run for about two seconds and the gauge should indicate pressure and hold steady.

7   Turn on the engine, allow it to warm up to its normal operating temperature, then measure the fuel pressure and compare your readings to the system pressure listed in this Chapter's Specifications.

a) *If the pressure is high, disconnect the vacuum hose from the fuel pressure*

regulator and connect a vacuum gauge to it. Make sure there is 12 in-Hg or more vacuum present at the hose. If there isn't, check the hose for a restriction or leak.

b) *If there is adequate vacuum to the regulator but the pressure is high, check for a restricted fuel return hose or line. If the return hose and line are clear, replace the pressure regulator (see Section 10).*

c) *If the pressure is low, pinch the fuel return hose. If the pressure goes up, replace the fuel pressure regulator (see Section 10). If the pressure does not increase, replace the fuel filter (see Chapter 1) and recheck the pressure. If it's still low, check the fuel supply hose and line for a restriction. If there is no restriction, replace the fuel pump module (see Section 7).* **Note:** *As the fuel pump is removed, check the inlet strainer on the bottom of the pump for clogging.*

8   To check the operation of the fuel pressure regulator, disconnect the vacuum hose from the regulator with the engine idling and watch the fuel pressure gauge - the fuel pressure should increase 3 to 10 psi as soon as the hose is disconnected. If it doesn't, check for vacuum at the hose. If vacuum is present, replace the fuel pressure regulator.

9   Relieve the system fuel pressure (see Section 3), then disconnect the cable from the negative battery terminal. Remove the fuel pressure gauge, then reconnect the fuel supply hose. Reconnect the cable to the negative battery terminal, then turn the ignition key to the On position and check for leaks.

5   Fuel lines and fittings - general information

Warning: *Gasoline is extremely flammable. See* **Fuel system warnings** *in Section 1.*

1   Relieve the fuel pressure before servicing fuel lines or fittings (see Section 3), then disconnect the cable from the negative battery terminal (see Chapter 5) before proceeding.

2   The fuel supply line connects the fuel pump in the fuel tank to the fuel rail on the engine. The Evaporative Emission (EVAP) system lines connect the fuel tank to the EVAP canister and connect the canister to the intake manifold.

3   Whenever you're working under the vehicle, be sure to inspect all fuel and evaporative emission lines for leaks, kinks, dents and other damage. Always replace a damaged fuel or EVAP line immediately.

4   If you find signs of dirt in the lines during disassembly, disconnect all lines and blow them out with compressed air. Inspect the fuel strainer on the fuel pump pick-up unit for damage and deterioration.

Steel tubing

5   It is critical that the fuel lines be replaced with lines of equivalent type and specification.

6   Some steel fuel lines have threaded fit-

tings. When loosening these fittings, hold the stationary fitting with a wrench while turning the tube nut.

Plastic tubing

7   When replacing fuel system plastic tubing, use only original equipment replacement plastic tubing. **Caution:** *When removing or installing plastic fuel line tubing, be careful not to bend or twist it too much, which can damage it. Also, plastic fuel tubing is NOT heat resistant, so keep it away from excessive heat.*

Flexible hoses

8   When replacing fuel system flexible hoses, use only original equipment replacements.

9   Don't route fuel hoses (or metal lines) within four inches of the exhaust system or within ten inches of the catalytic converter. Make sure that no rubber hoses are installed directly against the vehicle, particularly in places where there is any vibration. If allowed to touch some vibrating part of the vehicle, a hose can easily become chafed and it might start leaking. A good rule of thumb is to maintain a minimum of 1/4-inch clearance around a hose (or metal line) to prevent contact with the vehicle underbody.

6   Exhaust system servicing - general information

Refer to illustration 6.1

Warning: *Allow exhaust system components to cool before inspection or repair. Also, when working under the vehicle, make sure it is securely supported on jackstands.*

1   The exhaust system consists of the exhaust manifolds, catalytic converter, muffler, tailpipe and all connecting pipes, flanges and clamps. The exhaust system is isolated from the vehicle body and from chassis components by a series of rubber hangers **(see illustration)**. Periodically inspect these hangers for cracks or other signs of deterioration, replacing them as necessary.

2   Conduct regular inspections of the exhaust system to keep it safe and quiet. Look for any damaged or bent parts, open seams, holes, loose connections, excessive corrosion or other defects which could allow exhaust fumes to enter the vehicle. Do not repair deteriorated exhaust system components; replace them with new parts.

3   If the exhaust system components are extremely corroded, or rusted together, a cutting torch is the most convenient tool for removal. Consult a properly-equipped repair shop. If a cutting torch is not available, you can use a hacksaw, or if you have compressed air, there are special pneumatic cutting chisels that can also be used. Wear safety goggles to protect your eyes from metal chips and wear work gloves to protect your hands.

7.4a Fuel pump/fuel level sensor cover screws

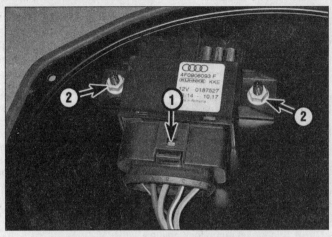

7.4b Fuel Pump Control Module (FPCM) details
(2006 and later models):

1   *Electrical connector*   2   *Mounting nuts*

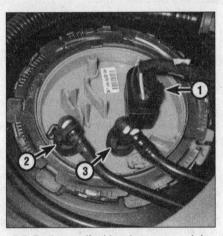

7.5 Fuel pump/fuel level sensor module
electrical, fuel and vent line connections:

1   *Fuel pump/fuel level sensor*
     electrical connector
2   *Fuel pump supply line*
3   *Fuel return line (from filter/pressure*
     regulator)

7.6a On models with a plastic fuel pump
module lock ring, a large pair of pliers can
usually be used to unscrew the lock ring

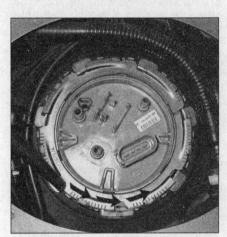

7.6b On models with a metal fuel pump
module lock ring, use a hammer and
brass punch to loosen the lock ring

4   Here are some simple guidelines to follow when repairing the exhaust system:

a) *Work from the back to the front when*
    removing exhaust system components.
b) *Apply penetrating oil to the exhaust sys-*
    tem component fasteners to make them
    easier to remove.
c) *Use new gaskets, hangers and clamps.*
d) *Apply anti-seize compound to the*
    threads of all exhaust system fasteners
    during reassembly.
e) *Be sure to allow sufficient clearance*
    between newly installed parts and all
    points on the underbody to avoid over-
    heating the floor pan and possibly dam-
    aging the interior carpet and insulation.
    Pay particularly close attention to the
    catalytic converter and heat shield.

7   Fuel pump/fuel level sensor module - removal and installation

FWD vehicles

*Refer to illustrations 7.4a, 7.4b, 7.5, 7.6a,
7.6b, 7.8 and 7.10*

Warning: *Gasoline is extremely flammable,
so take extra precautions when you work on
any part of the fuel system. See the* **Fuel system warnings** *in Section 1.*

1   Disconnect the cable from the negative
battery terminal (see Chapter 5).
2   Relieve the fuel system pressure (see
Section 3).
3   To access the fuel pump module inspection hole cover, remove the following components, depending on the model: On Sedan
and Cabriolet models, remove the carpet in
the luggage compartment (see Chapter 11);
fold forward the right backrest of the rear seat
if necessary. On Avant models, remove the

left seat back, the left side luggage compartment trim panel and the floor covering (see
Chapter 11).
4   Remove the fuel pump module access
cover retaining screws **(see illustration)** and
remove the cover. On 2006 and later models,
the Fuel Pump Control Module (FPCM) **(see
illustration)** is attached to the underside of
the cover, so handle the cover carefully. It's
not necessary to disconnect the electrical connector from the FPCM or remove the mounting
fasteners unless you're replacing the FPCM.
5   Disconnect the fuel pump module electrical connector and lines **(see illustration)**.
Mark the lines to prevent mix-ups when reconnecting them.
6   Remove the fuel pump module lock ring.
On models with a plastic lock ring, a special tool
(available at most auto parts stores) is available to unscrew the lock ring, but a large pair
of pliers will work **(see illustration)**. On models with a metal lock ring, use a brass punch to
loosen the lock ring **(see illustration)**.

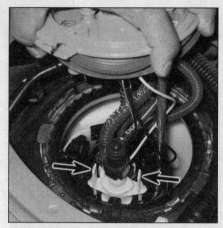

7.8 Suction jet pump locking lugs

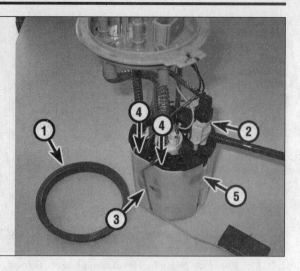

7.10 Typical fuel pump/fuel level sensor module details:

1 Flange seal
2 Suction jet pump
3 Fuel level sensor location (inside fuel module)
4 Fuel level sensor release tabs (depress and pull sensor straight up)
5 Fuel pump module assembly (no further disassembly possible)

7 Unscrew the lock ring and pull the fuel pump module up.

8 If you're just replacing the suction jet pump, the jet pump is secured to the fuel pump module by a pair of locking lugs. Lift up the fuel pump module slightly **(see illustration)**, reach through the fuel pump module access hole, disconnect the suction jet hose from the jet pump, then push the upper ends of the lugs toward each other and disconnect the suction jet pump from the pump module. Installation of the suction jet pump is the reverse of removal. Make sure that the pump locking lugs and the suction jet hose snap into place when installed.

9 If you're replacing the fuel pump module or the fuel level sensor, pull the fuel pump/fuel level sensor module out of the tank as a single assembly. Angle the module as necessary to protect the fuel level sensor float arm.

10 Inspect the flange seal **(see illustration)**. If the seal is damaged, replace it.

11 To remove the fuel level sensor, disconnect the sensor electrical connector, then use a small screwdriver to disengage the two sensor lock tabs that secure the sensor to the fuel pump module. Pull the sensor straight up out of the pump module.

12 When installing the fuel level sensor module on the fuel pump module, make sure that the locking tabs snap into place.

13 No further disassembly of the fuel pump/fuel level sensor module is possible.

14 Installation is the reverse of removal. Be sure to use a seal for the locking ring if the old seal is damaged.

AWD vehicles

Fuel pump module

15 Disconnect the cable from the negative battery terminal (see Chapter 5).

16 Relieve the fuel system pressure (see Section 3).

17 Remove the rear seat bench (see Chapter 11).

18 Remove the right fuel pump module access cover retaining screws **(see illustration 7.4a)** and remove the cover.

19 Disconnect the electrical connectors from the fuel pump module mounting flange.

20 Disconnect the fuel supply line and, on turbocharged models, the vent line.

21 Loosen and unscrew the fuel pump module lock ring **(see illustrations 7.6a and 7.6b)**.

22 Lift up the flange and disconnect the electrical connectors from the underside of the flange.

23 The fuel pump module is secured to the baffle housing by a bayonet-type mounting system. Using a screwdriver, carefully rotate the fuel pump module about 15 degrees in a counterclockwise direction until the V-shaped notch in the upper edge of the pump module is aligned with the mark on the baffle housing, then lift the pump module out of the baffle housing and out of the fuel tank.

24 Installation is the reverse of removal.

Fuel level sensors and suction jet pump

Note: On AWD models, the fuel tank is divided into two compartments to provide clearance in the center for the driveshaft and exhaust system. There are two fuel level sensors - one for each fuel tank compartment. Fuel level sensor 1, the fuel level sensor for the right fuel tank compartment, is located on the baffle for the fuel pump assembly. Fuel level sensor 2 and the suction jet pump are located in the left fuel tank compartment.

Fuel level sensor 1 (right fuel level sensor)

25 Unlock the fuel pump module locking flange and lift it up (see Steps 15 through 23).

26 Disconnect the fuel level sensor from the underside of the fuel pump module locking flange.

27 To release the fuel level sensor from the baffle housing, depress the retaining tab on the sensor.

28 Pull the fuel level sensor out of the fuel tank. Be careful not to damage the float arm. Alter the angle of the sensor as necessary to protect the float arm.

29 Installation is the reverse of removal.

Fuel level sensor 2 (left fuel level sensor)

30 Disconnect the cable from the negative battery terminal (see Chapter 5).

31 Relieve the fuel system pressure (see Section 3).

32 Remove the rear seat bench (see Chapter 11).

33 Remove the left fuel pump module access cover retaining screws and remove the cover.

34 Disconnect the electrical connector from the fuel level sensor locking flange.

35 Disconnect the fuel line from the left locking flange.

36 Loosen and unscrew the left locking ring with a hammer and brass punch.

37 Carefully lift up the locking flange and pull the fuel level sensor out of the fuel tank. Be careful not to damage the float arm. Alter the angle of the sensor as necessary to protect the float arm. Once you have pulled the fuel level sensor out of the fuel tank, unclip the suction jet pump from the lower end of the sensor.

38 The lower end of the fuel line extending down into the tank from the underside of the locking flange is connected to a Y-fitting. Squeeze the two locking lugs on the Y-fitting and disconnect the Y-fitting from the fuel line.

39 Carefully remove the locking flange and fuel level sensor 2 from the fuel tank. Alter the angle of the sensor as necessary to protect the float arm.

40 To release the fuel level sensor from its mounting bracket, depress the retaining tabs on the sensor.

41 Installation is the reverse of removal.

Suction jet pump

42 Unlock the fuel pump module locking flange and lift it up (see Steps 15 through 23).

43 Disconnect the two suction jet pipe lines from the distribution piece mounted on the side of the baffle housing

44 Remove fuel level sensor 2 (see Steps 30 through 40).

45 Reach into the left fuel tank access hole and pull the suction jet pump and lines to the left side of the tank and out through the left access hole.

46 Installation is the reverse of removal.

8.2a To remove the rear part of the fresh air intake duct, disconnect it from the air filter housing, then separate it from the front part

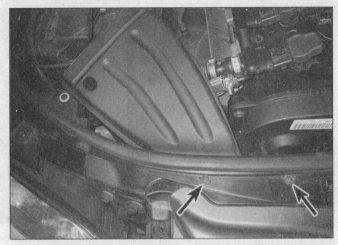

8.2b To remove the front part of the fresh air intake duct, remove these two screws and pull it out (2.0L model shown, others similar)

8 Air filter housing - removal and installation

Refer to illustrations 8.2a, 8.2b, 8.4a, 8.4b, 8.4c and 8.5

1   Remove the air filter housing cover, if equipped.
2   Detach the fresh air intake duct from the air filter housing (**see illustrations**).
3   Disconnect the electrical connector from the Mass Air Flow/Intake Air Temperature (MAF/IAT) sensor (see Chapter 6).
4   Loosen the clamps (**see illustrations**) that secure the air intake duct to the air filter housing, then detach the intake duct.
5   Remove the mounting fastener that secures the air filter housing to the right inner fender (**see illustration**).
6   On some models, you can now remove the air filter housing.

8.4a Loosen the clamp and detach the duct from the air filter housing (1.8L four-cylinder models)

8.4b Air intake duct hose clamps (2.0L four-cylinder models)

8.4c Typical air intake duct on V6 models (3.0L model shown, 3.2L models similar)

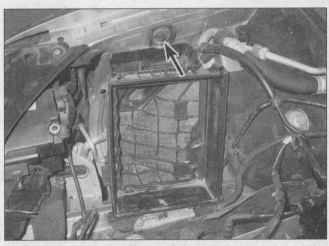

8.5 Typical air filter housing mounting fastener (2.0L four-cylinder model shown, other models similar)

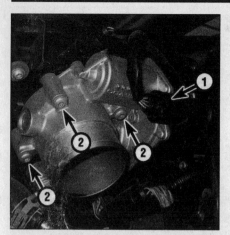

9.4 Throttle body details (2.0L four-cylinder model shown, other models similar):

1   *Electrical connector*
2   *Throttle body mounting fasteners (fourth fastener not visible)*

10.4 Remove the retaining clip and pull the fuel pressure regulator out of the fuel rail

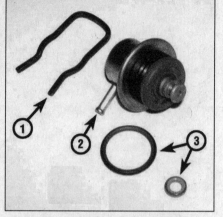

10.5 Fuel pressure regulator details (June 2003 and earlier 3.0L V6 engines)

1   *Retaining clip*
2   *Fuel pressure regulator*
3   *O-rings*

7   On other models, the filter housing is also secured to the right inner fender by additional fasteners inside the lower part of the filter housing. If the filter housing still feels like it's secured to the fender, remove the filter housing cover and the filter element (see Chapter 1), then remove the fasteners from the floor of the lower part of the filter housing and remove the housing.

8   While the air filter housing is out, inspect the condition of the rubber grommet for the filter housing locator pin.

9   Before reassembling and installing the air filter housing, thoroughly blow out all parts of the housing with compressed air.

10   Installation is the reverse of removal.

9   Throttle body - removal and installation

Refer to illustration 9.4

1   Disconnect the cable from the negative battery terminal (see Chapter 5).

2   Remove the engine cover.

3   Loosen the clamp and detach the air intake duct from the throttle body.

4   Disconnect the electrical connector from the throttle body **(see illustration).**

5   Remove the throttle body mounting fasteners and carefully remove the throttle body from the intake manifold.

6   Remove and inspect the throttle body gasket. If it's flattened, hardened or cracked, replace it. If it's in good condition, it can be re-used.

7   Cover the intake manifold opening with a clean shop towel to prevent anything from entering.

8   Installation is the reverse of removal. Tighten the throttle body fasteners to the torque listed in this Chapter's Specifications.

10   Fuel pressure regulator - replacement

Refer to illustrations 10.4 and 10.5

Warning: *Gasoline is extremely flammable, so take extra precautions when you work on any part of the fuel system. See the* **Fuel system warnings** *in Section 1.*

Note: *This Section applies only to June 2003 and earlier 3.0L V6 models. The pressure regulator used on all other models is an integral component of the fuel filter and cannot be replaced separately (see Chapter 1).*

1   Remove the engine cover (see Chapter 2).

2   Relieve the system fuel pressure (see Section 3).

3   Disconnect the vacuum hose from the fuel pressure regulator.

4   Remove the fuel pressure regulator retaining clip and remove the pressure regulator from the fuel rail **(see illustration).**

5   Be sure to replace the pressure regulator O-ring seals **(see illustration). Note:** *If you don't see the small O-ring seal on the pressure regulator, it might still be inside the fuel rail. Be sure to dig it out and discard it.*

6   Lubricate the new O-rings with a thin film of engine oil and install them on the regulator.

7   Insert the regulator into the fuel rail. Make sure that it's fully seated, then install the retaining clip.

8   Connect the vacuum hose to the regulator.

9   Start the engine and check for leaks.

10   Install the engine cover.

11   High-pressure fuel pump - removal and installation

Warning: *Wait until the engine is completely cool before performing this procedure.*

2.0L four-cylinder models

Refer to illustrations 11.3, 11.4 and 11.5

Warning: *Gasoline is extremely flammable,*

so take extra precautions when you work on any part of the fuel system. See the **Fuel system warnings** *in Section 1.*

1   Relieve the fuel system pressure (see Section 3).

2   Disconnect the cable from the negative battery terminal (see Chapter 5).

3   Disconnect the electrical connectors from the low fuel pressure sensor and fuel pressure regulator valve **(see illustration 3.7 and accompanying illustration).**

4   Disconnect both fuel lines from the high-pressure pump **(see illustration). Warning:** *Surround the fitting and wrenches with a rag before loosening the high-pressure fuel line fitting.*

5   Remove the three high-pressure pump mounting fasteners **(see illustration)** and remove the pump. **Note:** *The sleeve might remain in the cylinder head.*

6   Remove and discard the old pump

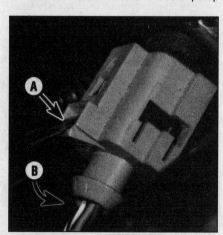

11.3 To disconnect the electrical connector from the low fuel pressure sensor, insert a small screwdriver (A) into the slot and pry in the direction of (B) to release the retainer.

O-ring. Always use a new O-ring when installing the pump.

7   Before installing the pump, insert the sleeve in the cylinder head, then rotate the crankshaft with a socket and breaker bar on the center bolt of the crankshaft pulley until the sleeve reaches its lowest point. **Note:** *Apply pressure with your fingertip to hold the sleeve down in its bore as you rotate the engine.*

8   Once the sleeve is at its lowest point, install the pump with a new O-ring. Install the pump mounting fasteners and tighten them, in a diagonal sequence, to the torque listed in this Chapter's Specifications. Reinstall the Schrader valve, if equipped, tightening it securely.

9   Reconnect the fuel lines and tighten them securely.

10   Connect the electrical connectors to the low fuel pressure sensor and the fuel pressure regulator valve.

3.2L V6 models

11   Drain the engine coolant (see Chapter 1).

12   Remove the front coolant pipe (see Chapter 3) and the upper intake manifold (see Chapter 2B).

13   Loosen the high-pressure fuel line fittings, remove the fuel line bracket fasteners and unscrew the fuel line fittings.

14   Remove the large lifting eye, if equipped.

15   Disconnect the electrical connector from the high-pressure pump.

16   Remove the high-pressure pump mounting fasteners, carefully lift the fuel lines and remove the pump and actuator. **Caution:** *Be extremely careful not to bend or kink the fuel lines.*

17   Remove and discard the old pump O-ring. Always use a new O-ring when installing the pump.

18   Carefully lift the fuel lines and install the high-pressure pump, with a new O-ring. **Caution:** *Be extremely careful not to bend or kink the fuel lines.*

19   Install the pump mounting fasteners and tighten them to the torque listed in this Chapter's Specifications.

11.4 High-pressure fuel line tube nut (1) and feed line fitting (2, disconnect whichever end is easier). Hold fitting (3) with a wrench while loosing fitting (1) to prevent it from turning (2.0L four-cylinder unit shown; V6 unit similar)

20   Hand tighten the threaded fittings for the fuel lines and make sure that none of the fuel lines are stressed. Install the fuel line bracket fasteners securely. Tighten the fuel line fittings to the torque listed in this Chapter's Specifications.

21   The remainder of installation is the reverse of removal. Refill the cooling system (see Chapter 1).

---

12   Fuel rail and injectors - removal and installation

Warning: *Gasoline is extremely flammable, so take extra precautions when you work on any part of the fuel system. See the Fuel system warnings in Section 1.*

1   Relieve the fuel system pressure (see Section 3). **Warning:** *On 2.0L four-cylinder and 3.2L V6 models, be sure to also relieve the high-pressure side of the fuel system.*

2   Disconnect the cable from the negative battery terminal (see Chapter 5).

11.5 High-pressure fuel pump mounting fasteners. The Schrader valve fitting (A, if equipped) will have to be removed to access the bolt underneath (2.0L four-cylinder unit shown; V6 unit similar)

1.8L four-cylinder and 3.0L V6 models

Removal

Refer to illustrations 12.4a, 12.4b, 12.6, 12.8 and 12.9

3   Remove the engine cover.

4   Place a rag around the fuel supply line fitting and, if equipped, fuel return line fitting, then disconnect the fittings **(see illustrations)**. **Note:** *June 2003 and earlier V6 models use a fuel supply and return line; July 2003 and later models have a returnless system and therefore have no fuel return line fitting at the fuel rail.*

5   On four-cylinder models, disconnect the electrical connectors from the Camshaft Position (CMP) sensor and the fuel injectors. On V6 models, disconnect the electrical connectors from the intake manifold change-over valve and the fuel injectors.

12.4b Fuel supply line and return line fittings (3.0L V6 models):

1   Fuel supply line fitting
2   Fuel return line fitting (June 2003 and earlier models only)

12.4a Fuel injection system details (1.8L four-cylinder models):

1   Fuel supply line fitting
2   Fuel injector electrical connectors
3   Camshaft Position (CMP) sensor electrical connector
4   Fuel rail mounting bolts

12.6 Fuel rail mounting fasteners (3.0L V6 models)

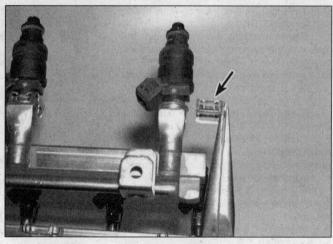

12.8 Remove each injector retaining clip, then pull the injector out of the fuel rail

6   Remove the fuel rail mounting fasteners **(see illustration)**.

7   To remove the fuel rail and injectors from the intake manifold, grasp the fuel rail firmly and pull the injectors out of the intake manifold.

8   Remove the retainer clip from each fuel injector **(see illustration)**, then pull the injectors out of the fuel rail.

9   Remove and discard the old injector O-rings **(see illustration). Note:** *Even if you only removed the fuel rail assembly to replace a single injector or a leaking O-ring, it's a good idea to remove all of the injectors from the fuel rails and replace all of the O-rings at the same time.*

Installation

10   Coat the new upper and lower O-rings with clean engine oil and slide them into place on the fuel injectors.

11   Coat each upper O-ring with clean engine oil, then insert the injector into its bore in the fuel rail and push it into the bore until the injector is fully seated in the fuel rail.

12   Secure each injector with its retainer clip.

13   Coat the lower injector O-rings with clean engine oil, then install the fuel rail assemblies on the intake manifold. Tighten the fuel rail mounting fasteners securely.

14   The remainder of installation is the reverse of removal.

15   When you're done, reconnect the battery, then turn the ignition switch to ON (but don't operate the starter). This activates the fuel pump for about two seconds, which builds up fuel pressure in the fuel lines and the fuel rail. Repeat this step two or three times, then check the fuel lines, fuel rails and injectors for fuel leaks.

2.0L four-cylinder models
Intake manifold/fuel rail removal

Refer to illustrations 12.18, 12.19, 12.25, 12.27a and 12.27b

Warning: *The fuel system on these models operates at very high pressure (in excess of 1500 psi) and can cause serious injury. Do not attempt to work on the fuel system until you are absolutely sure that the fuel pressure has been relieved (see Section 3).*

Note: *A special puller tool might be required to remove the injectors from the cylinder head if they're stuck, and a special press tool might be required to install the injectors. Special tools are also available to install and size the new Teflon O-ring on each injector, but we were able to devise a way to do this without them. Check on the availability of these tools before performing the following procedure.*

16   Remove the engine cover (see Chapter 2).

17   Detach the intake duct from the throttle body.

18   Wrap a shop rag around the threaded fuel supply line fitting and disconnect the fitting **(see illustration)**. Plug the supply line and the fuel rail.

19   Disconnect all electrical connectors from the intake manifold **(see illustration)** and the fuel rail.

20   Label and disconnect all hoses from the intake manifold. On vehicles with an automatic transaxle, disconnect the vacuum hose that connects the intake manifold to the vacuum pump.

21   Remove the fasteners from both coolant pipe support brackets. **Note:** *On some mod-*

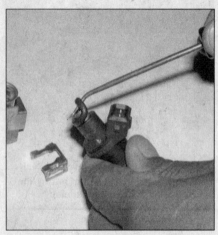

12.9 Replace the injector O-rings

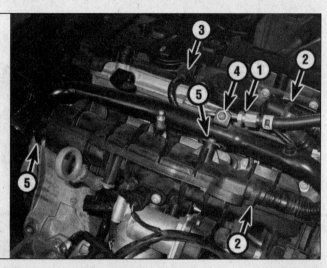

12.18 Intake manifold/fuel rail removal details (2.0L four-cylinder models):

1   Fuel supply line fitting
2   PCV hose fittings
3   EVAP line fitting
4   Fuel supply line bracket fastener
5   Coolant pipe bracket fasteners

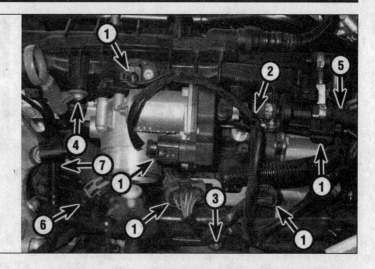

12.19 Intake manifold/fuel rail removal details (2.0L four-cylinder models):

1 *Electrical connectors*
2 *Harness cable tie (location and number of cable ties varies with model)*
3 *Coolant pipe mounting bracket bolt*
4 *Dipstick tube support bracket fastener*
5 *EVAP purge valve hose (disconnect from pipe on firewall)*
6 *Bracket fastener for turbocharger coolant return pipe*
7 *Turbocharger coolant return pipe*

els, it isn't necessary to disconnect the radiator hose from the coolant pipe; removing the pipe-to-manifold fasteners will allow the coolant pipe to be repositioned far enough from the manifold for removal. If you find that this is not the case on your vehicle, drain the coolant (see Chapter 1) and detach the radiator hose from the front of the coolant pipe.

22 Remove the dipstick, remove the fastener from the dipstick tube bracket, then pull out and remove the upper part of the dipstick tube.

23 Wrap a shop rag around each of the fuel line fittings at the high-pressure pump, then disconnect both fittings **(see illustration 11.4)**. Be prepared to catch the fuel spillage. Plug the open lines and the fuel pipes on the pump.

24 Remove the turbocharger coolant return hose from the return pipe, remove the return pipe bracket fasteners and set the return pipe aside.

25 Disconnect the electrical connector from the fuel pressure sensor **(see illustration)**.

26 Remove the intake manifold support bracket.

27 Remove the intake manifold fasteners **(see illustrations)**.

28 Remove the intake manifold and fuel rail as a single assembly. Some injectors might come out with the fuel rail, but it's unlikely; the injectors will probably remain in the cylinder head.

29 Remove and discard the old intake manifold gasket.

30 Place the intake manifold on a clean work surface. If any injectors came out of the cylinder head when you removed the intake manifold and fuel rail, remove them from the fuel rail by simply pulling them out.

Fuel injector removal and disassembly

Refer to illustrations 12.31a, 12.31b, 12.32 and 12.33

31 Most injectors probably did not come out of the cylinder head when you removed the fuel rail. To remove each injector from the cylinder head, disengage the tabs of the radial compensator from the support ring, remove the support ring and use a pair angled needle nose pliers to pull the injector out of the head

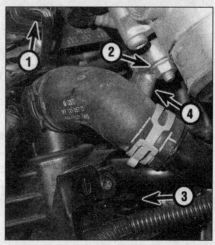

12.25 Lower intake manifold/fuel rail details (2.0L four-cylinder models)

1 *Fuel pressure sensor*
2 *Support bracket nut*
3 *Support bracket bolt*
4 *Support bracket*

12.27a Upper intake manifold fasteners (2.0L four-cylinder models)

12.27b Lower intake manifold fasteners (2.0L four-cylinder models)

12.31a Use a small screwdriver or pick to disengage the radial compensator tabs (A) from the support ring (B), remove the support ring . . .

12.31b . . . then carefully pry the injector out of its bore in the cylinder head

12.32 Fuel injector details (2.0L four-cylinder model shown, 3.2L V6 models similar):

1   *Combustion chamber Teflon sealing ring*
2   *Radial compensator*
3   *Support ring*
4   *Spacer ring*
5   *Injector upper O-ring*

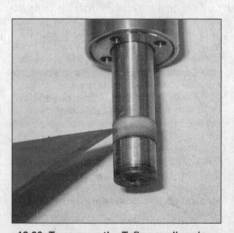

12.33 To remove the Teflon sealing ring, cut it off with a hobby knife (be careful not to scratch the injector groove)

(see illustrations). If any of the injectors are seriously stuck in the cylinder head, you might have to remove them with a special puller tool set.

32   Remove and inspect the condition of the radial compensator **(see illustration)**. If it's damaged, replace it. Also inspect the support ring. Again, if it's damaged, replace it.

33   Remove the old combustion chamber Teflon sealing ring and the upper O-ring from each injector **(see illustration)**. **Caution:** *Be extremely careful not to damage the groove for the seal or the rib in the floor of the groove. If you damage the groove or the rib, you must replace the injector.*

34   Inspect the condition of the upper spacer

ring; it only needs to be replaced if it's damaged.

Intake manifold disassembly and reassembly

Refer to illustrations 12.35a and 12.35b

Note: *No further disassembly of the intake manifold is necessary unless you're replacing some component on the manifold, or the manifold itself.*

35   Remove the EVAP line fasteners and clamps from the top and underside of the intake manifold, then pull the EVAP canister purge solenoid off its mounting bracket **(see illustrations)** and remove the EVAP assembly.

36   Remove the fuel line clamp, unscrew the line fittings and remove the lines from the intake manifold.

37   Carefully pry off the intake flap motor linkage, remove the intake flap motor mounting fasteners and remove the intake flap motor from the intake manifold.

38   If you're replacing the intake manifold, remove the throttle body from the intake man-

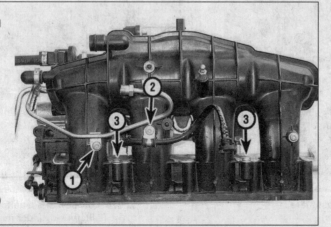

12.35a Intake manifold disassembly details (2.0L four-cylinder models):

1   *Fuel supply line bracket fastener*
2   *EVAP line bracket fastener*
3   *Fuel rail retaining fasteners (do not remove until you've removed everything in illustration 12.35b)*

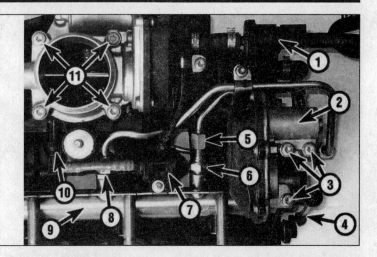

12.35b Intake manifold disassembly details (2.0L four-cylinder models):

1   EVAP canister purge solenoid valve
2   Intake flap motor
3   Intake flap motor mounting fasteners
4   Intake flap motor control rod
5   Low pressure fuel line fitting
6   Check valve
7   EVAP purge line
8   High pressure fuel line fitting
9   Fuel rail
10 EVAP purge line quick-connect fitting
11 Throttle body mounting fasteners

ifold. This step is not necessary if you are simply removing or replacing the fuel rail.

39   Remove the fuel rail mounting fasteners and remove the fuel rail from the intake manifold.

40   Reassembly is the reverse of disassembly.

Injector reassembly and installation

Refer to illustrations 12.45, 12.46, 12.47a, 12.47b, 12.48, 12.49a and 12.49b

41   Before installing the new Teflon seal on each injector, thoroughly clean the groove for the seal and the injector shaft. Remove all combustion residue and varnish with a clean shop rag.

Teflon seal installation using the special tools

42   The manufacturer recommends that you use the tools included in the special injector tool set described above to install the Teflon lower seals on the injectors: Install the special seal assembly cone on the injector, install the special sleeve on the injector and use the sleeve to push on the assembly cone, which pushes the Teflon seal into place on its groove. Do NOT use any lubricants to do so.

43   Pushing the Teflon seal into place in its groove expands it slightly. There are two siz-

12.45 Slide the new Teflon seal onto the end of a socket that's the same diameter as the end of the fuel injector . . .

ing sleeves in the special tool set with progressively smaller inside diameters. Using a clockwise rotating motion of about 180 degrees, install the slightly larger sleeve onto the injector and over the Teflon seal until the sleeve hits its stop, then carefully turn the sleeve counterclockwise as you pull it off the injector. Use the slightly smaller sizing sleeve the same way. The seal is now sized. Repeat this step for each injector.

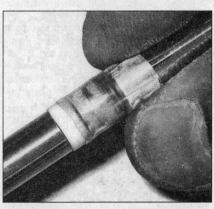

12.47a Use the socket to push a short section of plastic tubing onto the end of the injector and over the new seal . . .

12.47b . . . then leave the plastic tubing in place for several hours to compress the new seal

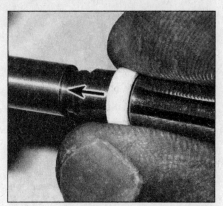

12.46 . . . align the socket with the end of the injector and slide the seal onto the injector and into its mounting groove

Teflon seal installation without special tools

44   If you don't have the special injector tool set, the Teflon seal can be installed using this method: First, find a socket that is equal or very close in diameter to the diameter of the end of the fuel injector.

45   Work the new Teflon seal onto the end of the socket (**see illustration**).

46   Place the socket against the end of the injector (**see illustration**) and slide the seal from the socket onto the injector. Do NOT use any lubricants to do so. Continue pushing the seal onto the injector until it seats into its mounting groove.

47   Because the inside diameter of the seal has to be stretched open to fit over the bore of the socket and the injector, its outside diameter is now slightly too large - it is no longer flush with the surface of the injector. It must be shrunk it back to its original size. To do so, push a piece of plastic tubing with an interference fit onto the end of the socket; a plastic straw that fits tightly on the injector will work. After pushing the plastic tubing onto the socket about an inch, snip off the rest of the tubing, then use the socket to push the tubing onto the end of the injector (**see illustration**) and slide it onto the injector until it completely covers the new seal (**see illustration**). Leave

12.48 Note that the upper O-ring (1) is installed *above* the spacer ring (2)

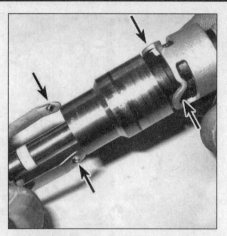

12.49a Make sure that the locking tabs on the radial compensator are correctly aligned with the openings in the support ring . . .

12.49b . . . then push the components together so the tabs snap into place

the tubing on for a few hours, then remove it. The seal should now be shrunk back its original outside diameter, or close to it.

Spacer ring and radial compensator installation

48   Install the new spacer ring at the upper end of the injector. Lubricate the new upper O-ring with clean engine oil and install it on the injector. Do NOT oil the new Teflon seal. Note that the seal is installed *above* the spacer **(see illustration)**.

49   Install the support ring on the top of the injector; note that the support ring can only go on the injector one way because its opening must fit around the electrical terminal. Once the support ring is in place, install the radial compensator so that the locking tabs are correctly aligned with the support ring, then push the compensator toward the upper end of the injector until the locking tabs snap into place **(see illustrations)**.

50   Repeat this procedure until all four injectors are reassembled.

Injector installation

51   Thoroughly clean the injector bores with

a small nylon brush. If any of the valves are in the way, carefully rotate the engine just enough to provide enough clearance to reach all of the bore.

52   Install the fuel injectors in the cylinder head (NOT in the fuel rail). You should be able to push each assembled injector into its bore in the cylinder head. The bore is tapered, so you will encounter some resistance as the Teflon seal nears the bottom of the bore. Press the injector into its bore until it stops.

Intake manifold/fuel rail installation

Refer to illustration 12.53

53   Install a new gasket on the reassembled intake manifold **(see illustration)**.

54   Install the assembled intake manifold/fuel rail assembly. Make sure that the holes in the fuel rail for the fuel injectors fit onto the injectors, then push the manifold firmly until it's seated against the cylinder head. Install the intake manifold mounting fasteners and tighten them to the torque listed in this Chapter's Specifications.

55   Installation is otherwise the reverse of removal.

3.2L V6 models

Warning: *The fuel system on these models operates at very high pressure (in excess of 1500 psi) and can cause serious injury. Do not attempt to work on the fuel system until you are absolutely sure that the fuel pressure has been relieved (see Section 3).*

Note: *A special puller tool might be required to remove the injectors from the cylinder head if they're stuck, and a special press tool might be required to install the injectors. Special tools are also available to install and size the new Teflon O-ring on each injector, but we were able to devise a way to do this without them. Check on the availability of these tools before performing the following procedure.*

56   Remove the engine cover and the upper intake manifold (see Chapter 2B).

57   Wrap a shop rag around the threaded fuel supply line fitting and disconnect the fitting. Be prepared to catch the fuel spillage and to plug the supply line and the fuel rail immediately.

58   Unscrew the fuel line fittings and remove the fuel line bracket fasteners.

59   Disconnect the electrical connectors for the intake manifold runner position sensor and the fuel pressure sensor.

60   Remove the intake manifold fasteners and nuts and remove the lower intake manifold and fuel rails as a single assembly.

61   Remove and discard the old intake manifold gasket, plug the cylinder head intake ports with clean shop rags and place the intake manifold on a clean work surface.

62   If any injectors are stuck in either cylinder head, you'll need to use a special puller like the one described in the **Note** above, or use the method described in Step 31 for the 2.0L four-cylinder engine.

63   Remove the fuel rail retaining bracket fasteners and remove the fuel rails from the lower intake manifold.

64   Carefully pull the injectors out of the fuel rail (if any came out with the fuel rail).

12.53 Install a new gasket on the intake manifold (2.0L four-cylinder models)

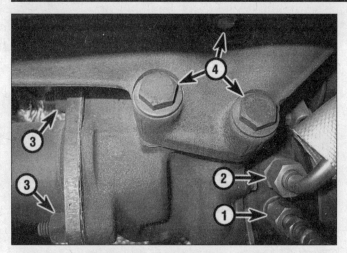

13.5 Turbocharger removal details (1.8L four-cylinder models):

1   *Oil supply line fitting*
2   *Coolant return line fitting*
3   *Catalytic converter-to-turbocharger nuts (third nut not visible)*
4   *Exhaust manifold-to-turbocharger bolts*

13.8 Turbocharger inlet duct (1), outlet duct (2) and support bracket fastener (3) (other support bracket fastener not visible in this photo) (1.8L four-cylinder models)

65   Replace all injector seals, then install the support ring and radial compensator on each injector (see Steps 32, 33, 34 and 41 through 50).

66   Thoroughly clean the injector bores. If any of the valves are in the way, carefully rotate the engine just enough so that the valves are safely out of the way.

67   Install the fuel injectors in the cylinder head (NOT in the fuel rail). You should be able to push each assembled injector into its bore in the cylinder head. The bore is tapered, so you will encounter some resistance as the combustion chamber Teflon seal nears the bottom of the bore. Press the injector into its bore until it stops.

68   Reattach the fuel rails to the lower intake manifold.

69   Using a new lower intake manifold gasket, install the lower manifold and fuel rails. Press the fuel rails evenly onto the fuel injectors. Install the lower intake manifold mounting fasteners, then slowly and evenly tighten the lower manifold fasteners in a crisscross fashion to the torque listed in this Chapter's Specifications.

70   Installation is otherwise the reverse of removal.

13   Turbocharger and intercooler(s) - check and replacement

Check

1   The turbocharger is a precision component which can be severely damaged by a lack of lubrication or from foreign material entering the air intake duct. Turbocharger failure may be indicated by poor engine performance, blue/gray exhaust smoke or unusual noises from the turbocharger. If a turbocharger failure is suspected, check the following areas:

a)   *Check the intake air duct for looseness or damage. Make sure there are no restrictions in the air intake system. Check for a dirty air filter element or damaged intercooler.*

b)   *Check the system vacuum hoses for restrictions or damage.*

c)   *Check the system wiring for damage and electrical connectors for looseness or corrosion.*

d)   *Make sure the wastegate actuator linkage is not binding.*

e)   *Check the exhaust system for damage or restrictions.*

f)   *Check the lubricating oil supply and drainback lines for damage or restrictions.*

g)   *Check the coolant supply and return lines for damage and restrictions.*

h)   *If the turbocharger requires replacement due to failure, be sure to change the engine oil and filter (see Chapter 1).*

2   Complete diagnosis of the turbocharger and control system requires special techniques and equipment. If the previous checks fail to identify the problem, take the vehicle to a dealership service department or other properly equipped repair facility for diagnosis.

Replacement

Turbocharger

1.8L models

Refer to illustrations 13.5, 13.8, 13.10 and 13.11

3   Remove the engine cover, the fresh air inlet duct, the air filter housing cover, the air intake duct and the air filter housing (see Chapter 4).

4   Warm up the engine and drain the engine oil, then allow the engine to cool off and drain the cooling system (see Chapter 1).

5   Disconnect the oil supply line and coolant return line fittings from the top of the turbocharger **(see illustration)**.

6   Raise the vehicle and support it securely on jackstands. Remove the engine compartment under-covers.

7   Remove the air conditioning compressor from its mounting bracket (see Chapter 3) and position the compressor aside without disconnecting the refrigerant hoses.

8   Loosen the hose clamps and disconnect the air inlet and outlet ducts from the turbocharger **(see illustration)**.

9   Remove the turbocharger support bracket fasteners and remove the support bracket.

10   Unbolt the oil return line from the oil pan **(see illustration)**. Have a drain pan ready to catch any residual oil in the turbocharger or

13.10 Typical oil return pipe at the oil pan (1.8L four-cylinder models)

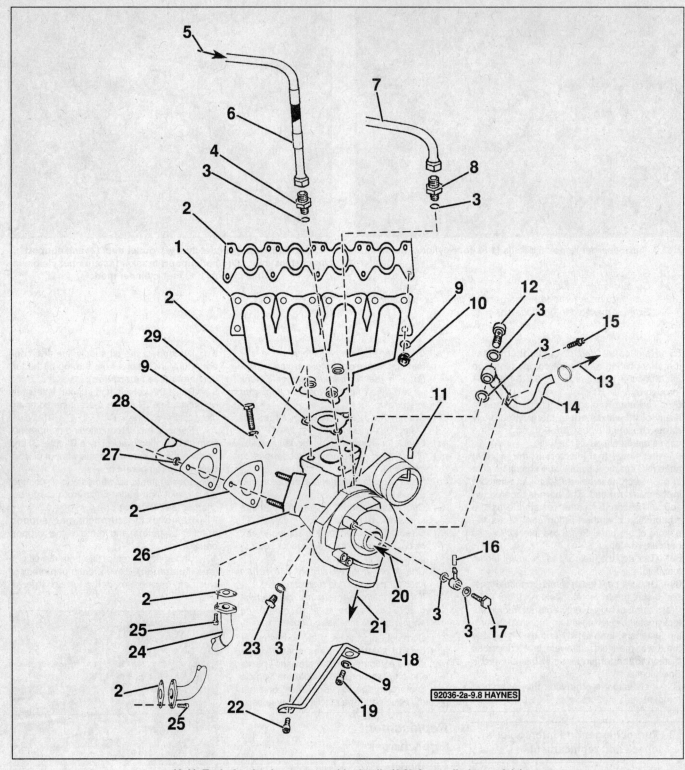

13.11 Typical turbocharger assembly details (1.8L four-cylinder models)

1	Exhaust manifold	9	Washer	17	Banjo bolt	24	Oil return pipe
2	Gasket	10	Nut	18	Turbocharger support	25	Bolt
3	Oil seal	11	Vacuum hose		bracket	26	Turbocharger
4	Fitting	12	Banjo bolt	19	Bolt	27	Nut
5	From oil filter adapter	13	From cylinder block	20	From air cleaner	28	Front exhaust pipe
6	Oil supply line	14	Coolant supply line	21	To intercooler	29	Bolt
7	Coolant return line	15	Bolt	22	Bolt		
8	Fitting	16	Hose	23	Plug		

13.23 Exhaust manifold heat shield fasteners (forwardmost fastener not visible in this photo) (2.0L four-cylinder models)

13.24 Turbocharger assembly details (2.0L four-cylinder models)

1   PCV crankcase ventilation line
2   EVAP hose (already disconnected from valve cover pipe)
3   Coolant return line banjo bolt
4   Oil supply line banjo bolt
5   Coolant supply line banjo bolt

the return line. Trace the return line up to the turbocharger, unbolt the oil return line flange from the underside of the turbocharger and remove the line. Remove and discard the old flange gaskets.

11   Remove the banjo bolt that secures the coolant supply line to the left (inner) upper side of the turbocharger **(see illustration)**.

12   Locate the secondary air injection line **(see illustration 8.4a)**. Remove the injection line retaining fasteners (near the lower end of the line) and remove the line.

13   Remove the heat shield on the right side of the cylinder head.

14   Disconnect the vacuum hose from the wastegate actuator.

15   Unfasten the catalytic converter from the turbocharger.

16   Unfasten the turbocharger from the exhaust manifold

17   Reposition the turbocharger to one side and loosen the retaining bracket. Rotate the turbocharger to access the remaining hose and disconnect the hose from the turbocharger.

18   Remove the turbocharger.

19   When installing the turbocharger assembly, be sure to:

a) Replace all gaskets, seals, banjo bolt sealing washers and self-locking nuts.
b) Tighten the turbocharger mounting fasteners to the torque listed in this Chapter's Specifications.
c) Refill the engine with new engine oil and install a new oil filter (see Chapter 1).
d) Refill the engine with new engine coolant (see Chapter 1).
e) Before starting the engine, remove the fuel pump fuse and crank the engine over until oil pressure builds.

13.28 Turbocharger-to-right intercooler air hose details (2.0L models):

1   Hose clamps
2   Air duct connecting turbocharger outlet to right intercooler
3   Turbocharger outlet
4   Right intercooler

f) After starting the engine, allow it to idle for about one minute to ensure that the turbocharger is properly lubricated.

20   Installation is otherwise the reverse of removal.

2.0L models

Refer to illustrations 13.23, 13.24, 13.28, 13.29a, 13.29b and 13.34

21   Warm up the engine and drain the engine oil, then allow the engine to cool off and drain the cooling system (see Chapter 1).

22   Remove the engine cover, the air intake duct between the air filter housing and the turbocharger **(see illustration 8.4b)** and the air filter housing (see Section 8).

23   Remove the exhaust manifold heat shield fasteners and remove the heat shield **(see illustration)**.

24   Disconnect and remove the PCV fresh air inlet hose and the EVAP hose from the engine valve cover and from the turbocharger **(see illustration)**.

25   Remove the coolant return, oil supply and coolant supply line banjo bolts from the turbocharger.

26   Remove the nuts and detach the catalytic converter from the turbocharger.

27   Raise the vehicle and place it securely on jackstands. Remove the engine compartment under-covers.

28   Disconnect and remove the air hose **(see illustration)** between the turbocharger and the right intercooler.

29   Disconnect the electrical connectors

13.29a Turbocharger lower details:

1   Recirculating valve electrical connector
2   Wastegate bypass regulator valve electrical connector
3   Oil return line flange bolts
4   Turbocharger support brace

13.29b Turbocharger lower details:

1   Oil supply line
2   Oil supply line banjo bolt
3   Coolant supply line
4   Coolant supply line banjo bolt
5   Coolant supply line bracket bolt
6   Oil return line flange bolts
7   Turbocharger support brace fasteners

from the wastegate bypass regulator valve and the turbocharger recirculating valve **(see illustrations)**.

30   Remove the oil return line flange fasteners and disconnect the return line from the turbocharger. Trace the return line down to the oil pan, remove the flange fasteners and disconnect the return line from the oil pan. Remove the oil return line.

31   Remove the lower oil supply line banjo bolt from the block and remove the oil supply line.

32   Remove the lower coolant supply line banjo bolt, remove the coolant supply line bracket fastener and remove the coolant supply line.

33   Remove the fastener from the lower end of the turbocharger support brace. It's not absolutely necessary to detach the upper end of the brace from the turbocharger until after

you have removed the turbo from the vehicle, but if you can remove it, and the brace, it will give you a little more maneuverability when removing the exhaust manifold/turbocharger assembly. The nut for the upper brace bolt is tough to access, but even loosening it a couple of turns will allow you to move the brace as necessary when removing the exhaust manifold/turbocharger assembly.

34   Remove the exhaust manifold mounting nuts and loosen, but do not remove, the lower clamping bar nuts **(see illustration)**.

35   Remove the exhaust manifold/turbocharger assembly.

36   If you're replacing the exhaust manifold/turbocharger assembly, place the assembly on a clean work bench and remove the components that don't come with the new or remanufactured exhaust manifold/turbocharger assembly and install them on the new unit.

37   When installing the turbocharger assembly, be sure to:

a)   Coat the threads of all exhaust manifold and turbocharger fasteners and all banjo fasteners with anti-seize compound

b)   Replace all seals, gaskets and self-locking nuts

c)   Set the bottom of the exhaust manifold flange on the clamping bar, then rotate the manifold up over the upper mounting studs and install the upper nuts. Tighten the fasteners evenly, a little at a time, to the torque listed in this Chapter's Specifications

d)   Use new sealing washers for all banjo fittings

e)   Tighten all turbocharger fasteners to the torque listed in this Chapter's Specifications (if no torque specification is listed, tighten the fastener securely)

f)   Add oil to the turbocharger through the oil supply line

g)   Make sure that all hoses are clean inside before installing them

h)   If you're replacing any hose clamps, the replacement clamps must be the same types as the old ones

i)   Make sure that the exhaust system is properly aligned before reconnecting it to the turbocharger

j)   Refill the engine coolant and top up the engine oil (see Chapter 1) before starting the engine

k)   After starting the engine, let it idle for about one minute to ensure an adequate oil supply to the turbocharger

38   Installation is otherwise the reverse of removal.

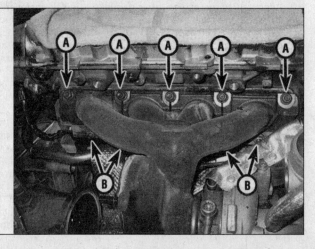

13.34 Exhaust manifold mounting nuts (A) and clamping bar nuts (B, inner nuts not visible).
Note: *Loosen the clamping bar nuts a few turns, but don't remove them*

13.43 Typical intercooler air intake scoop and approximate clip locations (lower clip not visible) (right scoop for 2.0L models shown; other scoops use various styles of mounting clips)

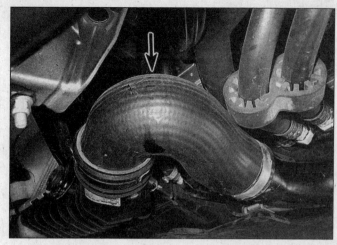

13.44a Air intake hose between the air tube in the radiator support and the intercooler (1.8L models)

Intercooler (1.8L and 2.0L models)

Refer to illustrations 13.43, 13.44a, 13.44b, 13.46a and 13.46b

Note: *On 1.8L models, a single intercooler is located at the left front corner of the vehicle, below the left headlight housing. On 2.0L models, there are two intercoolers; one at the left front corner of the vehicle and one at the right front corner of the vehicle.*

39   Raise the vehicle and support it securely on jackstands.

40   Remove the engine compartment undercovers.

41   If you're working on a 1.8L model, place the radiator support in the service position (see Chapter 11). If you're working on a 2.0L model, remove the front bumper cover (see Chapter 11).

42   On 2.0L models, also remove the left or right headlight housing (see Chapter 12).

43   Remove the air intake scoop from the front of the intercooler. To detach the air scoop from the intercooler, disengage the clips on the scoop from the plastic locator pins on the front of the intercooler **(see illustration)**.

44   Loosen the hose clamp and disconnect the inlet and outlet air ducts from the intercooler **(see illustrations)**.

45   Look for and disconnect any electrical connectors in the way, such as the charge air pressure sensor, which is located on the upper backside of the intercooler on some models.

46   Remove the intercooler from its mounting bracket by disengaging the mounting hooks on the intercooler from their corresponding grommets in the mounting bracket **(see illustrations)**. It's not necessary to remove the mounting bracket.

47   Installation is the reverse of removal. Be sure to replace any damaged ducts, hoses and/or hose clamps.

13.44b Air inlet hose between the left intercooler and the air tube in the lower radiator support (2.0L models)

13.46a Lower intercooler locator pin and mounting bracket grommet location (right intercooler for 2.0L model shown)

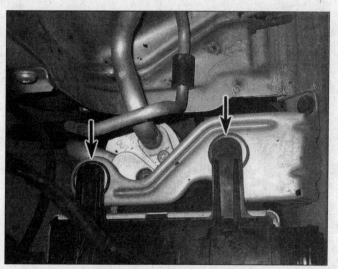

13.46b Upper intercooler locator pin and mounting bracket grommet locations (right intercooler for 2.0L model shown)

Notes

Chapter 5
Engine electrical systems

Contents

	Section		Section
Alternator - removal and installation	7	General information and precautions	1
Battery - disconnection	3	Ignition coils - removal and installation	6
Battery - removal and installation	4	Starter motor - removal and installation	8
Battery cables - replacement	5	Troubleshooting	2

1 General information and precautions

General information

Ignition system

The electronic ignition system consists of the Crankshaft Position (CKP) sensor, the Camshaft Position (CMP) sensor, the Knock Sensor (KS), the Powertrain Control Module (PCM), the ignition switch, the battery, the individual ignition coils or a coil pack, and the spark plugs. For more information on the CKP, CMP and KS sensors, as well as the PCM, refer to Chapter 6.

Charging system

The charging system includes the alternator (with an integral voltage regulator), the Powertrain Control Module (PCM), the Body Control Module (BCM), a charge indicator light on the dash, the battery, a fuse or fusible link and the wiring connecting all of these components. The charging system supplies electrical power for the ignition system, the lights, the radio, etc. The alternator is driven by a drivebelt.

Starting system

The starting system consists of the battery, the ignition switch, the starter relay, the Powertrain Control Module (PCM), the Body Control Module (BCM), the Transmission Range (TR) switch, the starter motor and solenoid assembly, and the wiring connecting all of the components.

Precautions

Always observe the following precautions when working on the electrical system:

a) *Be extremely careful when servicing engine electrical components. They are easily damaged if checked, connected or handled improperly.*

b) *Never leave the ignition switched on for long periods of time when the engine is not running.*

c) *Never disconnect the battery cables while the engine is running.*

d) *Maintain correct polarity when connecting battery cables from another vehicle during jump starting - see the "Booster battery (jump) starting" Section at the front of this manual.*

e) *Always disconnect the cable from the negative battery terminal before working on the electrical system, but read the battery disconnection procedure first (see Section 3).*

It's also a good idea to review the safety-related information regarding the engine electrical systems located in the *Safety first!* Section at the front of this manual before beginning any operation included in this Chapter.

Engine electrical system details (1.8L models):

1   Battery
2   Starter motor (right rear side of
    engine block)

3   Alternator
4   Ignition coils

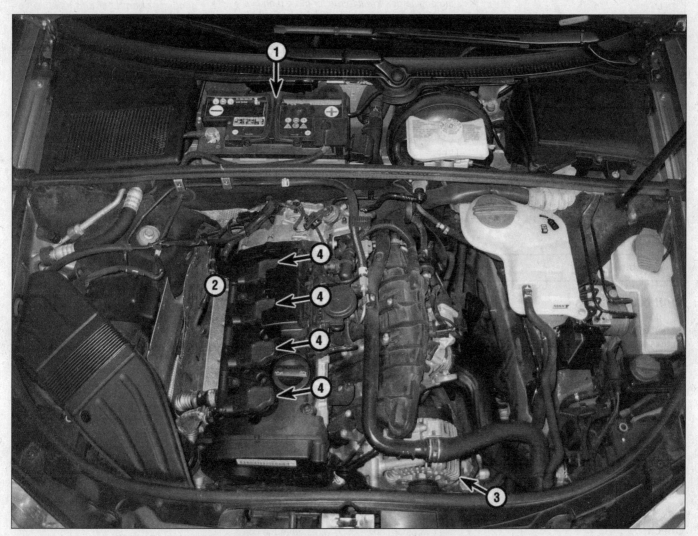

Engine electrical system details (2.0L models):

1 Battery
2 Starter motor (right rear side of engine block)
3 Alternator
4 Ignition coils

2.3 Spark tester

---

2   Troubleshooting

Ignition system

1   If a malfunction occurs in the ignition system, do not immediately assume that any particular part is causing the problem. First, check the following items:

a) Make sure that the cable clamps at the battery terminals are clean and tight.

b) Test the condition of the battery (see Steps 21 through 24). If it doesn't pass all the tests, replace it.

c) Check the ignition coil or coil pack connections.

d) Check any relevant fuses in the engine compartment fuse and relay box (see Chapter 12). If they're burned, determine the cause and repair the circuit.

Check

Refer to illustration 2.3

Warning: *Because of the high voltage generated by the ignition system, use extreme care when performing a procedure involving ignition components.*

Note 1: *The ignition system components on these vehicles are difficult to diagnose. In the event of ignition system failure that you can't diagnose, have the vehicle tested at a dealer service department or other qualified auto repair facility.*

Note 2: *You'll need a spark tester for the following test. Spark testers are available at most auto supply stores.*

2   If the engine turns over but won't start, verify that there is sufficient ignition voltage to fire the spark plugs as follows.

3   On models with a coil-over-plug type ignition system, remove a coil and install the tester between the boot at the lower end of the coil and the spark plug **(see illustration)**. On models with spark plug wires, disconnect a spark plug wire from a spark plug and install the tester between the spark plug wire boot and the spark plug.

4   Crank the engine and note whether or not the tester flashes. **Caution:** *Do NOT crank the engine or allow it to run for more than five seconds; running the engine for more than five seconds may set a Diagnostic Trouble Code (DTC) for a cylinder misfire.*

Models with a coil-over-plug type ignition system

5   If the tester flashes during cranking, the coil is delivering sufficient voltage to the spark plug to fire it. Repeat this test for each cylinder to verify that the other coils are OK.

6   If the tester doesn't flash, remove a coil from another cylinder and swap it for the one being tested. If the tester now flashes, you know that the original coil is bad. If the tester still doesn't flash, the PCM or wiring harness is probably defective. Have the PCM checked out by a dealer service department or other qualified repair shop (testing the PCM is beyond the scope of the do-it-yourselfer because it requires expensive special tools).

7   If the tester flashes during cranking but a misfire code (related to the cylinder being tested) has been stored, the spark plug could be fouled or defective.

Models with spark plug wires

8   If the tester flashes during cranking, sufficient voltage is reaching the spark plug to fire it.

9   Repeat this test on the remaining cylinders.

10   Proceed on this basis until you have verified that there's a good spark from each spark plug wire. If there is, then you have verified that the coils in the coil pack are functioning correctly and that the spark plug wires are OK.

11   If there is no spark from a spark plug wire, then either the coil is bad, the plug wire is bad or a connection at one end of the plug wire is loose. Assuming that you're using new plug wires or known good wires, then the coil is probably defective. Also inspect the coil pack electrical connector. Make sure that it's clean, tight and in good condition.

12   If all the coils are firing correctly, but the engine misfires, then one or more of the plugs might be fouled. Remove and check the spark plugs or install new ones (see Chapter 1).

13   No further testing of the ignition system is possible without special tools. If the problem persists, have the ignition system tested by a dealer service department or other qualified repair shop.

Charging system

14   If a malfunction occurs in the charging system, do not automatically assume the alternator is causing the problem. First check the following items:

a) Check the drivebelt tension and condition, as described in Chapter 1. Replace it if it's worn or deteriorated.

b) Make sure the alternator mounting bolts are tight.

c) Inspect the alternator wiring harness and the connectors at the alternator and voltage regulator. They must be in good condition, tight and have no corrosion.

d) Check the fusible link (if equipped) or main fuse in the underhood fuse/relay box. If it is burned, determine the cause, repair the circuit and replace the link or fuse (the vehicle will not start and/or the accessories will not work if the fusible link or main fuse is blown).

e) Start the engine and check the alternator for abnormal noises (a shrieking or squealing sound indicates a bad bearing).

f) Check the battery. Make sure it's fully charged and in good condition (one bad cell in a battery can cause overcharging by the alternator).

g) Disconnect the battery cables (negative first, then positive). Inspect the battery posts and the cable clamps for corrosion. Clean them thoroughly if necessary (see Chapter 1). Reconnect the cables (positive first, negative last).

Alternator - check

15   Use a voltmeter to check the battery voltage with the engine off. It should be at least 12.6 volts **(see illustration 2.21)**.

16   Start the engine and check the battery voltage again. It should now be approximately 13.5 to 15 volts.

17   If the voltage reading is more or less than the specified charging voltage, the voltage regulator is probably defective, which will require replacement of the alternator (the voltage regulator is not replaceable separately). Remove the alternator and have it bench tested (most auto parts stores will do this for you).

18   The charging system (battery) light on the instrument cluster lights up when the ignition key is turned to ON, but it should go out when the engine starts.

19   If the charging system light stays on after the engine has been started, there is a problem with the charging system. Before replacing the alternator, check the battery condition, alternator belt tension and electrical cable connections.

20   If replacing the alternator doesn't restore voltage to the specified range, have the charging system tested by a dealer service department or other qualified repair shop.

Battery - check

Refer to illustrations 2.21 and 2.23

21   Check the battery state of charge. Visually inspect the indicator eye on the top of the battery (if equipped with one); if the indi-

2.21 To test the open circuit voltage of the battery, touch the black probe of the voltmeter to the negative terminal and the red probe to the positive terminal of the battery; a fully charged battery should be at least 12.6 volts

2.23 Connect a battery load tester to the battery and check the battery condition under load following the tool manufacturer's instructions

cator eye is black in color, charge the battery as described in Chapter 1. Next perform an open circuit voltage test using a digital voltmeter. **Note:** *The battery's surface charge must be removed before accurate voltage measurements can be made. Turn on the high beams for ten seconds, then turn them off and let the vehicle stand for two minutes.* With the engine and all accessories Off, touch the negative probe of the voltmeter to the negative terminal of the battery and the positive probe to the positive terminal of the battery **(see illustration)**. The battery voltage should be 12.6 volts or slightly above. If the battery is less than the specified voltage, charge the battery before proceeding to the next test. Do not proceed with the battery load test unless the battery charge is correct.

22   Disconnect the negative battery cable, then the positive cable from the battery.

23   Perform a battery load test. An accurate check of the battery condition can only be performed with a load tester **(see illustration)**. This test evaluates the ability of the battery to operate the starter and other accessories during periods of high current draw. Connect the load tester to the battery terminals. Load test the battery according to the tool manufacturer's instructions. This tool increases the load demand (current draw) on the battery.

24   Maintain the load on the battery for 15 seconds and observe that the battery voltage does not drop below 9.6 volts. If the battery condition is weak or defective, the tool will indicate this condition immediately. **Note:** *Cold temperatures will cause the minimum voltage reading to drop slightly. Follow the chart given in the manufacturer's instructions to compensate for cold*

climates. Minimum load voltage for freezing temperatures (32 degrees F) should be approximately 9.1 volts.

Starting system

The starter rotates, but the engine doesn't

25   Remove the starter (see Section 8). Check the overrunning clutch and bench test the starter to make sure the drive mechanism extends fully for proper engagement with the flywheel ring gear. If it doesn't, replace the starter.

26   Check the flywheel ring gear for missing teeth and other damage. With the ignition turned off, rotate the flywheel so you can check the entire ring gear.

The starter is noisy

27   If the solenoid is making a chattering noise, first check the battery (see Steps 21 through 24). If the battery is okay, check the cables and connections.

28   If you hear a grinding, crashing metallic sound when you turn the key to Start, check for loose starter mounting bolts. If they're tight, remove the starter and inspect the teeth on the starter pinion gear and flywheel ring gear. Look for missing or damaged teeth.

29   If the starter sounds fine when you first turn the key to Start, but then stops rotating the engine and emits a zinging sound, the problem is probably a defective starter drive that's not staying engaged with the ring gear. Replace the starter.

The starter rotates slowly

30   Check the battery (see Steps 21 through 24).

31   If the battery is okay, verify all connections (at the battery, the starter solenoid and motor) are clean, corrosion-free and tight. Make sure the cables aren't frayed or damaged.

32   Check that the starter mounting bolts are tight so it grounds properly. Also check the pinion gear and flywheel ring gear for evidence of a mechanical bind (galling, deformed gear teeth or other damage).

The starter does not rotate at all

33   Check the battery (see Steps 21 through 24).

34   If the battery is okay, verify all connections (at the battery, the starter solenoid and motor) are clean, corrosion-free and tight. Make sure the cables aren't frayed or damaged.

35   Check all of the fuses in the underhood fuse/relay box.

36   Check that the starter mounting bolts are tight so it grounds properly.

37   Check for voltage at the starter solenoid "S" terminal when the ignition key is turned to the start position. If voltage is present, replace the starter/solenoid assembly. If no voltage is present, the problem could be the starter relay, the Transmission Range (TR) switch or clutch start switch (see Chapter 8), or with an electrical connector somewhere in the circuit (see the wiring diagrams at the end of Chapter 12). Also, on many modern vehicles, the Powertrain Control Module (PCM) and the Body Control Module (BCM) control the voltage signal to the starter solenoid; on such vehicles a special scan tool is required for diagnosis.

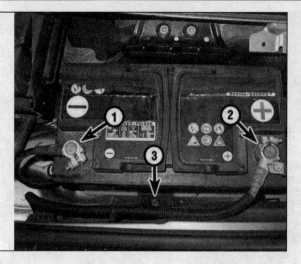

4.2 Battery removal details (2.0L model shown, other models similar):

1 *Battery negative terminal (disconnect FIRST, reconnect LAST)*
2 *Battery positive terminal*
3 *Battery hold-down clamp bolt*

3   Battery - disconnection

Caution: *Always disconnect the cable from the negative battery terminal FIRST and hook it up LAST or the battery may be shorted by the tool being used to loosen the cable clamps.*

Some systems on the vehicle require battery power to be available at all times, either to maintain continuous operation (alarm system, power door locks, etc.), or to maintain control unit memory (radio station presets, Powertrain Control Module and other control units). When the battery is disconnected, the power that maintains these systems is cut. So, before you disconnect the battery, please note that on a vehicle with power door locks, it's a wise precaution to remove the key from the ignition and to keep it with you, so that it does not get locked inside if the power door locks should engage accidentally when the battery is reconnected!

Devices known as "memory-savers" can be used to avoid some of these problems. Precise details vary according to the device used. The typical memory saver is plugged into the cigarette lighter and is connected to a spare battery. Then the vehicle battery can be disconnected from the electrical system. The memory saver will provide sufficient current to maintain audio unit security codes, PCM memory, etc. and will provide power to always hot circuits such as the clock and radio memory circuits. **Warning 1:** *Some memory savers deliver a considerable amount of current in order to keep vehicle systems operational after the main battery is disconnected. If you're using a memory saver, make sure that the circuit concerned is actually open before servicing it.* **Warning 2:** *If you're going to work near any of the airbag system components, the battery MUST be disconnected and a memory saver must NOT be used. If a memory saver is used, power will be supplied to the airbag, which means that it could accidentally deploy and cause serious personal injury.*

To disconnect the battery for service procedures requiring power to be cut from the vehicle, turn the ignition switch to the Off position, then loosen the cable end bolt and disconnect the cable from the negative battery terminal. Isolate the cable end to prevent it from coming into accidental contact with the battery terminal.

4   Battery - removal and installation

Refer to illustration 4.2

1 If equipped, remove the fasteners securing the battery cover, then remove the cover and set it aside.
2 Disconnect the cable from the negative battery terminal first, then disconnect the cable from the positive battery terminal **(see illustration)**.
3 Remove the battery hold-down clamp.
4 Lift out the battery. Be careful - it's heavy.
Note: *Battery straps and handlers are available at most auto parts stores for reasonable prices. They make it easier to remove and carry the battery.*
5 If you are replacing the battery, make sure you get one that's identical, with the same dimensions, amperage rating, cold cranking rating, etc.
6 Installation is the reverse of removal. Be sure to connect the positive cable first and the negative cable last.

5   Battery cables - replacement

1 When removing the cables, always disconnect the cable from the negative battery terminal first and hook it up last, or you might accidentally short out the battery with the tool you're using to loosen the cable clamps. Even if you're only replacing the cable for the positive terminal, be sure to disconnect the negative cable from the battery first.

2 Disconnect the old cables from the battery, then trace each of them to their opposite ends and disconnect them. Be sure to note the routing of each cable before disconnecting it to ensure correct installation.
3 If you are replacing any of the old cables, take them with you when buying new cables. It is vitally important that you replace the cables with identical parts.
4 Clean the threads of the solenoid or ground connection with a wire brush to remove rust and corrosion. Apply a light coat of battery terminal corrosion inhibitor or petroleum jelly to the threads to prevent future corrosion.
5 Attach the cable to the solenoid or ground connection and tighten the mounting nut/bolt securely.
6 Before connecting a new cable to the battery, make sure that it reaches the battery post without having to be stretched.
7 Connect the cable to the positive battery terminal first, *then* connect the ground cable to the negative battery terminal.

6   Ignition coils - removal and installation

1 Disconnect the cable from the negative battery terminal (see Section 3).

Four-cylinder models

Refer to illustrations 6.3a and 6.3b
Note: *This procedure applies to all four ignition coils.*
2 On 1.8L models, remove the engine cover.
3 Remove the screws securing the wiring harness and disconnect all four connectors from the ignition coils **(see illustrations)**.
4 To remove an ignition coil, grasp it firmly and pull it straight up.
5 Apply a little silicone dielectric compound to the inside of the spark plug boot before installing the coil. Installation is otherwise the reverse of removal.

V6 models

Note: *This procedure applies to all six ignition coils.*
6 If you're removing a coil or coils from the left valve cover of a 3.0L model, remove the left front engine compartment cover and remove the engine coolant reservoir (see Chapter 3). If you're removing a coil or coils on a 3.2L model, remove the front and rear engine covers and, if you're removing a coil or coils from the right valve cover, remove the fresh air inlet duct and the air intake duct (see Chapter 4).
7 Disconnect the electrical connectors from all components with harnesses that are in the way, then set the harnesses aside.
8 Remove the fasteners that secure the clips for the ignition coil harness, then disconnect all three electrical connectors from the

6.3a Ignition coil harness fasteners (2.0L model shown)

6.3b The ignition coil harness is rigid, so you have to disconnect all four electrical connectors to remove a coil. Depress the tabs to release the connectors

coils. You have to disconnect all three connectors in order to pull the harness back far enough so that the coil clears the connector.
9   To remove an ignition coil, grasp it firmly and pull it straight up.
10   Apply a little silicone dielectric compound to the inside of the spark plug boot before installing the coil.

7   Alternator - removal and installation

1   Disconnect the cable from the negative battery terminal (see Section 3).
2   Remove the engine cover.

Four-cylinder models

1.8L models only

Warning: *Wait until the engine is completely cool before performing this procedure.*
3   Unscrew the coolant reservoir cap.

4   Raise the vehicle and place it securely on jackstands.
5   Remove the engine under-covers (see Chapter 2A).
6   Remove the clip for the Engine Coolant Temperature (ECT) sensor electrical lead.
7   Put a drain pan under the ECT sensor, then unscrew the sensor and allow the coolant to drain.
8   Disconnect the upper radiator hose from the coolant pipe.
9   Remove the radiator fan control module mounting fastener and remove the module.

All four-cylinder models

Refer to illustration 7.11

10   Remove the drivebelt (see Chapter 1).
11   Disconnect the electrical connectors from the alternator **(see illustration)**.
12   Remove the two upper and two lower alternator mounting fasteners and remove the alternator, then reposition the alternator so

that you can access the electrical connectors on the backside of the alternator.

V6 models

3.0L V6 models

Refer to illustrations 7.20 and 7.21

13   Remove the front engine cover.
14   Remove the drivebelt (see Chapter 1).
15   Raise the vehicle and place it securely on jackstands.
16   Remove the engine under-covers.
17   Remove the cable ties that secure the starter cable harness guide and disengage the harness from the guide.
18   On models equipped with an automatic transmission, remove the fastener for the bracket that secures the automatic transmission fluid lines.
19   Unclip the air conditioning line from the bracket on the oil pan.
20   Disconnect the electrical connectors from the alternator **(see illustration)**.

7.11 Alternator electrical connectors and mounting bolts (2.0L model shown, 1.8L models similar)

7.20 Alternator electrical connectors (3.0L model shown, 3.2L models similar)

7.21 Alternator mounting fasteners (3.0L model shown; 3.2L models use four side bolts, like four-cylinder models)

8.4 Starter motor details (1.8L models):

1 Starter motor battery terminal
2 Starter solenoid electrical connector
3 Starter harness clamp and mounting bracket nut
4 Mounting bracket nut
5 Starter bracket mounting bolt

21 Remove the alternator mounting fasteners **(see illustration)** and remove the alternator.

3.2L V6 models
22 Remove the front engine cover.
23 Raise the vehicle and place it securely on jackstands.
24 Remove the engine under-covers.
25 Place the radiator support panel in the service position (see Chapter 11).
26 Remove the drivebelt (see Chapter 1).
27 Remove the two upper and two lower alternator mounting fasteners and reposition the alternator so that you can access the electrical connectors on the backside of the alternator.
28 Disconnect the electrical connectors from the alternator and remove the alternator.

All models
29 Installation is the reverse of removal. Be sure to tighten the alternator mounting fasteners securely.

30 Reconnect the cable to the negative terminal of the battery (see Section 3).
31 If you're working on a 1.8L four-cylinder model, refill the cooling system (see Chapter 1).
32 Check the charging voltage (see Section 2) to verify that the alternator is operating correctly.

---

8   Starter motor - removal and installation

---

1 Disconnect the cable from the negative terminal of the battery (see Section 3).
2 If you're working on a V6 model, loosen the right front wheel lug bolts.
3 Raise the vehicle and place it on jackstands. Remove the engine under-covers.

1.8L four-cylinder models
Refer to illustration 8.4
4 Disconnect the starter motor electrical connectors **(see illustration)**.

5 Remove the fastener that secures the harness clamp to the starter motor bracket.
6 Remove the starter bracket fastener and remove the bracket.
7 Remove the two starter motor mounting fasteners **(see illustrations 8.10 and 8.11)** and remove the starter from below.
8 Installation is the reverse of removal. Be sure to tighten the starter motor mounting fasteners securely.

2.0L four-cylinder models
Refer to illustrations 8.10 and 8.11
9 Remove the heat shield for the right driveaxle.
10 Disconnect the starter motor electrical connectors and remove the nut that secures the starter harness clamp to the starter **(see illustration)**.
11 Remove the starter motor mounting fasteners **(see illustration)**, pull out the starter and reposition it so that you can access the electrical connectors.

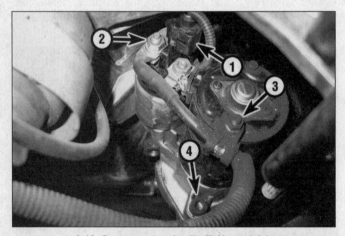

8.10 Starter motor details (2.0L models):

1 Starter solenoid electrical connector
2 Starter motor battery terminal
3 Starter harness clamp nut
4 Lower starter motor mounting bolt

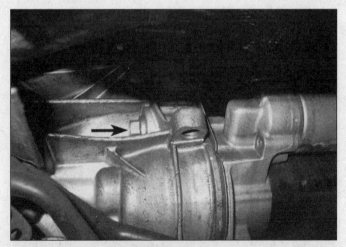

8.11 The upper bolt for the starter motor on 2.0L models is located on the bellhousing side

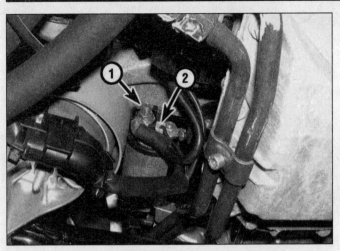

8.17 Starter motor details (3.0L model shown, 3.2L models similar)

1 *Starter motor battery terminal*
2 *Starter solenoid electrical connector*

8.19 Starter motor mounting fasteners (3.0L model shown; 3.2L models similar)

12 Remove the starter motor.
13 Installation is the reverse of removal. Be sure to tighten the starter motor mounting fasteners securely.

3.0L V6 models

Refer to illustrations 8.17 and 8.19

14 Remove the right front wheel.
15 Remove the alternator (see Section 7).
16 Remove the heat shield for the right driveaxle.
17 Disconnect the starter motor electrical connectors **(see illustration)**.
18 Remove the solenoid heat shield.

19 Remove the starter motor mounting fasteners **(see illustration)**.
20 Installation is the reverse of removal. Be sure to tighten the starter motor mounting fasteners securely.

3.2L V6 models

21 Remove the right front wheel.
22 Remove the engine under-covers.
23 Remove the heat shield for the right driveaxle.
24 On vehicles with an automatic transmission, disconnect the inner end of the right driveaxle from the axle flange (see Chapter 8).

25 Disconnect the starter motor electrical connectors.
26 Remove the starter motor mounting fasteners.
27 On vehicles with an automatic transmission, remove the starter through the opening at the rear of the wheel well.
28 On vehicles with a manual transmission, remove the starter through the opening between the transmission and the engine subframe.
29 Installation is the reverse of removal. Be sure to tighten the starter motor mounting fasteners securely.

Notes

Chapter 6
Emissions and engine control systems

Contents

	Section			Section
Accelerator Pedal Position (APP) sensor - replacement	4		Obtaining and clearing Diagnostic Trouble Codes (DTCs)	3
Camshaft Position (CMP) sensor - replacement	5		On Board Diagnosis (OBD) system	2
Catalytic converter - replacement	14		Oxygen sensors - replacement	11
Crankshaft Position (CKP) sensor - replacement	6		Positive Crankcase Ventilation (PCV) system -	
Engine Coolant Temperature (ECT) sensor - replacement	7		component replacement	16
Evaporative Emissions Control (EVAP) system -			Powertrain Control Module (PCM) - removal and installation	13
component replacement	15		Secondary Air Injection (AIR) system (1.8L and 3.0L models) -	
General information	1		component replacement	17
Knock sensor - replacement	8		Transmission speed sensors - replacement	12
Manifold Absolute Pressure/Intake Air Temperature (MAP/IAT)			Variable camshaft adjustment solenoid valve - replacement	18
sensor - replacement	9		Variable intake manifold - component replacement	19
Mass Air Flow/Intake Air Temperature (MAF/IAT)				
sensor - replacement	10			

Specifications

Torque specifications

	Ft-lbs	Nm
Knock sensor mounting fastener (all engines)	15	20
Oxygen sensors (all sensors, all models)	40	54

1   General information

To prevent pollution of the atmosphere from incompletely burned and evaporating gases, and to maintain good driveability and fuel economy, a number of emission control systems are incorporated. They include the:

Catalytic converter

A catalytic converter is an emission control device in the exhaust system that reduces certain pollutants in the exhaust gas stream. There are two types of converters: oxidation converters and reduction converters.

Oxidation converters contain a monolithic substrate (a ceramic honeycomb) coated with the semi-precious metals platinum and palla-dium. An oxidation catalyst reduces unburned hydrocarbons (HC) and carbon monoxide (CO) by adding oxygen to the exhaust stream as it passes through the substrate, which, in the presence of high temperature and the catalyst materials, converts the HC and CO to water vapor (H_2O) and carbon dioxide (CO_2).

Reduction converters contain a mono-lithic substrate coated with platinum and rho-dium. A reduction catalyst reduces oxides of nitrogen (NOx) by removing oxygen, which in the presence of high temperature and the catalyst material produces nitrogen (N) and carbon dioxide (CO_2).

Catalytic converters that combine both types of catalysts in one assembly are known as "three-way catalysts" or TWCs. A TWC can reduce all three pollutants.

Evaporative Emissions Control (EVAP) system

The Evaporative Emissions Control (EVAP) system prevents fuel system vapors (which contain unburned hydrocarbons) from escaping into the atmosphere. On warm days, vapors trapped inside the fuel tank expand until the pressure reaches a certain threshold. Then the fuel vapors are routed from the fuel tank through the fuel vapor vent valve and the fuel vapor control valve to the EVAP canister, where they're stored tempo-rarily until the next time the vehicle is oper-ated. When the conditions are right (engine warmed up, vehicle up to speed, moderate or heavy load on the engine, etc.) the PCM opens the canister purge valve, which allows fuel vapors to be drawn from the canister into the intake manifold. Once in the intake manifold, the fuel vapors mix with incoming air before being drawn through the intake ports into the combustion chambers where they're burned up with the rest of the air/fuel mixture. The EVAP system is complex and virtually impossible to troubleshoot without the right tools and training.

Exhaust Gas Recirculation (EGR) system

The EGR system reduces oxides of nitrogen by recirculating exhaust gases from the exhaust manifold, through the EGR valve and intake manifold, then back to the combustion chambers, where it mixes with the incoming air/fuel mixture before being consumed. These recirculated exhaust gases dilute the incoming air/fuel mixture, which cools the combustion chambers, thereby reducing NOx emissions.

The EGR system consists of the Powertrain Control Module (PCM), the EGR valve, the EGR valve position sensor and various other information sensors that the PCM uses to determine when to open the EGR valve. The degree to which the EGR valve is opened is referred to as "EGR valve lift." The PCM is programmed to produce the ideal EGR valve lift for varying operating conditions. The EGR valve position sensor, which is an integral part of the EGR valve, detects the amount of EGR valve lift

and sends this information to the PCM. The PCM then compares it with the appropriate EGR valve lift for the operating conditions. The PCM increases current flow to the EGR valve to increase valve lift and reduces the current to reduce the amount of lift. If EGR flow is inappropriate to the operating conditions (idle, cold engine, etc.) the PCM simply cuts the current to the EGR valve and the valve closes.

Secondary Air Injection (AIR) system

Some models are equipped with a secondary air injection (AIR) system. The secondary air injection system is used to reduce tailpipe emissions on initial engine start-up. The system uses an electric motor/pump assembly, relay, vacuum valve/solenoid, air shut-off valve, check valves and tubing to inject fresh air directly into the exhaust manifolds. The fresh air (oxygen) reacts with the exhaust gas in the catalytic converter to reduce HC and CO levels. The air pump and solenoid are controlled by the PCM through the AIR relay. During initial start-up, the PCM energizes the AIR relay, the relay supplies battery voltage to the air pump and the vacuum valve/solenoid, engine vacuum is applied to the air shut-off valve which opens and allows air to flow through the tubing into the exhaust manifolds. The PCM will operate the air pump until closed loop operation is

reached (approximately four minutes). During normal operation, the check valves prevent exhaust backflow into the system.

Powertrain Control Module (PCM)

The Powertrain Control Module (PCM) is the brain of the engine management system. It also controls a wide variety of other vehicle systems. In order to program the new PCM, the dealer needs the vehicle as well as the new PCM. If you're planning to replace the PCM with a new one, there is no point in trying to do so at home because you won't be able to program it yourself.

Positive Crankcase Ventilation (PCV) system

The Positive Crankcase Ventilation (PCV) system reduces hydrocarbon emissions by scavenging crankcase vapors, which are rich in unburned hydrocarbons. A PCV valve or orifice regulates the flow of gases into the intake manifold in proportion to the amount of intake vacuum available.

The PCV system generally consists of the fresh air inlet hose, the PCV valve or orifice and the crankcase ventilation hose (or PCV hose). The fresh air inlet hose connects the air intake duct to a pipe on the valve cover. The crankcase ventilation hose (or PCV hose) connects the PCV valve or orifice in the valve cover to the intake manifold.

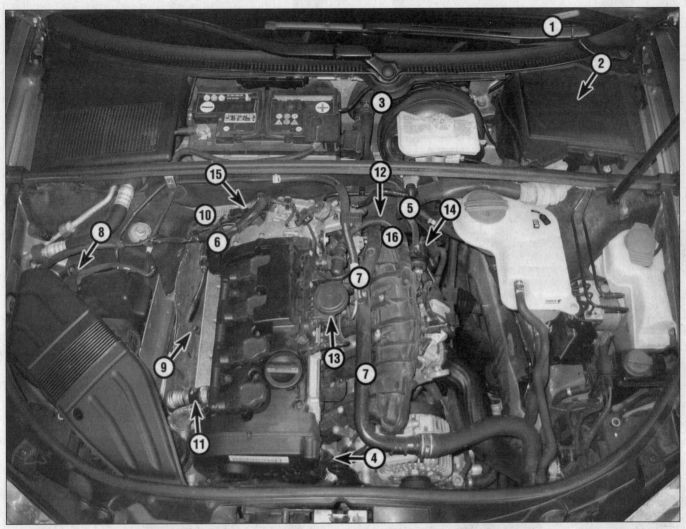

Typical information sensor and output actuator locations (2.0L four-cylinder model shown)

1   Data Link Connector (located inside vehicle, under left end of dash)
2   Powertrain Control Module (PCM)
3   Accelerator Pedal Position (APP) sensor (located at the top of the accelerator pedal assembly)
4   Camshaft Position (CMP) sensor
5   Crankshaft Position (CKP) sensor (located on the left side of the block at the transmission bellhousing)

6   Engine Coolant Temperature (ECT) sensor (located at the right rear corner of the cylinder head)
7   Knock sensors (located underneath the intake manifold, on left side of the engine block)
8   Mass Air Flow/Intake Air Temperature (MAF/IAT) sensor
9   Upstream oxygen sensor
10 Downstream oxygen sensor (at back end of catalytic converter)

11 PCV fresh air inlet hose and pipe
12 Positive Crankcase Ventilation (PCV) hose
13 Crankcase pressure regulator valve for PCV system
14 EVAP canister purge solenoid valve
15 Variable camshaft adjustment solenoid
16 Intake flap motor for variable intake manifold (located under back end of intake manifold)

Information Sensors

Accelerator Pedal Position (APP) sensor - as you press the accelerator pedal, the APP sensor alters its voltage signal to the PCM in proportion to the angle of the pedal, and the PCM commands a motor inside the throttle body to open or close the throttle plate accordingly

Camshaft Position (CMP) sensor - produces a signal that the PCM uses to identify the number 1 cylinder and to time the firing sequence of the fuel injectors

Crankshaft Position (CKP) sensor - produces a signal that the PCM uses to calculate engine speed and crankshaft position, which enables it to synchronize ignition timing with fuel injector timing, and to detect misfires

Engine Coolant Temperature (ECT) sensor - a thermistor (temperature-sensitive variable resistor) that sends a voltage signal to the PCM, which uses this data to determine the temperature of the engine coolant

Fuel tank pressure sensor - measures the fuel tank pressure and controls fuel tank pressure by signaling the EVAP system to purge the fuel tank vapors when the pressure becomes excessive

Intake Air Temperature (IAT) sensor - monitors the temperature of the air entering the engine and sends a signal to the PCM to determine injector pulse-width (the duration of each injector's on-time) and to adjust spark timing (to prevent spark knock)

Knock sensor - a piezoelectric crystal that oscillates in proportion to engine vibration which produces a voltage output that is monitored by the PCM. This retards the ignition timing when the oscillation exceeds a certain threshold

Manifold Absolute Pressure (MAP) sensor - monitors the pressure or vacuum inside the intake manifold. The PCM uses this data to determine engine load so that it can alter the ignition advance and fuel enrichment

Mass Air Flow (MAF) sensor - measures the amount of intake air drawn into the engine. It uses a hot-wire sensing element to measure the amount of air entering the engine

Oxygen sensors - generates a small variable voltage signal in proportion to the difference between the oxygen content in the exhaust stream and the oxygen content in the ambient air. The PCM uses this information to maintain the proper air/fuel ratio. A second oxygen sensor monitors the efficiency of the catalytic converter

Throttle Position (TP) sensor - a potentiometer that generates a voltage signal that varies in relation to the opening angle of the throttle plate inside the throttle body. Works with the PCM and other sensors to calculate injector pulse width (the duration of each injector's on-time)

Photos courtesy of Wells Manufacturing, except APP and MAF sensors.

2.4a Simple code readers are an economical way to extract trouble codes when the CHECK ENGINE light comes on

2.4b Hand-held scan tools like these can extract computer codes and also perform diagnostics

2   On Board Diagnosis (OBD) system

General description

1   All models are equipped with the second generation OBD-II system. This system consists of an on-board computer known as the Powertrain Control Module (PCM), and information sensors, which monitor various functions of the engine and send data to the PCM. This system incorporates a series of diagnostic monitors that detect and identify fuel injection and emissions control system faults and store the information in the computer memory. This system also tests sensors and output actuators, diagnoses drive cycles, freezes data and clears codes.

2   The PCM is the brain of the electronically controlled fuel and emissions system. It receives data from a number of sensors and other electronic components (switches, relays, etc.). Based on the information it receives, the PCM generates output signals to control various relays, solenoids (fuel injectors) and other actuators. The PCM is specifically calibrated to optimize the emissions, fuel economy and driveability of the vehicle.

3   It isn't a good idea to attempt diagnosis or replacement of the PCM or emission control components at home while the vehicle is under warranty. Because of a federally-mandated warranty which covers the emissions system components and because any owner-induced damage to the PCM, the sensors and/or the control devices may void this warranty, take the vehicle to a dealer service department if the PCM or a system component malfunctions.

Scan tool information

Refer to illustrations 2.4a and 2.4b

4   Because extracting the Diagnostic Trouble Codes (DTCs) from an engine management system is now the first step in troubleshooting many computer-controlled systems and components, a code reader, at the very

least, will be required **(see illustration)**. More powerful scan tools can also perform many of the diagnostics once associated with expensive factory scan tools **(see illustration)**. If you're planning to obtain a generic scan tool for your vehicle, make sure that it's compatible with OBD-II systems. If you don't plan to purchase a code reader or scan tool and don't have access to one, you can have the codes extracted by a dealer service department or an independent repair shop. **Note:** *Some auto parts stores even provide this service.*

3   Obtaining and clearing Diagnostic Trouble Codes (DTCs)

All models covered by this manual are equipped with on-board diagnostics. When the PCM recognizes a malfunction in a monitored emission or engine control system, component or circuit, it turns on the Malfunction Indicator Light (MIL) on the dash. The PCM will continue to display the MIL until the problem is fixed and the Diagnostic Trouble Code (DTC) is cleared from the PCM's memory. You'll need a scan tool to access any DTCs stored in the PCM.

Before outputting any DTCs stored in the PCM, thoroughly inspect ALL electrical connectors and hoses. Make sure that all electrical connections are tight, clean and free of corrosion. And make sure that all hoses are correctly connected, fit tightly and are in good condition (no cracks or tears).

Accessing the DTCs

Refer to illustration 3.1

1   The Diagnostic Trouble Codes (DTCs) can only be accessed with a code reader or scan tool. Professional scan tools are expensive, but relatively inexpensive generic code readers or scan tools **(see illustrations 2.4a and 2.4b)** are available at most auto parts stores. Simply plug the connector of the scan tool into the diagnostic connector **(see illustration)**. Then follow the instructions included

with the scan tool to extract the DTCs.

2   Once you have outputted all of the stored DTCs, look them up on the accompanying DTC chart.

3   After troubleshooting the source of each DTC, make any necessary repairs or replace the defective component(s).

Clearing the DTCs

4   Clear the DTCs with the code reader or scan tool in accordance with the instructions provided by the tool's manufacturer.

Diagnostic Trouble Codes

5   The accompanying tables are a list of the Diagnostic Trouble Codes (DTCs) that can be accessed by a do-it-yourselfer working at home (there are many, many more DTCs available to professional mechanics with proprietary scan tools and software, but those codes cannot be accessed by a generic scan tool). If, after you have checked and repaired the connectors, wire harness and vacuum hoses (if applicable) for an emission-related system, component or circuit, the problem persists, have the vehicle checked by a dealer service department or other qualified repair shop.

3.1 The Data Link Connector (DLC) is located under the lower left end of the instrument panel

Diagnostic trouble codes

Code	Possible cause
P0010	Intake camshaft position actuator circuit open (bank 1)
P0011	"A" Camshaft position - timing over-advanced (bank 1)
P0012	"A" Camshaft position - timing over-retarded (bank 1)
P0013	"B" Camshaft position - actuator circuit malfunction (bank 1)
P0020	Intake camshaft position actuator circuit open (bank 2)
P0021	Intake camshaft position-timing over-advanced (bank 2)
P0022	Intake camshaft position-timing over-retarded (bank 2)
P0023	"B" Camshaft position - actuator circuit (bank 2)
P0024	"B" Camshaft position - timing over-advanced or system performance problem (bank 2)
P0025	"B" Camshaft position - timing over-retarded (bank 2)
P0030	HO2S heater control circuit (bank 1, sensor 1)
P0031	HO2S heater control circuit low (bank 1, sensor 1)
P0032	HO2S heater control circuit high (bank 1, sensor 1)
P0036	HO2S heater control circuit (bank 1 sensor 2)
P0037	HO2S heater control circuit low (bank 1, sensor 2)
P0038	HO2S heater control circuit high (bank 1, sensor 2)
P0040	Upstream oxygen sensors swapped from bank to bank (HO2S - bank 1, sensor 1/bank 2, sensor 1)
P0041	Downstream oxygen sensors swapped from bank to bank (HO2S - bank 1, sensor 2/bank 2, sensor 2)
P0050	HO2S heater control circuit (bank 2, sensor 1)
P0051	HO2S heater control circuit low (bank 2, sensor 1)
P0052	HO2S heater control circuit high (bank 2, sensor 1)
P0056	HO2S heater control circuit malfunction (bank 2, sensor 2)
P0057	HO2S heater control circuit low (bank 2, sensor 2)
P0058	HO2S heater control circuit high (bank 2, sensor 2)
P0101	Mass air flow or volume air flow circuit, range or performance problem
P0102	Mass air flow or volume air flow circuit, low input
P0103	Mass air flow or volume air flow circuit, high input
P0106	Manifold absolute pressure or barometric pressure circuit, range or performance problem

Code	Possible cause
P0111	Intake air temperature circuit, range or performance problem
P0112	Intake air temperature circuit, low input
P0113	Intake air temperature circuit, high input
P0116	Engine coolant temperature circuit range/performance problem
P0117	Engine coolant temperature circuit, low input
P0118	Engine coolant temperature circuit, high input
P0121	Throttle position or pedal position sensor/switch circuit, range or performance problem
P0122	Throttle position or pedal position sensor/switch circuit, low input
P0123	Throttle position or pedal position sensor/switch circuit, high input
P0130	O2 sensor circuit malfunction (bank 1, sensor 1)
P0133	O2 sensor circuit, slow response (bank 1, sensor 1)
P0135	O2 sensor heater circuit malfunction (bank 1, sensor 1)
P0136	O2 sensor circuit malfunction (bank 1, sensor 2)
P0137	O2 sensor circuit, low voltage (bank 1, sensor 2)
P0138	O2 sensor circuit, high voltage (bank 1, sensor 2)
P0139	O2 sensor circuit, slow response (bank 1, sensor 2)
P0140	O2 sensor circuit - no activity detected (bank 1, sensor 2)
P0141	O2 sensor heater circuit malfunction (bank 1, sensor 2)
P0150	O2 sensor circuit malfunction (bank 2, sensor 1)
P0153	O2 sensor circuit, slow response (bank 2, sensor 1)
P0155	O2 sensor heater circuit malfunction (bank 2, sensor 1)
P0156	O2 sensor circuit malfunction (bank 2, sensor 2)
P0157	O2 sensor circuit, low voltage (bank 2, sensor 2)
P0158	O2 sensor circuit, high voltage (bank 2, sensor 2)
P0159	O2 sensor circuit, slow response (bank 2, sensor 2)
P0160	O2 sensor circuit - no activity detected (bank 2, sensor 2)
P0161	O2 sensor heater circuit malfunction (bank 2, sensor 2)
P0171	System too lean (bank 1)
P0172	System too rich (bank 1)

Diagnostic trouble codes (continued)

Code	Possible cause
P0174	System too lean (bank 2)
P0175	System too rich (bank 2)
P0201	Injector circuit malfunction - cylinder no. 1
P0202	Injector circuit malfunction - cylinder no. 2
P0203	Injector circuit malfunction - cylinder no. 3
P0204	Injector circuit malfunction - cylinder no. 4
P0205	Injector circuit malfunction - cylinder no. 5
P0206	Injector circuit malfunction - cylinder no. 6
P0207	Injector circuit malfunction - cylinder no. 7
P0208	Injector circuit malfunction - cylinder no. 8
P0221	Throttle position or pedal position sensor/switch B, range or performance problem
P0222	Throttle position or pedal position sensor/switch B circuit, low input
P0223	Throttle position or pedal position sensor/switch B circuit, high input
P0230	Fuel pump primary circuit malfunction
P0236	Turbocharger boost sensor A circuit, range or performance problem
P0237	Turbocharger boost sensor A circuit, low
P0238	Turbocharger boost sensor A circuit, high
P0243	Turbocharger wastegate solenoid A malfunction
P0245	Turbocharger wastegate solenoid A, low
P0246	Turbocharger wastegate solenoid A, high
P0261	Cylinder no. 1 injector circuit, low
P0262	Cylinder no. 1 injector circuit, high
P0264	Cylinder no. 2 injector circuit, low
P0265	Cylinder no. 2 injector circuit, high
P0267	Cylinder no. 3 injector circuit, low
P0268	Cylinder no. 3 injector circuit, high
P0270	Cylinder no. 4 injector circuit, low
P0271	Cylinder no. 4 injector circuit, high

Code	Possible cause
P0273	Cylinder no. 5 injector circuit, low
P0274	Cylinder no. 5 injector circuit, high
P0276	Cylinder no. 6 injector circuit, low
P0277	Cylinder no. 6 injector circuit, high
P0279	Cylinder no. 7 injector circuit, low
P0280	Cylinder no. 7 injector circuit, high
P0282	Cylinder no. 8 injector circuit, low
P0283	Cylinder no. 8 injector circuit, high
P0300	Random/multiple cylinder misfire detected
P0301	Cylinder no. 1 misfire detected
P0302	Cylinder no. 2 misfire detected
P0303	Cylinder no. 3 misfire detected
P0304	Cylinder no. 4 misfire detected
P0305	Cylinder no. 5 misfire detected
P0306	Cylinder no. 6 misfire detected
P0307	Cylinder no. 7 misfire detected
P0308	Cylinder no. 8 misfire detected
P0321	Crankshaft position (CKP) sensor/engine speed (RPM) sensor - range or performance problem
P0322	Crankshaft position (CKP) sensor/engine speed (RPM) sensor - no signal
P0324	Knock control system error
P0327	Knock sensor no. 1 circuit, low input (bank 1 or single sensor)
P0328	Knock sensor no. 1 circuit, high input (bank 1 or single sensor)
P0332	Knock sensor no. 2 circuit, low input (bank 2)
P0333	Knock sensor no. 2 circuit, high input (bank 2)
P0340	Camshaft position sensor "A" - circuit malfunction (bank 1)
P0341	Camshaft position sensor "A" - range or performance problem (bank 1)
P0342	Camshaft position sensor "A" - low input (bank 1)
P0343	Camshaft position sensor "A" - high input (bank 1)
P0345	Camshaft position sensor "A" - circuit malfunction (bank 2)

Diagnostic trouble codes (continued)

Code	Possible cause
P0346	Camshaft position sensor "A" - range/performance problem (bank 2)
P0347	Camshaft position sensor "A" - low input (bank 2)
P0348	Camshaft position sensor "A" - range/performance problem (bank 2)
P0351	Ignition coil A primary or secondary circuit malfunction
P0352	Ignition coil B primary or secondary circuit malfunction
P0353	Ignition coil C primary or secondary circuit malfunction
P0354	Ignition coil D primary or secondary circuit malfunction
P0355	Ignition coil E primary or secondary circuit malfunction
P0356	Ignition coil F primary or secondary circuit malfunction
P0357	Ignition coil G primary or secondary circuit malfunction
P0358	Ignition coil H primary or secondary circuit malfunction
P0365	Camshaft position sensor "B" - circuit malfunction (bank 1)
P0366	Camshaft position sensor "B" - range/performance problem (bank 1)
P0367	Camshaft position sensor "B" - low input (bank 1)
P0368	Camshaft position sensor "B" circuit high input (bank 1)
P0390	Camshaft position sensor "B" - circuit malfunction
P0391	Camshaft position sensor "B" - range/performance problem (bank 2)
P0392	Camshaft position sensor "B" - low input (bank 2)
P0393	Camshaft position sensor "B" - high input (bank 2)
P0411	Secondary air injection system, incorrect flow detected
P0412	Secondary air injection system switching valve A - circuit malfunction
P0413	Secondary air injection system switching valve A - open circuit
P0414	Secondary air injection system switching valve A - shorted circuit
P0418	Secondary air injection system, pump relay A - circuit malfunction
P0420	Catalyst system efficiency below threshold (bank 1)
P0421	Warm-up catalyst efficiency below threshold (bank 1)
P0431	Warm-up catalyst efficiency below threshold (bank 2)
P0440	Evaporative emission control system malfunction

Code	Possible cause
P0441	Evaporative emission control system, incorrect purge flow
P0442	Evaporative emission control system, small leak detected
P0443	Evaporative emission control system, purge control valve circuit malfunction
P0444	Evaporative emission control system, open purge control valve circuit
P0445	Evaporative emission control system, short in purge control valve circuit
P0455	Evaporative emission (EVAP) control system leak detected (no purge flow or large leak)
P0456	Evaporative emission (EVAP) control system leak detected (very small leak)
P0491	Secondary air injection system (bank 1)
P0492	Secondary air injection system (bank 2)
P0501	Vehicle speed sensor, range or performance problem
P0506	Idle control system, rpm lower than expected
P0507	Idle control system, rpm higher than expected
P0560	System voltage malfunction
P0562	System voltage low
P0563	System voltage high
P0571	Cruise control/brake switch A, circuit malfunction
P0600	Serial communication link malfunction
P0601	Internal control module, memory check sum error
P0604	Internal control module, random access memory (RAM) error
P0605	Internal control module, read only memory (ROM) error
P0606	PCM processor fault
P0638	Throttle actuator control range/performance problem (bank 1)
P0685	ECM power relay, control - circuit open
P0686	ECM power relay control - circuit low
P0687	Engine, control relay - short to ground
P0688	Engine, control relay - short to positive
P0704	Clutch switch input circuit malfunction

5.2 The CMP sensor is located on the front left corner of the cylinder head (2.0L four-cylinder engine shown, 1.8L engine similar)

6.3 The CKP sensor is located on the left side of the engine block, near the flywheel (2.0L four-cylinder engine shown; 1.8L models similar)

1   Electrical connector
2   CKP sensor (mounting bolt, which faces forward, not visible)

4   Accelerator Pedal Position (APP) sensor - replacement

The APP sensor is located at the top of (and is an integral component of) the accelerator pedal. There is no reason to remove the APP sensor except to replace it. But if the APP sensor is replaced, the new unit must be programmed with a factory scan tool. If you get a Diagnostic Trouble Code indicating a problem with the APP sensor, have the sensor replaced by a dealer service department or other qualified repair shop equipped with the necessary scan tool.

5   Camshaft Position (CMP) sensor - replacement

Four-cylinder models

Refer to illustration 5.2

1   Disconnect the cable from the negative battery terminal (see Chapter 5).
2   Locate the CMP sensor **(see illustration)**.
3   Remove the upper timing belt cover (see Chapter 2A).
4   Disconnect the CMP sensor electrical connector.
5   Remove the CMP sensor mounting fasteners and remove the CMP sensor.
6   Installation is the reverse of removal.

V6 models

3.0L models

Note: *There are four CMP sensors - one for each intake camshaft and one for each exhaust camshaft. The CMP sensors are located on the back end of the cylinder heads.*
7   Disconnect the cable from the negative battery terminal (see Chapter 5).

8   Remove the engine cover.
9   If you're replacing either CMP sensor on the left (driver's side) cylinder head, detach the coolant reservoir (see Chapter 3) and set it aside. Don't disconnect the coolant hoses.
10   Disconnect the CMP sensor electrical connector.
11   Remove the CMP sensor mounting fasteners and remove the sensor.
12   Installation is the reverse of removal.

3.2L models

Note: *There are four CMP sensors - one for each intake camshaft and one for each exhaust camshaft. The CMP sensors are located on the cylinder heads, adjacent to the upper and lower edges of the valve covers. The CMP sensors for the intake camshafts are on the upper middle part of the cylinder heads; the CMP sensors for the exhaust cams are located on the middle lower part of the heads.*
13   Disconnect the cable from the negative battery terminal (see Chapter 5).
14   Remove the engine cover.
15   Disconnect the CMP sensor electrical connector.
16   Remove the CMP sensor mounting fastener and remove the sensor.
17   Installation is the reverse of removal.

6   Crankshaft Position (CKP) sensor - replacement

Four-cylinder models

Refer to illustration 6.3

Note: *The CKP sensor is extremely difficult to access because it's directly behind the oil filter housing.*
1   Drain the engine oil (see Chapter 1).
2   Remove the oil filter housing.

3   Disconnect the electrical connector from the CKP sensor **(see illustration)**.
4   Remove the CKP sensor mounting fastener and remove the CKP sensor.
5   Installation is the reverse of removal.

V6 models

Refer to illustration 6.7

6   Raise the front of the vehicle and place it securely on jackstands.
7   Locate the CKP sensor on the transmission bellhousing, near the ring gear **(see illustration)**.
8   Trace the CKP sensor electrical lead to the sensor electrical connector and disconnect the connector.
9   Remove the CKP sensor mounting fastener and remove the sensor.
10   Installation is the reverse of removal.

6.7 The CKP sensor is located on the left front side of the transmission bellhousing (3.0L V6 shown; 3.2L V6 similar)

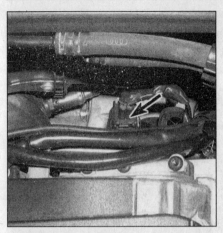

7.2a On 1.8L four-cylinder engines, the ECT sensor is located at the back end of the cylinder head

7.2b On 2.0L four-cylinder engines, the ECT sensor is located at the right rear corner of the cylinder head

7 Engine Coolant Temperature (ECT) sensor - replacement

Warning: *Wait until the engine has cooled completely before beginning this procedure.*

Four-cylinder models

Refer to illustrations 7.2a and 7.2b

1   Partially drain the cooling system (see Chapter 1).
2   Disconnect the electrical connector from the ECT sensor **(see illustrations)**.
3   Pull out the retaining clip and remove the sensor. Remove and discard the sensor O-ring.
4   Before installing the ECT sensor, install a new O-ring and apply some engine coolant to the O-ring.
5   Installation is otherwise the reverse of removal.
6   Refill the cooling system (see Chapter 1).

V6 models

Refer to illustration 7.10

Note: *The ECT sensor is located on the crossover pipe that connects the two cylinder heads. On 3.0L models, the coolant crossover pipe is located behind the engine; on 3.2L models, the coolant crossover pipe is located in front of the engine.*

7   Remove the engine cover (see Chapter 2B).
8   Partially drain the cooling system (see Chapter 1).
9   If you're replacing the ECT sensor on a 3.0L V6 model, remove the air intake duct (see *Air filter housing - removal and installation* in Chapter 4).
10   Disconnect the electrical connector from the ECT sensor **(see illustration)**.
11   Pull out the retaining clip and remove the sensor. Remove and discard the sensor O-ring.

12   Before installing the ECT sensor, install a new O-ring and apply some engine coolant to the O-ring.
13   Installation is otherwise the reverse of removal.
14   Refill the cooling system (see Chapter 1).

8 Knock sensor - replacement

Warning: *Don't attempt to remove a knock sensor when the engine is hot. If the engine has just been operated, allow sufficient time for it to cool down.*
1   Disconnect the cable from the negative battery terminal (see Chapter 5).

Four-cylinder models

Refer to illustration 8.3

Note: *This procedure applies to either knock sensor.*
2   Remove the intake manifold (on 1.8L models, see Chapter 2A; on 2.0L models, see Chapter 4),
3   Disconnect the knock sensor electrical connector **(see illustration)**.
4   Unscrew the knock sensor retaining fastener and remove the sensor.
5   Installation is the reverse of removal. Be sure to tighten the knock sensor fastener to the torque listed in this Chapter's Specifications. **Caution:** *Incorrectly tightening a knock sensor fastener can affect the performance of the sensor.*

V6 models

Refer to illustration 8.7

6   On 3.0L models, remove the intake manifold; on 3.2L models, remove the upper intake manifold (see Chapter 2B).

7.10 On 3.0L V6 engines, the ECT sensor is located on the coolant crossover pipe that connects the cylinder heads at the back of the engine

8.3 On four-cylinder engines, the knock sensors are located on the left side of the block, below the intake manifold (2.0L engine shown, 1.8L models similar)

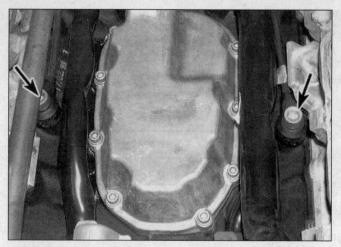

8.7 The two knock sensors are located in the valley between the cylinder heads (typical V6)

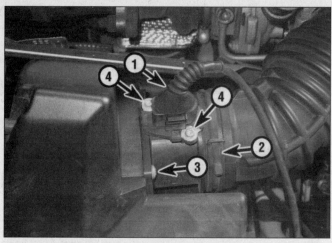

10.2 Typical MAF/IAT sensor details (2.0L model shown, other models similar):

1   MAF/IAT sensor electrical connector
2   Air intake duct hose clamp
3   MAF/IAT sensor tube mounting fasteners (other fastener not visible)
4   MAF/IAT sensor mounting fasteners

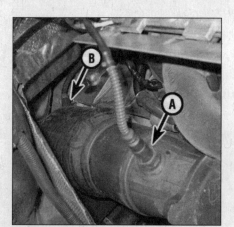

11.2 The upstream oxygen sensor (A) is located at the upper end of the catalytic converter. The downstream oxygen sensor (B) is located at the other end of the converter (2.0L four-cylinder model shown, other models similar)

7   Locate the knock sensors (see illustration), then trace the electrical lead for each sensor back to the sensor electrical connector and disconnect it.
8   Remove the knock sensor mounting fastener and remove the sensor.
9   When installing a knock sensor, be sure to tighten the sensor mounting fastener to the torque listed in this Chapter's Specifications. Caution: *Incorrectly tightening a knock sensor fastener can affect the performance of the knock sensor.*
10   Installation is otherwise the reverse of removal.

9   Manifold Absolute Pressure/ Intake Air Temperature (MAP/IAT) sensor - replacement

Note: *The MAP/IAT sensor, which is used only on 3.2L V6 models, is located at the back*

end of the intake manifold.
1   Remove the rear engine cover.
2   Disconnect the electrical connector from the MAP/IAT sensor.
3   Remove the MAP/IAT sensor mounting fastener and remove the sensor.
4   Remove and discard the old MAP/IAT sensor O-ring.
5   Installation is the reverse of removal. Be sure to use a new O-ring.

10   Mass Air Flow/Intake Air Temperature (MAF/IAT) sensor - replacement

Refer to illustration 10.2
Note: *The MAF/IAT sensor is used on all models except 3.2L V6 models.*
1   Remove the ambient (outside) air inlet duct (see *Air filter housing - removal and installation* in Chapter 4).
2   Loosen the hose clamp and disconnect the air intake duct from the MAF/IAT sensor (see illustration).
3   Disconnect the electrical connector from the MAF/IAT sensor.
4   Remove the MAF/IAT sensor mounting fasteners and remove the sensor from the air filter housing.
5   Installation is the reverse of removal.

11   Oxygen sensors - replacement

Note: *Because the oxygen sensors are installed in the catalytic converter(s), which*

contracts when cool, they can be difficult to loosen when the engine is cold. Rather than risk damage to an oxygen sensor or its mounting threads, start and run the engine for a minute or two, then shut it off. Be careful not to burn yourself during the following procedure.
1   Be particularly careful when servicing an oxygen sensor:

a) *Oxygen sensors have a permanently attached pigtail and an electrical connector that cannot be removed. Damaging or removing the pigtail or electrical connector will render the sensor useless.*
b) *Keep grease, dirt and other contaminants away from the electrical connector and the louvered end of the sensor.*
c) *Do not use cleaning solvents of any kind on an oxygen sensor.*
d) *Oxygen sensors are extremely delicate. Do not drop a sensor, throw it around or handle it roughly.*
e) *Make sure that the silicone boot on the sensor is installed in the correct position. Otherwise, the boot might melt and it might prevent the sensor from operating correctly.*

Upstream oxygen sensors
Refer to illustrations 11.2 and 11.3
2   Locate the upstream oxygen sensor (see illustration), then trace the wiring harness to its electrical connector and disconnect the connector. Disengage the sensor harness from any harness clips.
3   Unscrew the upstream oxygen sensor

11.3 An oxygen sensor socket will allow you to work in tight quarters where a wrench would be difficult to use (and might round-off the corners of the sensor's hex)

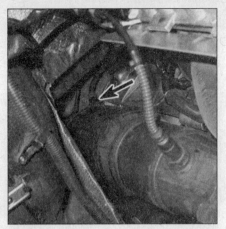

11.7 The downstream oxygen sensor is located at the exhaust end of the catalyst (2.0L model shown, other models similar)

14.4 Details of the forward end of the catalytic converter (2.0L model shown, other models similar):

1   *Upstream oxygen sensor*
2   *Catalytic converter-to-turbocharger nuts (one nut not visible)*

(see illustration).
4   If you're going to install the old sensor, apply anti-seize compound to the threads of the sensor to facilitate future removal. If you're going to install a new oxygen sensor, it's not necessary to apply anti-seize compound to the threads; the threads on new sensors already have anti-seize compound on them.
5   Installation is the reverse of removal. Be sure to tighten the oxygen sensor to the torque listed in this Chapter's Specifications.

Downstream oxygen sensors

Refer to illustration 11.7
6   Raise the vehicle and support it securely on jackstands.
7   Locate the downstream oxygen sensor **(see illustration)**, then trace the lead up to the electrical connector and disconnect the connector (refer to Step 2 regarding locations of the sensor electrical connectors).
8   Unscrew the downstream oxygen sensor.
9   If you're going to install the old sensor, apply anti-seize compound to the threads of the sensor to facilitate future removal. If you're going to install a new oxygen sensor, it's not necessary to apply anti-seize compound to the threads. The threads on new sensors already have anti-seize compound on them.
10   Installation is the reverse of removal. Be sure to tighten the oxygen sensor to the torque listed in this Chapter's Specifications.

12 Transmission speed sensors - replacement

Manual transmissions
1   Loosen the left front wheel lug nuts, raise the vehicle and place it securely on jackstands. Remove the left front wheel.
2   Remove the left wheel well splash shield (see Chapter 11).

3   On some models, there might be a small splash shield fastened to the differential housing. If so, remove the splash shield fasteners and remove the splash shield.
4   Disconnect the electrical connector from the speed sensor.
5   Remove the speed sensor retaining fastener and remove the speed sensor.
6   Remove and discard the speed sensor O-ring.
7   Installation is the reverse of removal. Be sure to use a new sensor O-ring.

Automatic transmissions
8   On automatic transmissions, speed sensors are integral components of the valve body/Transmission Control Module (TCM) assembly, which is located inside the transmission. Replacing one of these sensors is beyond the scope of the home mechanic.

13 Powertrain Control Module (PCM) - removal and installation

Note: *The Powertrain Control Module (PCM), which is housed within a waterproof box in the left end of the cowl area, cannot be replaced at home because the new unit must be reprogrammed with a proprietary scan tool. The PCM in many models is also housed inside a special metal anti-theft box and is extremely difficult to remove. This procedure is only intended for removing the PCM and electronics box for access to the clutch master cylinder.*
1   Disconnect the cable from the negative battery terminal (see Chapter 5).
2   Remove the cowl cover (see Chapter 11).
3   Remove the cover from the electronics box.
4   Pry off the retaining strap from the PCM, then move the PCM aside. **Note:** *Some models are equipped with an anti-theft housing in*

which the PCM is mounted. The housing is secured with shear-head bolts that must be heated with a heat gun, then unscrewed with locking pliers. Heat should only be applied to the bolts that do not thread into the PCM.
5   Unplug the electrical connectors near the firewall.
6   Pull back the release tabs and detach the relay carrier from the electronics box, then dislodge the grommet and pull the wiring harness through the opening in the electronics box.
7   Unscrew the fasteners and remove the electronics box from the cowl area.
8   Installation is the reverse of the removal procedure.

14 Catalytic converter - replacement

Four-cylinder models
Refer to illustrations 14.4 and 14.6
1   On 1.8L models, remove the engine cover. On all models, you can give yourself more room to work if you remove the air filter housing (see Chapter 4).
2   Disconnect the electrical connectors for the upstream and downstream oxygen sensors. To access the sensor connectors on some models, you might have to detach the coolant expansion tank (see Chapter 3). The tank has an electrical connector for the coolant level sensor underneath. Disconnect the connector, but don't disconnect the coolant hoses from the tank; just set the tank aside.
3   Remove the upstream and downstream oxygen sensors from the catalytic converter (see Section 11).
4   Remove the fasteners that secure the front exhaust pipe to the catalytic converter **(see illustration).**

**14.6 Front exhaust pipe support bracket
bolts (2.0L model shown,
1.8L models similar)**

5   Raise the vehicle and place it securely on jackstands.

6   Remove the front exhaust pipe support bracket bolts **(see illustration)** and remove the support bracket. This step isn't absolutely necessary, but the three lower fasteners that secure the flange at the lower end of the converter to the front exhaust pipe flange are extremely difficult to access with the bracket in place, and the bracket is easy to remove.

7   Remove the three fasteners that secure the lower catalytic converter flange to the front exhaust pipe.

8   Remove the catalytic converter.

9   Remove and discard the old flange gaskets.

10   Installation is the reverse of removal. Be sure to use new gaskets and self-locking nuts and tighten all fasteners securely.

V6 models

3.0L models

11   Remove the rear engine cover.

Left-side catalytic converter

12   Remove the small cover from the front left corner of the engine compartment.

13   Disconnect the electrical connector for the engine coolant level sensor, then detach the coolant expansion tank - don't disconnect any of the coolant hoses - and set it aside. You have to move the coolant expansion tank out of the way to access the oxygen sensor electrical connectors. On some models, you will also need to remove the power brake booster vacuum hose.

14   If the oxygen sensor electrical connectors on the firewall are protected by a heat shield, remove the shield. Disconnect the oxygen sensor electrical connectors, then push the wiring harnesses and connectors down toward the oxygen sensors.

Right-side catalytic converter

15   Remove the small cover from the right front corner of the engine compartment.

16   Remove the air filter housing and the air intake duct (see *Air filter housing - removal and installation* in Chapter 4).

17   Disconnect the oxygen sensor electrical connectors, then push the wiring harnesses and connectors down toward the oxygen sensors.

Either catalytic converter

18   Remove the upper nuts that secure the upper end of the converter/front exhaust pipe to the exhaust manifold. It's difficult to access the lower nuts from above; you'll have to remove the lower nuts from below, after you raise the vehicle.

19   Loosen the left or right front wheel lug nuts, raise the front of the vehicle and place it securely on jackstands. Remove the left or right front wheel.

20   Remove the engine compartment under-covers.

21   Remove the upstream and downstream oxygen sensors from the catalytic converter (see Section 11). You might not be able to extricate the sensors until you have removed the exhaust pipe support bracket.

22   Remove the four front crossmember fasteners and remove the front crossmember.

23   Detach the exhaust system from the underside of the vehicle at the two clamping sleeves.

24   On AWD models:

a) *Remove the heat shield above the exhaust system.*

b) *Remove the driveshaft heat shield from the differential cover.*

c) *Remove the fasteners from the transmission/driveshaft flange.*

d) *Slide the driveshaft toward the final drive.*

e) *Set the driveshaft aside.*

f) *Support the transmission with a floor jack just behind the oil pan.*

g) *Unbolt the subframe and slightly lower the transmission and subframe*

h) *Unbolt the transmission mounting bracket fasteners, remove the brackets and carefully lower the transmission just far enough to clear the front exhaust pipe/catalytic converters.*

25   On models equipped with a Multitronic transmission:

a) *Support the rear transmission crossmember with a floor jack.*

b) *Remove the four smaller rear bolts from the rear crossmember, then remove the two larger front bolts from the crossmember.*

c) *Carefully and slowly lower the rear transmission crossmember.*

d) *Remove the floor jack.*

e) *Remove the two nuts that secure the rear crossmember to the transmission and remove the crossmember.*

26   Remove the heat shield for the left or right driveaxle.

27   If you're removing the right catalytic converter on an AWD model, remove the right driveaxle (see Chapter 8).

28   Remove the exhaust pipe support bracket. If you were unable to remove the oxygen sensors previously because the sensor electrical harnesses were difficult to remove, you may now do so.

29   If you're removing the right catalytic converter on an AWD model, remove the fastener that secures the bracket for the automatic transmission fluid lines. Place a drain pan under the ATF line connection on the transmission, disconnect the lines, set them aside and secure them with a piece of wire.

30   Remove the lower nuts that secure the upper end of the converter/front exhaust pipe to the exhaust manifold and remove the converter/exhaust pipe. Remove and discard the old gaskets.

31   Installation is the reverse of removal. Be sure to use new gaskets and self-locking nuts and tighten the fasteners securely.

3.2L V6 models

Note: *There are two catalytic converters, one for each cylinder bank.*

32   Remove the rear engine cover.

33   If you're removing the catalytic converter for the left cylinder bank, disconnect the electrical connector for the engine coolant level sensor, then detach the coolant expansion tank - don't disconnect any of the coolant hoses - and set it aside. You have to move the coolant expansion tank out of the way to access the oxygen sensor electrical connectors.

34   Disconnect the electrical connector for the downstream oxygen sensor.

35   If you're removing the catalytic converter for the right cylinder bank, remove the air intake duct (see *Air filter housing - removal and installation* in Chapter 4).

Either catalytic converter

36   Remove the upper catalytic converter-to-exhaust manifold fastener. One of the three fasteners is easily accessible from above; you might find it easier to loosen two of the fasteners from underneath the vehicle.

37   Loosen the left or right front wheel lug nuts, raise the front of the vehicle and place it securely on jackstands. Remove the left or right front wheel.

38   Remove the engine compartment under-covers.

39   Remove the heat shield for the left or right driveaxle.

40   Remove the other catalytic converter-to-exhaust manifold fastener(s).

41   Remove the exhaust pipe bracket fasteners and detach the bracket from the transmission.

42   Detach the exhaust system at the clamping sleeve.

43   If you're removing the left catalytic converter/front exhaust pipe assembly on models with an automatic transmission:

a) *Remove the bolts for the left and right transmission mounts.*

b) *Support the transmission with a floor jack.*

c) *Lift the transmission slightly.*

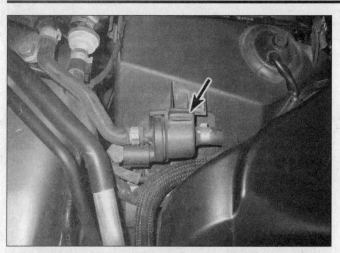

15.2a On 1.8L four-cylinder (shown) and 3.0L V6 models, the EVAP canister purge control solenoid valve is located on the back side of the air filter housing

15.2b On 2.0L four-cylinder models, the EVAP canister purge control solenoid valve is located at the left rear part of the intake manifold

d) Remove the heat shield for the left transmission support.
e) Remove the left transmission support and mounting bracket.
f) Carefully raise the transmission far enough to provide sufficient clearance to remove the catalytic converter/front exhaust pipe assembly

44   If you're removing the right catalytic converter/front exhaust pipe assembly on models with an automatic transmission:

a) Support the transmission with a floor jack.
b) Remove the four smaller subframe bolts (two on each side), then remove the two larger subframe bolts (one on each side).
c) Carefully and slowly lower the transmission and subframe about two inches (50 mm).
d) Remove the bolt that secures the bracket for the front part of the exhaust pipe.

45   On models equipped with a Multitronic transmission:

a) Support the rear transmission crossmember with a floor jack.

b) Remove the four smaller rear bolts from the rear crossmember, then remove the two larger front bolts from the crossmember.
c) Carefully and slowly lower the rear transmission crossmember.
d) Remove the floor jack.
e) Remove the two nuts that secure the rear crossmember to the transmission and remove the crossmember.

46   Remove the catalytic converter/front exhaust pipe assembly.
47   Installation is the reverse of removal. Be sure to use new gaskets and self-locking nuts and tighten all fasteners securely.

15   Evaporative Emissions Control (EVAP) system - component replacement

EVAP purge control solenoid valve

Refer to illustrations 15.2a and 15.2b

Note: *On 1.8L four-cylinder and 3.0L V6 models, the EVAP canister purge control solenoid*

valve is located at the back of the air filter housing. On 2.0L four-cylinder models, it's located on the left rear part of the intake manifold. On 3.2L V6 models, it's located on the throttle body.

1   Remove the air filter housing cover or engine cover.
2   Disconnect the electrical connector from the purge control solenoid valve **(see illustrations).**
3   Disconnect the hoses from the purge control solenoid valve.
4   Remove the purge control valve from its mounting bracket.
5   Installation is the reverse of removal.

EVAP canister

Refer to illustrations 15.7 and 15.8

Note: *The EVAP canister is located underneath the vehicle, in a recess below the spare tire well.*

6   Raise the vehicle and place it securely on jackstands.
7   Remove the EVAP canister cover **(see illustration).**
8   Disconnect the hoses **(see illustration)** from the canister. To disconnect each hose quick-connect fitting, press the release ring

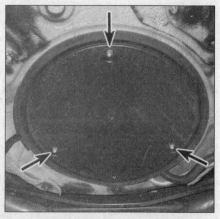

15.7 EVAP canister cover fasteners

15.8 EVAP canister details:

1   EVAP hose (to leak detection pump)
2   EVAP vent hose (from fuel tank)
3   EVAP purge line (to purge control solenoid valve in engine compartment)
4   Mounting nuts

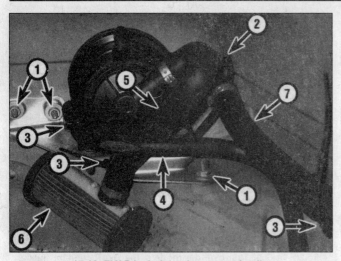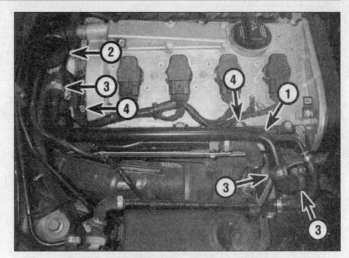

15.12 EVAP leak detection pump details:

1   Mounting bracket nuts
2   Electrical connector
    (not visible)
3   Cable ties
4   Vacuum hose
5   Air filter hose
6   Air filter
7   Hose from EVAP canister

**16.3   Typical PCV fresh air inlet pipe/hose assembly details
(1.8L models):**

1   PCV fresh air inlet pipe/hose assembly
2   Crankcase ventilation pressure regulator valve
3   Hose clamps
4   Mounting bracket fasteners

toward the canister (away from the hose) and simultaneously pull off the hose.
9   Remove the canister mounting fasteners and remove the canister.
10   Installation is the reverse of removal.

Leak detection pump

Refer to illustration 15.12
Note: *The leak detection pump is located inside the left rear wheel well.*
11   Loosen the left rear wheel lug nuts, raise the vehicle and place it securely on jackstands. Remove the left rear wheel. Remove the left rear wheel well splash shield (see Chapter 11).

16.11   PCV fresh air inlet pipe/hose assembly (2.0L models)

1   PCV fresh air inlet pipe
2   PCV fresh air inlet hose
3   Hose clamps

12   Remove the leak detection pump mounting bracket fasteners **(see illustration)**, pull down the pump and mounting bracket, then disconnect the electrical connector from the leak detection pump.
13   Cut the cable ties that secure the hoses to the leak detection pump or the pump mounting bracket. Disconnect the hoses from the leak detection pump. To disconnect a hose, press the release button on the quick-connect fitting.
14   Remove the fasteners that secure the leak detection pump to its mounting bracket.
15   Installation is the reverse of removal.

---

16   Positive Crankcase Ventilation (PCV) system - component replacement

---

1.8L four-cylinder models
PCV fresh air inlet hose

Refer to illustration 16.3
1   Remove the engine cover.
2   Remove the ambient (outside) air inlet duct from the air filter housing (see *Air filter housing - removal and installation* in Chapter 4).
3   The PCV fresh air inlet pipe/hose assembly **(see illustration)** connects the air intake duct (the outlet duct for the turbocharger) to a pipe at the left rear corner of the valve cover. To remove the fresh air pipe/hose assembly, loosen or cut all hose clamps.
4   Remove all mounting bracket fasteners for the PCV fresh air inlet pipe/hose assembly and remove the pipe and hose as a single assembly. If you're replacing the hose, cut the

clamp and remove the hose from the pipe.
5   Installation is the reverse of removal. Be sure to use new hose clamps.

PCV crankcase ventilation hose (PCV hose)

6   Remove the engine cover.
7   The PCV crankcase ventilation hose, or PCV hose, connects a pipe at the back of the valve cover to another pipe on the underside of the intake manifold.
8   Loosen the hose clamp and pull the hose off the pipe at the back of the valve cover.
9   Using a flashlight and a mirror, trace the PCV hose to the pipe on the underside of the intake manifold, loosen the hose clamp and pull the hose off the pipe.
10   Installation is the reverse of removal.

2.0L four-cylinder models
PCV fresh air inlet hose

Refer to illustrations 16.11 and 16.13
11   The PCV fresh air inlet pipe and hose assembly **(see illustration)** connects the inlet side of the turbocharger to a pipe at the right front corner of the valve cover.
12   Cut the hose clamp at the valve cover and pull off the rubber PCV fresh air inlet hose.
13   Remove the two Allen bolts **(see illustration)** that secure the lower PCV fresh air inlet pipe flange to the turbocharger.
14   If you're replacing the short hose at the upper end of the PCV fresh air inlet pipe, cut the other hose clamp and pull off the hose.
15   Installation is the reverse of removal. Be sure to use new hose clamps and tighten the two Allen bolts securely.

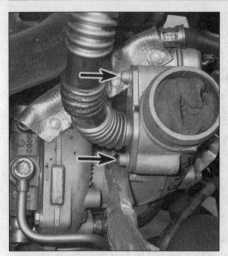

16.13 PCV fresh air inlet pipe flange bolts (2.0L models)

16.16 PCV crankcase ventilation hose (PCV hose) details:

1 *Quick-connect fittings for PCV hose*
2 *Crankcase pressure regulator valve*

PCV crankcase ventilation hose (PCV hose)

Refer to illustration 16.16

16 The PCV crankcase ventilation hose (PCV hose) assembly **(see illustration)** connects the crankcase pressure regulator valve on the valve cover to the intake manifold.
17 Disconnect the quick-connect fittings at each end of the PCV hose and remove the hose.
18 Installation is the reverse of removal.

V6 models

PCV fresh air inlet hose

19 Remove the engine cover.
20 The PCV fresh air inlet hose connects a pipe on the lower left side of the air inlet elbow to a pair of pipes on the back ends of the valve covers.
21 Remove the air intake duct, then remove the air inlet elbow (see *Air filter housing - removal and installation* in Chapter 4).
22 Disconnect the fresh air inlet hose from the air inlet elbow.
23 Disconnect the fresh air inlet hose from the left valve cover.
24 Disconnect the fresh air inlet hose from the right valve cover.
25 Installation is the reverse of removal.

PCV crankcase ventilation hose (PCV hose)

26 Remove the engine cover.
27 The PCV hose connects the crankcase ventilation pressure regulator valve, which is located behind the intake manifold, to the intake manifold.
28 Disconnect the PCV hose from the crankcase ventilation pressure regulator valve.
29 Disconnect the PCV hose from the intake manifold.
30 Installation is the reverse of removal.

17 Secondary Air Injection (AIR) system (1.8L and 3.0L models) - component replacement

Secondary air injection pump

Note: *The secondary air injection pump motor is located in the lower right front corner of the engine compartment.*

1 Remove the air filter housing (see Chapter 4).
2 Remove the upper air injection pump mounting bracket bolts.
3 Raise the vehicle and place it securely on jackstands.
4 Remove the engine compartment under covers.
5 Disconnect the electrical connector from the secondary AIR pump.
6 Disconnect the two air hoses from the secondary AIR pump.
7 Remove the lower secondary AIR pump mounting bracket fasteners.
8 Remove the secondary air pump and mounting bracket as a single assembly.
9 Detach the secondary air pump from its mounting bracket.
10 Installation is the reverse of removal.

Secondary air combination valve

1.8L models

Note: *The secondary air combination valve is located at the back end of the cylinder head.*

11 Remove the engine cover.
12 Disconnect the electrical connector from the Engine Coolant Temperature (ECT) sensor and set aside the wiring harness.
13 Disconnect the vacuum hose from the combination valve.
14 Remove the four combination valve mounting fasteners and remove the combination valve. Remove and discard the old seals.
15 Installation is the reverse of removal. Be sure to use new seals and tighten the combination valve mounting fasteners securely.

3.0L models

Left combination valve

Warning: *Wait until the engine is completely cool before performing this procedure.*

16 Remove the rear engine cover.
17 Remove the three solenoid valve retaining plate fasteners and remove the solenoid valve retaining plate.
18 Remove the air intake duct (see *Air filter housing - removal and installation* in Chapter 4).
19 Remove the air inlet elbow from the throttle body. The air inlet elbow is secured to the throttle body by one fastener. Remove the fastener, pull up the inlet elbow and disconnect the PCV hose from the elbow.
20 Remove the front left engine compartment cover.
21 Clamp off the upper rear coolant hose connected to the coolant expansion tank and disconnect it. Remove the coolant expansion tank fasteners, lift up the tank and disconnect the electrical connector from the coolant level sensor. Set the tank aside. Do not disconnect the other two coolant hoses.
22 Disconnect the electrical connectors from the two Camshaft Position (CMP) sensors.
23 Disconnect the PCV fresh air inlet hose from the back end of the left valve cover.
24 Remove the two fasteners that secure the vacuum hose flange to the left combination valve, then loosen the hose bracket fastener so that the hose can be moved slightly to clear the combination valve.
25 Remove the three left combination valve mounting fasteners and remove the valve. Remove and discard the old seals.
26 Installation is the reverse of removal. Be sure to use new seals

Right combination valve

27 Remove the rear engine cover and the air filter housing cover.
28 Remove the three solenoid valve retaining plate fasteners and remove the solenoid valve retaining plate.
29 Remove the air intake duct (see *Air filter*

18.2 Variable camshaft adjustment solenoid valve details (2.0L four-cylinder models):

1   Harness clip bracket (clip already disengaged from bracket)
2   Camshaft adjustment solenoid valve electrical connector
3   Solenoid valve mounting bolt

19.4 Connector bracket fasteners (2.0L four-cylinder models) (intake manifold removed for clarity)

housing - removal and installation in Chapter 4).

30   Remove the air inlet elbow from the throttle body. The air inlet elbow is secured to the throttle body by one fastener. Remove the fastener, pull up the inlet elbow and disconnect the PCV hose from the elbow.

31   Remove the two fasteners that secure the vacuum hose flange to the right combination valve.

32   Remove the three right combination valve mounting fasteners and pull up the valve to access the other vacuum hose.

33   Loosen or cut off the hose clamp and disconnect the other hose from the combination valve.

34   Remove the right combination valve. Remove and discard the old seals.

35   Installation is the reverse of removal. Be sure to use new seals.

18   Variable camshaft adjustment solenoid valve - replacement

Note: On 1.8L four-cylinder models and 3.0L V6 models, the variable camshaft adjustment solenoid valves are integral with the camshaft timing chain sprocket. If you need to replace a variable camshaft adjustment solenoid valve on one of these models, refer to Chapter 2A (1.8L models) or Chapter 2B (3.0L models).

2.0L models

Refer to illustration 18.2

Note: The variable camshaft adjustment solenoid is located on the back end of the cylinder head.

1   Remove the engine cover.
2   Detach the engine harness clip from its bracket (see illustration) and push the harness aside.

3   Disconnect the electrical connector from the camshaft adjustment solenoid valve.

4   Remove the camshaft adjustment solenoid valve mounting bolt and pull the valve out of the valve cover.

5   Remove and discard the solenoid valve O-ring.

6   Installation is the reverse of removal. Be sure to use a new O-ring.

3.2L V6 models

Note: The variable camshaft adjustment solenoid valves are located on the valve covers. There are four solenoid valves - one for each camshaft. The two solenoid valves for the cams on the left cylinder head are both located on top of the left valve cover, near the back end of the cover. The two solenoid valves for the cams on the right cylinder head are located on top of the right valve cover. The solenoid valve for the intake cam is located at the upper, inner edge of the valve cover, just ahead of the PCV hose; the solenoid for the exhaust cam is in the same spot as the exhaust cam solenoid valve on the left valve cover, in the center of and near the back end of the right valve cover. This procedure applies to all four solenoid valves.

7   Remove the front and rear engine covers.

8   If you're removing a camshaft adjustment solenoid valve from the left cylinder head, detach the coolant expansion tank, lift it up, disconnect the electrical connector from the coolant level sensor on the underside of the tank and set the tank aside. You can disconnect the upper coolant hose from the tank if necessary, but don't disconnect the lower hose.

9   If you're removing a camshaft adjust-

ment solenoid valve from the right cylinder head, remove the ambient (outside) air inlet duct and the air intake duct (see Air filter housing - removal and installation in Chapter 4).

10   Disconnect the electrical connector from the solenoid valve.

11   Remove the solenoid valve mounting bolt and remove the solenoid valve.

12   Remove and discard the old solenoid valve O-ring.

13   Installation is the reverse of removal. Be sure to use a new O-ring.

19   Variable intake manifold - component replacement

2.0L four-cylinder models

Refer to illustrations 19.4, 19.5 and 19.8

Warning: Wait until the engine is completely cool before performing this procedure.

1   Remove the engine cover.
2   Remove the coolant expansion tank (see Chapter 3).
3   Remove the air intake hose between the left intercooler and the throttle body (see Chapter 4).
4   Remove the two fasteners (see illustration) that secure the electrical connector bracket to the coolant pipe.
5   Disconnect all electrical connectors from the area adjacent to the intake flap motor (see illustration).
6   Cut the cable ties that secure the wiring harnesses to the coolant pipe, move the harnesses out of the way and remove the connector bracket.
7   Remove the bolt that secures the coolant pipe bracket (see illustration 19.5) and push the coolant pipe out of the way.

19.5 Intake flap motor details (2.0L four-cylinder models):

1   *Electrical connectors*
2   *Harness cable tie (other cable ties not visible in this photo)*
3   *Coolant pipe mounting bracket bolt*

19.8 Intake flap motor removal details (2.0L four-cylinder models) (intake manifold removed for clarity):

1   *Control rod connection to crank arm on intake manifold*
2   *Intake flap motor mounting fasteners*

8   Using a screwdriver, disengage the intake flap motor control rod from the crank arm on the intake manifold **(see illustration)**.
9   Remove the intake flap motor mounting fasteners and remove the motor.
10 Installation is the reverse of removal.

V6 models

3.0L models

Note: *The vacuum actuator and intake manifold change-over valve are located on the front of the intake manifold.*
11 Remove the engine cover.
12 Disconnect the electrical connector from the intake manifold change-over valve.

13 Disconnect the vacuum lines from the intake manifold change-over valve and from the vacuum actuator.
14 Remove the intake manifold change-over valve from the vacuum actuator.
15 Remove the two vacuum actuator mounting fasteners and remove the actuator from the intake manifold.
16 Installation is the reverse of removal.

3.2L models

Note: *The intake manifold tuning valve position sensor, the intake manifold change-over actuator and the change-over valve for the intake manifold flap are all located on the front of the intake manifold.*

17 Remove the front engine cover.
18 Disconnect the electrical connectors from the intake manifold tuning valve position sensor and from the change-over valve for the intake manifold flap.
19 Disconnect the vacuum lines from the actuator and from the change-over valve for the intake manifold flap.
20 To remove the actuator or the sensor, remove the mounting fasteners.
21 To remove the change-over valve for the intake manifold flap, simply pull it off its bracket.
22 Installation is the reverse of removal.

Notes

Chapter 7 Part A
Manual transaxle

Contents

	Section			Section
Back-up light switch - removal and installation	5	Manual transaxle overhaul - general information		4
General information	1	Oil seals - replacement		6
Manual transaxle - removal and installation	3	Shift linkage - adjustment		2
Manual transaxle lubricant change	See Chapter 1	Transaxle mount replacement		See Chapter 7B
Manual transaxle lubricant level check	See Chapter 1			

Specifications

General

Lubricant type and capacity	See Chapter 1

Torque specifications

	Ft-lbs	Nm
Transaxle-to-engine bolts		
M10	33	45
M12	48	65
Shift adjustment bolt	18	25
Lubricant level filler/check plug and drain plug		
5-speed	18	25
6-speed (OA3)	29	40
6-speed (O2X)	33	45
Back-up light switch	18	25

1 General information

Two manual transmissions are available in the vehicles covered by this manual: a five-speed and a six-speed. The manual transmission is bolted to the rear of the engine. The transaxle on front-wheel drive models transmits the power to a differential unit located at the front of the transaxle, through driveaxles, to the front wheels. On all-wheel drive models, power is also transmitted through a transfer gearbox to a driveshaft, which turns the rear differential, driveaxles and wheels. All gears including reverse incorporate a synchromesh engagement.

2 Shift linkage - adjustment

Refer to illustration 2.5

1   Hold the shift knob while turning the plastic ferrule below it clockwise to remove it. Slide the shift knob from the shifter stalk.

2   Remove the shifter cover from the console and remove the ashtray (see Chapter 11).

3   Remove the large washer and insulation.

4   Remove two bolts and take out the larger, rigid insulation plate.

5   Loosen the bolt for the pushrod **(see illustration)**.

6   Measure the distance between the centers of the two studs **(B and C in illustration 2.5)**. Adjust the distance until it is 3-23/64 inches (85 mm), then tighten the pushrod bolt.

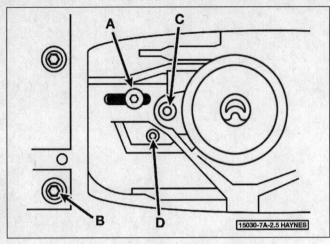

2.5 Shifter adjustment details

A *Pushrod bolt*
B *Assembly front mounting stud*
C *Stud on shifter*
D *Selector rod bolt*

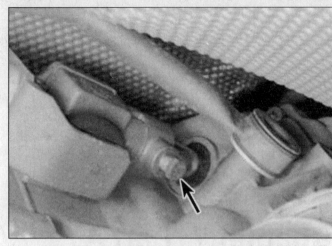

3.15 Shift rod connection at the rear of the transaxle

7   Remove the bolt for the selector rod and center the shifter (held straight UP) so that it is radially the same distance all around to the ball housing. Hold the shifter in that position and tighten the selector rod bolt.

8   Reinstall all components and test-drive to check that the shifter operates correctly in all gears.

---

3   Manual transaxle - removal and installation

Removal

Refer to illustration 3.15

1   Select a solid, level surface to park the vehicle upon. Give yourself enough space to move around it easily. Apply the parking brake and chock the rear wheels. Support the engine from above with an engine support fixture.

2   Remove the transaxle-to-engine bolts accessible from above.

3   Raise the front of the vehicle and support it securely on jackstands. Remove the splash guard from under the engine compartment.

4   Disconnect the cable from the negative terminal of the battery (see Chapter 5).

5   Remove the air cleaner assembly (see Chapter 4).

6   Disconnect the downstream oxygen sensor electrical connectors.

7   Remove the front portion of the exhaust system (see Chapter 4). Take care not to excessively bend the flexible section of the front pipe.

8   Detach the inner ends of the driveaxles from the transaxle (see Chapter 8). Support the driveaxles with lengths of wire.

9   If you are working on an all-wheel drive model, remove the driveshaft (see Chap-

ter 8).

10   Support the transaxle on a jack, preferably one made for this purpose. Secure the transaxle to the jack with a safety chain. Unbolt the transaxle mount complete with rubber bushing.

11   Disconnect the electrical connector from the back-up light switch on the transaxle.

12   Disconnect the electrical connector from the speedometer sensor. Check that all wiring and ground straps have been disconnected from the transaxle.

13   Remove the starter motor (see Chapter 5).

14   Unbolt the release cylinder from the transaxle, and tie it to one side without disconnecting the hydraulic line. **Note:** *Do not depress the clutch pedal with the release cylinder removed.*

15   Unscrew the bolt and disconnect the shift rod from the rear of the transaxle **(see illustration)**. Also detach the other shift rod from the transaxle.

16   If you are working on a Cabriolet model, remove the torque reaction supports and drop the stabilizer bar from its mounts. Loosen the engine mount lower nuts to the end of their studs, then use the support fixture to raise the engine until the nuts just touch the bottom of the mounts.

17   Make sure that the transaxle is adequately supported, then unscrew the remaining bolts securing the transaxle to the engine.

18   Unscrew the bolts from the transaxle mount, then remove the transaxle crossmember (see Chapter 7B). Remove the bolts and the rear subframe crossmember.

19   With the help of an assistant, withdraw the transaxle from the locating dowels on the rear of the engine, making sure that the input shaft does not hang on the clutch. Make sure that the driveshafts are supported clear of

the transaxle. **Warning:** *Make sure that the transaxle remains steady on the jack head. Keep the transaxle level until the input shaft is fully withdrawn from the clutch friction plate.*

20   Lower the transaxle to the ground.

Installation

21   Before installing the transaxle, make sure that the location dowels are correctly positioned in the engine cylinder block rear face. Also make sure that the starter motor lower mounting bolt is positioned in the transaxle, as it cannot be inserted with the transaxle in its normal position.

22   Installation of the transaxle is a reversal of the removal procedure, but note the following points:

a) *Check the rear rubber mounts and replace them if necessary.*

b) *Apply a little high-melting-point grease to the splines of the transaxle input shaft.*

c) *Tighten all fasteners to the specified torque where given.*

d) *On completion, refer to Section 2 and check the shift linkage adjustment.*

---

4   Manual transaxle overhaul - general information

1   Overhauling a manual transaxle unit is a difficult and involved job for the home mechanic. In addition to dismantling and reassembling many small parts, clearances must be precisely measured and, if necessary, changed by selecting shims and spacers. Internal transaxle components are also often difficult to obtain and in many instances, extremely expensive. Because of this, if the transaxle develops a fault or becomes noisy, the best course of action is to have the unit

overhauled by a transmission specialist or to obtain an exchange reconditioned unit.

2   Nevertheless, it is not impossible for the more experienced mechanic to overhaul the transaxle if the special tools are available and the job is carried out in a deliberate step-by-step manner, to ensure that nothing is overlooked.

3   The tools necessary for an overhaul include internal and external snap-ring pliers, bearing pullers, a slide hammer, a set of pin punches, a dial test indicator and possibly a hydraulic press. In addition, a large, sturdy workbench and a vise will be required.

4   During dismantling of the transaxle, make careful notes of how each component is fitted to make reassembly easier and accurate.

5   Before disassembling the transaxle, it will help if you have some idea of where the problem lies. Certain problems can be closely related to specific areas in the transaxle which can make component examination and replacement easier. Refer to the *Troubleshooting* Section in this manual for more information.

5   Back-up light switch - removal and installation

1   Apply the parking brake, then raise the front of the vehicle and support it on jackstands.

2   Remove the under-vehicle splash shield.

3   Disconnect the back-up light switch electrical connector.

4   Unscrew the back-up light switch from the transaxle, or remove the bolts securing the switch to the transaxle, depending on design.

5   Installation is the reverse of the removal.

6   Oil seals - replacement

Drive flange oil seals

1   Loosen the wheel bolts. Apply the parking brake, then raise the front of the vehicle and support it securely on jackstands. Remove the wheel.

2   Refer to Chapter 8 and unbolt the heat shield, then unscrew the bolts and detach the relevant driveaxle from the transaxle drive flange. Tie the driveaxle away from the transaxle, and wrap the inner joint in a plastic

bag in order to prevent entry of dust and dirt. Turn the steering as necessary to move the driveshaft away from the flange.

3   Position a suitable container beneath the transaxle to catch spilled oil.

4   The drive flange is held in position by a circlip, and in order to remove the flange, it is necessary to release the circlip from its groove. To do this, locate a suitable distance piece (such as a chisel) between the flange and the final drive cover or transaxle casing, then screw a bolt through the flange onto the distance piece. As the bolt is tightened, the flange will be forced outwards and the circlip released from its groove. If the flange is tight, turn it 180-degrees and repeat the removal procedure.

5   With the flange out, note the installed depth of the oil seal in the housing, then pry it out using a large flat-bladed screwdriver.

6   Clean all traces of dirt from the area around the oil seal aperture, then apply a smear of grease to the lips of the new oil seal.

7   Ensure the seal is correctly positioned, with its sealing lip facing inwards, and tap it squarely into position, using a suitable tubular drift (such as a socket) which bears only on the hard outer edge of the seal. If the surface of the flange is good, make sure the seal is installed at the same depth in its housing as originally noted; it should be 7/32-inch (5.5 mm) below the outer edge of the transaxle. If the surface of the flange is worn, install the oil seal at a depth of 1/4-inch (6.5 mm).

8   Clean the oil seal and apply a smear of multi-purpose grease to its lips.

9   It is recommended that the circlip on the inner end of the drive flange is replaced whenever the flange is removed. To do this, mount the flange in a soft-jawed vise, then pry off the old circlip and install the new one. Lightly grease the circlip.

10   Insert the drive flange through the oil seal and engage it with the differential gear. Using a suitable drift, drive the flange fully into the gear until the circlip is felt to engage.

11   Install the driveaxle (see Chapter 8).

12   Install the wheel, then lower the vehicle to the ground. Check, and if necessary top up, the transaxle oil level.

Input shaft oil seal

13   The transaxle must be removed for access to the input shaft oil seal. Refer to Section 3 of this Chapter.

14   Remove the clutch release bearing and

lever (see Chapter 8).

15   Unscrew the bolts and remove the guide sleeve from inside the bellhousing. Recover the gasket. Do not disturb any shims located on the input shaft.

16   Note the installed depth of the oil seal in the transaxle housing, then use a screwdriver to pry it out, taking care not to damage the input shaft.

17   Wipe clean the oil seal seating and input shaft.

18   Smear a little multi-purpose grease on the lips of the new oil seal, then locate the seal over the input shaft with its sealing lip facing inwards. Tap the oil seal squarely into position, using a suitable tubular drift which bears only on the hard outer edge of the seal. Make sure the seal is fitted at the same depth in its housing as originally noted; it should be 3/16-inch (4.5 mm) below the guide sleeve mounting surface.

19   Install the guide sleeve together with a new gasket and new bolts, and tighten the bolts to the torque listed in this Chapter's Specifications.

20   Install the clutch release bearing and lever (see Chapter 8).

21   Install the transaxle (see Section 3).

Selector shaft oil seal

22   Apply the parking brake, then raise the front of the vehicle and support it securely on jackstands.

23   Unscrew the locking bolt and slide the gearshift coupling from the transaxle selector shaft.

24   Using a small screwdriver, carefully pry the oil seal from the transaxle housing, taking care not to damage the surface of the selector shaft or housing.

25   Wipe clean the oil seal seating and selector shaft, then smear a little multi-purpose grease on the new oil seal lips and locate the seal over the end of the shaft. Make sure the closed side of the seal faces outwards. To prevent damage to the oil seal, temporarily wrap some adhesive tape around the end of the shaft.

26   Tap the oil seal squarely into position, using a suitable tubular drift which bears only on the hard outer edge of the seal. The seal should be inserted until it is 1/32-inch (1.0 mm) below the surface of the transaxle.

27   Install the gearshift coupling and tighten the locking bolt.

28   Lower the vehicle to the ground.

Notes

Chapter 7 Part B
Automatic transaxle

Contents

	Section		Section
Automatic transaxle - removal and installation	5	General information	1
Automatic transaxle fluid change	See Chapter 1	Shift cable - removal, installation and adjustment	3
Automatic transaxle fluid level check	See Chapter 1	Shift interlock system - description, check and	
Automatic transaxle overhaul - general information	6	component replacement	4
Diagnosis - general	2	Transaxle mounts - check and replacement	7
Drive flange oil seals - replacement	See Chapter 7A		

Specifications

General

5-speed automatic designation	01V
6-speed automatic designations	09L
CVT automatic designation	01J
Automatic transaxle fluid and type	See Chapter 1

Torque specifications

Note: *One foot-pound (ft-lb) of torque is equivalent to 12 inch-pounds (in-lbs) of torque. Torque values below approximately 15 foot-pounds are expressed in inch-pounds, because most foot-pound torque wrenches are not accurate at these smaller values.*

	Ft-lbs (unless otherwise indicated)	Nm
Automatic selector cable support bolt	80 in-lbs	9
Auxiliary cooler filter (CVT transmission)		
Filter-to-bracket	177 in-lbs	20
Filter bracket-to-transmission	30	40

Torque specifications (continued)

	Ft-lbs (unless otherwise indicated)	Nm
Note: One foot-pound (ft-lb) of torque is equivalent to 12 inch-pounds (in-lbs) of torque. Torque values below approximately 15 foot-pounds are expressed in inch-pounds, because most foot-pound torque wrenches are not accurate at these smaller values.

	Ft-lbs	Nm
Bracket for fluid pipe	17	23
Driveplate-to-converter (new bolts)	63	85
Fluid pipes-to-transmission	16	21
Fluid line union nuts	21	29
Transaxle-to-engine mounting bolts		
M12 and M10x115	48	65
M10x80, M10x60, and M10x45	33	45
M10x30	30	40
M10x22	88 in-lbs	10
Transaxle mount bolts		
Left		
M10x30	30	40
M10x22	88 in-lbs	10
Right		
M8	17	23
M10	37	50
Rear mount-to-crossmember (nuts/bolts)	17	23
Rear crossmember-to-frame bolts	41	55

1   General information

The automatic transmissions on the covered models include a five-speed, a six-speed, and a CVT (Continuously Variable Transmission).

Some V6 models have a dampening disc between the driveplate and the converter, similar to the clutch disc on a manual transmission. The dampener is designed to reduce the transfer of engine vibrations to the transmission.

The identification of the transmission designation is the first three digits of the transmission number. On five-speed transmissions, the numbers are on the left side of the bellhousing. On six-speed transmissions, the numbers are on the bottom of the left-side driveaxle flange at the transaxle, and on CVT transmissions, the numbers are on a pad underneath the transmission.

The overall operation of the transaxle is managed by the Engine Control Module (ECM) and the Transmission Control Module (TCM). Comprehensive troubleshooting can therefore only be carried out using dedicated electronic test equipment such as a factory scan tool.

Due to the complexity of the transaxle and its control system, major repairs and overhaul operations should be left to a dealer service department or other qualified repair facility, who will be equipped to carry out troubleshooting and repair. The information in this Chapter is therefore limited to a description of the removal and installation of the transaxle as a complete unit. The removal, installation and adjustment of the shift cable and key interlock cable is also described.

2   Diagnosis - general

Automatic transaxle malfunctions may be caused by five general conditions:

a) Poor engine performance
b) Improper adjustments
c) Hydraulic malfunctions
d) Mechanical malfunctions
e) Malfunctions in the computer or its signal network

Diagnosis of these problems should always begin with a check of the easily repaired items: fluid level and condition (see Chapter 1) and shift cable adjustment. Next, perform a road test to determine if the problem has been corrected or if more diagnosis is necessary. If the problem persists after the preliminary tests and corrections are completed, additional diagnosis should be done by a dealer service department or transmission repair shop. Refer to the *Troubleshooting* Section at the front of this manual for information on symptoms of transaxle problems.

Preliminary checks

1   Drive the vehicle to warm the transaxle to normal operating temperature.
2   Check the fluid level as described in Chapter 1.

a) *If the fluid level is unusually low, add enough fluid to bring it up to the proper level, then check for external leaks (see below).*

b) *If the fluid level is abnormally high, drain off the excess, then check the drained fluid for contamination by coolant. The presence of engine coolant in the automatic transmission fluid indicates that a failure has occurred in the transaxle fluid cooler.*

c) *If the fluid is foaming, drain it and refill the transaxle, then check for coolant in the fluid.*

3   Look for a CHECK ENGINE light glowing on the instrument panel (see Chapter 6 for information). **Note:** *If the engine or its control network is malfunctioning, do not proceed with the preliminary checks until it has been repaired and runs normally.*
4   Inspect the shift cable (see Section 3). Make sure that it's properly adjusted and that it operates smoothly.

Fluid leak diagnosis

5   Most fluid leaks are easy to locate visually. Repair usually consists of replacing a seal or gasket. If a leak is difficult to find, the following procedure may help.
6   Identify the fluid. Make sure it's transmission fluid and not engine oil or brake fluid.
7   Try to pinpoint the source of the leak. Drive the vehicle several miles, then park it over a large sheet of cardboard. After a minute or two, you should be able to locate the leak by determining the source of the fluid dripping onto the cardboard.
8   Make a careful visual inspection of the suspected component and the area immediately around it. Pay particular attention to gasket mating surfaces. A mirror is often

helpful for finding leaks in areas that are hard to see.

9   If the leak still cannot be found, clean the suspected area thoroughly with a degreaser or solvent, then dry it.

10   Drive the vehicle for several miles at normal operating temperature and varying speeds. After driving the vehicle, visually inspect the suspected component again.

11   Once the leak has been located, the cause must be determined before it can be properly repaired. If a gasket is replaced but the sealing flange is bent, the new gasket will not stop the leak. The bent flange must be straightened.

12   Before attempting to repair a leak, check to make sure that the following conditions are corrected or they may cause another leak. **Note:** *Some of the following conditions cannot be fixed without highly specialized tools and expertise. Such problems must be referred to a transmission shop or a dealer service department.*

Gasket leaks

13   Check the pan periodically. Make sure the bolts are tight, no bolts are missing, the gasket is in good condition and the pan is flat (dents in the pan may indicate damage to the valve body inside).

14   If the pan gasket is leaking, the fluid level may be too high, the vent may be plugged, the pan bolts may be too tight, the pan sealing flange may be warped, the sealing surface of the transaxle housing may be damaged, the gasket may be damaged or the transaxle casting may be cracked or porous. If sealant instead of gasket material has been used to form a seal between the pan and the transaxle housing, it may be the wrong sealant.

Seal leaks

15   If a transaxle seal is leaking, the fluid level may be too high, the vent may be plugged, the seal bore may be damaged, the seal itself may be damaged or improperly installed, the surface of the shaft protruding through the seal may be damaged or a loose bearing may be causing excessive shaft movement.

16   Make sure the fluid drain/check plug in the transmission fluid pan is in good condition. If leaking transmission fluid is evident, replace the O-ring on the drain plug.

Case leaks

17   If the case itself appears to be leaking, the casting is porous and will have to be repaired or replaced.

18   Make sure the oil cooler hose fittings are tight and in good condition. **Note:** *The CVT transmission's case is made of magnesium, check it for signs of corrosion. Replace any corroded bolts with new, factory-coated bolts to prevent electrolysis.*

Fluid comes out vent pipe

19   If this condition occurs, the transaxle is overfilled, there is coolant in the fluid, the

vent is plugged or the drain-back holes are plugged.

---

3   Shift cable - removal, installation and adjustment

Removal

1   On models with a PRND legend, shift the lever to the D position. On models with a PRNDS legend, place the lever in the S position.

2   Apply the parking brake, then raise the front of the vehicle and support it securely on jackstands.

3   Working under the vehicle, remove the screws and lower the heat shield from the shifter mounting bracket onto the exhaust. Slide the heat shield forwards. On V6 models, remove the left exhaust pipe and the left transmission mount for access to the shift control.

4   Unbolt the cable bracket from the transmission case.

5   At the transmission end of the cable, use a screwdriver to pry the end of the inner cable up from the transmission lever.

6   Unscrew the bolt and detach the support bracket and cable from the side of the transmission.

7   Loosen the locknuts and detach the cable from the bracket. Withdraw the cable from under the vehicle.

Installation

8   Installation is a reversal of removal, but lightly grease the cable end fittings.

9   Before lowering the vehicle to the ground and before reconnecting the cable to the transmission lever, adjust the cable as follows.

Adjustment

10   On models with a PRND legend, shift the lever to the D position. On models with a PRNDS legend, place the lever in the S position.

11   Using a hex tool, loosen the selector lever bolt at the front of the shift mechanism by one full turn.

12   Move the shifter slightly fore and aft, without changing gears. The correct position is assured by pushing the lever slightly toward the driver's seat. Tighten the selector lever bolt.

13   If the shifter still does not operate correctly, a scan tool may be necessary to coordinate the transmission range selector with the shifter.

14   Check the adjustment by selecting P. With the brake pedal released, check that the selector lever cannot be moved out of the P position with the lever button pressed. Now depress the brake pedal and check that the lock solenoid releases, enabling the selector lever to be moved to any position with the lever button pressed. Check that the display agrees with the actual position of the lever.

15   Select position N. With the brake pedal released, check that the selector lever is locked. Depress the pedal and check that the selector lever can be moved to any position. Note that it is only possible to select R with the button pressed.

16   Check that it is only possible to operate the starter motor in positions P and N with the button released.

---

4   Shift interlock system - description, check and component replacement

Warning: *These models are equipped with airbags. Always disable the airbag system before working in the vicinity of any airbag system component to avoid the possibility of accidental deployment of the airbag(s), which could cause personal injury (see Chapter 12).* **Warning:** *Do not use a memory saving device to preserve the ECM's memory when working on or near airbag system components.*

Description

1   The shift lock system prevents the shift lever from being shifted out of Park or Neutral until the brake pedal is applied and the button on the lever is pushed in. It also prevents the ignition key from being turned to the Lock position until the shift lever has been placed in the Park position.

Solenoid check

2   Remove the center console (see Chapter 11).

3   Follow the wiring harness from the shift lock solenoid back to the electrical connector, then unplug the connector. Using a pair of jumper wires, momentarily apply battery voltage and ground to the solenoid terminals and verify that there's an audible click. **Caution:** *Don't apply battery voltage any longer than necessary to perform this check.*

4   If the shift lock solenoid doesn't click when energized, replace it.

Component replacement

Shift lock solenoid

01V and 01J transaxles

5   Remove the center console (see Chapter 11).

6   The solenoid is located at the front of the shifter mechanism. Disconnect the electrical connector. Release the clips and pull the solenoid forward out of the shifter housing.

7   Installation is the reverse of removal.

09L transaxle

Refer to illustration 4.10

8   Remove the center console (see Chapter 11).

9   Pull the lock button out of the shifter handle and keep it in this position by attaching a plastic cable tie around the button. Twist and

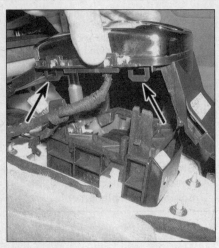

4.10 The shift housing cover/gear position indicator is secured by two locking tabs on each side

lift off the shift knob.

10   Release the four clips and pull up the shifter cover to access the solenoid **(see illustration)**.

11   Push back the plastic clip securing the solenoid and push down and twist the solenoid to release the plastic ball-end at the bottom.

12   Installation is the reverse of removal.

Key interlock cable

Replacement

Refer to illustrations 4.20 and 4.21

13   Disconnect the cable from the negative terminal of the battery (see Chapter 5).

14   Remove the steering wheel (see Chapter 10).

15   Remove the steering column cover (see Chapter 11).

16   Remove the shift knob (see Step 9).

17   Remove the center console and the trim panel from around the radio (see Chapter 11). Remove the HVAC control panel (see Chapter 3) and the ashtray.

18   Disengage the locking tabs and remove the cover and gear position indicator from the shift lever housing **(see illustration 4.10)**.

19   Turn the ignition key to the On position and place the shift lever in the Park position.

20   Pull out the clip that retains the cable to the key lock cylinder housing, then detach the cable from the housing **(see illustration)**.

21   Remove the clamp bolt, then pull up on the retaining spring and detach the interlock cable from the locking lever at the shifter housing **(see illustration)**.

22   Remove the cable from the instrument panel, noting how it's routed. To ease installation of the new cable, it's a good idea to attach a length of wire to the end of the old cable; as you remove the old cable, the length of wire will occupy its place. Then attach the wire to the new cable and use it to help pull the new cable into place.

23   To install the cable, reverse the removal procedure, then adjust the cable as described in the next Step.

Adjustment

24   Remove the center console, if not already done (see Chapter 11).

25   Place the shift lever in the Park position, then turn the ignition key to Lock and remove it from the lock cylinder (see Chapter 12).

26   Loosen the cable clamp bolt at the shifter housing **(see illustration 4.21)**.

27   Place the steering column to the lowest position (closest position to the driver).

28   An adjustment tool (Audi T3352A) must be used to adjust the locking cable at the shifter assembly. Insert the tool over the pin in the shifter end of the locking cable eye. The factory tool is long enough that the console must be removed to use it, but the tool

can be cut off just at the end of its flattened notch. This allows use for this purpose without removing the console. With the tool in place, pull the cable housing towards the rear of the vehicle to remove any slack, then tighten the bolt at the shifter assembly and remove the tool. **Note:** *If you can't obtain this tool, you can try to approximate the position of the pin in the cable eye by holding the cable eye as centralized as possible over the pin while pulling back on the cable housing.*

29   Turn the ignition key on, depress the brake pedal and move the shift lever to D, then back to P. Make sure it is now possible to remove the ignition key.

---

5   Automatic transaxle - removal and installation

Removal

Refer to illustrations 5.3, 5.4 and 5.17

1   Select a solid, level surface to park the vehicle upon. Give yourself enough space to move around it easily. Apply the parking brake and chock the rear wheels.

2   Disconnect the cable from the negative terminal of the battery (see Chapter 5). Remove the engine covers (see Chapter 2A or 2B).

3   Support the engine with a three-bar engine support locating on the front fender inner channels **(see illustration)**. The engine should be supported using both the front and rear lifting eyes. Depending on the engine, temporarily remove components as necessary to attach the support fixture.

4   Unscrew and remove the transaxle-to-engine mounting bolts accessible from the engine compartment or through the fenderwells **(see illustration)**. Loosen the four bolts

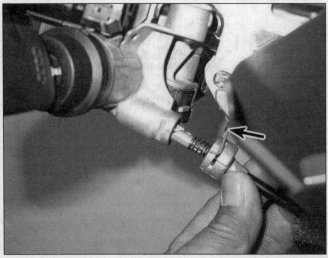

4.20 Remove this clip to detach the key interlock cable from the lock cylinder housing

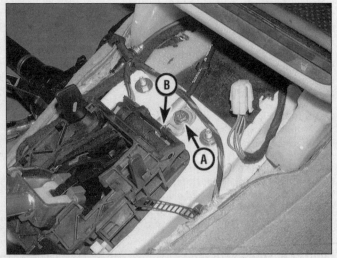

4.21 Details of the key interlock cable at the shifter housing

A   Clamp bolt   B   Retaining spring

5.3 An engine support fixture can be obtained at most equipment rental yards.

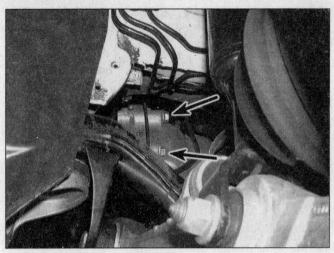

5.4 These transaxle mounting bolts are accessible through the left wheel well

securing the front torque rod mount to the bottom of the radiator support panel to allow engine movement, and loosen the engine mount nuts until they are flush with their studs. This allows raising the engine until the nuts are against the engine brackets.

5   Loosen the front wheel bolts, then raise the front of the vehicle and support it on jackstands. Remove both front wheels.

6   Remove the under-vehicle splash shield and its bracket.

7   Remove the exhaust system (see Chapter 4). **Note:** *On some models, there are two body crossmembers under the transmission tunnel that must be removed in order to remove the exhaust system. Do not confuse these with the actual transmission crossmember, which is a large casting.*

8   Disconnect the wiring from the sensors on the transmission (see Chapter 6).

9   Identify the wiring connections on the transaxle, then unplug them. Loosen and detach the wiring support, and position the wiring to one side.

10   With the selector lever in position P, carefully disconnect the inner cable from the shift lever, then unbolt the support bracket. Position the cable to one side.

11   Remove the heat shields from over the inner end of the driveaxles.

12   Refer to Chapter 8 and detach the driveaxles from the transaxle flanges. Tie the driveaxles away from the transaxle. If you are working on an all-wheel drive model, remove the driveshaft.

13   Position a suitable container beneath the transaxle to collect spilled fluid.

14   Detach the cooler lines from the transaxle, and recover the sealing rings. Plug the openings in the transaxle housing to prevent entry of dust and dirt.

15   Support the transaxle on a jack, preferably one made for this purpose. Secure the transaxle to the jack with a safety chain. Unbolt the right-hand transaxle mount complete with rubber bushing.

16   Remove the left and right-hand transaxle mounts, keeping track of the location of various-length bolts (see Section 7). At the rear of the transmission, remove the nuts securing the rear mount to the crossmember, then remove the rear crossmember.

17   Unscrew the transaxle-to-engine mounting bolts accessible from under the car **(see illustration)**.

18   Remove the starter motor (see Chapter 5). **Caution:** *On models with CVT transmission, do not remove the starter until the weight of the transmission is being carried by the transmission jack, not the lower transmission-to-engine bolts.*

19   Turn the engine to locate one of the torque converter-to-driveplate nuts or bolts in the starter motor aperture. Unscrew and remove the nuts or bolts while preventing the engine from turning using a wide-bladed screwdriver engaged with the ring gear teeth on the driveplate. Unscrew the remaining two fasteners, turning the engine a third of a turn at a time to locate them. Mark the relationship of the torque converter to the driveplate so balance will be preserved when reinstalling the transaxle. **Note:** *On 3.2L engines, a special socket adapter (Audi # T40058) is necessary to rotate the crankshaft pulley center bolt.*

20   Mark the location of the subframe beneath the engine compartment, then loosen the front subframe bolts. Support the rear of the subframe with a floor jack. Remove the remaining subframe bolts and lower the rear of the subframe. This allows access to remove the two side mounts on the transaxle. **Note:** *It is important that the subframe is reinstalled in its correct position otherwise the handling of the car will be affected and excessive wear will occur.*

21   With the help of an assistant, withdraw the transaxle from the locating dowels on the rear of the engine, making sure that the torque converter remains fully engaged with the transaxle input shaft. If necessary, use a lever to release the torque converter from the driveplate.

22   When the locating dowels are clear of their mounting holes, lower the transaxle to the ground using the jack. Strap a restraining bar across the front of the bellhousing to keep

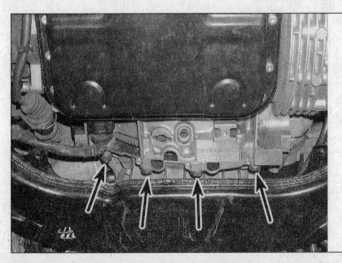

5.17 From below, these four transaxle mounting fasteners can be removed (V6 engine shown)

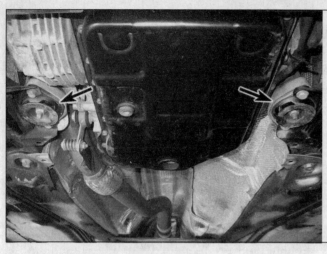

7.5 Transaxle side mounts - remove the center nuts and the two frame bolts at each side

the torque converter in position. **Warning:** *Make sure that the transaxle remains steady on the jack head.*

23   Where necessary, remove the intermediate plate from the locating dowels.

Installation

24   Installation of the transaxle is a reversal of the removal procedure, but note the following points:

a)   *As the torque converter is reinstalled, ensure that the drive pins at the center of the torque converter hub engage with the recesses in the automatic transaxle fluid pump inner wheel.*

b)   *When installing the transaxle, make sure the marks on the torque converter and driveplate are in alignment.*

c)   *Tighten the bellhousing bolts and torque converter-to-driveplate nuts to the specified torque. Always replace self-locking nuts and bolts.*

d)   *Replace the O-ring seals on the fluid pipes and filler tube attached to the transaxle casing.*

e)   *Tighten the transaxle mounting bolts to the correct torque.*

f)   *Tighten the driveaxle inner CV joint bolts and, on all-wheel drive models, the driveshaft-to-center differential flange bolts, to the torque values listed in the Chapter 8 Specifications.*

g)   *Check the final drive oil level and transaxle fluid level as described in Chapter 1.*

h)   *On completion, refer to Section 4 and check the shift cable adjustment.*

6   Automatic transaxle overhaul - general information

In the event of a fault occurring, it will be necessary to establish whether the fault is electrical, mechanical or hydraulic in nature, before repair work can be contemplated. Diagnosis requires detailed knowledge of the transaxle's operation and construction, as well as access to specialized test equipment, and

so is deemed to be beyond the scope of this manual. It is therefore essential that problems with the automatic transaxle are referred to a dealer service department or other qualified repair facility for assessment.

Note that a faulty transaxle should not be removed before the vehicle has been assessed by a knowledgeable technician equipped with the proper tools, as trouble-shooting must be performed with the transaxle installed in the vehicle.

7   Transaxle mounts - check and replacement

Check

1   Raise the vehicle and support it securely on jackstands.

2   Insert a large screwdriver or prybar between the transaxle and the subframe and try to pry the transaxle up slightly.

3   The transmission should not move much at all - if the mount is cracked or torn, replace it.

Replacement

Refer to illustration 7.5

4   Support the transaxle with a floor jack. Place a block of wood on the jack head to act as a cushion.

5   Remove the bolts and nuts attaching the mount to the subframe and transaxle **(see illustration)**.

6   Raise the transaxle slightly with the jack and remove the mount.

7   Installation is the reverse of the removal procedure. Be sure to tighten all fasteners securely.

Chapter 8
Clutch and driveline

Contents

	Section
Clutch - description and check	2
Clutch components - removal, inspection and installation	6
Clutch hydraulic system - bleeding	5
Clutch master cylinder - removal and installation	3
Clutch pedal and over-center spring - removal and installation	8
Clutch pedal switch and clutch pedal starter interlock switch - removal and installation	9
Clutch release bearing and lever - removal, inspection and installation	7

	Section
Clutch release cylinder - removal and installation	4
Driveaxle - removal and installation	11
Driveaxle boot replacement and CV joint inspection	12
Driveaxles - general information and inspection	10
Driveshaft (all-wheel drive models) - removal and installation	13
General information	1
Rear differential assembly - removal and installation	15
Rear differential oil seals - replacement	14

Specifications

Torque specifications

Note: *One foot-pound (ft-lb) of torque is equivalent to 12 inch-pounds (in-lbs) of torque. Torque values below approximately 15 ft-lbs are expressed in inch-pounds, since most foot-pound torque wrenches are not accurate at these smaller values.*

	Ft-lbs (unless otherwise indicated)	Nm
Clutch master cylinder retaining bolts	15	20
Clutch release cylinder retaining bolts	17	23
Clutch release lever leaf spring fastener	18	24
Clutch pressure plate bolts	16	22
Flywheel bolts	See Chapter 2A or 2B	
Driveaxle flange bolts (front and rear)		
M8 bolts	30	40
M10 bolts	51	69
Driveaxle/hub bolt*		
M14 bolt		
Step 1	85	115
Step 2	Tighten an additional 180-degrees (1/2-turn)	
M16 bolt		
Step 1	148	201
Step 2	Tighten an additional 180-degrees (1/2-turn)	
Driveshaft CV joint bolts*	41	56
Driveshaft center support bearing bracket/heat shield bolts	18	24
Differential companion flange		
Step 1	133 in-lbs	15
Step 2		
M8 bolts	30	40
M10 bolts	51	69
Rear differential crossmember-to-body bolts		
Step 1	81	110
Step 2	Tighten an additional 90-degrees (1/4-turn)	
Rear differential mounting bolts	30	40
Rear driveaxle heat shield	18	24

Replace with new bolt(s)

1   General information

The information in this Chapter deals with the components from the rear of the engine to the drive wheels, except for the transaxle, which is dealt with in Chapters 7A and 7B. Included in this Chapter is service information on the clutch and its release system, driveaxles, and, on all-wheel drive models, the driveshaft and rear differential. Information on the center differential on all-wheel drive models can be found in Chapter 7.

Since nearly all the procedures covered in this Chapter involve working under the vehicle, make sure it's securely supported on sturdy jackstands or a hoist where the vehicle can be easily raised and lowered.

2   Clutch - description and check

1   All models with a manual transaxle use a single dry plate, diaphragm spring type clutch. The clutch disc has a splined hub which allows it to slide along the splines of the transaxle input shaft. The clutch and pressure plate are held in contact by spring pressure exerted by the diaphragm in the pressure plate.

2   The clutch release system is hydraulically operated. The release system consists of the clutch pedal, the clutch master cylinder, the clutch release cylinder, the hydraulic line between the master cylinder and release cylinder.

3   When pressure is applied to the clutch pedal to release the clutch, the clutch master cylinder transmits this movement to the clutch release cylinder, which moves the clutch release lever. As the lever pivots, the release bearing pushes against the fingers of the diaphragm spring of the pressure plate assembly, which in turn releases the clutch plate.

4   Terminology can be a problem regarding the clutch components because common names have in some cases changed from that used by the manufacturer. For example, the clutch release cylinder is sometimes referred to as a slave cylinder, the driven plate is also called the clutch plate or disc, the pressure plate assembly is also known as the clutch cover, and the clutch release bearing is sometimes called a throw-out bearing.

5   Other than replacing components that have obvious damage, some preliminary checks should be performed to diagnose a clutch system failure.

a) *To check clutch spin down time, run the engine at normal idle speed with the transaxle in Neutral (clutch pedal up, engaged). Disengage the clutch (pedal down), wait several seconds and shift the transaxle into Reverse. No grinding noise should be heard. A grinding noise would most likely indicate a problem in the pressure plate or the clutch disc.*

b) *To check for complete clutch release, run the engine (with the parking brake applied to prevent movement) and hold the clutch pedal approximately 1/2-inch from the floor. Shift the transaxle between 1st gear and Reverse several times. If the shift is not smooth, component failure is indicated.*

c) *Visually inspect the clutch pedal pivot at the top of the clutch pedal to make sure there is no sticking or excessive wear.*

d) *Make sure that the hydraulic lines aren't leaking at either the master cylinder or the release cylinder (see Sections 3 and 4). Bleed the system if necessary (see Section 5).*

3   Clutch master cylinder - removal and installation

Warning: *The models covered by this manual are equipped with Supplemental Restraint Systems (SRS), more commonly known as airbags. Always disable the airbag system before working in the vicinity of any airbag system components to avoid the possibility of accidental deployment of the airbags, which could cause personal injury (see Chapter 12, Section 23).*

Removal

Refer to illustrations 3.5 and 3.16

1   Disconnect the cable from the negative terminal of the battery (see Chapter 5).

2   Remove the cowl cover (see Chapter 11).

3   Remove the electronic box that houses the PCM and auxiliary relay center (see Chapter 6), to gain access to the hydraulic lines.

4   Place enough rags on the floor under the clutch pedal to absorb any brake fluid that may spill. **Note:** *Do not allow brake fluid to get into the plenum chamber or on the transmission. If this does happen, clean the area thoroughly.*

5   Working in the cowl chamber, detach the fluid supply hose from the clutch master cylinder **(see illustration)**. Have a plug ready and

immediately plug the line.

6   Detach the pressure line fitting from the clutch master cylinder. Pull out the clip to separate the line from the master cylinder. Plug the line to prevent excessive fluid loss and the entry of contaminants.

7   Remove the brake master cylinder reservoir retaining bolt and disconnect the electrical connector from the fluid level sensor (this will allow the reservoir to be tilted enough for access to the upper brake master cylinder/booster mounting bolt).

8   Unscrew the two long bolts that hold the brake master cylinder/booster to the pedal assembly bracket.

9   Working inside the vehicle, remove the left-side under-dash panel.

10   Remove the clutch pedal and over-center spring (see Section 8).

11   Disconnect the brake pedal from the booster (see Chapter 9).

12   Remove the pinch bolt securing the steering column shaft universal to the steering gear input shaft and separate the universal joint from the steering gear input shaft (see Chapter 10).

13   Disconnect the electrical connectors to the clutch pedal switch (see Section 9), brake light switch (see Chapter 10) and accelerator pedal module (see Chapter 6).

14   Remove the pedal assembly upper mounting fastener and lower the pedal assembly.

15   Release the clutch master cylinder operating rod by depressing the sides of the retaining clip through the open recesses of the master cylinder. **Caution:** *Do not allow the clutch pedal to swing freely; it may damage the clutch pedal switch.*

16   Unclip the pin securing the clutch master cylinder to the clutch pedal **(see illustration)** and slide the clutch pedal out.

17   Unscrew the mounting bolts and detach the master cylinder from the pedal assembly. Be careful not to spill fluid on the carpet.

Installation

18   Installation is the reverse of removal, with the following points:

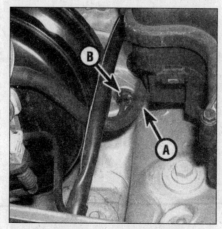

3.5 Clutch master cylinder feed hose (A) and pressure line fitting (B)

3.16 Unclip the pushrod pin and slide it out

a) *Tighten all fasteners to the torque values listed in this Chapter's Specifications.*
b) *Bleed the clutch hydraulic system (see Section 5).*
c) *Check the brake fluid level in the brake fluid reservoir, adding as necessary to bring it to the appropriate level (see Chapter 1).*

4 Clutch release cylinder - removal and installation

Removal

Refer to illustration 4.6

1 Place the shift lever in Neutral and remove the key from the ignition switch.
2 Apply the parking brake and block the rear wheels to prevent the vehicle from rolling. Raise the front of the vehicle and support it securely on jackstands.
3 Remove the lower splash shield.
4 On some V6 models, it may be necessary to disconnect the front of the exhaust system (see Chapter 4) and remove the left side driveaxle from the flange shaft (see Section 11) and move the driveaxle out of the way, to gain access to the clutch release cylinder.
5 Remove the shift selector mounting nut and separate the lever from the selector shaft.
6 Detach the pressure line from the release cylinder. Pull out the clip to separate the line from the cylinder **(see illustration)**. Have some rags handy, as some fluid will be spilled when the line is disconnected. Plug the line to prevent excessive fluid loss and the entry of contaminants.
7 Remove the release cylinder mounting bolt and pull the cylinder straight out of the transaxle.

Installation

8 Lubricate the end of the pushrod with copper grease. Apply lithium-base grease to the area of the boot that seats in the bore in the transaxle. Install the release cylinder, inserting it straight into its bore (otherwise

the pushrod may not seat in its pocket in the release lever).
9 Connect the pressure line to the cylinder. Insert the clip and make sure the line is completely attached and won't pull off.
10 Attach the bracket for the hydraulic line (if equipped), install the release cylinder mounting bolt and tighten it to the torque listed in this Chapter's Specifications.
11 The remainder of installation is the reverse of removal, with the additional following points:

a) *Bleed the system (see Section 5).*
b) *Check the fluid level in the brake fluid reservoir, adding as necessary to bring it to the appropriate level (see Chapter 1).*
c) *Wash off any spilled brake fluid with water.*

5 Clutch hydraulic system - bleeding

1 The hydraulic system should be bled of all air whenever any part of the system has been removed or if the fluid level has been allowed to fall so low that air has been drawn into the master cylinder. The procedure is similar to bleeding a brake system.
2 Fill the brake master cylinder with new brake fluid conforming to DOT 4 specifications. **Warning:** *Do not re-use any of the fluid coming from the system during the bleeding operation or use fluid which has been inside an open container for an extended period of time.*
3 Apply the parking brake and block the rear wheels to prevent the vehicle from rolling. Raise the front of the vehicle and support it securely on jackstands. Locate the bleeder screw on the clutch release cylinder **(see illustration 4.6)**. Remove the dust cap from the bleeder screw and push a length of snug-fitting (preferably clear) hose over the screw. Place the other end of the hose into a clear container with about two inches of brake fluid in it. The hose end must be submerged in the fluid.
4 Have an assistant depress the clutch pedal and hold it. Open the bleeder screw

on the release cylinder, allowing fluid to flow through the hose. Close the bleeder screw when fluid stops flowing from the hose. Once closed, have your assistant release the pedal.
5 Continue this process until all air is evacuated from the system, indicated by a full, solid stream of fluid being ejected from the bleeder screw each time and no air bubbles in the hose or container. Keep a close watch on the fluid level inside the brake master cylinder reservoir; if the level drops too low, air will be sucked back into the system and the process will have to be started over again.
6 Install the dust cap on the bleeder screw. Check carefully for proper operation before placing the vehicle in normal service.
7 Lower the vehicle.
8 Recheck the brake fluid level.

6 Clutch components - removal, inspection and installation

Warning: *Dust produced by clutch wear and deposited on clutch components is hazardous to your health. DO NOT blow it out with compressed air and DO NOT inhale it. DO NOT use gasoline or petroleum-based solvents to remove the dust. Brake system cleaner should be used to flush the dust into a drain pan. After the clutch components are wiped clean with a rag, dispose of the contaminated rags and cleaner in a labeled, covered container.*

Removal

Refer to illustrations 6.4 and 6.6

1 Access to the clutch components is normally accomplished by removing the transaxle, leaving the engine in the vehicle. If, of course, the engine is being removed for major overhaul, then the opportunity should always be taken to check the clutch for wear and replace worn components as necessary. However, the relatively low cost of the clutch components compared to the time and labor involved in gaining access to them warrants their replacement any time the engine or transaxle is removed, unless they are new or in near-perfect condition. The following procedures assume that the engine will stay in place.
2 Remove the transaxle from the vehicle (see Chapter 7A). Support the engine while the transaxle is out. Preferably, an engine hoist or support fixture should be used to support it from above. However, if a jack is used underneath the engine, make sure a piece of wood is used between the jack and oil pan to spread the load.
3 The release lever and release bearing can remain attached to the transaxle; however, you should inspect them (see Section 7) while the transaxle is removed.
4 Carefully inspect the flywheel and pressure plate for indexing marks. If they cannot be found, scribe marks yourself so the pressure plate and the flywheel will be in the same

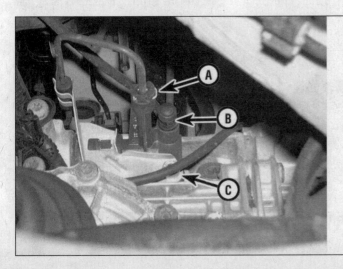

4.6 Clutch release cylinder details

A *Hydraulic line fitting*
B *Bleeder screw*
C *Mounting bolt*

6.4 Mark the relationship of the pressure plate to the flywheel (in case you're going to re-use the same pressure plate)

6.6 When removing the pressure plate, be careful not to let the clutch disc fall out

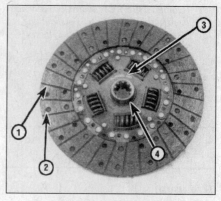

6.11 The clutch disc

1　*Lining* - this will wear down in use
2　*Rivets* - these secure the lining and will damage the flywheel or pressure plate if allowed to contact the surfaces
3　*Markings* - "Flywheel side" or something similar
4　*Hub* - be sure this is installed facing the proper direction (see the text)

alignment during installation **(see illustration)**. Of course, this won't be necessary if you're planning on replacing the pressure plate with a new one.

5　Slowly loosen the pressure plate-to-flywheel bolts. Work in a criss-cross pattern and loosen each bolt a little at a time until all spring pressure is relieved.

6　Hold the pressure plate securely and completely remove the bolts, followed by the pressure plate and clutch disc **(see illustration)**.

Inspection

Refer to illustrations 6.11, 6.13a and 6.13b

7　Inspect the pilot bearing recessed into the end of the crankshaft for wear or damage. If the needle bearings are good, clean the area and apply new grease to the needle bearings. If the bearing is damaged, insert a puller (available at most auto parts stores) and pull the bearing out from the crankshaft.

8　Using a brass drift or equivalent, drive the pilot bearing into the crankshaft with the letters on the needle bearing to the outside. The bearing should be inserted 1/8-inch below the edge of the crankshaft.

9　Ordinarily, when a problem occurs in the clutch, it can be attributed to wear of the clutch driven plate assembly (clutch disc). However, all components should be inspected at this time.

10　Inspect the flywheel for cracks, heat checking, score marks and other damage. If the imperfections are slight, a machine shop can resurface it to make it flat and smooth. Refer to Chapter 2A for the flywheel removal procedure.

11　Inspect the lining on the clutch disc. There should be at least 1/16-inch of lining above the rivet heads. Check for loose rivets, distortion, cracks, broken springs and other obvious damage **(see illustration)**. As mentioned above, ordinarily the clutch disc is replaced as a matter of course, so if in doubt about the condition, replace it with a new one.

12　The release bearing should be replaced along with the clutch disc (see Section 7).

13　Check the machined surface and the diaphragm spring fingers of the pressure plate **(see illustrations)**. If the surface is grooved or otherwise damaged, replace the pressure plate assembly. Also check for obvious damage, distortion, cracking, etc. Light glazing can be removed with emery cloth or sandpa-

per. If a new pressure plate is indicated, new or factory rebuilt units are available.

Adjustment

Refer to illustrations 6.14 and 6.15

Note 1: *This procedure applies only to models equipped with a Self-adjusting clutch (SAC).*

Note 2: *If installing the original pressure plate and a new clutch disc is being installed, before installation, the self-adjusting pressure plate must be preadjusted, and to do so requires a hydraulic press. If you don't have a press, take the pressure plate to an automotive machine shop for adjustment. Disregard Steps 14 through 19 if you're replacing the pressure plate with a new one.*

14　Insert three pressure plate bolts into the pressure plate securing holes **(see illustration)**.

15　Place the pressure plate on the press making sure the bolts heads are the only part to make contact with the surface of the press, then depress the clutch diaphragm fingers until the adjusting rings move freely **(see illustration)**.

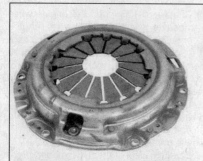

NORMAL FINGER WEAR

EXCESSIVE WEAR →

EXCESSIVE FINGER WEAR

BROKEN OR BENT FINGERS

6.13a Replace the pressure plate if excessive wear is noted

6.13b Examine the pressure plate friction surface for score marks, cracks and evidence of overheating

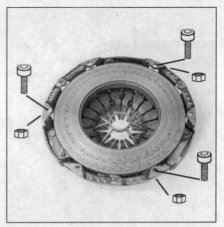

6.14 Insert the three pressure plate bolts as shown, then tighten the nuts slightly

6.15 Using a suitable adapter, depress the clutch diaphragm until the adjusting rings can be moved against their stops

16   Using two screwdrivers, move both the adjusting rings counterclockwise until the tension springs reach the limit stop.

17   Holding the adjusting rings in place, release pressure on the diaphragm fingers.

18   Remove the pressure plate from the press.

19   Remove the three pressure plate bolts.

Installation

Refer to illustration 6.22

20   Position the clutch disc and pressure plate with the clutch held in place with an alignment tool. Make sure the disc is installed properly. If your vehicle is equipped with a one-piece flywheel, the spring cage must face the pressure plate. If the vehicle is equipped with a two-piece flywheel, the shorter hub end must face the pressure plate. You may find the word "Getriebeseite" stamped on the hub of the disc; if so, this side must face the pressure plate. Also, if the vehicle is equipped with a two-piece flywheel, the white mark on the flywheel must line-up with the white mark on the pressure plate.

21   Tighten the pressure plate-to-flywheel bolts only finger tight, working around the pressure plate.

22   Center the clutch disc by ensuring the alignment tool is through the splined hub and into the recess in the crankshaft **(see illustration)**. Wiggle the tool up, down or side-to-side as needed to bottom the tool. Tighten the pressure plate-to-flywheel bolts a little at a time, working in a criss-cross pattern to prevent distortion of the cover. After all of the bolts are snug, tighten them to the torque listed in this Chapter's Specifications. Remove the alignment tool.

23   Using moly-base grease, lubricate the inner surface of the release bearing and the face of the bearing where it contacts the fingers of the pressure plate diaphragm spring. Also place grease on the release lever contact areas and the transaxle input shaft. **Caution:** *Don't use too much grease.*

24   Install the clutch release bearing (see Section 7).

25   Install the transaxle and all components removed previously, tightening all fasteners to the proper torque specifications.

7   Clutch release bearing and lever - removal, inspection and installation

Refer to illustrations 7.3, 7.4, 7.6 and 7.8

Warning: *Dust produced by clutch wear and deposited on clutch components is hazardous to your health. DO NOT blow it out with compressed air and DO NOT inhale it. DO NOT use gasoline or petroleum-based solvents to remove the dust. Brake system cleaner should be used to flush it into a drain pan. After the clutch components are wiped clean with a rag, dispose of the contaminated rags and cleaner in a labeled, covered container.*

Removal

1   Remove the transaxle as described in Chapter 7A.

2   Remove the leaf spring mounting bolt at the end of the clutch release lever and remove the spring.

3   Push the detent spring back at the pivot

7.3 Push the detent back to release the lever

6.22 Center the clutch disc with a clutch alignment tool, then tighten the pressure plate bolts a little at a time, in a criss-cross pattern, to the torque listed in this Chapter's Specifications

end to release lever by pushing it through the hole **(see illustration)**. This will release the pivot end of the lever. Withdraw the lever together with the release bearing from the guide sleeve.

4   Use a screwdriver to depress the tabs and separate the bearing from the lever **(see illustration)**.

7.4 Pry inward on the plastic tabs retaining the bearing to the lever, then separate the bearing from the lever

7.6 To check the bearing, hold it by the outer race and rotate the inner race while applying pressure; if the bearing doesn't turn smoothly or if it's noisy, replace it

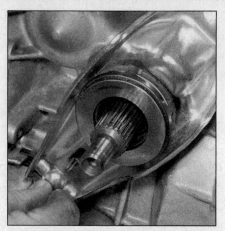

7.8 Press the release lever onto the ballstud until the spring clip holds it in position

5   Remove the plastic pivot from the ball-stud. The release lever locates on the plastic pivot.

Inspection

6   Hold the bearing by the outer race and rotate the inner race while applying pressure **(see illustration)**. If the bearing doesn't turn smoothly, or if it's noisy, replace the bearing with a new one. Wipe the bearing with a clean rag and inspect it for damage, wear and cracks. Don't immerse the bearing in solvent; it's sealed for life and to do so would ruin it. Also check the release lever for cracks and bends.

Installation

7   Begin installation by lubricating the ballstud and plastic pivot with a little copper grease. Smear a little grease on the release bearing surface which contacts the diaphragm spring fingers and the release lever, and also on the guide sleeve.
8   Install the spring onto the release lever, making sure the plastic pivot is in place on the ballstud. Position the lever and bearing and press the release lever onto the ballstud until the spring holds it in position **(see illustration)**.
9   Install the transaxle (see Chapter 7A).

8   Clutch pedal and over-center spring - removal and installation

Note: *A special spring retaining clamp is needed to hold the over-center spring in the compressed position; if this tool is not available, this job should be left to a professional mechanic.*
1   Remove the driver's side knee bolster (see Chapter 11).
2   Remove the clutch pedal switch (see Section 9).
3   Depress the clutch pedal and install the

center spring retaining clamp.
4   Release the clip securing the clutch master cylinder pushrod pin from the pedal by twisting it upwards, then pulling it from the pedal. Pull up the pedal to disconnect it from the pushrod.
5   Pry the pedal retaining clip from the groove in the left end of the pivot shaft.
6   Remove the clip from the pedal pivot shaft, then push the shaft to the right until the clutch pedal can be removed from the bracket.
7   Remove the over-center spring from the slots in the pedal bracket.
8   Installation is the reverse of removal. When installing the over-center spring, install the black end of the spring toward the clutch pedal.

9   Clutch pedal switch and clutch pedal starter interlock switch - removal and installation

1   Remove the driver's side knee bolster for access (see Chapter 11).

Clutch pedal switch

Note: *For the purpose of a secure fit, the manufacturer recommends installing the clutch pedal switch only once.*
2   The clutch pedal switch is located on the front side of the clutch pedal. Disconnect the clutch pedal switch electrical connector.
3   Rotate the switch about 45 degrees counterclockwise, then carefully remove it from the bracket.
4   Before installing the switch, pull the plunger on the switch out fully.
5   With the clutch pedal fully released (up), install the switch in its bracket in the opposite manner that it was removed. The switch will self-adjust by design when installed correctly.
6   Connect the electrical connector.
7   Install the knee bolster.

Clutch pedal starter interlock switch

8   The clutch pedal starter interlock switch is located on the back side of the clutch pedal. Disconnect the clutch pedal starter interlock switch electrical connector.
9   Press and hold the clutch pedal all the way down, then rotate the switch about 45 degrees clockwise, and carefully remove it from the bracket.
10   Before installing the switch, pull the plunger on the switch out fully.
11   With the clutch pedal fully pressed down, install the switch in its bracket in the opposite manner that it was removed. The switch will self-adjust by design when installed correctly.
12   Connect the electrical connector.
13   Install the knee bolster.

10   Driveaxles - general information and inspection

1   Power is transmitted from the transaxle to the front wheels through a pair of driveaxles. On all-wheel drive models, power is also transmitted to the rear wheels through two driveaxles. The inner end of each driveaxle is bolted to a drive flange protruding from the differential; the outer end of each driveaxle has a stub shaft that is splined to the hub and bearing assembly and locked in place with a large bolt.
2   The inner ends of the driveaxles are equipped with sliding constant velocity (CV) joints, which are capable of both angular and axial motion. Each inner CV joint assembly consists of a either a triple rotor-type bearing or a ball-and-cage type bearing and a housing in which the joint is free to slide in-and-out as the driveaxle moves up-and-down with the wheel.
3   The outer ends of the driveaxles are equipped with ball-and-cage type CV joints, which are capable of angular but not axial movement. Each outer CV joint consists of six ball bearings running between an inner race and an outer cage.
4   The boots should be inspected periodically for damage and leaking lubricant. Torn CV joint boots must be replaced immediately or the joints will be damaged. If either boot of a driveaxle is damaged, that driveaxle must be removed in order to replace the boot (see Section 11).
5   Should a boot be damaged, the CV joint can be disassembled and cleaned, but if any parts are damaged, the entire driveaxle assembly may have to be replaced as a unit - check with your local auto parts store regarding the availability of replacement parts and CV joints (see Section 12).
6   The most common symptom of worn or damaged CV joints, besides lubricant leaks, is a clicking noise in turns, a clunk when accelerating after coasting and vibration at highway speeds. To check for wear in the CV joints and driveaxle shafts, grasp each axle (one at a time) and rotate it in both directions while

11.3 Mark the relationship of the inner CV joint to the drive flange and remove the mounting fasteners

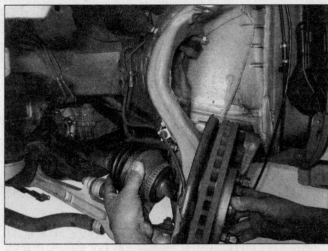

11.8 Carefully slide the outer CV joint from the hub and remove the axle assembly from the vehicle

holding the CV joint housings, feeling for play indicating worn splines or sloppy CV joints. Also check the driveaxle shafts for cracks, dents and distortion.

11 Driveaxle - removal and installation

Warning: *The manufacturer recommends replacing the driveaxle/hub bolt with a new one whenever it is removed.*

Front
Removal
Refer to illustrations 11.3 and 11.8

1   Remove the wheel trim/hub cap (as applicable) and loosen the driveaxle/hub bolt 1/4-turn with the vehicle resting on its wheels. Also loosen the wheel bolts.
2   Raise the front of the vehicle and support it securely on jackstands. Block the rear wheels to prevent the vehicle from rolling off the stands. Remove the wheel.
3   Unscrew the bolts securing the inner CV joint to the transaxle drive flange and remove the retaining plates from underneath the bolts **(see illustration)**. Support the driveaxle by suspending it with wire or string - do not allow it to hang under its weight, or the joint may be damaged.
4   Pull the ABS wheel speed sensor partially out of its mounting hole in the steering knuckle (see Chapter 9). This will prevent it from becoming damaged as the driveaxle is withdrawn from the hub.
5   Remove the driveaxle/hub bolt.
6   Detach the upper control arms from the steering knuckle (see Chapter 10).
7   Carefully swing the steering knuckle outwards and withdraw the driveaxle outer constant velocity joint from the hub. If the splines of the outer joint are stuck in the hub, tap the joint out of the hub using a brass drift. If this fails to free it from the hub, the joint will

have to be pressed out using a puller which is bolted to the hub.
8   Maneuver the driveaxle out from underneath the vehicle **(see illustration)**. Remove the gasket from the end of the inner constant velocity joint, if present. Discard the gasket; a new one should be used on installation.
9   Don't allow the vehicle to rest on its wheels with one (or both) driveaxle(s) removed, as damage to the wheel bearing(s) may result. If moving the vehicle is unavoidable, temporarily insert the outer end of the driveaxle(s) in the hub(s) and tighten the driveaxle/hub bolt(s); in this case, the inner end(s) of the driveaxle(s) must be supported, for example by suspending with string from the vehicle underbody. Do not allow the driveaxle to hang down, as the joint may be damaged.

Installation
10   Ensure that the transaxle drive flange and inner joint mating surfaces are clean and dry.
11   Ensure that the outer joint and hub splines and threads are clean, then lubricate the splines with a light coat of multi-purpose grease.
12   Maneuver the driveaxle into position and engage the outer joint with the hub. Install a new bolt and tighten it to draw the joint fully into position. Don't tighten it completely yet (wait until the wheel is installed and the vehicle has been lowered to the ground).
13   Connect the control arms to the steering knuckle, tightening the pinch bolt nut to the torque listed in the Chapter 10 Specifications.
14   Align the driveaxle inner joint with the transaxle flange and install the retaining bolts and plates. Tighten the bolts to the torque listed in this Chapter's Specifications.
15   Ensure that the outer joint is drawn fully into position, then install the wheel and lower the vehicle to the ground.
16   The remainder of installation is the reverse of removal, with the following points:

a) *Tighten the driveaxle/hub bolt to the torque and angle of rotation listed in this Chapter's Specifications.*

b) *Once the driveaxle/hub bolt is correctly tightened, tighten the wheel lug bolts to the torque listed in the Chapter 1 Specifications and install the wheel trim/hub cap.*

Rear (all-wheel drive models)
Removal
Refer to illustration 11.22

17   Remove the wheel trim/hub cap (as applicable) and loosen the driveaxle/hub bolt 1/4-turn with the vehicle resting on its wheels. Also loosen the wheel bolts.
18   Raise the rear of the vehicle and support it securely on jackstands. Block the front wheels to prevent the vehicle from rolling off the stands. Remove the wheel.
19   Remove the rear coil spring (see Chapter 10).
20   Partially remove the ABS wheel speed sensor to prevent damaging it when the driveaxle is removed (see Chapter 9).
21   Remove the driveaxle heat shield fasteners and heat shield (if equipped).
22   Unscrew the bolts securing the inner CV joint to the differential drive flange and remove the retaining plates from underneath the bolts **(see illustration)**. Support the driveaxle by

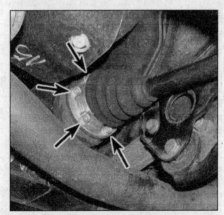

11.22 Rear driveaxle inner CV joint bolts - four of six shown

12.2 Cut the CV joint boot clamps off with a pair of diagonal cutters and discard them

12.4 Drive the outer CV joint off the shaft with a hammer and a brass punch

suspending it with wire or string - do not allow it to hang under its weight, or the joint may be damaged.

23   Remove the driveaxle/hub bolt.

24   Lower the inner end of the driveaxle and slide the outer end of the driveaxle out of the hub and through the lower control arm. If the splines of the outer joint are stuck in the hub, tap the joint out of the hub using a brass drift. If this fails to free it from the hub, the joint will have to be pressed out using a puller which is bolted to the hub.

25   Pull down by hand on the rear portion of the exhaust system and maneuver the driveaxle out from underneath the vehicle. Recover the gasket from the end of the inner CV joint, if present. Discard the gasket - a new one should be used on installation.

26   Don't allow the vehicle to rest on its wheels with one (or both) driveaxle(s) removed, as damage to the wheel bearing(s) may result. If moving the vehicle is unavoidable, temporarily insert the outer end of the driveaxle(s) in the hub(s) and tighten the driveaxle/hub bolt(s); in this case, the inner end(s) of the driveaxle(s) must be supported, for example by suspending with string from the vehicle underbody. Do not allow the driveaxle to hang down, as the joint may be damaged.

Installation

27   Ensure that the differential drive flange and inner joint mating surfaces are clean and dry. Install a new gasket to the joint by peeling off its backing foil and sticking it in position.

28   Ensure that the outer joint and hub splines and threads are clean, then lubricate the splines with a light coat of multi-purpose grease.

29   Maneuver the driveaxle into position and engage the outer joint with the hub. Install a new bolt and tighten it to draw the joint fully into position. Don't tighten it completely yet (wait until the wheel is installed and the vehicle has been lowered to the ground).

30   Align the driveaxle inner joint with the dif-

ferential flange and install the retaining bolts and plates. Tighten the bolts to the torque listed in this Chapter's Specifications.

31   Install the coil spring (see Chapter 10).

32   Ensure that the outer joint is drawn fully into position, then install the wheel and lower the vehicle to the ground.

33   The remainder of installation is the reverse of removal, with the following points:

a) Tighten the driveaxle/hub bolt to the torque and angle of rotation listed in this Chapter's Specifications.

b) Once the driveaxle/hub bolt is correctly tightened, tighten the wheel lug bolts to the torque listed in the Chapter 1 Specifications and install the wheel trim/hub cap.

---

12   Driveaxle boot replacement and CV joint inspection

Note: If the CV joints exhibit signs of wear indicating need for an overhaul (usually due to torn boots), explore all options before beginning the job. Complete rebuilt driveaxles are available on an exchange basis, which eliminates much time and work. Whichever route you choose to take, check on the cost and availability of parts before disassembling the driveaxle.

1   Remove the driveaxle from the vehicle as described in Section 11.

Outer CV joint (all models)

Refer to illustrations 12.2, 12.4, 12.5a, 12.5b, 12.5c, 12.7, 12.8, 12.9, 12.10, 12.17, 12.20a, 12.20b, 12.22a and 12.22b

2   Secure the driveaxle in a vise equipped with soft jaws, then cut the two outer joint boot retaining clamps off (see illustration).

3   Slide the boot down the shaft to expose the constant velocity (CV) joint and wipe off as much grease as possible.

4   Using a hammer and a brass punch, tap

the joint off the end of the driveaxle (see illustration). **Caution:** Place the punch on the inner race of the CV joint only.

5   Remove the circlip from the driveaxle groove (see illustration), then slide the thrust washer and dished washer (if equipped), noting which way they are installed (see illustrations).

6   Slide the boot off the driveaxle and discard it.

7   Clean the outer CV joint assembly to remove as much grease as possible. Mark the relative position of the bearing cage, inner race and housing (see illustration).

8   Mount the outer CV joint in a vise equipped with soft jaws. Push down on one side of the cage and remove the ball bearing from the opposite side. Repeat this procedure until all of the balls are removed (see illustration). If the joint is tight, tap on the inner race (not the cage) with a hammer and brass punch.

9   Remove the cage and inner race assembly from the housing by tilting it vertically and aligning two opposing cage windows in the area between the ball grooves (see illustration).

10   Turn the inner race 90-degrees to the cage and align one of the spherical lands with a cage window. Raise the land into the window and swivel the inner race out of the cage (see illustration).

11   Clean all of the parts with solvent and dry them off.

12   Inspect the housing, splines, balls and races for damage, corrosion, wear and cracks. Check the inner race for wear and scoring in the races. If any of the components are not serviceable, the entire CV joint assembly must be replaced with a new one. If the joint is in satisfactory condition, obtain a boot replacement kit; kits usually contain a new boot and retaining clamps, a constant velocity joint snap-ring and the correct type of grease. If grease isn't included in the kit, be sure to obtain some CV joint grease.

13   Coat all of the CV joint components with

12.5a Remove the circlip from the end
of the shaft . . .

12.5b . . . the thrust washer . . .

12.5c . . . and the dished washer

12.7 Mark the relationship of the bearing
cage, inner race and housing

12.8 If necessary, pry the balls out
with a screwdriver

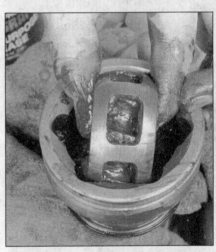

12.9 Tilt the inner race and cage
90-degrees, then align the windows in the
cage with the lands and rotate the inner
race up and out of the outer race

CV joint grease before beginning reassembly.

14   Install the inner race in the cage and align the marks made in Step 7.

15   Install the inner race and cage assembly into the CV joint housing, aligning the marks on the inner race and cage assembly with the mark on the housing.

16   Install the balls into the holes, one at a time, until they are all in place.

17   Apply CV joint grease through the hole in the inner race, then force a wooden dowel down through the hole **(see illustration)**. This will force the grease into the joint. Continue this procedure until the joint is completely packed. Joints with an outer diameter of 88 mm (3.5 inches) will require 90 grams (3 ounces) of grease; joints with an outer diameter of 100 mm (3.9 inches) will require 120 grams (4.2 ounces) of grease. Pack the joint with as much grease as you can, then place the remainder of the grease in the boot.

18   Place the axleshaft in the vise. Clean the end of the axleshaft, then slide the new

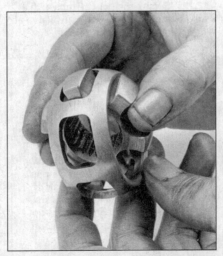

12.10 Align the inner race with the cage
windows and rotate the inner race out
of the cage

12.17 Apply grease through the splined
hole, then insert a wooden dowel into the
hole and push down - the dowel will force
the grease into the joint

clamp and boot into place. **Note:** *It's a good idea to wrap the axleshaft splines with electri-* cal tape to prevent damage to the boot. Apply the remainder of the grease from the kit into the CV joint boot.

19   Remove the protective tape from the driveaxle splines.

20   Install a new circlip in the groove on the driveaxle **(see illustrations)**, use a small screwdriver to depress the circlip, then tap the joint onto the driveaxle until the circlip engages with the groove in the inner race. Make sure the joint is securely retained by the circlip.

21   Ease the boot over the joint, making sure that the boot lips are correctly located on both the driveaxle and CV joint. Lift the outer sealing lip of the boot to equalize air pressure within the boot.

22   Install the large retaining clamp on the boot. Pull the small clamp as tight as possible and locate the hooks on the clamp in their slots **(see illustration)**. Tighten the clamp by crimping the raised area with a special boot clamp tool **(see illustration)**. Due to the relatively hard composition of the boots, this type of tool is required to apply adequate crimping force on the clamps. Secure the large retaining clamp using the same procedure.

23   Make sure the constant velocity joint moves freely in all directions, then install the driveaxle as described in Section 11.

12.20a Install a new circlip in the driveaxle groove . . .

12.20b . . . push the circlip in and tap the joint into place

12.22a Pull the small clamp as tight as possible and locate the hooks on the clamp in their slots

12.22b Secure the boot clamps with a clamp crimping tool like this, available at most auto parts stores

Inner CV joint

Triple-roller type joint (non-peened)

Refer to illustrations 12.24, 12.25a, 12.25b, 12.26, 12.27, 12.28, 12.36, 12.37 and 12.38

24   Remove the boot clamps and discard them, then pull the boot back on the shaft **(see illustration)**.

25   Mount the driveaxle in a vise equipped with soft jaws, then pry the cover off the inner end of the joint and remove the O-ring from the groove **(see illustrations)**. Discard the cover and O-ring - it isn't necessary to install a new cover or O-ring, as a square-section O-ring will take its place.

26   Mark the relationship of the housing, triple-roller spider and the end of the axleshaft **(see illustration)**, then remove the axleshaft from the vise and slide it down the shaft.

27   Mark the relationship of the rollers to the spider **(see illustration)**.

28   Remove the snap-ring from the end of the axleshaft with a pair of snap-ring pliers, then slide the spider off the shaft **(see illustration)**. **Note:** *If the spider won't slide off or tap off easily, it will be necessary to push it off with a hydraulic press.*

29   Remove the housing from the shaft, then clean all of the components with solvent. Inspect all components for pitting and other signs of wear (shiny, polished spots are normal and won't affect operation). If any signs of wear are found, replace the entire joint.

30   Slide the joint housing onto the shaft, then place the shaft back in the vise.

31   Install the small clamp and the boot onto the shaft. It's a good idea to wrap the splines of the shaft with electrical tape to prevent damage to the boot.

32   Install the spider on the shaft, aligning the marks made in Step 26. **Note:** *The cham-*

12.24 Cut the CV joint boot clamps off with a pair of diagonal cutters, then pull the boot back on the shaft

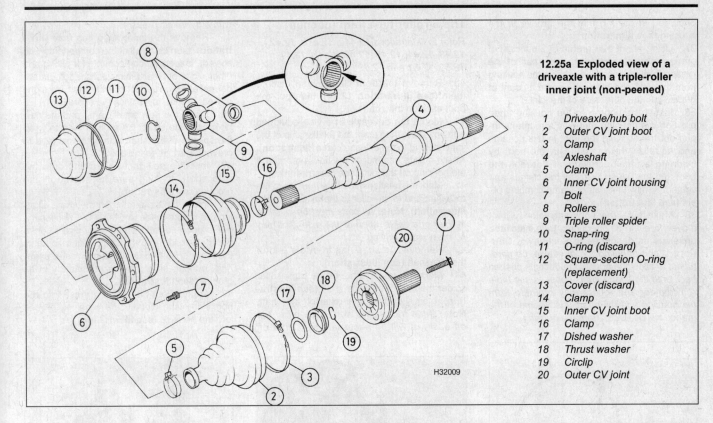

12.25a Exploded view of a driveaxle with a triple-roller inner joint (non-peened)

1   Driveaxle/hub bolt
2   Outer CV joint boot
3   Clamp
4   Axleshaft
5   Clamp
6   Inner CV joint housing
7   Bolt
8   Rollers
9   Triple roller spider
10   Snap-ring
11   O-ring (discard)
12   Square-section O-ring (replacement)
13   Cover (discard)
14   Clamp
15   Inner CV joint boot
16   Clamp
17   Dished washer
18   Thrust washer
19   Circlip
20   Outer CV joint

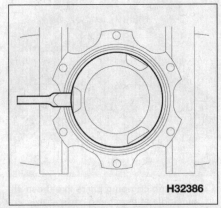

12.25b If this is the first time the inner boot is being replaced, you'll have to pry off this cover and remove the O-ring from the groove underneath

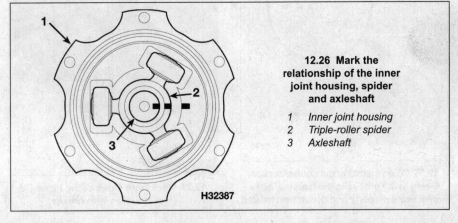

12.26 Mark the relationship of the inner joint housing, spider and axleshaft

1   Inner joint housing
2   Triple-roller spider
3   Axleshaft

fered side of the spider splines face the opposite side of the shaft. If necessary, use a deep socket or a piece of pipe to drive the spider onto the shaft until it contacts its stop. Install a new snap-ring, making sure it seats completely in its groove.

33   Lubricate the posts of the spider with CV joint grease, then install the rollers onto their respective posts. Now coat the outside of the rollers with CV joint grease.

34   Release the shaft from the vise, then slide the housing up onto the triple-rotor spider, aligning the marks made in Step 26.

35   Clamp the housing in the vise, allowing the shaft to hang straight down.

36   Install the square-section O-ring

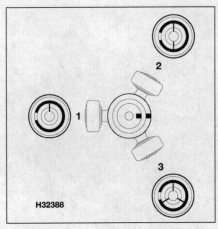

12.27 Use a permanent marker to mark the position of each roller to its post on the spider

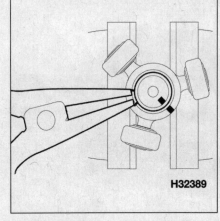

12.28 Remove the snap-ring from the end of the axleshaft, then remove the spider

(included in the kit) into the groove in the housing **(see illustration)**.

37 Using about 120 grams (4.2 ounces) of grease **(see illustration)**, apply half of the grease from the top, then remove the housing from the vise and place the same amount of grease into the other side of the joint.

38 Install the boot onto the housing, then position the housing mid-way through its in-and-out travel. Hold the joint in this position and equalize the pressure in the boot by inserting a small screwdriver between the boot and the housing. Install the clamps and tighten them with a pair of clamp crimping pliers **(see illustration)**.

39 Make sure the constant velocity joint moves freely in all directions, then install the driveaxle as described in Section 11. **Caution:** *When handling the driveaxle, be careful not to allow the housing to become pushed back onto the shaft - if this happens, the triple rotor spider and rollers may protrude from the housing and fall apart. Also, some of the grease will be forced from the housing.*

Triple-roller type joint (peened)

Refer to illustrations 12.41a, 12.41b, 12.42, 12.43, 12.44, 12.45, 12.47, 12.48, 12.49, 12.50, 12.51 and 12.52

40 Remove the boot clamps and discard them **(see illustration 12.24)**, then pull the boot back on the shaft

41 Mount the driveaxle in a vise equipped with soft jaws, then mark the relationship of the joint housing to the axleshaft **(see illustration)**. Attach a slide hammer to the housing and pull the housing off the joint **(see illustration)**.

42 Mark the relationship of the housing to the axleshaft and triple-roller to the axleshaft **(see illustration)**. **Note:** *All parts must be installed in their original location or the axle joint may be noisy when driving.*

43 Remove the snap-ring from the end of the axleshaft **(see illustration)**.

44 Mark the relationship of the triple-roller spider the end of the axle shaft **(see illustration)**, then slide the triple-roller off the shaft. **Note:** *If the triple-roller won't slide off or tap off easily, it will be necessary to push it off*

with a hydraulic press.

45 Remove the inner snap-ring **(see illustration)**, then clean all of the components with solvent. Inspect all components for pitting and other signs of wear (shiny, polished spots are normal and won't affect operation). If any signs of wear are found, replace the entire joint.

46 Install the new small clamp and the new boot onto the shaft. It's a good idea to wrap the splines of the shaft with electrical tape to prevent damage to the boot.

47 Install a new inner snap-ring onto the axle shaft, making sure its seated in the groove **(see illustration)**.

48 Install the triple-roller on the shaft, aligning the marks made in Step 44. If necessary, use a deep socket or a piece of pipe to drive the triple-roller onto the shaft until it contacts the inner snap-ring. Install a new outer snap-ring, making sure it seats completely in its groove **(see illustration)**.

49 Apply about half of the grease into the boot side of the joint and the remaining grease into the housing **(see illustration)**.

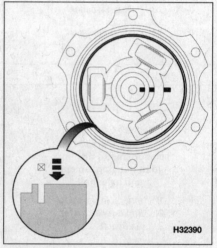

12.36 When installing the square-section O-ring in the groove in the housing, make sure it seats properly and doesn't get twisted

12.37 Pack both sides of the inner CV joint housing with grease

12.38 Clamp crimping pliers like these are available at most auto parts stores

12.41a Mark the joint housing to the axleshaft

12.41b Attach a slide hammer to the triple-roller housing and pull the housing straight off the triple roller

12.42 Mark the triple-roller spider the axleshaft

50   Mount the driveaxle in a vise equipped with soft jaws, using a block of wood and hammer, tap the housing onto the triple-roller **(see illustration)**. **Caution:** *Do not let the housing tilt while installing it, as it could be damaged.*

51   Install the boot onto the housing, then position the housing mid-way through its in-and-out travel. Hold the joint in this position and equalize the pressure in the boot by inserting a small screwdriver between the boot and the housing **(see illustration)**.

52   Place the crimp part of the large clamp in between the bolt hole flanges, then tighten both clamps with a pair of clamp crimping pliers **(see illustration)**.

53   Make sure the CV joint moves freely, then install the driveaxle as described in Section 11.

12.43   Using a pair of snap-ring pliers, remove the outer snap-ring from the axleshaft end

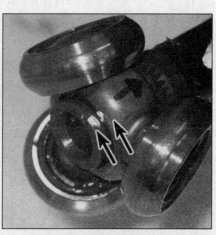

12.44   Mark the triple-roller splines to the axleshaft splines

12.45   Using a pair of snap-ring pliers, remove the inner snap-ring from the axleshaft groove

12.47   Install the new inner snap-ring, making sure the snap-ring is seated into the groove

12.48   The triple-roller should be seated against both snap-rings

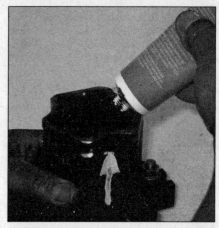

12.49   Apply half of the CV joint grease directly into the housing before installing it onto the axle shaft

12.50   Use a block of wood and hammer to reinstall the housing over the rollers

12.51   Position the housing mid-way through its travel, then insert a screwdriver between the housing and boot to equalize the pressure

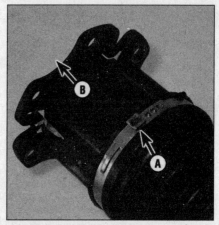

12.52   Make sure the crimped part of the clamp (A) is centered between the bolt hole flanges (B)

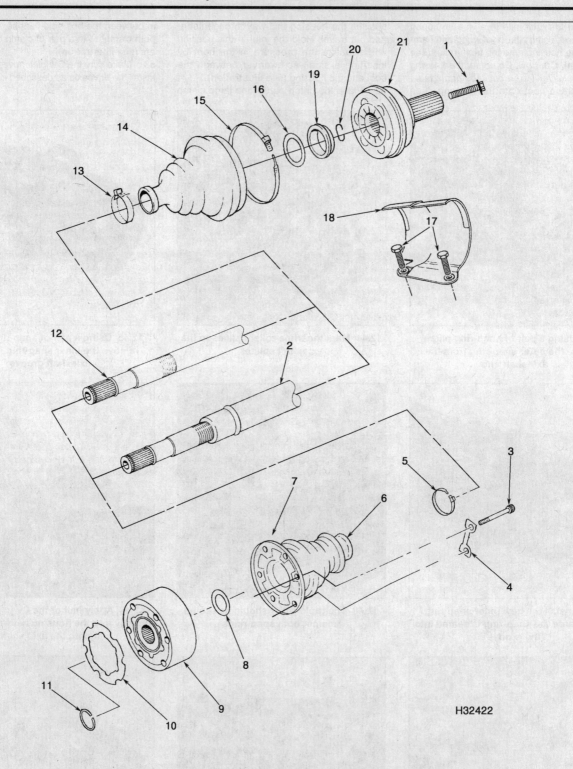

12.56 Exploded view of a driveaxle with a ball-and-cage inner joint

1	Driveaxle/hub bolt	8	Dished washer	16	Dished washer
2	Axleshaft (right side)	9	Inner CV joint	17	Bolt
3	Bolt	10	Gasket	18	Heat shield
4	Retaining plate	11	Snap-ring	19	Thrust washer
5	Clamp	12	Axleshaft (left side)	20	Circlip
6	Inner CV joint boot	13	Clamp	21	Outer CV joint
7	Inner CV joint boot	14	Outer CV joint boot		
	metal collar	15	Clamp		

H32422

Ball-and-cage type joint

Refer to illustrations 12.56, 12.59, 12.66 and 12.67

54   Remove the boot clamp and discard it.

55   Mount the driveaxle in a vise equipped with soft jaws. Using a hammer and a punch, knock the boot cap off the inner CV joint.

56   Using a pair of snap-ring pliers, remove the snap-ring from its groove in the end of the driveaxle **(see illustration)**.

57   Pull the inner joint off the end of the axle-shaft. If it is stuck, use a hammer and a brass punch to drive it off the shaft; apply force to the inner race of the joint only. If it still won't come off, it'll be necessary to push it off with a hydraulic press. Remove the dished washer from the shaft, then pull off the boot.

58   Wipe the grease off the joint and mark the relationship of the inner race, cage and housing.

59   Rotate the cage and inner race 90-degrees and remove it from the housing **(see illustration)**.

60   Remove each ball bearing from the cage,

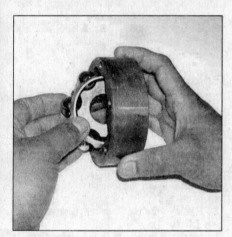

12.59   Turn the cage and inner race 90-degrees and rotate it out of the housing

keeping track of their positions so they can be reinstalled in the same spot.

61   Turn the inner race 90-degrees in the cage, align one of the grooves with the edge of the cage and rotate the inner race out.

62   Clean all of the components and inspect for worn or damaged splines, race grooves, ball bearings and cage. Shiny spots are normal and won't affect operation. Replace the joint with a new one if any of the components show signs of wear.

63   Coat the components of the joint with CV joint grease, then assemble the inner race and cage, aligning the marks made in Step 58.

64   Press the ball bearings into their openings, then insert the inner race, cage and balls into the housing. The chamfered side of the splines must face the larger diameter side of the housing. When the components are rotated into place, the wide-spaced grooves of the inner race must be lined up with the wide-spaced grooves in the housing.

65   Install the new boot and clamp on the axleshaft. It's a good idea to wrap the splines of the axleshaft with electrical tape to prevent damage to the boot.

66   Remove the tape and install the dished washer on the axleshaft with the concave side facing the end of the shaft **(see illustration)**.

67   If you're replacing the boot, seat the inner end of the boot in between the smaller diameter portion of the axleshaft **(see illustration)**.

68   Place the inner joint assembly on the axleshaft and install a new snap-ring. Make sure the snap-ring seats in its groove completely.

69   Pack the CV joint with CV joint grease, approximately 120 grams (4.2 ounces) of grease. Place 1/3 of the grease in the joint and the other 2/3 on the inner side of the joint and in the boot.

70   Seat the cap of the boot on the joint housing, aligning the bolt holes. Make sure the boot is not twisted or deformed in any way.

71   Clean the surface of the joint housing, then stick a new gasket onto the housing.

72   Make sure the constant velocity joint moves freely in all directions, then install the driveaxle as described in Section 11.

13   Driveshaft (all-wheel drive models) - removal and installation

Refer to illustrations 13.4 and 13.5

Caution: *The driveshaft must not be bent at an angle of more than 25-degrees. The manufacturer recommends the use of a holding fixture that secures the two sections of the driveshaft so they are held straight. A similar fixture can be constructed from a 2x4 cut to the proper length, and a block of wood of the correct height at each end. The fixture can then be strapped to the driveshaft before removal or installation. If such a fixture is not used, be sure to support the driveshaft in a level plane either by the use of a floor jack or with the help of an assistant.*

Note: *At the time of writing, replacement parts for the driveshaft were not available. If the CV joints, U-joint or center support bearing are worn-out, the entire driveshaft must be replaced as an assembly. Before replacing the driveshaft with a new one, however, it would be a good idea to check with a driveline specialist to see if they can carry out repairs to the shaft.*

1   Raise the vehicle and support it securely on jackstands.

2   Remove the rear section of the exhaust system (see Chapter 4).

3   Pry the heat shield front rivets/mounting fasteners off and discard them. The center support bearing (located under the heat shield), is supported by the heat shield rear mounting fasteners. Remove one side of

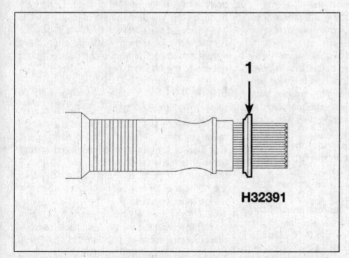

12.66   The concave side of the dished washer (1) must face the end of the axleshaft (ball-and-cage inner CV joint)

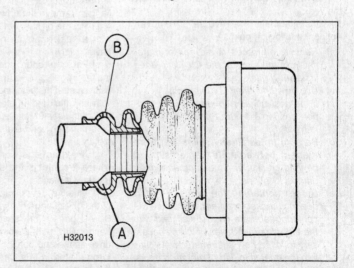

12.67   The inner end of the right inner CV joint boot must be positioned on the axleshaft like this, so the edge of the vent chamber (A) seats on the tube; the vent hole (B) must not be obstructed

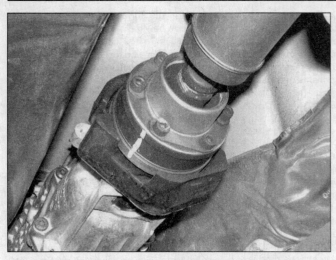

13.4 Mark the relationship of the driveshaft CV joints to their respective flanges

13.5 Using a chain wrench to prevent the driveshaft from turning as the bolts are removed

the heat shield fasteners at a time. Pull the removed side of the shield down and reinstall the mounting fastener by hand, then remove the opposite side and reinstall the mounting fastener. **Note:** *Make sure the center support bearing bracket alignment tabs are centered in the outer holes of the floor pan.*

4   Mark the relationship of the constant velocity (CV) joints to their corresponding flanges at each end of the driveshaft **(see illustration)**.

5   Support each end of the driveshaft, then remove the bolts securing the CV joints to their corresponding companion flanges **(see illustration)**.

6   Remove the fasteners securing the center support bearing bracket to the floorpan (see Step 3). Retrieve any shims that may be present between the bracket and the floorpan, noting their installed positions. Carefully lower the driveshaft and remove it out from under the vehicle.

7   Installation is the reverse of removal, noting the following points:

a) *Remove all traces of old gasket material from the ends of the CV joints, then install new gaskets.*

b) *Use **new** driveshaft CV joint bolts.*

c) *If the heat shield above the center support bearing fell out of place, be sure to reinstall it.*

d) *Be sure to install any shims that were present between the center support bearing bracket and the floorpan in their original locations.*

e) *Before tightening the center support bearing bracket fasteners, make sure the centering tabs are correctly aligned with the outer floorpan holes. It will be necessary to insert new sheetmetal rivets/clips into the heat shield front mounting holes.*

f) *Tighten all fasteners to the torque values listed in this Chapter's Specifications.*

14   Rear differential oil seals - replacement

Drive flange (side gear shaft) seals

1   Raise the rear of the vehicle and support it securely on jackstands. Block the front wheels to prevent the vehicle from rolling off the stands.

2   Remove the heat shields from the differential and unbolt the driveaxle from the drive flange (see Section 11). Position the driveaxle out of the way and support it with a piece of wire.

3   Place a drain pan under the differential. Thread two of the driveaxle securing bolts into the drive flange and brace the flange with a large screwdriver to prevent it from turning, then remove the bolt from the center of the flange. Remove the drive flange.

4   Pry the oil seal out of the differential bore with a seal removal tool or a large screwdriver.

5   Pack the open side of the new seal with multi-purpose grease, then drive it into its bore using a seal installation tool or a large socket with an outside diameter slightly smaller than that of the seal. Make sure the seal enters the bore squarely, and is driven in until it is completely seated.

6   If a groove is worn in the drive flange where it contacts the seal, the drive flange must be replaced.

7   Install a new circlip on the splined area of the drive flange.

8   Lubricate the seal contact area of the flange with multi-purpose grease. Install the drive flange and bolt, tightening the bolt to the torque listed in this Chapter's Specifications. If the drive flange will not go on by hand, slight tapping with a hammer may be required to seat it.

9   Reconnect the driveaxle to the drive

flange, tightening the bolts to the torque listed in this Chapter's Specifications.

10   Check the differential lubricant, adding as necessary to bring it to the appropriate level (see Chapter 1).

Pinion seal

Note: *There are two types of rear differentials used on these models: Models 01R and 0AR (the identification numbers are stamped on the passenger's side of the differential just behind the pinion flange).*

11   Raise the rear of the vehicle and support it securely on jackstands. Block the front wheels to prevent the vehicle from rolling off the stands.

12   Remove the rear section of the exhaust (see Chapter 4).

13   Mark the driveshaft to the pinion flange, and unbolt the driveshaft from the pinion flange. Support the driveshaft from the underbody with a piece of wire or rope. Don't let it hang, as this will damage the U-joint.

14   Support the differential with a floor jack. Remove the bolts from the differential front mount and lower the front of the differential for access to the pinion flange.

Model 01R

Refer to illustration 14.15

15   Measure the distance from the flange mating surface to the end of the pinion shaft and also to the pinion nut **(see illustration)**. Write these measurements down, as they'll be used during reassembly. Also write down the number of turns when removing the pinion flange mounting nut.

16   Thread two of the driveshaft CV joint bolts into the pinion flange and brace a screwdriver across them to prevent the shaft from turning, then unscrew the pinion nut.

17   Place a drip pan underneath the differential. Using a puller, draw the flange off the pinion shaft.

18   Using a slide hammer and a hook-type

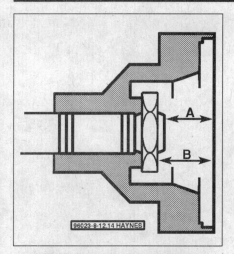

14.15 Measure the distance from the surface of the flange to the end of the pinion shaft (A) and to the pinion nut (B)

seal removal adapter, pull the seal out of the differential housing.

19   Remove the O-ring from the pinion shaft and install a new one.

20   Lubricate the outer edge and lips of the new seal with multi-purpose grease. Also pack the area between the seal lips with grease. Drive the new seal squarely into the bore with a seal driver or a piece of pipe with an outside diameter slightly less than that of the seal.

21   Install the pinion flange and nut. Tighten the nut until the distance from the end of the pinion shaft to the surface of the flange, and the distance from the nut to the surface of the flange, are the same as recorded in Step 15 (within 0.020-inch [0.5 mm]).

22   Stake the collar of the nut to the shaft.

23   Clean off all gasket material from the driveshaft CV joint and attach a new one to it. Connect the driveshaft CV joint to the pinion flange, tightening the bolts to the torque listed in this Chapter's Specifications.

24   Check the differential lubricant and add as necessary to bring it to the appropriate level (see Chapter 1).

Model 0AR

25   Remove the pinion flange circlip and install a puller with two M8 x 30 bolts screwed into the flange, then pull the flange off the shaft.

26   Carefully push the seal in at the top and pry the seal out from the bottom.

27   Lubricate the outer edge and lips of the new seal with multi-purpose grease. Also pack the area between the seal lips with grease. Drive the new seal squarely into the bore with a seal driver or a piece of pipe with an outside diameter slightly less than that of the seal.

28   Warm the flange to 80-degrees F and drive the pinion flange onto the shaft far enough to install the circlip. **Note:** *If the circlip is stretched or damaged it must be replaced.*

29   Raise the front of the differential and install the crossmember-to-body bolts. Tighten the bolts to the torque listed in this Chapter's Specifications.

30   Clean off all gasket material from the driveshaft CV joint and attach a new one to it. Connect the driveshaft CV joint to the differential flange, tightening the bolts to the torque listed in this Chapter's Specifications.

31   Check the differential lubricant and add as necessary to bring it to the appropriate level (see Chapter 1).

15   Rear differential assembly - removal and installation

1   Raise the rear of the vehicle and support it securely on jackstands. Block the front wheels to prevent the vehicle from rolling off the stands.

2   Remove the rear portion of the exhaust system (see Chapter 4).

3   Unscrew the bolts securing the inner CV joints to the drive flanges and remove the retaining plates from underneath the bolts. Support the driveaxles by suspending them with wire or string - do not allow them to hang under their weight, or the joints may be damaged.

4   Unbolt the driveshaft from the differential pinion flange. Support the driveshaft from the underbody with a piece of wire or rope. Don't let it hang, as this will damage the U-joint.

5   Remove the heat shield from above the driveshaft.

6   Support the differential with a jack. Preferably, a transaxle jack with safety chains should be used; these can be obtained at most equipment rental yards. If one is not available a floor jack can be used, but you'll have to be extra careful not to let the assembly topple off the jack.

7   Unbolt the front and rear mounting brackets from the differential assembly.

8   With the help of an assistant, carefully lower the differential assembly and remove it from under the vehicle.

9   Installation is the reverse of the removal procedure. Tighten all fasteners to the torque values listed in this Chapter's Specifications. Check the lubricant level in the rear differential and add, as necessary, to bring it to the appropriate level.

Notes

Chapter 9 Brakes

Contents

	Section
Anti-lock Brake System (ABS) and	
Electronic Stability Program (ESP) - general information	2
Brake caliper - removal and installation	5
Brake disc - inspection, removal and installation	6
Brake hoses and lines - inspection and replacement	8
Brake hydraulic system - bleeding	9
Brake light switch - removal and installation	13

	Section
Brake pedal - removal and installation	12
Disc brake pads (front) - replacement	3
Disc brake pads (rear) - replacement	4
General information	1
Master cylinder - removal and installation	7
Parking brake - check and adjustment	11
Power brake booster - check, removal and installation	10

Specifications

General

Brake fluid type	See Chapter 1
Pushrod length	6.26 inches (159 mm)
Parking brake adjustment gap	0.060 inch (1.5 mm)

Disc brakes

Minimum brake pad thickness	See Chapter 1
Disc minimum thickness	Cast into disc
Disc runout limit	Not specified (see Section 6 of this Chapter)

Torque specifications

	Ft-lbs	Nm
Caliper mounting bolts		
Front		
All except Brembo	22	30
Brembo	81	110
Rear	26	35
Caliper mounting bracket bolts		
Front	140	190
Rear	56	75
Brake hose-to-caliper inlet fitting bolt (rear)	28	38
Master cylinder-to-brake booster nuts	37	50
Brake booster bolts	18	25
Wheel bolts	See Chapter 1	

1   General information

The vehicles covered by this manual are equipped with hydraulically operated front and rear disc brake systems. These brakes are self-adjusting and automatically compensate for pad wear.

Hydraulic system

The hydraulic system consists of two separate circuits. In the event of a leak or failure in one hydraulic circuit, the other circuit will remain operative.

Power brake booster

The power brake booster is mounted in the cowl compartment between the engine firewall and the bulkhead. It uses engine manifold vacuum and atmospheric pressure to provide assistance to the hydraulically operated brakes.

Parking brake

The parking brake lever actuates the rear brake caliper mechanically using cables. The parking brake cable requires no routine adjustment except after service to the rear brake system.

Service

After completing any operation involving disassembly of any part of the brake system, always test-drive the vehicle to check for proper braking performance before resuming normal driving. When testing the brakes, perform the tests on a clean, dry, flat surface. Conditions other than these can lead to inaccurate test results.

Test the brakes at various speeds with both light and heavy pedal pressure. The vehicle should stop evenly without pulling to one side or the other. Extreme braking will initiate the ABS system.

Tires, vehicle load and wheel alignment are other factors that affect braking performance as well.

Precautions

There are some general cautions and warnings concerning brake system components:

a) *Use only the proper type of brake fluid (see Chapter 1).*
b) *The brake pads and linings contain fibers which are hazardous to your health if inhaled. Whenever you work on brake system components, clean all parts with brake system cleaner. Do not allow the fine dust to become airborne. Also, wear an approved filtering mask.*
c) *Safety should be paramount whenever any servicing of the brake components is performed. Do not use parts or fasteners which are not in perfect condition, and be sure that all clearances and torque specifications are adhered to. If you are at all unsure about a certain procedure, seek professional advice. Upon*

2.2 Typical ABS (ESP) actuator assembly

completion of any brake system work, test the brakes carefully in a controlled area before putting the vehicle into normal service. If a problem is suspected in the brake system, don't drive the vehicle until it's fixed.
d) *Used brake fluid is considered a hazardous waste and it must be disposed of in accordance with federal, state and local laws. **DO NOT pour it down the sink, into septic tanks or storm drains, or on the ground.***
e) *Clean up any spilled brake fluid immediately and wash the area with large amounts of water. This is especially true for any finished or painted surfaces.*

2   Anti-lock Brake System (ABS) and Electronic Stability Program (ESP) - general information

1   The Anti-lock Brake System (ABS) and Electronic Stabilization Program (ESP) are designed to help maintain vehicle steerability, directional stability and optimum deceleration under severe braking or maneuvering conditions and on most road surfaces. The ABS system is primarily designed to prevent wheel lockup during heavy or panic braking situations. It works by monitoring the rotational speed of each wheel and controlling the brake line pressure to each wheel when engaged. Data provided by the ABS wheel speed sensors is shared with the Electronic Stabilization Program. This very sophisticated system helps with traction control, over/under-steering and acceleration control under all driving conditions. Overall, these systems aid in vehicle control and handling. Other systems added to vehicles with ESP are Electronic Differential Lock (EDL) and Acceleration Slip Regulation (ASR).

Components

Actuator assembly

Refer to illustration 2.2

2   The actuator assembly is mounted in the engine compartment and consists of an electric hydraulic pump and solenoid valves **(see illustration)**.

a) *The electric pump provides hydraulic pressure to charge the reservoirs in the actuator, which supplies pressure to the braking system. The pump and reservoirs are housed in the actuator assembly.*
b) *The solenoid valves modulate brake line pressure during ABS, ESP or ASR operation.*

Wheel speed sensors

3   There is a wheel speed sensor for each wheel. Each sensor generates a signal in the form of a low-voltage electrical current or a frequency when the wheel is turning. A variable signal is generated as a result of a square-toothed ring (tone-ring, exciter-ring, reluctor, etc.) that rotates very close to the sensor. The signal is directly proportional to the wheel speed and is interpreted by an electronic module (computer).
4   The front sensors are mounted to the wheel bearing assemblies.
5   The rear sensors are mounted in the rear suspension knuckles.

ABS/ESP computer

6   The ABS/ESP computer is mounted with the actuator and is the brain of these systems. The function of the computer is to accept and process information received from the wheel speed sensors to control the hydraulic line pressure, avoiding wheel lock up or wheel spin. The computer also constantly monitors the system, even under normal driving conditions, to find faults within the system.

Diagnosis and repair

7   If a dashboard warning light comes on and stays on while the vehicle is in operation, the ABS or ESP system requires attention. Although special electronic diagnostic testing tools are necessary to properly diagnose the system, you can perform a few preliminary checks before taking the vehicle to a dealer service department.

a) *Check the brake fluid level in the reservoir.*
b) *Verify that the computer electrical connectors are securely connected.*
c) *Check the electrical connectors at the hydraulic control unit.*
d) *Check the fuses.*
e) *Follow the wiring harness to each wheel and verify that all connections are secure and that the wiring is undamaged.*

8   If the above preliminary checks do not rectify the problem, the vehicle should be diagnosed by a dealer service department or other qualified repair shop. Due to the complexity of this system, all actual repair work must be done by a qualified automotive technician.
Warning: *Do NOT try to repair an ABS/ESP*

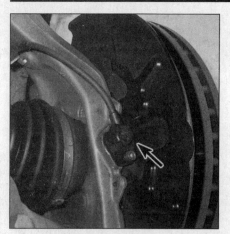

2.12a The front wheel speed
sensor location

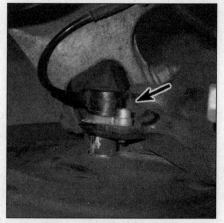

2.12b The rear wheel speed
sensor location

3.4 Before disassembling the brake, wash
it thoroughly with brake system cleaner
and allow it to dry - position a drain pan
under the brake to catch the residue - DO
NOT use compressed air to blow off the
brake dust!

wiring harness. These systems are sensitive
to even the smallest changes in resistance.
Repairing the harness could alter resistance
values and cause the system to malfunction.
If the wiring harness is damaged in any way,
it must be replaced. **Caution:** *Make sure the
ignition is turned off before unplugging or reat-
taching any electrical connections.*

Wheel speed sensor - removal and installation

Refer to illustrations 2.12a and 2.12b

9   Loosen the wheel lug nuts, raise the
vehicle and support it securely on jackstands.
Remove the wheel.
10   Make sure the ignition key is turned to
the "OFF" position.
11   Trace the wiring back from the sensor,
detaching all brackets and clips while noting
its correct routing, then disconnect the electrical connector.
12   Remove the mounting bolt and carefully pull the sensor out from the knuckle **(see
illustrations)**.
13   Installation is the reverse of the removal
procedure. Tighten the mounting fastener
securely.
14   Install the wheel and bolts, tightening
them securely. Lower the vehicle and tighten
the bolts to the torque listed in the Chapter 1
Specifications.

3   Disc brake pads (front) - replacement

Refer to illustration 3.4

Warning: *Disc brake pads must be replaced
on both front wheels at the same time - never
replace the pads on only one wheel. Also, the
dust created by the brake system is harmful to
your health. Never blow it out with compressed
air and don't inhale any of it. An approved fil-*

*tering mask should be worn when working on
the brakes. Do not, under any circumstances,
use petroleum-based solvents to clean brake
parts. Use brake system cleaner only!*
Warning: *All bolts used to mount the brake
calipers are self-locking and designed to be
used only once. The manufacturer states to
replace caliper mounting bolts any time they
are removed.*

1   Remove the cap from the brake fluid reservoir. Remove about two-thirds of the fluid
from the reservoir, reinstall the cap. **Warning:** *Brake fluid is poisonous - never siphon
it by mouth. Use a suction gun or old poultry
baster. If a baster is used, never again use it
for the preparation of food.* **Caution:** *Brake
fluid will damage paint. If any fluid is spilled,
wash it off immediately with plenty of clean,
cold water.*
2   Loosen the front wheel bolts, raise the
front of the vehicle and support it securely on
jackstands. Block the wheels at the opposite
end.

3.5 Insert a screwdriver through the
caliper and pry outward to push the caliper
piston back into the bore, just enough to
allow the caliper to be easily removed

3   Remove the wheels. Work on one brake
assembly at a time, using the assembled
brake for reference if necessary.
4   Before removing anything, thoroughly
clean the caliper and disc with brake system
cleaner **(see illustration)**.

Removal

Models with FNR-G 60 front brakes

*Refer to illustrations 3.5, 3.6, 3.7, 3.8, 3.9,
3.10a and 3.10b*

5   Push the piston back into the bore to
allow the caliper to be removed easily **(see
illustration)**.
6   Carefully unclip the pad retaining spring
and remove it from the brake caliper **(see
illustration)**.
7   Remove the protective end caps to gain

3.6 Pry the center of the retaining spring
up enough for the tab to clear the bracket.
Then pull the outer ends of the spring
down and out to remove the spring

3.7 Remove the protective end caps from the guide pins and remove the pins (arrows)

3.8 Disconnect the brake pad wear indicator sensor and rotate the sensor connector from the bracket to remove it

access to the caliper guide pins **(see illustration)**.

8   Disconnect the brake pad wear indicator electrical connector **(see illustration)**, turn

the connector and remove it from the bracket.

9   Unscrew the caliper guide pins, and lift the caliper away from the mounting bracket. Tie the caliper to the suspension strut using a

suitable piece of wire; do not allow it to hang unsupported from the flexible brake hose **(see illustration)**.

10   Unclip the inner pad from the caliper piston and remove the outer pad from the caliper housing relief **(see illustrations)**. Proceed to Step 22.

Models with FN3 front brakes

Refer to illustrations 3.11, 3.12, 3.13a, 3.13b, 3.13c, 3.14a and 3.14b

11   Carefully unclip the pad retaining spring and remove it from the brake caliper **(see illustration)**. Disconnect the brake pad wear indicator electrical connector **(see illustration 3.8)**, turn the connector and remove it from the bracket.

12   Remove the end caps from the guide bushing to gain access to the caliper guide pins **(see illustration)**.

13   Unscrew the caliper guide pins, then lift the caliper away from the mounting bracket **(see illustrations)**. Tie the caliper to the suspension strut using a suitable piece of wire; do not allow it to hang unsupported

3.9 Remove the caliper from the mounting bracket and support it with a length of wire

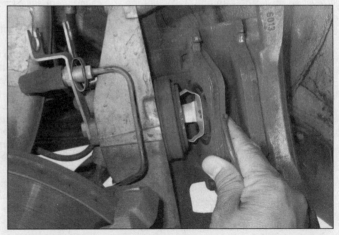

3.10a Unclip and remove the inner pad from the piston . . .

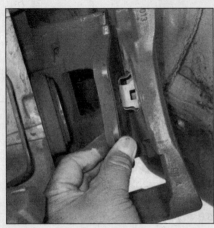

3.10b . . . and the outer pad from the relief in the caliper housing

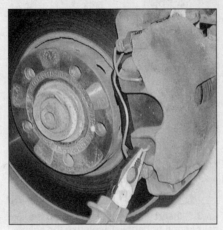

3.11 Unclip the pad retaining spring and remove it from the caliper

3.12 Remove the end caps from the guide bushings to gain access to the caliper guide pins

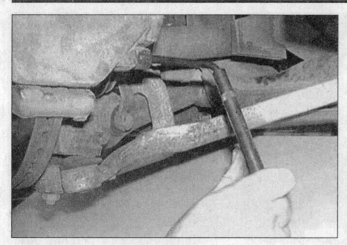

3.13a Loosen . . .

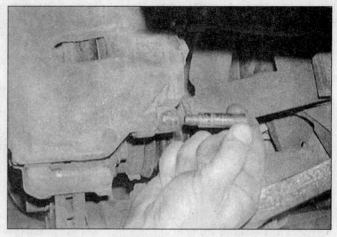

3.13b . . . and remove the caliper guide pins . . .

from the flexible brake hose **(see illustration 3.9)**.

14   Unclip the inner pad from the caliper piston and remove the outer pad from the mounting bracket **(see illustrations)**. Proceed to Step 22.

Models with C54 front brakes

Refer to illustrations 3.15, 3.17a, 3.17b and 3.17c

15   Disconnect the brake pad wear indicator electrical connector **(see illustration 3.8)**,

turn the connector and remove it from the bracket. Unscrew the caliper upper and lower mounting bolts while preventing the guide pins from turning with an open-end wrench **(see illustration)**. **Note:** *New bolts must be used on installation.*

3.13c . . . then lift the caliper off the mounting bracket

3.14a Unclip the inner pad from the caliper piston . . .

3.14b . . . and remove the outer pad from the mounting bracket

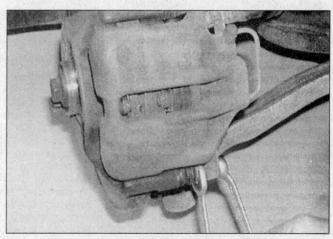

3.15 Hold the guide pins with an open-end wrench while loosening the caliper mounting bolts

3.17a Remove the inner . . .

3.17b . . . and outer pads from the caliper mounting bracket

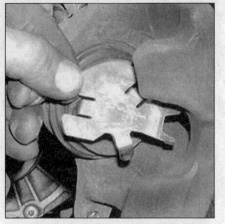

3.17c Make sure the circular heat shield plate remains clipped into the end face of the piston

16 Remove the caliper from the mounting bracket and hang it from the coil spring with a length of wire **(see illustration 3.9)**.
17 Remove the inner and outer pads from the caliper mounting bracket. Ensure that the circular heat shield plate remains clipped into the end face of the piston **(see illustrations)**.

Models with Brembo front brakes
18 Disconnect the brake pad wear indicator electrical connector **(see illustration 3.8)**, turn the connector and remove it from the bracket.
19 Starting from the outer side of the caliper, drive the brake pad retaining pins out using a hammer and a pin punch.
20 Remove the brake pad retaining springs.
21 Using a screwdriver, press the pistons back into the bore just enough to free the brake pads. Remove and replace the pads one at a time (don't remove both pads at once, because when the pistons on one side of the caliper are depressed into their bores, the pistons on the other side of the caliper will be pushed out).

Inspection (all models)
22 Inspect the brake disc carefully as outlined in Section 6. If machining is necessary, follow the information in that Section to remove the disc, at which time the pads can be removed as well.
23 Prior to fitting the pads, check that the guide pins are free to slide easily in the caliper body bushings, and are a reasonably tight fit. On models with C54 front brakes, pull the guide pins out and inspect them for signs of wear. If they're OK, lubricate them with high-temperature brake grease and reinstall them. Use brake system cleaner to clean the caliper and piston. Inspect the dust seal around the piston for damage, and the piston for evidence of fluid leaks, corrosion or damage. If any of these components require attention, the caliper should be replaced.

Installation
Refer to illustration 3.24
24 To make room for the new pads, the caliper piston(s) must be pushed back into the cylinder. Either use a piston retraction tool or a C-clamp. Connect a brake bleeding kit to the caliper bleed screw. Open the bleed screw as the piston is retracted; the surplus brake fluid will then be collected in the bleed kit container **(see illustration)**. Tighten the bleed screw as soon as the piston is retracted to prevent air from being drawn into the system. **Note:** *The ABS unit contains hydraulic components that are very sensitive to impurities in the brake fluid. Even the smallest particles can cause the system to fail through blockage. The pad retraction method described here prevents any debris in the brake fluid expelled from the caliper from being passed back to the ABS hydraulic unit.*

Models with FNR-G 60 front brakes
25 Clip the inner pad into the caliper piston and the outer pad into the caliper housing relief.
26 Lubricate the caliper guide pins with a light coat of high-temperature brake grease. Maneuver the caliper into position, then install the caliper guide pins and tighten them to the torque listed in this Chapter's Specifications.
27 Install the protective end caps over the caliper guide pins.
28 Lock the brake pad wear indicator electrical connector into the bracket and connect the electrical connector.

Models with FN3 front brakes
29 Clip the inner pad into the caliper piston and fit the outer pad to the mounting bracket, ensuring its friction material is against the brake disc. Note that the outer pad has an arrow stamped onto its outer lower edge; this should point in the normal direction of rotation of the brake disc. Remove the adhesive foil backing from the outer pad.
30 Lubricate the caliper guide pins with a light coat of high-temperature brake grease. Maneuver the caliper into position, then install the caliper guide pins and tighten them to the torque listed in this Chapter's Specifications.
31 Install the end caps to the caliper guide bushings.

32 Install the pad retaining spring, ensuring its ends are correctly located in the caliper body holes. Press the inner edge of the spring into position so that its ends are firmly in contact with the surface of the brake pad.
33 Lock the brake pad wear indicator electrical connector into the bracket and reconnect the electrical connector.

Models with C54 front brakes
34 Install the new pads in the caliper mounting bracket ensuring the friction material is against the brake disc.
35 Fit the caliper over the brake pads, ensuring that the butterfly springs on the outer edge of the brake pads bear against the inner surface of the caliper body without jamming in the caliper inspection aperture. **Note:** *New caliper mounting bolts must be used.*
36 Install the new caliper mounting bolts and tighten them to the torque listed in this Chapter's Specifications, holding the guide pins with an open-end wrench, just like during removal.
37 Lock the brake pad wear indicator elec-

3.24 Connecting a bleeder bottle and opening the bleeder screw while pushing the piston into the caliper will prevent contaminated fluid from being pushed back into the hydraulic system

4.2a Remove the parking brake cable retaining clip ...

4.2b ... and slide the cable ball end from the lever

trical connector into the bracket and reconnect the electrical connector.

Models with Brembo front brakes

38   Install the new pads into the caliper housing, ensuring the friction material is against the brake disc. **Note:** *The brake pads are directional and specific to each side. Check the marking on each pad to prevent mixing the pads up.*
39   Install the brake pad retaining springs.
40   Press and hold the return springs down, then drive the brake pad retaining pins in, to the stop, using a hammer and a pin punch.
41   Lock the brake pad wear indicator electrical connector into the bracket and connect the electrical connector.

All models

42   Depress the brake pedal repeatedly, until the pads are pressed into contact with the brake disc, and a firm brake pedal feel is obtained.
43   Repeat the above procedure on the remaining front brake caliper.
44   Install the wheels and wheel bolts, then lower the vehicle to the ground and tighten the bolts to the torque listed in the Chapter 1 Specifications.
45   Once again, firmly depress the brake

pedal a few times to bring the pads into contact with the disc.
46   Check and, if necessary, top-up the brake fluid level as described in Chapter 1.
47   Test the operation of the brakes carefully before placing the vehicle into normal service.
Warning: *New pads will not give full braking efficiency until they have bedded in. Be prepared for this, and avoid hard braking as much as possible for the first hundred miles or so after pad replacement.*

4   Disc brake pads (rear) - replacement

Refer to illustrations 4.2a, 4.2b, 4.3, 4.4, 4.5a, 4.5b and 4.7

Warning: *Disc brake pads must be replaced on both rear wheels at the same time - never replace the pads on only one wheel. Also, the dust created by the brake system is harmful to your health. Never blow it out with compressed air and don't inhale any of it. An approved filtering mask should be worn when working on the brakes. Do not, under any circumstances, use petroleum-based solvents to clean brake*

parts. Use brake system cleaner only!
Warning: *All bolts used to mount the brake calipers are self-locking and designed to be used only once. The manufacturer states to replace caliper mounting bolts any time they are removed.*

1   Loosen the rear wheel bolts. Block the front wheels, then raise the rear of the vehicle and support it securely on jackstands. Remove the rear wheels.
2   Remove the parking brake cable and retaining clip, and disengage the cable from the parking brake lever **(see illustrations)**.
3   Unscrew the caliper mounting bolts, while holding the guide pins with an open-end wrench to prevent them from rotating **(see illustration)**. Discard the mounting bolts - new bolts must be used on installation. **Note:** *On RS4 models, do not remove the upper damper bolt; remove the lower bolt and swing the caliper up to change the brake pads. If the damper is removed it must be replaced.*
4   Lift the caliper away from the brake pads **(see illustration)**, and tie it to the suspension strut using a length of wire. Do not allow the caliper to hang unsupported on the flexible brake hose.
5   Remove the brake pads and guide clips

4.3 When removing the mounting bolts, use an open-end wrench to hold the guide pins and prevent them from rotating

4.4 Remove the caliper from the mounting bracket and support it with a length of wire ...

4.5a . . . then remove the inner pad . . .

4.5b . . . and outer pad from the caliper mounting bracket

4.7 Using a retraction tool to push the piston back into the caliper

from the caliper mounting bracket **(see illustrations)**.

6   Prior to installing the new pads, check that the anti-rattle springs are not damaged and fit tightly to the caliper mounting bracket, check that the guide pins are free to slide easily in the caliper bracket, and check that the rubber guide pin boots are undamaged. Pull the guide pins out and inspect them for signs of wear. If they're OK, lubricate them with high-temperature brake grease and reinstall them. Clean the caliper and piston with brake system cleaner. Inspect the dust seal around the piston for damage, and the piston for evidence of fluid leaks, corrosion or damage. If necessary, replace the caliper.

7   To make room for the new brake pads, it will be necessary to retract the piston fully into the caliper bore by rotating it in a clockwise direction using a retraction tool, or a pair of needle-nose pliers **(see illustration)**. Connect a brake bleeding kit to the caliper bleed screw. Open the bleed screw as the piston is retracted; the surplus brake fluid will then be collected in the bleed kit container **(see illustration 3.24)**. Tighten the bleed screw as soon as the piston is retracted to prevent air from being drawn into the system. **Note:** *The ABS unit contains hydraulic components that are very sensitive to impurities in the brake fluid. Even the smallest particles can cause the system to fail through blockage. The pad retraction method described here prevents any debris in the brake fluid expelled from the caliper from being passed back to the ABS hydraulic unit.*

8   Peel the protective sheet from the pad backing plates, then install the pads in the mounting bracket, ensuring that each pad's friction material is facing the brake disc.

9   Slide the caliper back into position over the pads, making sure the pad anti-rattle springs are correctly positioned against the inner surface of the caliper body and are not jammed in the inspection aperture. **Note:** *New mounting bolts must be used when the caliper is installed.*

10   Press the caliper into position, then install

the new mounting bolts, tightening them to the torque listed in this Chapter's Specifications while preventing the guide pins from turning with an open-end wrench.

11   Repeat the above procedure on the remaining rear brake caliper.

12   Connect the parking brake cable and adjust the parking brake cables (see Section 11).

13   Depress the brake pedal repeatedly to force the pads into firm contact with the discs. Once normal pedal feel has returned, check that the discs rotate freely.

14   Install the wheels and wheel bolts, then lower the vehicle to the ground and tighten the wheel bolts to the torque listed in the Chapter 1 Specifications.

15   Check and, if necessary, top-up the brake fluid level as described in Chapter 1.

16   Test the operation of the brakes carefully before placing the vehicle into normal service. **Warning:** *New pads will not give full braking efficiency until they have bedded in. Be prepared for this, and avoid hard braking as much as possible for the first hundred miles or so after pad replacement.*

---

5   Brake caliper - removal and installation

Refer to illustrations 5.3, 5.4a and 5.4b

Warning: *Dust created by the brake system is harmful to your health. Never blow it out with compressed air and don't inhale any of it. An approved filtering mask should be worn when working on the brakes. Do not, under any circumstances, use petroleum-based solvents to clean brake parts. Use brake system cleaner only!*

Warning: *All bolts used to mount the brake calipers are self-locking and designed to be used only once. The manufacturer states to replace caliper mounting bolts any time they are removed.*

Note: *Always replace the calipers in pairs - never replace just one of them.*

Removal

1   Loosen the front or rear wheel bolts, raise the front or rear of the vehicle and support it securely on jackstands. Block the wheels at the opposite end. Remove the front or rear wheel.

2   If you are removing a rear caliper, remove the cable retaining clip and disengage the cable from the parking brake lever **(see illustrations 4.2a and 4.2b)**.

3   If you're removing a front caliper, unscrew the brake line fitting from the caliper, using a flare-nut wrench to prevent rounding-off the corners of the fitting. Unbolt the brake line bracket **(see illustration)** from the caliper and pull the line away, then plug the fitting to prevent fluid loss and the entry of contaminants.

4   If you're removing a rear caliper, remove the inlet fitting bolt and discard the old sealing washers **(see illustration)**. Disconnect the brake hose from the caliper. Plug the brake hose to keep contaminants out of the brake system and to prevent losing any more brake fluid than is necessary **(see illustration)**. **Note:** *If you're removing the caliper for access to other components, don't disconnect the hose. Suspend the caliper with a piece of wire*

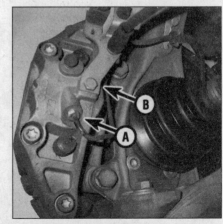

5.3 On front calipers, unscrew the brake line (A), cap the line and hole, then remove the brake line bracket (B)

to prevent damaging the brake hose.

5   Remove the caliper guide pins or the mounting bolts and detach the caliper (see Section 3 [front] or 4 [rear]).

Installation

6   Installation is the reverse of removal. If you're installing a rear caliper, don't forget to use new sealing washers on each side of the brake hose inlet fitting, and tighten the fitting bolt to the torque listed in this Chapter's Specifications. Be sure to tighten the mounting fasteners to the torque listed in this Chapter's Specifications.

7   Bleed the brake system (see Section 9). Make sure there are no leaks from the hose connections. Pump the brake pedal several times before driving the vehicle, and test the brakes carefully before returning the vehicle to normal service.

6   Brake disc - inspection, removal and installation

Warning: *All bolts used to mount the brake calipers are self-locking and designed to be used only once. The manufacturer states to replace caliper mounting bolts any time they are removed.*

Note: *Some models may be equipped with cross-drilled brake discs. These discs have a series of holes through them to help with cooling during extreme braking. Drilled discs cannot be resurfaced (machined) on typical brake lathes used by automotive brake repair shops. If a cross-drilled disc is warped or defective, replacement may be the easiest and most cost effective solution.*

Inspection

Refer to illustrations 6.4, 6.5a, 6.5b, 6.6a and 6.6b

1   Loosen the wheel bolts, raise the vehicle and support it securely on jackstands. Remove the wheel.

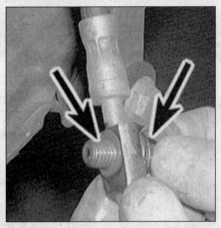

5.4a There is a sealing washer on either side of the rear brake hose inlet fitting; be sure to replace these with new ones when reconnecting the hose

5.4b The rear brake hose can be plugged using a snug-fitting piece of tubing

2   Remove the brake caliper as outlined in Section 5. It's not necessary to disconnect the brake hose for this procedure. After removing the caliper bolts, suspend the caliper out of the way with a piece of wire. Don't let the caliper hang by the hose and don't stretch or twist the hose.

3   Reinstall the wheel bolts to hold the disc securely against the hub, if necessary. It may be necessary to install washers between the disc and the wheel bolts to take up space.

4   Visually check the disc surface for score marks, cracks and other damage. Light scratches and shallow grooves are normal after use and may not always be detrimental to brake operation. Deep score marks or cracks may require disc refinishing by an automotive machine shop or disc replacement **(see illustration)**. On cross-drilled discs, hairline cracks that are 10 mm (25/64-inch) or less in length can be considered acceptable. Be sure to check both sides of the disc. If pulsating has been noticed during application of the brakes, suspect disc runout. **Note:** *The most common symptoms of damaged or worn brake discs are pulsation in the brake pedal when the brakes are applied or loud grinding noises caused from severely worn brake pads. If these symptoms are extreme, it is very likely that the discs will need to be replaced.*

5   To check disc runout, place a dial indicator at a point about 1/2-inch from the outer edge of the disc **(see illustration)**. Set the indicator to zero and turn the disc. Although the manufacturer doesn't give a runout specification, an indicator reading that exceeds 0.003 of an inch could cause pulsation upon brake application and will require disc refinishing by an automotive machine shop or disc replacement. **Note:** *If disc refinishing or replacement is not necessary, you can deglaze the brake pad surface on the disc with emery cloth or sandpaper (use a swirling motion to ensure a non-directional finish)* **(see illustration).**

6.4 The brake pads on this vehicle were obviously neglected, as they wore down completely and cut deep grooves into the disc - wear this severe means the disc must be replaced

6.5a Use a dial indicator to check disc runout; if the reading exceeds the maximum allowable runout limit, the disc will have to be machined or replaced

6.5b Using a swirling motion, remove the glaze from the disc surface with sandpaper or emery cloth

6.6a   The minimum wear dimension is typically cast or etched into the disc. Inspect all areas (front, back, edges, etc.) of the disc closely to find this information

6.6b   Use a micrometer to measure disc thickness

6.7a   Remove the caliper mounting bracket fasteners and detach the mounting bracket - this is a typical front caliper mounting bracket . . .

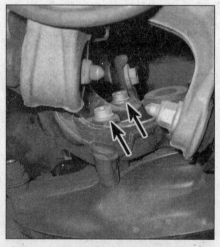

6.7b   . . . and this is a typical rear caliper mounting bracket - as viewed from below

6   It's absolutely critical that the disc not be machined to a thickness under the specified minimum thickness. The minimum (or discard) thickness is cast or stamped into the disc (**see illustration**). The disc thickness can be checked with a micrometer (**see illustration**).

Removal and installation

Refer to illustrations 6.7a, 6.7b, 6.8, 6.9a and 6.9b

7   Remove the brake caliper and suspend it out of the way with a piece of wire (don't disconnect the line/hose). Remove the caliper mounting bracket (**see illustrations**).

8   Remove the disc retaining screw and any wheel bolts installed during inspection, and remove the disc (**see illustration**). If it's stuck, use a mallet to loosen it from the hub.

9   Clean the hub flange and the inside of the brake disc thoroughly; removing any rust

6.8   A disc retaining screw holds the disc to the hub flange

6.9a   Clean any rust and corrosion from the areas of the hub flange that contact the disc. A wire brush or sanding tool, designed to be used with a power drill, can make the job a lot easier

6.9b   Clean any rust or corrosion from the area inside the disc that contacts the hub flange. Again, power tools are very useful for this job

8.3 Front brake hose frame bracket (A) and strut bracket and grommet (B)

8.12 Rear brake hose (A) and mounting bracket (B)

or corrosion **(see illustrations)**. Apply a thin film of anti-seize compound between the hub flange and inside of the disc to prevent rust and corrosion prior to the next brake service.

10   Install the disc onto the hub and tighten the retaining screw securely.

11   Install the brake caliper mounting bracket and tighten the bolts to the torque listed in this Chapter's Specifications.

12   Install the brake pads and caliper, tightening the bolts to the torque listed in this Chapter's Specifications.

13   Install the wheel, then lower the vehicle to the ground. Tighten the wheel bolts to the torque listed in the Chapter 1 Specifications. Depress the brake pedal a few times to bring the brake pads into contact with the disc. Bleeding of the system will not be necessary unless the brake hose was disconnected from the caliper. Check the operation of the brakes carefully before placing the vehicle into normal service. Also, check the parking brake operation and adjust if necessary.

7   Master cylinder - removal and installation

The master cylinder is removed along with the power brake booster and separated after they are removed. Refer to Section 10 for master cylinder removal and installation.

8   Brake hoses and lines - inspection and replacement

Inspection

1   Once a year, with the vehicle raised and supported securely on jackstands, the rubber hoses which connect the steel brake lines with the front and rear brake assemblies should be inspected for cracks, chafing of the outer cover, leaks, blisters and other damage. These are important and vulnerable parts of the brake system and inspection should be complete. A light and mirror will be helpful for

a thorough check. If a hose exhibits any of the above conditions, replace it with a new one.

Replacement

Front brake hose

Refer to illustration 8.3

2   Loosen the wheel bolts, raise the vehicle and support it securely on jackstands. Remove the wheel.

3   At the frame bracket **(see illustration)**, note how the small tabs of the hose fitting sit in the bracket and keep it from rotating.

4   Support the hose fitting with an open-end wrench, and unscrew the brake line fitting from the hose. Use a flare-nut wrench to prevent rounding off the corners of the nut and be careful not to lose the spring on the end of the hose fitting.

5   At the caliper end of the hose, use a flare nut wrench to separate the hose fitting from the caliper.

6   Remove the grommet from the bracket at the lower end of the strut, then pull the hose through the bracket.

7   To install the hose, place the grommet on the hose, thread the hose through the bracket on the strut, then connect the hose fitting to the caliper and tighten it with a flare-nut wrench. Seat the grommet back into the bracket on the strut.

8   Place the brake hose fitting into the frame bracket while making sure the hose isn't twisted between the caliper and the frame bracket.

9   Place the small spring on the line fitting and connect it to the hose fitting, starting the threads by hand, then tighten the fitting securely.

10   Bleed the caliper (see Section 9).

11   Install the wheel and bolts, lower the vehicle and tighten the bolts to the torque listed in the Chapter 1 Specifications.

Rear brake hose

Refer to illustration 8.12

12   The rear brake hose has a fitting and a bracket that is fastened to the rear frame **(see illustration)**.

13   Support the hose fitting with an open-end wrench, and unscrew the brake line fitting from the hose, being careful not to lose the spring clip on the end of the hose. Use a flare-nut wrench to prevent rounding off the corners of the nut.

14   At the caliper end of the hose, remove the inlet fitting bolt and discard the old sealing washers **(see illustration 5.4a)**. Disconnect the brake hose from the caliper.

15   Install the hose by reversing the removal procedure, using new sealing washers and making sure the hose isn't twisted. Tighten the inlet fitting bolt to the torque listed in this Chapter's Specifications.

16   Bleed the caliper (see Section 9).

17   Install the wheel and bolts, then lower the vehicle and tighten the bolts to the torque listed in the Chapter 1 Specifications.

Metal brake lines

18   When replacing brake lines, be sure to use the correct parts. Don't use copper tubing for any brake system components. Purchase genuine steel brake lines from a dealer or auto parts store.

19   Prefabricated brake line, with the tube ends already flared and fittings installed, is available at auto parts stores and dealer parts departments.

20   When installing the new line, make sure it's securely supported in the brackets and has plenty of clearance between moving or hot components.

21   After installation, check the master cylinder fluid level and add fluid as necessary. Bleed the brake system (see Section 9) and test the brakes carefully before driving the vehicle in traffic.

9   Brake hydraulic system - bleeding

Refer to illustration 9.8

Warning: *Wear eye protection when bleeding the brake system. If the fluid comes in contact*

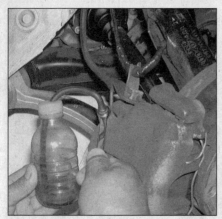

9.8 When bleeding the brakes, a hose is connected to the bleeder valve at the caliper and the other end is submerged in brake fluid. Air will be seen as bubbles in the tube and container. All air must be expelled before moving to the next wheel

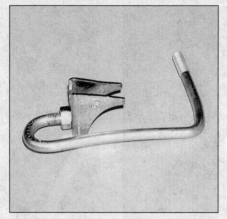

10.9a A tool, fabricated from a modified exhaust clamp, can be used to detach the booster pushrod from the brake pedal

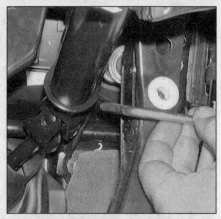

10.9b The tool is used to push on the plastic retaining lugs to release the brake pedal

with your eyes, immediately rinse them with water and seek medical attention.

Note: Bleeding the hydraulic system is necessary to remove any air that manages to find its way into the system when it's been opened during removal and installation of a hose, line, caliper or master cylinder.

1   You'll probably have to bleed the system at all four brakes if air has entered it due to low fluid level, or if the brake lines have been disconnected at the master cylinder.

2   If a brake line was disconnected only at a wheel, then only that caliper must be bled. If a brake line is disconnected at a fitting located between the master cylinder and any of the brakes, that part of the system served by the disconnected line must be bled.

3   Raise the vehicle about one foot and support it securely on jackstands.

4   Remove any residual vacuum from the brake power booster by pressing the brake pedal several times with the engine off.

5   Remove the master cylinder reservoir cap and fill the reservoir with brake fluid. Reinstall the cover. **Note:** Continue to add fluid while bleeding the system to prevent the fluid level from dropping too low; if this happens, air will enter the master cylinder.

6   Have an assistant on hand, as well as a supply of new brake fluid, a clear container partially filled with clean brake fluid, a length of clear tubing to fit over the bleeder valve and a wrench to open and close the bleeder valve.

7   Beginning at the left front wheel, loosen the bleeder valve slightly, then tighten it to a point where it's snug but can still be loosened quickly and easily. **Note:** Use a six-point box-end wrench or socket to loosen the bleeder valve. For bleeder valves that appear to be stuck, clean the area where the valve screws into the caliper with a small wire brush, then apply penetrating oil to the threads and allow it to soak in for awhile.

8   Place one end of the tubing over the bleeder valve and submerge the other end in

brake fluid in the container **(see illustration)**.

9   Have the assistant depress the brake pedal slowly, then hold the pedal down firmly.

10   While the pedal is held down, open the bleeder valve just enough to allow a flow of fluid to leave the valve. Watch for air bubbles to exit the submerged end of the tube. When the fluid flow slows after a couple of seconds, close the valve and have your assistant release the pedal.

11   Repeat Steps 9 and 10 until no more air is seen leaving the tube, then carefully tighten the bleeder valve and proceed to the right front wheel, the left rear wheel and the right rear wheel, in that order, and perform the same procedure. Be sure to check the fluid in the master cylinder reservoir frequently.

12   Never use old brake fluid. It contains moisture that can boil, rendering the brake system inoperative.

13   Refill the master cylinder with fluid at the end of the operation.

14   Check the operation of the brakes. The pedal should feel solid when depressed, with no sponginess. If necessary, repeat the entire process. **Warning:** Do not operate the vehicle if you are in doubt about the effectiveness of the brake system. It's possible for air to become trapped in the ABS hydraulic control unit, so, if the pedal continues to feel spongy after repeated bleedings or the BRAKE or ABS light stays on, have the vehicle towed to a dealer service department or other qualified repair shop to be bled.

---

10   Power brake booster - check, removal and installation

Note: On models equipped with an automatic transmission, a vacuum pump supplies vacuum to the power brake booster in addition to manifold vacuum. The pump is mounted near the ABS/ESP hydraulic unit and has a vacuum hose routed to the brake booster. Vehicles equipped with a brake booster vacuum pump require diagnosis by a dealer service department if the system appears to be defective.

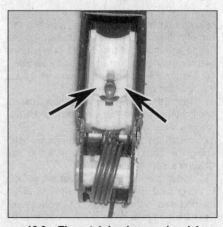

10.9c The retaining lugs and pedal assembly viewed from the rear

Note: The master cylinder is removed along with the power brake booster as an assembly. They are separated after they are removed.

Operating check

1   Depress the brake pedal several times with the engine off and make sure there's no change in the pedal reserve distance.

2   Depress the pedal and start the engine. If the pedal goes down slightly, operation is normal.

Airtightness check

3   Start the engine and turn it off after one or two minutes. Depress the brake pedal slowly several times. If the pedal depresses less each time, the booster is airtight.

4   Depress the brake pedal while the engine is running, then stop the engine with the pedal depressed. If there's no change in the pedal reserve travel after holding the pedal for 30 seconds, the booster is airtight.

Removal

Refer to illustrations 10.9a, 10.9b, 10.9c, 10.11 and 10.13

Caution: Brake fluid will damage paint or fin-

10.11 Brake booster check valve

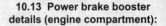
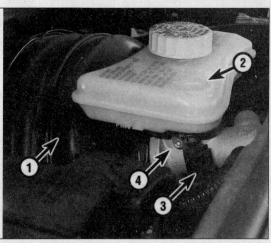

10.13 Power brake booster details (engine compartment):

1 Brake booster/master cylinder assembly
2 Fluid removal service port
3 Warning sensor and electrical connector
4 Brake fluid reservoir retaining bolt

ished surfaces. Refer to the Precautions in Section 1.

Note: *The power brake booster is not serviceable; replace it with a new or rebuilt unit if it's defective.*

5   With the engine off, press the brake pedal several times to remove any stored vacuum in the power brake booster.

6   Disconnect the cable from the negative battery terminal (see Chapter 5).

7   Remove the driver's side knee bolster (see Chapter 11).

8   Remove the brake light switch (see Section 13).

9   Detach the booster pushrod from the brake pedal **(see illustrations)**.

10   Working inside the engine compartment, remove the engine cover.

11   Pull the check valve from the brake booster while leaving the vacuum hose attached **(see illustration)**.

12   Remove as much fluid as possible from the reservoir with a syringe or equivalent. **Note:** *The small port at the corner of the reservoir is designed for this.*

13   Unplug the electrical connector for the brake fluid level warning switch **(see illustration)**.

14   Remove the brake fluid reservoir retaining bolt **(see illustration 10.13)**, and detach the reservoir from the master cylinder.

15   Clean the area around the brake line fittings at the master cylinder and the ABS/ESP actuator assembly thoroughly with brake cleaner. Place rags beneath the fittings to catch fluid, then detach the brake lines. Cap or plug all openings to prevent contamination.

16   Remove the suspension cross-brace from above the booster, if equipped.

17   Unscrew the booster mounting bolts until they're completely loose (you won't be able to remove them until the booster and master cylinder are removed from the cowl compartment). **Note:** *Do not remove the master cylinder mounting nuts yet.*

18   Carefully remove the booster and master cylinder out from the cowl compartment.

19   Pull out the booster mounting bolts, remove the master cylinder mounting nuts, then detach the master cylinder from the power booster.

Installation

Refer to illustrations 10.20, 10.21 and 10.22

20   If a replacement brake booster is being used, check and, if necessary, adjust the pushrod length **(see illustration)** to the measurement listed in this Chapter's Specifications.

21   Replace the O-ring seal between the master cylinder and the power booster **(see illustration)**, then assemble the master cylinder to the power brake booster. Make sure to match the pushrod to the master cylinder correctly during assembly. Also, replace the seals between the master cylinder and the reservoir.

22   The remainder of the installation procedures are essentially the reverse of removal.

 a) Tighten all mounting fasteners to the torque values listed in this Chapter's Specifications.

 b) To bleed the master cylinder on the vehicle, have an assistant pump the brake pedal several times slowly, and hold the pedal to the floor. Loosen the line fittings one at a time to allow air and fluid to escape. Repeat this procedure on both fittings until the fluid is clear of air bubbles **(see illustration)**. **Caution:** *Have plenty of rags on hand to catch the fluid - brake fluid will ruin painted surfaces.*

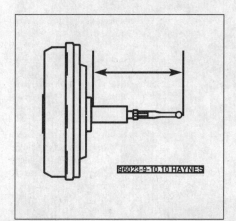

10.20 Measure the distance from the booster mounting surface (without the gasket) to the end of the pushrod

10.21 Replace the seal on the master cylinder any time the cylinder is removed (typical shown)

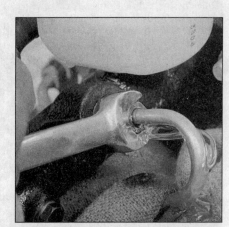

10.22 With the brake pedal depressed, loosen a fitting on the master cylinder to bleed it when it is installed on the vehicle. Bleed the lines one at a time (typical shown)

11.5 Measure the distance between the parking brake lever and the stop on the rear caliper

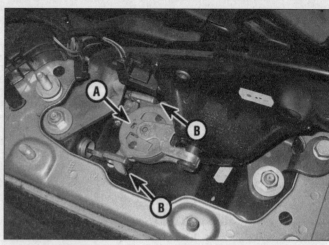

11.6 Press and hold the cable release button (A) and allow the cables to equalize, making sure both spring-loaded hooks (B) are still connected to the eyelets on both parking brake cables

c) *Bleed the brake system (see Section 9) and test the operation of the brakes before putting the vehicle into normal service.* **Warning:** *Do not operate the vehicle if you are in doubt about the effectiveness of the brake system. It's possible for air to become trapped in the ABS hydraulic control unit, so, if the pedal continues to feel spongy after repeated bleedings or the BRAKE or ABS light stays on, have the vehicle towed to a dealer service department or other qualified repair shop to be bled.*

---

11   Parking brake - check and adjustment

Check

1   Pulling up the parking brake lever five clicks should engage the parking brake fully.

If the number of clicks is much less, there's a chance the parking brake might not be releasing completely resulting in brake drag. If the number of clicks is much more, the parking brake may not hold the vehicle on an incline.

2   One method of checking the parking brake is to park the vehicle on a steep hill with the parking brake set and the transmission in Neutral (be sure to stay in the vehicle for this check!). If the parking brake cannot prevent the vehicle from rolling, it's in need of adjustment.

Adjustment

Refer to illustrations 11.5 and 11.6

Note: *The rear brakes are self-adjusting, and do not require normal maintenance adjustments. Adjustment is only required after replacing brake discs, brake pads, brake calipers or parking brake cables.*

3   Block the front wheels, raise the rear of the vehicle and support it securely on

jackstands. Remove the rear wheels.

4   Remove the parking brake handle covers (see Chapter 11, Section 20).

5   Insert a 1.5 mm feeler gauge between each rear caliper lever and the stop **(see illustration)**.

6   Using a small screwdriver, press and hold the cable release button **(see illustration)** and allow the cables to be equalized. Make sure both spring-loaded hooks are still connected to the eyelets on both parking brake cables, then release the button.

7   Remove the feeler gauges and set the parking brake fully. Release the parking brake and confirm the gap between the caliper lever and the stop is between 0 to 1.5 mm.

8   Apply the parking brake and confirm the brake holds.

9   Release the parking brake and confirm that the brakes don't drag when the rear wheels are turned.

10   Installation is the reverse of removal.

12.4 Remove the small socket head anti-rotational bolt from the back of the brake pedal bracket

12.5 Carefully pry the circlip from the right side of the pedal pivot pin and slide the pin out

12   Brake pedal - removal and installation

Refer to illustrations 12.4 and 12.5

1   Remove the driver's side knee bolster for access (see Chapter 11).
2   Disconnect the brake light switch electrical connector (see Section 13).
3   Disconnect the brake booster from the brake pedal (see Section 10).
4   Remove the small socket head anti-rotational bolt **(see illustration)**.
5   Remove the brake pedal pivot pin circlip from the right side of the pedal **(see illustration)**.
6   Slide the pivot pin back through the bracket far enough to allow the brake pedal to be lowered from the bracket and remove the pedal from the vehicle.
7   Place the pedal back up into the bracket and slide the pivot pin through the bracket and pedal. Install the circlip and tighten the anti-rotational bolt securely.
8   Installation is the reverse of removal.
9   Replace the knee bolster.

13   Brake light switch - removal and installation

Refer to illustration 13.2
Note: *For the purpose of a secure fit, the*

13.2 Typical brake light switch mounting details

1   *Electrical connector*
2   *Brake light switch*
3   *Mounting bracket*
4   *Switch plunger and brake pedal*

manufacturer recommends installing the brake light switch only once.
1   Remove the driver's side knee bolster for access (see Chapter 11).
2   Disconnect the brake light switch electrical connector **(see illustration)**.
3   Rotate the switch about 45 degrees counterclockwise, then carefully remove it from the bracket.
4   Before installing the switch, pull the plunger on the switch out fully.

5   With the brake pedal fully released (up), install the switch in its bracket in the opposite manner that it was removed. The switch will self-adjust by design when installed correctly.
6   Connect the electrical connector. Confirm that the brake lights are operating properly.
7   Replace the knee bolster.

Notes

Chapter 10
Suspension and steering systems

Contents

	Section			Section
Balljoints - check and replacement	8		Shock absorber/coil spring assembly (front) - removal inspection and installation	2
Coil spring (rear) - removal and installation	10		Stabilizer bar and bushings (front) - removal and installation	6
Control arms (front) - removal, bushing replacement and installation	7		Stabilizer bar and bushings (rear) - removal and installation	13
General information and precautions	1		Steering and suspension check	See Chapter 1
Hub and wheel bearing (front) - removal, bearing replacement and installation	5		Steering column - removal and installation	16
			Steering gear - removal and installation	19
Hub and wheel bearing assembly (rear) - removal and installation	11		Steering gear boots - replacement	18
			Steering knuckle - removal and installation	4
Knuckle (rear) - removal and installation	12		Steering wheel - removal and installation	15
Power steering fluid level check	See Chapter 1		Tie-rod ends (front) - removal and installation	17
Power steering pump - removal and installation	20		Tire and tire pressure checks	See Chapter 1
Power steering system - bleeding	21		Tire rotation	See Chapter 1
Rear suspension arms - removal and installation	14		Wheel alignment - general information	23
Shock absorber (rear) - removal and installation	9		Wheels and tires - general information	22
Shock absorber or coil spring (front) - replacement	3			

Specifications

Torque specifications

Note: *One foot-pound (ft-lb) of torque is equivalent to 12 inch-pounds (in-lbs) of torque. Torque values below approximately 15 ft-lbs are expressed in inch-pounds, since most foot-pound torque wrenches are not accurate at these smaller values.*

	Ft-lbs (unless otherwise indicated)	**Nm**
Front suspension		
Driveaxle/hub bolt	See Chapter 8	
Stabilizer bar		
Connecting link bolts		
Step 1	30	40
Step 2	Tighten an additional 1/4-turn (90-degrees)	
Clamp nuts	18	24
Upper balljoint clamp bolt/nut	30	40
Upper front and rear control link pivot bolt/nut		
Step 1	37	50
Step 2	Tighten an additional 1/4-turn (90-degrees)	
Upper front and rear control link balljoint clamp bolt/nut	29	39
Lower control arm and guide link balljoint nut	81	110
Lower control arm and guide link pivot bolt		
Step 1	51	69
Step 2	Tighten an additional 1/2-turn (180-degrees)	
Shock absorber damper shaft nut	37	50
Shock absorber mounting bracket bolts	55	75
Shock absorber-to-lower control arm bolt/nut	66	89
Subframe mounting bolts		
Step 1	81	110
Step 2	Tighten an additional 1/4-turn (90-degrees)	
Subframe front supports	55	75
Subframe rear supports	40	54
Tie-rod end pinch bolt	33	45
Track adjusting bolt	62 in-lbs	7
Wheel bearing assembly mounting bolts		
Step 1	59	80
Step 2	Tighten an additional 1/4-turn (90-degrees)	

Torque specifications (continued)

Note: One foot-pound (ft-lb) of torque is equivalent to 12 inch-pounds (in-lbs) of torque. Torque values below approximately 15 ft-lbs are expressed in inch-pounds, since most foot-pound torque wrenches are not accurate at these smaller values.

	Ft-lbs (unless otherwise indicated)	**Nm**
Rear suspension		
Diagonal brace bolts (convertible)	48	65
Driveaxle/hub bolt	See Chapter 8	
Control arms (transverse link)		
Lower control arm/tie-rod-to-subframe bolt/nut	62	84
Lower control arm/tie-rod-to-knuckle bolt/nut	62	84
Lower control arm-to-knuckle bolt/nut	62	84
Upper control arm-to-subframe	62	84
Upper control arm-to-knuckle eccentric bolt/nut	70	95
Rock guard (lower control arm)	18	24
Shock absorber upper mounting bolts	26	35
Shock absorber-to-lower control arm bolt/nut		
Step 1	110	149
Step 2	Tighten an additional 1/4-turn (90-degrees)	
Stabilizer bar		
Connecting link-to-stabilizer bolt	33	45
Connecting link-to-control arm bolts	18	24
Clamp bolts	18	24
Subframe bolts		
Step 1	81	110
Step 2	Tighten an additional 1/4-turn (90-degrees)	
Wheel bearing assembly bolts (aluminum knuckle)		
Step 1	59	80
Step 2	Tighten an additional 1/4-turn (90-degrees)	
Steering		
Driver's airbag module mounting fasteners	62 in-lbs	7
Steering column		
Mounting bolts	16	22
Universal joint pinch bolt/nut	22	30
Steering gear		
Mounting bolts		
Step 1	30	40
Step 2	Tighten an additional 1/4-turn (90-degrees)	
Pressure line banjo fitting bolt	26	35
Return line banjo fitting bolt	35	47
Tie-rod end	74	100
Tie-rod end (lock nut)	30	40
Steering wheel bolt	37	50
Power steering pump		
Mounting bolts	17	23
Pressure line banjo fitting bolt	37	50
Wheels		
Wheel bolts	See Chapter 1	

1   General information and precautions

Front suspension

Refer to illustration 1.1

The front suspension is made up of four transverse control arms (two upper and two lower) in an unequal-length, double-wishbone configuration, a steering knuckle/hub assembly, coil-over shock absorbers and a stabilizer bar **(see illustration)**.

Rear suspension

Refer to illustration 1.2

The rear suspension incorporates upper and lower control arms, knuckle and hub assemblies, track rods connected to the knuckles, shock absorbers, coil springs and a stabilizer bar **(see illustration)**.

Steering

The steering column is connected to the steering gear by a universal joint.

The steering gear is mounted on the front subframe, and is connected by two tie-

1.1 Front suspension components

1	Stabilizer bar	4	Front lower control arm	7	Tie-rod end
2	Stabilizer bar clamp	5	Shock absorber lower mount	8	Steering knuckle
3	Stabilizer bar link	6	Rear lower control arm	9	Subframe

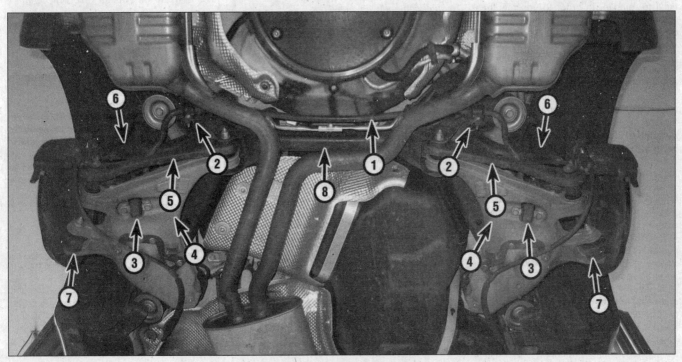

1.2 Rear suspension components

1	Stabilizer bar	4	Lower control arm	7	Steering knuckle
2	Stabilizer bar clamp	5	Rear tie-rod	8	Subframe
3	Stabilizer bar link	6	Upper rear control arm		

rods, with balljoints at their outer ends, to the steering arms projecting rearwards from the steering knuckles.

Power-assisted steering is standard equipment. The hydraulic steering system is powered by a belt-driven pump, which is driven off the crankshaft pulley.

Special manufacturer equipment

Dynamic Ride Control

Some models are equipped with Dynamic Ride Control (DRC, DRC II) as an option. There are no driver controls for this system. You can easily determine if your vehicle is equipped with DRC by looking for hydraulic lines attached to the shock absorbers. This system connects the front and rear shock absorbers hydraulically to improve handling. It consists of two diagonal circuits: the left-front and right-rear shocks are in one circuit and the right-front and left-rear shocks are in the other circuit. Other components include central and extraction/filling valves, hoses and joints connecting the system together. Special tools and expertise are required to service this system.

Precautions

Frequently, when working on the suspension or steering system components, you may come across fasteners which seem impossible to loosen. These fasteners on the underside of the vehicle are continually subjected to water, road grime, mud, etc., and can become rusted or frozen, making them extremely difficult to remove. In order to unscrew these stubborn fasteners without damaging them (or other components), be sure to use lots of penetrating oil and allow it to soak in for a while. Using a wire brush to clean exposed threads will also ease removal of the nut or bolt and prevent damage to the threads. Sometimes a sharp blow with a hammer and punch will break the bond between a nut and bolt threads, but care must be taken to prevent the punch from slipping off the fastener and ruining the threads. Heating the stuck fastener and surrounding area with a torch sometimes helps too, but isn't recommended because of the obvious dangers associated with fire. Long breaker bars and extension, or cheater, pipes will increase leverage, but never use an extension pipe on a ratchet - the ratcheting mechanism could be damaged. Sometimes tightening the nut or bolt first will help to break it loose. Fasteners that require drastic measures to remove should always be replaced with new ones. Many of the fasteners (nuts and bolts) that are used to mount the suspension components are self-locking (prevailing torque) and designed to be used only once. The manufacturers require replacement of self-locking fasteners whenever they are loosened or removed.

Since most of the procedures dealt with in this Chapter involve jacking up the vehicle and working underneath it, a good pair of jackstands will be needed. A hydraulic floor jack is the preferred type of jack to

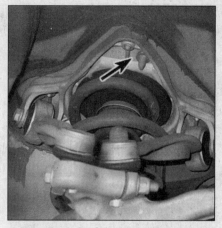

2.6 Cut and discard the factory mounting clip - it is not necessary to install a new clip

lift the vehicle, and it can also be used to support certain components during various operations. **Warning:** *Never, under any circumstances, rely on a jack to support the vehicle while working on it. Whenever any of the suspension or steering fasteners are loosened or removed they must be inspected and, if necessary, replaced with new ones of the same part number or of original equipment quality and design. Torque specifications must be followed for proper reassembly and component retention. Never attempt to heat or straighten any suspension or steering components. Instead, replace any bent or damaged part with a new one.*

---

2   Shock absorber/coil spring assembly (front) - removal, inspection and installation

Removal

Refer to illustrations 2.6, 2.10, 2.14a and 2.14b

Caution: *DO NOT disconnect hydraulic hoses from the shock absorbers or related components on vehicles equipped with the Dynamic Ride Control (DRC) system (see Section 1).*

1   Remove the wheel trim/hub cap (as applicable) and loosen the wheel bolts by half a turn with the vehicle resting on its wheels.

2   Chock the rear wheels of the car, firmly apply the parking brake, then raise the front of the vehicle and support it securely on jackstands. Remove the wheel.

3   On vehicles equipped with automatic leveling headlamps, disconnect the vehicle level sensor linkage from the front lower control arm.

4   Remove the ABS wheel speed sensor harness from its mounting bracket and position it away from the shock absorber (see Chapter 9).

5   Remove the brake caliper and support it with a length of wire (see Chapter 9). **Caution:** *Don't let the caliper hang by the brake hose.*

2.10 Remove the shock absorber lower mounting fastener

6   Remove the clip from the stud underneath the shock absorber upper mount and discard it **(see illustration)**. **Note:** *The clip does not need to be replaced.*

7   Place cardboard or equivalent around the steering gear boot to protect it from damage during shock removal.

8   Support the steering knuckle with a floor jack.

9   Separate the upper control arms from the steering knuckle (see Section 7).

10   Remove the shock absorber lower mounting fasteners **(see illustration)** and carefully turn the steering knuckle to the side.

11   Loosen the coolant reservoir connections.

12   Remove the cowl cover that is below the windshield and adjacent to the engine compartment.

13   Remove the small bolt cover(s) **(see illustrations 2.14a and 2.14b)** to gain access to the mounting fasteners.

14   Remove the shock absorber upper mounting fasteners **(see illustrations)** while noting the washer locations, and carefully guide the unit from the wheelwell. **Note:** *Leave the upper control arms attached to the shock absorber's upper mount. They can remain in place unless the entire shock absorber/coil assembly is going to be replaced.*

Installation

Refer to illustration 2.15

Note: *The manufacturer states to replace the mounting fasteners whenever they are removed.*

15   Guide the shock absorber/coil spring unit into position and install the mounting bolts, tightening them to the torque listed in this Chapter's Specifications. Reinstall any rubber bolt covers. Ensure that the alignment hole in the coil spring lower seat, faces inwards towards the vehicle **(see illustration)**.

16   Connect the shock absorber to the lower control arm, place the mounting bolt in rear to front, then install a new mounting nut, but hand-tighten it only at this stage.

17   Reconnect the upper control arms to the

2.14a Shock absorber upper mounting fastener cover (A) and fasteners - right side shown

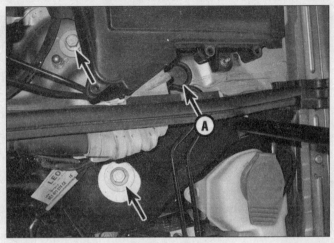

2.14b Shock absorber upper mounting fastener cover (A) and fasteners - left side shown

steering knuckle as described in Section 7. Install a new clamp bolt and self-locking nut, then tighten the nut to the torque listed in this Chapter's Specifications. Press down on both control arms as you tighten the nut, to ensure that the balljoint studs are properly seated in the steering knuckle.

18   Reattach the ABS wheel speed sensor harness and install the brake caliper (see Chapter 9).

19   On vehicles equipped with automatic leveling headlamps, reconnect the vehicle level sensor connecting rod to the front lower control arm.

20   Using a floor jack positioned under the outer ends of the lower control arms, raise the suspension to simulate normal ride height. Now tighten the shock absorber lower mounting nut to the torque listed in this Chapter's Specifications.

21   Install the wheel and wheel bolts, tightening the bolts as securely as possible with the wheel off the ground. Lower the vehicle and tighten the wheel bolts to the torque listed in the Chapter 1 Specifications.

3   Shock absorber or coil spring (front) - replacement

Refer to illustrations 3.3, 3.4, 3.5a, 3.5b, 3.5c, 3.6a, 3.6b, 3.6c, 3.7a, 3.7b, 3.12a, 3.12b, 3.13, 3.14a, 3.14b, 3.14c, 3.14d and 3.14e
Warning: *Always replace the shock absorbers or coil springs in pairs - never replace just one of them, as handling peculiarities may result.*

1   If the shock absorbers or coil springs exhibit the telltale signs of wear (leaking fluid, loss of damping capability, chipped, sagging or cracked coil springs) explore all options before beginning any work. The shock absorber itself is not serviceable and must be replaced if a problem develops. However, shock absorber/coil spring assemblies complete with springs may be available on an exchange basis, which eliminates much time and work. Whichever route you choose to take, check on the cost and availability of parts before disassembling your vehicle. **Warning:** *Disassembling a coil-over type shock absorber is potentially dangerous and utmost atten-*

tion must be directed to the job, or serious injury may result. Use only a high-quality spring compressor and carefully follow the manufacturer's instructions furnished with the tool. After removing the coil spring from the shock absorber, set it aside in a safe, isolated area.

2   Remove the shock absorber and spring assembly following the procedure described in the previous Section. Mount the assembly in a vise. Line the vise jaws with wood or rags to prevent damage to the unit and don't tighten the vise excessively. **Note:** *Leave the upper control arms attached to the shock absorber's upper mount. They can remain in place unless the entire shock absorber/coil assembly is going to be replaced.*

3   Following the tool manufacturer's instructions, install the spring compressor (which can be obtained at most auto parts stores or equipment yards on a daily rental basis) on the spring and compress it sufficiently to relieve all pressure from the upper spring seat **(see illustration).** This can be verified by wiggling the spring.

2.15 Ensure that the alignment hole in the spring seat faces towards the center of the vehicle

3.3 Compress the coil spring evenly and progressively until tension is relieved from the spring seats

3.4 Loosen the damper shaft nut while preventing the shaft from turning with an Allen wrench

3.5a Remove the nut and lift off the mounting plate . . .

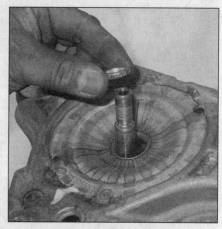

3.5b . . . followed by the washer . . .

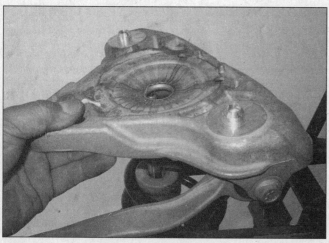

3.5c . . . the upper spring seat and upper spring support

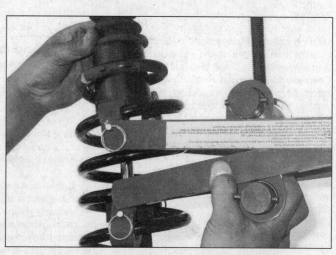

3.6a Remove the dust boot and rubber bump stop . . .

4   Make a mark between the upper spring seat and mounting plate. Loosen the shock absorber damper shaft nut while preventing the damper shaft from turning with an Allen wrench or hex bit **(see illustration)**.

5   Remove the nut, then lift off the mounting plate followed by the washer, the upper spring seat and upper spring support **(see illustrations)**. Mark the upper spring support to the spring seat.

6   Remove the dust boot and rubber bump stop, then lift off the compressed coil spring and protective cap from the shock absorber piston **(see illustrations)**. **Warning:** *Keep the ends of the spring away from your body.*

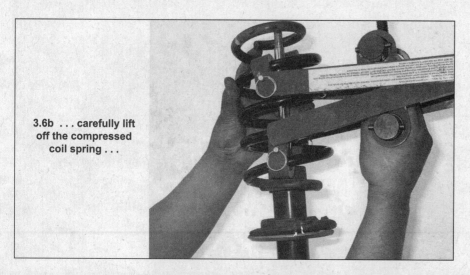

3.6b . . . carefully lift off the compressed coil spring . . .

3.6c . . . and the protective cap from the shock absorber

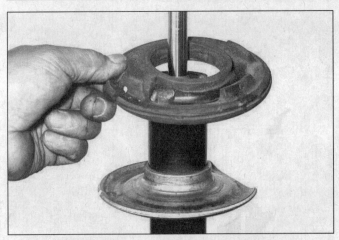

3.7a Remove the lower spring support . . .

3.7b . . . and slide the lower spring seat up from the shock absorber body

7   Make an alignment mark between the lower spring seat support and the spring seat, then remove the lower spring support, and if required, loosen the lower spring seat from the shock absorber body **(see illustrations)** by tapping it lightly with a soft-faced mallet. **Note:** *Do not remove the lower spring seat unless the shock absorber is being replaced.*

8   With the shock absorber now completely disassembled, examine all the components for wear, damage or deformation, and check the bearing for smoothness of operation. Replace any of the components as necessary.

9   Examine the shock for signs of fluid leakage (a slight amount of seepage is normal). Check the shock damper shaft for signs of pitting along its entire length, and check the body for signs of damage. While holding it in an upright position, test the operation of the shock by moving the damper shaft through a full stroke, then through several short strokes. In both cases, the resistance felt should be smooth and continuous. If the resistance is jerky or uneven, or if there is any visible sign of wear or damage to the shock, replacement is necessary.

10   If any doubt exists about the condition of the coil spring, carefully remove the spring compressor and check the spring for distortion and signs of cracking. Replace the spring if it is damaged or distorted, or if there is any doubt as to its condition.

11   Inspect all other components for signs of damage or deterioration, and replace any that are suspect.

12   Slide the lower spring seat (if removed) into the correct position **(see illustrations)**, lower spring support, protective cap, bump stop and boot onto the damper shaft.

13   Install the coil spring onto the shock absorber, making sure its end is correctly located against the spring seat stop **(see illustration).**

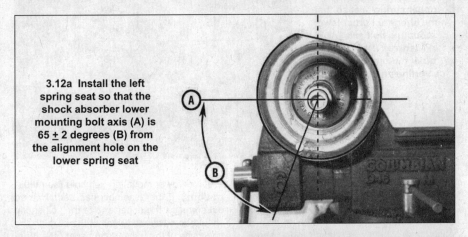

3.12a Install the left spring seat so that the shock absorber lower mounting bolt axis (A) is 65 ± 2 degrees (B) from the alignment hole on the lower spring seat

3.12b Install the right spring seat so that the shock absorber lower mounting bolt axis (A) is 87 ± 2 degrees (B) from the alignment hole on the lower spring seat

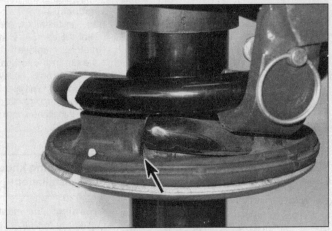

3.13 Ensure that the end of the coil spring bears against the stop on the spring support

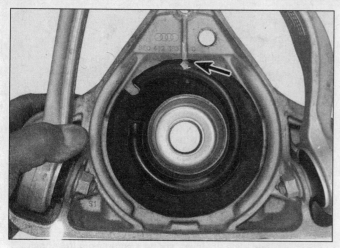

3.14a Install the upper spring seat, ensuring the alignment marks are matching

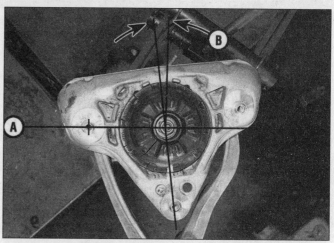

3.14b Install the left upper spring seat so that the shock absorber lower mounting bolt axis (A) is 7 degrees (B) from the outer mounting bolt hole centerline on the spring seat

3.14c Install the right upper spring seat so that the shock absorber lower mounting bolt axis (A) is 7 degrees (B) from the outer mounting bolt hole centerline on the spring seat

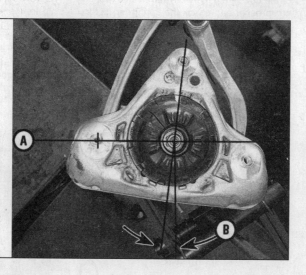

3.14d The upper end of the coil spring should be positioned against the upper stop . . .

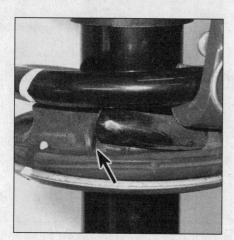

3.14e . . . and the lower end of the spring against the lower stop

14   Install the upper spring support and spring seat **(see illustration)**, washer and upper mounting to the top of the shock, so that the spring seat front mounting hole is positioned correctly in relation to the shock absorber lower mounting bolt hole **(see illustrations)**. If the assembly has been carried out correctly, the upper end of the coil spring should be positioned against the stop on the underside of the upper spring seat **(see illustrations)**.

15   Install a new damper shaft nut, then prevent the damper shaft from turning using the method employed during removal. Tighten the nut to the torque listed in this Chapter's Specifications. Slowly loosen the spring compressor and remove it, making sure the ends of the spring are still properly situated.

16   Install the shock absorber assembly (see Section 2).

4   Steering knuckle - removal and installation

Warning: *The manufacturer recommends replacing the driveaxle/hub bolt, control arm pivot bolts and nuts and all other self-locking nuts with new ones whenever they are removed (see Section 1).*

Note: *Remove the hub and wheel bearing assembly if the steering knuckle is going to be replaced. Refer to Section 5.*

Removal

1   Remove the wheel cover and loosen the driveaxle/hub bolt with the vehicle resting on its wheels. Also loosen the wheel bolts.

2   Chock the rear wheels of the car, firmly apply the parking brake, then raise the front of the car and support it securely on jackstands. Remove the front wheel.

3   Remove the driveaxle/hub bolt.

4   Remove the ABS wheel speed sensor as described in Chapter 9.

5   Remove the brake caliper (don't disconnect the hose) and brake disc (see Chapter 9). Using a piece of wire or string, tie the caliper to the coil spring - don't let the caliper hang by the hose.

6   Detach the tie-rod end from the steering knuckle (see Section 17).

7   Detach the lower balljoints from the

5.4 Remove the shield mounting bolts

5.7 Location of the hub bearing mounting bolts

steering knuckle (see Section 7).

8   Detach the upper control arms from the steering knuckle (see Section 7).

9   Carefully pull the hub assembly outwards while pushing the driveaxle from the hub. If necessary, tap the CV joint out of the hub using a soft-faced hammer. If this fails to free it from the hub, the joint will have to be pressed out using a puller. Support the driveaxle with wire or an equivalent and never let it hang. **Caution:** *Be careful not to overextend the inner CV joint.*

Installation

10   Lubricate the splines of the driveaxle with multi-purpose grease.

11   Maneuver the knuckle/hub assembly into position and engage it with the driveaxle stub shaft. Install a new driveaxle/hub bolt, but don't attempt to tighten it yet.

12   Connect the upper control arms to the knuckle, pushing the balljoints into their bores as far as possible. Install the pinch bolt and a new nut, and tighten the nut to the torque listed in this Chapter's Specifications.

13   Connect the lower control arms to the knuckle. Install new nuts and tighten them to the torque listed in this Chapter's Specifications.

14   Engage the tie-rod end with the steering knuckle, install the retaining bolt, clamp bolt and a new clamp bolt nut. Tighten these fasteners to the torque values listed in this Chapter's Specifications.

15   Install the brake disc and caliper, tightening the caliper mounting bracket bolts (if equipped) and caliper guide pins to the torque values listed in Chapter 9 Specifications.

16   Install the ABS wheel speed sensor as described in Chapter 9.

17   Install the wheel and lower the vehicle to the ground.

18   Tighten the driveaxle/hub bolt to the torque listed in the Chapter 8 Specifications, then tighten the wheel bolts to the torque listed in the Chapter 1 Specifications.

---

5   Hub and wheel bearing (front) - removal, bearing replacement and installation

---

Removal

Refer to illustrations 5.4 and 5.7

Warning: *The manufacturer recommends replacing the driveaxle/hub bolt, control arm pivot bolts and nuts and all other self-locking nuts with new ones whenever they are removed (see Section 1).*

1   Loosen the driveaxle/hub bolt (see Chapter 8).

2   Loosen the wheel bolts, raise the vehicle and support it securely on jackstands. Remove the wheel.

3   Remove the brake caliper, the caliper mounting bracket and the brake disc from the hub (see Chapter 9). **Caution:** *Be sure to support the brake caliper with a length of wire or rope.*

4   Remove the shield from the steering knuckle **(see illustration)**.

5   Detach the upper control arms from the steering knuckle (see Section 7).

6   Carefully pull the knuckle assembly outwards while pushing the driveaxle from the hub. If necessary, tap the CV joint out of the hub using a soft-faced hammer. If this fails to free it from the hub, the joint will have to be pressed out using a puller. Support the driveaxle with wire or an equivalent and never let it hang. **Caution:** *Be careful not to overextend the inner CV joint.*

7   Remove the hub/bearing assembly mounting bolts from the rear of the steering knuckle **(see illustration)**.

8   Remove the hub/bearing assembly from the steering knuckle.

Bearing replacement

9   Due to the special tools and expertise required to press the hub from the bearing, this job should be left to a professional

mechanic. Take the hub and bearing assembly to an automotive machine shop or other qualified repair facility for service.

Installation

10   Make sure that the mounting surfaces inside the steering knuckle and on the driveaxle splines are smooth and free of burrs and nicks prior to installing the hub/bearing assembly.

11   Install the hub/bearing assembly to the steering knuckle and tighten the bolts to the torque listed in this Chapter's Specifications.

12   Lubricate the driveaxle splines with multi-purpose grease, then place it into the hub/bearing assembly. Install a new driveaxle/hub bolt, but don't attempt to tighten it yet.

13   Reconnect the upper control arms to the steering knuckle as described in Section 7. Install a new clamp bolt, self-locking nut, and tighten the nut to the torque listed in this Chapter's Specifications. Press down on both control arms as you tighten the nut, to ensure that the balljoint studs are properly seated in the steering knuckle.

14   Install the brake disc, the caliper mounting bracket and the caliper; tighten the fasteners to the torque values listed in the Chapter 9 Specifications.

15   Install the wheel, remove the jackstands and lower the vehicle.

16   Tighten the driveaxle/hub bolt to the torque listed in the Chapter 8 Specifications. **Note:** *Have an assistant apply the brakes while tightening the driveaxle/hub bolt.*

17   Tighten the wheel bolts to the torque listed in the Chapter 1 Specifications.

---

6   Stabilizer bar and bushings (front) - removal and installation

---

Refer to illustration 6.3

Warning: *The manufacturer recommends replacing the stabilizer bar link nuts and bushing clamp nuts with new ones whenever they*

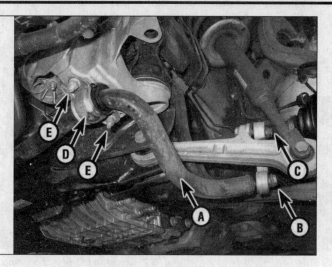

6.3 Front stabilizer bar details

A   *Stabilizer bar*
B   *Stabilizer bar link-to lower arm bolt*
C   *Stabilizer bar link-to-bar bolt*
D   *Stabilizer bar clamp*
E   *Stabilizer bar clamp mounting fasteners*

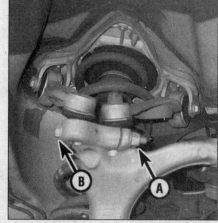

7.6 Remove the nut (A) and pull the clamp bolt (B) out of the top of the steering knuckle, then separate the balljoints from the steering knuckle

are removed (see Section 1).

1   Raise the front of the vehicle and support it securely on jackstands.
2   Remove the under-vehicle splash shield.
3   Remove the mounting fasteners and detach the stabilizer bar links from the stabilizer bar **(see illustration)**. **Note:** *Early models use balljoint-type stabilizer bar links; you may have to remove the link-to-control arm nut and fully detach the link in order to detach it from the stabilizer bar.*
4   Remove the mounting fasteners and detach the stabilizer bar bushing clamps from the subframe.
5   Remove the stabilizer bar. If necessary, unbolt the stabilizer bar links from the control arms.
6   Inspect the clamp bushings and the link bushings. If they're cracked, hardened or deteriorated in any way, replace them.
7   Installation is the reverse of the removal procedure. Be sure to tighten the fasteners to the torque values listed in this Chapter's Specifications.

7   Control arms (front) - removal, bushing replacement and installation

Warning: *The manufacturer recommends replacing the control arm pivot bolts and nuts, the lower balljoint nuts, the upper control arm balljoint clamp bolt nut and the shock absorber lower mounting nut with new ones whenever they are removed (see Section 1).*

Upper control arms (upper links)

Removal

Refer to illustrations 7.6 and 7.8

1   Remove the wheel trim/hub cap (as applicable) and loosen the wheel bolts by half a turn with the vehicle resting on its wheels.
2   Chock the rear wheels of the car, firmly apply the parking brake, then raise the front

of the vehicle and support it securely on jackstands. Remove the wheel.
3   On vehicles equipped with automatic leveling headlamps, disconnect the vehicle level sensor linkage from the front lower control arm.
4   Remove the ABS wheel speed sensor harness from its mounting bracket and position it away from the shock absorber (see Chapter 9).
5   Remove the brake caliper and position it aside (see Chapter 9).
6   Remove the securing nut and extract the clamp bolt from the top of the steering knuckle **(see illustration)**. Separate the front and rear upper control arm balljoints from the top of the steering knuckle, but do not force the slots apart with a screwdriver or chisel in an attempt to free the balljoint studs. Take care to avoid damaging the balljoint rubber boots.
7   Remove the shock absorber and coil spring assembly (see Section 2).
8   Mount the lower end of the shock absorber in a bench vise, then loosen and remove the nut and bolt securing the appropriate upper control arm to the mounting bracket **(see illustration)**.

Bushing replacement

Refer to illustration 7.10

9   Thoroughly clean the arm, removing all traces of dirt, thread locking compound and undercoating if necessary, then check carefully for cracks, distortion or any other signs of wear or damage, paying particular attention to the inner pivot bushing and balljoint. The balljoint is an integral part of the arm and cannot be replaced separately. If the arm or balljoint are damaged, the complete assembly must be replaced.
10   Replacement of the inner pivot bushing will require the use of a hydraulic press and several spacers and is therefore best entrusted to an automotive machine shop with access to the necessary equipment. If such equipment is available, press out the old bushing and install the new one using a spacer, which bears only on the bushing outer edge. Ensure the bushing is correctly positioned so that the cavities are aligned with the center axis of the arm **(see illustration)**.

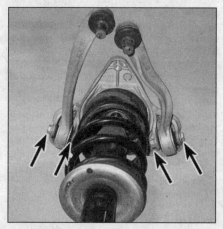

7.8 Location of the upper control arm bracket fasteners

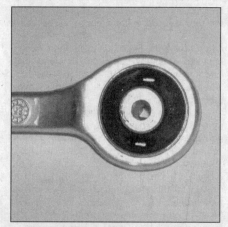

7.10 Make sure the bushing is correctly positioned so that the cavities are aligned with the center axis of the arm

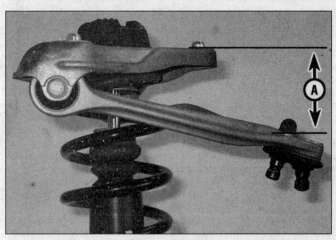

7.12a Position the front upper control arm so that the distance between the front edge of the mounting bracket (A) and the arm is 81 mm ± 2 mm, then tighten the mounting bolt nuts

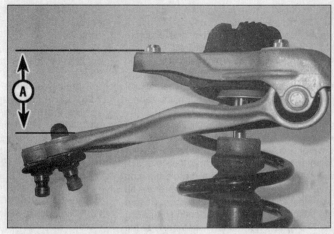

7.12b Position the rear control arm so that the distance between the front edge of the mounting bracket (A) and the arm is 70 mm ± 2 mm, then tighten the mounting bolt nuts

Installation

Refer to illustrations 7.12a and 7.12b

11   Place the control arm on the mounting bracket, insert a new securing bolt and screw on a new securing nut.

12   Position the arm such that the vertical distance between the front edge of the mounting bracket and the arm is 81 mm ± 2 mm for the upper front control arm and 70 mm ± 2 mm for the upper rear control arm **(see illustrations)**. Hold the arm in this position and tighten the securing nut to the specified stage 1 and 2 torque settings. This ensures that the rubber bushing is not stressed when the vehicle is lowered onto its wheels.

13   Install the shock absorber and coil spring assembly while leaving the new lower mounting fasteners hand tight (see Section 2).

14   Reconnect the upper control arm balljoints to the top of the steering knuckle, inserting the balljoints as far as they will go. Install a new clamp bolt and self-locking nut, tightening it to the torque listed in this Chapter's Specifications. Press down on both control arms as you tighten the nut, to ensure that the balljoints

are properly seated in the steering knuckle.

15   Reinstall the ABS wheel speed sensor and secure the wiring harness.

16   On vehicles equipped with automatic leveling headlamps, fasten the clip to reconnect the vehicle level sensor connecting rod to the front lower control arm.

17   Using a floor jack, raise the outer ends of the lower control arms to simulate normal ride height, then tighten the shock absorber lower mounting nut to the torque listed in this Chapter's Specifications.

18   Install the wheel and tighten the bolts as securely as possible, then lower the vehicle to the ground and tighten the bolts to the torque listed in the Chapter 1 Specifications.

19   On completion, have the front wheel alignment checked and, if necessary, adjusted.

Rear lower control arm (lower guide link)

Removal

Refer to illustrations 7.22 and 7.23

20   Loosen the wheel bolts. Chock the rear wheels, firmly apply the parking brake, then

raise the front of the vehicle and support it securely on jackstands. Remove the wheel.

21   Remove the ABS wheel speed sensor and brake caliper, then secure the caliper aside (see Chapter 9).

22   Remove the balljoint nut, then separate the control arm from the base of the steering knuckle using a balljoint separator **(see illustration)**.

23   Remove the nut from the bolt at the inner end of the control arm. To allow the bolt to be withdrawn, the corner of the subframe must be lowered slightly. To do this, support the subframe with a floor jack, unscrew and remove the two support plate bolts, then loosen and withdraw the subframe securing bolt. Note that the bolt is threaded through the inner of the two sets of subframe bolt holes **(see illustration)**.

24   Lower the subframe slightly, withdraw the control arm inner pivot bolt, then remove the arm from the vehicle.

Bushing replacement

25   Thoroughly clean the arm, removing all traces of dirt, thread locking compound and

7.22 This type of balljoint separator won't damage the balljoint boot

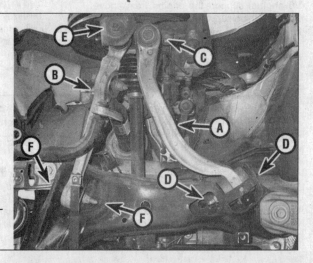

7.23 Front lower control arm details

A   Rear lower control arm (lower guide link)
B   Front lower control arm (lower control link)
C   Rear lower control arm balljoint
D   Rear control arm-to-subframe mounting fasteners
E   Front lower control arm mounting nut
F   Front lower control arm-to-subframe mounting fasteners

undercoating if necessary, then check carefully for cracks, distortion or any other signs of wear or damage, paying particular attention to the inner pivot bushing and balljoint. Note that the inner bushing has a hydraulic action; fluid leakage indicates that the bushing has been damaged and must be replaced. The balljoint is an integral part of the lower arm and cannot be replaced separately.

26   Replacement of the inner pivot bushing will require the use of a hydraulic press and several spacers and is therefore best entrusted to an automotive machine shop. If such equipment is available, press out the old bushing and install the new one using a spacer which bears only on the bushing outer edge. Ensure the bushing is correctly positioned so that the cavities are aligned with the center axis of the arm (see illustration 7.10).

Installation

27   Installation is the reverse of removal, noting the following points:

a) *Use new control arm and subframe securing nuts and bolts.*

b) *Ensure that the control arm inboard securing bolt passes through the inner of the two sets of subframe bolt holes.*

c) *Raise the outer ends of the control arms with a floor jack to simulate normal ride height before tightening the inner pivot bolt/nut.*

d) *Tighten all suspension fasteners to the torque values listed in this Chapter's Specifications.*

e) *Tighten the brake caliper mounting fasteners to the torque values listed in the Chapter 9 Specifications.*

f) *Lower the vehicle and tighten the wheel bolts to the torque listed in the Chapter 1 Specifications.*

g) *Have the front end alignment checked and, if necessary, adjusted.*

Front lower control arm (front control link)

Removal

28   If you're working on a model with a 3.2L V6 engine, support the engine from above with an engine support fixture.

29   Loosen the wheel bolts. Chock the rear wheels, firmly apply the parking brake, then raise the front of the vehicle and support it securely on jackstands. Remove the wheel.

30   On vehicles equipped with automatic leveling headlamps, release the clip and disconnect the vehicle level sensor connecting rod from the front lower control arm.

31   Support the steering knuckle by placing a floor jack beneath the hub flange. **Note:** *Don't lift the flange, just support the steering knuckle by placing the floor jack under the flange.*

32   Remove the nut, and separate the front lower control arm from the steering knuckle with the aid of a balljoint separator (see illustration 7.22).

33   Unscrew the nut and remove the shock absorber lower mounting bolt from the front control arm.

34   Remove the nut and detach the stabilizer bar link from the control arm (see Section 6).

35   Unscrew the nut and withdraw the control arm inner pivot bolt (see illustration 7.23), then remove the control arm from the vehicle. **Warning:** *When removing the inner pivot bolt on vehicles with a 3.2L FSI engine, you'll have to remove the engine mount/stabilizer bar bracket (with the engine supported by a support fixture from above), then pull the bracket downward to remove the pivot bolt.*

Bushing replacement

36   Thoroughly clean the arm, removing all traces of dirt, thread locking compound and undercoating if necessary, then check carefully for cracks, distortion or any other signs of wear or damage, paying particular attention to the inner and shock absorber pivot bushings and balljoint. The balljoint is an integral part of the lower arm and cannot be an replaced separately.

37   Replacement of the inner and shock absorber mount bushings will require the use of a hydraulic press and several spacers and is therefore best entrusted to an automotive machine shop. If such equipment is available, press out the old bushing and install the new one using a spacer which bears only on the bushing outer edge. Ensure the bushing is correctly positioned so that the cavities are aligned with the center axis of the arm (see illustration 7.10).

Installation

38   Installation is the reverse of the removal procedure, noting the following points:

a) *Use new control arm and shock absorber nuts and bolts.*

b) *Ensure that the control arm inboard securing bolt passes through the inner of the two sets of subframe bolt holes.*

c) *Raise the outer ends of the control arms with a floor jack to simulate normal ride height before tightening the inner pivot bolt/nut.*

d) *Tighten all fasteners to the torque values listed in this Chapter's Specifications.*

e) *Lower the vehicle and tighten the wheel bolts to the torque listed in the Chapter 1 Specifications.*

f) *Have the front end alignment checked and, if necessary, adjusted.*

8   Balljoints - check and replacement

Check

1   Inspect the control arm balljoints for looseness anytime either of them is separated from the steering knuckle. See if you can turn the ballstud in its socket with your fingers. If the balljoint is loose, or if the ballstud can be turned, replace the balljoint. You can

also check the balljoints with the suspension assembled as follows.

Upper balljoint

2   Raise the front of the vehicle and support it securely on jackstands placed under the frame rails. Place a floor jack under the lower control arm and raise it slightly.

3   Attempt to move the upper control arm up and down; a prybar may be helpful. If any play is felt, replace the upper control arm and balljoint as an assembly (the balljoint is not replaceable separately).

4   Also try to move the steering knuckle in-and-out. If any play is felt, replace the upper control arm/balljoint assembly.

5   Check the balljoint boot for cracks and tears. If any are present, replace the upper control arm/balljoint assembly.

Lower balljoint

6   Raise the front of the vehicle and support it securely on jackstands placed under the frame rails.

7   Place a floor jack under the front lower control arm and raise it slightly. Attempt to move the steering knuckle up and down; a large prybar underneath the tire, or a prybar placed between the end of the control arm and the steering knuckle will be helpful. If any play is felt, replace the control arm and balljoint as an assembly (the balljoint is not replaceable separately).

8   Also try to move the steering knuckle in-and-out. If any play is felt, replace the control arm/balljoint assembly.

9   Check the balljoint boot for cracks and tears. If any are present, replace the upper control arm/balljoint assembly.

Replacement

10   As stated previously, the balljoints are integral parts of the control arms and are not available separately. The entire control arm must be replaced.

9   Shock absorber (rear) - removal and installation

Refer to illustrations 9.3 and 9.4

Warning: *The manufacturer recommends replacing the shock absorber lower mounting bolt and nut with new ones whenever they are removed.*

Warning: *Always replace the shock absorbers in pairs - never replace just one of them, as handling peculiarities may result.*

Caution: *DO NOT disconnect hydraulic hoses from the shock absorbers or related components on vehicles equipped with the Dynamic Ride Control (DRC) system (see Section 1).*

1   Loosen the rear wheel bolts. Chock the front wheels to keep the vehicle from rolling, then raise the rear of the vehicle and support it securely on jackstands. Remove the rear wheel.

2   Remove the coil spring (see Section 10).

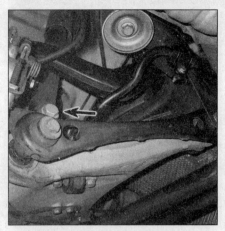

9.3 Rear shock absorber lower mounting fastener

9.4 Rear shock absorber upper mounting bolts

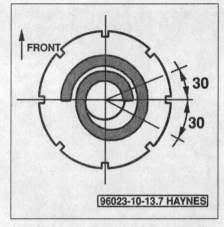

10.4 Make sure the ends of the coil spring are positioned in their spring seats like this when installed

3   Remove the shock absorber lower mounting fastener **(see illustration)**. Note how the longer end of the collar (in the lower bushing) fits with the rear knuckle.

4   Remove the shock absorber upper mounting fasteners and remove the shock absorber **(see illustration)**.

5   Guide the shock absorber into position and install the upper mounting bolts and a new lower mounting bolt and nut. Don't tighten the lower mounting bolt/nut yet.

6   Tighten the upper mounting bolts to the torque listed in this Chapter's Specifications.

7   Raise the rear axle to simulate normal ride height, then tighten the lower mounting bolt/nut to the torque listed in this Chapter's Specifications. **Note:** *The long collar of the shock absorber must face to the rear and sit into the center of the knuckle housing arm seat.*

8   Repeat the procedure to replace the other rear shock absorber.

9   Install the wheels and lower the vehicle. Tighten the wheel bolts to the torque listed in the Chapter 1 Specifications.

---

10 Coil spring (rear) - removal and installation

Refer to illustration 10.4

Warning: *Always replace the coil springs in pairs - never replace just one of them.*

1   Loosen the wheel bolts. Chock the front wheels to prevent the vehicle from rolling, then raise the rear of the vehicle and support it securely on jackstands placed under the rocker panel flanges. Remove the wheels.

2   Following the tool manufacturer's instructions, install a spring compressor (which can be obtained at most auto parts stores or equipment yards on a daily rental basis) on the spring and compress it enough to relieve the tension on the other suspension components. This can be verified by wiggling the spring. **Warning:** *Removing a coil spring is potentially dangerous. Use only a high-quality*

spring compressor and carefully follow the manufacturer's instructions furnished with the tool. After removing the coil spring, set it aside in a safe, isolated area.

3   Remove the spring and the upper and lower spring seats. Check the spring for cracks and chips, replacing the springs as a set if any defects are found. Also check the upper and lower seats for damage and deterioration, replacing them as necessary. **Note:** *If the lower spring seat is removed, it has a location pin that must be inserted back into the lower control arm to center the seat.*

4   Installation is the reverse of the removal procedure, but make sure the coil springs and seats are positioned properly, and the conical end of the spring points downward **(see illustration)** and into the spring seat stop.

5   Lower the vehicle and tighten the wheel bolts to the torque listed in the Chapter 1 Specifications.

---

11 Hub and wheel bearing assembly (rear) - removal and installation

---

1   On AWD models, loosen the driveaxle bolt (see Chapter 8).

2   Loosen the rear wheel bolts, raise the rear of the vehicle and support it securely on jackstands. Remove the wheel.

3   Remove the brake caliper (don't detach the hose), mounting bracket and disc (see Chapter 9). Hang the caliper with a piece of wire - don't let it hang by the brake hose.

Bolt-on

Note: *The hub and wheel bearing are press-fit together and removed as an assembly. The assembly can be removed and taken to an automotive repair facility for service.*

4   Remove the hub and bearing assembly mounting bolts from the back of the rear knuckle.

5   Remove the hub and bearing assembly from the knuckle. If it is stuck, tap on it from

side-to-side to free it.

6   On AWD models, carefully pull the assembly outwards while pushing the driveaxle inwards. If necessary, tap the CV joint out of the hub using a soft-faced hammer. If this fails to free it from the hub, the driveaxle will have to be pressed out using a puller (see Chapter 8). Support the driveaxle with wire or an equivalent and never let it hang. **Caution:** *Be careful not to overextend the inner CV joint.*

7   Installation is the reverse of removal, noting the following points:

a) *Make sure the mating surfaces on the knuckle and the hub and bearing assembly are clean before installation.*

b) *Tighten the mounting bolts to the torque listed in this Chapter's Specifications.*

c) *Install the brake caliper (see Chapter 9), tightening the mounting bolts to the torque listed in the Chapter 9 Specifications.*

d) *Install the wheel and wheel bolts. Lower the vehicle and tighten the bolts to the torque listed in the Chapter 1 Specifications.*

Pressed

8   Due to the special tools and expertise required to press the hub and bearing from the rear knuckle, this job should be left to a professional mechanic. However, the rear knuckle and hub may be removed and the assembly taken to an automotive machine shop or other qualified repair facility. See Section 12 for the rear knuckle removal procedure.

---

12 Knuckle (rear) - removal and installation

Warning: *The manufacturer recommends replacing all self-locking fasteners.*

1   Loosen the wheel bolts and the rear driveaxle/hub bolt, raise the rear of the vehicle

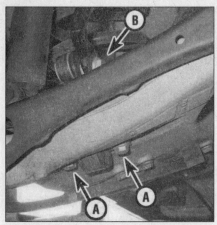

13.2 Remove the stabilizer lower mounting fasteners (A), then remove the upper fastener (B), and separate the links from the bar - left side shown, right side is identical

13.3 The rear stabilizer bar mounting fastener locations - left side shown, right side is identical

and support it securely on jackstands. **Note:** *Only loosen the driveaxle/hub bolt 1/4 turn while the wheel is on the ground.* Remove the wheel and loosen the driveaxle/hub bolt a few turns, then tap the bolt with a soft-faced hammer to loosen the axle from the hub. Remove the bolt.

2   Remove the rear brake caliper, caliper mounting bracket and brake disc (see Chapter 9). Support the caliper with a length of wire - don't let it hang by the hose.

3   Remove the ABS rear wheel speed sensor (see Chapter 9).

4   Remove the rear coil spring (see Section 10).

5   Detach the shock absorber from the knuckle (see Section 9).

6   Detach the lower control arm from the knuckle (see Section 14).

7   Detach the tie-rod from the knuckle (see Section 14).

8   Detach the upper control arm from the knuckle (see Section 14), then remove the knuckle. **Note:** *Be sure to make reference marks on the adjusting fasteners before removing the arm.*

9   Installation is the reverse of removal, noting the following points:

a) *Use a new driveaxle/hub bolt (AWD), upper control arm-to-rear knuckle bolt, washer and nut, the lower control arm-to-rear knuckle nut, and the tie-rod bar-to-rear knuckle nut. Tighten the driveaxle/ hub bolt securely, but don't try to tighten it completely until the wheels are on the ground.*

b) *Don't tighten any of the suspension fasteners until the rear suspension has been raised to simulate normal ride height (this will prevent bushing distortion). Tighten all suspension fasteners to the torque values listed in this Chapter's Specifications.*

c) *Install the brake disc, caliper mounting bracket and caliper (see Chapter 9).*

Tighten the brake fasteners to the torque values listed in the Chapter 9 Specifications.

d) *Install the wheel and tighten the bolts securely, then lower the vehicle and tighten the bolts to the torque listed in the Chapter 1 Specifications. Tighten the driveaxle/hub bolt to the torque listed in the Chapter 8 Specifications with the wheels on the ground.*

13   Stabilizer bar and bushings (rear) - removal and installation

Refer to illustrations 13.2 and 13.3

Warning: *The manufacturer recommends replacing all self-locking nuts whenever they are removed.*

1   Loosen the rear wheel bolts, raise the rear of the vehicle and support it securely on jackstands. Block the front wheels to keep the vehicle from rolling off the stands. Remove the rear wheels and lower control arm stone trim protector (if equipped).

2   Remove the mounting fasteners from the stabilizer bar links, then separate the links

from the bar **(see illustration)**. **Note:** *On convertible models, remove the rear cross brace fasteners and brace.*

3   Remove the stabilizer bar clamp mounting fasteners **(see illustration)** and remove the stabilizer bar. **Note:** *On models equipped with dual rear mufflers, it may be necessary to remove the rear portion of the exhaust system for removal of the stabilizer bar.*

4   Inspect the stabilizer bar bushings and link bushings for cracks, tears and other signs of deterioration. Replace as necessary. Also check the ballstuds at the ends of the links for looseness, replacing the links if necessary.

5   Installation is the reverse of removal. Be sure to tighten all fasteners to the torque values listed in this Chapter's Specifications.

6   Tighten the wheel bolts to the torque listed in the Chapter 1 Specifications.

14   Rear suspension arms - removal and installation

Warning: *The manufacturer recommends replacing all fasteners that are removed or loosened.*

Note: *The lower control arms and the tie-rods may have protective covers mounted on them. Remove covers as necessary.*

1   Loosen the rear wheel bolts, raise the rear of the vehicle and support it securely on jackstands. Block the front wheels to keep the vehicle from rolling off the stands. Remove the rear wheel.

Upper control arm (transverse link)

Refer to illustration 14.5, 14.6 and 14.9

2   On AWD models, remove the driveshaft from the rear final drive and secure it to the underside of the vehicle (see Chapter 8).

3   Remove the coil spring (see Section 10).

4   Using a floor jack, support the subframe on the same side from which the upper arm will be removed.

5   Loosen the subframe mounting bolts **(see illustration)**, then carefully lower the subframe just enough to access the upper

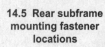

14.5 Rear subframe mounting fastener locations

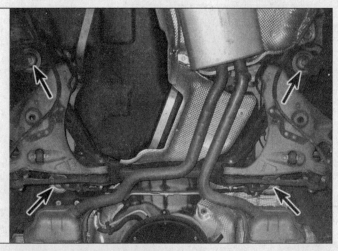

14.6 Rear upper control arm (transverse link) details

A   Rear upper control arm (transverse link)
B   Rear subframe
C   Cam adjuster
D   Upper control arm-to-knuckle fastener
E   Upper control arm-to-subframe fastener

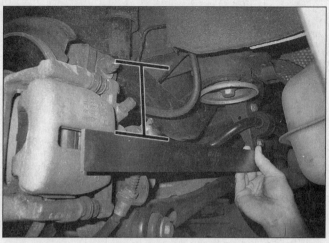

14.9 Place a straightedge flat against the bottom of the stabilizer bar bracket and measure to the center of the control arm bushing. Adjust this dimension to 142 mm ± 1 mm, then tighten the upper control arm fasteners

arm-to-subframe mounting fasteners. Support the subframe with jackstands. **Caution:** *Lowering the subframe can damage other components. Make sure that no wiring harnesses, brake lines or any other components will be damaged when lowering the subframe.*

6   Mark the relationship of the cam adjuster on the upper control arm-to-knuckle fasteners **(see illustration)**, and remove the fasteners.
7   Remove the upper control arm-to-subframe fasteners, then remove the arm.
8   Inspect the bushings for damage and wear. The bushings can be replaced, but a press and special adapters are required. If the bushings need to be replaced, take the arm to an automotive machine shop.
9   Installation is the reverse of removal, noting the following points:

a) *Use new fasteners as indicated in the* **Warning** *above.*
b) *Attach the upper control arm to the subframe and position it so that the center of the arm's bushing collar (that attaches to the knuckle) is 142 mm ± 1 mm to a straight line drawn from the bottom of the stabilizer bar bracket outward* **(see illustration)**. *A straightedge placed flat against the stabilizer bar mounting bracket can be used as a measuring point.*
c) *Align the cam adjuster with its mark made during removal, then tighten the control arm fasteners to the torque listed in this Chapter's Specifications.*
d) *Install the wheel and wheel bolts, then lower the vehicle and tighten the wheel bolts to the torque listed in the Chapter 1 Specifications.*
e) *Have the rear wheel alignment checked and, if necessary, adjusted.*

Lower control arm

Note: *On AWD models or 2WD right lower control arms, refer to Steps 3 through 5 in this Section to lower the subframe to remove the lower control arm mounting fasteners.*

10   Remove the lower control arm stone guard fasteners and remove the guards (if equipped). Also remove the diagonal brace fasteners and brace (convertible models).
11   Remove the bolts and detach the ABS wheel speed sensor harness from the lower arm. Also detach the parking brake cable from the lower arm.
12   On vehicles equipped with automatic leveling headlamps, disconnect the vehicle level sensor linkage from the lower control arm.
13   Detach the stabilizer bar link from the stabilizer bar (see Section 13).
14   Remove the rear coil spring (see Section 10).

AWD models

15   Detach the driveaxle from the rear final drive (see Chapter 8), allow it to hang down a little ways, then secure it to the underside of the vehicle in this position.
16   Detach the shock absorber lower mounting fasteners from the rear knuckle (see Section 9).
17   Remove the parking brake cable from the bracket at the fuel tank.
18   Remove the brake caliper (see Chapter 9).
19   Remove the cover for the right driveaxle.
20   Lower the subframe slightly (see Steps 3 through 5).

2WD model left control arm

21   Detach the shock absorber lower mounting fasteners from the rear knuckle (see Section 9).
22   Remove the brake caliper (see Chapter 9).
23   Lower the subframe slightly (see Steps 3 through 5).

All models

Refer to illustrations 14.24, 14.25 and 14.26

24   Mark the relationship of the cam adjuster to the lower control arm at the subframe **(see illustration)**.
25   Remove the lower control arm rear mounting fastener, the front mounting nut,

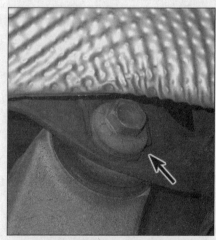

14.24 Mark both the eccentric washer (opposite side) and eccentric bolt to the subframe for proper installation

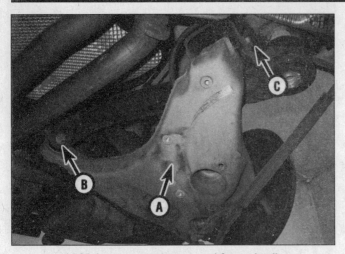

14.25 Lower control arm-to-subframe details

A   Lower control arm
B   Lower control arm-to-subframe rear mounting fastener
C   Lower control arm-to-subframe front eccentric mounting bolt

14.26 Lower control arm-to-rear knuckle details

A   Lower control arm
B   Lower control arm-to-knuckle front mounting fastener
C   Lower control arm-to-knuckle rear mounting fastener

eccentric washer and the eccentric bolt **(see illustration)**.

26   Remove the lower control arm pivot bolts and detach the arm from the vehicle **(see illustration)**.

27   Inspect the bushings for damage and wear. The bushings can be replaced, but special tools are required. If the bushings need to be replaced, take the arm to an automotive machine shop.

28   Installation is the reverse of removal, noting the following points:

a) Use new fasteners as indicated in the **Warning** above.
b) Bleed the brake system as described in Chapter 9.
c) Align the marks on the cam adjuster and the lower arm.
d) Don't tighten the control arm pivot bolt/nuts, the control arm-to-rear knuckle bolt/nut or the shock absorber lower mounting bolt/nut until the suspension has been raised to simulate normal ride height.

e) Tighten the wheel bolts to the torque listed in the Chapter 1 Specifications.
f) Have the rear wheel alignment checked and, if necessary, adjusted.

Tie-rod

Refer to illustration 14.30

29   Remove the coil spring (see Section 10).

30   Remove the lower control arm rear mounting fasteners **(see illustration)**, then remove the tie-rod.

31   Inspect the bushings for damage and wear. The bushings are not replaceable separately; if they are damaged, the tie-rod must be replaced

32   Installation is the reverse of removal, noting the following points:

a) Use new fasteners as indicated in the **Warning** above.
b) Don't tighten the tie-rod mounting fasteners until the suspension has been raised to simulate normal ride height.

c) Tighten the wheel bolts to the torque listed in the Chapter 1 Specifications.
d) Have the rear wheel alignment checked and, if necessary, adjusted.

15   Steering wheel - removal and installation

Warning: *These models are equipped with airbags. Always disable the airbag system before working in the vicinity of any airbag system component to avoid the possibility of accidental deployment of the airbag(s), which could cause personal injury (see Chapter 12).*
Warning: *Do not use a memory saving device to preserve the ECM's memory when working on or near airbag system components.*

Removal

Refer to illustrations 15.3, 15.4, 15.7, 15.8, 15.10a, 15.10b and 15.11

1   Park the vehicle with the wheels pointing straight ahead. Disconnect the cable from the negative battery terminal (see Chapter 5).

2   Refer to Chapter 12 and disable the airbag system.

3   To detach the airbag module from the steering wheel, use a small screwdriver to pry back the fastener covers and remove the two Torx mounting fasteners from each side **(see illustration)**. **Note:** *It may be necessary to turn the steering wheel a half turn to access both Torx fasteners. Make sure the steering wheel is centered after removing the final Torx fastener.*

4   Disconnect the airbag module and horn electrical connectors **(see illustration)**. **Note:** *To disconnect the airbag electrical connectors, first pry up the center locking portion of each connector.*

5   Set the module aside in a safe, isolated

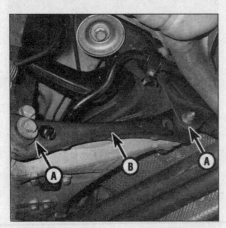

14.30 Remove the lower control arm rear fasteners (A) and remove the tie-rod (B)

15.3 Pry the trim covers back to access the airbag mounting fasteners

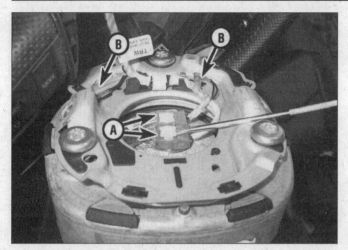

15.4 Typical airbag module electrical connection details

A   Airbag module electrical connectors
B   Horn electrical connectors

15.7 Remove the electrical connectors (A), then remove the steering wheel mounting fastener (B); a 12 mm, 12-point spline-drive bit is required

area, with the airbag side of the module facing UP. **Warning:** *When carrying the airbag module, keep the driver's (trim) side of it away from your body and, when you set it down, make sure the driver's side is facing up.*

6   Disconnect any other electrical connectors needed for removal **(see illustration 15.7)**.

7   Remove the steering wheel bolt using a 12 mm 12-point spline-drive bit **(see illustration)**.

8   Mark the position of the steering wheel to the steering shaft if marks don't already exist or don't line up **(see illustration)**.

9   Lift the steering wheel from the shaft, noting how any electrical wire harnesses are routed. If the steering wheel is tight, tap it up near the center using the palm of your hand, or twist it from side-to-side while pulling upwards. **Caution:** *Don't hammer on the shaft to remove the wheel.* **Warning:** *Don't allow the steering shaft to turn after the steer-*ing wheel is removed or damage to the airbag clockspring could occur.

Clockspring

10   If it is necessary to remove the clockspring, remove the steering column covers (see Chapter 11), disconnect the electrical connector, then disengage the clockspring retaining clips and detach it from the steering column **(see illustrations)**. **Caution:** *Do not allow the clockspring to rotate.*

Steering angle sensor

Note: *The new steering angle sensor must be calibrated with a factory scan tool. For this reason, if a new sensor is needed, it is best to have an Audi dealer perform this job.*

11   If it is necessary to remove the steering angle sensor, remove the steering column covers (see Chapter 11) and the steering column switch assembly (see Chapter 12).

15.8 After removing the bolt, check for alignment marks on the steering wheel and steering shaft - if there aren't any, make your own

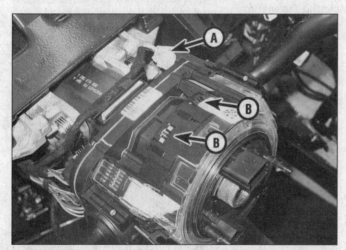

15.10a Disconnect the clockspring electrical connector (A), then carefully pry up the clockspring upper retaining clips (B)

15.10b Check for center marks (A) on the clockspring - if there aren't any, make your own, then disconnect the remaining clockspring retaining clips (B) and remove the clockspring

15.11 Carefully disengage the steering angle sensor from the steering column switch assembly

15.12 Before installing the steering wheel, make sure the center marks (A) are aligned

Depress the tabs and slide the steering gear sensor from the switch **(see illustration)**. Installation is the reverse of removal.

Installation

Refer to illustration 15.12

12   Before installing the steering wheel, make sure the airbag clockspring is centered **(see illustration)** and all of the clip fasteners are locked into place.

13   Install the wheel onto the steering shaft, aligning the index marks and routing any wiring harnesses.

14   Install a *new* steering wheel bolt and tighten it to the torque listed in this Chapter's Specifications. **Warning:** *Do not reuse the steering wheel bolt.*

15   Connect the electrical connectors for the horn and the airbag module.

16   Position the airbag module onto the steering wheel. Install the Torx mounting fasteners and tighten them to the torque listed in this Chapter's Specifications.

17   Refer to Chapter 12 for the procedure to enable the airbag system.

16   Steering column - removal and installation

Warning: *These models are equipped with airbags. Always disable the airbag system before working in the vicinity of any airbag system component to avoid the possibility of accidental deployment of the airbag(s), which could cause personal injury (see Chapter 12).* **Warning:** *Do not use a memory saving device to preserve the ECM's memory when working on or near airbag system components.*

Removal

Refer to illustrations 16.8 and 16.10

1   Park the vehicle with the wheels pointing straight ahead. For models with an automatic transmission, place the shift lever in PARK. Disconnect the cable from the negative battery terminal (see Chapter 5). Disable the airbag system (see Chapter 12).

2   Remove the steering column cover (see Chapter 11). **Note:** *It may be necessary to remove the tilt lever mounting fastener to*

remove the cover.

3   Remove the steering wheel (see Section 15). Prevent the steering shaft from turning. **Caution:** *If this is not done, the airbag clockspring could be damaged.*

4   Remove the lower instrument panel trim (under the steering column) (see Chapter 11).

5   Remove the airbag system clockspring (see Section 15).

6   Remove the multi-function switch (see Chapter 12).

7   On models equipped with an automatic transmission, detach the shift interlock cable from the ignition switch (see Chapter 12).

8   Secure the lower section of the steering column to the upper section by passing a length of wire through the hole in the lower section of the column and through the spring on the upper section **(see illustration)**.

9   Mark the relationship of the steering shaft lower universal joint to the steering gear input shaft, then remove the pinch bolt securing the universal joint **(see illustration 19.6)**.

10   Remove the steering column mounting bolts **(see illustration)**, then separate the universal joint from the steering gear input shaft

16.8 Secure the lower portion of the shaft to the upper portion by passing a length of wire through the hole and spring

16.10 Steering column mounting bolts

17.2 Hold the tie-rod still with a wrench, then break loose the jam nut

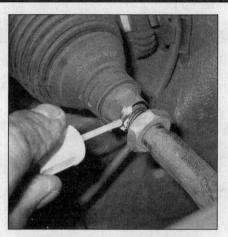

17.3 Mark the exposed threads, then unscrew the tie-rod end. If you're installing a new tie-rod end, make a corresponding mark on the new part in the same location so it can be installed in the same position as the old one

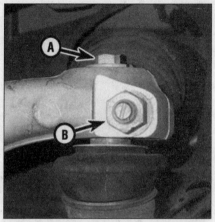

17.4 Remove the tie-rod end-to-steering knuckle bolt (A), followed by the nut and pinch bolt (B), then detach the tie-rod end from the knuckle

and guide the column out from the instrument panel.

Installation

11   Guide the column into position, connecting the U-joint with the steering gear input shaft. Install the pinch bolt loosely.

12   Install the steering column mounting bolts, but don't tighten them yet.

13   Remove the wire installed in Step 8. If a new steering column was installed, remove the protective materials used for transport from the column.

14   The remainder of installation is the reverse of the removal procedure, noting the following points:

a) *When installing the steering wheel, be sure the airbag clockspring is centered (see Section 15), and tighten the steering wheel bolt to the torque listed in this Chapter's Specifications.*

b) *With the steering column in position, tighten the column mounting bolts to the torque listed in this Chapter's Specifications.*

c) *Be sure to reconnect the shift interlock cable (see Chapter 12).*

d) *Tighten the U-joint pinch bolt to the torque listed in this Chapter's Specifications after the steering column mounting fasteners have been tightened.*

17   Tie-rod ends (front) - removal and installation

Warning: *The manufacturer recommends replacing the tie-rod end-to-steering knuckle pinch bolt nut with a new one whenever it is removed.*

Removal

Refer to illustrations 17.2, 17.3 and 17.4

1   Loosen the wheel bolts, raise the front of the vehicle and support it securely on jackstands. Apply the parking brake and block the rear wheels to keep the vehicle from rolling off the jackstands. Remove the wheel.

2   Loosen the tie-rod end jam nut **(see illustration)**.

3   Make a mark on the threads of the tie-rod end. If you're removing the tie-rod end to install a new steering gear boot, this will allow you to install the tie-rod end in the same position as before. If you're installing a new tie-rod end, make a corresponding mark in the same spot on the threads of the new tie-rod end, so the new part can be installed in the same location. This will help to restore the toe-in setting when reassembled **(see illustration)**.

4   Remove the tie-rod to steering knuckle bolt and the pinch bolt/nut **(see illustration)**. Push the tie-rod end out of the steering knuckle.

5   Unscrew the tie-rod end from the tie-rod.

Installation

6   Thread the tie-rod end into the tie-rod using the index mark made in Step 3.

7   Connect the tie-rod end to the steering knuckle. Install the tie-rod end-to-steering knuckle bolt and tighten it to the torque listed in this Chapter's Specifications.

8   Install the pinch bolt and a new nut, tightening the nut to the torque listed in this Chapter's Specifications.

9   Tighten the jam nut securely and install the wheel. Lower the vehicle and tighten the wheel bolts to the torque listed in the Chapter 1 Specifications.

10   Have the front end alignment checked and, if necessary, adjusted.

18   Steering gear boots - replacement

Refer to illustration 18.3

Warning: *The manufacturer recommends replacing the tie-rod end-to-steering knuckle pinch bolt nut with a new one whenever it is removed.*

1   Loosen the wheel bolts, raise the front of the vehicle and support it securely on jackstands. Remove the wheels.

2   Remove the tie-rod end from the tie-rod (see Section 17).

3   Remove the inner and outer boot clamps and discard them **(see illustration)**. The clamps can be pried apart at the crimped area, or cut off with a pair of cutting pliers.

4   Remove the boot.

5   Install a new clamp on the inner end of the boot.

18.3 Pry open or cut off the steering gear boot clamps

19.6 Locate the pinch bolt at the base of the steering column, and remove the bolt

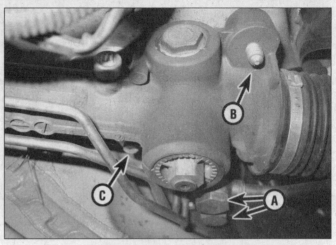

19.16 Typical power steering gear details

A   Power steering line banjo bolts
B   Left-side upper mounting fastener
C   Left-side lower mounting fastener

6   Slide the boot into place, making sure each end of the boot seats in its groove.
7   Make sure the boot isn't twisted, then tighten the inner clamp with a pair of clamp crimping pliers.
8   Install and tighten the outer clamp.
9   Install the tie-rod end (see Section 17).
10   Have the front end alignment checked and, if necessary, adjusted.

19   Steering gear - removal and installation

Warning: *These models are equipped with airbags. Always disable the airbag system before working in the vicinity of any airbag system component to avoid the possibility of accidental deployment of the airbag, which could cause personal injury (see Chapter 12). Also, don't allow the steering wheel to turn after the steering gear has been removed. To prevent this, pass the seat belt through the steering wheel and plug it into its latch.*
Warning: *Do not use a memory saving device to preserve the ECM's memory when working on or near airbag system components.*

Removal

Refer to illustrations 19.6 and 19.16

1   Park the vehicle with the front wheels pointing straight ahead. Apply the parking brake and chock the rear wheels, then loosen the front wheel bolts. Raise the front of the vehicle and support it securely on jackstands. Remove both front wheels.
2   Remove the battery from the engine compartment (see Chapter 5).
3   Turn the steering wheel to the center position, then remove the ignition key to engage the steering lock. **Caution:** *Ensure that the steering column remains in the*
straight-ahead position throughout the remainder of this procedure, or the airbag contact unit may become misaligned, leading to the failure of the airbag system.
4   Remove the driver's side under-dash panel (see Chapter 11).
5   Secure the lower section of the steering column to the upper section as described in Section 16. **Caution:** *Do not allow the upper and lower sections of the steering column to become separated while the steering column is detached from the steering gear, as this can cause the internal components to become detached and misaligned.*
6   Remove the pinch bolt securing the universal joint to the input shaft of the steering gear **(see illustration)**.
7   Pull the steering column universal joint off the steering gear input shaft and move it to one side. Pull the input shaft cover from the firewall and into the vehicle.
8   Siphon the fluid from the power steering fluid reservoir. If a suitable implement is not readily available to siphon the fluid from the system, it can be drained into a container when the hydraulic lines are detached from the steering gear.
9   To minimize fluid leakage, apply hose clamps to the fluid lines leading to and from the steering gear. Take care to avoid causing damage to the hoses by pinching.
10   Remove the front lower shock absorber mounting fastener (see Section 2) from the left-side. Move the shock absorber over and in front of the lower control arm.
11   Working on the left side of the vehicle, disconnect the top of the steering knuckle upper control arms (see Section 4).
12   Refer to Section 17 and detach the tie-rod ends from the steering knuckles.
13   Secure the knuckle assembly to the front shock absorber assembly using a piece of wire or string.

14   Remove the liner nut, pry out the clips and remove the section of plastic inner wheel well liner that shrouds the point where the tie-rod end enters the engine compartment.
15   On V6 engine models, remove the front catalytic converter from the driver's side (see Chapter 4), the power steering gear heat shield mounting fasteners (from the driver's side only) and the shield.
16   Unscrew the fittings and disconnect the fluid supply and return lines from the steering gear **(see illustration)**. Clean the connections before they are detached. Drain any fluid remaining in the system into a container for disposal. Tie the lines back away from the work area, and seal off their ends to prevent further leakage and keep dirt from entering the system.
17   From the top, loosen the passenger side steering gear upper mounting fastener one full turn, then loosen the driver's side upper mounting fastener one full turn.
18   From under the vehicle, remove the lower steering gear mounting fastener **(see illustration 19.16)**, then remove both upper fasteners.
19   Check that all connections are free and clear of the steering gear, rotate the left-side of the steering gear forward and withdraw the steering gear from the vehicle through the left-side wheel well.
20   If the steering gear is known to be damaged or worn beyond an acceptable level, it may have to be replaced. However, it is possible to have the steering gear overhauled - consult a dealer service department or other qualified repair shop for further advice.

Installation

Refer to illustration 19.21

21   Before the steering gear can be installed, it must be centered as follows. Remove the

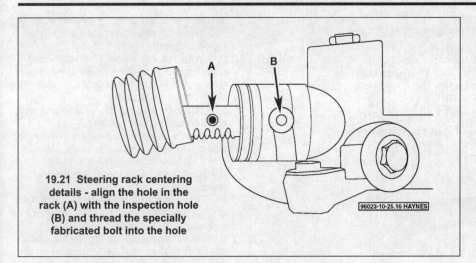

19.21 Steering rack centering details - align the hole in the rack (A) with the inspection hole (B) and thread the specially fabricated bolt into the hole

96023-10-25.16 HAYNES

socket head bolt from the tapped inspection hole at the side of the input shaft housing. Move the right-side tie-rod by hand until the alignment hole - drilled into the surface of the steering rack - is visible through the inspection hole. Obtain a bolt of the same thread as that removed from the inspection hole and file the end of it to a conical point. Thread the bolt into the inspection hole and turn it until the pointed end engages with the drilled alignment hole in the steering rack; check that the rack is immobilized by trying to move the right-hand tie-rod end. The steering gear is now locked in the center position **(see illustration)**.

22   Maneuver the steering gear into position in the engine compartment. Insert the three securing fasteners, and tighten the one accessible from underneath to the torque listed in this Chapter's Specifications. Now tighten the two upper mounting fasteners to the torque listed in this Chapter's Specifications. On completion, remove the locking bolt from the alignment hole, and reinstall the original plug to seal the steering gear.

23   The remainder of the installation procedure is a reversal of removal, noting the following points:

a) *Connect the pressure and return line fittings to the steering gear, using new sealing washers. Tighten the banjo bolts to the torque listed in this Chapter's Specifications.*

b) *Refer to Section 17 to reconnect the tie-rod ends.*

c) *Top up the fluid level as described in Chapter 1 and bleed the system as described in Section 21.*

d) *Tighten the wheel bolts to the torque listed in the Chapter 1 Specifications.*

e) *Finally, have the wheel alignment checked and, if necessary, adjusted.*

20 Power steering pump - removal and installation

1   Disconnect the cable from the negative terminal of the battery (see Chapter 5).
2   Remove the drivebelt (see Chapter 1).

Four-cylinder models

Refer to illustrations 20.11

3   Raise the front of the vehicle and support it securely on jackstands.
4   Remove the under-vehicle splash shield (see Chapter 11).
5   Remove the front bumper (see Chapter 11), then move the radiator support panel to the service position (see Chapter 11).
6   Remove the power steering pump drivebelt (see Chapter 1).
7   Using brake hose clamps, clamp both the supply and return hoses near the power steering fluid reservoir. This will minimize fluid loss during subsequent operations.
8   Wipe clean the area around the power steering pressure and return line fittings.
9   Unscrew the banjo bolt **(see illustration 20.11)** and disconnect the pressure line from the pump; be prepared for fluid spillage, and position a container beneath the pipe while unscrewing the fitting bolt. Disconnect the line and recover the sealing washers; discard the washers (new ones must be used when reassembling). Plug the end of the line and the steering pump orifice, to minimize fluid leakage and to keep dirt out of the hydraulic system.
10   Loosen the clamp and disconnect the

fluid supply hose from the rear of the power steering pump. Plug the end of the hose and cover the pump fluid port to prevent contamination.
11   Remove the pump mounting fasteners and detach the pump from its bracket. On some models, it may be necessary to remove the mounting fasteners and detach the pulley from the pump first. A strap wrench or equivalent can be used to prevent the pulley from turning as the bolts are loosened. On other models, you can access mounting bolts through holes in the pulley **(see illustration)**.
12   If the power steering pump is faulty, it must be replaced. The pump is a sealed unit and cannot be overhauled.
13   If a new pump is to be installed, it must be primed with fluid first, to ensure adequate lubrication during its initial stages of operation. Failure to do this could cause noisy operation and may lead to early pump failure. To prime the pump, pour the specified grade of hydraulic fluid into the fluid supply port on the pump, and simultaneously rotate the pump pulley. When the fluid exits from the pressure port, it is primed and ready for use.
14   Maneuver the pump into position, then install it's mounting bolts and tighten them to the torque listed in this Chapter's Specifications.
15   Using new sealing washers, connect the pressure line to the pump. Ensure the line is correctly routed, then tighten the banjo bolt to the torque listed in this Chapter's Specifications.
16   Reconnect the supply hose to the pump and secure it in position with the retaining clip. Remove the hose clamps used to minimize fluid loss.
17   Install the power steering pump pulley, if removed.
18   Install the power steering pump drivebelt (see Chapter 1).
19   Install the radiator support panel and front bumper (see Chapter 11).
20   Install the under-vehicle splash shield. Reconnect the negative battery cable.
21   Top up the hydraulic system (see Chapter 1), then bleed the system as described in Section 21.

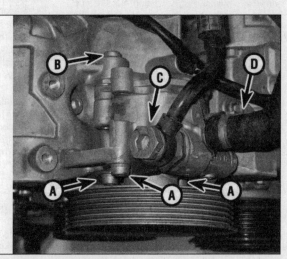

20.11 Typical power steering pump details - alternator removed for clarity

A   *Power steering pump front fasteners (access through the pulley holes)*
B   *Power steering pump rear fastener*
C   *High pressure line and banjo bolt*
D   *Power steering suction line*

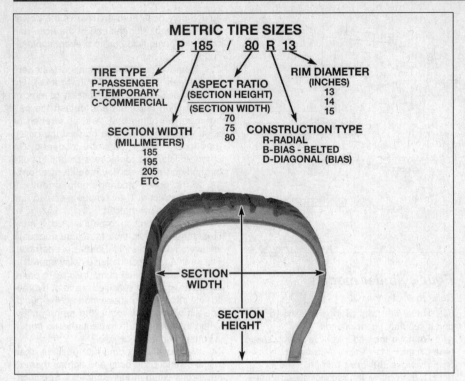

METRIC TIRE SIZES

P 185 / 80 R 13

TIRE TYPE
P-PASSENGER
T-TEMPORARY
C-COMMERCIAL

ASPECT RATIO
(SECTION HEIGHT)
—————————
(SECTION WIDTH)
70
75
80

RIM DIAMETER
(INCHES)
13
14
15

SECTION WIDTH
(MILLIMETERS)
185
195
205
ETC

CONSTRUCTION TYPE
R-RADIAL
B-BIAS - BELTED
D-DIAGONAL (BIAS)

SECTION WIDTH

SECTION HEIGHT

22.1 Metric tire size code

V6 models

22   Remove the top engine cover (see Chapter 2B).

23   Remove the mounting fasteners and detach the pulley from the pump. A strap wrench or equivalent can be used to prevent the pulley from turning as the fasteners are loosened.

24   Remove the power steering pump rear mounting fastener using a long extension and socket from above. **Note:** *Some models have a threaded pin through the rear mounting fastener; it may be necessary to remove the intake manifold to remove the pin and fastener (see Chapter 2B).*

25   Unscrew the banjo bolt and disconnect the pressure line from the pump; be prepared for fluid spillage. Disconnect the line and recover the sealing washers; discard the washers (new ones must be used when reassembling). Plug the end of the line and the steering pump orifice to minimize fluid leakage and to keep dirt out of the hydraulic system.

26   Loosen the clamp and disconnect the fluid supply hose from the pump. Plug the end of the hose and cover the pump fluid port to prevent contamination.

27   Remove the pump bracket mounting fasteners and detach the pump and bracket from the engine. The pump can now be separated from the mounting bracket by removing the fasteners.

28   If the power steering pump is faulty, it must be replaced. The pump is a sealed unit and cannot be overhauled.

29   If a new pump is to be installed, it must be primed with fluid first, to ensure adequate lubrication during its initial stages of operation. Failure to do this could cause noisy operation and may lead to early pump failure. To prime the pump, pour the specified grade of power steering fluid into the fluid supply port on the pump, and simultaneously rotate the pump pulley. When the fluid exits from the pressure port, it is primed and ready for use.

30   Maneuver the pump and bracket into position, install the mounting fasteners and tighten them to the torque listed in this Chapter's Specifications.

31   Using new sealing washers, connect the pressure line to the pump. Ensure the line is correctly routed, and tighten the banjo bolt to the torque listed in this Chapter's Specifications.

32   Reconnect the supply hose to the pump and secure it in position with the retaining clip. Remove the hose clamps used to minimize fluid loss.

33   Install the pulley, tightening the bolts to the torque listed in this Chapter's Specifications.

34   Install the ignition coil assembly (see Chapter 5) and the engine top cover.

35   Reconnect the negative battery cable, top up the power steering fluid (see Chapter 1), then bleed the system as described in Section 21.

21   Power steering system - bleeding

1   Following any operation in which the power steering fluid lines have been disconnected, the power steering system must be bled to remove all air and obtain proper steering performance.

2   With the front wheels in the straight ahead position, check the power steering fluid level and, if low, add fluid until it is up to the MIN mark on the dipstick.

3   Raise the front of the vehicle and support it securely on jackstands.

4   Turn the steering wheel back-and-forth repeatedly, lightly hitting the stops. **Caution:** *Don't hold the steering wheel in the full-right or full-left position, as this could damage the pump.*

5   Start the engine and allow it to run at fast idle. Recheck the fluid level and add more if necessary until it is up to the MIN mark.

6   Bleed the system by turning the wheels from side to side, just barely contacting the stops. This will work the air out of the system. Keep the reservoir full of fluid as this is done.

7   When the air is worked out of the system and the fluid level stabilizes, return the wheels to the straight ahead position and leave the vehicle running for several more minutes before shutting it off. Lower the vehicle.

8   Road test the vehicle to be sure the steering system is functioning normally and noise-free.

9   Recheck the fluid level to be sure it is up to the HOT mark on the dipstick while the engine is at normal operating temperature. Add fluid if necessary (see Chapter 1).

22   Wheels and tires - general information

Refer to illustration 22.1

1   All vehicles covered by this manual are equipped with metric-sized steel belted radial tires **(see illustration)**. Use of other size or type of tires may affect the ride and handling of the vehicle. Don't mix different types of tires, such as radials and bias belted, on the same vehicle as handling may be seriously affected. It's recommended that tires be replaced in pairs on the same axle, but if only one tire is being replaced, be sure it's the same size, structure and tread design as the other.

2   Because tire pressure has a substantial effect on handling and wear, the pressure on all tires should be checked at least once a month or before any extended trips (see Chapter 1).

3   Wheels must be replaced if they are bent, dented, leak air, have elongated bolt holes, are heavily rusted, out of vertical symmetry or if the wheel bolts won't stay tight. Wheel repairs that use welding or peening are not recommended.

4   Tire and wheel balance is important in the overall handling, braking and performance of the vehicle. Unbalanced wheels can adversely affect handling and ride characteristics as well as tire life. Whenever a tire is installed on a wheel, the tire and wheel should be balanced by a shop with the proper equipment.

23   Wheel alignment - general information

Refer to illustration 23.2

A wheel alignment refers to the adjustments made to the wheels so they are in proper angular relationship to the suspension and the ground. Wheels that are out of proper alignment not only affect vehicle control, but also increase tire wear.

The angles normally measured are camber, caster and toe-in **(see illustration)**. Camber and caster are not always adjustable but are usually checked to see if any suspension components are worn or damaged. The toe-in angle is commonly adjusted on all vehicles in the front and on the rear of vehicles with independent rear suspension.

Getting the proper wheel alignment is a very exacting process, one in which complicated and expensive machines are necessary to perform the job properly. Because of this, you should have a technician with the proper equipment perform these tasks. We will, however, use this space to give you a basic idea of what is involved with a wheel alignment so you can better understand the process and deal intelligently with the shop that does the work.

Toe-in is the turning in of the wheels. The purpose of a toe specification is to ensure parallel rolling of the wheels. In a vehicle with zero toe-in, the distance between the front edges of the wheels will be the same as the distance between the rear edges of the wheels. The actual amount of toe-in is normally only a fraction of an inch. On the front end, toe-in is controlled by the tie-rod end position on the tie-rod. Incorrect toe-in will cause the tires to wear improperly by making them scrub against the road surface.

Camber is the tilting of the wheels from vertical when viewed from one end of the vehicle. When the wheels tilt out at the top, the camber is said to be positive (+). When the wheels tilt in at the top the camber is negative (-). The amount of tilt is measured in degrees from vertical and this measurement is called the camber angle. This angle affects the amount of tire tread that contacts the road and compensates for changes in the suspension geometry when the vehicle is cornering or traveling over an undulating surface.

Caster is the tilting of the front steering axis from the vertical. A tilt toward the rear is positive caster and a tilt toward the front is negative caster.

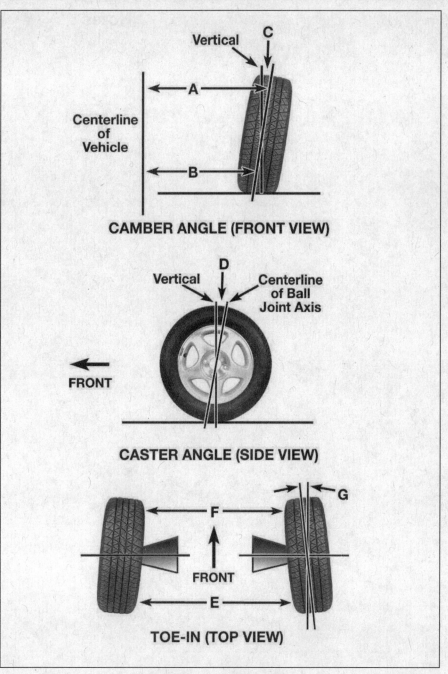

CAMBER ANGLE (FRONT VIEW)

CASTER ANGLE (SIDE VIEW)

TOE-IN (TOP VIEW)

23.2 Wheel alignment details

A minus B = C (degrees camber)
D = degrees caster

E minus F = toe-in (measured in inches)
G = toe-in (expressed in degrees)

Notes

Chapter 11 Body

Contents

	Section
Body repair - major damage	4
Body repair - minor damage	3
Bumper covers - removal and installation	12
Center console - removal and installation	26
Convertible top - general information	31
Cowl cover - removal and installation	15
Dashboard trim panels - removal and installation	27
Door - removal, installation and adjustment	21
Door latch, lock cylinder and outside handle - removal and installation	22
Door trim panels - removal and installation	20
Door window glass - removal and installation	23
Door window glass frame and regulator - removal and installation	24
Fastener and trim removal	6
Front fender - removal and installation	14
Front grille - removal and installation	13
General information	1
Hinges and locks - maintenance	7
Hood - removal, installation and adjustment	10

	Section
Hood latch, release cable and support struts - removal and installation	11
Instrument panel - removal and installation	29
Liftgate (wagon models) - removal, installation and adjustment	18
Liftgate latch, lock cylinder and support struts (wagon models) - removal and installation	19
Mirrors - removal and installation	25
Radiator support panel - repositioning, removal and installation	9
Repair minor paint scratches	2
Seat belts - removal and installation	33
Seats - removal and installation	30
Steering column covers - removal and installation	28
Sunroof - adjustment	32
Trunk lid (sedan and convertible models) - removal, installation and adjustment	16
Trunk lid latch, lock cylinder and support struts - removal and installation	17
Upholstery, carpets and vinyl trim - maintenance	5
Windshield and fixed glass - replacement	8

1   General information

Warning: *The models covered by this manual are equipped with Supplemental Restraint Systems (SRS), more commonly known as airbags. Always disable the airbag system before working in the vicinity of any airbag system components to avoid the possibility of accidental deployment of the airbags, which could cause personal injury (see Chapter 12).*

Certain body components are particularly vulnerable to accident damage and can be unbolted and repaired or replaced. Among these parts are the hood, doors, tailgate, liftgate, bumpers and front fenders.

Only general body maintenance practices and body panel repair procedures within the scope of the do-it-yourselfer are included in this Chapter.

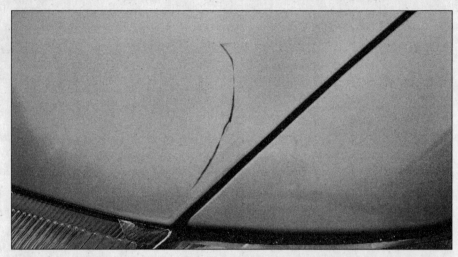

Make sure the damaged area is perfectly clean and rust free. If the touch-up kit has a wire brush, use it to clean the scratch or chip. Or use fine steel wool wrapped around the end of a pencil. Clean the scratched or chipped surface only, not the good paint surrounding it. Rinse the area with water and allow it to dry thoroughly

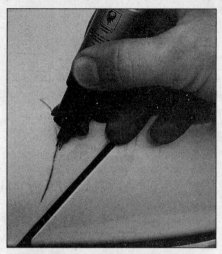

Thoroughly mix the paint, then apply a small amount with the touch-up kit brush or a very fine artist's brush. Brush in one direction as you fill the scratch area. Do not build up the paint higher than the surrounding paint

2   Repair minor paint scratches

No matter how hard you try to keep your vehicle looking like new, it will inevitably be scratched, chipped or dented at some point. If the metal is actually dented, seek the advice of a professional. But you can fix minor scratches and chips yourself. Buy a touch-up paint kit from a dealer service department or an auto parts store. To ensure that you get the right color, you'll need to have the specific make, model and year of your vehicle and, ideally, the paint code, which is located on a special metal plate under the hood or in the door jamb.

3   Body repair - minor damage

Plastic body panels

The following repair procedures are for minor scratches and gouges. Repair of more serious damage should be left to a dealer service department or qualified auto body shop. Below is a list of the equipment and materials necessary to perform the following repair procedures on plastic body panels.

Wax, grease and silicone removing solvent
Cloth-backed body tape
Sanding discs
Drill motor with three-inch disc holder
Hand sanding block
Rubber squeegees
Sandpaper
Non-porous mixing palette
Wood paddle or putty knife
Curved-tooth body file
Flexible parts repair material

Flexible panels (bumper trim)

1   Remove the damaged panel, if necessary or desirable. In most cases, repairs can be car-

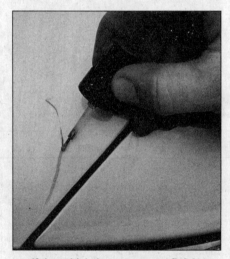

If the vehicle has a two-coat finish, apply the clear coat after the color coat has dried

ried out with the panel installed.
2   Clean the area(s) to be repaired with a wax, grease and silicone removing solvent applied with a water-dampened cloth.
3   If the damage is structural, that is, if it extends through the panel, clean the backside of the panel area to be repaired as well. Wipe dry.
4   Sand the rear surface about 1-1/2 inches beyond the break.
5   Cut two pieces of fiberglass cloth large enough to overlap the break by about 1-1/2 inches. Cut only to the required length.
6   Mix the adhesive from the repair kit according to the instructions included with the kit, and apply a layer of the mixture approximately 1/8-inch thick on the backside of the panel. Overlap the break by at least 1-1/2 inches.
7   Apply one piece of fiberglass cloth to the adhesive and cover the cloth with additional adhesive. Apply a second piece of fiberglass

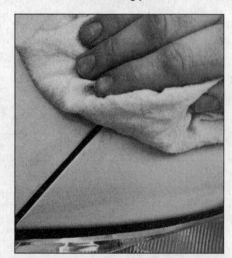

Wait a few days for the paint to dry thoroughly, then rub out the repainted area with a polishing compound to blend the new paint with the surrounding area. When you're happy with your work, wash and polish the area

cloth to the adhesive and immediately cover the cloth with additional adhesive in sufficient quantity to fill the weave.
8   Allow the repair to cure for 20 to 30 minutes at 60-degrees to 80-degrees F.
9   If necessary, trim the excess repair material at the edge.
10   Remove all of the paint film over and around the area(s) to be repaired. The repair material should not overlap the painted surface.
11   With a drill motor and a sanding disc (or a rotary file), cut a "V" along the break line approximately 1/2-inch wide. Remove all dust and loose particles from the repair area.
12   Mix and apply the repair material. Apply a light coat first over the damaged area; then continue applying material until it reaches a level

slightly higher than the surrounding finish.

13   Cure the mixture for 20 to 30 minutes at 60-degrees to 80-degrees F.

14   Roughly establish the contour of the area being repaired with a body file. If low areas or pits remain, mix and apply additional adhesive.

15   Block sand the damaged area with sandpaper to establish the actual contour of the surrounding surface.

16   If desired, the repaired area can be temporarily protected with several light coats of primer. Because of the special paints and techniques required for flexible body panels, it is recommended that the vehicle be taken to a paint shop for completion of the body repair.

Steel body panels

See photo sequence

Repair of dents

17   When repairing dents, the first job is to pull the dent out until the affected area is as close as possible to its original shape. There is no point in trying to restore the original shape completely as the metal in the damaged area will have stretched on impact and cannot be restored to its original contours. It is better to bring the level of the dent up to a point that is about 1/8-inch below the level of the surrounding metal. In cases where the dent is very shallow, it is not worth trying to pull it out at all.

18   If the backside of the dent is accessible, it can be hammered out gently from behind using a soft-face hammer. While doing this, hold a block of wood firmly against the opposite side of the metal to absorb the hammer blows and prevent the metal from being stretched.

19   If the dent is in a section of the body which has double layers, or some other factor makes it inaccessible from behind, a different technique is required. Drill several small holes through the metal inside the damaged area, particularly in the deeper sections. Screw long, self-tapping screws into the holes just enough for them to get a good grip in the metal. Now pulling on the protruding heads of the screws with locking pliers can pull out the dent.

20   The next stage of repair is the removal of paint from the damaged area and from an inch or so of the surrounding metal. This is easily done with a wire brush or sanding disk in a drill motor, although it can be done just as effectively by hand with sandpaper. To complete the preparation for filling, score the surface of the bare metal with a screwdriver or the tang of a file or drill small holes in the affected area. This will provide a good grip for the filler material. To complete the repair, see the Section on filling and painting.

Repair of rust holes or gashes

21   Remove all paint from the affected area and from an inch or so of the surrounding metal using a sanding disk or wire brush mounted in a drill motor. If these are not available, a few sheets of sandpaper will do the job just as effectively.

22   With the paint removed, you will be able to determine the severity of the corrosion and decide whether to replace the whole panel, if possible, or repair the affected area. New body panels are not as expensive as most people think and it is often quicker to install a new panel than to repair large areas of rust.

23   Remove all trim pieces from the affected area except those which will act as a guide to the original shape of the damaged body, such as headlight shells, etc. Using metal snips or a hacksaw blade, remove all loose metal and any other metal that is badly affected by rust. Hammer the edges of the hole in to create a slight depression for the filler material.

24   Wire-brush the affected area to remove the powdery rust from the surface of the metal. If the back of the rusted area is accessible, treat it with rust inhibiting paint.

25   Before filling is done, block the hole in some way. This can be done with sheet metal riveted or screwed into place, or by stuffing the hole with wire mesh.

26   Once the hole is blocked off, the affected area can be filled and painted. See the following subsection on filling and painting.

Filling and painting

27   Many types of body fillers are available, but generally speaking, body repair kits which contain filler paste and a tube of resin hardener are best for this type of repair work. A wide, flexible plastic or nylon applicator will be necessary for imparting a smooth and contoured finish to the surface of the filler material. Mix up a small amount of filler on a clean piece of wood or cardboard (use the hardener sparingly). Follow the manufacturer's instructions on the package, otherwise the filler will set incorrectly.

28   Using the applicator, apply the filler paste to the prepared area. Draw the applicator across the surface of the filler to achieve the desired contour and to level the filler surface. As soon as a contour that approximates the original one is achieved, stop working the paste. If you continue, the paste will begin to stick to the applicator. Continue to add thin layers of paste at 20-minute intervals until the level of the filler is just above the surrounding metal.

29   Once the filler has hardened, the excess can be removed with a body file. From then on, progressively finer grades of sandpaper should be used, starting with a 180-grit paper and finishing with a 600-grit wet-or-dry paper. Always wrap the sandpaper around a flat rubber or wooden block, otherwise the surface of the filler will not be completely flat. During the sanding of the filler surface, the wet-or-dry paper should be periodically rinsed in water. This will ensure that a very smooth finish is produced in the final stage.

30   At this point, the repair area should be surrounded by a ring of bare metal, which in turn should be encircled by the finely feathered edge of good paint. Rinse the repair area with clean water until all of the dust produced by the sanding operation is gone.

31   Spray the entire area with a light coat of primer. This will reveal any imperfections in the surface of the filler. Repair the imperfections with fresh filler paste or glaze filler and once more smooth the surface with sandpaper. Repeat this spray-and-repair procedure until you are satisfied that the surface of the filler and the feathered edge of the paint are perfect. Rinse the area with clean water and allow it to dry completely.

32   The repair area is now ready for painting. Spray painting must be carried out in a warm, dry, windless and dust free atmosphere. These conditions can be created if you have access to a large indoor work area, but if you are forced to work in the open, you will have to pick the day very carefully. If you are working indoors, dousing the floor in the work area with water will help settle the dust that would otherwise be in the air. If the repair area is confined to one body panel, mask off the surrounding panels. This will help minimize the effects of a slight mismatch in paint color. Trim pieces such as chrome strips, door handles, etc., will also need to be masked off or removed. Use masking tape and several thickness of newspaper for the masking operations.

33   Before spraying, shake the paint can thoroughly, then spray a test area until the spray painting technique is mastered. Cover the repair area with a thick coat of primer. The thickness should be built up using several thin layers of primer rather than one thick one. Using 600-grit wet-or-dry sandpaper, rub down the surface of the primer until it is very smooth. While doing this, the work area should be thoroughly rinsed with water and the wet-or-dry sandpaper periodically rinsed as well. Allow the primer to dry before spraying additional coats.

34   Spray on the top coat, again building up the thickness by using several thin layers of paint. Begin spraying in the center of the repair area and then, using a circular motion, work out until the whole repair area and about two inches of the surrounding original paint is covered. Remove all masking material 10 to 15 minutes after spraying on the final coat of paint. Allow the new paint at least two weeks to harden, then use a very fine rubbing compound to blend the edges of the new paint into the existing paint. Finally, apply a coat of wax

4   Body repair - major damage

1   Major damage must be repaired by an auto body shop specifically equipped to perform body and frame repairs. These shops have the specialized equipment required to do the job properly.

2   If the damage is extensive, the frame must be checked for proper alignment or the vehicle's handling characteristics may be adversely affected and other components may wear at an accelerated rate.

3   Due to the fact that all of the major body components (hood, fenders, etc.) are separate and replaceable units, any seriously damaged components should be replaced rather than repaired. Sometimes the components can be found in a wrecking yard that specializes in used vehicle components, often at considerable savings over the cost of new parts.

These photos illustrate a method of repairing simple dents. They are intended to supplement *Body repair - minor damage* in this Chapter and should not be used as the sole instructions for body repair on these vehicles.

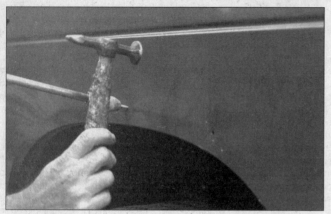

1 If you can't access the backside of the body panel to hammer out the dent, pull it out with a slide-hammer-type dent puller. Tap with a hammer near the edge of the dent to help 'pop' the metal back to its original shape, about 1/8-inch below the surface of the surrounding metal

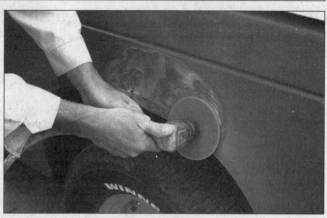

2 Using coarse-grit sandpaper, remove the paint down to the bare metal. Clean the repair area with wax/silicone remover.

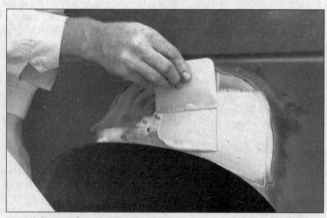

3 Following label instructions, mix up a batch of plastic filler and hardener, then quickly press it into the metal with a plastic applicator. Work the filler until it matches the original contour and is slightly above the surrounding metal

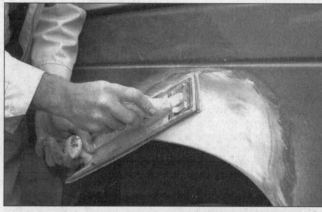

4 Let the filler harden until you can just dent it with your fingernail. File, then sand the filler down until it's smooth and even. Work down to finer grits of sandpaper - always using a board or block - ending up with 360 or 400 grit

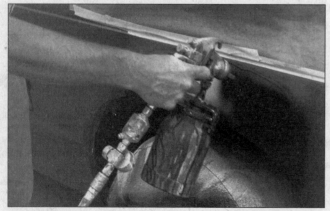

5 When the area is smooth to the touch, clean the area and mask around it. Apply several layers of primer to the area. A professional-type spray gun is being used here, but aerosol spray primer works fine

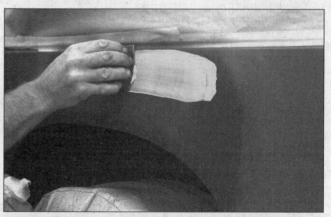

6 Fill imperfections or scratches with glazing compound. Sand with 360 or 400-grit and re-spray. Finish sand the primer with 600 grit, clean thoroughly, then apply the finish coat. Don't attempt to rub out or wax the repair area until the paint has dried completely (at least two weeks)

5 Upholstery, carpets and vinyl trim - maintenance

Upholstery and carpets

1   Every three months remove the floormats and clean the interior of the vehicle (more frequently if necessary). Use a stiff whiskbroom to brush the carpeting and loosen dirt and dust, then vacuum the upholstery and carpets thoroughly, especially along seams and crevices.

2   Dirt and stains can be removed from carpeting with basic household or automotive carpet shampoos available in spray cans. Follow the directions and vacuum again, then use a stiff brush to bring back the "nap" of the carpet.

3   Most interiors have cloth or vinyl upholstery, either of which can be cleaned and maintained with a number of material-specific cleaners or shampoos available in auto supply stores. Follow the directions on the product for usage, and always spot-test any upholstery cleaner on an inconspicuous area (bottom edge of a backseat cushion) to ensure that it doesn't cause a color shift in the material.

4   After cleaning, vinyl upholstery should be treated with a protectant. **Note:** *Make sure the protectant container indicates the product can be used on seats - some products may make a seat too slippery.* **Caution:** *Do not use protectant on vinyl-covered steering wheels.*

5   Leather upholstery requires special care. It should be cleaned regularly with saddle-soap or leather cleaner. Never use alcohol, gasoline, nail polish remover or thinner to clean leather upholstery.

6   After cleaning, regularly treat leather upholstery with a leather conditioner, rubbed in with a soft cotton cloth. Never use car wax on leather upholstery.

7   In areas where the interior of the vehicle is subject to bright sunlight, cover leather seating areas of the seats with a sheet if the vehicle is to be left out for any length of time.

Vinyl trim

8   Don't clean vinyl trim with detergents, caustic soap or petroleum-based cleaners. Plain soap and water works just fine, with a soft brush to clean dirt that may be ingrained. Wash the vinyl as frequently as the rest of the vehicle.

9   After cleaning, application of a high-quality rubber and vinyl protectant will help prevent oxidation and cracks. The protectant can also be applied to weather-stripping, vacuum lines and rubber hoses, which often fail as a result of chemical degradation, and to the tires.

6 Fastener and trim removal

Refer to illustration 6.4

1   There is a variety of plastic fasteners used to hold trim panels, splash shields and other parts in place in addition to typical screws, nuts and bolts. Once you are familiar with them, they can usually be removed without too much difficulty.

2   The proper tools and approach can prevent added time and expense to a project by minimizing the number of broken fasteners and/or parts.

3   The following illustration shows various types of fasteners that are typically used on most vehicles and how to remove and install them **(see illustration)**. Replacement fasten-

Fasteners

This tool is designed to remove special fasteners. A small pry tool used for removing nails will also work well in place of this tool

A Phillips head screwdriver can be used to release the center portion, but light pressure must be used because the plastic is easily damaged. Once the center is up, the fastener can easily be pried from its hole

Here is a view with the center portion fully released. Install the fastener as shown, then press the center in to set it

This fastener is used for exterior panels and shields. The center portion must be pried up to release the fastener. Install the fastener with the center up, then press the center in to set it

This type of fastener is used commonly for interior panels. Use a small blunt tool to press the small pin at the center in to release it . . .

. . . the pin will stay with the fastener in the released position

Reset the fastener for installation by moving the pin out. Install the fastener, then press the pin flush with the fastener to set it

This fastener is used for exterior and interior panels. It has no moving parts. Simply pry the fastener from its hole like the claw of a hammer removes a nail. Without a tool that can get under the top of the fastener, it can be very difficult to remove

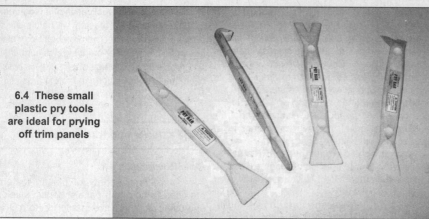

6.4 These small plastic pry tools are ideal for prying off trim panels

ers are commonly found at most auto parts stores, if necessary.

4   Trim panels are typically made of plastic and their flexibility can help during removal. The key to their removal is to use a tool to pry the panel near its retainers to release it without damaging surrounding areas or breaking-off any retainers. The retainers will usually snap out of their designated slot or hole after force is applied to them. Stiff plastic tools designed for prying on trim panels are available at most auto parts stores **(see illustration)**. Tools that are tapered and wrapped in protective tape, such as a screwdriver or small pry tool, are also very effective when used with care.

7   Hinges and locks - maintenance

Once every 3000 miles, or every three months, the hinges and latch assemblies on the doors, hood and trunk should be given a few drops of light oil or lock lubricant. The door latch strikers should also be lubricated with a thin coat of grease to reduce wear and ensure free movement. Lubricate the door and trunk locks with spray-on graphite lubricant.

8   Windshield and fixed glass - replacement

Replacement of the windshield and fixed glass requires the use of special fast-setting adhesive/caulk materials and some specialized tools and techniques. These operations should be left to a dealer service department or a shop specializing in glass work.

9   Radiator support panel - repositioning, removal and installation

1   The radiator support panel is the section of bodywork that is mounted across the front of the vehicle. The radiator support panel and its associated components can be removed as an assembly; the radiator support panel can also be moved forward several inches to the service position without having to disconnect all the components mounted on it. Once the radiator support panel is placed in the service position, access to components at the front of the engine are greatly improved.

Placing the radiator support panel in the service position
Refer to illustration 9.3, 9.7, 9.8a, 9.8b, 9.9, 9.10, 9.11 and 9.15

Note: *To carry out this procedure, it will be necessary to fabricate two service tools, using two 10 inch lengths of threaded rod and a selection of hex nuts.*

2   Raise the front of the vehicle and support it securely on jackstands.

3   Working under the vehicle, remove the lower splash shield fasteners and remove the shield **(see illustration)**. **Note:** *On models equipped with an auxiliary heater, remove the three fasteners from the splash shield.*

4   Remove the engine cover(s) if equipped.

5   Remove the front bumper (see Section 12).

6   Remove the intake air duct (see Chapter 4).

7   Disconnect the air duct from the air cooler **(see illustration)**.

8   On turbo models, remove the air duct hoses to the intercooler and unclip the A/C hose from the bracket **(see illustrations)**.

9   Disconnect the electrical harness connectors **(see illustration)**.

10   Remove the upper fasteners for the radiator support panel to the fenders. Also remove the fasteners securing the radiator support panel to the side of each front fender (one on each side, located underneath the front turn signal housing) **(see illustration)**.

11   Thread the homemade service tools into the threaded holes **(see illustration)**, then thread the hex nuts onto the end of the service tools.

12   Remove the remainder of the bumper support bracket fasteners **(see illustration 9.11)**.

13   Carefully draw the radiator support panel away from the front of the engine compartment as far as possible without disconnecting the coolant hoses.

14   Secure the service position by aligning the rear bolt holes at the top with the front bolt

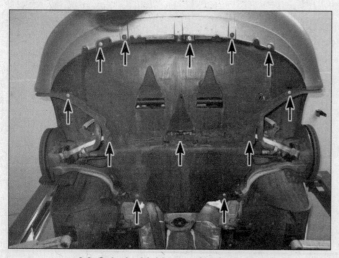

9.3 Splash shield mounting fasteners

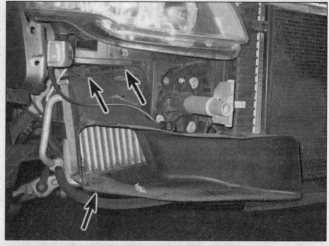

9.7 Remove the mounting fasteners and detach the lower air intake duct

9.8a On turbo models, remove the right air duct hose to the intercooler . . .

9.8b . . . and the left air duct hose (A) and unclip the A/C hose from the bracket (B)

holes and inserting the bolts to retain the lock carrier in position.

15 The radiator support panel can be refitted by following the repositioning procedure in reverse. Ensure that the torque support is properly aligned **(see illustration)** and all fasteners are tightened securely. On completion, check the positioning of the headlights and adjust if necessary (see Chapter 12).

Removal and installation

Warning: *Wait until the engine is completely cool before beginning this procedure.*

16 Remove the A/C condenser from the radiator (refer to Chapter 3 for mounting details), but do not disconnect the A/C lines. Tie the condenser to the lower corners of the fenders using a suitable piece of wire; do not allow it to hang unsupported from the flexible hoses. **Warning:** *The air conditioning system is under high pressure. DO NOT loosen any fittings or remove any components until after the system has been discharged. Air conditioning refrigerant should be properly discharged into an EPA-approved container at a*

dealership service department or an automotive air conditioning facility. Always wear eye protection when disconnecting air conditioning system fittings. **Caution:** *If the condenser cannot be properly secured prior to removal, have the air conditioning system discharged by a dealership service department or an automotive air conditioning facility.*

17 Refer to Steps 1 through 15 and place the radiator support panel in the service position.

18 Drain the coolant as described in Chapter 1.

19 Disconnect the coolant hoses from the radiator as described in Chapter 3. On models with air conditioning, also unbolt the refrigerant lines from the condenser and disconnect the electrical connectors from the A/C high pressure switch (see Chapter 3).

20 Disconnect the hood release cable from the hood latch mechanism (see Section 11).

21 Disconnect the electrical connectors for the headlights, the side marker lights and, if equipped, the headlight aiming control motors. Also disconnect the electrical con-

nectors located at the left hand corner of the engine compartment.

22 Disconnect the power steering lines to the oil cooler and remove the cooler.

9.9 Disconnect the electrical connectors from the mounting bracket

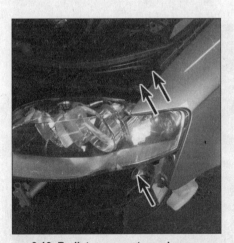

9.10 Radiator support panel upper fasteners and radiator support panel-to-fender fasteners

9.11 Bumper support bracket mounting details

A Bumper support bracket fasteners
B Threaded rod installation location

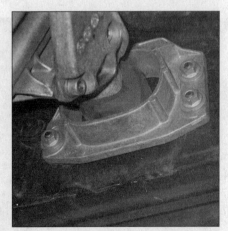

9.15 Proper alignment of the torque support

10.2 Disconnect the windshield washer jet hose and electrical connector and remove the spray nozzle assembly

10.4 Use a marking pen to outline the hinge plate and mounting nuts

9   Loosen the nuts and move the hood into correct alignment. Move it only a little at a time. Tighten the hinge nuts and carefully lower the hood to check the alignment.

10   Adjust the hood bumpers on the hood by turning them in or out to make the hood flush with the fenders when closed **(see illustration)**.

11   The safety latch assembly can also be adjusted up-and-down and side-to-side after loosening the nuts.

12   Adjust the buffer stops on each side of the radiator support by screwing the stop in or out.

23   On models equipped with an automatic transmission, disconnect the transmission cooler lines and cap the ends of the lines.

24   With the help of an assistant to support the panel, remove the nuts from the ends of the service tools, then withdraw the radiator support panel from the front of the vehicle.

25   Installation is the reverse of removal. Check the operation of the front lights, and the hood lock and safety catch. Refill and bleed the cooling system as described in Chapter 1, and have the headlights checked for correct alignment.

10   Hood - removal, installation and adjustment

Note: *The hood is awkward to remove and install - at least two people should perform this procedure.*

Removal and installation

Refer to illustrations 10.2, 10.4 and 10.6

1   Use blankets or pads to cover the cowl area of the body and the fenders.

2   Remove the wiper washer cover; disconnect the windshield washer hose and electrical connector **(see illustration)**.

3   Remove the harness cover from the hood hinge by sliding the locking tab to the left, then pull the cover off and disconnect the electrical harness.

4   Make alignment marks around the hinge plates using a permanent marker to insure the same installation **(see illustration)**.

5   Have an assistant support the hood and detach the upper end of the hood support strut (see Section 11).

6   Remove the hinge-to-hood bolts and lift off the hood **(see illustration)**.

7   Installation is the reverse of removal.

Adjustment

Refer to illustration 10.10

8   Fore-and-aft and side-to-side adjustment of the hood is done by moving the hood in relation to the hinge plates after loosening the nuts.

11   Hood latch, release cable and support struts - removal and installation

Latch

Refer to illustrations 11.2 and 11.3

1   Open the hood.

2   Remove the fasteners from the back side of the latch, disconnect the electrical connector and detach the latch assembly **(see illustration)**.

3   Disconnect the retaining clip and detach the cable from the latch assembly **(see illustration)**, then remove the front side fasteners and latch.

4   Installation is the reverse of removal.

Cable

Refer to illustration 11.8

5   Raise the vehicle and support it securely on jackstands. Remove the driver's side inner fender liner.

6   Remove the driver's knee bolster (see Section 27).

7   Detach the cable case from the bracket and release the cable end from the latch in

10.6 Support the hood with your shoulder while removing the hood bolts

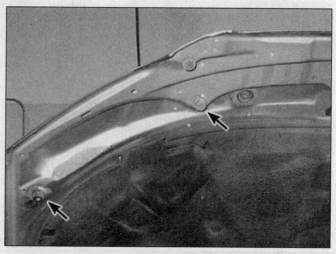

10.10 Adjust the hood height by screwing the hood bumpers in or out

11.2 Latch assembly mounting fasteners (A) and latch electrical connector (B)

11.3 Pry the cable retaining clip end back and detach the cable from the latch

11.8 Hood release handle mounting fastener

11.14 Pry the clip off to release the hood support strut

the engine compartment following Steps 1 through 3.

8   From inside the vehicle, remove the hood release handle mounting fastener and detach the cable from the lever **(see illustration)**.

9   Attach a wire or string to the end of the old cable in the engine compartment.

10   Working inside the passenger compartment, pull the cable through the cowl and into the passenger compartment.

11   Connect the string or wire to the new cable and pull it through the cowl into the engine compartment.

12   The remainder of installation is the reverse of removal. Be sure to fasten all of the cable retaining clips in their original locations.

Support strut

Refer to illustration 11.14

13   Open the hood and support it securely.

14   Use a small screwdriver to carefully lift the retaining springs **(see illustration)** at both ends of the support strut. Then pry or pull the

strut from the ball stud to detach it from the vehicle.

15   Installation is the reverse of removal.

12   Bumper covers - removal and installation

1   Front and rear bumpers are composed of a fascia, or bumper (exterior) cover, and a metal structural beam.

Front bumper cover

Refer to illustrations 12.4, 12.6, and 12.9

2   Raise the front of the vehicle and support it securely on jackstands.

3   Remove the splash shield from below the engine **(see illustration 9.3)**.

4   Open the hood and remove the upper mounting fasteners **(see illustration)**.

5   Detach the front section of the inner fender splash shield and pull it back.

6   Working at each front wheelwell, remove the fasteners from the bumper cover **(see**

illustration) and unclip the rear edge of the bumper cover.

7   From the lower front, release the retaining tab using a screwdriver and remove the

12.4 Bumper cover upper mounting fasteners

12.6 Remove the fasteners securing the bumper cover to the front fenderwells

12.9 Remove the fasteners securing the structural beam to the bumper support brackets

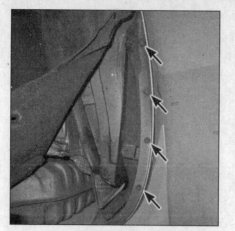

12.13 Rear bumper cover-to-wheelwell fasteners

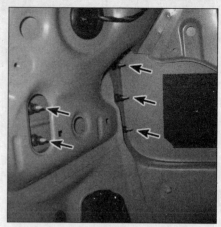

12.15 Rear bumper cover mounting nuts in the trunk

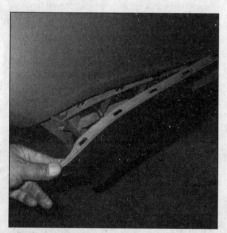

12.16 Unclip the trailing edge of the bumper cover from its retaining bracket, then pull the rear bumper away from the vehicle

lower grilles from both sides of the bumper.

8   If equipped, remove the foglights from the bumper, referring to Chapter 12, if necessary. On certain models, the ambient temperature sensor is mounted on the rear surface of the bumper; disconnect the electrical connector.

9   Remove the two bumper retaining bolts from below **(see illustration)**.

10   Carefully withdraw the bumper assembly by sliding it squarely away from the front of the vehicle. If equipped with headlight wipers, pull the bumper out to the point where the washer hose can be detached from its bumper-to-cross panel connection before fully withdrawing the bumper. **Note:** *The height of the bumper can be altered by adjusting the position of the threaded sleeves inside the bumper mounting tubes.*

11   If the bumper cover needs to be removed from the metal bumper, simply remove the fasteners and release catches and separate the two components.

12   Installation is the reverse of removal.

Loosely fit all fasteners before fully tightening them.

Rear bumper cover

Refer to illustration 12.13, 12.15 and 12.16

13   Working at the rear wheelwells, remove the fasteners for the liner to the lower rear corner, fold the wheelwell liner back and remove the fasteners securing the bumper cover to the wheelwell **(see illustration)**.

14   Working in the trunk area, fold back the floor covering for access, then remove the side storage compartment and navigation tuner, if equipped.

15   Remove the mounting nuts at each side **(see illustration)** and the bumper support bracket mounting bolts. On Avant models, it will be necessary to remove the floor sill plate and the side trim panels in the rear cargo area in order to peel back the floor carpet and gain access to the support bracket bolts.

16   Carefully withdraw the bumper cover assembly by sliding it squarely away from the rear of the vehicle. Disengage the locking tabs from the edges one at a time by grasping the lower edge of the bumper just to the rear of the wheelwell and pivoting it upwards and away from the rear quarter panel to release it **(see illustration)**.

17   The bumper support brackets can be removed from the bumper by removing the fasteners.

18   Installation is the reverse of removal. Loosely fit all fasteners before fully tightening them.

13   Front grille - removal and installation

1   Remove the front bumper cover (see Section 12).

2   Remove the grille fasteners from the inside of the bumper cover.

3   Remove the license plate holder by pressing the plastic locks to the free position and pulling the plate from the grille.

4   Installation is the reverse of removal. Loosely fit all fasteners before fully tightening them.

14   Front fender - removal and installation

Refer to illustrations 14.4, 14.6, 14.8 and 14.9

1   Loosen the wheel bolts, raise the vehicle, support it securely on jackstands and remove the front wheel.

2   Refer to Section 12 and remove the front bumper cover.

3   Remove the inner fender splash shield fasteners and remove the inner fender splash shield.

4   Working at the rear of the front wheelwell, remove the end panel fasteners between the fender and the door **(see illustration)**. This will allow access to the fasteners securing the fender to the "A" pillar.

5   Remove the fasteners for the fender to the "A" pillar, then open the door and remove the upper fender-to-door pillar fastener in the doorjamb.

14.4 Remove the end panel fasteners to gain access to the fender-to-A pillar fasteners

14.6 Remove the rocker panel fasteners (one of six shown) and lower the panel to remove the lower fender fasteners

14.8 Remove the fender support brace and front fender fasteners

14.9 Fender top mounting fasteners

6 Remove the rocker panel fasteners **(see illustration)**, lower the rocker panel and detach the two fasteners for the lower half of the fender to the rocker panel.

7 Remove the headlight/side marker light assembly (see Chapter 12).

8 Remove the fasteners for the fender to the front support brace and the lower inner fenderwell brace **(see illustration)**.

9 Remove the fasteners securing the top of the fender **(see illustration)**. Detach the hood release cable from the fender.

10 Detach the fender. It's a good idea to have an assistant support the fender while it's being moved away from the vehicle to prevent damage to the surrounding body panels.

11 Installation is the reverse of the removal procedure. Tighten all fasteners securely.

12 Tighten the wheel bolts to the torque listed in the Chapter 1 Specifications.

15 Cowl cover - removal and installation

Refer to illustration 15.3

1 Open the hood, then refer to Chapter 12 and remove the windshield wiper arms.

2 Remove the battery cover weather strip, start on one side and pull the strip forward until it reaches the opposite side. Remove the strip and cover.

3 Remove the cowl cover retaining clips **(see illustration)**.

4 Lift the plastic cowl cover upwards and out.

5 Installation is the reverse of removal.

16 Trunk lid (sedan and convertible models) - removal, installation and adjustment

Refer to illustrations 16.3, 16.4 and 16.7
Note: *The trunk lid is heavy and somewhat*

awkward to remove and install - at least two people should perform this procedure.

1 Open the trunk lid and cover the edges of the trunk compartment with pads or cloths to protect the painted surfaces when the lid is removed.

2 Remove the warning triangle from the trunk lid, then remove the warning triangle holder (if equipped). Remove the screw securing the grab handle to the trunk lid (if equipped).

3 Separate the trunk emergency release handle halves and remove the cable from the handle **(see illustration)**. Pull the release handle from the socket and remove the mounting screw and cover.

4 Remove the flock-covered screw and trim panel from the trunk lid **(see illustration)**.

5 Disconnect the electrical harness connectors and pull the harness out from the trunk lid.

6 Remove the trunk lid support struts (see Section 17).

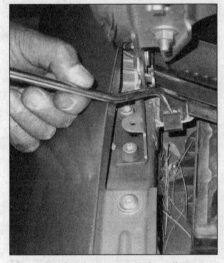

15.3 Cowl cover retaining clips (one of three shown)

16.3 Separate the trunk release handle halves, remove the cable end and pop the handle out of the socket

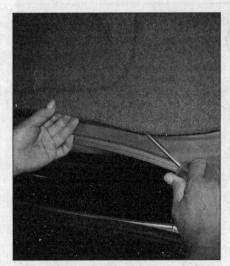

16.4 Remove the flock-covered screw then unclip the trim panel from the trunk lid

16.7 Trunk lid retaining nuts

17.2 Trunk latch mounting details

A   *Actuating cables/rods*
B   *Retaining nuts*

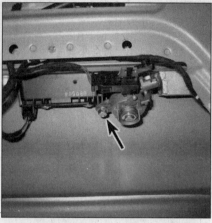

17.7 Lock cylinder mounting fastener

7   Mark the relationship between the trunk lid and the hinges by drawing around the outside of each hinge with a marker **(see illustration)**.
8   With the help of an assistant to support the trunk lid, remove the hinge-to-trunk lid retaining nuts **(see illustration 16.7)**, and lift the lid clear.
9   Installation is the reverse of removal. Check the trunk lid for correct alignment, and if necessary, loosen the hinge nuts to adjust, then retighten them; there should be an even gap of approximately 1/8 inch (3 mm) between the outside edge of the trunk lid and the surrounding bodywork. Adjust the trunk lid height (if necessary) by removing rubber caps on the buffer stops on each side of the trunk lid and screwing the stop in or out as necessary.

17   Trunk lid latch, lock cylinder and support struts - removal and installation

Latch

Refer to illustration 17.2

1   Refer to Section 16 and remove the inner trim panel from the trunk lid.
2   Disconnect the lock operating cables from the latch **(see illustration)**.
3   Mark the fitted position of the latch with a marker, remove the retaining nuts and withdraw the lock unit from the trunk lid. As it is withdrawn, unplug the electrical connector from the lock.
4   Installation is the reverse of removal.
Note: *When reinstalling the trunk lid latch, align the bolt heads with the marks made during removal.*

Lock cylinder

Refer to illustration 17.7

5   Detach the operating rod from the joint by unclipping the plastic fastener and rotating the joint while pulling the rod from the lever.

6   Disconnect the wiring from the lock cylinder unit as it becomes accessible.
7   Remove the lock cylinder mounting fastener **(see illustration)**.
8   Rotate the lock 90-degrees and remove the lock cylinder from the handle.
9   Installation is the reverse of removal.

Support struts

10   The trunk lid supports are removed in the same manner as the hood support struts. Refer to Section 11 for this procedure.

18   Liftgate (wagon models) - removal, installation and adjustment

Note: *The liftgate is heavy and somewhat awkward to remove and install - at least two people should perform this procedure.*

1   Open the liftgate, then remove the trim panel/grab handle fasteners at the center of the lower edge of the liftgate.
2   Remove the fasteners at the left and right hand sides, then carefully pry the lower section of the trim panel from the liftgate using just enough force to overcome the spring clips. Similarly, unclip the upper section of the trim panel from the liftgate rear window opening.
3   Disconnect the wiring from the liftgate components (lock switch, wiper motor, and rear light units) at the connectors. Note the routing and attachment locations of the wires.
4   Mark the relationship between the liftgate and its hinges using a marker.
5   With an assistant to help support the liftgate, use a small screwdriver to carefully lift the retaining springs **(see illustration 11.14)** at both ends of the support strut.
6   Pry or pull the strut from the ball stud to detach it from the vehicle.
7   Carefully pry the hinge covers off and remove the covers.
8   Remove the liftgate-to-hinge fasteners, and lift the liftgate clear of the vehicle.
9   Installation is the reverse of removal.

Check that the liftgate is correctly aligned before fully tightening the liftgate hinge bolts.
10   The latch assembly can also be adjusted up-and-down after loosening the nuts.
11   The closed position of the liftgate can be adjusted by altering the positions of the rubber liftgate stops towards the top of the liftgate opening.
12   Unclip the plastic cover from the liftgate stop and adjust the center adjusting screw in or out as necessary.

19   Liftgate latch, lock cylinder and support struts (wagon models) - removal and installation

The liftgate latch, lock cylinder and support struts are removed in the same manner as the trunk lid latch, lock cylinder and support struts. Refer to Section 17 for this procedure.

20   Door trim panels - removal and installation

Refer to illustrations 20.1, 20.2, 20.3a, 20.3b, 20.4, 20.5, 20.6 and 20.9

1   Open the door and carefully pry the upper trim from the door panel **(see illustration)**.
2   Carefully pry the lower armrest cover off and remove the fastener **(see illustration)**.
3   On models with manual front windows, insert a flat bladed screwdriver underneath the winder handle knob and pry against the trim to detach it from the winder handle. Remove the securing screw and the handle from its shaft, together with its spacer **(see illustrations)**.
4   Remove the door trim panel mounting fasteners **(see illustration)**.
5   Lift the trim panel up squarely to disengage the fasteners on the rear of the panel from the door **(see illustration)**.
6   Unhook the operating cable from the rear of the interior handle as it becomes accessible **(see illustration)**.

20.1 Start from the front of the door and carefully pry the trim back towards the rear

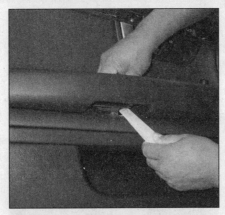

20.2 Lower armrest fastener cover

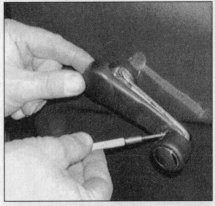

20.3a On models with manual windows, lever against the trim cover to detach it from the handle

20.3b Undo the handle retaining screw and remove the handle from its shaft

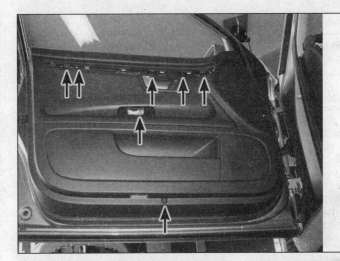

20.4 Door panel mounting fasteners

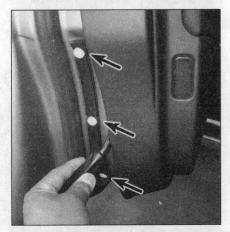

20.5 Pull the door trim panel back to disengage the fasteners

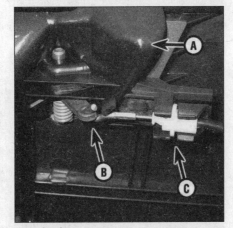

20.6 Interior door handle details

A Interior handle
B Operating cable
C Operating cable mounting clip

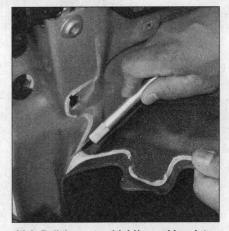

20.9 Pull the watershield/sound insulator back and separate it from the adhesive

7   Unplug the wiring from the electric window/mirror/central locking switches (where applicable) and the door speakers. Release the wiring from its retaining clips on the rear of the door panel.

8   Lift the trim panel away from the door,

noting the fitted positions of the molded clips mounted along the sides.

9   If required, the watershield/sound insulator can be carefully separated from the door using a utility knife **(see illustration)**.

10   Installation is the reverse of removal.

Guide the door locking knob through the hole at the upper edge of the trim panel, and ensure that the wiring and connections are secure and correctly routed, clear of the window regulator and latch/lock components.

21.5 Pull off the trim cap and remove the retaining screw from the upper hinge

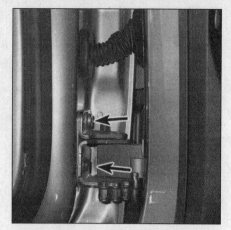

21.7 Remove the lower hinge fasteners and lift the door off

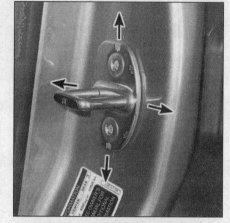

21.9 The striker can be loosened and moved slightly to achieve secure latch engagement

21 Door - removal, installation and adjustment

Refer to illustrations 21.5, 21.7 and 21.9

1   Remove the door trim panel (see Section 20).
2   If you're removing the front doors, refer to Section 27 and remove the kick panel, then disconnect the top two electrical connectors from the multi-terminal connector.
3   If you're removing the rear doors, detach the trim panel from the door pillar and disconnect the electrical connectors from the multi-terminal connector.
4   Pull the rubber harness boot out of the body and feed the harness connectors out.
5   Pull off the trim cap and remove the screw from the upper hinge **(see illustration)**.
6   Place a jack under the door or have an assistant on hand to support it when the lower hinge bolts are removed. **Note:** *If a jack is used, place a rag between it and the door to protect the door's painted surfaces.*
7   Scribe a line around the lower hinge with a marking pen, remove the lower hinge bolts **(see illustration)** and carefully lift off the door.
8   Installation is the reverse of removal, making sure to align the hinge with the marks made during removal before tightening the bolts.
9   Following installation of the door, check the alignment and adjust it if necessary as follows:

a) *Up-and-down and in-and-out adjustments are made by loosening the hinge-to-door bolts/nuts and moving the door as necessary.*
b) *Forward-and-backward adjustments are made by loosening the hinge-to-body bolts and moving the door as necessary.*
c) *The door lock striker can also be adjusted both up-and-down and sideways to provide positive engagement with the lock mechanism. This is done by loosening the fasteners and moving the striker as necessary* **(see illustration)**.

22 Door latch, lock cylinder and outside handle - removal and installation

Latch

Refer to illustration 22.5

1   Remove the door trim panel and watershield (see Section 20).
2   Refer to Section 24 and remove the window glass regulator from the door.
3   Disconnect the electrical harness connector at the door lock.
4   Disconnect the operating rod from the door handle and unclip the rod from the lock assembly. Make a note of the rod location.
5   Remove the two fasteners, and withdraw the lock unit, together with its base plate from the door **(see illustration)**.
6   Disconnect the operating cable housing from the lock unit.
7   Unhook the interior handle operation cable from the lock unit by rotating the cable end 90 degrees and unclip the cable.
8   Installation is the reverse of the removal.

Lock cylinder

Refer to illustration 22.9

9   Open the driver's door and remove the lock cylinder cover cap **(see illustration)**.
10   Turn the Torx bolt counterclockwise until it stops. This moves the locking arm to the rear and releases the lock cylinder.
11   Remove the lock cylinder from the outside door handle.
12   Installation is the reverse of removal.

Outside handle

13   Fully close the window. Refer to Section 20 and remove the door trim panel and the watershield.
14   Refer to Section 24 and remove the window glass regulator from the door.
15   Disconnect the operating rod from the lower clip, then rotate the rod and remove it from the outside handle clip.
16   Rotate the locking element to release it from the rear of the handle and lock cylinder.
17   Insert a screwdriver through the door plate and insert the screwdriver tip into the release slider.
18   Slide the release towards the latch end.
19   Remove the handle and trim from the

22.5 Door latch mounting fasteners

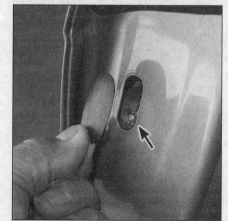

22.9 Remove the lock cylinder cover cap on the driver's door

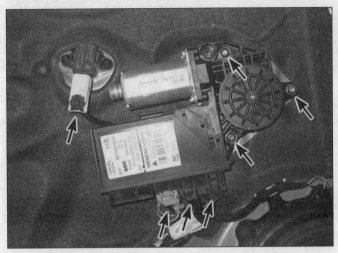

24.2 Power window motor mounting details

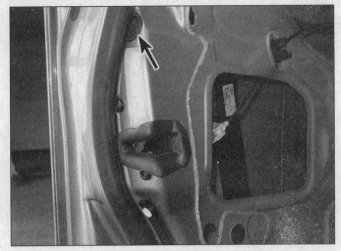

24.3 Remove the regulator fastener cover cap to gain access to the mounting fastener

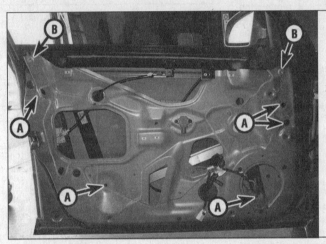

24.4 Window regulator mounting details:

A   Window regulator mounting fasteners
B   Shoulder fasteners

outer surface of the door.

20   If required, the door handle trim can be removed from the handle using a small flat bladed screwdriver. Insert the screwdriver at the front of the handle and push the release tab towards the opposite side and detach the trim panel.

21   Installation is the reverse of removal.

23   Door window glass - removal and installation

Front door glass

1   Remove the door trim panel (see Section 20).

2   Refer to Section 24 and remove the window regulator and window glass as an assembly from the door.

3   Remove the window glass fasteners and remove the glass from the window regulator.

4   Install the glass and mounting fasteners onto the regulator but do not fully tighten.

5   Raise the window up into the frame and tighten once the window glass is in the frame.

6   Check that the window glass moves properly in the window frame. The remainder of installation is the reverse of the removal procedure.

Rear door glass

7   Remove the door trim panel (see Section 20).

8   Refer to Section 24 and remove the window regulator and the rear window glass as an assembly from the door.

9   Lower the window down in the regulator carrier.

10   Remove the glass retaining fasteners and remove the rear window from the regulator carrier.

11   The remainder of the installation is the reverse of the removal procedure.

24   Door window glass frame and regulator - removal and installation

Removal

Refer to illustration 24.2, 24.3 and 24.4

1   Remove the door trim panel (see Sec-

tion 20) and exterior mirror trim cover (see Section 25).

2   Remove the power window motor fasteners, unplug the electrical connectors and remove the motor **(see illustration)**.

3   Remove the watershield/insulator and access plug to the hidden regulator mounting fastener **(see illustration)**.

4   Remove the fasteners for the window regulator carrier to the door **(see illustration)**. **Note:** *Some models are equipped with a regulator mounting fastener hidden under the exterior mirror trim cover* **(see illustration 25.5)**.

5   Remove the window regulator and window glass as an assembly from the door.

6   Remove the window glass from the window regulator (see Section 23).

Installation

7   Install the window glass in the window regulator assembly (see Section 23).

8   Carefully insert the assembly into the door, push the upper halves of the door-side gasket into the window frame and loosely install the regulator fasteners.

9   Hand tighten the shoulder fasteners **(see illustration 24.4),** then lightly move the window frame in at the top and tighten all the window regulator mounting fasteners securely except the shoulder fasteners. **Note:** *The glass should move up the frame without binding.*

10   Tighten the shoulder fasteners securely. The remainder of installation is the reverse of the removal procedure.

25   Mirrors - removal and installation

Interior mirror

Refer to illustrations 25.1 and 25.2

1   Rotate the mirror 60 to 90 degrees until the retaining spring disengages and remove the mirror from the retaining plate **(see illus-**

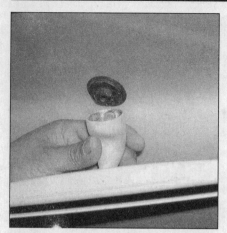

25.1 Pull the inside mirror off its retaining bracket at an angle

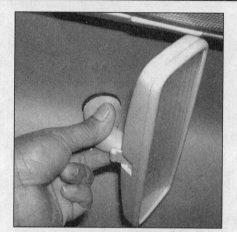

25.2 Align the mirror vertically in the vehicle and rotate it 90 degrees until it locks into place

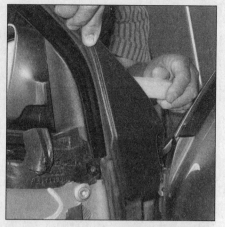

25.4 Carefully pry the trim cover off of the door

ration). If the vehicle is equipped with an automatic mirror, unclip the cover and detach wiring harness and mirror connector, then

25.5 Exterior mirror mounting details

A   *Mirror mounting fastener*
B   *Window regulator frame mounting fastener*

rotate the mirror 90 degrees and remove the mirror.

2   To install the mirror, align it 90 degrees from the installed position (vertical with the front and rear of the vehicle) and engage the mirror with the retaining plate, then rotate it clockwise until the mirror locks in place **(see illustration)**.

3   If the vehicle is equipped with an automatic mirror, connect the wiring harness, mirror connector and the mirror trim cover.

Exterior mirror

Refer to illustrations 25.4 and 25.5

4   With the door open, carefully pry the trim cover from the door **(see illustration)**.

5   Remove the mirror mounting fasteners and detach the mirror from the door **(see illustration)**. Work the mirror harness through the hole in the door.

6   Disconnect the electrical connector for the mirror and carefully withdraw the connector.

7   Installation is the reverse of removal.

26 Center console - removal and installation

Refer to illustrations 26.3, 26.4, 26.5, 26.6, 26.9, 26.10, 26.11, 26.13, 26.15a and 26.15b

Warning: *The models covered by this manual are equipped with Supplemental Restraint Systems (SRS), more commonly known as airbags. Always disable the airbag system before working in the vicinity of any airbag system components to avoid the possibility of accidental deployment of the airbags, which could cause personal injury (see Chapter 12).*

1   Carefully pry out the rear ashtray and remove it. Disconnect the electrical connectors for the door lock switch and seat heater switch (if equipped).

2   Remove the rear switch mount by pressing both corner tabs towards the sides and rotate the mount down and out. Disconnect the electrical connectors.

3   From the rear of the console, remove the center armrest mounting nut **(see illustration)** and lift the armrest out of the console.

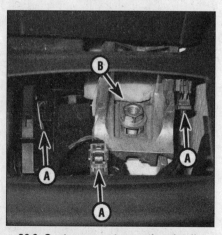

26.3 Center armrest mounting details

A   *Electrical connectors*
B   *Center armrest mounting nut*

26.4 Use a trim to tool to carefully pry the parking brake trim cover out

26.5 Working from the front of the shift cover, pry the cover up and out

26.6 Use a small screwdriver to remove the button trim from the top of the console

26.9 Remove the fastener cover and fastener - right side shown

26.10 Press down on the parking brake lever handle retaining clip with a small screwdriver

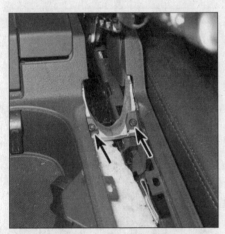

26.11 Parking brake carrier mounting fasteners

26.13 Remove the front ashtray fasteners

If equipped with a center armrest phone, depress the tab on the connector and separate the harness.

4   Carefully remove the parking brake trim cover from the center console, starting at the front and working your way to the back (see illustration).

5   Pry up the shift cover from the sides and remove the cover and boot (see illustration).

6   Carefully pry the button trim away from the top of the console and remove the trim cover (see illustration).

7   Remove the radio assembly (see Chapter 12).

8   Remove the air conditioning control assembly (see Chapter 3).

9   Remove the plastic access plugs from both lower edges (see illustration) at the front of the console and remove the fasteners.

10 With the handbrake lever applied, depress the retaining clip (see illustration) and release the clip at the base of the parking brake grip and pull the lever grip from the lever.

11 Remove the parking brake carrier fasteners (see illustration) and carrier.

12 On vehicles equipped with automatic

transmissions, move the shift selector all the way to the back.

13 Remove the front ashtray fasteners and ashtray (see illustration). Once the ashtray is removed, disconnect the electrical connector.

14 Disconnect the center console lighter by

depressing the two corner tabs with a small screwdriver. Remove the assembly and disconnect the electrical connector.

15 Remove the fasteners at the top front and sides of the console (see illustration). Remove the rear mounting nuts (see illustration).

26.15a Remove the center console and front mounting fasteners . . .

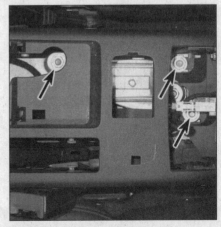

26.15b . . . then the rear mounting nuts

27.2 End cap retaining clips (left side shown, right side similar)

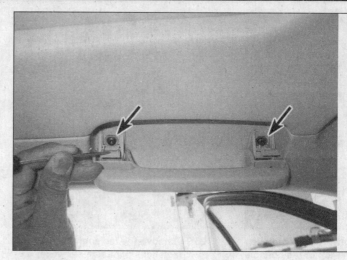

27.5 Use a small screwdriver to pry open the fastener covers

16   Partially withdraw the console, disconnect the navigation control head wiring, then remove the console, by lifting it from the rear up and over the brake lever.

17   Installation is the reverse of the removal. Ensure that the ashtray/cigar lighter, navigation control head wiring is reconnected and that the center armrest phone connector is installed in the correct position. Ensure that the clips at the front lower edges of the console engage with the instrument panel support framework.

27 Dashboard trim panels - removal and installation

Warning: *The models covered by this manual are equipped with Supplemental*

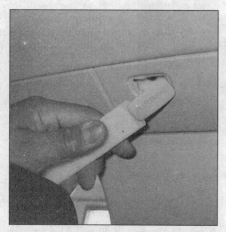

27.6 Remove the A-pillar trim panel airbag fastener covers

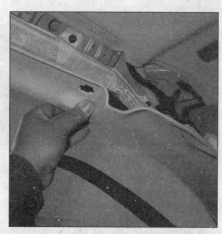

27.7 Remove the A-pillar trim panel

27.9 With the end cap removed, pull the trim to release the mounting clips

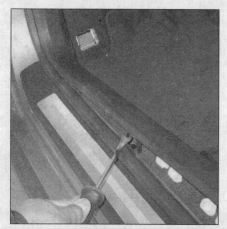

27.11 Using a trim tool, pry up on the kick panel to release the retaining clips

27.14 Remove the knee bolster lower fasteners and pull the bolster back and out

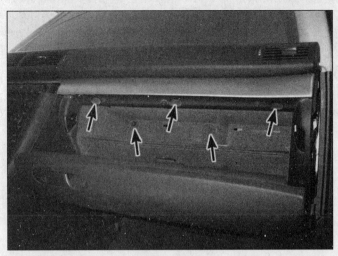

27.20 Remove the fasteners from inside of the glove box (five of seven shown)

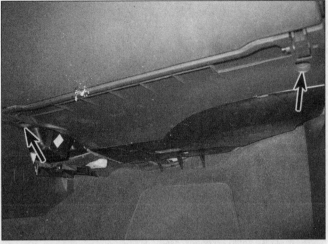

27.23 Remove the lower fasteners and lower the glove box down

Restraint Systems (SRS), more commonly known as airbags. Always disable the airbag system before working in the vicinity of any airbag system components to avoid the possibility of accidental deployment of the airbags, which could cause personal injury (see Chapter 12).

Dashboard end caps

Refer to illustration 27.2

1   The end caps are held in place by clips.
2   Pry the cover out with a trim tool to release the mounting clips **(see illustration)**.
3   Installation is the reverse of removal.

A-pillar trim panels

Refer to illustrations 27.5, 27.6 and 27.7

4   Rotate the sun visor to the side. Use a small screwdriver to remove the sun visor screw cap located at the base of the visor and remove the fastener. Carefully pull the visor away from the headliner to disconnect the electrical connector and remove the visor.
5   Remove the handle mounting fasteners and the handle **(see illustration)**.
6   Carefully pry the airbag trim fastener covers from the A-pillar trim **(see illustration)**.
7   Pull the A-pillar trim panel away from the windshield back to the door **(see illustration)**. **Note:** *The A-pillar trim starts from the windshield and stops at the rear door.*
8   Installation is the reverse of removal.

Kick panels

Refer to illustrations 27.9 and 27.11

9   Remove the dashboard end caps **(see illustration 27.2)**, pull the kick panel away from the A-pillar **(see illustration)** and unclip the lower section of the trim panel.
10   On the driver's side, remove the footrest mounting fastener and footrest.
11   Pry the kick panel up **(see illustration)**. **Note:** *The kick panels are long, one-piece panels that must be removed as a unit.*
12   Installation is the reverse of removal.

Driver's knee bolster (driver's side storage compartment)

Refer to illustration 27.14

13   Remove the left dashboard end cap to access two side fasteners **(see illustration 27.2)**.
14   Remove the fasteners retaining the bottom of the bolster to the instrument panel **(see illustration)**.
15   Pull backward on the top of the bolster to release it from the clips, disconnect the electrical connectors and unclip the diagnostic socket.
16   If the bolster reinforcement panel needs to be removed to perform a repair procedure, remove the reinforcement panel fasteners.
17   Installation is the reverse of removal.

Glove box

Refer to illustrations 27.20 and 27.23

18   Remove the right dashboard end cap **(see illustration 27.2)**.
19   Remove the knee airbag on the passenger's side (if equipped) (see Chapter 12).
20   Open the glove box, remove the fasteners at the top in each depression and at the back of the glove box **(see illustration)**.
21   On models equipped with a glovebox

cover brake, disconnect the electrical connector and squeeze the joint pin from the hinge through the end cap opening.
22   Rotate the brake cylinder in a clockwise rotation and remove it from the pin and out of the glovebox.
23   Remove the lower glovebox fasteners from the outside bottom of the glove box **(see illustration)**. Remove the CD changer mounting fasteners if equipped.
24   On models equipped with an insulating box, disconnect the vent.
25   Lower the glove box and disconnect the electrical connector. Remove the glove box from the instrument panel.
26   Installation is the reverse of removal.

28   Steering column covers - removal and installation

Refer to illustration 28.2 and 28.3

1   Remove the steering wheel (see Chapter 10).
2   Pull down on the steering column tilt lever, lower the column and remove the upper trim and fasteners **(see illustration)**.
3   Remove the fasteners from the lower

28.2 Carefully pull back on the upper trim and remove the trim and fasteners (one of two shown)

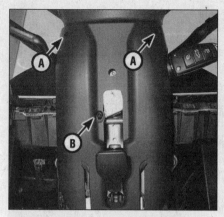

28.3 Steering column cover fasteners

  A   Upper column cover fasteners
  B   Lower column cover fastener

29.9 Pry the optical sensor trim out using a small screwdriver

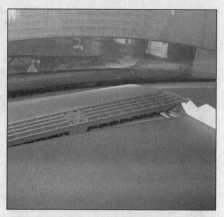

29.10 Pry the defrost vent out from the instrument panel

steering column cover **(see illustration)**, and remove the upper and lower covers.

4   Remove the tilt lever mounting screw and lever. **Note:** *The lower cover can be maneuvered over the tilt lever on some models.*

5   Installation is the reverse of removal.

29   Instrument panel - removal and installation

Refer to illustrations 29.9, 29.10, 29.12, 29.13, 29.14 and 29.16

Warning: *The models covered by this*

manual are equipped with Supplemental Restraint Systems (SRS), more commonly known as airbags. Always disable the airbag system before working in the vicinity of any airbag system components to avoid the possibility of accidental deployment of the airbags, which could cause personal injury (see

29.12 Remove the vent sensors from each end of the instrument panel - left side shown

A   Vent temperature sensors   B   Instrument panel end fasteners

29.13 Remove the left side center instrument panel fasteners

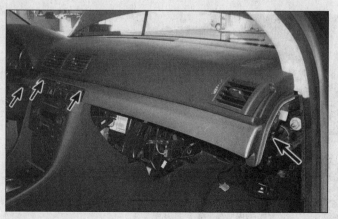

29.14 Remove the right side center instrument panel fasteners

29.16 Remove the panel fasteners

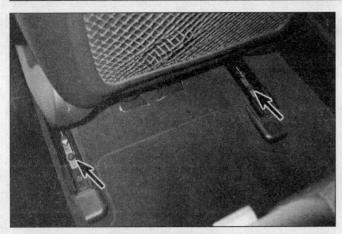

30.2 Remove the plastic buttons in the seat track covers, then remove the rear mounting fasteners

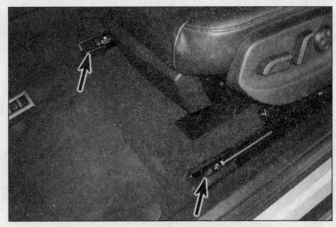

30.3 Remove the front seat mounting fasteners

Chapter 12).

Caution: *This is a difficult procedure for the home mechanic, involving tedious disassembly and the disconnection/reconnection of numerous electrical connectors. If you do attempt this procedure, make sure you take good notes and mark all matching connectors (and their mounting points) to aid reassembly.*

1   Disconnect the negative battery cable (see Chapter 5).

2   Remove the center console (see Section 26).

3   Remove the steering wheel (see Chapter 10).

4   Remove the steering column covers (see Section 28).

5   Remove all of the dashboard trim panels (see Section 27).

6   Remove the audio components, the multi-function switch and the instrument cluster (see Chapter 12)

7   Disconnect the electrical connector for the passenger's side airbag (see Chapter 12). **Note:** *The passenger's side airbag remains in the vehicle as the panel is removed.*

8   Remove the headlight switch (see Chapter 12).

9   Carefully pry the optical photo sensor cover at the top of the instrument panel **(see illustration)**, disconnect the sensor from the electrical connector and remove the sensor.

10   Remove the defrost vent fastener and remove the vent **(see illustration)**.

11   Remove the center speaker fasteners and remove the speaker (see Chapter 12).

12   Remove the instrument panel end caps (see Section 27), and remove the left and right vent temperature sensor connectors **(see illustration)**.

13   Remove the fasteners for the left side center panel trim and disengage the clips **(see illustration)**.

14   Remove the fasteners for the right side center panel trim and disengage the clips **(see illustration)**, then pry the trim out.

15   Remove the fasteners securing the ends of the instrument panel **(see illustration 29.12)**.

16   Remove any remaining fasteners securing the instrument panel **(see illustration)**, and disconnect any electrical connectors still attached to the panel. Have an assistant help you pull the panel back and out of the vehicle.

17   Installation is the reverse of removal.

---

30   Seats - removal and installation

Warning: *The models covered by this manual are equipped with Supplemental Restraint Systems (SRS), more commonly known as airbags. Always disable the airbag system before working in the vicinity of any airbag system components to avoid the possibility of accidental deployment of the airbags, which could cause personal injury (see Chapter 12).*

Front

Refer to illustrations 30.2 and 30.3

1   The front seats on some models are equipped with side-impact airbags at the upper outside of the seat back. Refer to Chapter 12 to disable the airbag system before working

on front seats.

2   Slide the seat forward and remove the seat track covers, remove the rear seat track fasteners and unplug any electrical connectors attached to the seat **(see illustration)**.

3   Slide the seat all the way to the back, remove the seat track covers, unplug any electrical connectors and remove the front seat track fasteners **(see illustration)**. Remove the seat from the vehicle.

4   Installation is the reverse of removal.

Rear

Sedan

Refer to illustrations 30.5 and 30.6

5   Remove the seat bottom cushion by pushing in on the front edge of the cushion in the vicinity of the clips, to disengage part of the seat's wire frame from the clips **(see illustration)**. With the clips unhooked, lift up and disconnect any electrical connectors and remove the seat bottom from the vehicle.

6   Remove the seat back lower mounting fasteners **(see illustration)**, remove the head rests and lift the seat back up and off the mounting pin. Disconnect any electrical con-

30.5 Pull up the center tab of the rear seat cushion to disengage the cushion from the clips

30.6 Remove the seat back mounting fasteners - left side shown

30.8 Pry the trim cover up and remove the seat back fastener

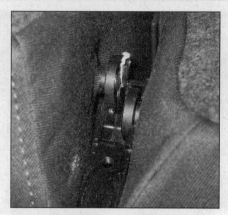

30.9 Lift the seat back off the center support

nectors and remove the seat back from the vehicle.

7   Installation is the reverse of removal. Tighten the seat back fasteners securely.

Wagon

Refer to illustrations 30.8 and 30.9

8   Pry the trim up between the seat cushions and remove the seat back mounting fastener **(see illustration)**.

9   Lift the seat back off the center support, slide the seat off of the rotating pin and remove it from the vehicle **(see illustration)**.

10   Installation is the reverse of removal. Tighten the seat back fasteners securely.

---

31   Convertible top - general information

Note: *This information is general in nature, as it is intended to apply to all vehicle types, years and models.*

Adjustments

Note: *The following are typical adjustments. Some of these adjustments may not be applicable to your vehicle.*

The latches secure the convertible top frame to the upper edge of the windshield frame. If the latches are too loose, the top will rattle and move side to side. If the latches are too tight, they will be difficult or impossible to secure. The hooks on some latches are threaded so they can be screwed in or out to tighten or loosen the latch; pliers are often necessary, so make sure you protect the finish of the hook with a rag. Other latches have set-screws that lock the hooks in place - loosen the set-screws (usually with an Allen or Torx wrench), position the hooks as desired, then tighten the set-screws.

Also keep in mind that a weatherstrip is attached to the front edge of the top. As this weatherstrip deteriorates over time, it will cause the latches and the front edge of the convertible top to become loose. The proper

fix for this problem is to replace the deteriorated weatherstrip, which will also reduce wind noise.

Power-top troubleshooting

Power tops are operated by hydraulic cylinders that are mounted between the vehicle body and the convertible-top framework. The cylinders receive hydraulic pressure from an electric motor/pump assembly that is located in the luggage compartment. When the switch is pressed to raise the top, the motor drives the pump in a direction that sends hydraulic pressure to the bottom of each hydraulic cylinder, driving the pistons out of the cylinders, which raises the top. When the switch is pressed to lower the top, the motor turns in the opposite direction, sending hydraulic pressure to the top of each cylinder, driving the pistons down and lowering the top.

As a first step in troubleshooting, listen for the whirring sound of the motor as the switch is pressed. If there is no sound from the motor, proceed to *Electrical troubleshooting*. If you can hear the motor running but the top does not raise, proceed to *Hydraulic/ mechanical troubleshooting*.

Hydraulic/mechanical troubleshooting

Mechanical and hydraulic problems will cause the top to not open (or close) or to get stuck part-way through the process. If the motor is operating normally, there are generally two possible causes for these problems: 1) A hydraulic system malfunction (low fluid level, air in the system, inadequate pump pressure) or 2) A mechanical binding in the top framework.

Hydraulic system fluid level check

Note: *The fluid level should only be checked when the top is in the open position.*

Locate the hydraulic motor/pump behind the trim panel in the right-rear corner of the luggage compartment. It will have an electrical connector and hoses attached to it. On the side or end of the motor/pump assembly will be a screw-type check plug. The fluid level

is seen through the side of the reservoir. The level should be between the Min and Max marks. If necessary, add fluid through the check-plug hole to bring the fluid level to normal, but do not exceed the Max mark.

Check your owner's manual for specific fluid recommendations, but generally, DEXRON III Automatic Transmission Fluid (ATF) is used. If you find a low fluid level, check for leaks at the pump, hoses and hydraulic cylinders.

Hydraulic system bleeding

Air can get into the hydraulic system through leaks, and if the fluid level is too low. Air in the system will generally cause excess noise and, in extreme cases, will cause the top to raise or lower only part-way.

To bleed the hydraulic system, first check the fluid level, then start the engine and raise and lower the top. If the fluid has excessive air, the top might not raise or lower, so you will need an assistant to hold the switch while you raise and lower the top slowly by hand. Raise and lower the top several times to work out all the air. Check the fluid level again, since it will likely drop as the air is expelled.

Checking for binding

If the hydraulic system seems to be operating properly, disconnect the hydraulic cylinders from the top framework and operate the top by hand. The top should go up and down smoothly, without excessive effort.

If the top binds during manual operation, make sure all adjustments are correct and spray penetrating lubricant on all framework joints.

If the top is operating smoothly during manual operation but will not raise properly with the hydraulic cylinders connected, suspect a pump/motor assembly that is not providing adequate pressure.

Electrical troubleshooting

If you cannot hear the motor running when the switch is pressed, first check for blown fuses and fusible links. If the fuses and fusible links are all OK, disconnect the electrical connector at the motor. Connect a 12-volt test-light to ground and probe each terminal of the disconnected wiring-harness connector while an assistant operates the switch. There should be power (light will illuminate) at one terminal with the switch in the TOP UP position and power at the other terminal with the switch in the TOP DOWN position.

If there is power, but the motor does not operate, check the ground circuit. On most models, there is a third wire from the motor that is attached to ground somewhere near the motor. It is common for this ground connection to become loose or corroded, causing the motor to stop functioning. If the motor is receiving power and has a good ground, but it is still not functioning, the motor itself is the problem. **Note:** *On some vehicles there is no separate ground connection. A relay in the system alternately grounds one wire and pow-*

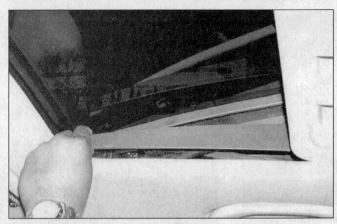

32.3a Unsnap and pull out the first sunroof track plastic cover . . .

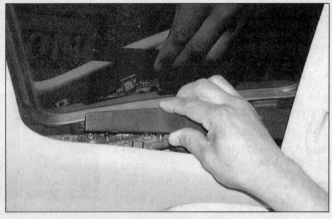

32.3b . . . then the second cover to reveal the tracks

ers the other, depending on switch position. On models with this type of system, check for a solid ground at the relay.

If there is no power at the motor, check for power at the three switch terminals by backprobing with the electrical connector still attached. There should be power at one of the switch terminals with the switch in the neutral position, and power at two of the terminals with the switch in either the TOP UP or TOP DOWN position. If there is no power at the switch, the problem lies in the wiring between the battery and the switch. If there is power at only one terminal in the TOP UP or TOP DOWN position, the switch is bad. If the switch tests are OK, the problem lies in the relay(s) (if equipped) or the wiring.

32.4 The sunroof glass has three fasteners on each side (arrows) used to adjust the fit of the glass to the roof

32 Sunroof - adjustment

Refer to illustrations 32.3a, 32.3b and 32.4

1   The position of the glass panel can be adjusted in the following manner.
2   Open the interior sunshade all the way back and operate the sunroof until it is tilted open.
3   There are glass fasteners on each side of the sunroof opening, inside the vehicle. Remove the plastic covers **(see illustrations)**.
4   Loosen the front fasteners and lower the sunroof **(see illustration)**. Set the front edge of the glass approximately 0.039-inch (1 mm) below the surface of the roof when closed. Tighten the front fasteners.
5   Loosen the rear glass adjustment fasteners and adjust the glass approximately 0.039-inch (1 mm) above the roof at the rear. Tighten the rear fasteners.
6   When the adjustment is correct, tilt the sunroof open and reinstall the plastic covers over the glass rails.

33 Seat belts - removal and installation

Warning: *The models covered by this manual are equipped with Supplemental Restraint*

Systems (SRS), more commonly known as airbags. Always disable the airbag system before working in the vicinity of any airbag system components to avoid the possibility of accidental deployment of the airbags, which could cause personal injury (see Chapter 12).
Warning: *Do not use electrical test equipment on the belt tensioner system; it could cause the pyrotechnic belt tensioner to discharge.*
Warning: *An auxiliary voltage input device (memory saver) must not be used when working near airbag system components.*
Caution: *Never strike the pillars or floorpan with a hammer or use an impact-driver tool in these areas unless the system is disabled.*
Caution: *Disconnecting the battery can cause driveability problems that require a scan tool to rectify. Additionally, disconnecting the battery may cause one or more warning lights on the instrument panel to illuminate, which will also require the use of a scan tool to turn off. Most scan tools available to the public do not have the capability to perform either of these tasks, which will necessitate taking the vehicle to a dealer service department or other properly equipped repair facility after service work has been performed. See Chapter 5, Section 1 for other precautions related to battery disconnection.*
Caution: *These models are equipped with an anti-theft radio. Before performing a procedure that requires disconnecting the battery, make sure you have the proper activation code.*

Front seat belts

Refer to illustrations 33.4 and 33.7

1   Raise the seat to the highest point.
2   Disconnect the negative battery cable (see Chapter 5).
3   Remove the seat anchor cover from the outer side of the seat and push the anchor end down and off the anchor point. Slide the belt through the belt guide and off the seat.
4   Remove the A-pillar and B-pillar trim (see Section 27) and remove the height adjuster trim **(see illustration)**.
5   Remove the belt tensioner fastener

33.4 Loosen the side curtain airbag fastener and unclip the height adjuster trim

from the base of the B-pillar and remove the belt tensioner.

6   Use a small screwdriver to open the yellow/blue wire retainer and disconnect the electrical connector from the belt module.

7   Remove the upper belt fastener from the height adjuster **(see illustration)** and remove the belt. **Note:** *To replace the height adjuster, remove the adjuster mounting fastener and remove the adjuster assembly.*

8   Installation is the reverse of removal. Make sure the belt is not twisted before installing the lower seat mount side.

Belt latch

9   Remove the latch fastener and latch from the base of the seat.

10   Disconnect the electrical connector to the seat latch. **Note:** *On some models, the driver's side electrical connector will need to be removed at the connector housing. Use a small screwdriver to depress the connector housing hooks and press the connector out of the housing. Open the connector and separate the wires from the back side of the connector, noting their locations.*

11   Installation is the reverse of removal.

Rear seat belts

Refer to illustrations 33.13 and 33.15

12   Disconnect the negative battery cable (see Chapter 5).

13   Remove the seat (see Section 30) and remove the lower anchor point fastener **(see illustration)** and belt end.

14   Remove the C-pillar trim and rear parcel shelf trim on sedans (see Chapter 12, Section 11).

15   From inside the rear luggage compartment, remove the trim and loosen the belt tensioner fastener. Slide the tensioner assembly back, up and out **(see illustration)**.

16   Use a small screwdriver to open the yellow retainer and disconnect the electrical connector from the belt module.

17   Installation is the reverse of removal. Make sure the belt is not twisted before installing the lower seat mount side.

33.7 Height adjuster and seat belt mounting details

A   *Upper seat belt mounting bolt*
B   *Height adjuster assembly mounting bolt*

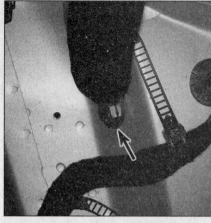

33.13 Remove the lower seat belt fastener and belt

33.15 Loosen the rear seat belt tensioner fastener from the luggage compartment and slide the assembly back, up and out into the interior

Belt latch

Refer to illustration 33.18

18   Remove the latch fastener and latch

33.18 Remove the rear seat belt latch fastener and latch

from the floorpan **(see illustration)**.

19   Installation is the reverse of removal. Make sure the belt is not twisted before installing the lower mount side.

Chapter 12
Chassis electrical system

Contents

	Section
Airbag system - general information and system component removal and installation	23
Antenna - removal and installation	12
Bulb - replacement	17
Cruise control system - description and check	20
Electrical connectors - general information	5
Electrical troubleshooting - general information	2
Fuses, fusible links and circuit breakers - general information	3
General information	1
Headlight bulb - replacement	15
Headlight housing - replacement	14
Headlights - adjustment	16
Horn - replacement	18

	Section
Ignition switch and key lock cylinder - replacement	7
Instrument cluster - removal and installation	10
Instrument panel switches - replacement	9
Key fob - battery replacement and transmitter programming	6
Power door lock system - general information	22
Power window system - general information	21
Radio and speakers - removal and installation	11
Rear window defogger - check and repair	13
Relays - general information	4
Steering column switches - replacement	8
Wiper motor - replacement	19
Wiring diagrams - general information	24

1   General information

The electrical system is a 12-volt, negative ground type. Power for the lights and all electrical accessories is supplied by a lead/acid-type battery that is charged by the alternator.

This Chapter covers repair and service procedures for the various electrical components not associated with the engine. Information on the battery, alternator, ignition system and starter motor can be found in Chapter 5.

It should be noted that when portions of the electrical system are serviced, the negative cable should be disconnected from the battery to prevent electrical shorts and/or fires.

2   Electrical troubleshooting - general information

Refer to illustrations 2.5a, 2.5b, 2.6 and 2.9

A typical electrical circuit consists of an electrical component, any switches, relays, motors, fuses, fusible links or circuit breakers related to that component and the wiring and connectors that link the component to both the battery and the chassis. To help you pinpoint an electrical circuit problem, wiring diagrams are included at the end of this Chapter.

Before tackling any troublesome electrical circuit, first study the appropriate wiring diagrams to get a complete understanding of what makes up that individual circuit. Trouble spots, for instance, can often be narrowed down by noting if other components related to the circuit are operating properly. If several components or circuits fail at one time, chances are the problem is in a fuse or ground connection, because several circuits are often routed through the same fuse and ground connections.

Electrical problems usually stem from simple causes, such as loose or corroded connections, a blown fuse, a melted fusible link or a failed relay. Visually inspect the condition of all fuses, wires and connections in a problem circuit before troubleshooting the circuit.

If test equipment and instruments are going to be utilized, use the diagrams to plan ahead of time where you will make the necessary connections in order to accurately pinpoint the trouble spot.

The basic tools needed for electrical troubleshooting include a circuit tester or voltmeter (a 12-volt bulb with a set of test leads can also be used), a continuity tester, which includes a bulb, battery and set of test leads, and a jumper wire, preferably with a circuit breaker incorporated, which can be used to bypass electrical components **(see illustrations)**. Before attempting to locate a problem with test instruments, use the wiring diagram(s) to decide where to make the connections.

Voltage checks

Voltage checks should be performed if a circuit is not functioning properly. Connect one lead of a circuit tester to either the negative battery terminal or a known good ground. Connect the other lead to a connector in the circuit being tested, preferably nearest to the battery or fuse **(see illustration)**. If the bulb of the tester lights, voltage is present, which means that the part of the circuit between the connector and the battery is problem free. Continue checking the rest of the circuit in the same fashion. When you reach a point at which no voltage is present, the problem lies between that point and the last test point with voltage. Most of the time the problem can be traced to a loose connection. **Note:** *Keep in mind that some circuits receive voltage only when the ignition key is in the Accessory or Run position.*

Finding a short

One method of finding shorts in a circuit is to remove the fuse and connect a test light or voltmeter in place of the fuse terminals. There should be no voltage present in the circuit. Move the wiring harness from side-to-side while watching the test light. If the bulb goes on, there is a short to ground somewhere in that area, probably where the insulation has rubbed through. The same test can be performed on each component in the circuit, even a switch.

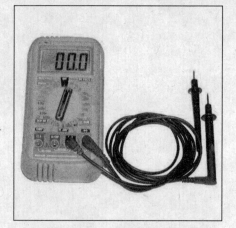

2.5a The most useful tool for electrical troubleshooting is a digital multimeter that can check volts, amps, and test continuity

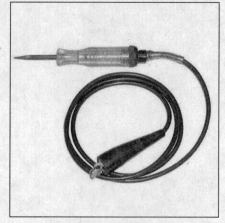

2.5b A test light is a very handy tool for checking voltage

Ground check

Perform a ground test to check whether a component is properly grounded. Disconnect the battery and connect one lead of a continuity tester or multimeter (set to the ohms scale), to a known good ground. Connect the other lead to the wire or ground connection being tested. If the resistance is low (less than 5 ohms), the ground is good. If the bulb on a self-powered test light does not go on, the ground is not good.

Continuity check

A continuity check is done to determine if there are any breaks in a circuit - if it is passing electricity properly. With the circuit off (no power in the circuit), a self-powered continuity tester or multimeter can be used to check the circuit. Connect the test leads to both ends of the circuit (or to the power end and a good ground), and if the test light comes on the

circuit is passing current properly **(see illustration)**. If the resistance is low (less than 5 ohms), there is continuity; if the reading is 10,000 ohms or higher, there is a break somewhere in the circuit. The same procedure can be used to test a switch, by connecting the continuity tester to the switch terminals. With the switch turned On, the test light should come on (or low resistance should be indicated on a meter).

Finding an open circuit

When diagnosing for possible open circuits, it is often difficult to locate them by sight because the connectors hide oxidation or terminal misalignment. Merely wiggling a connector on a sensor or in the wiring harness may correct the open circuit condition. Remember this when an open circuit is indicated when troubleshooting a circuit. Intermittent problems may also be caused by oxidized

2.6 In use, a basic test light's lead is clipped to a known good ground, then the pointed probe can test connectors, wires or electrical sockets - if the bulb lights, the part being tested has battery voltage

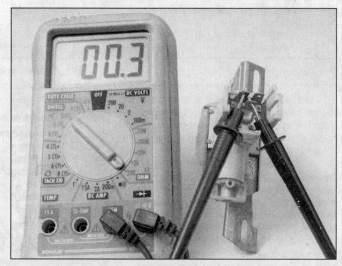

2.9 With a multimeter set to the ohms scale, resistance can be checked across two terminals - when checking for continuity, a low reading indicates continuity, a high reading indicates lack of continuity

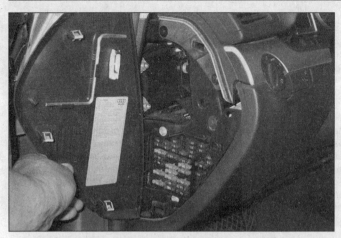

3.1a The interior fuse box is located at the left end of the instrument panel, under a cover

3.1b There are more fuses in the electronics box under the left side of the cowl

or loose connections.

Electrical troubleshooting is simple if you keep in mind that all electrical circuits are basically electricity running from the battery, through the wires, switches, relays, fuses and fusible links to each electrical component (light bulb, motor, etc.) and to ground, from which it is passed back to the battery. Any electrical problem is an interruption in the flow of electricity to and from the battery.

3 Fuses, fusible links and circuit breakers - general information

Fuses

Refer to illustrations 3.1a, 3.1b and 3.3

The electrical circuits of the vehicle are protected by a combination of fuses, circuit breakers and fusible links. The main fuse/relay panel is in the engine compartment **(see illustration)**, while the interior fuse/relay panel is located inside the passenger compartment **(see illustration)**. Each of the fuses is designed to protect a specific circuit, and the various circuits are identified on the fuse panel itself.

Several sizes of fuses are employed in the fuse blocks. There are small, medium and large sizes of the same design, all with the same blade terminal design. The medium and large fuses can be removed with your fingers, but the small fuses require the use of pliers or the small plastic fuse-puller tool found in most fuse boxes.

If an electrical component fails, always check the fuse first. The best way to check the fuses is with a test light. Check for power at the exposed terminal tips of each fuse. If power is present at one side of the fuse but not the other, the fuse is blown. A blown fuse can also be identified by visually inspecting it **(see illustration)**.

Be sure to replace blown fuses with the correct type. Fuses (of the same physical size) of different ratings may be physically interchangeable, but only fuses of the proper rating should be used. Replacing a fuse with one of a higher or lower value than specified is not recommended. Each electrical circuit needs a specific amount of protection. The amperage value of each fuse is molded into the top of the fuse body.

If the replacement fuse immediately fails, don't replace it again until the cause of the problem is isolated and corrected. In most cases, this will be a short circuit in the wiring caused by a broken or deteriorated wire.

Fusible links

Some circuits are protected by fusible links. The links are used in circuits which are not ordinarily fused, or which carry high current, such as the circuit between the alternator and the starter motor. Fusible links, which are usually several wire gauges smaller in size than the circuit that they protect, are designed to melt if the circuit is subjected to more current than it was designed to carry. If you have to replace a blown fusible link, make sure that you replace it with one of the same specification. If the replacement fusible link blows in the same circuit, make sure that you troubleshoot the circuit in which the fusible link melted BEFORE installing another fusible link.

Circuit breakers - general information

Circuit breakers protect certain circuits, such as the power windows or heated seats. Depending on the vehicle's accessories, there may be one or two circuit breakers, located in the fuse/relay box in the engine compartment.

Because the circuit breakers reset automatically, an electrical overload in a circuit breaker-protected system will cause the circuit to fail momentarily, then come back on. If the circuit does not come back on, check it immediately.

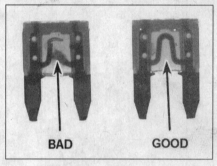

3.3 When a fuse blows, the element between the terminals melts

For a basic check, pull the circuit breaker up out of its socket on the fuse panel, but just far enough to probe with a voltmeter. The breaker should still contact the sockets. With the voltmeter negative lead on a good chassis ground, touch each end prong of the circuit breaker with the positive meter probe. There should be battery voltage at each end. If there is battery voltage only at one end, the circuit breaker must be replaced.

Some circuit breakers must be reset manually.

4 Relays - general information

Several electrical accessories in the vehicle, such as the fuel injection system, horns, starter, and fog lamps use relays to transmit the electrical signal to the component. Relays use a low-current circuit (the control circuit) to open and close a high-current circuit (the power circuit). If the relay is defective, that component will not operate properly. Most relays are mounted under the left end of the instrument panel.

5   Electrical connectors - general information

Most electrical connections on these vehicles are made with multiwire plastic connectors. The mating halves of many connectors are secured with locking clips molded into the plastic connector shells. The mating halves of some large connectors, such as some of those under the instrument panel, are held together by a bolt through the center of the connector.

To separate a connector with locking clips, use a small screwdriver to pry the clips apart carefully, then separate the connector halves. Pull only on the shell, never pull on the wiring harness as you may damage the individual wires and terminals inside the connectors. Look at the connector closely before trying to separate the halves. Often the locking clips are engaged in a way that is not immediately clear. Additionally, many connectors have more than one set of clips.

Each pair of connector terminals has a male half and a female half. When you look at the end view of a connector in a diagram, be sure to understand whether the view shows the harness side or the component side of the connector. Connector halves are mirror images of each other, and a terminal shown on the right side end-view of one half will be on the left side end-view of the other half.

It is often necessary to take circuit voltage measurements with a connector connected. Whenever possible, carefully insert a small straight pin (not your meter probe) into the rear of the connector shell to contact the terminal inside, then clip your meter lead to the pin. This kind of connection is called "back-probing." When inserting a test probe into a terminal, be careful not to distort the terminal opening. Doing so can lead to a poor connection and corrosion at that terminal later. Using the small straight pin instead of a meter probe results in less chance of deforming the terminal connector

Most electrical connectors have a single release tab that you depress to release the connector

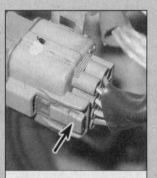

The single release tab might be on the side of the connector instead of on top (or on bottom!)

Some connectors have two release tabs that you must squeeze to release the connector

Some connectors use wire retainers that you squeeze to release the connector

Critical connectors often employ a sliding lock (1) that you must pull out before you can depress the release tab (2)

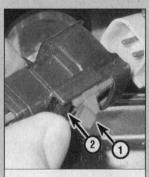

Here's another sliding-lock style connector, with the lock (1) and the release tab (2) on the side of the connector

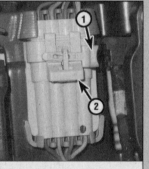

On some connectors the lock (1) must be pulled out to the side and removed before you can depress the release tab (2)

Some critical connectors, like the multi-pin connectors at the Powertrain Control Module employ pivoting locks that must be flipped open

6   Key fob - battery replacement and transmitter programming

Battery replacement

Refer to illustrations 6.3 and 6.4

1   Replace the battery when the key fob transmitter doesn't operate the locks at a distance of 10 feet. Normal range should be about 30 feet.
2   Before replacing the key fob battery, open the driver's door with the key.
3   Use a small screwdriver to carefully separate the case halves **(see illustration)**.
4   Replace the transmitter battery with a new battery **(see illustration)**.
5   Snap the case halves together and perform the synchronization procedure.

Transmitter programming (synchronization)

6   Open the door with the key.
7   Press the unlock button of the key fob.
8   Insert the key into the ignition lock and turn the ignition to the "ON" position.
9   Turn the ignition off and remove the key.
10   Press the unlock button on the key fob.
Note: *The synchronization procedure should be completed within 30 seconds.*
11   The locking system should respond - if not, remove and install the key fob battery and begin again.

7   Ignition switch and key lock cylinder - replacement

Refer to illustration 7.1

Warning: *The models covered by this manual are equipped with Supplemental Restraint Systems (SRS), more commonly known as airbags. Always disable the airbag system before working in the vicinity of any airbag system components to avoid the possibility of accidental deployment of the airbags, which*

6.3 Use a small screwdriver to separate the fob halves

could cause personal injury (see Section 23).
1   The ignition switch, located under the steering column (switch on the left, key lock cylinder on the right), is comprised of a cast-metal housing, an ignition lock cylinder and an electrical component, the switch device **(see illustration)**.
2   Disconnect the cable from the negative terminal of the battery (see Chapter 5).
3   Remove the steering column covers (see Chapter 11) and steering column switch assembly (see Section 8).

Key lock cylinder

Refer to illustrations 7.5, 7.6 and 7.7

4   On models with automatic transmissions, the shift linkage must be in Park before removing/installing the ignition switch. Insert the key into the lock and turn to the "ON" position.
5   Lift up the retaining clip and disconnect the park/lock cable from the ignition switch **(see illustration)**.
6   To remove the key lock cylinder, keep the key in the lock and rotated to the "ON" position and align the access hole with the

6.4 Remove the battery; note which way the battery is facing before you remove it

mark on the trim **(see illustration)**.
7   Insert the straightened end of a large paper clip into the hole in the cylinder **(see illustration)** and pull the key, lock cylinder and reader coil from the lock cylinder hous-

7.1 Lock housing assembly

A   *Ignition switch*
B   *Immobilizer reader coil*
C   *Key lock cylinder*

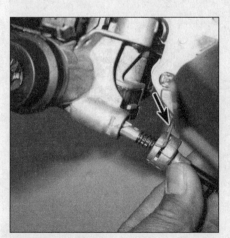

7.5 Lift up the retaining clip and slide the park/lock cable out

7.6 Access hole location

7.7 Insert a paper clip into the access hole and pull the assembly out

7.10 Disconnect the electrical connector from the ignition switch

7.11 Chip off the coating of the ignition switch fasteners and loosen (but do not remove) them

ing as an assembly. **Note:** *The reader coil is integrated into the lock cylinder and can't be replaced separately.*

8   When installing the key lock cylinder, align the cylinder as it was (still in "ON" position with the key in), then push the cylinder in until it snaps into position. Remove the paper clip, turn the key to the Lock position and remove the key.

9   Installation is the reverse of removal.

Ignition switch

Refer to illustrations 7.10 and 7.11

10   Disconnect the large electrical connector on the left side **(see illustration)**.

11   The switch retaining screw heads are coated with a special locking coating **(see illustration)**. Chip off the coating and loosen, but do not remove, the screws. Pull the switch out of the ignition assembly.

12   Installation is the reverse of removal.

Lock housing

13   Loosen the steering column mounting bolts and lower the steering column (see

Chapter 10). **Caution:** *The mounting brackets are easily damaged; do not use a chisel to remove the shear bolt heads.*

14   To remove the housing, cut slots into the heads of the shear bolts and use a blade screwdriver to remove the bolts, or drill the bolt heads out from the steering column bracket.

15   Installation is the reverse of removal. Tighten the new shear bolts until their heads break off.

---

8   Steering column switches - replacement

Refer to illustrations 8.5 and 8.7

Warning: *The models covered by this manual are equipped with Supplemental Restraint Systems (SRS), more commonly known as airbags. Always disable the airbag system before working in the vicinity of any airbag system components to avoid the possibility of accidental deployment of the airbags, which*

could cause personal injury (see Section 23).

1   The steering column switch module is located on the top of the steering column. It incorporates into one switch the turn signal, headlight dimmer, windshield wiper/washer, steering angle sensor and, if equipped, cruise control functions.

2   Disconnect the cable from the negative terminal of the battery (see Chapter 5). Remove the airbag module and steering wheel (see Chapter 10).

3   Remove the steering column covers (see Chapter 11).

4   Remove clockspring (see Chapter 10, Section 15).

5   Remove the fastener at the bottom of the steering column switch module **(see illustration)**.

6   Pull the steering column switch module out from the steering column enough to disconnect the electrical connectors.

7   Remove the individual switch fasteners **(see illustration)** and disconnect the switch(es) from the module.

8   Installation is the reverse of removal.

8.5 Steering column switch retaining fastener

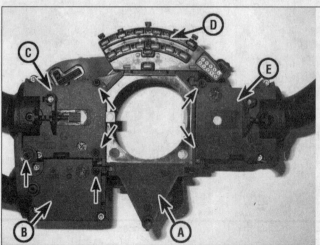

8.7 Remove the individual fasteners for the switch(es) and pull the switch from the module

A   Steering column switch module
B   Cruise control switch
C   Turn signal switch
D   Steering angle sensor - do not remove for switch replacement
E   Windshield wiper switch

9.1 Push in on the switch and twist it to the right (clockwise), then withdraw it from the instrument panel

9.5 With the headlight switch removed, pull the dimmer switch out from the dash

9   Instrument panel switches - replacement

Warning: *The models covered by this manual are equipped with Supplemental Restraint Systems (SRS), more commonly known as airbags. Always disable the airbag system before working in the vicinity of any airbag system components to avoid the possibility of accidental deployment of the airbags, which could cause personal injury (see Section 23).*

Headlight switch

Refer to illustration 9.1

1   Turn the headlight switch knob counterclockwise until it stops at the zero position. Push in on the switch and twist it to the right (clockwise), then withdraw it from the instrument panel **(see illustration)**.
2   Pull the switch out far enough to disconnect the electrical connector and remove the switch.
3   Installation is the reverse of removal.

Dash light dimmer switch

Refer to illustration 9.5

4   Remove the headlight switch as described in Steps 1 and 2.
5   Pull the dimmer switch out from the dashboard trim panel **(see illustration)** and disconnect the electrical connector.
6   Remove the dimmer switch.
7   Installation is the reverse of removal.

On/Off switches

Refer to illustrations 9.10 and 9.11

8   Depending on the options of the vehicle, there may be one or more switches on the instrument panel, including seat heaters, hazard flasher and rear window defogger.
9   All of the aforementioned switches are located in the switch panel at the center of the dashboard.
10   Remove the switch button cover **(see illustration)**
11   All of the switches are removed the same way. Use a pair of screwdrivers **(see illustra-**

tion) or trim tools to press the lock tabs in and release them from the switch panel, then pull them out far enough to disconnect the electrical connector.
12   Installation is the reverse of removal.

10   Instrument cluster - removal and installation

Refer to illustrations 10.3 and 10.6

Warning: *The models covered by this manual are equipped with Supplemental Restraint Systems (SRS), more commonly known as airbags. Always disable the airbag system before working in the vicinity of any airbag system components to avoid the possibility of accidental deployment of the airbags, which could cause personal injury (see Section 23).*
Note: *The instrument cluster is not serviceable and must be replaced as a complete unit. The new cluster must be programmed with a factory scan tool. For this reason it is*

9.10 Carefully pry the button switch cover off

9.11 Using two screwdrivers, push down on the locking tabs to release the switch

10.3 Instrument cluster fasteners

10.6 Lift up the lock lever to release the instrument cluster electrical connector

best to have an Audi dealer perform this job if replacement of the unit is required.

1   Disconnect the negative cable from the battery (see Chapter 5).

2   Remove the steering column upper trim cover (see Chapter 11).

3   Remove the screws securing the cluster to the instrument panel **(see illustration)**.

4   Remove the dashboard end cap (see Chapter 11).

5   Reach through the opening in the dashboard end and push the cluster forward from the back.

6   Disconnect the electrical connector(s) at the back **(see illustration)**, then pull the cluster out, tilting the top out first.

7   Installation is the reverse of removal.

---

11   Radio and speakers - removal and installation

Warning: *The models covered by this manual are equipped with Supplemental Restraint*

Systems (SRS), more commonly known as airbags. Always disable the airbag system before working in the vicinity of any airbag system components to avoid the possibility of accidental deployment of the airbags, which could cause personal injury (see Section 23).

Note: *The audio system is part of the diagnostic network of the vehicle. Any problems with the radio, antenna or speakers may set a trouble code that can be retrieved with a scan tool.*

Radio

Refer to illustrations 11.3, 11.4a and 11.4b

Caution: *On models equipped with the "Symphony II+" radio the transport mode must be activated before removing and deactivated after installation.*

1   Turn the ignition switch to the Off position and remove the key. Also turn the radio to Off.

2   On models with a Symphony II+ radio, press and hold buttons 3, 5 and Tone at the same time. After 5 seconds, "TRANSPORT" will appear in the radio display.

3   Two special tools, available at most auto parts stores, must be used to remove the radio **(see illustration)**. These tools can be fabricated from pieces of sheetmetal (like feeler gauges) if you can't purchase them.

4   Push the two tools into the slots on either side of the radio, pull the radio out of the instrument panel, disconnect the connectors, then remove the radio from the vehicle **(see illustrations)**.

5   To disengage the plastic tools from the radio before installation, depress the lugs on the side of the radio.

6   Installation is the reverse of removal. To cancel the "TRANSPORT" display, press and hold the CANCEL button until the display goes out.

Satellite Radio

Refer to illustration 11.9

7   Turn the ignition switch to the Off position and remove the key.

8   Open the trunk or liftgate and open the side storage compartment door.

9   Carefully pry open the face plate **(see**

11.3 Radio removal tools for the "Symphony II+" shown - others similar

11.4a Push the tools into the slots and pull the radio out

11.4b Disconnect the connectors from the rear of the radio

11.9 Carefully pry the face plate from the satellite radio cover

11.17 Disconnect the electrical connector and unscrew the fasteners

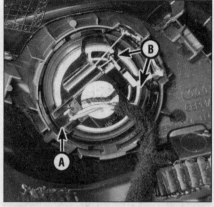

11.21 Midrange speaker details

A   Electrical connector
B   Retaining tabs

illustration) and remove the radio fasteners.
10   Slide the radio out enough to disconnect the electrical connectors and remove the unit.
11   Installation is the reverse of the removal procedure.

CD Changer

12   Turn the ignition switch to the Off position and remove the key.
13   Open the glove box.
14   Push the two tools into the slots on either side of the CD changer, pull the changer out of the glove box, disconnect the connectors, then remove it from the vehicle.
15   Installation is the reverse of the removal procedure.

Speakers

Door bass speakers

Refer to illustration 11.17

16   Remove the door panel (see Chapter 11).
17   Disconnect the electrical connector at the speaker, then remove the fasteners and remove the speaker **(see illustration)**.
18   Installation is the reverse of the removal procedure.

Door midrange speakers

Refer to illustration 11.21

19   On front doors, carefully pry the speaker off. **Note:** *If the front door bass speaker is being removed, do not remove the midrange speaker cover, and access the speaker from the back of the door panel.*
20   On rear doors, remove the door panel (see Chapter 11).
21   Disconnect the electrical connector at the speaker, release the retaining tabs and remove the speaker **(see illustration)**.
22   Installation is the reverse of the removal procedure.

Subwoofer

Sedans

Refer to illustrations 11.23a, 11.23b, 11.25, and 11.27

23   Remove the rear headliner trim panel, handle and "D" pillar trim **(see illustrations)**.
24   Pry the subwoofer cover off using a trim tool.
25   Remove the fasteners **(see illustration)** from the rear parcel shelf and remove the shelf.

26   Disconnect the electrical connector and the front mounting fasteners.
27   Open the trunk and remove the lower fastener **(see illustration)**.
28   Remove the subwoofer from inside. Installation is the reverse of the removal procedure.

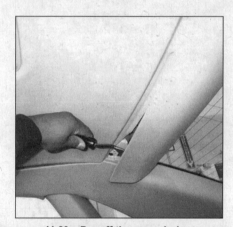

11.23a Pry off the rear window trim panel . . .

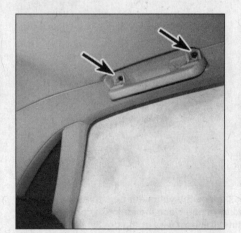

11.23b . . . remove the upper handle and remove the rear side trim

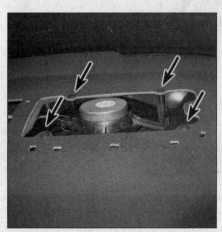

11.25 Remove the upper fasteners and remove the parcel shelf

11.27 Remove the lower subwoofer fastener

11.34 Center dashboard speaker fasteners

13.5 When measuring the voltage at the rear window defogger grid, wrap a piece of aluminum foil around the positive probe of the voltmeter and press the foil against the wire with your finger

Avant and Cabriolet

29   Open the liftgate or trunk and remove the passengers side trim panel.
30   Disconnect the electrical connectors.
31   Remove the four fasteners, then remove the amplifier and the subwoofer.
32   Installation is the reverse of the removal procedure.

Center dashboard speaker

Refer to illustration 11.34

33   Remove the optical sensor and defrost vent (see Chapter 11, Section 29).
34   Remove the fasteners **(see illustration)** and rotate the speaker down and out enough to disconnect the electrical connector.
35   Remove the speaker from the dash.
36   Installation is the reverse of the removal procedure.

12   Antenna - removal and installation

Note: *There are two types of antennas used on these models, a grid type and roof mounted type. The grid type is an integral component of the rear windshield on coupes and sedans and an integral part of the rear side windows on wagons. To replace these antennas you must replace the rear windshield or side window(s).*

1   Remove the rear headliner trim and "D" pillar trim from both sides **(see illustrations 11.23a and 11.23b)**.
2   Remove rear reading light or luggage compartment light (wagons) housing (see Section 17).
3   Disconnect the antenna cable(s).
4   Carefully pull down the headliner at the rear.

5   Remove the mounting nut and antenna from the roof.
6   Installation is reverse of removal.

13   Rear window defogger - check and repair

1   The rear window defogger consists of a number of horizontal heating elements baked onto the inside surface of the glass. Power is supplied through a large fuse from the fuse/relay box in the dash area. Refer to the wiring diagrams at the end of Chapter 12. The heater is controlled by the instrument panel switch.
2   Small breaks in the element can be repaired without removing the rear window.

Check

Refer to illustrations 13.5, 13.6 and 13.8

3   Turn the ignition switch and defogger switch to the ON position.
4   Using a voltmeter, place the positive probe against the defogger grid positive terminal and the negative probe against the ground terminal. If battery voltage is not indicated, check the fuse, defogger switch, defogger relay and related wiring. If voltage is indicated, but all or part of the defogger doesn't heat, proceed with the following tests.
5   When measuring voltage during the next two tests, wrap a piece of aluminum foil around the tip of the voltmeter positive probe and press the foil against the heating element with your finger **(see illustration)**. Place the negative probe on the defogger grid ground terminal.
6   Check the voltage at the center of each heating element **(see illustration)**. If the voltage is 5 to 6 volts, the element is okay (there

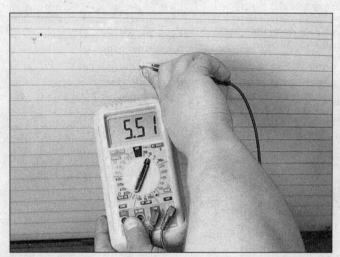

13.6 To determine if a heating element has broken, check the voltage at the center of each element - if the voltage is 6-volts, the element is unbroken

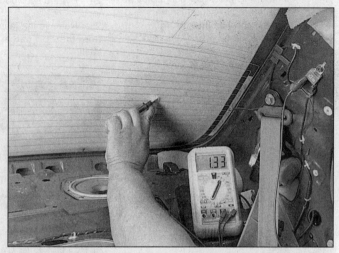

13.8 To find the break, place the voltmeter negative lead against the defogger ground terminal, place the voltmeter positive lead with the foil strip against the heat wire at the positive terminal end and slide it toward the negative terminal end - the point at which the voltmeter deflects from several volts to zero volts is the point at which the wire is broken

is no break). If the voltage is 0 volts, the element is broken between the center of the element and the positive end. If the voltage is 10 to 12 volts, the element is broken between the center of the element and the ground side. Check each heating element.

7   If none of the elements are broken, connect the negative probe to a good chassis ground. The voltage reading should stay the same - if it doesn't, the ground connection is bad.

8   To find the break, place the voltmeter negative probe against the defogger ground terminal. Place the voltmeter positive probe with the foil strip against the heating element at the positive side and slide it toward the negative side. The point at which the voltmeter deflects from several volts to zero is the point where the heating element is broken **(see illustration)**.

Repair

Refer to illustration 13.14

9   Repair the break in the element using a repair kit specifically for this purpose, such as DuPont paste No. 4817 (or equivalent). The kit includes conductive plastic epoxy.

10   Before repairing a break, turn off the system and allow it to cool for a few minutes.

11   Lightly buff the element area with fine steel wool, then clean it thoroughly with rubbing alcohol.

12   Use masking tape to mask off the area being repaired.

13   Thoroughly mix the epoxy, following the kit instructions.

14   Apply the epoxy material to the slit in the masking tape, overlapping the undamaged area by about 3/4-inch on either end **(see illustration)**.

15   Allow the repair to cure for 24 hours before removing the tape and using the system.

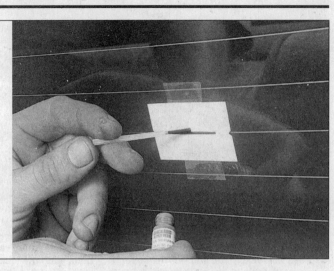

13.14 To use a defogger repair kit, apply masking to the inside of the window at the damaged area, then brush on the special conductive coating

14   Headlight housing - replacement

Models with halogen bulbs

Models built 10/2004 and before

1   Remove the engine compartment covers depending on which headlight is going to be removed.

2   On the passenger's side headlight only, remove the air intake (see Chapter 4).

3   Apply masking tape onto the body areas surrounding the headlight housing to prevent damage.

4   Remove the upper fasteners and loosen, but do not remove, the lower bolt.

5   Disconnect the electrical connector.

6   Rotate the housing towards the fender and pull the headlight housing all the way out.

7   The remainder of installation is the reverse of the removal procedure. Refer to Section 16 for adjusting procedures after the headlight housing is installed.

Models built 11/2004 and after

Refer to illustrations 14.9 and 14.10

8   Remove the bumper cover (see Chapter 11).

9   Remove the center headlight housing fastener (A) and loosen, but do not remove, the inner and outer fasteners (B) and (C) **(see illustration)**. **Note:** *Loosen the outer fastener (C) through the access hole in the fender.*

10   Slide the headlight housing forward, disconnect the wiring from the headlight and remove the housing **(see illustration)**.

11   Install the housing but do not fully tighten the fasteners. Install the bumper cover (see Chapter 11).

12   Check for a proper gap between the headlight housing and the bumper cover. If the gap is correct, securely tighten the housing mounting fasteners.

13   The remainder of installation is the reverse of removal.

14.9 Headlight housing details

A   *Center mounting fastener (remove)*
B   *Inner mounting fastener (loosen only)*
C   *Outer mounting fastener access hole (loosen fastener only)*

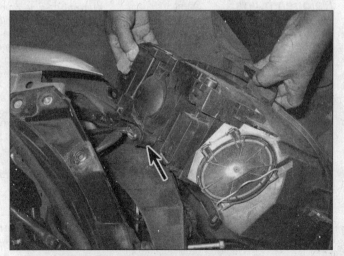

14.10 Slide the headlight housing out and disconnect the electrical connector

15.6a If you're replacing a low-beam bulb, depress the locking tab and pull the cover back (headlight housing removed for clarity)

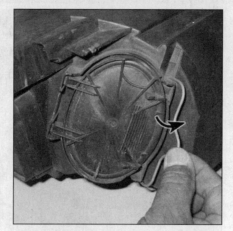

15.6b If you're replacing a high-beam bulb, snap the lock spring over and open the cover (headlight housing removed for clarity)

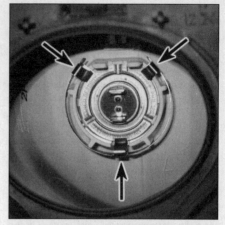

15.8 Depress the spring clips starting at the top and remove the spring - low beam shown, high beam similar

Models with xenon (HID) bulbs

Warning: *Some models use High Intensity Discharge (HID) bulbs instead of halogen bulbs. These can be identified by the high-voltage warning sticker on the headlight housing. According to the manufacturer, the high voltages produced by this system can be fatal in the event of a shock. Also, the voltage can remain in the circuit even after the headlight switch has been turned to OFF and the ignition key has been removed. Therefore, for your safety, we don't recommend that you try to remove one these headlight housings. Instead, have this service performed by a dealer service department or other qualified repair shop.*

---

15   Headlight bulb - replacement

Halogen bulbs

Warning: *Halogen bulbs are gas-filled and under pressure and may shatter if the surface is scratched or the bulb is dropped. Wear eye protection and handle the bulbs carefully, grasping only the base whenever possible. Don't touch the surface of the bulb with your fingers because the oil from your skin could cause it to overheat and fail prematurely. If you do touch the bulb surface, clean it with rubbing alcohol.*

Models built 10/2004 and earlier

1   Refer to Section 14 and remove the headlight housing.
2   Disconnect the bulb electrical connectors.
3   Remove the outer (low beam) or inner (high beam) bulb holder from the back of the headlight housing. Remove the old bulb from the holder.
4   Handling the new bulb only with gloves or a clean rag, insert the new bulb in the holder.

5   Installation of the housing is the reverse of the removal procedure.

Models built 11/2004 and later Halogen bulbs

Refer to illustrations 15.6a, 15.6b and 15.8

6   Remove any interfering engine compartment covers/air intake ducts for access to the headlight housing. Open the plastic cover from the back of the headlight housing **(see illustrations)**.
7   Disconnect the electrical connector.
8   Push the retaining spring clips in towards the center to release the bulb **(see illustration)**.
9   Pull the bulb straight out of the socket. Make sure to avoid touching the new bulb with your fingers (see **Warning** in this Section).
10   Installation is the reverse of removal.

Xenon (HID) bulbs

Warning: *Some models use High Intensity Discharge (HID) bulbs instead of halogen bulbs. These can be identified by the high-voltage warning sticker on the headlight housing. According to the manufacturer, the high voltages produced by this system can be fatal in the event of a shock. Also, the voltage can remain in the circuit even after the headlight switch has been turned to OFF and the ignition key has been removed. Therefore, for your safety, we don't recommend that you try to replace one of these bulbs yourself. Instead, have this service performed by a dealer service department or other qualified repair shop.*

---

16   Headlights - adjustment

Refer to illustrations 16.1 and 16.2

Warning: *The headlights must be aimed correctly. If adjusted incorrectly, they could temporarily blind the driver of an oncoming*

vehicle and cause an accident or seriously reduce your ability to see the road. The headlights should be checked for proper aim every 12 months and any time a new headlight is installed or front-end bodywork is performed. The following procedure is only an interim step to provide temporary adjustment until the headlights can be adjusted by a properly equipped shop.

Note: *Some models are equipped with a headlight leveling system. This adjustment procedure will not apply to those models. Have the headlights adjusted by a dealer service department or other qualified repair shop.*

1   These models are equipped with headlight housings with two adjustment screws, one controlling left-and-right movement and one for up-and-down movement **(see illustration)**.
2   There are several methods of adjusting the headlights. The simplest method requires an open area with a blank wall and a level

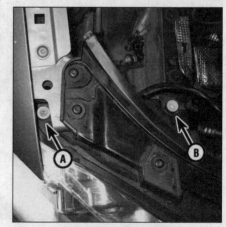

16.1 Headlight adjustment screws

A   *Horizontal (side-to-side) adjuster*
B   *Vertical (up-and-down) adjuster*

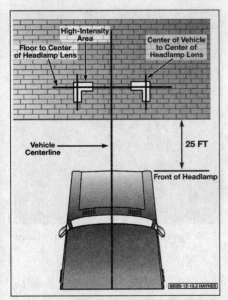

16.2 Headlight adjustment details

floor **(see illustration)**.

3   Position masking tape vertically on the wall in reference to the vehicle centerline and the centerlines of both headlights.

4   Position a horizontal tape line in reference to the centerline of all the headlights. **Note:** *It may be easier to position the tape on the wall with the vehicle parked only a few inches away.*

5   Adjustment should be made with the vehicle parked 25 feet from the wall, sitting level, the gas tank half-full and no unusually heavy load in the vehicle.

6   Starting with the low beam adjustment, position the high intensity zone so it is two inches below the horizontal line and two inches to the side of the vertical headlight line, away from oncoming traffic. Twist the adjustment screws until the desired level has been achieved.

7   With the high beams on, the high intensity zone should be vertically centered with the exact center just below the horizontal line. **Note:** *It may not be possible to position the headlight aim exactly for both high and low beams. If a compromise must be made, keep in mind that the low beams are the most used and have the greatest effect on driver safety.*

8   Have the headlights adjusted by a dealer service department at the earliest opportunity.

17   Bulb - replacement

Warning: *Bulbs can remain hot for up to twenty minutes after they're turned off. Be sure bulbs are off and cool before you touch them.*

Front turn signal light

Models built 10/2004 and before

1   Refer to Section 14 and remove the headlight housing.
2   Disconnect the bulb electrical connectors.
3   Installation of the housing is the reverse of the removal procedure.

Models built 11/2004 and after

Refer to illustration 17.5

4   Remove the fasteners from the front section of the inner fender liner (see Chapter 11) and pull the liner back.
5   Reach up and twist the bulb holder counterclockwise and remove it from the headlight housing **(see illustration)**. Replace the bulb by pulling the bulb straight out of the bulb holder. Installation is the reverse of removal.

Front parking light

6   Remove any interfering engine compartment covers/air intake ducts for access to the headlight housing.
7   Open the plastic cover for the high-beam bulb on the back of the headlight housing **(see illustration 15.6b)**.
8   Pull the parking light bulb holder out of the headlight housing, then pull the bulb

from the holder. Installation is the reverse of removal.

Side-marker lights

Refer to illustration 17.9

9   Push the back of the marker light housing forward and lift it out of the fender **(see illustration)**.
10   Twist the bulb holder counterclockwise to remove it, then replace the bulb.
11   Installation is the reverse of the removal procedure. Make sure the hook (forward) end of the light housing goes in first, then snap the housing in place until the tab is engaged.

Tail/stop/turn/back-up lights

Refer to illustrations 17.12, 17.13 and 17.15

12   Open the trunk or liftgate, pull the fastener cover back and remove the housing fastener **(see illustration)**.
13   Swing the inboard part of the light housing outward, disengage the locking pins and remove the housing **(see illustration)**.
14   Pull the taillight housing out and disconnect the electrical connectors.

17.5 Rotate the bulb holder counterclockwise and pull the holder from the housing - headlight housing removed for clarity

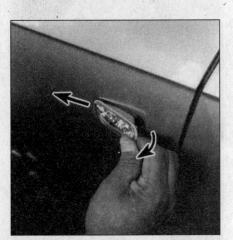

17.9 Push the side-marker light housing forward and remove the housing from the fender, back end first

17.12 Pull the taillight housing access cover down and remove the mounting fastener

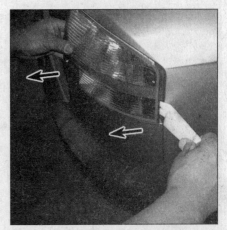

17.13 Carefully pry on the ballstud side of the housing while pulling from the opposite side

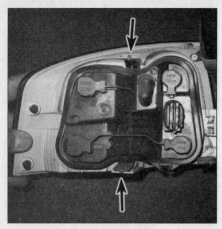

17.15 Squeeze the two tabs to release the bulb holder

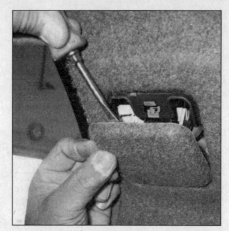

17.18 Use a screwdriver to disengage the mounting clip and cover

17.19 Spread the retaining tabs to release the bulb assembly

15   Squeeze the release tabs to unlock the bulb assembly **(see illustration)** and remove the bulb holder from the housing.

16   Twist the bulbs counterclockwise to remove them for replacement.

17   Installation is the reverse of removal.

Tail/rear fog light

Refer to illustrations 17.18 and 17.19

18   The tail/rear fog lights are located on the trunk lid. Open the trunk lid and locate the door cover; use a screwdriver to pry the door open **(see illustration)**.

19   Spread the release clips to unlock the bulb assembly **(see illustration)**.

20   Pull the housing out and disconnect the electrical connectors. Twist the bulb counterclockwise to remove the bulb.

21   Installation is the reverse of removal.

High-mount brake light

Sedans

Refer to illustration 17.23

22   Refer to Chapter 11 and remove the inner trim panel from the rear shelf, directly

against the rear window.

23   Disconnect the electrical connector and press the retaining clips away from the light assembly **(see illustration)**.

24   Rotate the assembly back and guide it through the access hole. **Note:** *The high-mount brake light must be replaced as a unit; the individual LED lights are not serviceable.*

Wagons

25   Refer to Chapter 11 and remove the inner trim panel from the rear hatch.

26   Insert a screwdriver through the same hole that the brake light harness runs through and press the light assembly down and towards the right, releasing the spring tabs.

27   Pull the housing from the hatch and disconnect the electrical connector. **Note:** *The high-mount brake light must be replaced as a unit; the individual LED lights are not serviceable.*

Cabriolet

28   Remove the rear trunk lid trim.

29   Remove the six retaining fasteners, remove the light assembly from the body cutout and disconnect the electrical connector.

Note: *The high-mount brake light must be replaced as a unit; the individual LED lights are not serviceable.*

All models

30   Installation is the reverse of the removal procedure.

License plate light bulb

Refer to illustration 17.31

31   Use a small screwdriver to remove the mounting screw of the license plate light, then tilt and pull out the light housing **(see illustration)**.

32   Remove the bulb from the bulb holder.

33   Installation is the reverse of removal.

Interior lights

Instrument cluster lights

34   The instrument cluster is illuminated by LEDs that are part of the printed circuit board. There are no user-replaceable bulbs behind the instrument cluster. Consult with a dealer service department or other qualified repair shop; some facilities might be equipped to repair the cluster, or might offer an exchange

17.23 High-mount brake light details

A   Electrical connector
B   Locking clips

17.31 License plate light retaining screw

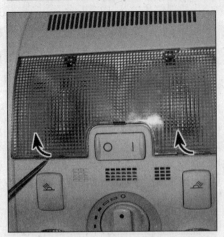

17.35a Carefully pry the lens cover off, using a small flat-blade screwdriver

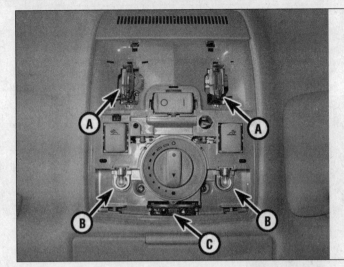

17.35b Front overhead lighting assembly details

A   Front dome light bulbs
B   Front reading light bulbs
C   Ambient light LEDs

program. If the instrument cluster is replaced, it will have to be programmed with a proprietary Audi scan tool.

Front dome lights

Refer to illustrations 17.35a and 17.35b

35   Remove the dome light lens (**see illustration**), then remove the bulb(s) by pulling straight out (**see illustration**).
36   Installation is the reverse of removal.

Front reading lights

Refer to illustration 17.37

37   Remove the front light cover trim (**see illustration**). Remove the bulb(s) (**see illustration 17.35b**).
38   Installation is the reverse of removal.

Vanity lights

Refer to illustration 17.39

39   Pry the light out of the headliner carefully with a small screwdriver (**see illustration**).
40   Unhook the bulb cover, then remove the bulb by pulling it straight out.
41   Installation is the reverse of removal.

Glovebox light

42   Open the glovebox door and pry the light out of the glovebox carefully with a small screwdriver.
43   Remove the bulb by pulling it straight out of the bulb holder.
44   Installation is the reverse of removal.

Rear reading lights

Refer to illustrations 17.45 and 17.46

45   Pry the light assembly out of the headliner carefully with a trim tool (**see illustration**).
46   Replace the bulb by twisting it counterclockwise and pulling it out (**see illustration**).
47   Installation is the reverse of removal.

Luggage compartment lights

48   Pry the light assembly from the trunk lid, liftgate or trunk floor opening depending on the model and disconnect the electrical connector.
49   Remove the bulb by pulling it straight out of the light assembly.
50   Installation is the reverse of removal.

18   Horn - replacement

Models built 10/2004 and before

Note: *There are two horns; one mounted behind each headlight.*

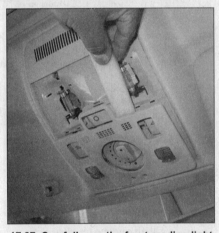

17.37 Carefully pry the front reading light trim out

17.39 Pry out the vanity light housing using a small screwdriver

17.45 Carefully pry the rear reading light assembly from the headliner

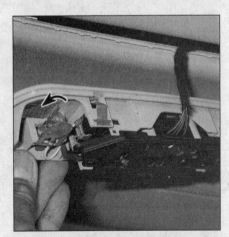

17.46 Rotate the bulb counterclockwise and pull it straight out of the holder

1   Remove the headlight housing (see Section 14).
2   Disconnect the electrical connector, remove the fasteners and detach the horn.
3   Installation is the reverse of removal.

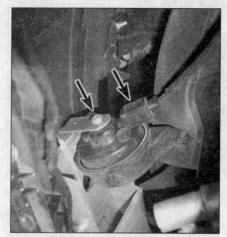

18.5 Disconnect the electrical connector and unscrew the bolt, then remove the horn

19.2 Pry the cover off the wiper arm, then remove the nut

Models built 11/2004 and after

Refer to illustration 18.5

Note: *The horn is bolted to the end of the front bumper reinforcement bar.*

4   If you're working on a V6 model, remove the forward under-vehicle splash shield. If you're working on a four-cylinder model, remove the bumper cover (see Chapter 11).
5   Disconnect the electrical connector **(see illustration)**, remove the fastener and detach the horn.
6   Installation is the reverse of removal.

---

19   Wiper motor - replacement

Front wiper motor

Refer to illustrations 19.2, 19.6 and 19.7

1   Turn the ignition switch to the Off position and remove the key.
2   Mark the positions of the wiper arm(s) on the windshield, remove the nuts, then remove the wiper arm using a rocking motion **(see illustration)**.
3   Remove the windshield cowl cover and weatherstrip (see Chapter 11).
4   Remove the cover from the ECM (see Chapter 6).
5   Remove the ECM housing mounting nuts and push the housing forward for added clearance.
6   Remove the windshield wiper motor/linkage assembly fasteners **(see illustration)**.
7   Disconnect the wiper motor electrical connector and pry off the wiper link from the ballstud **(see illustration)**.
8   Lift the windshield wiper motor assembly from the cowl area.
9   Remove the wiper motor fasteners and separate the motor from the assembly.
10   Installation is the reverse of removal.

Rear wiper motor

11   Turn the ignition switch to the Off position and remove the key.

12   Mark the position of the wiper arm on the windshield, then carefully pry the base cap apart and lift off.
13   Detach the rear spray jet and loosen, but do not remove, the wiper arm nut.
14   Carefully rock the wiper arm back and forth until it is loose and remove nut and wiper arm.
15   Remove the inner trim panel from the hatch area (see Chapter 11).
16   Disconnect the wiper motor harness connector and remove the windshield wiper motor mounting bolts.
17   Lift the windshield wiper motor assembly from the hatch area.
18   Installation is the reverse of removal.

---

20   Cruise control system - description and check

These vehicles have an electrically controlled throttle body. The accelerator pedal communicates with the throttle body through the Powertrain Control Module (PCM) (see Chapters 4 and 6 for more information about the electronic throttle control system). The PCM also controls the cruise control system, which is now an integral function of the electronic throttle control system. If the system malfunctions, begin diagnosis by checking to see if any trouble codes have been set (see Chapter 6). If that doesn't lead to the problem, take it to a dealer service department or other qualified repair shop for further diagnosis.

---

21   Power window system - general information

Note: *These vehicles are equipped with various control modules that govern the door locks, the power windows, the ignition lock and security system, the interior and exterior lights, the headlights, the horn, the windshield wipers/washers, the heating/air conditioning*

19.6 Wiper linkage fastener locations

19.7 Pry off the wiper link from the ballstud

system, the audio system and the power mirrors. In the event of a malfunction with one of these systems, have the vehicle diagnosed by a dealership service department or other qualified automotive repair facility if no obvious problems are found.

The power window system operates electric motors, mounted on the doors, which lower and raise the windows. The system consists of the control switches, the motors, regulators, glass mechanisms and associated wiring.

The power windows can be lowered and raised from the master control switch by the driver or by the switch located at the passenger window. Each window has a separate motor that is reversible. The position of the control switch determines the polarity and therefore the direction of operation.

The circuit is protected by fuses and a circuit breaker. Check the fuses in the fuse panel at the left end of the instrument panel. Each motor is equipped with an internal circuit breaker; this prevents one stuck window from disabling the whole system. Refer to the wiring diagrams at the end of Chapter 12. Problems within this system can only be diagnosed with a professional-grade scan tool. If you have eliminated the obvious causes of a problem, have the vehicle checked at a dealership service department or other properly equipped repair shop.

22 Power door lock system - general information

Note: *These vehicles are equipped with various control modules that govern the door locks, the power windows, the ignition lock and security system, the interior and exterior lights, the headlights, the horn, the windshield wipers/washers, the heating/air conditioning system, the audio system and the power mirrors. In the event of a malfunction with one of these systems, have the vehicle diagnosed by a dealership service department or other qualified automotive repair facility if no obvious problems are found.*

The central locking system uses two actuators (motors) integrated into each door lock. The actuators are not serviceable separately and if one is bad the entire lock assembly must be replaced. The power door lock systems operate bi-directional motors. The first motor locks the exterior door and the second motor locks the interior door latch assembly, called the safe function. This no longer allows the doors to open from the interior door handles when the doors are locked. **Note:** *In the event of an accident in which the airbags have been deployed, the locking system control module will open all locked doors.*

The central locking system control module is located on the driver's side floor, directly in front of the driver's seat under the floor mat. Problems within this module can only be diagnosed with a factory scan tool. If you have eliminated the obvious causes of a problem,

have the vehicle checked at a dealership service department or other properly equipped repair shop.

23 Airbag system - general information and system component removal and installation

1   These models are equipped with a Supplemental Restraint System (SRS), more commonly known as airbags, designed to protect the driver and the passenger from serious injury in the event of a head-on or side collision. All models have a diagnostic control unit, located on the floor under the center console **(see illustration 23.11)**. **Warning:** *If your vehicle is ever involved in a flood, or the interior carpeting is soaked for any reason, disconnect the battery and do not start the vehicle until the airbag system can be checked by your dealer. If the SRS system is subjected to flooding, the airbags could go off upon starting the vehicle, even without an accident taking place.*

Airbag modules

2   The airbag modules consist of a housing incorporating the cushion (airbag) and inflator unit. The inflator assembly is mounted on the back of the housing over a hole through which gas is expelled, inflating the bag almost instantaneously when an electrical signal is sent from the system. The specially-wound wire on the driver's side that carries this signal to the driver's module is called a clockspring. The clockspring is a flat, ribbon-like electrically conductive tape that is wound many times so that it can transmit an electrical signal regardless of steering wheel position. Airbag modules are located in the steering wheel, on the passenger side above the glovebox, at the upper side of each front seat (side-impact airbags) and head-level airbags located along the roof rails (side curtain airbags).

Control unit and sensors

3   The sensing/diagnostic control unit contains an on-board microprocessor which monitors the operation of the system, and the crash sensors. The crash sensors are located in the front and sides of the vehicle. It checks this system every time the vehicle is started, causing the "AIRBAG" light to illuminate for five seconds, then go off, if the system is operating properly. If there is a fault in the system, the light may not come on at all, or the light will come on and stay on, either illuminated steadily or blinking, and the unit will store fault codes indicating the nature of the fault.

Operation

4   For the airbag(s) to deploy, the impact sensor(s) must be activated. When this condition occurs, the circuit to the airbag inflator is closed and the airbag inflates.

Self-diagnosis system

5   A self-diagnosis circuit in the control unit displays a light on the instrument panel when the ignition switch is turned to the On position. If the system is operating normally, the light should go out after about five seconds. If the light doesn't come on, or doesn't go out after a short time, or if it comes on while you're driving the vehicle, or if it blinks at any time, there's a malfunction in the SRS system. Have it inspected and repaired as soon as possible. Do not attempt to troubleshoot or service the SRS system yourself. Even a small mistake could cause the SRS system to malfunction when you need it.

Servicing components near the SRS system

6   Nevertheless, there are times when you need to remove the steering wheel or radio, or service other components on or near the dashboard. At these times, you'll be working around components and wire harnesses for the SRS system. **Warning:** *Do not use electrical test equipment on airbag system wires; it could cause the airbag(s) to deploy.* **ALWAYS DISABLE THE SRS SYSTEM BEFORE WORKING NEAR THE SRS SYSTEM COMPONENTS OR RELATED WIRING.**

Disabling the SRS system

Warning: *Any time you are working in the vicinity of airbag wiring or components, DISABLE THE SRS SYSTEM.*
Warning: *An auxiliary voltage input device (memory saver) must NOT be used when working near airbag system components.*

7   To disable the airbag system, perform the following steps:

a)   *Turn the steering wheel to the straight-ahead position and turn the ignition switch to the Lock position, then remove the key.*
b)   *Disconnect the negative battery cable (see Chapter 5).*
c)   *Before touching any airbag system component, ground yourself to a metal part of the vehicle to discharge any static electricity built up in your body.*

Enabling the system

8   To enable the airbag system, perform the following steps:

a)   *Turn the ignition switch to the On position.*
b)   *Make sure nobody is inside the vehicle.*
c)   *Connect the battery cable.*
d)   *Turn the ignition to the Off position, then with your body out of the path of the airbag, turn the ignition switch to the On position. Confirm that the airbag warning light is functioning properly.*
e)   *Take the vehicle to a dealer service department or other qualified repair facility and have the airbag system checked and the diagnostic light canceled, if it remains lit.*

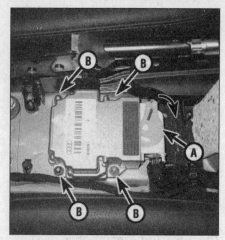

23.11 Rotate the airbag control unit harness lock (A) to disconnect the harness, then remove the mounting fasteners (B) and carefully remove the control unit

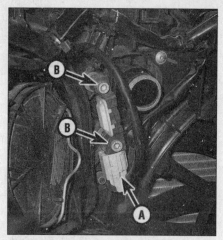

23.14a Driver's side front impact sensor details

A Electrical connector
B Mounting fasteners

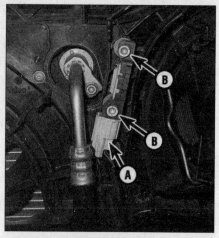

23.14b Passenger's side front impact sensor details

A Electrical connector
B Mounting fasteners

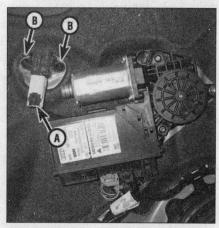

23.18 Side-front impact sensor details (models produced after 11/2004)

A Electrical connector
B Mounting fasteners

Removal and installation
Control unit

Refer to illustration 23.11

9   Disable the airbag system as described earlier in this Section.
10   Remove the center console (see Chapter 11).
11   Swing open the electrical connector lock, then disconnect the control unit connector and remove the mounting fasteners **(see illustration)**. Carefully remove the control unit from the vehicle.
12   Installation is the reverse of the removal procedure.

Impact (crash) sensors
Front

Refer to illustrations 23.14a and 23.14b

13   Disable the airbag system as described earlier in this Section.

14   Working under the hood, disconnect the impact sensor connector **(see illustrations)**, remove the mounting fasteners and carefully remove the sensor(s).
15   Installation is the reverse of the removal procedure.

Side-front

Refer to illustration 23.18

16   Disable the airbag system as described earlier in this Section.
17   Remove the front door panel (see Chapter 11). **Note:** *On some earlier models (vehicles built from 2002 to 10/2004), the side-front impact sensors are located at the bottom of the "B" pillar.*
18   Disconnect the impact sensor connector **(see illustration)**, remove the mounting fasteners and carefully remove the sensor from the door.
19   Installation is the reverse of the removal procedure.

23.21 Loosen the nut, then remove the latch bolt

23.22 Remove the lower side seat pad fasteners and pad

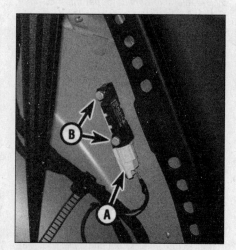

23.23 Side-rear impact sensor details

A Electrical connector
B Mounting fasteners

23.28 Disconnect the passenger's side airbag connector

23.29 Remove the dash support brace fasteners

Side-rear

Refer to illustrations 23.21, 23.22 and 23.23

20   Remove the rear seat (see Chapter 11).
21   Remove the rear seat latch bolt **(see illustration)** and remove the bolt. **Note:** *On some earlier models, the side-rear impact sensors are located at the bottom of the "C" pillar.*
22   Remove the lower side seat pad fastener **(see illustration)** and pull the pad off.
23   Disconnect sensor connector **(see illustration)**, remove the mounting fasteners and carefully remove the sensor from the door.
24   Installation is the reverse of the removal procedure.

Driver's airbag

25   Refer to Chapter 10 for removal and installation of the driver's airbag located in the steering wheel.

Passenger's airbag

Refer to illustrations 23.28, 23.29 and 23.30

26   Disable the airbag system as described earlier in this Section.
27   Remove the glovebox and its dash panel (see Chapter 11).
28   From under the instrument panel, disconnect the passenger airbag connector **(see illustration)**.
29   Remove the dash support brace fasteners **(see illustration)** and slide the braces out from the dash.
30   Remove the airbag mounting nuts and the mounting bracket fasteners **(see illustration)**.
31   Gently pry the airbag module from the brackets on the dash support and remove the airbag from the dash. **Warning:** *Whenever handling an airbag module, always carry the airbag module with the trim panel side facing*

away from your body. Place the airbag module in a safe location with the trim panel side facing up. **Caution:** *The airbag assembly is heavier than it looks; use both hands when removing it from the dash.*
32   Installation is the reverse of the removal procedure.

Side curtain airbags

Refer to illustrations 23.35, 23.36a and 23.36b

33   Disable the airbag system as described earlier in this Section.
34   The side curtain airbags are concealed beneath the door pillar trim pieces. Refer to Chapter 11 and remove the side covers of the door pillars.
35   Disconnect the airbag wiring **(see illustration)**.
36   The side curtain airbag is a long one-

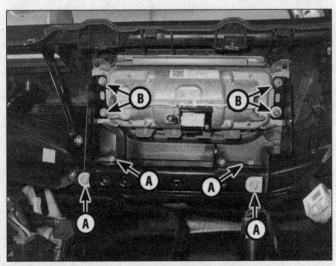

23.30 Passenger's side airbag mounting details

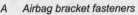

A   Airbag bracket fasteners
B   Airbag mounting nuts

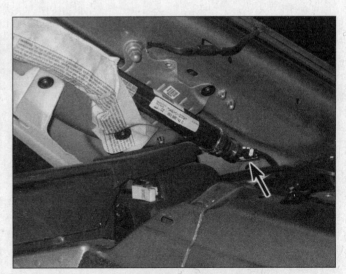

23.35 Disconnect the side curtain airbag connector

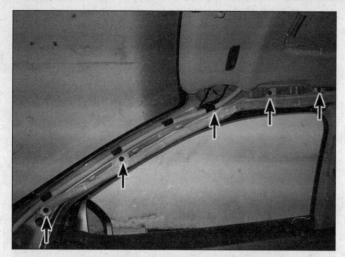

23.36a Remove the side curtain airbag fasteners starting from the front . . .

23.36b . . . then remove the remaining fasteners and lift the entire assembly out

piece unit. Remove the screws and detach the airbag from the retaining clips **(see illustrations)**. **Warning:** *Be sure to ground your body using a special wrist strap or a similar device connected to a solid ground on the vehicle's body. Place the airbag module in a safe place with the trim panel side facing up.*

37   Installation is the reverse of removal.

Impact seat belt retractors

38   All models are equipped with pyrotechnic (explosive) units in the front seat belt retracting mechanisms for both the lap and shoulder belts. During an impact that would trigger the airbag system, the airbag control unit also triggers the seat belt retractors. When the pyrotechnic charges go off, they accelerate the retractors to instantly take up any slack in the seat belt system to more fully secure the driver and front seat passenger for impact.

39   The airbag system should be disabled any time work is done on or around the seats. **Caution:** *Never strike the pillars or floorpan with a hammer or use an impact-driver tool in these areas unless the system is disabled.*

---

24 Wiring diagrams - general information

Since it isn't possible to include all wiring diagrams for every year and model covered by this manual, the following diagrams are those that are typical and most commonly needed.

Prior to troubleshooting any circuits, check the fuses and circuit breakers (if equipped) to make sure they're in good condition. Make sure the battery is properly charged and check the cable connections (see Chapter 1).

When checking a circuit, make sure that all connectors are clean, with no broken or loose terminals. When disconnecting a connector, do not pull on the wires. Pull only on the connector housings themselves.

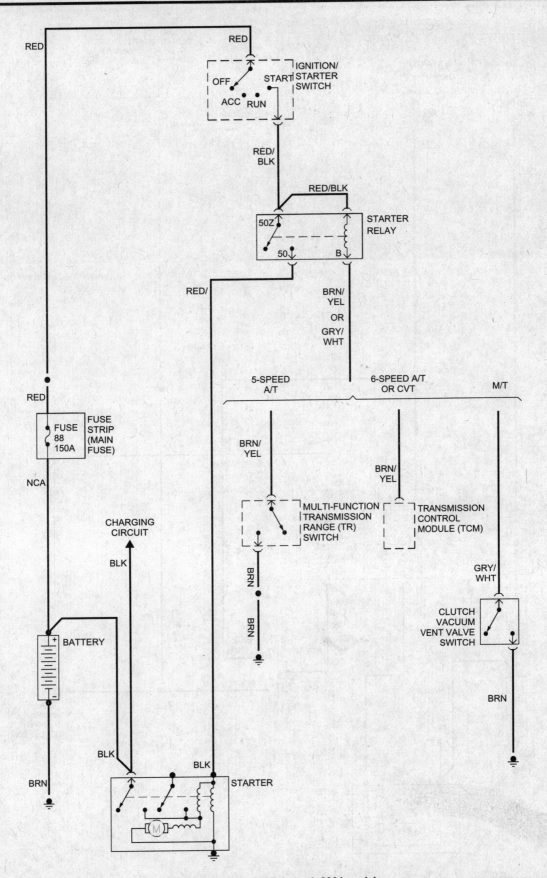

Starting system - 2002 through 2004 models

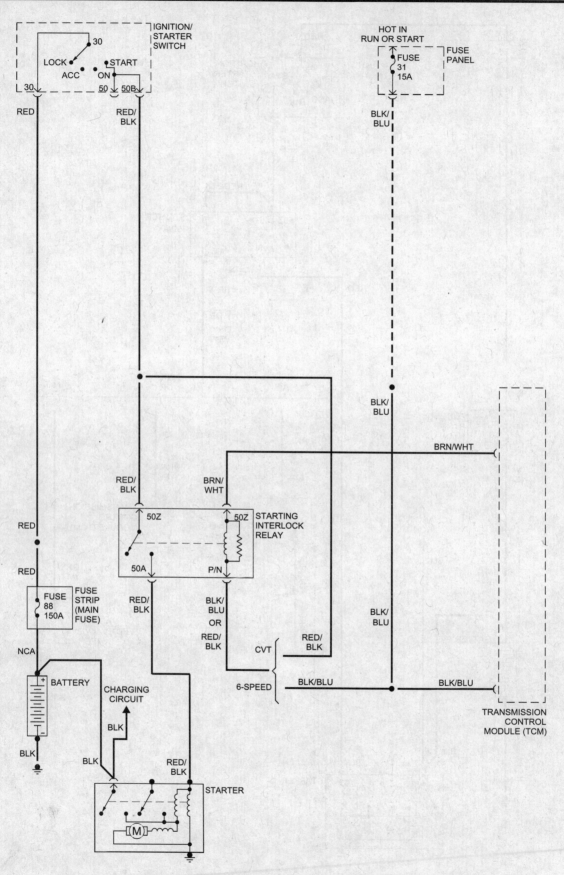

Starting system - 2005 and later 2.0L four-cylinder models with an automatic or CVT transaxle

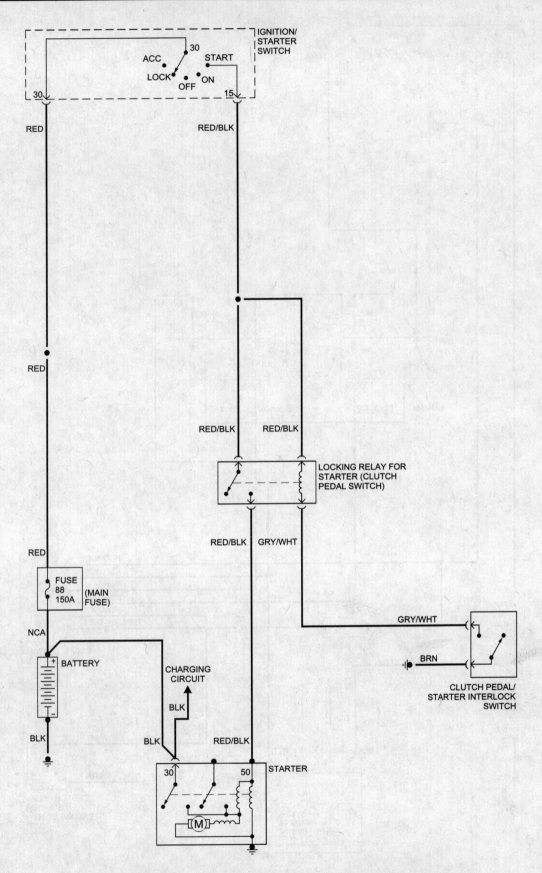

Starting system - 2005 and later 2.0L four-cylinder models with a manual transaxle

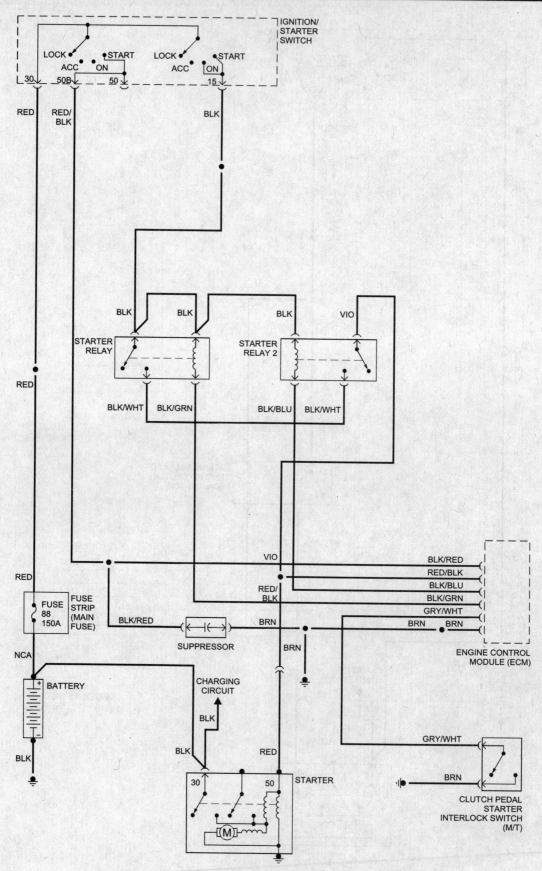

Starting system - 2005 and later 3.2L V6 models with a manual transaxle

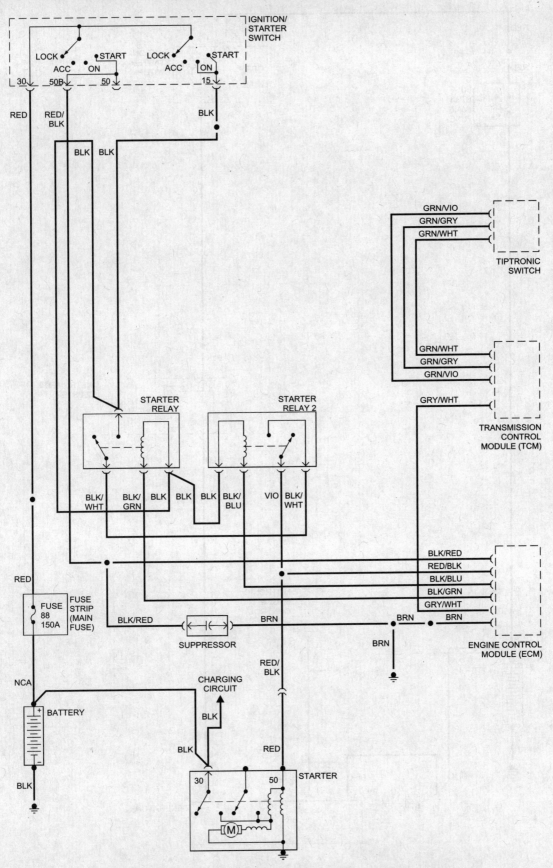

Starting system - 2005 and later 3.2L V6 models with an automatic transaxle

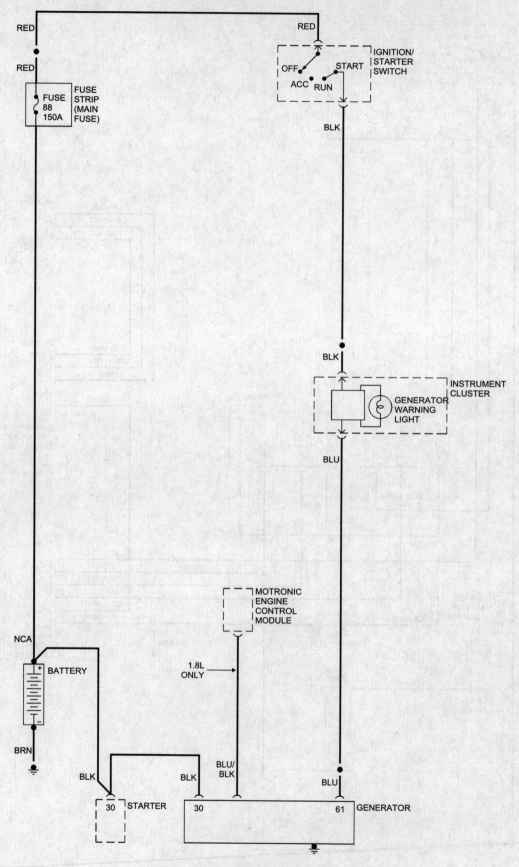

Charging system - 2002 through 2004 models

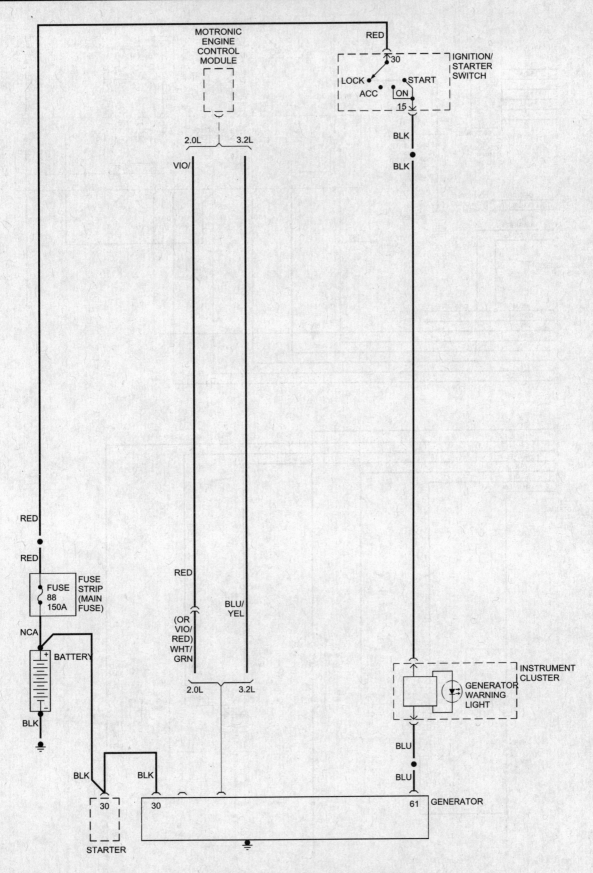

Charging system - 2005 and later models

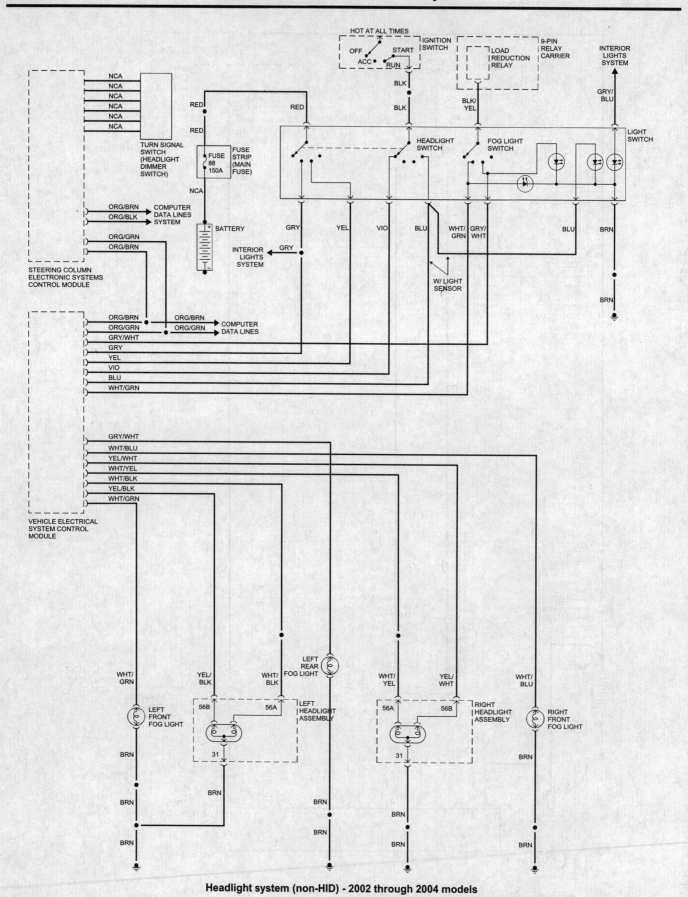

Headlight system (non-HID) - 2002 through 2004 models

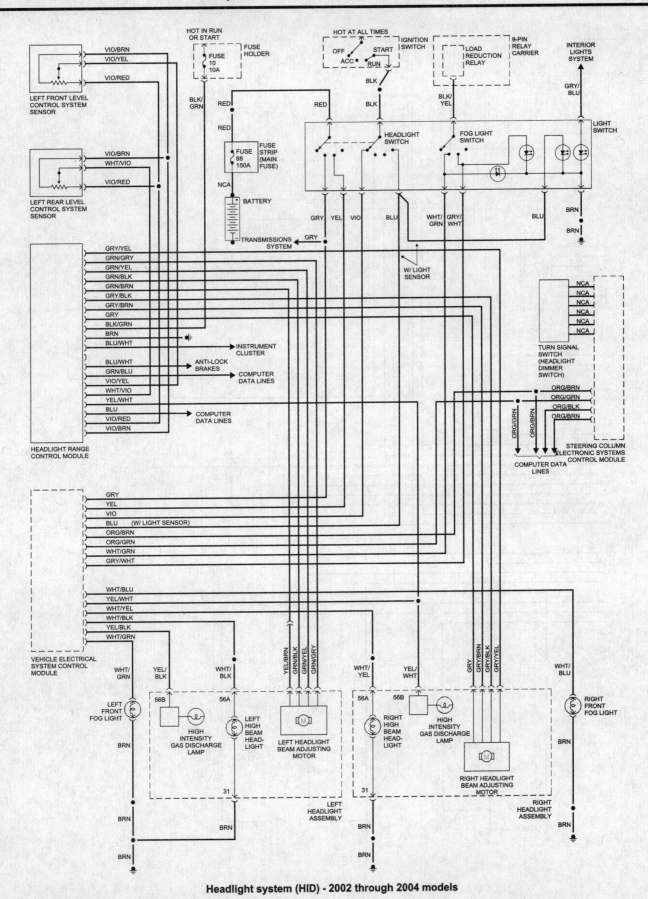

Headlight system (HID) - 2002 through 2004 models

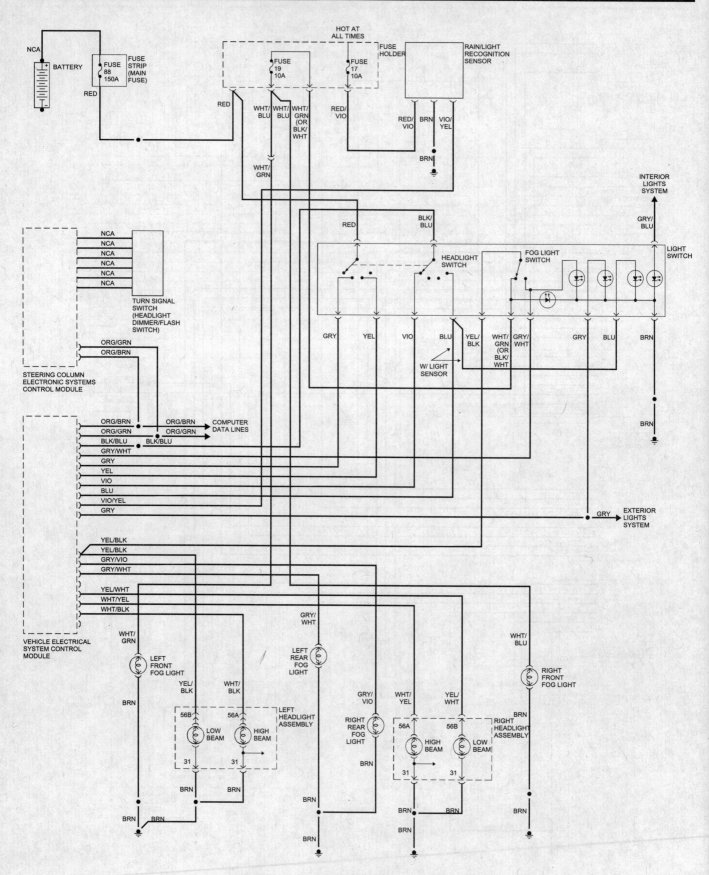

Headlight system (non-HID) - 2005 and later models

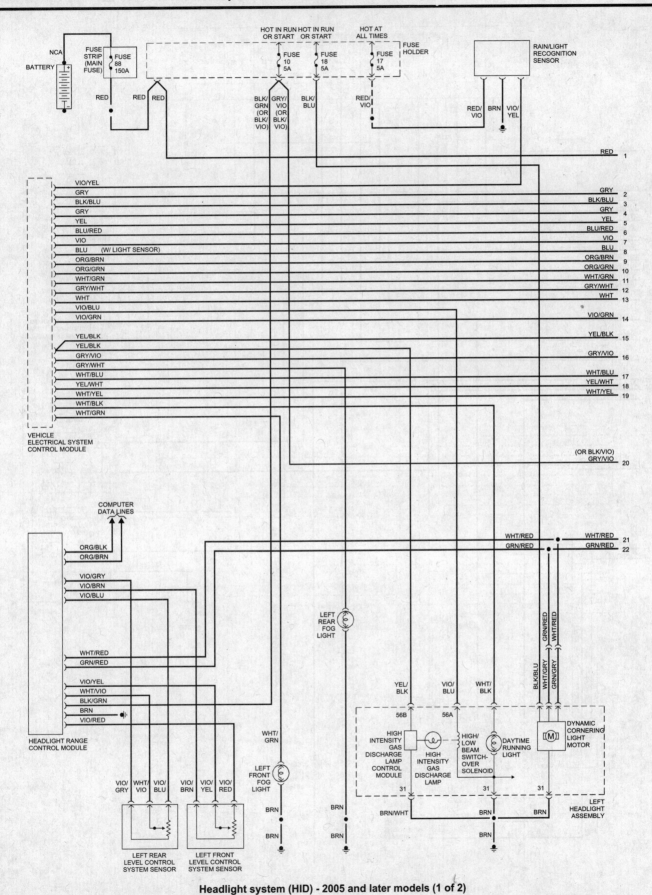

Headlight system (HID) - 2005 and later models (1 of 2)

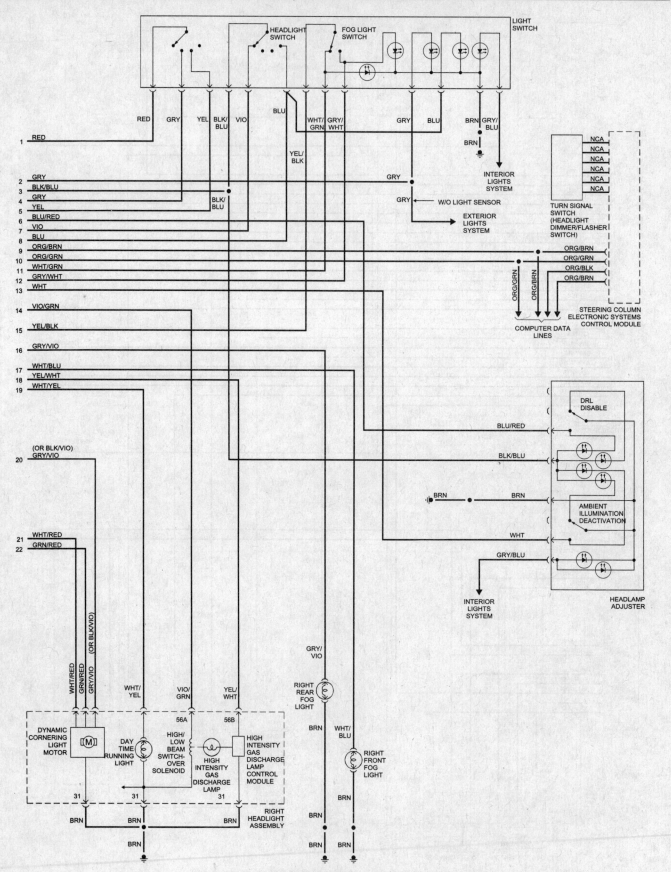

Headlight system (HID) - 2005 and later models (2 of 2)

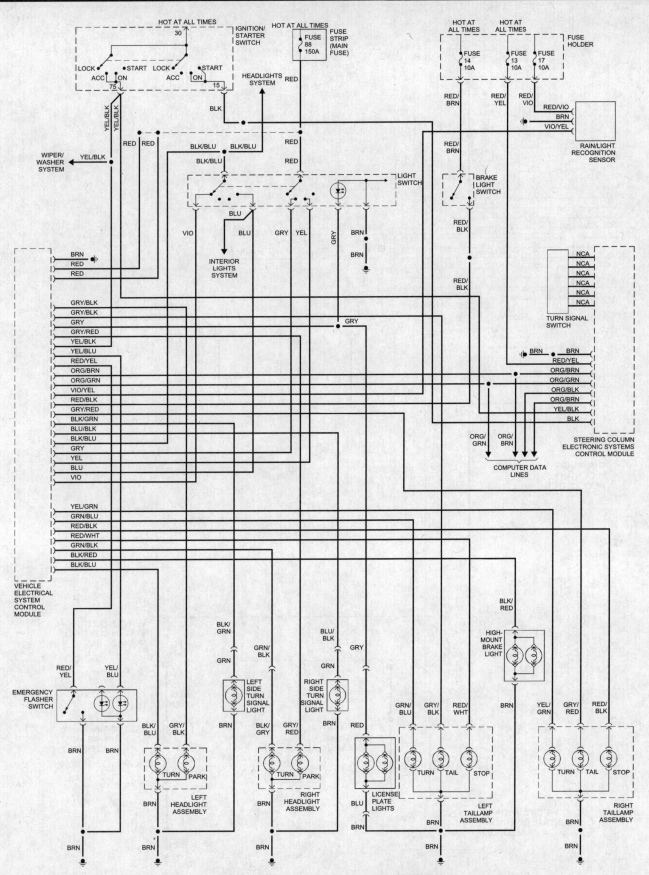

Exterior lighting system (except back-up lights)

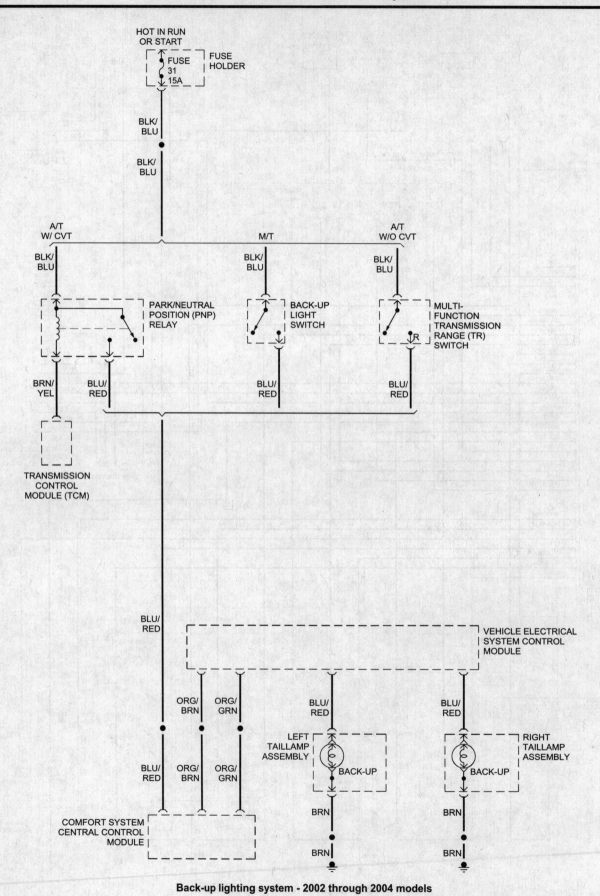

Back-up lighting system - 2002 through 2004 models

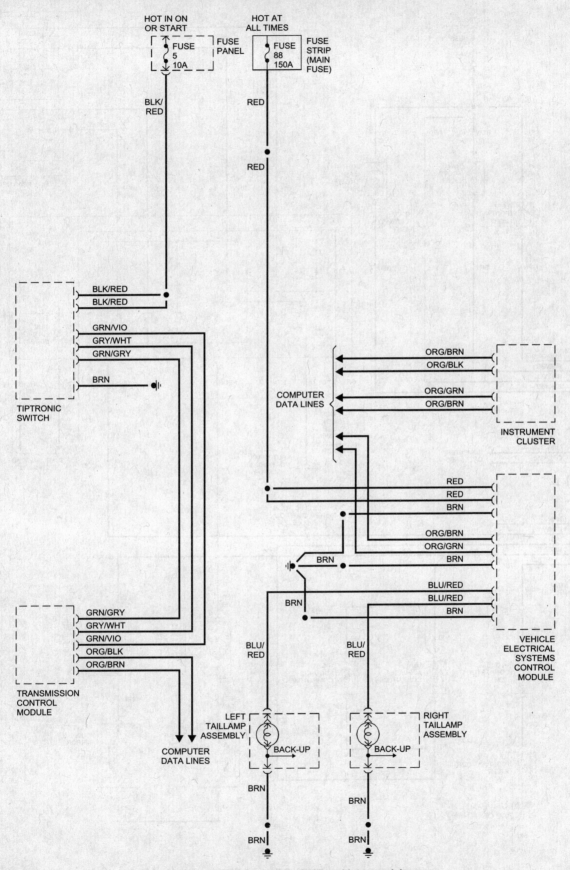

Back-up lighting system - 2005 and later models

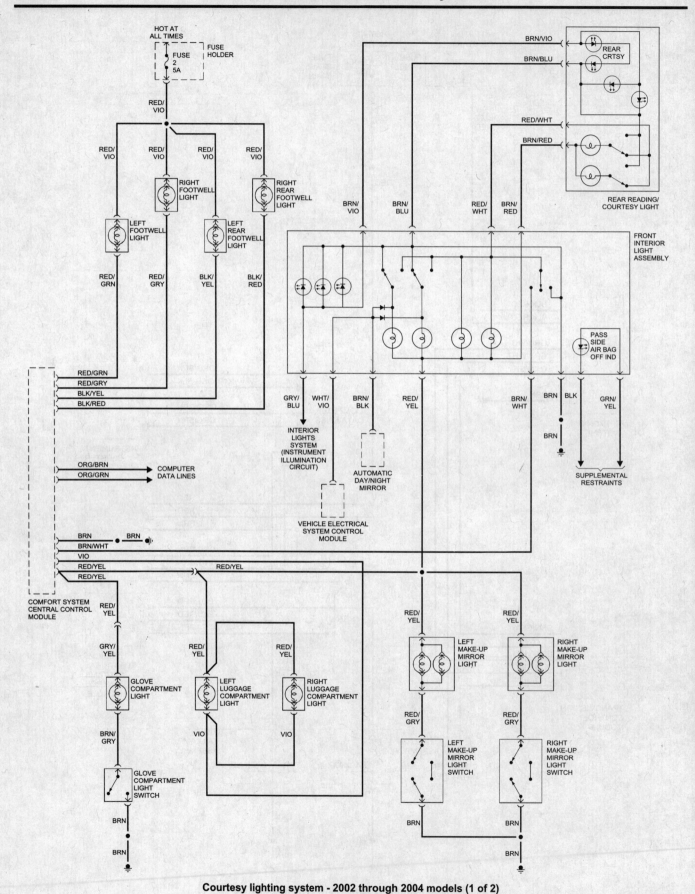

Courtesy lighting system - 2002 through 2004 models (1 of 2)

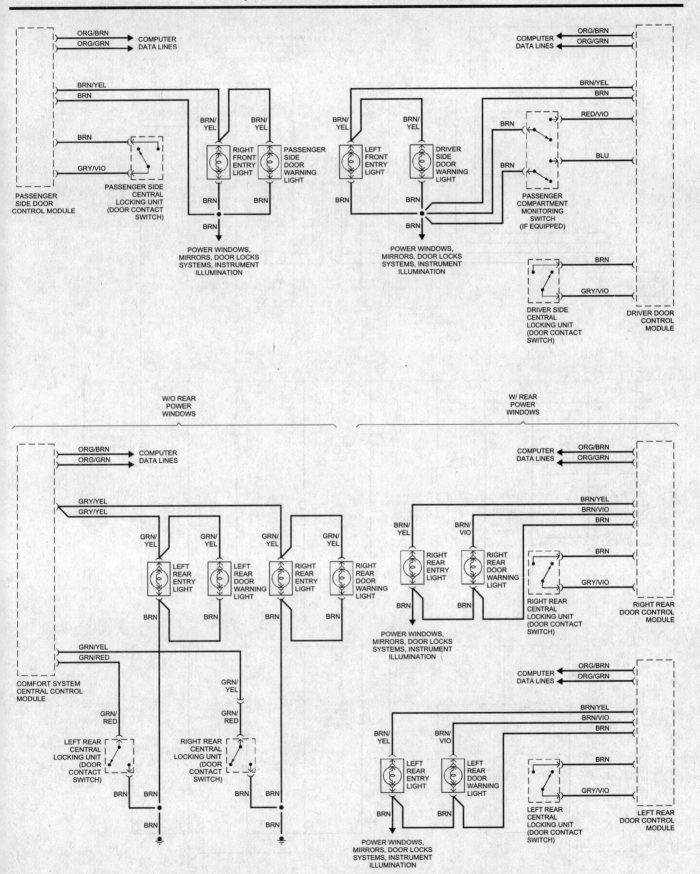

Courtesy lighting system - 2002 through 2004 models (2 of 2)

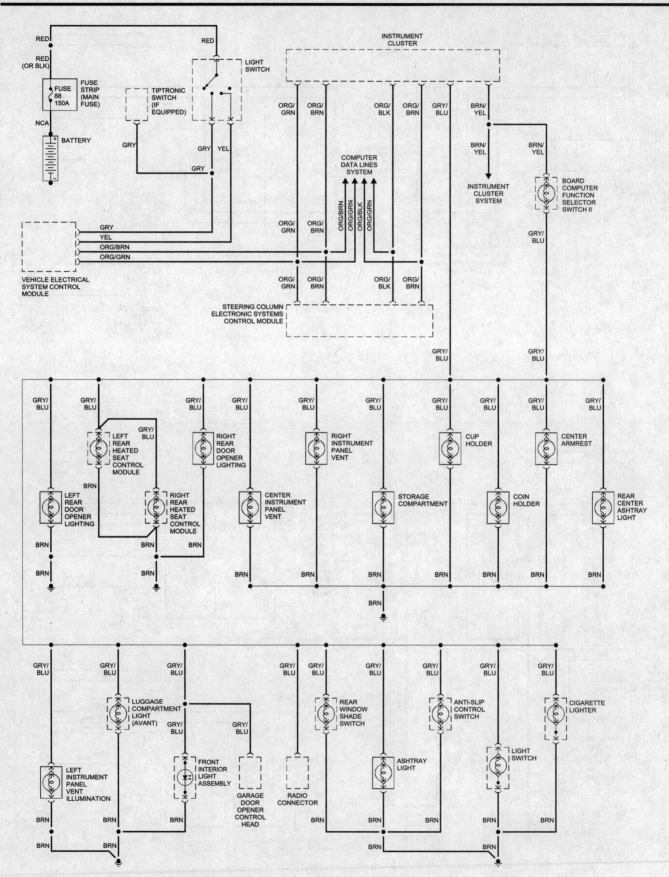

Instrument panel and switch illumination - 2002 through 2004 models (1 of 2)

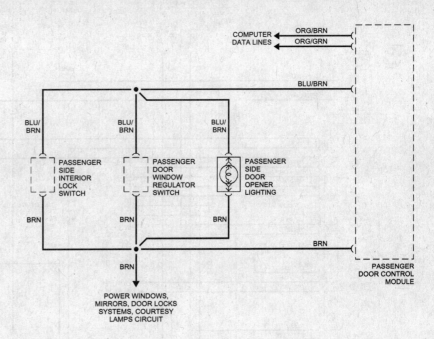

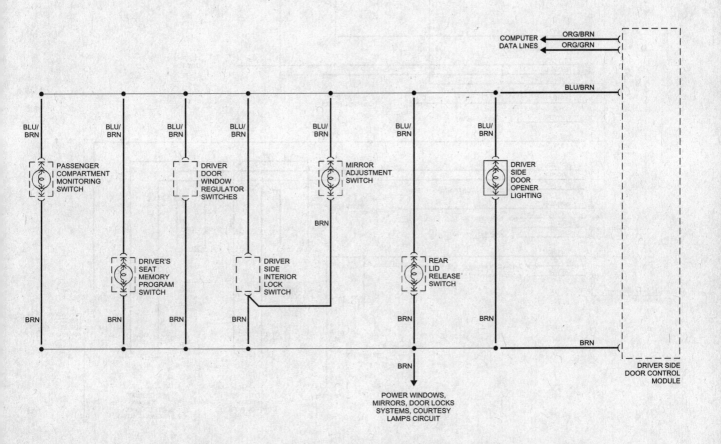

Instrument panel and switch illumination - 2002 through 2004 models (2 of 2)

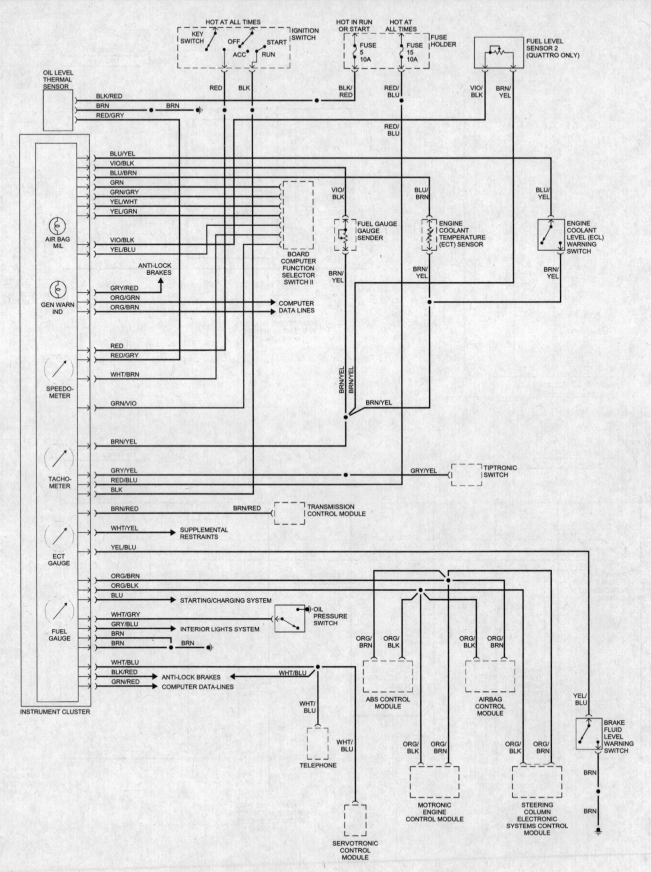

Gauges and warning lights system - 2002 through 2004 models

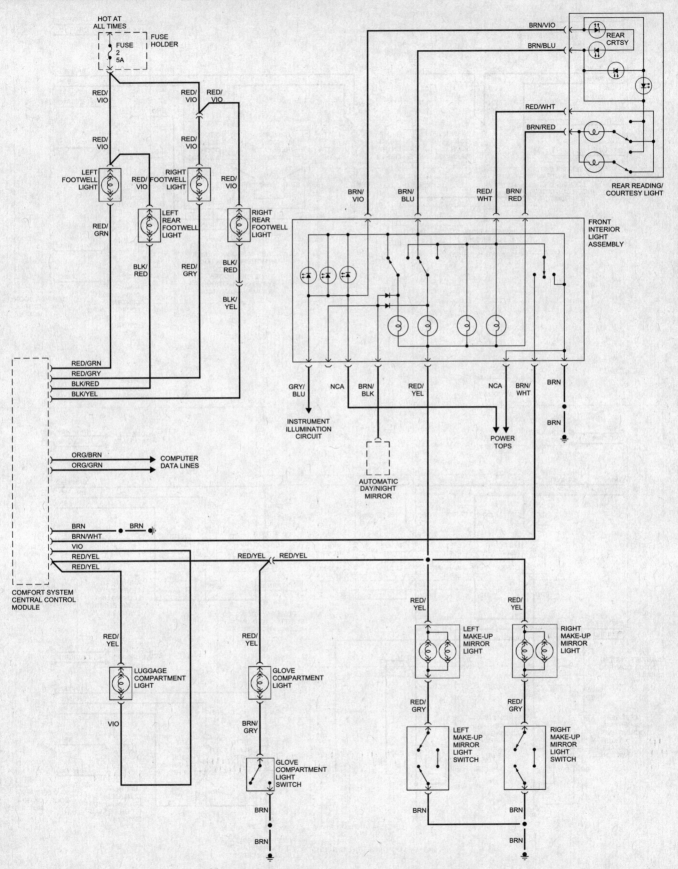

Courtesy lighting system - 2005 and later models (1 of 2)

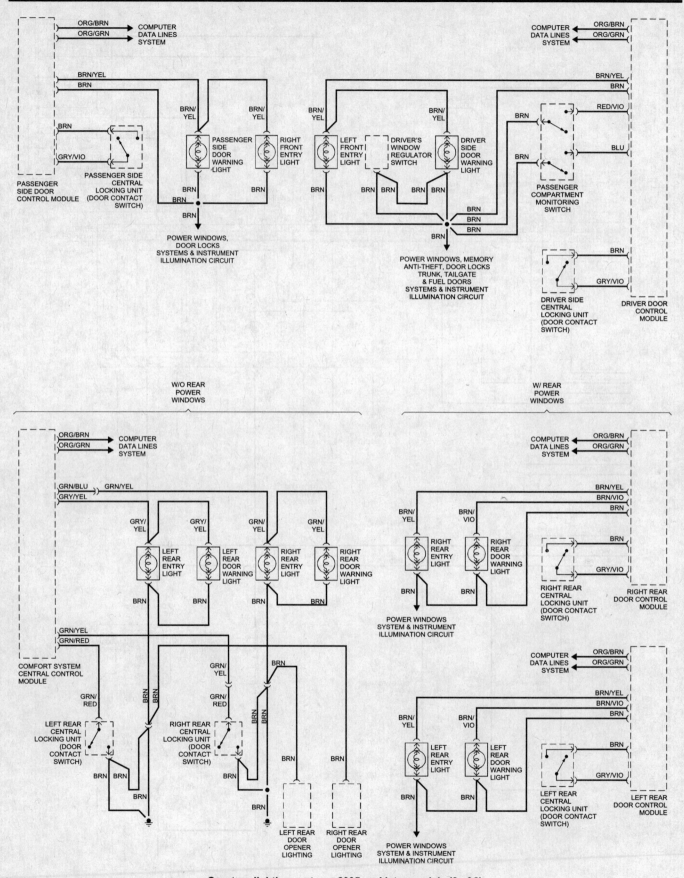

Courtesy lighting system - 2005 and later models (2 of 2)

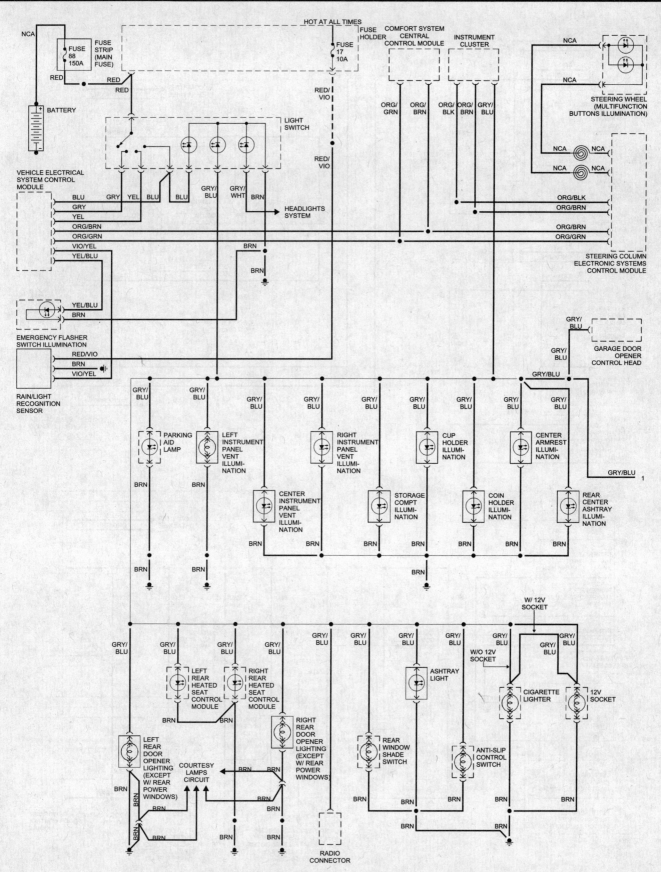

Instrument panel and switch illumination - 2005 and later models (1 of 2)

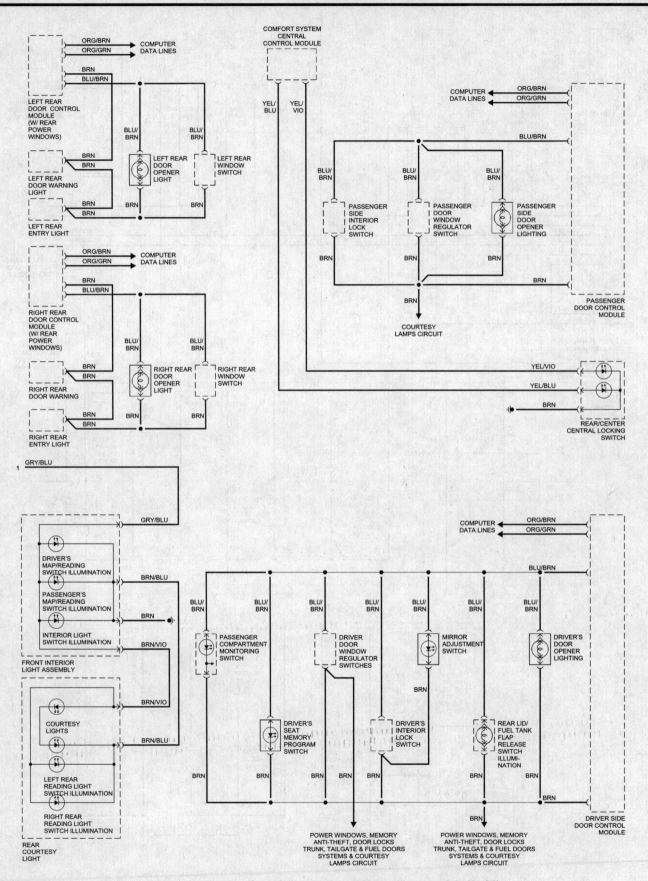

Instrument panel and switch illumination - 2005 and later models (2 of 2)

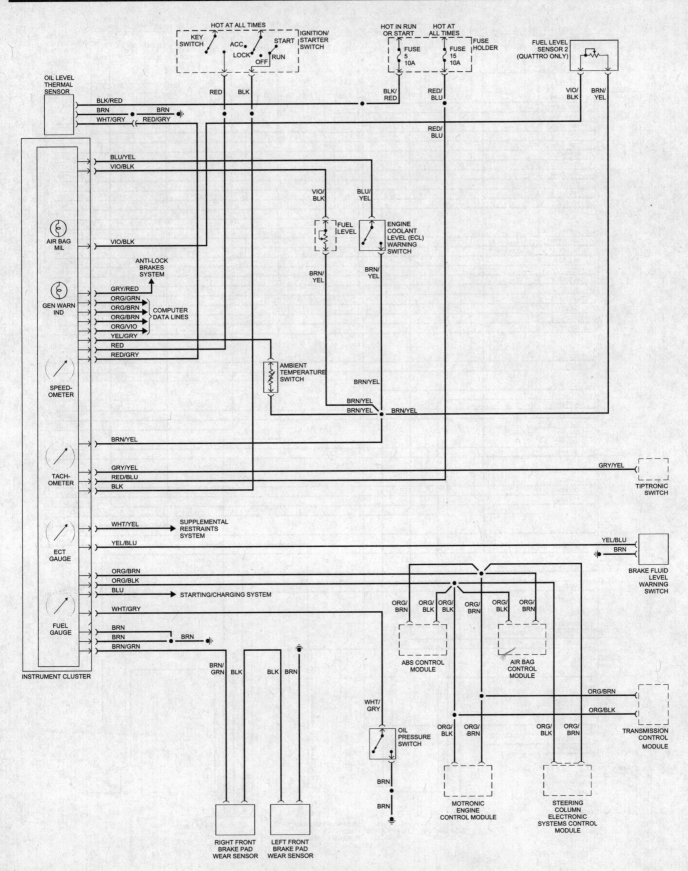

Gauges and warning lights system - 2005 and later models

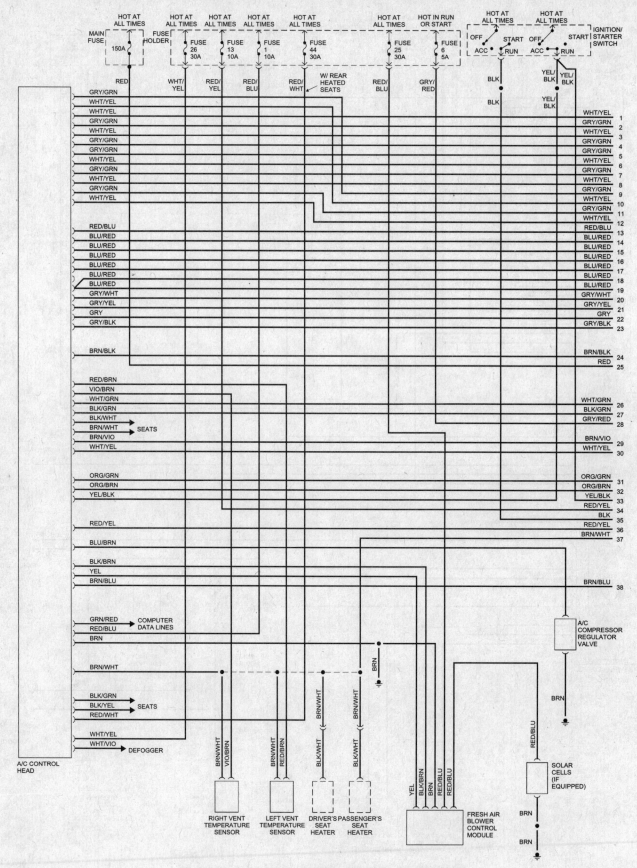

Climate control system - 2002 through 2004 models (1 of 2)

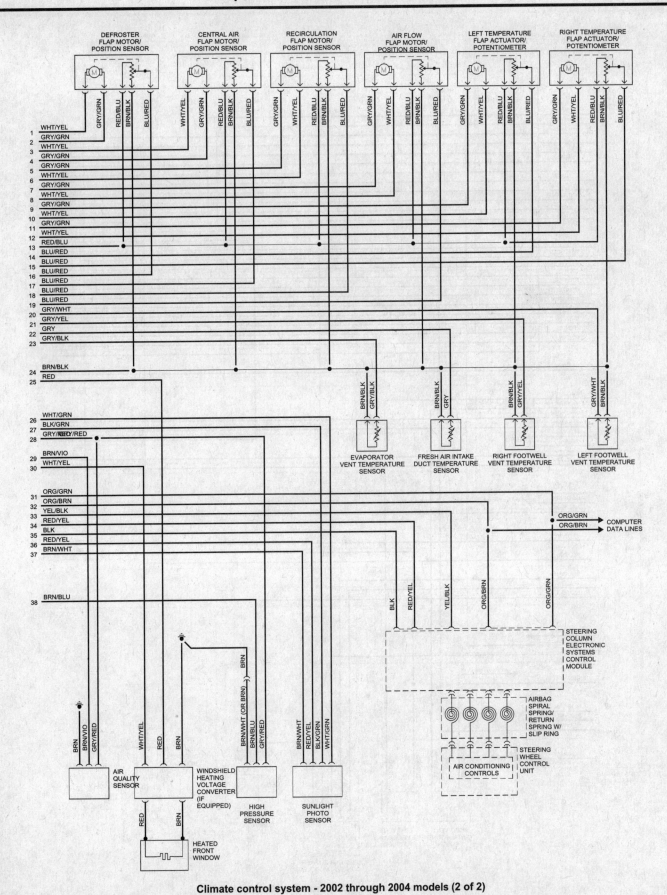

Climate control system - 2002 through 2004 models (2 of 2)

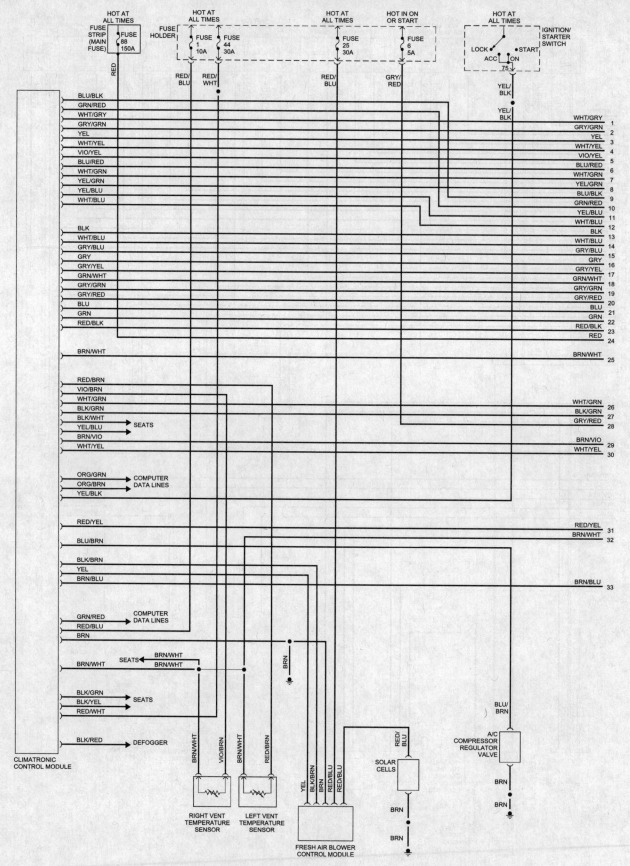

Climate control system - 2005 and later models (1 of 3)

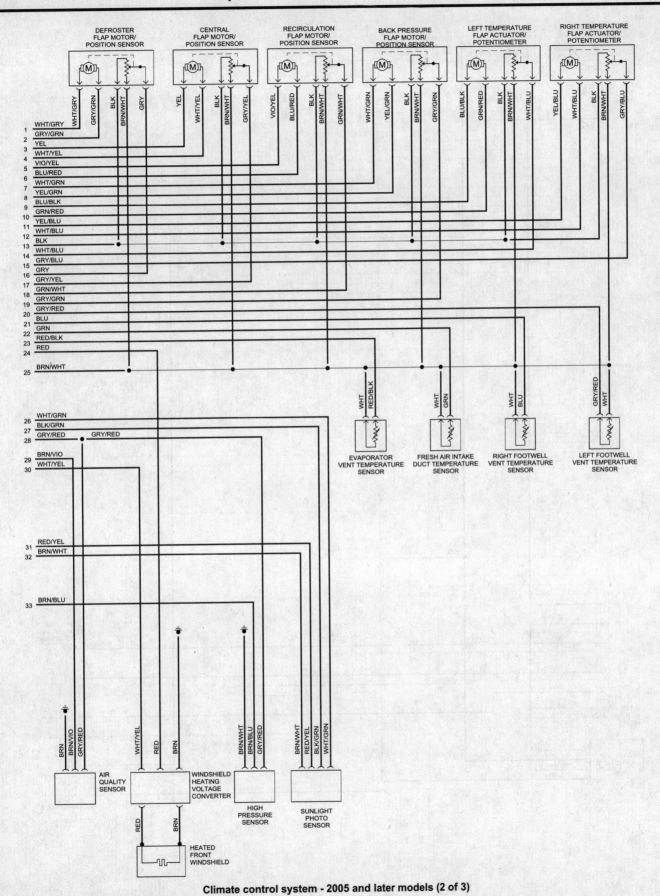

Climate control system - 2005 and later models (2 of 3)

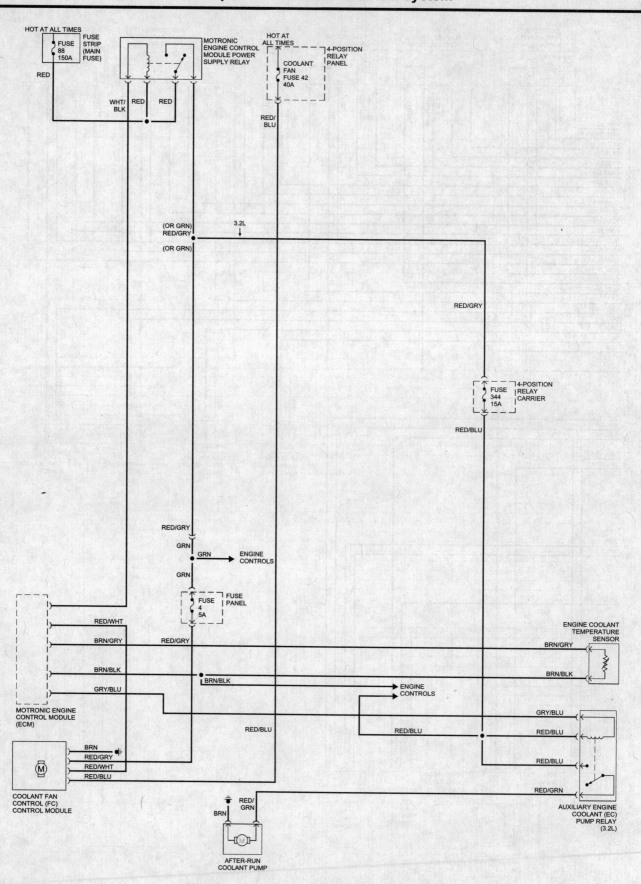

Climate control system - 2005 and later models (3 of 3)

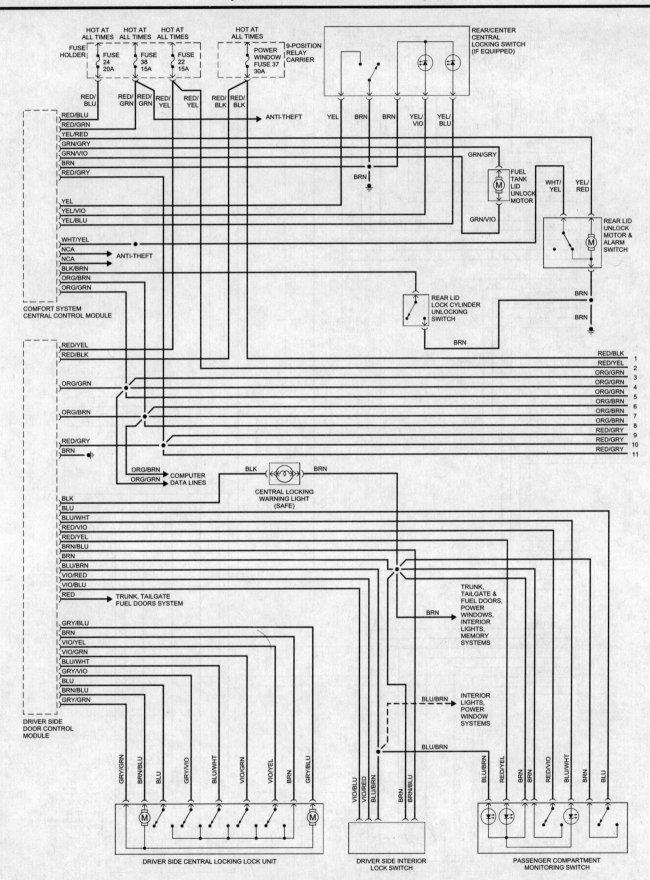

Power door lock system (1 of 2)

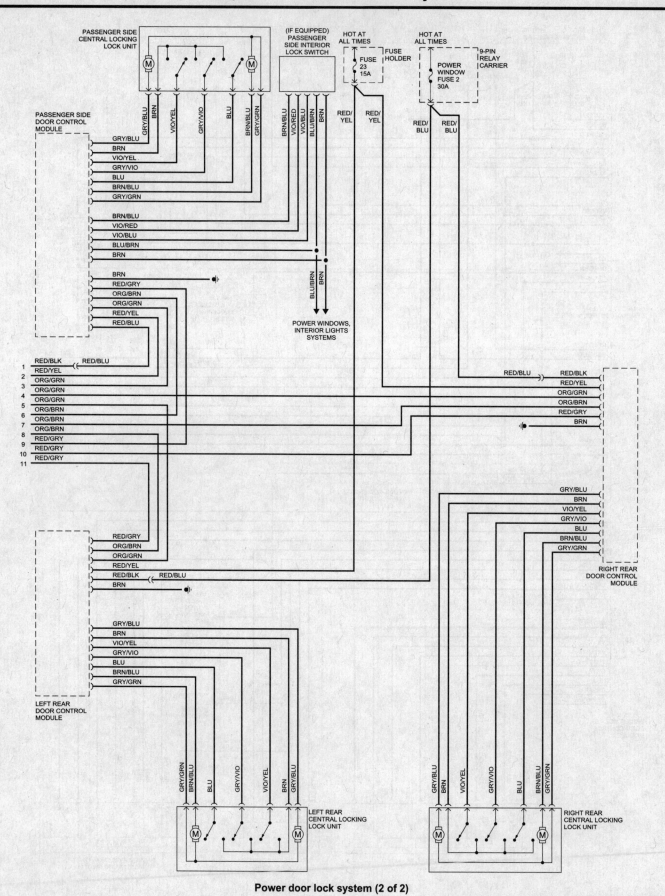

Power door lock system (2 of 2)

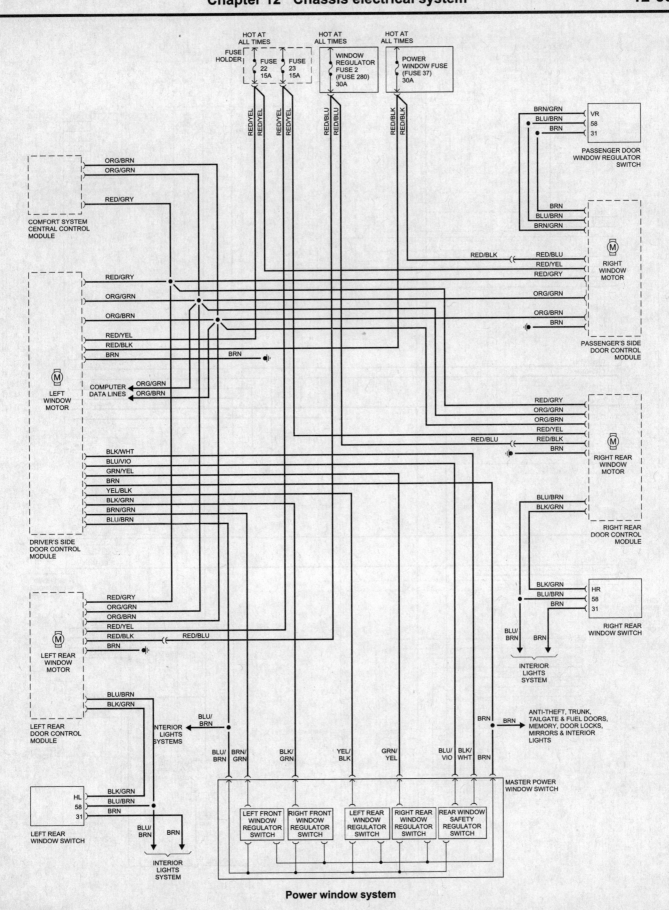

Power window system

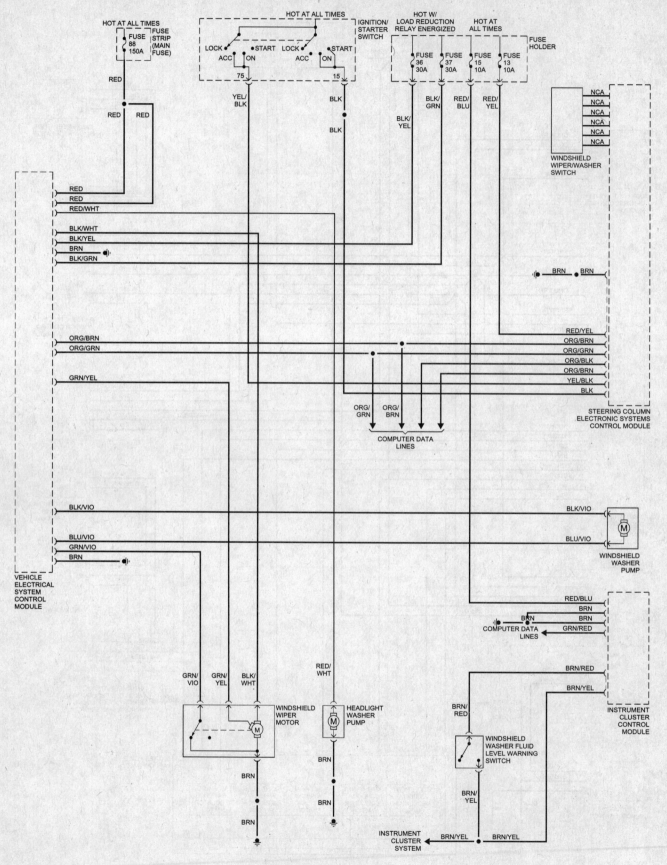

Wiper/washer system

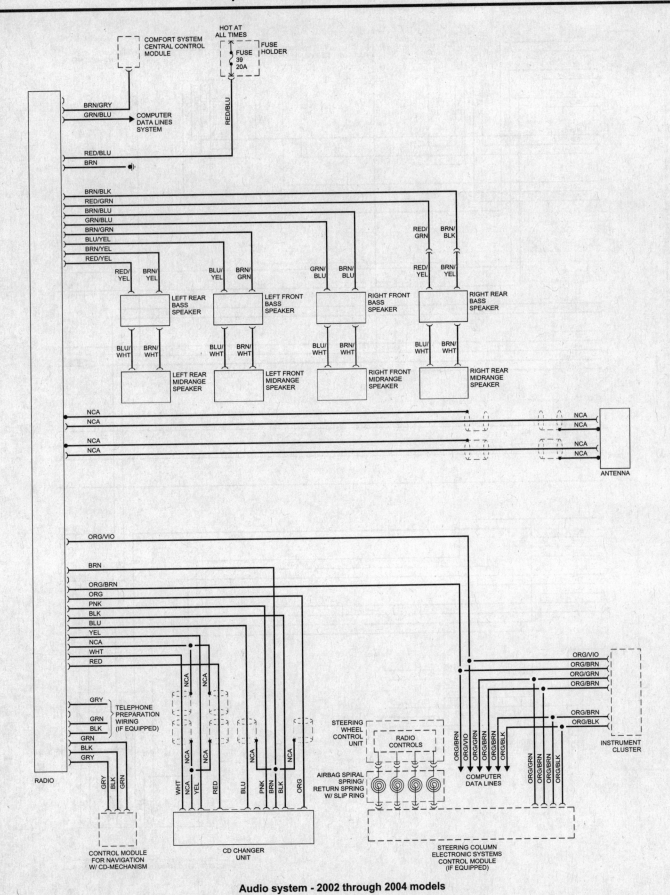

Audio system - 2002 through 2004 models

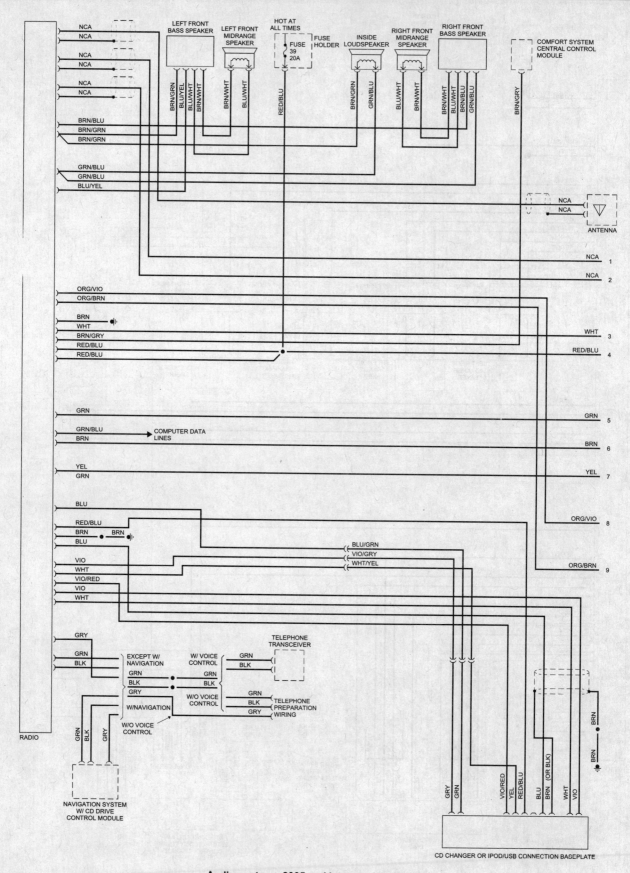

Audio system - 2005 and later models (1 of 2)

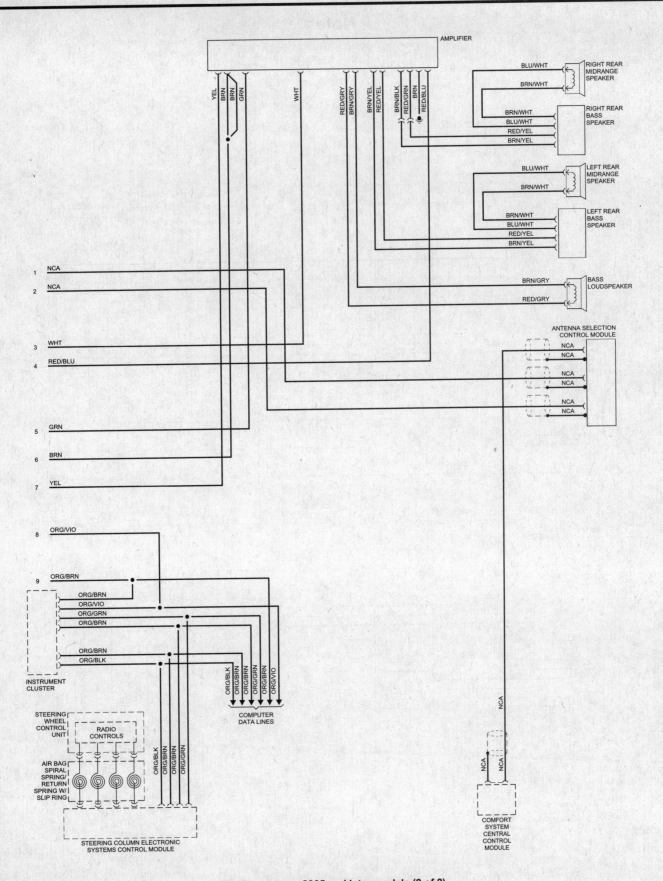

Audio system - 2005 and later models (2 of 2)

Notes

Index

A

About this manual, 0-5
Accelerator Pedal Position (APP) sensor,
    replacement, 6-12
Accumulator, air conditioning, removal and
    installation, 3-14
Acknowledgements, 0-2
After-run coolant pump, replacement, 3-9
Air conditioning
    accumulator, removal and installation, 3-14
    and heating system, check and maintenance, 3-4
    compressor, removal and installation, 3-14
    condenser, removal and installation, 3-15
    evaporator core, removal and installation, 3-16
    expansion (orifice) tube, removal and installation, 3-14
Air filter
    element, replacement, 1-16
    housing, removal and installation, 4-9
Airbag system, general information and system
    component removal and installation, 12-17
Alternator, removal and installation, 5-7
Antenna, removal and installation, 12-10
Anti-lock Brake System (ABS) and Electronic
    Stability Program (ESP), general information, 9-2
Anti-theft audio system, 0-15
Automatic transaxle
    diagnosis, general, 7B-2
    fluid
        change, 1-26
        type, 1-1
    general information, 7B-2
    overhaul, general information, 7B-6
    removal and installation, 7B-4
    shift
        cable, removal, installation and
            adjustment, 7B-3
        interlock system, description, check and
            component replacement, 7B-3
Automotive chemicals and lubricants, 0-17

B

Back-up light switch, removal and
    installation, 7A-3
Balljoints, check and replacement, 10-12
Battery
    cables, replacement, 5-6
    check, maintenance and charging, 1-17
    disconnection, 5-6
    removal and installation, 5-6
Blower motor, removal and installation, 3-11
Body repair
    major damage, 11-3
    minor damage, 11-2
    minor paint scratches, 11-2
Body, 11-1
Booster battery (jump) starting, 0-16

Brakes
Anti-lock Brake System (ABS) and Electronic Stability Program (ESP), general information, 9-2
caliper, removal and installation, 9-8
disc, inspection, removal and installation, 9-9
fluid
change, 1-24
level check, 1-11
type, 1-1
general information, 9-2
hoses and lines, inspection and replacement, 9-11
hydraulic system, bleeding, 9-11
light switch, removal and installation, 9-15
master cylinder, removal and installation, 9-11
pads, replacement
front, 9-3
rear, 9-7
parking brake, check and adjustment, 9-14
pedal, removal and installation, 9-15
power brake booster, check, removal and installation, 9-12
system check, 1-21
Bulb replacement, 12-13
Bumper covers, removal and installation, 11-9
Buying parts, 0-8

C

Cabin air filter replacement, 1-21
Cable replacement
battery, 5-6
hood release, 11-8
Caliper, disc brake, removal and installation, 9-8
Camshaft Position (CMP) sensor, replacement, 6-12
Camshafts and lifters, removal, inspection and installation
3.0L and 3.2 L V6 engines, 2B-6
four-cylinder engines, 2A-9
Capacities, fluids and lubricants, 1-2
Carpets, maintenance, 11-5
Catalytic converter, replacement, 6-15
Center console, removal and installation, 11-16
Charging system
alternator, removal and installation, 5-7
general information and precautions, 5-1
Chassis electrical system, 12-1
Chemicals and lubricants, 0-17
Circuit breakers, general information, 12-3
Clutch
components, removal, inspection and installation, 8-3
description and check, 8-2

fluid
level check, 1-11
type, 1-1
hydraulic system, bleeding, 8-3
master cylinder, removal and installation, 8-2
pedal
and over-center spring, removal and installation, 8-6
starter interlock switch, removal and installation, 8-6
switch, removal and installation, 8-6
release bearing and lever, removal, inspection and installation, 8-5
release cylinder, removal and installation, 8-3
Coil spring, removal and installation
front, 10-5
rear, 10-13
Coils, ignition, removal and installation, 5-6
Compressor, air conditioning, removal and installation, 3-14
Condenser, air conditioning, removal and installation, 3-15
Control arms, front, removal, bushing replacement and installation, 10-10
Control arms, rear, removal and installation
lower, 10-15
upper, 10-14
Conversion factors, 0-18
Convertible top, general information, 11-22
Coolant
expansion tank, removal and installation, 3-9
level check, 1-11
Temperature (ECT) sensor, replacement, 6-13
temperature gauge sending unit, check and replacement, 3-10
type, 1-1
Cooling system
check, 1-20
general information, 3-2
servicing (draining, flushing and refilling), 1-28
Cooling, heating and air conditioning systems, troubleshooting, 3-2
Cowl cover, removal and installation, 11-11
Crankshaft front oil seal and housing, replacement
3.0L and 3.2L V6 engines, 2B-10
four-cylinder engines, 2A-18
Crankshaft Position (CKP) sensor, replacement, 6-12
Crankshaft pulley, removal and installation
3.0L and 3.2L V6 engines, 2B-10
four-cylinder engines, 2A-18
Crankshaft, removal and installation, 2C-13
Cruise control system, description and check, 12-16
Cylinder compression check, 2C-5
Cylinder head, removal and installation
3.0L and 3.2L V6 engines, 2B-9
four-cylinder engines, 2A-17

D

Dashboard trim panels, removal and installation, 11-18
Defogger, rear window, check and repair, 12-10
Diagnosis, 0-21
Diagnostic Trouble Codes (DTCs)
　P0 code list, 6-6
　obtaining and clearing, 6-5
Differential
　lubricant level check
　　center (all-wheel drive models with automatic
　　　transaxles), 1-27
　　front, 1-27
　lubricant type, 1-1
Differential, rear
　lubricant change, 1-27
　oil seals, replacement, 8-16
　removal and installation, 8-17
Disc brake
　caliper, removal and installation, 9-8
　disc, inspection, removal and installation, 9-9
　pads, replacement
　　front, 9-3
　　rear, 9-7
Door
　latch, lock cylinder and outside handle, removal
　　and installation, 11-14
　removal, installation and adjustment, 11-14
　trim panels, removal and installation, 11-12
　window glass frame and regulator, removal
　　and installation, 11-15
　window glass, removal and installation, 11-15
Driveaxle
　boot check, 1-22
　boot replacement, 8-8
　CV joint inspection, 8-8
　general information and inspection, 8-6
　removal and installation, 8-7
Drivebelt
　check and replacement, 1-23
　tensioner replacement, 1-24
**Driveshaft (all-wheel drive models), removal
　and installation, 8-15**

E

Electrical connectors, general information, 12-4
Electrical troubleshooting, general information, 12-1
**Electronic Stability Program (ESP), general
　information, 9-2**
Emissions and engine control systems, 6-1
**Engine Coolant Temperature (ECT) sensor,
　replacement, 6-13**
Engine coolant, level check, 1-11

Engine cooling fans, removal and installation, 3-8
Engine electrical systems
　general information and precautions, 5-1
　troubleshooting, 5-4
Engine mounts, check and replacement
　3.0L and 3.2L V6 engines, 2B-12
　four-cylinder engines, 2A-23
Engine oil
　and filter change, 1-14
　level check, 1-10
　type and viscosity, 1-1
Engine overhaul
　disassembly sequence, 2C-9
　reassembly sequence, 2C-17
Engine rebuilding alternatives, 2C-6
Engine removal, methods and precautions, 2C-7
Engine, general overhaul procedures
　crankshaft, removal and installation, 2C-13
　cylinder compression check, 2C-3, 2C-5
　engine overhaul
　　disassembly sequence, 2C-9
　　reassembly sequence, 2C-17
　engine rebuilding alternatives, 2C-6
　engine removal, methods and precautions, 2C-7
　engine, removal and installation, 2C-8
　initial start-up and break-in after overhaul, 2C-18
　oil pressure check, 2C-4
　pistons and connecting rods, removal and
　　installation, 2C-10
　vacuum gauge diagnostic checks, 2C-5
Engine, in-vehicle repair procedures
Four-cylinder engines
　camshafts and lifters, removal, inspection and
　　installation, 2A-9
　crankshaft front oil seal and housing,
　　replacement, 2A-18
　crankshaft pulley, removal and installation, 2A-18
　cylinder head, removal and installation, 2A-17
　engine mounts, check and replacement, 2A-23
　exhaust manifold, removal and installation, 2A-15
　flywheel/driveplate, removal and installation, 2A-21
　intake manifold, removal and installation, 2A-15
　intermediate shaft oil seal, replacement, 2A-23
　oil pan, removal and installation, 2A-19
　oil pump, removal, inspection and
　　installation, 2A-21
　rear main oil seal, replacement, 2A-22
　repair operations possible with the engine in
　　the vehicle, 2A-4
　timing belt and sprockets, removal, inspection and
　　installation, 2A-6
　Top Dead Center (TDC) for number 1 piston,
　　locating, 2A-4
　valve cover, removal and installation, 2A-5
　valve springs, retainers and seals,
　　replacement, 2A-14

3.0L and 3.2L V6 engines
  camshafts and lifters, removal, inspection and installation, 2B-6
  crankshaft front oil seal and housing, replacement, 2B-10
  crankshaft pulley, removal and installation, 2B-10
  cylinder head, removal and installation, 2B-9
  engine mounts, check and replacement, 2B-12
  exhaust manifold, removal and installation, 2B-8
  flywheel/driveplate, removal and installation, 2B-12
  intake manifold, removal and installation, 2B-8
  oil pan, removal and installation, 2B-11
  oil pump, removal, inspection and installation, 2B-11
  rear main oil seal, replacement, 2B-12
  repair operations possible with the engine in the vehicle, 2B-4
  timing belt and sprockets (3.0L V6 engine), removal, inspection and installation, 2B-5
  timing chain and sprockets (3.2L V6 engine), removal, inspection and installation, 2B-6
  Top Dead Center (TDC) for number 1 piston, locating, 2B-4
  valve covers, removal and installation, 2B-4
Engine, removal and installation, 2C-8
Evaporative emissions control (EVAP) system, component replacement, 6-17
Evaporator core, air conditioning, removal and installation, 3-16
Exhaust manifold, removal and installation
  3.0L and 3.2L V6 engines, 2B-8
  four-cylinder engines, 2A-15
Exhaust system
  check, 1-20
  servicing, general information, 4-6
Expansion (orifice) tube, air conditioning, removal and installation, 3-14
Expansion tank, coolant, removal and installation, 3-9

F

Fans, engine cooling, removal and installation, 3-8
Fastener and trim removal, 11-5
Fault finding, 0-21
Fender, front, removal and installation, 11-10
Filter replacement
  engine air, 1-16
  engine oil, 1-14
  fuel, 1-28
  interior ventilation, 1-21

Firing order, 1-3
Fluid level checks, 1-10
  brake fluid, 1-11
  clutch fluid, 1-11
  differential
    center ,1-27
    front, 1-27
    rear, 1-27
  engine coolant, 1-11
  engine oil, 1-10
  power steering, 1-12
  transaxle
    automatic, 1-26
    manual, 1-27
  windshield washer, 1-12
Fluids and lubricants
  capacities, 1-2
  recommended, 1-1
Flywheel/driveplate, removal and installation
  3.0L and 3.2L V6 engines, 2B-12
  four-cylinder engines, 2A-21
Four-cylinder engines
  camshafts and lifters, removal, inspection and installation, 2A-9
  crankshaft front oil seal and housing, replacement, 2A-18
  crankshaft pulley, removal and installation, 2A-18
  cylinder head, removal and installation, 2A-17
  engine mounts, check and replacement, 2A-23
  exhaust manifold, removal and installation, 2A-15
  flywheel/driveplate, removal and installation, 2A-21
  intake manifold, removal and installation, 2A-15
  intermediate shaft oil seal, replacement, 2A-23
  oil pan, removal and installation, 2A-19
  oil pump, removal, inspection and installation, 2A-21
  rear main oil seal, replacement, 2A-22
  repair operations possible with the engine in the vehicle, 2A-4
  timing belt and sprockets, removal, inspection and installation, 2A-6
  Top Dead Center (TDC) for number 1 piston, locating, 2A-4
  valve cover, removal and installation, 2A-5
  valve springs, retainers and seals, replacement, 2A-14
Fraction/decimal/millimeter equivalents, 0-19
Front hub and wheel bearing, removal, bearing replacement and installation, 10-9
Fuel
  high-pressure fuel pump, removal and installation, 4-10
  lines and fittings, disconnecting, 4-5
  lines and fittings, general information, 4-6
  pressure, check, 4-4
  pressure regulator, removal and installation, 4-10
  pressure relief procedure, 4-3

pump/fuel level sensor module, removal and installation, 4-7

rail and injectors, removal and installation, 4-11

system check, 1-23

system warnings, 4-2

troubleshooting, 4-3

Fuel filter replacement, 1-28

Fuses, general information, 12-3

Fusible links, general information, 12-3

G

General engine overhaul procedures

crankshaft, removal and installation, 2C-13

cylinder compression check, 2C-3, 2C-5

engine overhaul

disassembly sequence, 2C-9

reassembly sequence, 2C-17

engine rebuilding alternatives, 2C-6

engine removal, methods and precautions, 2C-7

engine, removal and installation, 2C-8

initial start-up and break-in after overhaul, 2C-18

oil pressure check, 2C-4

pistons and connecting rods, removal and installation, 2C-10

vacuum gauge diagnostic checks, 2C-5

Grille, radiator, removal and installation, 11-10

H

Headlight

adjustment, 12-12

bulb, replacement, 12-12

housing, replacement, 12-11

Heater and air conditioning

control assembly, removal and installation, 3-11

housing, removal and installation, 3-12

Heater core, removal and installation, 3-11

Heating and air conditioning system, check and maintenance, 3-4

High-pressure fuel pump, removal and installation, 4-10

Hinges and locks, maintenance, 11-6

Hood latch, release cable and support struts, removal and installation, 11-8

Hood, removal, installation and adjustment, 11-8

Horn, replacement, 12-15

Hub and wheel bearing assembly, removal and installation

front, 10-9

rear, 10-13

I

Ignition

coils, removal and installation, 5-6

key lock cylinder, replacement, 12-5

switch and key lock cylinder, replacement, 12-5

Information sensors, description, 6-4

Initial start-up and break-in after overhaul, 2C-18

Injectors, fuel, removal and installation, 4-11

Instrument

cluster, removal and installation, 12-7

panel, removal and installation, 11-20

panel switches, replacement, 12-7

Intake Air Temperature (IAT) sensor, replacement

MAF/IAT, 6-14

MAP/IAT, 6-14

Intake manifold, removal and installation

3.0L and 3.2L V6 engines, 2B-8

four-cylinder engines, 2A-15

Intercooler(s), check and replacement, 4-17

Interior ventilation filter replacement, 1-21

Intermediate shaft oil seal, four-cylinder engines, replacement, 2A-23

Introduction to the Audi A4, 0-5

J

Jacking and towing, 0-15

Jump starting, 0-16

K

Key fob, battery replacement and transmitter programming, 12-5

Key lock cylinder and latch, removal and installation

door, 11-14

liftgate, 11-12

trunk, 11-12

Key lock cylinder, ignition, replacement, 12-5

Knock sensor, replacement, 6-13

Knuckle (rear), removal and installation, 10-13

L

Liftgate

latch, lock cylinder and support struts, removal and installation, 11-12

removal, installation and adjustment, 11-12

Lock carrier, repositioning, removal and installation, 11-6

Lubricants and chemicals, 0-17
Lubricants and fluids
   capacities, 1-2
   recommended, 1-1

M

Maintenance
   schedule, 1-5
   techniques, tools and working facilities, 0-8
Manifold Absolute Pressure/Intake Air Temperature (MAP/IAT) sensor, replacement, 6-14
Manual transaxle
   back-up light switch, removal and installation, 7A-3
   lubricant
      change, 1-27
      type, 1-1
   oil seals, replacement, 7A-3
   overhaul, general information, 7A-2
   removal and installation, 7A-2
   shift linkage, adjustment, 7A-1
Mass Air Flow/Intake Air Temperature (MAF/IAT) sensor, replacement, 6-14
Master cylinder, removal and installation
   brake, 9-11
   clutch, 8-2
Mirrors, removal and installation, 11-15

O

Obtaining and clearing Diagnostic Trouble Codes (DTCs), 6-5
Oil, engine, level check, 1-10
Oil, engine, type and viscosity, 1-1
Oil pan, removal and installation
   3.0L and 3.2L V6 engines, 2B-11
   four-cylinder engines, 2A-19
Oil pressure check, 2C-4
Oil pump, removal, inspection and installation
   3.0L and 3.2L V6 engines, 2B-11
   four-cylinder engines, 2A-21
Oil seals (manual transaxle), replacement, 7A-3
On-Board Diagnosis (OBD) system, 6-5
Orifice tube, air conditioning, removal and installation, 3-14
Oxygen sensors, replacement, 6-14

P

Pads, disc brake, replacement
   front, 9-3
   rear, 9-7

Parking brake, check and adjustment, 9-14
Parts, replacement, buying, 0-8
Pistons and connecting rods, removal and installation, 2C-10
Positive Crankcase Ventilation (PCV) system, component replacement, 6-18
Power brake booster, check, removal and installation, 9-12
Power door lock system, general information, 12-17
Power steering
   fluid level check, 1-12
   fluid type, 1-1
   pump, removal and installation, 10-21
   system, bleeding, 10-22
Power window system, general information, 12-16
Powertrain Control Module (PCM), removal and installation, 6-15

R

Radiator
   grille, removal and installation, 11-10
   support panel, repositioning, removal and installation, 11-6
Radiator and expansion tank, removal and installation, 3-9
Radio and speakers, removal and installation, 12-8
Rear differential
   assembly, removal and installation, 8-17
   oil seals, replacement, 8-16
Rear hub and wheel bearing assembly, removal and installation, 10-13
Rear main oil seal, replacement
   3.0L and 3.2L V6 engines, 2B-12
   four-cylinder engines, 2A-22
Rear suspension arms, removal and installation, 10-14
Rear window defogger, check and repair, 12-10
Recall information, 0-7
Recommended lubricants and fluids, 1-1
Relays, general information, 12-3
Release bearing and lever, clutch, removal, inspection and installation, 8-5
Release cylinder, clutch, removal and installation, 8-3
Repair minor paint scratches, 11-2
Repair operations possible with the engine in the vehicle
   3.0L and 3.2L V6 engines, 2B-4
   four-cylinder engines, 2A-4
Replacement parts, buying, 0-8
Rotating the tires, 1-19
Rotor, brake, inspection, removal and installation, 9-9
Routine maintenance schedule, 1-5

S

Safety first!, 0-20
Safety recall information, 0-7
Scheduled maintenance, 1-1
Seat belt
    check, 1-19
    removal and installation, 11-23
Seats, removal and installation, 11-21
Secondary Air Injection (AIR) system (1.8L and
    3.0L models), component replacement, 6-19
Service record, 1-4, 1-30, 1-31
Shift linkage, manual transaxle, adjustment, 7A-1
Shift cable, automatic transaxle, removal, installation
    and adjustment, 7B-3
Shift interlock system, automatic transaxle,
    description, check and component
    replacement, 7B-3
Shock absorber, replacement
    front, 10-5
    rear, 10-12
Shock absorber/coil spring assembly (front),
    removal, inspection and installation, 10-4
Slave cylinder, clutch, removal and installation, 8-3
Spare tire, installing, 0-15
Spark plug
    check and replacement, 1-25
    torque, 1-3
    type and gap, 1-2
Speakers, removal and installation, 12-8
Stabilizer bar and bushings, removal and installation
    front, 10-9
    rear, 10-14
Starter motor, removal and installation, 5-8
Starting system, general information and
    precautions, 5-1
Steering
    column
        covers, removal and installation, 11-19
        switches, replacement, 12-6
        removal and installation, 10-18
    gear boots, removal and installation, 10-19
    gear, removal and installation, 10-20
    knuckle, removal and installation, 10-8
    wheel, removal and installation, 10-16
Stop light switch, removal and installation, 9-15
Sunroof, adjustment, 11-23
Suspension and steering systems, general
    information and precautions, 10-2
Suspension, steering and driveaxle boot check, 1-22

T

Temperature gauge sending unit, check and
    replacement, 3-10

Tensioner, drivebelt, replacement, 1-24
Thermostat, check and replacement, 3-7
Throttle body, removal and installation, 4-10
Tie-rod ends (front), removal and installation, 10-19
Timing belt and sprockets, removal, inspection
    and installation
    3.0L V6 engine, 2B-5
    four-cylinder engines, 2A-6
Timing chain and sprockets, 3.2L V6 engine,
    removal, inspection and installation, 2B-6
Tire and tire pressure checks, 1-12
Tire rotation, 1-19
Tire, spare, installing, 0-15
Tools and working facilities, 0-8
Top Dead Center (TDC) for number 1 piston, locating
    3.0L and 3.2L V6 engines, 2B-4
    four-cylinder engines, 2A-4
Torque specifications
    brake caliper mounting bolts, 9-1
    cylinder head bolts
        1.8L four-cylinder engines, 2A-2
        2.0L four-cylinder engines, 2A-3
        3.0L V6 engines, 2B-2
        3.2L V6 engines, 2B-3
    spark plugs, 1-3
    thermostat housing fasteners, 3-1
    water pump fasteners, 3-1
    wheel bolts, 1-3
    Other torque specifications can be found in the
        Chapter that deals with the component
        being serviced.
Towing, 0-15
Transaxle mounts, check and replacement, 7B-6
Transaxle, automatic
    diagnosis, general, 7B-2
    fluid
        change, 1-26
        type, 1-1
    general information, 7B-2
    overhaul, general information, 7B-6
    removal and installation, 7B-4
    shift
        cable, removal, installation and adjustment, 7B-3
        interlock system, description, check and
            component replacement, 7B-3
Transaxle, manual
    back-up light switch, removal and installation, 7A-3
    lubricant
        change, 1-27
        type, 1-1
    oil seals, replacement, 7A-3
    overhaul, general information, 7A-2
    removal and installation, 7A-2
    shift linkage, adjustment, 7A-1
Transmission speed sensors, replacement, 6-15
Trim panels, removal and installation, door, 11-12

Trouble codes
   P0 code list, 6-6
   obtaining and clearing, 6-5
Troubleshooting, 0-21
   cooling, heating and air conditioning systems, 3-2
   engine electrical systems, 5-4
   fuel and exhaust systems, 4-3
Trunk lid
   latch, lock cylinder and support struts, removal and
      installation, 11-12
   removal, installation and adjustment, 11-11
Tune-up and routine maintenance, 1-1
Tune-up general information, 1-10
Turbocharger and intercooler(s), check and
   replacement, 4-17

U

Underhood hose check and replacement, 1-19
Upholstery, carpets and vinyl trim, maintenance, 11-5

V

V6 engines
   camshafts and lifters, removal, inspection and
      installation, 2B-6
   crankshaft front oil seal and housing,
      replacement, 2B-10
   crankshaft pulley, removal and installation, 2B-10
   cylinder head, removal and installation, 2B-9
   engine mounts, check and replacement, 2B-12
   exhaust manifold, removal and installation, 2B-8
   flywheel/driveplate, removal and installation, 2B-12
   intake manifold, removal and installation, 2B-8
   oil pan, removal and installation, 2B-11
   oil pump, removal, inspection and installation, 2B-11
   rear main oil seal, replacement, 2B-12

repair operations possible with the engine in
   the vehicle, 2B-4
timing belt and sprockets (3.0L V6 engine), removal,
   inspection and installation, 2B-5
timing chain and sprockets (3.2L V6 engine), removal,
   inspection and installation, 2B-6
Top Dead Center (TDC) for number 1 piston,
   locating, 2B-4
valve covers, removal and installation, 2B-4
Vacuum gauge diagnostic checks, 2C-5
Valve cover, removal and installation
   3.0L and 3.2L V6 engines, 2B-4
   four-cylinder engines, 2A-5
Valve springs, retainers and seals,
   replacement, 2A-14
Variable camshaft adjustment solenoid valve,
   replacement, 6-20
Variable intake manifold, component
   replacement, 6-20
Vehicle identification numbers, 0-6
Vinyl trim, maintenance, 11-5

W

Water pump and after-run coolant pump,
   replacement, 3-9
Wheel alignment, general information, 10-23
Wheels and tires, general information, 10-22
Window glass frame and regulator, removal and
   installation, 11-15
Window glass, door, removal and installation, 11-15
Windshield
   and fixed glass, replacement, 11-6
   washer fluid, level check, 1-12
   wiper blade inspection and replacement, 1-17
Wiper motor, replacement, 12-16
Wiring diagrams, general information, 12-20
Working facilities, 0-8

Manuales automotrices Haynes

NOTA: Si usted no puede encontrar su vehículo en esta lista, consulte con su distribuidor Haynes, para información de la producción más moderna.

ACURA
12020 **Integra** '86 thru '89 **& Legend**
'86 thru '90
12021 **Integra** '90 thru '93 **& Legend**
'91 thru '95
12050 **Acura TL** all models '99 thru '08

AMC
Jeep CJ - *see JEEP (50020)*
14020 **Mid-size models** '70 thru '83
14025 **(Renault) Alliance & Encore**
'83 thru '87

AUDI
15020 **4000** all models '80 thru '87
15025 **5000** all models '77 thru '83
15026 **5000** all models '84 thru '88
15030 **Audi A4** '02 thru '08

AUSTIN-HEALEY
Sprite - *see MG Midget (66015)*

BMW
18020 **3/5 Series** not including diesel or
all-wheel drive models '82 thru '92
18021 **3-Series** incl. Z3 models '92 thru '98
18022 **3-Series, E46 chassis** '99 thru '05,
Z4 models '03 thru '05
18025 **320i** all 4 cyl models '75 thru '83
18050 **1500 thru 2002** except Turbo
'59 thru '77

BUICK
19010 **Buick Century** '97 thru '05
Century (front-wheel drive) -
see GM (38005)
19020 **Buick, Oldsmobile & Pontiac
Full-size (Front-wheel drive)**
'85 thru '05, **Buick** Electra, LeSabre
and Park Avenue; **Oldsmobile**
Delta 88 Royale, Ninety Eight and
Regency; **Pontiac** Bonneville
19025 **Buick, Oldsmobile & Pontiac
Full-size (Rear wheel drive)**
Buick Estate '70 thru '90, Electra
'70 thru '84, LeSabre '70 thru '85,
Limited '74 thru '79, **Oldsmobile**
Custom Cruiser '70 thru '90, Delta 88
'70 thru '85, Ninety-eight '70 thru '84,
Pontiac Bonneville '70 thru '81,
Catalina '70 thru '81, Grandville '70
thru '75, Parisienne '83 thru '86
19030 **Mid-size Regal & Century**
all rear-drive models with V6, V8 and
Turbo '74 thru '87
Regal -
see GENERAL MOTORS (38010)
Riviera -
see GENERAL MOTORS (38030)
Roadmaster -
see CHEVROLET (24046)

Skyhawk -
see GENERAL MOTORS (38015)
Skylark - *see GM (38020, 38025)*
Somerset -
see GENERAL MOTORS (38025)

CADILLAC
21030 **Cadillac Rear Wheel Drive**
'70 thru '93
Cimarron -
see GENERAL MOTORS (38015)
DeVille - *see GM (38031 & 38032)*
Eldorado - *see GM (38030 & 38031)*
Fleetwood - *see GM (38031)*
Seville -
see GM (38030, 38031 & 38032)

CHEVROLET
10305 **Chevrolet Engine Overhaul Manual**
24010 **Astro & GMC Safari Mini-vans**
'85 thru '05
24015 **Camaro V8** all models '70 thru '81
24016 **Camaro** all models '82 thru '92
24017 **Camaro & Firebird** '93 thru '02
Cavalier -
see GENERAL MOTORS (38016)
Celebrity -
see GENERAL MOTORS (38005)
24020 **Chevelle, Malibu & El Camino**
'69 thru '87
24024 **Chevette & Pontiac T1000**
'76 thru '87
Citation -
see GENERAL MOTORS (38020)
24027 **Colorado & GMC Canyon**
'04 thru '08
24032 **Corsica/Beretta** all models
'87 thru '96
24040 **Corvette** all V8 models '68 thru '82
24041 **Corvette** all models '84 thru '96
24045 **Full-size Sedans** Caprice, Impala,
Biscayne, Bel Air & Wagons
'69 thru '90
24046 **Impala SS & Caprice and
Buick Roadmaster** '91 thru '96
Impala - *see LUMINA (24048)*
Lumina '90 thru '94 -
see GM (38010)
24047 **Impala & Monte Carlo** all models
'06 thru '08
24048 **Lumina & Monte Carlo** '95 thru '05
Lumina APV - *see GM (38035)*
24050 **Luv Pick-up** all 2WD & 4WD
'72 thru '82
Malibu '97 thru '00 - *see GM (38026)*
24055 **Monte Carlo** all models '70 thru '88
Monte Carlo '95 thru '01 -
see LUMINA (24048)
24059 **Nova** all V8 models '69 thru '79
24060 **Nova and Geo Prizm** '85 thru '92
24064 **Pick-ups '67 thru '87** - Chevrolet
& GMC, all V8 & in-line 6 cyl, 2WD &
4WD '67 thru '87; Suburbans, Blazers
& Jimmys '67 thru '91

24065 **Pick-ups '88 thru '98** -
Chevrolet & GMC, full-size pick-
ups '88 thru '98, C/K Classic '99 &
'00, Blazer & Jimmy '92 thru '94;
Suburban '92 thru '99; Tahoe &
Yukon '95 thru '99
24066 **Pick-ups '99 thru '06** -
Chevrolet Silverado & GMC Sierra
'99 thru '06, Suburban/Tahoe/Yukon/
Yukon XL/Avalanche '00 thru '06
24067 **Chevrolet Silverado &GMC Sierra**
'07 thru '09
24070 **S-10 & S-15 Pick-ups** '82 thru '93,
Blazer & Jimmy '83 thru '94,
24071 **S-10 & Sonoma Pick-ups** '94 thru
'04, **Blazer & Jimmy** '95 thru '04,
Hombre '96 thru '01
24072 **Chevrolet TrailBlazer, GMC Envoy
& Oldsmobile Bravada** '02 thru '09
24075 **Sprint** '85 thru '88 **& Geo Metro**
'89 thru '01
24080 **Vans - Chevrolet & GMC** '68 thru '96
24081 **Chevrolet Express & GMC Savana**
Full-size Vans '96 thru '07

CHRYSLER
10310 **Chrysler Engine Overhaul Manual**
25015 **Chrysler Cirrus, Dodge Stratus,
Plymouth Breeze** '95 thru '00
25020 **Full-size Front-Wheel Drive**
'88 thru '93
K-Cars - *see DODGE Aries (30008)*
Laser - *see DODGE Daytona (30030)*
25025 **Chrysler LHS, Concorde, New
Yorker, Dodge** Intrepid, **Eagle**
Vision, '93 thru '97
25026 **Chrysler LHS, Concorde, 300M,
Dodge** Intrepid, '98 thru '04
25027 **Chrysler 300, Dodge Charger &
Magnum** '05 thru '09
25030 **Chrysler & Plymouth Mid-size**
front wheel drive '82 thru '95
Rear-wheel Drive - *see Dodge (30050)*
25035 **PT Cruiser** all models '01 thru '09
25040 **Chrysler** Sebring, **Dodge** Avenger '95
thru '05 **Dodge** Stratus '01 thru 05

DATSUN
28005 **200SX** all models '80 thru '83
28007 **B-210** all models '73 thru '78
28009 **210** all models '79 thru '82
28012 **240Z, 260Z & 280Z** Coupe
'70 thru '78
28014 **280ZX** Coupe & 2+2 '79 thru '83
300ZX - *see NISSAN (72010)*
28018 **510 & PL521 Pick-up** '68 thru '73
28020 **510** all models '78 thru '81
28022 **620 Series Pick-up** all models
'73 thru '79
720 Series Pick-up -
see NISSAN (72030)
28025 **810/Maxima** all gasoline models
'77 thru '84

(Continuación)

Haynes North America, Inc., 861 Lawrence Drive, Newbury Park, CA 91320-1514 • (805) 498-6703 • http://www.haynes.com

Manuales automotrices Haynes (continuacíon)

NOTA: Si usted no puede encontrar su vehículo en esta lista, consulte con su distribuidor Haynes, para información de la producción más moderna.

DODGE

400 & 600 - see CHRYSLER (25030)

30008 **Aries & Plymouth Reliant** '81 thru '89

30010 **Caravan & Plymouth Voyager** '84 thru '95

30011 **Caravan & Plymouth Voyager** '96 thru '02

30012 **Challenger/Plymouth Saporro** '78 thru '83

30013 **Caravan, Chrysler Voyager, Town & Country** '03 thru '07

30016 **Colt & Plymouth Champ** '78 thru '87

30020 **Dakota Pick-ups** all models '87 thru '96

30021 **Durango '98 & '99, Dakota** '97 thru '99

30022 **Durango '00 thru '03 Dakota** '00 thru '04

30023 **Durango '04 thru '06, Dakota** '05 and '06

30025 **Dart, Demon, Plymouth Barracuda, Duster & Valiant** 6 cyl models '67 thru '76

30030 **Daytona & Chrysler Laser** '84 thru '89

Intrepid - *see CHRYSLER (25025, 25026)*

30034 **Neon** all models '95 thru '99

30035 **Omni & Plymouth Horizon** '78 thru '90

30036 **Dodge and Plymouth Neon** '00 thru '05

30040 **Pick-ups** all full-size models '74 thru '93

30041 **Pick-ups** all full-size models '94 thru '01

30042 **Pick-ups Full-size** '02 thru '08

30045 **Ram 50/D50 Pick-ups & Raider and Plymouth Arrow Pick-ups** '79 thru '93

30050 **Dodge/Plymouth/Chrysler** RWD '71 thru '89

30055 **Shadow & Plymouth Sundance** '87 thru '94

30060 **Spirit & Plymouth Acclaim** '89 thru '95

30065 **Vans - Dodge & Plymouth** '71 thru '03

EAGLE

Talon - *see MITSUBISHI (68030, 68031)*

Vision - *see CHRYSLER (25025)*

FIAT

34010 **124 Sport Coupe & Spider** '68 thru '78

34025 **X1/9** all models '74 thru '80

FORD

10320 **Ford Engine Overhaul Manual**

10355 **Ford Automatic Transmission Overhaul**

36004 **Aerostar Mini-vans** all models '86 thru '97

36006 **Contour & Mercury Mystique** '95 thru '00

36008 **Courier Pick-up** all models '72 thru '82

36012 **Crown Victoria & Mercury Grand Marquis** '88 thru '10

36016 **Escort/Mercury Lynx** all models '81 thru '90

36020 **Escort/Mercury Tracer** '91 thru '02

36022 **Escape & Mazda Tribute** '01 thru '07

36024 **Explorer & Mazda Navajo** '91 thru '01

36025 **Explorer/Mercury Mountaineer** '02 thru '10

36028 **Fairmont & Mercury Zephyr** '78 thru '83

36030 **Festiva & Aspire** '88 thru '97

36032 **Fiesta** all models '77 thru '80

36034 **Focus** all models '00 thru '07

36036 **Ford & Mercury Full-size** '75 thru '87

36044 **Ford & Mercury Mid-size** '75 thru '86

36048 **Mustang V8** all models '64-1/2 thru '73

36049 **Mustang II** 4 cyl, V6 & V8 models '74 thru '78

36050 **Mustang & Mercury Capri** all models Mustang, '79 thru '93; Capri, '79 thru '86

36051 **Mustang** all models '94 thru '04

36052 **Mustang** '05 thru '07

36054 **Pick-ups & Bronco** '73 thru '79

36058 **Pick-ups & Bronco** '80 thru '96

36059 **F-150 & Expedition** '97 thru '09, **F-250** '97 thru '99 & **Lincoln Navigator** '98 thru '09

36060 **Super Duty Pick-ups, Excursion** '99 thru '10

36061 **F-150** full-size '04 thru '09

36062 **Pinto & Mercury Bobcat** '75 thru '80

36066 **Probe** all models '89 thru '92

36070 **Ranger/Bronco II** gasoline models '83 thru '92

36071 **Ranger** '93 thru '10 & **Mazda Pick-ups** '94 thru '09

36074 **Taurus & Mercury Sable** '86 thru '95

36075 **Taurus & Mercury Sable** '96 thru '05

36078 **Tempo & Mercury Topaz** '84 thru '94

36082 **Thunderbird/Mercury Cougar** '83 thru '88

36086 **Thunderbird/Mercury Cougar** '89 thru '97

36090 **Vans** all V8 Econoline models '69 thru '91

36094 **Vans** full size '92 thru '05

36097 **Windstar Mini-van** '95 thru '07

GENERAL MOTORS

10360 **GM Automatic Transmission Overhaul**

38005 **Buick Century, Chevrolet Celebrity, Oldsmobile Cutlass Ciera & Pontiac 6000** all models '82 thru '96

38010 **Buick Regal, Chevrolet Lumina, Oldsmobile Cutlass Supreme & Pontiac Grand Prix (FWD)** '88 thru '07

38015 **Buick Skyhawk, Cadillac Cimarron, Chevrolet Cavalier, Oldsmobile Firenza & Pontiac J-2000 & Sunbird** '82 thru '94

38016 **Chevrolet Cavalier & Pontiac Sunfire** '95 thru '05

38017 **Chevrolet Cobalt & Pontiac G5** '05 thru '09

38020 **Buick Skylark, Chevrolet Citation, Olds Omega, Pontiac Phoenix** '80 thru '85

38025 **Buick Skylark & Somerset, Oldsmobile Achieva & Calais and Pontiac Grand Am** all models '85 thru '98

38026 **Chevrolet Malibu, Olds Alero & Cutlass, Pontiac Grand Am** '97 thru '03

38027 **Chevrolet Malibu** '04 thru '07

38030 **Cadillac Eldorado** '71 thru '85, **Seville** '80 thru '85, **Oldsmobile Toronado** '71 thru '85, **Buick Riviera** '79 thru '85

38031 **Cadillac Eldorado & Seville** '86 thru '91, **DeVille** '86 thru '93, **Fleetwood & Olds Toronado** '86 thru '92, **Buick Riviera** '86 thru '93

38032 **Cadillac DeVille** '94 thru '05 & **Seville** '92 thru '04, Cadillac DTS '06 thru '10

38035 **Chevrolet Lumina APV, Olds Silhouette & Pontiac Trans Sport** all models '90 thru '96

38036 **Chevrolet Venture, Olds Silhouette, Pontiac Trans Sport & Montana** '97 thru '05

General Motors Full-size Rear-wheel Drive - see BUICK (19025)

38040 **Chevrolet Equinox** '05 thru '09 **Pontiac Torrent** '06 thru '09

GEO

Metro - see CHEVROLET Sprint (24075)

Prizm - '85 thru '92 see CHEVY (24060), '93 thru '02 see TOYOTA Corolla (92036)

40030 **Storm** all models '90 thru '93

Tracker - see SUZUKI Samurai (90010)

GMC

Vans & Pick-ups - see CHEVROLET

Haynes North America, Inc., 861 Lawrence Drive, Newbury Park, CA 91320-1514 • (805) 498-6703 • http://www.haynes.com

Manuales automotrices Haynes

HONDA

42010 Accord CVCC all models '76 thru '83
42011 Accord all models '84 thru '89
42012 Accord all models '90 thru '93
42013 Accord all models '94 thru '97
42014 Accord all models '98 thru '02
42015 Accord models '03 thru '07
42020 Civic 1200 all models '73 thru '79
42021 Civic 1300 & 1500 CVCC '80 thru '83
42022 Civic 1500 CVCC all models '75 thru '79
42023 Civic all models '84 thru '91
42024 Civic & del Sol '92 thru '95
42025 Civic '96 thru '00, **CR-V** '97 thru '01, **Acura Integra** '94 thru '00
42026 Civic '01 thru '10, **CR-V** '02 thru '09
42035 Odyssey all models '99 thru '04
42037 Honda Pilot '03 thru '07, **Acura MDX** '01 thru '07
42040 Prelude CVCC all models '79 thru '89

HYUNDAI

43010 Elantra all models '96 thru '06
43015 Excel & Accent all models '86 thru '09
43050 Santa Fe all models '01 thru '06
43055 Sonata all models '99 thru '08

ISUZU

Hombre - *see CHEVROLET S-10 (24071)*
47017 Rodeo '91 thru '02; **Amigo** '89 thru '94 and '98 thru '02; **Honda Passport** '95 thru '02
47020 Trooper & Pick-up '81 thru '93

JAGUAR

49010 XJ6 all 6 cyl models '68 thru '86
49011 XJ6 all models '88 thru '94
49015 XJ12 & XJS all 12 cyl models '72 thru '85

JEEP

50010 Cherokee, Comanche & Wagoneer Limited all models '84 thru '01
50020 CJ all models '49 thru '86
50025 Grand Cherokee all models '93 thru '04
50026 Grand Cherokee '05 thru '09
50029 Grand Wagoneer & Pick-up '72 thru '91
Grand Wagoneer '84 thru '91, Cherokee & Wagoneer '72 thru '83, Pick-up '72 thru '88
50030 Wrangler all models '87 thru '08
50035 Liberty '02 thru '07

KIA

54070 Sephia '94 thru '01, **Spectra** '00 thru '09

LEXUS

ES 300 - *see TOYOTA Camry (92007)*

LINCOLN

Navigator - *see FORD Pick-up (36059)*
59010 Rear-Wheel Drive all models '70 thru '10

MAZDA

61010 GLC Hatchback (rear-wheel drive) '77 thru '83
61011 GLC (front-wheel drive) '81 thru '85
61015 323 & Protegé '90 thru '00
61016 MX-5 Miata '90 thru '09
61020 MPV all models '89 thru '98
Navajo - *see Ford Explorer (36024)*
61030 Pick-ups '72 thru '93
Pick-ups '94 thru '00 - *see Ford Ranger (36071)*
61035 RX-7 all models '79 thru '85
61036 RX-7 all models '86 thru '91
61040 626 (rear-wheel drive) all models '79 thru '82
61041 626/MX-6 (front-wheel drive) '83 thru '92
61042 626 '93 thru '01, **MX-6/Ford Probe** '93 thru '01

MERCEDES-BENZ

63012 123 Series Diesel '76 thru '85
63015 190 Series four-cyl gas models, '84 thru '88
63020 230/250/280 6 cyl sohc models '68 thru '72
63025 280 123 Series gasoline models '77 thru '81
63030 350 & 450 all models '71 thru '80
63040 C-Class: C230/C240/C280/C320/C350 '01 thru '07

MERCURY

64200 Villager & Nissan Quest '93 thru '01
All other titles, see FORD Listing.

MG

66010 MGB Roadster & GT Coupe '62 thru '80
66015 MG Midget, Austin Healey Sprite '58 thru '80

MITSUBISHI

68020 Cordia, Tredia, Galant, Precis & Mirage '83 thru '93
68030 Eclipse, Eagle Talon & Ply. Laser '90 thru '94
68031 Eclipse '95 thru '05, **Eagle Talon** '95 thru '98
68035 Galant '94 thru '03
68040 Pick-up '83 thru '96 & **Montero** '83 thru '93

NISSAN

72010 300ZX all models including Turbo '84 thru '89

72011 350Z & Infiniti G35 all models '03 thru '08
72015 Altima all models '93 thru '06
72020 Maxima all models '85 thru '92
72021 Maxima all models '93 thru '04
72030 Pick-ups '80 thru '97 **Pathfinder** '87 thru '95
72031 Frontier Pick-up '98 thru '04, **Xterra** '00 thru '04, **Pathfinder** '96 thru '04
72032 Frontier & Xterra '05 thru '08
72040 Pulsar all models '83 thru '86
Quest - *see MERCURY Villager (64200)*
72050 Sentra all models '82 thru '94
72051 Sentra & 200SX all models '95 thru '06
72060 Stanza all models '82 thru '90
72070 Titan pick-ups '04 thru '09
Armada '05 thru '10

OLDSMOBILE

73015 Cutlass V6 & V8 gas models '74 thru '88
For other OLDSMOBILE titles, see BUICK, CHEVROLET or GENERAL MOTORS listing.

PLYMOUTH

For **PLYMOUTH** titles, see **DODGE** listing.

PONTIAC

79008 Fiero all models '84 thru '88
79018 Firebird V8 models except Turbo '70 thru '81
79019 Firebird all models '82 thru '92
79025 G6 all models '05 thru '09
79040 Mid-size Rear-wheel Drive '70 thru '87
For other PONTIAC titles, see BUICK, CHEVROLET or GENERAL MOTORS listing.

PORSCHE

80020 911 except Turbo & Carrera 4 '65 thru '89
80025 914 all 4 cyl models '69 thru '76
80030 924 all models including Turbo '76 thru '82
80035 944 all models including Turbo '83 thru '89

RENAULT

Alliance & Encore - *see AMC (14020)*

SAAB

84010 900 all models including Turbo '79 thru '88

SATURN

87010 Saturn all S-series models '91 thru '02
87011 Saturn Ion '03 thru '07

(Continuacion)

Manuales automotrices Haynes (continuacíon)

NOTA: Si usted no puede encontrar su vehículo en esta lista, consulte con su distribuidor Haynes, para información de la producción más moderna.

87020 **Saturn** all L-series models '00 thru '04
87040 **Saturn VUE** '02 thru '07

SUBARU
89002 **1100, 1300, 1400 & 1600** '71 thru '79
89003 **1600 & 1800** 2WD & 4WD '80 thru '94
89100 **Legacy** all models '90 thru '99
89101 **Legacy & Forester** '00 thru '06

SUZUKI
90010 **Samurai/Sidekick & Geo Tracker** '86 thru '01

TOYOTA
92005 **Camry** all models '83 thru '91
92006 **Camry** all models '92 thru '96
92007 **Camry, Avalon, Solara, Lexus ES 300** '97 thru '01
92008 **Toyota Camry, Avalon and Solara and Lexus ES 300/330** all models '02 thru '06
92015 **Celica Rear Wheel Drive** '71 thru '85
92020 **Celica Front Wheel Drive** '86 thru '99
92025 **Celica Supra** all models '79 thru '92
92030 **Corolla** all models '75 thru '79
92032 **Corolla** all rear wheel drive models '80 thru '87
92035 **Corolla** all front wheel drive models '84 thru '92
92036 **Corolla & Geo Prizm** '93 thru '02
92037 **Corolla** models '03 thru '08
92040 **Corolla Tercel** all models '80 thru '82
92045 **Corona** all models '74 thru '82
92050 **Cressida** all models '78 thru '82
92055 **Land Cruiser** FJ40, 43, 45, 55 '68 thru '82
92056 **Land Cruiser** FJ60, 62, 80, FZJ80 '80 thru '96
92060 **Matrix & Pontiac Vibe** '03 thru '08
92065 **MR2** all models '85 thru '87
92070 **Pick-up** all models '69 thru '78
92075 **Pick-up** all models '79 thru '95
92076 **Tacoma** '95 thru '04, **4Runner** '96 thru '02, & **T100** '93 thru '98
92077 **Tacoma** all models '05 thru '09
92078 **Tundra** '00 thru '06 & **Sequoia** '01 thru '07
92079 **4Runner** all models '03 thru '09
92080 **Previa** all models '91 thru '95
92081 **Prius** all models '01 thru '08
92082 **RAV4** all models '96 thru '05
92085 **Tercel** all models '87 thru '94
92090 **Sienna** all models '98 thru '09
92095 **Highlander & Lexus RX-330** '99 thru '06

TRIUMPH
94007 **Spitfire** all models '62 thru '81
94010 **TR7** all models '75 thru '81

VW
96008 **Beetle & Karmann Ghia** '54 thru '79
96009 **New Beetle** '98 thru '05
96016 **Rabbit, Jetta, Scirocco & Pick-up** gas models '75 thru '92 & Convertible '80 thru '92
96017 **Golf, GTI & Jetta** '93 thru '98 & **Cabrio** '95 thru '02
96018 **Golf, GTI, Jetta** '99 thru '05
96020 **Rabbit, Jetta & Pick-up** diesel '77 thru '84
96023 **Passat** '98 thru '05, **Audi A4** '96 thru '01
96030 **Transporter 1600** all models '68 thru '79
96035 **Transporter 1700, 1800 & 2000** '72 thru '79
96040 **Type 3 1500 & 1600** all models '63 thru '73
96045 **Vanagon** all air-cooled models '80 thru '83

VOLVO
97010 **120, 130 Series & 1800 Sports** '61 thru '73
97015 **140 Series** all models '66 thru '74
97020 **240 Series** all models '76 thru '93
97040 **740 & 760 Series** all models '82 thru '88
97050 **850 Series** all models '93 thru '97

TECHBOOK MANUALS
10205 **Automotive Computer Codes**
10206 **OBD-II & Electronic Engine Management Systems**
10210 **Automotive Emissions Control Manual**
10215 **Fuel Injection Manual, 1978 thru 1985**
10220 **Fuel Injection Manual, 1986 thru 1999**
10225 **Holley Carburetor Manual**
10230 **Rochester Carburetor Manual**
10240 **Weber/Zenith/Stromberg/SU Carburetors**
10305 **Chevrolet Engine Overhaul Manual**
10310 **Chrysler Engine Overhaul Manual**
10320 **Ford Engine Overhaul Manual**
10330 **GM and Ford Diesel Engine Repair Manual**
10333 **Engine Performance Manual**
10340 **Small Engine Repair Manual, 5 HP & Less**
10341 **Small Engine Repair Manual, 5.5 - 20 HP**
10345 **Suspension, Steering & Driveline Manual**
10355 **Ford Automatic Transmission Overhaul**

10360 **GM Automatic Transmission Overhaul**
10405 **Automotive Body Repair & Painting**
10410 **Automotive Brake Manual**
10411 **Automotive Anti-lock Brake (ABS) Systems**
10415 **Automotive Detaiing Manual**
10420 **Automotive Electrical Manual**
10425 **Automotive Heating & Air Conditioning**
10430 **Automotive Reference Manual & Dictionary**
10435 **Automotive Tools Manual**
10440 **Used Car Buying Guide**
10445 **Welding Manual**
10450 **ATV Basics**
10452 **Scooters 50cc to 250cc**

SPANISH MANUALS
98903 **Reparación de Carrocería & Pintura**
98904 **Carburadores para los modelos Holley & Rochester**
98905 **Códigos Automotrices de la Computadora**
98910 **Frenos Automotriz**
98913 **Electricidad Automotriz**
98915 **Inyección de Combustible 1986 al 1999**
99040 **Chevrolet & GMC Camionetas** '67 al '87 Incluye Suburban, Blazer & Jimmy '67 al '91
99041 **Chevrolet & GMC Camionetas** '88 al '98 Incluye Suburban '92 al '98, Blazer & Jimmy '92 al '94, Tahoe y Yukon '95 al '98
99042 **Chevrolet & GMC Camionetas Cerradas** '68 al '95
99043 **Chevrolet/GMC Camionetas** '94 thru '04
99055 **Dodge Caravan & Plymouth Voyager** '84 al '95
99075 **Ford Camionetas y Bronco** '80 al '94
99077 **Ford Camionetas Cerradas** '69 al '91
99088 **Ford Modelos de Tamaño Mediano** '75 al '86
99091 **Ford Taurus & Mercury Sable** '86 al '95
99095 **GM Modelos de Tamaño Grande** '70 al '90
99100 **GM Modelos de Tamaño Mediano** '70 al '88
99106 **Jeep Cherokee, Wagoneer & Comanche** '84 al '00
99110 **Nissan Camioneta** '80 al '96, **Pathfinder** '87 al '95
99118 **Nissan Sentra** '82 al '94
99125 **Toyota Camionetas y 4Runner** '79 al '95

Sobre 100 manuales de motocicletas también están incluidos

8-10